Sheldon Johnson

ISBN: 0-8010-0037-8

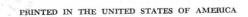

PRINTED IN THE UNITED STATES OF AMERICA

THE OLD TESTAMENT
Its Claims and Its Critics

by

OSWALD T. ALLIS

THE PRESBYTERIAN AND REFORMED
PUBLISHING COMPANY
1972

THE OLD TESTAMENT
Its Claims and Its Critics

To the Memory of
Rev. Samuel G. Craig, D.D.
Pastor, Author, Editor, Publisher,
valiant Defender of the Faith

CONTENTS

PREFACE

Two centuries have passed since the rise of the movement generally known as higher criticism, which is commonly dated from the publication in 1753 of Jean Astruc's little volume dealing with the sources of Genesis. In the year in which the present writer graduated from Princeton Seminary the Bross Prize was awarded to Professor James Orr of the United Free College of Glasgow for his volume, *The Problem of the Old Testament*. This was more than half a century ago (1905). And there were those who hoped and even expected that this volume would prove a convincing and conclusive answer to the critical attack upon the Old Testament, and serve as a quietus to it. Professor Orr clearly did not share this view. On the title page of the volume he placed these significant words, *Nubecula est, quae cito evanescet*. He saw quite plainly that the critical attack upon the Old Testament was not *a little cloud which would quickly disappear* and therefore might be lightly regarded, not a skirmish, not a mere local uprising which would be easily suppressed, but that it represented an attitude toward Scripture which could not easily or quickly be met and overcome. He was right. The problem of the Old Testament is still with us and each new generation must face it for itself.

Basically, the problem is not literary. It is historical and theological. It has its root in Theism. Is the biblical portrayal of God a true one? Has God spoken to men? Has he wrought wonders of old? Is sacred history true history? In a word, the whole problem centers in the supernatural. The Bible deals with spiritual things; and only the spiritual man is able to understand and interpret them aright; and it is the supernatural in the Bible which is supremely precious to him. If the words of the Psalmist, "He showed his word unto Jacob, his statutes and his judgments unto Israel. He hath not dealt so with any nation: and as for his judgments, they have not known them," are true and are to be taken in their obvious sense and as meaning what they say, then the history recorded in the Old Testament is a unique history and is to be studied as such. It is not to be measured and tested as to its correctness and accuracy by the course of history among the

vii

neighboring nations. The record of their development, or lack of it, is not a *pattern* by which the correctness of the biblical record and revelation is to be tested but rather is it to be regarded as a foil or background which will serve to exhibit the uniqueness of God's dealings with his Chosen People. The issue thus raised is not a minor one. It is of basic and supreme importance. This is illustrated by the claim that has often been made that "the Bible is to be read like any other book." For to do this means, only too often, that the redemptive supernaturalism which the Bible represents as factually true and fundamentally important is to be regarded with suspicion and even rejected out of hand if it does not conform to the natural pattern which is to be found in the histories of other peoples, especially those with which Israel came into close association like the Canaanites. For it is those very features of the biblical record which are most offensive to the student of comparative religion, because they do not fit into his pattern, that are of supreme value to those who accept and rejoice in the biblical record, with its account of a unique revelation and a unique history which points forward to a unique event, the coming of a unique Person in whom Israel's unique history was to find its world-changing fulfilment.

It was the privilege of the writer to study at Princeton Seminary under men who held firmly to the great tradition on which that institution was founded, men who not merely believed but gloried in that pervasive supernaturalism which alone can be called truly biblical. And he has felt that in striving to defend the heritage of unfeigned faith in the Holy Scriptures which dwelt in that noble succession of teachers, among whom Joseph Addison Alexander, William Henry Green and Robert Dick Wilson were so eminent, he was repaying in some measure the debt which he owed these mighty men of God.

Two decades have elapsed since the writer was invited by the Faculty of Fuller Theological Seminary to deliver the annual lectures on the Peyton Foundation in 1952. The general theme of the lectures was Old Testament Introduction. And the subject of each lecture is indicated by the main divisions of this book, except that the chapter on Chronology has been added because of the writer's interest in the defense made a century ago by George Smith of the traditional (Ussher) Chronology of the Old Testament kingdom period against the Assyrian Chronology proposed by Schrader and widely accepted today. Needless to say the present size of the volume indicates quite clearly that there has been much expansion as well as revision in the preparation of the lectures for publication. The writer wishes to express to the Faculty of the Seminary his appreciation of the honor conferred upon him by the invitation to deliver these lectures and it is his hope and prayer that this volume in its final form may promote the cause for which the lectureship was established.

The indexes have been prepared by Mr. Barry Traver, a graduate student at Westminster Theological Seminary. The writer wishes to express his thanks to him for his careful performance of this arduous task which forms for the reader a very helpful addition to the book.

Oswald T. Allis

Bryn Mawr, Pa.

ABBREVIATIONS

ABH	*Archaeology and Bible History*, by J. P. Free
AJA	*American Journal of Archaeology*
AJSLL	*American Journal of Semitic Languages and Literature*
ANEP	*Ancient Near Eastern Pictures*, ed. by J. B. Pritchard
ANET	*Ancient Near Eastern Texts*, ed. by J. B. Pritchard
ANTIQ.	*Antiquities of Josephus*
AOT	*Archaeology and the O.T.*, by M. F. Unger
AOOT	*Ancient Orient and the O.T.*, by K. A. Kitchen
ARAK	*Ancient Records of Assyrian Kings*, by D. D. Luckenbill
ARI	*Archaeology and the Religion of Israel,* by W. F. Albright
ARV	*American Revised Version*
AT	*American Translation of the Bible,* ed. by Smith and Goodspeed
AV	*Authorized (King James) Version*
BA	*The Biblical Archaeologist*
BANE	*The Bible and the Ancient Near East,* ed. by G. E. Wright
BASOR	*Bulletin of the American Schools of Oriental Research*
BCBS	*Bible Commentary for Bible Students*, ed. by Ellicott
BDB	*A Hebrew and English Dictionary of O.T.,* by Brown, Driver, Briggs
BETS	*Bulletin of the Evangelical Theological Society*
BJRL	*Bulletin of the John Ryland Library*
BS	*Bibliotheca Sacra*
BV	*Berkeley Version of the Bible*
CT	*Cuneiform Texts*, published by the British Museum
D	*Deuteronomy*
DDB	*Davis Dictionary of the Bible*
D	*The Deuteronomist*
DOTT	*Documents from O.T. Times*, D. W. Thomas
E	*The Elohist*
EA	*The El Amarna Letters*
EB	*Encyclopaedia Britannica*

EBi	*Encyclopaedia Biblica*
EQ	*Evangelical Quarterly*
FBM	*Five Books of Moses*, by O. T. Allis
FJJ	*From Joseph to Joshua*, by H. H. Rowley 1950
FSAC	*From the Stone Age to Christianity*, by W. F. Albright
HAE	*A History of Ancient Egypt*, by J. H. Breasted
HC	*Hammurabi Codex*
HDB	*Hastings Dictionary of the Bible*
IAD	*Israel and the Aramaens of Damascus*, by M. F. Unger
IBA	*Illustrations from Biblical Archaeology*, by D. J. Wiseman
ICC	*International Critical Commentary*
ILN	*Illustrated London News*
IOT	*Introduction to the O.T.*, by Young, or Pfeiffer or Eichrodt (as indicated) by the context.
ISBE	*International Standard Bible Encyclopaedia*, ed. by James Orr
JEDP	*Documents of the Pentateuch as defined by the Critics*
JBL	*Journal of Biblical Literature*
J	*The Jehovist*
JFB	*Critical and Expository Commentary*, by Jameison, Fausset and Brown
JNES	*Journal of Near Eastern Studies*
JQR	*Jewish Quarterly Review*
LAP	*Light on the Ancient Past*, by Jack Finegan
LOT	*Introduction to the Literature of the O.T.*, by S. R. Driver
LXX	*Septuagint Version of the O.T.*
MAR	*Myth and Ritual*, ed. by S. H. Hooke
MT	*Massoretic Texts* of Hebrew O.T.
NBC	*The New Bible Commentary*
NBCR	*The New Bible Commentary, Revised*
NBD	*New Bible Dictionary*
NEB	*New English Bible*
NSHERK	*New Schaff-Herzog Encyclopedia of Religious Knowledge*
OLZ	*Orientalisch Literatur Zeitung*
OTMS	*Old Testament and Modern Studies*, ed. by H. H. Rowley
P	*Prolegoma Priestly Documents According to the Critics*, by J. Wellhausen

ABBREVIATIONS (continued)

PAC	*Prophecy and the Church,* by O. T. Allis
POT	*Problem of the O.T.,* by James Orr
PTR	*Princeton Theological Review*
R	*Cuneiform Texts of Western Asia,* ed. by H. C. Rawlinson
RAR	*Record and Revelation,* ed. by H. W. Robinson
RMBA	*Rand, McNally Bible Atlas*
RNI	*Religion in Israel,* by R. H. Pfeiffer
RSV	*Revised Standard Version*
RV	*Revised Version*
Sam.	*Samaritan Text of the O.T.*
SIOT	*Scientific Introduction to the O.T.,* by R. D. Wilson
SYR	*Syriac Peshitto Versions*
TOT	*Theology of the Old Testament,* by Oehler or Eichrodt
VULG	*Latin Vulgate*
WBC	*Wycliffe Bible Commentary*
WTJ	*Westminster Theological Journal*
WDB	*Westminster Dictionary of the Bible*
ZAW	*Zeitschrift für die Alttestamentliche Wissenschaft*
ZPBD	*Zondervan Pictorial Bible Dictionary*

CHAPTER I

THE OLD TESTAMENT FROM WITHIN
ITS FACTS AND ITS DOCTRINES

The subject of biblical, or more specifically Old Testament, Introduction has been dealt with in so many ways, by so many writers, from so many different viewpoints, that it is well for us to remind ourselves at the outset of such a study as this that the Old Testament is a book which has neither foreword, preface, nor introduction. It begins with a brief and dogmatic affirmation: "In the beginning God created the heaven and the earth"; and everything that follows is in a broad sense the amplification of that majestic declaration. Anything in the nature of "introduction" is man-made. It is man's effort to account for, explain, and commend this Word of the Creator God who speaks through this Book to the man whom he has made in his image and to whom he makes known his will. This is a distinction which is often ignored and therefore needs constant emphasis.

THE SUFFICIENCY OF THE HOLY SCRIPTURES

It is a constitutional rule of the great Bible Societies that they are to circulate the Bible "without note or comment." This is a noteworthy and significant fact. It indicates that the Bible is a self-contained and a self-explanatory book, a book which does not have and cannot have an authoritative introduction; and untold thousands have found the Saviour and been built up in our most holy faith by the simple reading and study of the Word, under the guidance and illumination of the Holy Spirit. It is true of the Bible, as of no other book, that "the infallible rule of interpretation of Scripture is the Scripture itself."[1] Consequently, there are two things which are indispensable for most Bible students.

The first is a dependable, because accurate, translation into the vernacular. Relatively few Christians are in a position to go directly to the original, the Hebrew[2] and the Greek. Consequently, for most Bible students a good translation into their mother tongue is of prime importance. For English-speaking people, for many generations, this has meant the King James Version. But today a veritable spate of translations threatens to flood the market. Hardly a year passes without the appearance of a new translation, usually of the New Testament

1

or some part of it. This is an important matter. For some of the new translations, especially those which are described as "modern speech" versions, are paraphrase rather than translation; and with a view to clarifying or simplifying the meaning of the text, they at times introduce into it meanings which are at least questionable.[3] Sometimes they even change the text to bring out of it a meaning which is not clearly there. Hence, a dependable, because accurate, translation is a primary and indispensable aid to Bible study; and since no translation can do full justice to the original it goes without saying that an adequate knowledge of the original languages is one of the great assets of the Bible student and especially of the Bible teacher.

The second important, and in a sense indispensable, aid is a good concordance, preferably an analytical one.[4] It is just because the Bible is its own interpreter, that the concordance is so important; and the acceptance of this fact by the vast majority of Christians, is responsible for their extensive use. It has been well stated as follows: "The utility of concordances in the way of exegesis, is based on the position that the several parts of divine revelation are consistent with each other and form harmonious elements in one grand system of spiritual truth, so that by comparing together parallel passages, what is clear may be exemplified and confirmed, and what is dark may be expounded."[5] Every first-hand student of the Bible will testify out of his own experience that a good analytical concordance is perhaps the most generally useful "help" which the Bible student, whether minister or layman, professor or student, can possess. And, of course, the fuller and more complete the concordance, the greater is its value. Careful use of the concordance is the best way to find out what the Bible itself has to say about any subject with which it deals. Such use of the concordance will not of course be mechanical. It will take into account the progressive character of the biblical revelation (Mark 4:28; John 1:17). It will not seek to find clearly stated in the beginning teachings which are not fully revealed until toward the end.[6]

But while, as has been stated, the Old Testament has no introduction, it is a familiar and obvious fact that there is no book today which is thought to need so much "introducing" as the Bible. Every decade, almost every year, "introductions," some ponderous and erudite, others simple and popular, are published; some of them almost as large as the Bible itself, if not larger; and the number of Bible dictionaries, commentaries, histories, geographies, helps of every kind, is almost countless. Introducing and explaining the Bible is a major task of the Bible teacher today.

Why is this the case? There are two main reasons. One is that the Bible is a very old book and it covers a long period of time. It speaks of men and nations long forgotten, of events and transactions which happened many centuries ago; and consequently, other records, whether long known or recently discovered, may and do supply valuable information bearing upon it. Josephus has been recognized for centuries as an important contributor to our understanding of the Bible.[7] From him we learn, for example, much about the Herods: about Herod the Great (one lurid yet terribly characteristic episode in his life is recorded to his shame in the New Testament), that Herod the Tetrarch, the murderer of John the Baptist, was his son, that the Herod who killed James the brother of John with the sword and was eaten of worms was his grandson, and that king Agrippa before whom Paul testified at Caesarea was his great-grandson. First Maccabees, which has formed a part of the Apocrypha for centuries, throws valuable light on the most critical period between the two Testaments, the Maccabean Wars. And now, during the past century and a half, the spade of the archaeologist and the skill of the philologist and historian have made us acquainted with records from the days of such "forgotten men" as mighty Sargon, such ancient cities as Ur and Harran, No and On, and nations such as the Hittites, names which would have passed into oblivion centuries ago but for their mention in the Bible. Names and persons, laws, customs and events, languages and systems of writing, long forgotten, but known and familiar to the men who wrote the Bible records, have come to light. And all this information, while not indispensable, since for generations Christians have gotten along without it, is of great interest and value to the student of the Bible. Every Bible student should welcome and use all the light which historical research has thrown upon the Sacred Text. The service which secular history and archaeology render the modern reader of the Bible is to place him in possession of information regarding Bible times which was known to those to whom these writings were originally addressed or for whom they were primarily intended. But our use of the new data should always be with a view to getting light on what the Bible *says for itself*, the correct understanding of the sacred text.

We need however to remember that while in many cases the biblical writers assume and presuppose, on the part of their readers, knowledge which we of today do not possess and which we must obtain, if at all, from extra-biblical sources, the reason that much of the information of this nature is not recorded in the Bible itself is that, however interesting and even valuable it may be, it is not of vital importance. In First Corinthians, Paul associates a certain Sosthenes with himself in the salutation. Who was this Sosthenes? The name was a not uncommon one. But the only Sosthenes, mentioned elsewhere in the Bible, is the ruler of the synagogue at Corinth, who apparently was conspicuous among the Jewish leaders who opposed Paul and brought him before the Roman court; and we read that Sosthenes himself received a beating in consequence (Acts 18:12-17). Are the two Sosthenes one and the same person? The question has been much discussed. But definite proof is lacking. A well-known commentator who opposes the identification, concludes his discussion of 1 Corinthians 1:1 with the significant and rather obvious remark: "The *particulars* of the position of Sosthenes were well-known to the readers."[8] This is probably true. But it does not follow that we of today need to know these particulars which were more or less familiar to the original readers.[9] Were all such information, however relevant and interesting, included in the Bible, it would not be a book but a library or encyclopedia. It is because the Bible is so concerned to tell us the things of vital importance, that it fails to enlighten us as to many matters which are of mere human interest today. It constantly piques our curiosity without gratifying it. Yet it is unfortunately true that there are Bible students who become so interested in the things which the Bible does not tell us, its silence as to matters of secondary interest, that they almost lose sight of the far more important things which it not only tells us, but even reiterates and emphasizes.

Another point to be borne in mind is that while archaeology and secular history may assist and confirm faith, faith is not dependent on archaeology. We do not believe what the Bible tells us about men and events of ancient times because its statements have been confirmed by archaeological evidence. As we shall see later, the spade of the archaeologist has raised quite as many problems as it has solved. Furthermore, archaeology cannot and should not be expected to prove the supernatural. It is limited to the study of natural events, while biblical history is supernatural to the core. It is in the Bible alone that we find the record of those unique facts which constitute God's special dealings in words and works with his people of old. The Bible claims to speak with the authority of God; and the Bible-believing Christian accepts it on His authority and not because ancient records, recently brought to light have told him that he may do so. This needs to be said, not to minimize the value of archaeology or the importance of its results, but merely to place it in its proper place as the handmaid of the Bible and not its master.

There is a second reason for the plethora of introductions to which reference has just been made. It is to be found in the criticism, "higher criticism" as it is usually called, of the Bible which is so popular today. It is largely for the purpose of propounding and popularizing the often radical conclusions of this relatively modern science that so much time has to be devoted to the subject of introduction.

One of the most influential "critical" treatments of the Old Testament has been Wellhausen's *Prolegomena to the History of Israel*. In the English edition (1895) it is a volume of 425 pages. Yet Wellhausen called it "Prolegomena," a word which the dictionary explains as meaning "preliminary remarks, observations, preface," or we might call it "introduction" to the history of Israel, which shows that he realized the immense task of reconstruction and revising which this theory regarding the history of Israel involved. Thus when we meet as almost the first sentence in this work the words: "For the earliest period of the history of Israel, all that precedes the building of the temple, not a trace can be found of any sanctuary of exclusive legitimacy," it must be obvious to anyone at all familiar with the contents of the Old Testament, that this statement proceeds, that it must proceed, upon the assumption that the account of "the place of worship" in Israel set forth in this book will be quite different from the one given in the Pentateuch itself, and one which will necessitate the treating of the bulk of the Mosaic legislation as late and undependable. For if the statements contained in Exodus-Deuteronomy are accepted as reliable and taken at their face value and in their obvious sense, it must be clear to the most casual reader that the above statement is absolutely irreconcilable with the facts set forth in the Bible itself.[10] Yet it is the *considered* judgment of the members of this influential school of critics, the *assured* result of their investigations, that the *tabernacle* which is described in such detail in the latter part of the Book of Exodus and so clearly "purports" to be Mosaic, was never actually constructed, but was simply a figment of the pious imaginings of the priests of the exilic or post-exilic period, nearly a millennium after the time of Moses; and that the only tabernacle which can properly be called Mosaic, if that is not itself an overstatement, was the little temporary tent described in Exodus 33:7-11, which Moses used to take and pitch "without the camp."

The Book of Deuteronomy "purports" to consist in the main of discourses delivered by Moses to all Israel shortly before his death and in anticipation of the conquest of the land by Joshua. So understood it is a relatively simple and easy book to understand. But when the attempt is made to treat it as a product of the seventh century, a document written to justify a radical program unknown either to Moses or the Prophets, such as the centralization of the worship at Jerusalem by Josiah, much explaining is needed to justify so radical a position. For the late date of Deuteronomy is one of the most essential, as it is also one of the most vulnerable, of the hypotheses of the higher criticism.

How influential this theory still is, is illustrated by the fact that the members of what is now called the "Biblical Theology School," while claiming that the Bible is to be studied "from within," still hold that "from within" means, as seen through "critical" spectacles. Thus Gabriel Hebert in his book, *The Bible from Within,* accepts and defends Wellhausen's claim that the tabernacle described in such detail in the Pentateuch never existed and in arguing for the Maccabean date of Daniel he tells us: "This book purports to be a story of events in the time of Nebuchadnezzar, four centuries before: but its actual reference is to this persecution."[11] Such an attitude toward Scripture makes the title, *The Bible from Within,* sound rather paradoxical to say the least.

Is it any wonder that massive volumes have to be written and oceans of ink spilled in the attempt to make the Bible say exactly the opposite of what it does say? Is it any wonder that the critics find it difficult to find a satisfactory and edifying explanation for what they believe to have been a deliberate falsification of history, a "pious fraud"?[12]

The fact that the critical introduction is both the organ and the product of critical speculation is illustrated by a striking statement made a hundred years ago. Alluding to the fact that introductions to Isaiah were a phenomenon of relatively recent date, Alexander remarked: "Hence it is that in the older writers on Isaiah, even down to the middle of the eighteenth century, the place now occupied by *criticism,* in the modern sense, is wholly blank. No one of course thought it necessary to defend what had never been attacked, or to demonstrate what had never been disputed."[13] The fact that as A. B. Davidson admitted many years ago, "For about twenty-five centuries no one dreamt of doubting that Isaiah the son of Amoz was the author of every part of the book that goes under his name,"[14] made elaborate discussions of the authorship of this prophetic volume quite superfluous until its unity of authorship was seriously challenged.

Since so many critics of the Old Testament are so concerned to "introduce" it and to explain it and because the explanations which they give are so often quite inconsistent with the statements of the biblical record itself, it will be well for us at the outset and as a basis for all that is to follow to consider carefully what the Old Testament actually has to say for itself, what it claims to be and claims to teach.

Having pointed out that the Old Testament has and needs no introduction, that it is a self-contained book in the sense that it contains all the information which is necessary for the achieving of its great objective, which is to declare the will of God for the saving of men under the Old Dispensation, as the preparation for the coming of the Saviour to whom both Moses and the Prophets bear witness, we need to observe also that it is unique in a further and even more important sense. It is the *one* book and the *only* book which gives to men this all-important information.[15] The great theme of the Bible is Jesus Christ our Lord, the crucified and risen Saviour of the world. He is the One who was to come; and the Old Testament tells us of the ages-long preparation for his advent. He is the One who came; and the Gospels tell us the story of his life here on earth. He is the One who is to come again; and Gospels and Epistles and Apocalypse thrill with the promise of the fulfillment of that blessed hope. But we need to remember that secular history is almost wholly silent about him and about the mighty events which prepared the way for his coming. Countless volumes have been written about the Jesus of the Bible. But they all derive their information, insofar as it is true information, directly or indirectly from it. It is this which makes the Bible so uniquely precious to the Christian. For it is the Written Word through which he learns to know the Incarnate Word.[16]

When we come then to study the contents of this unique volume, we observe at once that it is concerned primarily with the recording of historical facts and events. All of the great creeds of Christendom recognize and assume that Christianity is a *historical* religion, whose great doctrines set forth the meaning of its great historical facts. We are now speaking of what the Bible, in its natural and obvious sense, claims to be. We shall later consider some of the ways in which this claim is treated in critical circles.

The Witness of the Old Testament to Itself

In the first place we observe that the Old Testament is a book *about God* and *from God*. It begins with the simple and yet immensely impressive declaration: "In the beginning God created the heaven and the earth."[17] Some 10,000 times in the Old Testament one or other of the names of God appears in its 23,000 verses, an average of once in about every two and a half verses. Consequently, God is the great and the pervasive theme.[18] The Bible is the Book of God because it is constantly telling us about God. And what it tells us about God is largely concerned with what he has done and with what he has said. The first chapter of Genesis is not strictly an account of the creation, but rather of God as the Creator. A little more than once a verse, on the average, the word "God" appears in it. Second causes and processes are largely ignored. God "spake and it was *done*" (Ps. 33:9) is the Psalmist's summary of this great introductory chapter. And the Old Testament is constantly declaring the mighty acts of God in the course of history.

Since the Bible is constantly speaking about God, it is and indeed must be characterized and pervaded by the supernatural. It is concerned to tell us again and again of the mighty acts of God. Secular history tends to confine itself to the recording of what is *humanly* possible. Anything which goes beyond the humanly possible it rejects, regards with suspicion, or relegates to the realm of myth, folklore or legend. Not so with sacred history. Its great concern is to tell us of the mighty acts of God, his wonders of old. Consequently it is only to be expected that the things which the Bible presents with great clearness and emphasis as of supreme importance, as being the surest evidence that God has spoken, that his mighty arm has wrought wonders, are the very things which the secular historian, who wishes to edit or rewrite the Bible so that it will read like any other book of history, must proceed at once to blue-pencil or delete. The amazing increase of Israel in Egypt, the plagues, the crossing of the Red Sea, the pillar of cloud and of fire, the manna, the water from the rock, the overthrow of Sihon and Og, the crossing of the Jordan, the capture of Jericho — all the unique events which made the deliverance from Egyptian bondage a momentous epoch in Israel's history and the great type of the deliverance from sin wrought on Calvary — become in the eyes of the secular historian a glorification of a series of significant but perhaps rather commonplace events which find frequent parallels elsewhere on the pages of history.

In concluding an essay on "Christian Supernaturalism," and published in 1897, B. B. Warfield tells us: "The confession of a supernatural God, who may and does act in a supernatural mode, and who acting in a supernatural mode has wrought out for us a supernatural redemption, interpreted in a supernatural revelation, and applied by the supernatural operations of His Spirit — this confession constitutes the core of the Christian profession."[19]

Not God's *works* only but also his *words*. Beginning with the first command imposed upon man in the garden (Gen. 2:16), the Old Testament is to a large degree the record of the revelations of his will made by God to man. God "spake" to Adam, to Cain, to Noah, to Abraham, to Moses. Thus in the Book of Leviticus about thirty passages begin with the words, "and the Lord spake [or "said"] unto Moses." Seventeen chapters of this book begin in the AV in this way. Hence we observe that there is in the Bible a pervasive supernaturalism. It is the book which contains the record of the *works* and *words* of God. It is not the story of man's agelong quest after and progressive discovery of God, but the record of God's revelation of himself, through instruments of his own choosing and at times and seasons of his own appointing, to a world which by its wisdom knew him not and could not find him.

In the second place we observe that the Bible is the *Book of Man,* a book written *by* man, *about* man, and *for* man. That the Bible is written by men and in human language is obvious. But it is important to observe that this fact does not make it any less the very Word of God. No one has emphasized this more strongly than Dr. Warfield. The illustration which he uses is a striking one. The truth of God, so the critics tell us, is like light passing through a stained glass window. The pure light of the sun is broken up and colored in a great variety of ways as it passes through its myriad panes. In like manner, the truth of God is colored and even distorted by passing through the minds of men and being expressed in the language of men, which means that the Bible is of necessity a very human and even a very fallible book, because the word of God comes through the minds and lips of fallible men. So runs the argument. But suppose, says Dr. Warfield, God so formed and trained and guided these fallible men as to make them just the instruments for the declaration of his truth to their fellow-men which he wished them to be. What if he designed and intended the diversities of style and diction, of temperament and training, of knowledge and experience, which we find in their writings so to blend together, as do the many colors in the stained glass window, in order to form that lovely and complete picture which in the case of the window, so beautifully exhibits the skill and artistry of the artist! The very beauty of the stained glass window should make the illustration refute the theory it is offered to prove.[20]

The faculty of speech which is the organ which expresses the intelligence of man as made in the image of God, is a wonderful and amazing instrument, as we realize when we read the words of a great writer or listen to the words that fall like pearls from the lips of a gifted orator. And if man can use this faculty so effectively, must we not believe that God can use it far better? When Moses alleged his inability to speak as an excuse for not undertaking the seemingly hopeless task proposed to him, God's word to him was, "Who hath made man's mouth? or who maketh the dumb or deaf or the seeing, or the blind? have not I the Lord? Now therefore go, and I will be with thy mouth and teach thee what thou shalt say" (Exod. 4:11-12). Before Jeremiah could fully express his sense of inadequacy for the prophetic office, the Lord said to him: "Before I formed thee in the belly I knew thee; and before thou camest forth out of the womb I sanctified thee, I ordained thee a prophet unto the nations" (Jer. 1:5).

Using a familiar analogy, we may say that the Bible is not a solo piece, it is orchestral music; and the variety which characterizes it greatly enhances its charm and its interest for us. It needs a full orchestra, a great chorus and gifted soloists to render the Hallelujah

Chorus at all adequately. The voices and instruments are different and so are the voices of the prophets of old — Isaiah and Haggai, Jeremiah and Ezekiel. But they all speak the word which the Lord gives them to speak and the harmony of their sayings is a proof of their inspiration. A man can make and control an automaton, a robot as we call it today. But only God can control a free agent. Within the sovereign control of an infinite God, the wisdom, affections, and self-determination of finite man find full room for self-expression. Like their fellow men, the prophets and other authors of our Bible were free men. They were not robots. But God so used and controlled and inspired them that what they said was in very truth the Word of the living God for sin-cursed, needy men. "Thus saith the Lord God" declared the authority of which they were conscious and with which they spoke.

Just as Jesus' perfect humanity did not destroy or defile his perfect Deity, so the human element in the Bible does not prevent it from being in a unique sense the Word of God. It is God's word to man through man: and, therefore, it is both *divine* and *human*. And all of it is God's word. Trustworthiness must be plenary, not general. Only an inspiration which includes phrases, words and letters is adequate. It is a mere commonplace to say that the change of a single letter may make a vast difference in the meaning of a word or of an entire sentence. Yet there are those who maintain that it is only the ideas of the Bible which are inspired, that the writers were allowed to express the "divine" truth as best they could in human words. The fallacy of such an argument and the disastrous results of its acceptance is illustrated by that word which figured so prominently centuries ago in the Arian controversy. Athanasius insisted that the Son is of the *same* essence (*homo-ousios*) as the Father. The Semi-Arians held that he is of *like* essence (*homoi-ousios*) — just the difference of a single letter — a diphthong for a vowel — but a difference of meaning which involves the very essence of orthodox, trinitarian Christianity.[21]

This Bible which is the Word of God spoken through men to men, not only tells us about God; it also tells us about *man*. It tells us first of all of his splendid origin, thus hinting at his glorious destiny. It tells us that man was created by God, the climax of his creative work, a being made in the image of God, made for communion with God, a being distinct from the lower animals and given dominion over them. Then, having told us of this entire creation of which man was the masterpiece, and having declared that in the sight of God it was "very good," the record proceeds to tell of the *relation* which God has established between himself and the man whom he has formed in his image. That relationship is very simply stated: "and the Lord God commanded the man saying" (Gen. 2:16). The permission to eat of the fruit of all of the trees of the garden save one, the prohibition of the eating of the fruit of the one, indicate very clearly the relationship in which man stands to God and the obligation which that relationship imposes upon him. He is to obey God's every command, to do what God requires and not to do what God forbids — unquestioning obedience!

The laying down of this basic law for man is speedily followed by the breaking of that law. The question, "Hast thou eaten of the tree whereof I commanded thee that thou shouldest not eat?" shows the nature of man's act. It was disobedience to, a challenging of God's sovereign will. It was rebellion and by this act man "fell from his high estate by sinning against God";[22] and the enormity and utter groundlessness of the act is well shown in Milton's familiar words, "For one restraint, lords of the world besides."[23] No attempt is made to describe the enormity of the sin and the greatness of the fall. This is made to appear, and only too plainly, in the tragic consequences which followed it, which may be summed up in the two words, *apostasy* and *judgment*.

Apostasy. The first consequence of disobedience was alienation from God. The evil root of disobedience developed quickly. All of man's relationships were affected: toward God, alienation and fear instead of love and joyous communion; toward his wife, fault-finding, domination, passion, instead of unselfish love; toward nature, arduous toil instead of pleasant labor, thorns and thistles instead of bounteous fruit; and finally, expulsion from the garden of Eden, which was the place of communion with God. The first-born of Adam and Eve became a murderer, a fratricide, and his line culminated in Lamech who composed a song of hate. Then, following the genealogy of the antediluvians, we read of the cause of the flood: "And God saw that the wickedness of man was great in the earth, and that every imagination of the thoughts of his heart was only evil continually" (Gen. 6:5), a terrible and terrifying picture of the depth of depravity of the state of fallen man as the result of sin: Sodom and Gomorrah, the selling of Joseph into slavery by his brethren, Aaron's golden calf, the refusal to go up and possess the land, the revolt of Dathan and Abiram, the sin of Baal-peor, the repeated apostasies of the period of the Judges, Micah's idolatry and the Danites, the sin at Gibeah, Saul's disobedience, David's great sin, Solomon's idolatry, Rehoboam's folly, the schism and Jeroboam's calves, Joash's ingratitude, Uzziah's sacrilege, Manasseh's apostasy, Jehoiakim's knifing of the prophetic word, foreign wives in the days of Ezra! These are some evidences, and there are many others, of the depravity and apostasy of man and particularly of the chosen people from the God who made man in his own image, the perversion of a creation which he had declared to be "very good." Again and again in the long course of Old Testament history it is made plain that the inevitable trend and tendency of the human heart, when left to itself, is downward. Isaiah's "Great Arraignment," as his first chapter has been fitly called, gathers up the charges of the "men of God" who preceded and is echoed by those who followed him. And the New Testament tells us that Jesus' arraignment of the Scribes and Pharisees — the great Woe-chapter of the New Testament (Matt. 23) — was speedily followed by Israel's crowning infamy, the crucifying of her Messiah.

"The heart of man is deceitful above all things and desperately wicked," declares Jeremiah (17:9); and the Psalmist tells us that "the dark places of the earth are full of the habitations of cruelty" (Ps. 74:20). The terrible confirmation these words have received in recent years is an answer to those who not so long ago confidently assured us that man had been steadily climbing the heights, that the superman would soon appear, and that a man-made millennium would shortly be realized! Never was it more plainly recorded on the page of history for the eyes of all to read, that the wages of sin is death, both moral and physical, that what we call "culture" is like the grass and flowers which grow on the sides of a slumbering volcano, which may look beautiful and suggest peace and safety but which will perish and be swept away in an instant when the slumbering giant awakes.

Judgment. In view of the importance which is attached from the very beginning to obedience to the revealed will of God and the picture which is very speedily given us of the sinfulness of man and the proneness of the human heart to disobedience, it follows as an obvious corollary, that *judgment*, exhibiting itself in *catastrophies*, will be one of the conspicuous features of Old Testament history throughout its entire course. Of this the Bible gives us many and terrible examples. Death was the penalty of disobedience (Gen. 2:17), and the first death recorded was a fratricidal murder. Almost immediately we read in Chapter 5 the mournful cadence of antediluvian history, "and he died." The flood was a judgment on the sin of man, and so severe was it that only a few were saved from the universal destruction. The exodus was a mighty deliverance of an entire nation from cruel bondage. But the entire generation which had witnessed the deliverance at the Red Sea, which had heard the voice of God at Sinai, which was fed daily with manna and drank of the water of the rock, perished — all but two, Caleb and Joshua — perished outside the land because of disobedience and unbelief. Listen to these terrible words which sum up the census taken in the plains of Moab at the end of the forty years:

But among these there was not a man of them whom Moses and Aaron the priest numbered, when they numbered the children of Israel in the wilderness of Sinai. For the Lord had said of them, They shall surely die in the wilderness. And there was not left a man of them, save Caleb the son of Jephunneh, and Joshua the son of Nun (Num. 26:64f.).

Again and again in the Book of Judges we are told how the Lord "sold" the people into the hands of their enemies. Early in the narrative we read: "And the children of Israel did evil in the sight of the Lord and served Baalim. . . . And they forsook the Lord, and served Baal and Ashtaroth" (Judg. 2:11f.). Jephthah was one of the prominent Judges of Israel. He was the kind of leader such an age might be expected to produce. He was ill-begotten and an outcast, self-taught, a leader of outlawed men. We cannot judge his conduct by the Law of Moses. We must rather estimate his ignorance of that law by his words and actions. If he offered his daughter as a sacrifice to the Lord, which is the most natural interpretation of the narrative, we must conclude that he did not know and understand the Sixth Commandment, and not that there was no Decalogue in his day. In one of the appendices, as we may call them, to that book, we read how the great tribe of Benjamin was almost exterminated because instead of punishing a shocking crime against the Law of God and against what we might call common decency, it came to the defense of the guilty. The great achievement of David's reign was the binding together of all the tribes of Israel and the healing of the wounds resulting from the sinful folly of Saul. But the idolatries of the wise king who succeeded him were followed by the Great Schism, the breaking away of the Ten Tribes and the calf worship of Jeroboam. Assyria was called by the Lord the "rod of mine anger" for destroying the Northern Kingdom and bringing the Southern Kingdom to its knees in penitence before God. But the sins of Manasseh filled up the cup of judgment; and Nebuchadnezzar made an end of the Southern Kingdom. The restoration under Cyrus, Ezra and Nehemiah did not cure the people of their sinful disobedience; and centuries later their crowning sin, the crucifying of their Messiah, was followed by the destruction of their Holy City and their dispersion among the nations.

The sinfulness of the people, their failure to keep the law, is referred to again and again in the Bible, by the prophets especially. We have referred to Isaiah's "Great Arraignment." No less striking are Jeremiah's words: "Run ye to and fro through the streets of Jerusalem, and see now, and know, and seek in the broad places thereof, if ye can find a man, if there be any that executeth judgment, that seeketh the truth; and I will pardon it" (5:1). Clearly, the religion of the Old Testament, the true religion, as given by God to Israel, was always the faith and life of a *minority*. Referring to one of the most remarkable features of Old Testament religion, prophetism, Stephen in his "great arraignment," as we may well call it, closes with this terrible indictment: "Which of the prophets have not your fathers persecuted? and they have slain them which showed before of the coming of the Just One; of whom ye have now been the betrayers and murderers: who received the law by the disposition of angels and have not kept it" (Acts 7:52f.). Such statements, and there are many of them in the Bible, expose the fallacy of the claim which is so often made that the Jews had a genius for religion, that they were the discoverers of that ethical monotheism which was their unique possession. Far otherwise, their genius as a people was for apostasy from that religion which God revealed to them and imposed upon them through his servants, Moses and the prophets.

Abnormality. A further consequence of the sinful apostasy of the people and of the resulting judgments of God upon them is what we may perhaps best describe by the word abnormality — the abnormal conditions and practices which so often interrupted and perverted what should have been the normal and harmonious life and the orderly progress of the Israelites from the time when they were made the particular objects of the Lord's favor. These abnormalities, as we shall call them, are responsible for many of the difficulties which the student encounters in his study of biblical history.

For example, when we read in the Pentateuch the elaborate account of the construction of the tabernacle, the ordaining of its priesthood, and the variety and complexity of the ritual which was to be performed in it, we are surprised that speaking generally so little is said about it in the records of the centuries which follow. Only a few of the hundreds of passover celebrations are mentioned, those of Joshua, Hezekiah, Josiah, and Zerubbabel. Yet the way in which the passover is referred to would indicate that the instructions for its annual celebration were observed, and that the pious in Israel, among whom Elkanah is a shining example, rejoiced in the keeping of the law which had been given them through Moses.

The extent to which the frequently occurring apostasies of the Israelites and the severe punishments which were visited upon them for their sins interfered with and even prevented the strict performance of the duties required by the Mosaic law, is strikingly illustrated by the history of the *ark of the covenant*. The ark was the most sacred vessel in the entire worship of Israel. Except when Israel was on the march, its place was in the Holy of Holies. It was unapproachable, except on one day of the year, the day of atonement, and then only by the high priest who was to envelop himself in a cloud of incense. On that supremely important day, it was the very center of the ritual (Lev. 16:2, 13, 14, 15).[24] A day of atonement without the ark would seem to be impossible, an anomaly. Yet we know that from the day when Hophni and Phineas carried forth the ark from Shiloh to use it as a fetish against the Philistines, the ark was never again in the tabernacle.[25] We read of its being at Ashdod and Ekron in the land of the Philistines for seven months (1 Sam. 6:1). When it returned it was first at Bethshemesh, then at Kirjath-jearim, in the house of Abinadab for twenty years (7:2). There it remained during the entire reign of Saul and until David's first ill-advised attempt to bring it to Jerusalem (2 Sam. 6:4). Then it was for three months in the house of Obed-edom the Gittite (6:11) until David succeeded in bringing it to Jerusalem and placing it in a tent on Mount Zion which he had pitched for it. As regards this anomalous situation, we are further told that "the tabernacle of the Lord which Moses made in the wilderness, and the altar of the burnt offering" were, at the time when David numbered the people, "in the high place at Gibeon" (1 Chron. 21:29), although several, perhaps many years had elapsed since the bringing up of the ark to Jerusalem. We read that Solomon went to sacrifice at Gibeon, "for that was the great high place" (1 Kings 3:4), which refers of course to the tabernacle and the altar of burnt offerings, where Zadok and his brethren officiated (1 Chron. 16:39). Consequently, at the close of the reign of David, and before the building of the temple by Solomon, there were at least two distinct places of sacrifice and worship, Jerusalem and Gibeon, the one apparently presided over by Abiathar, the other by Zadok; and at or near Jerusalem there was also the altar which David erected on Mt. Moriah. This was anomalous. It was in a sense illegal. But it was permitted apparently and even sanctioned because of the course of events. Furthermore, we know that the ark was carried away to Babylon and disappeared there. There was no ark in Zerubbabel's temple, nor in Herod's. Yet the worship of the faithful at these sanctuaries was acceptable to the Lord (cf. 2 Chron. 30:18ff.).

Such a survey of the history of the ark, as it is given to us in the Old Testament, helps us to understand the reference to the *repairing* of "the altar of the Lord" on Mount Carmel by Elijah (1 Kings 18:30) in order that he might there demonstrate to the men of the Northern Kingdom the uniqueness of Israel's God, as well as Elijah's words when the Lord spoke to him in the cave at Horeb, "For the children of Israel have forsaken thy covenant, thrown down thine altars, and slain thy prophets with the sword" (19:10). They have been interpreted as meaning that the idea of a central sanctuary for all Israel was unknown as yet. But Elijah's acts and words are readily understandable when we think of the situation which had developed in the Northern Kingdom through the setting up of the idolatrous worship of the golden calves and the attempts of Jezebel to force the worship of the Tyrian

Baal upon the people. It may well be that the "altars" referred to were places of worship which had been used centuries before by the Patriarchs, and were consequently naturally resorted to during this time of apostasy when worship at the temple at Jerusalem was all but impossible.[26]

Redemption. The picture of the apostasies of Israel and the divine judgments which followed and played such havoc with the ordered life of God's people is a sad and tragic one. Yet it is one which must neither be minimized nor ignored if we are to obtain a true under-standing of the course of Israel's history. But the Bible does not con-fine itself to telling us of the splendid origin of man and of his tragic fall from his original righteousness into an estate of sin and misery, and of the terrible punishments which a righteous God visited on his sins. Were such the case, it would be the most pessimistic book in the world. Far otherwise, the Bible is the book of *hope* for man, the book which tells of God's way of salvation for man. It is the book of the promises. Even before man is driven from the presence of God in the garden, the promise of redemption, of ultimate victory is made to him. For in the Protevangel (Gen. 3:15) as it is called, the victory of the seed of the woman over the enemy of souls is foretold in cryptic terms; and the meaning of this promise is made clearer and clearer as the story of redemption unfolds.

Covenant. The relation in which man stands to his Creator is, as we have seen, made clear at the very beginning. It is expressed in terms of obedience to a Divine command (Gen. 2:16; 3:11, 17, cf. 6:22). Since death and misery are threatened and imposed as the penalty of disobedience, it is obvious that life and blessedness are promised as the reward of obedience. Consequently, this relationship is called "the covenant of works." The word covenant is used first of the promise to Noah. It is comprehensive, embracing "all flesh," and it concerns the stability of the natural order under which man is to live (Gen. 9:8-17). The next covenant is with Abraham (Gen. 17) and it concerns his seed, the land, and the nations. This covenant was confirmed to Abra-ham's seed at Mt. Sinai (Exod. 19) and was the basis of all God's future dealings with Israel. It was in fulfilment of this covenant that Israel came into possession of the land of Canaan, and was to enjoy its possession on condition of obedience. A special application of the covenant is the Davidic-Messianic kingship (2 Sam. 7; Ps. 89:3f.). This is called "an everlasting covenant, the sure mercies of David" (Isa. 55:3), and is fulfilled in great David's Greater Son; it is the new and everlasting covenant foretold by Jeremiah (31:31-34).

In this redemption, the element of selection and exclusion is very prominent. The line of Cain is traced for six generations and dis-

missed. Of the Sethites, only Noah and his family are saved from the waters of the flood. Of the sons of Noah, Japheth and Ham and their descendants are mentioned and dismissed. Then the line of Shem is traced to Terah and his three sons. Abram is then called to *separate* himself from his kindred and from his father's house; and for centuries the hope of humanity is centered in the seed of Abraham. The faith of Abraham is tried and tested in respect of three things: the promise of the seed, of the land, and of blessing for the nations.

During the entire Old Testament period the promise of the "seed" and of the "land" are conspicuous. The Israelites are the "seed of Abraham." They are a chosen covenant people, claimed as peculiarly his own by Jehovah, by virtue of the promise to Abram and the deliverance from Egypt. They are in a peculiar sense "the people" of God. Their land is the land promised to Abraham. Its peaceful possession is a token of Jehovah's favor. Bondage in it and expulsion from it are the consequence of his displeasure, the punishment for their sins of disobedience to his law.

Separation and Distinctiveness. A necessary result of the apostasy of mankind is the separation between the good and the evil, or, to state it more precisely, the sundering of good from evil. This appears in the deluge, the saving of a righteous remnant from the destroying waters of the Flood. It appears next in the call of Abram to separate himself from his environment, clearly a pagan one, and to go forth into an unknown and strange land. It shows itself in the call of Israel to be a "peculiar treasure," "a kingdom of priests and a holy nation" on the condition that they *obey* God's voice and keep his covenant (Exod. 19:5f.). And the solemn responsibility resulting from that unique status is pointed out again and again; by no one more emphatically than by Amos: "You only have I known of all the families of the earth: therefore I will punish you for all your iniquities" (3:2).

This separation from the nations of the earth was not only designed to keep them from the moral corruption of these nations, but even more to preserve in Israel those true forms of faith and worship which were revealed by God to Israel as the divine pattern for a people of his own choosing. This is made clear in many ways. We read that Moses twice spent forty days in the Mount alone with God (Exod. 24:18; 34:28; Deut. 9:9, 11, 18, 25; 10:10); and there he received the command "See that thou make everything according to the pattern showed thee in the mount" (Exod. 25:9, 40; 26:30; Acts 7:44; Heb. 8:5). It is quite proper for us to recognize and stress the special providence by which Moses became "learned in all the wisdom of the Egyptians" (Acts 7:22). But it is the heavenly origin of the pattern which is stressed again and again (Exod. 31:1-11; 35:30-35; 36:1f.; 37:1; 38:22). And what is said regarding the tabernacle is equally true of the cultus as a whole. As we read that the tabernacle was constructed and erected "as the Lord commanded Moses" (this phrase occurs fifteen times in Exodus 39-40), so the laws of Moses are constantly introduced by such words as "and the Lord spake unto Moses, saying." Consequently, Moses might well ask, "What nation is there so great that hath statutes and judgments so righteous as all this law, which I set before you this day?" (Deut. 4:8). Both in their source and in their nature the institutions and laws of Israel were essentially distinctive and unique (Ps. 147:19f.), despite the fact that in many ways they resembled the customs and practices of other nations. It is quite correct to say that this revelation was not given in a vacuum. It was given to a people which had had contacts, immediately or historically, with the great nations of antiquity, Egypt and Babylon. Much of the culture of these peoples had undoubtedly influenced them in many ways. But the call of Abram and of his seed was to separation and uniqueness.

In this connection we note two further and somewhat similar characteristics of the biblical revelation.

(1) *The Channel of Revelation a Narrow One.* As the story of redemption lies before us in the Old Testament it is in large measure the story of a few conspicuous men, of God's dealings with them, and of his use of them as leaders and teachers of his people. The second quarter of the Book of Genesis is the life story of Abraham; and the second half of the book deals chiefly with Jacob and Joseph. In the other four books of the Pentateuch, Moses is the pre-eminent figure. Joshua is the leader in conquering the Land. Samuel is the king-maker. David and Solomon tower above all the other kings of Israel. Isaiah, Jeremiah and Ezekiel are conspicuous among the prophets. In fact if we add together those portions of the Old Testament which deal with the careers or consist of the writings of or concerning seven men, Abraham, Moses, David, Solomon, Isaiah, Jeremiah and Ezekiel, we find that we have included about half of the Old Testament. There are very many other individuals named in it; and some of them are more or less conspicuous. But it still remains true that Old Testament history and religion is largely set forth in terms of the biographies, the words and deeds, of a few men who were signally used of God in shaping the course of his dealings with his chosen people. This is a feature which is important when we come to deal with critical questions, especially with the claim that anonymity is characteristic of the Old Testament, and that its books are made up of a multitude of anonymous documents and sources. On the contrary the claim that has been made by secular historians that the history of a nation is the history of its great men is particularly true of Israel.

(2) *Selective and Episodal.* The history which the Bible gives us is of necessity both *selective* and *episodal.* A quarter of Genesis (12:1 – 25:10) is concerned, as we have seen, with Abraham, a considerable portion of the entire book! But when we observe that the story of his life, from his arrival in Canaan to his death, is spread over a period of one hundred years, it is quite obvious that only a few important events and episodes are recorded. This fact seems to be stressed by the dates which are given from time to time in the brief account. Long periods of Abraham's life are passed over in silence.

Of many of the obviously important and influential figures in biblical history we know very little, only a single incident in what may have been a long and an eventful life. Yet these brief episodes, as we might call them, are most revealing. For example, Abigail the wife of David is known to us only through a single incident (1 Sam. 25); we might almost call it an anecdote. Yet it is one of the most beautiful and suggestive of the insights into the personal life of David and his household given to us in Scripture; and it is told with consummate skill.

THE GREAT FIGURES IN OLD TESTAMENT HISTORY
Abraham

The first of the conspicuous figures in the Old Testament is Abraham. Like many other figures he appears rather suddenly. The long list of the descendants of Shem may be regarded as simply the ancestry of Abraham. It is with the call of Abram that Old Testament history, in its narrower sense, as the history of the chosen people, begins. By obeying the call of God to separate himself, he became the heir of the promise, and the unfolding of the promise is the great theme of the Old Testament. The importance of Abraham is shown by the number of times (more than sixty) that his name appears in the New Testament. It is his obedience which secures for his descendants, for all who are of the faith of Abraham, the fulfillment of the promises. It is his obedient faith, in contrast to the disobedience and unbelief of so many of his descendants, which is celebrated in the New Testament. That the call of Abraham was a definite preparation for the giving of the law is made plain by such a passage as Genesis 18:19, "For I have known him, to the end that he may command his children and his household after him, that they may keep the way of Jehovah to do righteousness and justice" (ARV); and while the law is never called the law of Abraham, the word "law" appears already in 26:5 where we read that the blessing promised to Abraham will be fulfilled to his descendants "because that Abraham obeyed my voice, and kept my charge, my commandments, my statutes, and my laws." It was to his "children" that the Lord fulfilled his promises by making known his Law at Sinai and establishing his Covenant with them, a covenant relationship which is referred to frequently in the Old Testament and even more frequently in the New. The call of Abraham and his obedience to that call and the blessings which followed are of prime importance in the history of Israel.

Moses

Moses is the second of the great figures in the Old Testament. He was the deliverer of his people from the bondage of Egypt. He was their leader during the forty years of Wandering. At Sinai he became their lawgiver. The Decalogue, spoken by the voice of God himself (Exod. 20:1, 19; Deut. 4:12, 33; 18:16), was recorded on two tables which were entrusted to Moses. It is the summary of the moral law and the basic law for Israel. The Book of the Covenant (Exod. 21:1 — 23:19) and all the statutes and ordinances of the law are designed to make it clear that God's law and his demands apply to the whole of life, that "the soul that sinneth it shall die" and that "without the shedding of blood there is no remission." According to the Pentateuchal record this great body of laws was given through Moses, and later generations have so regarded it. "The law was given by Moses" (John 1:17). Moses as the lawgiver is referred to frequently in the Old Testament, especially in the Historical Books, and almost as often in the New Testament.

When we speak of Moses as the lawgiver, it is well to remember that Moses exercised the office of judge before the giving of the Law at Sinai. We first read of his judging the people at Rephidim after the defeat of Amalek (Exod. 18:13); it is noteworthy that it was at Jethro's suggestion that he delegated much of this task to "able men out of all Israel" and organized them as "heads over the people, rulers of thousands, rulers of hundreds, rulers of fifties, and rulers of tens" reserving for himself the supreme authority (vs. 25f.). That the seventy (24:1) were to perform judicial functions is indicated by Numbers 11:16f. The fact that in New Testament times the Council (Sanhedrin) numbered seventy, indicates it to be patterned after, even if it was not the legitimate successor of the Seventy first appointed by Moses.[27] In ancient times the superhuman authority vested in the judge was very real and generally recognized. God is referred to by Abraham as "the Judge of all the earth" (Gen. 18:25); and the divine authority conferred on judges is strikingly indicated by the fact that they are even called "gods" (Exod. 21:6; Ps. 82:6; John 10:34f.). Hence the sanctity of the judicial oath taken in the name of God.[28] The importance of the judgeship in Israel is further illustrated, and impressively, by the fact that in the long interval between Joshua and Saul, Israel was governed or as it is called "judged" by a succession of Judges. It was only when the divinely raised up judges proved unable to judge justly and acceptably to God or to Israel that the kingship was introduced.

The most important office which Moses instituted was the priesthood (Lev. 8). The priestly laws are nearly all given through Moses.[29] The close connection between the law and the ritual of sacrifice which forms a part of the law is shown by the fact that the commandment regarding the building of the altar follows immediately on the pronouncing of the Ten Commandments (Exod. 20:24-26). For with the law came the knowledge of sin and of the need for its expiation (Rom. 3:20). But sacrifice goes back, of course, to the very beginning. Abel brought of the firstlings of his flock, Noah offered sacrifices on leaving the ark. The Patriarchs built altars in the land of Canaan. Several kinds of sacrifices are mentioned. It was probably to the place of sacrifice that Rebekah went to inquire of the Lord (Gen. 25:22). But before Sinai very little is said as to the meaning of sacrifice.[30] The Covenant at Sinai was ratified by sacrifice and the sprinkling of blood (Exod. 24:8). The Book of Exodus concludes with the erection and dedication of the tabernacle. Leviticus begins with a lengthy section (chaps. 1-7) dealing with the sacrifices which are to be offered there. Then it proceeds at once to the induction of Aaron and his sons to the priestly office. The "seven days" (8:35) and the "eighth day" (9:1) are obviously dated from "the first day of the first month" when the tabernacle was set up. The induction of Aaron and his sons took place as soon after the erection of the tabernacle as was possible (Exod. 29:35-37, cf. vs. 30). In all of this Moses was the agent and representative of God. A distinguishing mark of Jeroboam's apostasy was his opening up the ‛priesthood to all who applied (1 Kings 12:31; 13:33; 2 Chron. 13:9). Prominent among the priests were Aaron, Eleazar, Phineas, Eli, Abiathar, Zadok, Jehoiada, Jeshua and Ezra.

An important part of the priests' duties was instruction. They were to teach the people the Law of God (Lev. 10:11; Deut. 33:8-11; 2 Kings 12:2). They were to read the Law to Israel once every seven years at the feast of tabernacles (Deut. 31:10-13). They were also to act as judges (Deut. 17:8-13). Their failure to instruct the people in the law was largely responsible for the ignorance and disobedience which so frequently manifested itself in Israel. What is stated in 2 Chronicles 15:3 about the people being for a long season "without the true God and without a teaching priest and without law" (cf. Micah 3:11) was probably tragically true of much of Israel's history, despite the efforts of certain reforming kings and of the prophets (2 Chron. 17:7-9).

The unique position occupied by Moses is further indicated by the fact that he provided for and himself typified in a unique degree two other institutions which were to become of great importance in the history of Israel: *prophecy* (Deut. 18:9-22) and the *kingship* (Deut. 17:14-20). As a *prophet* Moses enjoyed a "mouth to mouth," "face to face," relationship with God (Num. 12:8; Deut. 34:10), which set him apart from all other mortal men and made him in a unique sense the type of Him who was to come (Deut. 18:18; John 1:21, 26).

The *kingship* foretold by Moses was not instituted until the time of Samuel. But even if the words, "and he was king in Jeshurun" (Deut. 33:5) do not refer to Moses but to God, as Numbers 23:21; Judges 8:23; 1 Samuel 8:7; 10:19, seem to indicate, it is clear that Moses exercised all the prerogatives of a king. He was the supreme ruler of Israel under God.[31]

Moses had no successor. This is shown by the fact that Joshua who followed him as leader and whose task it was to lead the people in the conquest of the land of promise was commanded to observe to do according to all that was written in the Law of Moses (Josh. 1:8) and also to inquire of the priest through "the judgment of the Urim" the will of the Lord for Israel (Num. 27:20f.). The uniqueness of Moses is further illustrated by the closing injunction to Israel of the last of the prophets: "Remember ye the law of Moses my servant, which I commanded unto him in Horeb, *with* the statutes and judgments" (Mal. 4:4).

"Faithful in all my house" (Num. 12:7) are the words with which the Lord describes the extent of the authority vested in Moses and his fidelity in exercising it. The final judge (Exod. 18:26), the unique prophet (Deut. 18:15), the priest who instituted the priesthood (Lev. 8), the ruler who was king in all but name — in Hebrews 3:5 we find these words echoed, "faithful in all his house," where it is pointed out that while Moses was faithful as a servant, his fidelity was only a type of the faithfulness of Christ as "a son over his own house."

The *kingship* was not instituted until the time of Samuel. The demand made of him by the people for the establishing of the kingship was lawful. But the reason given by the people, "we will have a king over us, that we also may be like all the nations" (1 Sam. 8:5, 20), showed how sadly the people, since the days of Moses, had failed to realize and to enjoy the blessings of the theocratic rule of their God (Num. 23:21; Deut. 33:5), how little they valued the honor and privilege of having "the Lord rule over them," as Gideon, that rugged old theocrat expressed it (Judg. 8:23). It also showed how far short the

Judges had fallen of being true representatives of the Lord (Judg. 18:1; 21:25). So the people were allowed to have their way. They were given a king and they were made to suffer under their kings as Samuel said they would (1 Sam. 8:10-18).

David

The first king of Israel by divine initiative was David (1 Sam. 16:1, 13).[32] With him begins that theocratic kingship which is to endure "for ever" (2 Sam. 7:13, 16, 25, 26, 29). It is a kingship, which shows both the good and evil in the heart of rulers and the potent consequences for good and evil which follow from a *human* rule. Only *four* kings in Judah are commended for their goodness, for following in the footsteps of David; and nearly all of the rulers of the schismatic Northern Kingdom are specifically condemned for sharing in the sin of Jeroboam the son of Nebat.[33] But the kingship points forward to that perfect rule which Isaiah describes as "the sure mercies of David" (55:3), to the king whom Hosea (3:5) and Ezekiel (34:23-25) speak of as David.

With David we have the beginning of *Psalmody*. This does not mean that poetry, both sacred and secular, was unknown before the time of David. Moses' triumph ode after the destruction of Pharaoh's host in the Red Sea, his Song, his Blessing, and his Prayer, and Deborah's paean over the victory at the Kishon are sufficient proof that psalmody did not originate with David. Yet about half of the Psalms are assigned by the titles to him;[34] and Chronicles is particularly concerned to make it clear that the appointing of singers was an important part of the preparation which David made for the worship of the temple which he was not permitted to build. This is partly accounted for by the singular gift of song with which the Lord endowed David.[35] He was pre-eminently, "the sweet psalmist of Israel" (2 Sam. 23:1). But why this service of song was not made a part of the tabernacle worship as instituted and arranged by Moses we are not told; and any speculation regarding it would be both idle and fruitless.

Solomon

In the reign of Solomon we have, despite the fact that its close was marred by apostasy and an oppression which sowed the seeds of rebellion and schism, the type of the great and prosperous ruler, both wise and just. His greatest act was the building of the temple. His wealth became proverbial. But it is especially his God-given wisdom (1 Kings 3:5-14) for which Solomon was famous. Consequently we find that the *Wisdom Literature* of the Old Testament is associated with his name. As the name David personifies Poetry, so the name Solomon stands for Wisdom.[36] Proverbs is largely his; and we not only read of his wisdom but also that "he spake three thousand proverbs and his songs were a thousand and five" (1 Kings 4:32). Since the Book of Proverbs has only 915 verses, it can contain only part of the wise sayings of this monarch, even if we include Ecclesiastes. And a still smaller portion of his songs is represented by the Song of Songs and the few psalms (Ps. 72, 127) which are probably to be attributed to him. The date of Job is problematical. It has been assigned to various periods and numerous authors. The age of Solomon would seem an appropriate one for its production. But that is all that can be said. It may be earlier or later.

There were other devout kings beside David and Solomon. Asa, Jehoshaphat, Hezekiah and Josiah, are the best. But none of them contributed as did David and Solomon to the corpus of Sacred Scripture.

The Prophets

A conspicuous and distinctive feature of the religion of Israel, which, as we have seen, became prominent about the time of and, it would seem, in preparation for the establishment of the monarchy, was *Prophetism*. Not that prophecy was new and strange in Israel. Abraham is called a prophet (Gen. 20:7) and justly. For he was a man of God and had communion with the Most High, and received promises from God which are still marching on to complete fulfillment. Moses, when he speaks of the prophet who is to come, describes him as "like unto me" (Deut. 18:15), and the obituary appended to the Book of Deuteronomy declares that "There hath not arisen a prophet since in Israel like unto Moses whom the Lord knew face to face." Jeremiah is very emphatic in tracing prophecy back to the time of the Exodus (7:25). Yet it is true that this great movement may be broadly described in the phrase, "Samuel and the prophets." For it was in connection with the kingship that the prophets appeared most prominently. They were in a special sense the counsellors of the kings.

In the case of the prophets, there are relatively few conspicuous figures. Samuel, Elijah and Elisha are the most prominent non-literary prophets. But the fact that it was Elijah who appeared with Moses on the Mount of Transfiguration seems to indicate that he was pre-eminently the man of God, the embodiment of the spirit of prophecy. Among the literary prophets, Isaiah, Jeremiah and Ezekiel, have left us the fullest record, about one-fourth of the Old Testament being devoted to the writings of these three men; and we have briefer records from the Twelve and from Daniel. Yet it is significant that in the case of most of them we know little or nothing about them as individuals. They are "men of God." They are "voices."

In dealing even briefly with the subject of Prophecy[37] there are several matters which need attention. First, the *magnitude* of this movement. When we observe that less than forty prophets are mentioned by name in the entire Old Testament, and nearly half of them rather briefly, we might be tempted to think of prophecy as a rare and occasional phenomenon in Israel.[38] But such was by no means the case. The reason for the importance of the office of prophet given in Deuteronomy 18 is that he is to take the place in Israel of those crude and evil practices — divination, incantation, exorcism, witchcraft — by means of which the heathen endeavored to ascertain the future; and since that desire was an ever present one, the office of the prophet was important in every age, not merely to the nation as a whole in times of crisis, but to all classes of the people and in all the experiences of their lives. There are clear indications that the prophets constituted a numerous body. We read of companies of the "sons of the prophets" in the days of Samuel (I Sam. 10:5; 19:20) and also that in the time of Elijah, Obadiah hid a hundred of them from the fury of Jezebel (1 Kings 18:4, 13).[39] The terrible judgments visited on Israel and on Judah for their sins did not come without ample and repeated warning: "Yet the Lord testified against Israel, and against Judah, by all the prophets, and by all the seers, saying, Turn ye from your evil ways, and keep my commandments and my statutes, according to all the law which I commanded your fathers, and which I sent unto you by my servants the prophets" (2 Kings 17:13). How frequently and earnestly the Lord warned and admonished his people is indicated by the picturesque phrase which appears a dozen times in Jeremiah, "daily rising up early and sending" (e.g., 7:25).

The *divine authority* with which the prophets spoke is very striking. Some of them are not even identified by name. Most of those whose names are given are introduced very briefly: Elijah the Tishbite, who was of the sojourners of Gilead, Elisha the son of Shaphat, Micah the Morashtite, Isaiah the son of Amoz, Joel the son of Pethuel. Their authority was, "Thus saith the Lord God" (cf. Ezek. 2:4). They were "voices" as John the Baptist described himself (Matt. 3:3) appealing to Isaiah 40:3; and the voice of God carried its own authority, and should have needed no proof of its heavenly origin.

Four words are used with varying frequency to designate and describe the prophet: (1) "man of God" (used about 75 times) describes his status and authority; we may call it the honor title of the prophets; the other three indicate the manner in which he received his message: (2) "seer" (*roeh*, 12 times), using the participle of the usual Hebrew word "to see," which occurs 1315 times in the Old Testament and suggests a manifestation as clear as sight; (3) "seer" (*chozeh*, 16 times), from a comparatively rare verb, also meaning "to see," but chiefly used in poetry; (4) "prophet" (*nabi,* 306 times) from a root the exact meaning of which is uncertain, but such passages as Deuteronomy 18:18b and Exodus 7:1 make it plain that a *nabi* is a spokesman for God.[40]

Nevertheless, because of the hardness of men's hearts, the prophets were accredited to the people as men of God both by the signs and wonders which they performed and by the fulfillment of prophecies which they uttered concerning the immediate future. Moses was given certain accrediting signs (Exod. 4:1-9); and the deliverance from the bondage of Egypt which had been the tremendous challenge of his personal faith and obedience (Exod. 3:12) was the incontestable proof that God had sent him (14:31). Elijah's prophecy of the drought (1 Kings 17:1), Elisha's prediction of the raising of the siege of Samaria (2 Kings 7:1-3), Isaiah's prophecy that Sennacherib would not succeed in capturing Jerusalem (37:33-35), Jeremiah's prediction of its capture by Nebuchadnezzar (21:10; 26:6, 9; 32:3; 38:3), proved to the men of their respective generations the divine authority with which these men spoke and supplied the test of fulfillment required by Deuteronomy 18:22.[41] Then, when the prophet had been fully accredited in these two ways, it was only to be expected that his utterances regarding events lying in the distant future should be believed by his own generation and recorded that they might be a witness to the generations following.[42]

The divine origin and the compulsive power of the message is shown by the attitude of the prophet toward the divine word which came to him (Isa. 8:11; Jer. 6-11; 20:9). It appears very clearly in the utterances of the unwilling prophet Balaam (Num. 22:20, 35, 38; 23:12, 26). Ezekiel stresses it by his use of the words "the hand of the Lord was upon me" (1:3; 3:14, 22; 8:1; 33:22; 37:1) as describing this divine compulsion. Especially noteworthy are the passages which describe the divine call of the prophets which is given such graphic expression in Isaiah 6:5-13; Jeremiah 1:7-10; Ezekiel 2:1 – 3:11. Clearly the phrase, "Thus saith the Lord" was not empty rhetoric; it was literal fact. The account of the rejection of Saul in 1 Samuel 15 is instructive in this connection. The divine revelation and the command as to its execution both angered and grieved Samuel (vs. 10f.). He "cried unto the Lord all night." But he executed the commission which the Lord gave him without hesitation and thoroughly.[43]

2 Samuel 7 is an especially striking example. The event described here is one of the greatest events in Israel's history: David's desire to build a house for the Lord, which is made the occasion and basis for the great Messianic promise regarding David's house. It is highly sig-

nificant that Nathan's brief statement of approval of David's plan is not introduced by any prophetic phrase or formula. We read simply that "Nathan said to the king, Go, do all that is in thine heart; for the Lord is with thee." Nathan here speaks as a man and a courtier. Then we are told "And it came to pass that night, that the word of the Lord came unto Nathan saying, Go and tell my servant David, Thus saith the Lord"; and the message which Nathan is to deliver is a reversal of his own words of approval. This is a most significant passage. It is amazing that the Lord introduces a wonderful promise to David by first discrediting, as it seems, the very messenger through whom he gives it. It must have been humiliating to Nathan to be obliged to confess to David that his words of approval of David's project were only his own personal opinion, that he had not spoken as a man of God but as a mere man.[44]

The prophets were primarily *preachers of righteousness.* Their great task was to exhort and persuade the people to keep the law, and to warn them of the certain punishment which must follow their failure to do this. Of the intrepid courage and superhuman authority with which the prophets spoke and of the mighty influence which they exerted we have a number of striking examples. An unnamed "man of God" rebuked the high priest Eli for his failure to discipline his wicked sons and foretold the downfall of his house (1 Sam. 2:27-36). Samuel declared to Saul that God had rejected him (1 Sam. 15). Nathan rebuked David for his great sin with the terrible words, "Thou art the man" (2 Sam. 12:7); and after the birth of Solomon, Nathan pronounced the blessing of the Lord upon him (2 Sam. 12:25). Ahijah might be called the king-maker. He played a somewhat similar role to that of Samuel. Yet the incident of the new mantle (1 Kings 11:29-39) and the prediction of the death of Jeroboam's son Abijah (14:1-18: cf. 15:29) are all that we are told about him. Jehu the son of Hanani we know only for his prediction of the death of Baasha (1 Kings 16:1-4, 7) and his reproof of Jehoshaphat (2 Chron. 19:2) of whom he became the biographer (20:34); Micaiah the son of Imlah only for his prophecy of Ahab's defeat and death (1 Kings 22:8-28). Huldah appears only because she was consulted regarding the significance of the finding of the book of the law in the days of Josiah (2 Kings 22:14). Haggai's brief series of prophecies cover only seven months. Of the prophet Joel we know only his name and that his father's name was Pethuel, of Amos only that he was among the herdsmen of Tekoah. Only in the case of one prophet, Zephaniah, are we given an extended family tree. Yet the little which is told suffices to indicate to us the powerful influence which these servants of the Lord, some of whose names are not even recorded, exerted upon the men and events of their day, not only in special crises but even during long periods of time. Shemaiah prevented a fratricidal war between Rehoboam and Jeroboam (1 Kings 12:22-24) and preached repentance when Shishak came up against Jerusalem (2 Chron. 12:5-8). Azariah called to repentance in the days of Asa (2 Chron. 15); and king and people hearkened. Elisha prevented the slaughter of the Syrians who were stricken with blindness (2 Kings 6:21-23); Jahaziel promised Jehoshaphat victory over Moab and Ammon (2 Chron. 20:14f.); Eliezer, son of Dodavah, foretold misfortune to the same monarch (vs. 37).

While most of these prophets are mentioned only once or twice and only in connection with some important event, it seems quite clear that the incidents recorded are merely a few of many examples which might have been mentioned; and it is not to be supposed that it was solely to the events recorded in Scripture that the prophets owed their reputation as men of God. We have noted that Nathan, the prophet, forbade David to build the temple (2 Sam. 7), that he rebuked him for his sin with Bathsheba (chap. 12), that he blessed the infant, Solomon. We read elsewhere that he secured the succession for Solomon (1 Kings 1), that he wrote a history of the reigns of David and Solomon (1 Chron. 29:29; 2 Chron. 9:29), and that he was partly responsible for the service of song which David ordained for the temple worship (2 Chron. 29:25). These items suggest to us the influence which Nathan exerted during a period of at least twenty years, as counselor of David and Solomon his son. And what is true of Nathan, could probably be said of many others, whose voices are heard in Scripture only once or twice, if at all, but who speak with an authority which causes even kings to tremble.

The role which the prophets played as counselors of kings was a spectacular one. But it is to be noted that they also figured prominently in the life of the common people. Saul's appeal to Samuel to enable him to find his father's asses (1 Sam. 9:6-10) is significant. It shows that a seer or prophet of the Lord was regarded as one who might properly be called upon by the people for help in solving the problems and difficulties of their daily life. Elijah's fiery denunciation of the judicial murder of Naboth (I Kings 21), and Elisha's supplying the need of the widow by the miraculous supply of oil (2 Kings 4:1-7) may be regarded as conspicuous examples of what may have been a relatively frequent occurrence. The zeal of the prophets for social justice meets us again and again in the utterances of the writing prophets: e.g., in the terrible denunciation of Israel by Amos (2:6-8), in the woes pronounced by Isaiah (1:17), by Micah (2:1-6), by Jeremiah (22:3), by Zechariah (7:9f.). In this the prophets were only demanding that the people carry out the letter and the spirit of the Law of Moses (e.g.,

Deut. 15:7-11; Lev. 19:9f.). For justice and mercy was the ideal set before the people of God and before the righteous king as the type of the Messianic king (Ps. 72; Isa. 61:1-3).

When Elisha paid the widow's debt and caused the borrowed axe-head to float he was just as much a type of him who in his ministry of mercy and healing fulfilled the mission of the Divine Servant set forth in Isaiah 61:1-3, as Elijah was when he defied the priests of Baal at Carmel. The God of the Bible is not only the God who puts down the mighty from their seats, but also the One who exalts them of low degree (Luke 1:52); and Elijah and Elisha as "men of God" both exhibited, though in varying degrees, the power and the compassion of One who cares for the widow and orphan and feeds the young ravens when they cry. The God of Elisha was the friend and protector of the widow, as the Law of Moses required, and so was Elijah (cf. 1 Kings 17:17-24 with 2 Kings 4:18-37). The assertion that the Elijah narratives "stand on a distinctly higher level than the Elisha narratives" and that the latter are "almost puerile"[45] in comparison is an expression of opinion which shows how prejudice against the supernatural can bias the critic and prevent him from understanding the nature and scope, the real character of that redemptive supernaturalism which is the pervasive feature of the Bible.

It is to be remembered that this ministry to the people of their own day was one which the prophets shared with the priests and Levites. It was, as we have seen, the task of the priests to instruct the people in the law as well as to make atonement for their sins (Deut. 33:10, cf. 31:9-13). Their failure to do this was largely responsible for the ignorant and apostate condition into which the people so readily and frequently lapsed (2 Chron. 15:1-4). There was, of course, also the failure of parental instruction (Deut. 6:1-9). The "eye-witness" generation failed to impress upon those who rose up after it "all the great works of the Lord" in the great days of the Exodus and the Conquest; and they lapsed into ignorance and sin (Judg. 2:6-13). So the prophets were the living voices which again and again reminded and exhorted the people: "Remember ye the law of Moses my servant, which I commanded unto him in Horeb for all Israel, with the statutes and judgments" (Mal. 4:4).

We are often told today that a great achievement of modern scholars has been the discovery that the Prophets were men of flesh and blood, men who took a vital interest in the people of their own time and spoke to them about events and matters which were of immediate interest and concern to them. If the critics have made the discovery that the prophets were the great preachers, teachers, spiritual leaders of the people among whom they lived, the reason for it lies in the simple fact that this is made so unmistakably plain in the Scriptures themselves. If the prophets had been mere visionaries, idealists, men who had visions of things in the clouds but who were blind to what was going on about them — men who, like the caricature of the true minister, were "invisible for six days of the week and incomprehensible on the seventh" — they would never have aroused the bitter hatred of the enemies of God as they did. But their mission was very different. They were men whose message to the people of their days was like the final message of Moses to the nation which he had brought out of Egypt: "See, I set before thee this day life and good, and death and evil . . . therefore choose life that both thou and thy seed may live" (Deut. 30:19); and they declared that message with the same passionate earnestness which was vibrant in Moses' words. This is both very true and very important, and should neither be minimized nor forgotten.

Very significant is the *mistreatment* of the prophets by the people and their leaders. The stoning of Zechariah, the son of Jehoiada, is a signal example of this (2 Chron. 24:21); Asa's imprisoning of Hanani (2 Chron. 16:10), and Ahab's similar treatment of Micaiah the son of Imlah (1 Kings 22:26f.), may have had many parallels, the most familiar being the mistreatment of Jeremiah and the threats upon his life (26:8; 38:6f.).[46] In the New Testament we have the testimony of the Lord himself, "O Jerusalem, Jerusalem, that killest the prophets and stonest them which are sent unto thee" (Matt. 23:34-39), and of the first Christian martyr who asked the fearfully revealing question, "Which of the prophets have not your fathers persecuted?" (Acts 7:5lf.). This proves conclusively that true prophecy was not a natural and spontaneous development in Israel, the expression of her religious life, her quests after God. It was God's word to an often disobedient and rebellious people who resented his messages and mistreated the messengers.

Hardly less significant is the prominence of *false* prophecy in the history of Israel. That there would be false prophecy is pointed out very plainly in Deuteronomy 13:1-5 and 18:20. This is especially evident in the writings of Jeremiah. The ministry of this prophet was a constant battle with the false prophets — both those who professed to be prophets of the Lord and those who did not — the men who prophesied "the deceit of their own hearts" (Jer. 23:26), who "healed the hurt of the daughter of my people slightly, saying, Peace, peace; when there is no peace" (Jer. 6:14, 8:11; Micah 3:5), who declared that the city of Jerusalem was impregnable, who defied Nebuchadnezzar and the hosts of hated Babylon. No wonder Jeremiah had a fearful struggle with such seeming patriots. He mentions four of them by name: Hananiah, Ahab, Zedekiah, and Shemaiah. But this was probably the experience of all the prophets. Elijah in his memorable encounter with the prophets of Baal on Mt. Carmel is the most thrilling example. Isaiah in foretelling the deliverance of Jerusalem from Sennacherib had advocated a popular cause. But he had had to warn the people against pagan practices (8:19); and in chapters 40-48 his great polemic is against the gods of the heathen who can neither foretell nor perform, who are impotent to save. It is of course only to be expected that in the case of a people which was noted for its apostasies (Jer. 2:13), this opposition to their God should manifest itself most markedly in the treatment which they gave to his representatives, to the "men of God" who rebuked them for their disobedience, warned them of the inevitable consequences of their sin, and called them to repentance.

The Prophets and the Nations. In stressing as we have done and are entitled to do the particularism of the Covenant, its primary application to Israel as the chosen people, we must bear in mind, what Israel often failed to do, that the very covenant which is made so definitely with Abram and his seed is also universal in its scope: "in thy seed shall all the nations of the earth be blessed" (Gen. 22:18; cf. 18:18; 26:4). While the emphasis in the Old Testament is on Israel as God's chosen people, it is made clear again and again by prophet and psalmist that the hope of Israel is the hope of the world because the God of Israel is the Creator and Ruler of the whole earth.

The world-embracing character of the religion of which Israel is at first the sole beneficiary is made clear in many ways. It is most strikingly illustrated by the fact that Abram received the blessing of Melchizedek, king of Salem, who is described as "priest of God Most High" (*El Elyon*); and the writer of the Epistle to the Hebrews reminds us that "without all contradiction the less is blessed of the better" (7:7). That in Canaan, the land of his separation, Abram should encounter a servant and priest of the one true God is most significant; also when Abraham sends his servant to distant Mesopotamia to secure a wife for Isaac from his own kindred, he causes his servant to swear by "the Lord, the God of heaven and the God of the earth" (Gen. 24:3). The deliverance from Egypt is a conflict between the God of Israel and Pharaoh (Exod. 5:1-3) who is in a sense a puppet king and who refused to recognize the authority of the God of Israel (9:16) over the Egyptians (10:2)[47] and over the gods of Egypt (12:12). The world-embracing outlook of the prophets is illustrated most impressively by Isaiah's treatment of Assyria. This mighty and invincible nation is quite unconsciously (10:7), so he tells his people, "the rod" of the Lord's anger (10:5); yet even if it were

like the forest of Lebanon" it shall "fall by a mighty one" (vs. 34).[48]
Yea "all nations before him are as nothing; and they are counted to
him less than nothing and vanity" (40:17). This fact that Jehovah is
sovereign over all the nations is stressed in the Psalms (e.g., the 2d,
72d, 96th, 100th, 148th), which close with the words: "Let everything
that hath breath praise the Lord (150:6)."[49] In the Prophets large
sections deal with the nations: Isaiah 13-23, Jeremiah 46-51, Ezekiel
25-32 are prophecies directed against the nations which had shown
their hostility to Israel in various ways. It is true that these prophecies
regarding the nations are in the main prophecies of punishment, but
they contain promises of blessing which prepare the way for the
gospel, notably Isaiah 2:2-5; 19:23-25; 55:1-5. Even so denunciatory a
prophecy as that of Obadiah ends with the words, "and the kingdom
shall be the Lord's."

Finally, and following logically on what has just been said, it
was the unique and distinctive function of the prophets to disclose the
future. The prophets did not merely *forth*tell or instruct; it was their
special function to *fore*tell, to declare things to come, both things
near at hand and things of the distant future; and while it was by the
fulfillment of the former[50] that they were approved to the people of
their own day as truly men of God, it is this *eschatological* or
Messianic aspect of Old Testament prophecy which has been of
supreme interest and concern to believers of every succeeding age,
and which unites Old Testament and New Testament into one book.
This emphasis on the future is illustrated by such phrases as "in that
day," "in the latter days," "behold the days come," and "the day of
the Lord."[51]

Messianic Prophecy has two main aspects. (1) The Coming of the
Lord, both in judgment and in grace (e.g., Ps. 50:3; 96:13; 98:9; Isa.
40:10; Zech. 14:5; Mal. 3:1-3). The Old Testament speaks of many
such comings of the Lord. Indeed we may say with Fairbairn regarding prophecy, "Everything of moment in the dispensations of God, is
there connected with His presence and working."[52] But the two great
and climactic Comings are the first and second Advent of the Messiah,
which are not clearly distinguished in the Old Testament. (2) The
fulfillment of the promise regarding the Seed of the Woman (Gen.
3:15). This has three aspects: the promise of the *prophet* of whom
Moses is the type (Deut. 18:15), of the *priest* who is typified in the
Levitical priesthood (Lev. 16:33) and is himself both priest and sacrifice as set forth most plainly in the Suffering Servant (Isa. 53), and of
the *king* of the house of David whose kingdom shall endure forever
(2 Sam. 7). These predictions of the deity and humanity of the
Messiah and of his three great offices blend already in the Old Testa-

ment. The child who is to sit on David's throne (Isa. 9:7) is "Immanuel" ("God with us," Isa. 7:14). His name is "Wonder" — all that concerns him is marvelous. "Counsellor" suggests his prophetic office, "mighty God" and "everlasting Father," his divine omnipotence, eternity and creative power, while "Prince of peace" points forward to his atoning work, for he shall make peace through the blood of his cross (53:5; cf. Col. 1:20).[53] Zechariah combines his priestly and his kingly offices, "a priest upon his throne" (6:13). These few passages serve to suggest to us the rich content of our Lord's discourse on the road to Emmaus: "And beginning at Moses and all the prophets he expounded unto them in all the Scriptures the things concerning himself" (Luke 24:27).[54] For it is in the Christ of the New Testament that all the rays of Old Testament prophecy focus and have their fulfilment. The enduring value and importance of the Old Testament lies in the fact that it is the preparation for and foundation of the New Testament. This is shown by the hundreds of quotations from and allusions to the Old Testament which are met with in the New Testament. The low view of the Old Testament which is entertained in many influential circles today finds no support in the New Testament itself. The words of Abraham in the parable of the Rich Man and Lazarus illustrate this most convincingly, "If they hear not Moses and the prophets neither will they be persuaded though one rose from the dead" (Luke 16:31).

The Old Testament Is Interpreted by the New

The statement was made at the beginning of this chapter that the Old Testament is a self-interpreting book, that it contains no introduction and needs none. This is perfectly true. But it is also true and equally important to remember that the Old Testament does have an inspired and authoritative interpreter, the New Testament; and it is in the light of the New Testament that the mysteries of the Old Testament are made plain. Augustine summed it up in his oft-quoted words: "In the Old Testament the New is concealed (*latet*); in the New the Old is revealed (*patet*)." And every interpretation which we or other men may place upon the Old Testament must be tested and tried by this authoritative interpreter, the New Testament. Only when it has stood that test can we feel assured of its correctness.

The importance of this witness of the New Testament to the Old should never be minimized or disregarded. It has often been pointed out that statements in the Old Testament, which have been seriously challenged or rejected by modern rationalistic critics, are referred to as facts of history in the New Testament. The words of Abram as recorded in Genesis 22:5, "I and the lad will go yonder and sacrifice, and come again to you," are taken by some critics to mean either that Abram lied to his servants, since he fully intended to sacrifice Isaac, or that the words "and will return unto you" are a later embellishment or gloss, regarded as appropriate in view of the outcome. Yet Hebrews 11:19 confirms the narrative as it stands and refers to this incident as evidence of the invincible faith of the patriarch.

It is most instructive and illuminating to study the New Testament use of passages which modern scholars would regard as myth, legend or folklore and seek to "demythologize," in order to find in them some element of truth which the modern mind can regard as profitable. The appeal to the account of the creation of woman (Gen. 2:21f.) by Paul (1 Cor. 11:8; 1 Tim. 2:13), to a primitive monogamy (Gen. 2:23f.) by Jesus (Matt. 19:5), to the flood by Jesus (Matt. 24:37f.) and by Peter 1 Peter 3:20; 2 Peter 2:5), to the brazen serpent (Num. 21:8) by Jesus (John 3:14), to the speaking ass (Num. 22:28) by Peter (2 Peter 2:16), to Jonah in the belly of the great fish (Jonah 2:1) by Jesus (Matt. 12:40), illustrate the striking difference between the two methods of interpretation. What the one treats as difficulties to be gotten rid of, the other appeals to as significant evidences of God's activity in human affairs. Especially significant is the importance which the New Testament writers attach to the fulfillment of prophecy in the person of Jesus Christ. It is in him that the types and prophecies of the Old Testament have their focus and fulfillment. Again and again Jesus quoted it with the words "It is written" and applied it to himself. His disciples did the same and they have been followed by a multitude of Bible students and teachers in every age.

In discussing the arguments which were advanced in defense of Christianity by the Apologists of the Early Church, Philip Schaff, the eminent church historian, places prophecy first: "The great argument, not only with the Jews, but with heathens also, was the PROPHECIES; since the knowledge of future events can come only from God. The first appeal of the apologists was, of course, to the prophetic writings of the Old Testament, in which they found, by a very liberal interpretation, every event of the gospel history and every lineament of our Saviour's character and work."[55] This was merely the consequence of following the Apostolic method which is used in the New Testament, where the appeal to Old Testament prophecy is constantly made. The hesitation or refusal of so many scholars and leaders in the church today to use this great argument illustrates very clearly how widely the attitude of the modern "critic" differs from that which has characterized the church throughout the centuries until relatively recent times. Prophecy and miracle are in the New Testament the great proofs of the truth of

Christianity. The tendency to minimize or ignore them is responsible for much of the weakness and ineffectiveness of the modern church when brought face to face with evils which only a supernatural religion can overcome.[56]

The fact that the account which the Old Testament gives of itself is so fully confirmed by the interpretation which the New Testament places upon it, is for the Christian the strongest proof of its correctness.[57] Yet it is this very self-testimony which, as the Jews at Rome said to the Apostle Paul, "is everywhere spoken against" today. In the following chapters it will be our aim to show that criticism has no worthy substitute to offer for the account which the Bible gives of itself, that it is destructive and not constructive; and that recent archaeological research has made it increasingly clear that the religion of the Old Testament is unique and must have a superhuman, a divine origin.

We need to study the Bible with the thought of its self-evidencing unity and harmony constantly in mind: to study Scripture in the light of Scripture, to interpret Scripture by Scripture. Failure to do this leads to disaster. The "consent of all the parts,"[58] the agreement of our interpretation of any single passage of Scripture with all the relevant data to be found elsewhere in Scripture is the best and surest evidence of its correctness. It is the great error of the higher critics that they adopt a divisive, antithetic, hair-splitting system of interpretation which leads to all sorts of strange and disastrous conclusions. All Scripture is given by inspiration of God; and the God of truth cannot lie.

The Higher Criticism has been to no small degree a quest for differences and contradictions. The harmonistic method of interpreting the Bible is much decried today. It has two obvious advantages. The one is that it does justice to the intelligence and common sense of the writers of the Bible. To claim that the writers, compilers, editors of the biblical records would introduce or combine conflicting accounts of the same event into a narrative is to challenge their intelligence, or their honesty, or their competence to deal with the data which they record. The second is that it is the biblical method of interpretation. The many times and various ways in which the biblical writers quote or refer to one another implies their confidence in the sources quoted. Their method is a harmonistic method. Most important of all, this method of interpretation is the only one which is consistent with the high claims of the Bible to be the Word of God.

The writer remembers hearing his teacher, Dr. David J. Burrell,[59] once say to the class that the attitude of the Christian toward the trustworthiness of Scripture should be the same as he would take toward the question of the fair name and virtue of his own mother. He will and must admit that all human beings are sinful, that the best of them have sometimes, like David, fallen into grievous sin. But if his mother is a worthy and godly woman, if she has given him abundant reason to love her and honor her, and if her example and influence have been a benediction to him, then he will not listen to any idle word of scandal; and if serious charges are levelled at her he will demand the most conclusive evidence and will investigate it with the utmost care and do his utmost to refute it. He will do this because he knows and honors and loves his mother. Such, Dr. Burrell told us, should be the attitude of the Christian to his Bible. He will not ignore charges which are brought against its truthfulness. He will examine and test them, and do his utmost to disprove them, especially if they are brought by those who reject its high claims and look with ill-disguised scorn on the wonders which it records. For those wonders — like the beauty of his mother's character — are the things which make the Bible most precious to him and make him so unwilling to admit the cavils of the unfriendly critic.

CHAPTER II

THE OLD TESTAMENT FROM WITHIN —
ITS LITERARY FORM

If we accept the principle that the Bible is its own best interpreter, it becomes, of course, of prime importance that we should have as clear an understanding as possible not only of its factual content, but also of its literary forms, of the language and style of the Bible, or what is covered broadly by the words, biblical rhetoric. The content of the Old Testament is very varied. We have in it simple prose, even the driest kind of prose, genealogies. We have prose narratives which contain figures of speech. We have poetical passages, which contain both fact and fancy, visions of spiritual realities, as well as simple facts of history. We have law codes which state what the law is and the penalty of disobeying it; objective, impersonal, inexorable. And we have words of passionate exhortation and appeal in which the personal equation, the solemnizing thought that man may make or wreck his career, is presented with the utmost earnestness. We have the beautiful figures of parable and poetry; we have dreams, symbolic actions, predictions which explain themselves and others which require interpretation. We must recognize these differences; and not apply the same measuring stick to all alike.

LITERALISM

Those who believe in the plenary inspiration and divine authority of Scripture are often accused of being *literalists* or biblicists. It must be confessed that there are literalists who greatly injure the cause which they love by failure to recognize that the Bible is a harp of many strings and that while it is more than mere literature, more than a mere human book, being the Word of God, it has the qualities and characteristics of the best literature which man has produced. And the reverent student of the Bible will both recognize and rejoice in its literary beauty and perfection.

One of the most beautiful of all the Psalms is the brief 114th, which gives a poetical summary of the entire Exodus period: the drying up of the *hindering* waters of Red Sea and Jordan, the awe-inspiring theophany at Sinai, the pouring forth of the *life-giving* waters at Horeb and Kadesh. It describes it "in miniature"; and it has been well said that "For perfection of form and dramatic vividness it is almost if not quite unrivalled in the Psalter."[1] This is quite true. But it must be recognized that the language is highly poetic and figurative. We cannot take it with entire literalness. If we say, "I believe the mountains actually skipped like rams because the Bible says so," how shall we deal with the words, "The sea saw it and fled" (cf. Ps. 77:16)? As an example of personification it is a striking and beautiful figure. Taken literally it would make the sea a sentient being and introduce pagan mythology or folklore into this beautiful psalm. We must be careful not to injure our cause by misrepresenting it.[2]

David's lament over Saul and Jonathan (2 Sam. 1:19-27) is a striking illustration of the importance of distinguishing between the literal and the figurative or poetic. We read in 1 Samuel 31:9 regarding the tragic death of Saul and the dishonoring of his body that the Philistines "cut off his head, and stripped off his armor, and sent into the land of the Philistines round about, to publish it in the house of their idols and among the people."[3] That is what actually happened; and no one knew better than David that it would happen. Yet in his lament he cries, "Tell it not in Gath, publish it not in the streets of Ashkelon; lest the daughters of the Philistines rejoice, lest the daughters of the uncircumcised triumph." "How utterly absurd!" cries the prosaic historian. "How could anyone have imagined that the news of the Philistine victory could be kept from the Philistine cities? What possible use was there in David's exhorting those of his friends and followers who were listening to his lament, not to carry the news of Saul's death to the cities of his enemies, or, in case there were any Philistine sympathizers among his followers, exhorting them to hush the matter up? How utterly absurd!" Yet, pause a moment. How could David have better expressed his sense of the humiliation, the tragedy, the national dishonor that had befallen Israel than by these words which have become proverbial, "Tell it not in Gath"?[4] It is just as important to interpret poetry as poetry, as it is to interpret prose as prose.

A striking example of the danger of a false literalism is given us in the *Birth Narrative* in Matthew 1. In verse 21 we read the announcement of the angelic messenger: "and she shall bring forth a son and thou shalt call his name Jesus." In verse 23 we are told that the birth of this child will be the fulfillment of an ancient prophecy: "Behold a virgin shall be with child, and shall bring forth a son, and they shall call his name Emmanuel." Each name is explained or translated: Jesus by "for he shall save his people from their sins," Immanuel by "God with us." It thus appears that Jesus which means literally "Jehovah is salvation" being a contraction of Joshua is, we may say, a more precise expression of the purpose of the incarnation than Immanuel. It states definitely what Immanuel implies, that in the incarnation God is with us as Saviour. Jesus is therefore a richer and more precious name than Immanuel, because it speaks definitely of salvation from sin. So the narrative in Matthew brings the two names together as if it were obvious that they are so nearly identical that Jesus is really the proper name for Immanuel. We meet the name Jesus either alone or in combination (e.g., Jesus Christ, Christ Jesus) nearly a thousand times in the New Testament. But we never meet the name Immanuel there. Consequently the Jews, who in this respect are strict literalists, can deny that the birth of Jesus was the fulfillment of Isaiah 7:14 and they are still looking for the coming of Immanuel.[5]

FIGURES OF SPEECH

If rhetoric may be broadly defined as the art of the effective use of language, then figures of speech will naturally play a prominent part in it. For language takes its terminology and subject-matter largely from the material, physical and phenomenal world; and hence it happens necessarily that in dealing with words we are often dealing with figures and that our use of them in speaking and writing may be far more figurative than we realize. We speak of the literal and figurative use of words and expressions as if the difference were perfectly clear and obvious. It often happens that figures of speech appear even in the most ordinary and commonplace statements.

A number of years ago a leading metropolitan daily in reporting the proceedings of a presidential convention made this statement regarding an important moment in the session: "At this point Senator _____ came upon the platform with the platform in his hands."[6] The account was not intended to be humorous. And probably most of those who read the statement saw nothing strange in it. The two uses of the word "platform" are so familiar that we scarcely notice the ambiguity. But a foreigner, who knows only the primary meaning of the word, might have difficulty with the sentence and fail to recognize that according to established usage the word "platform" refers first to material things and then to immaterial principles.

The most usual figures of speech are: simile, metaphor, metonymy, synecdoche, allegory, parable, fable; apostrophe, personification, anthropomorphism; epigram, irony and sarcasm, innuendo; litotes, hyperbole, rhetorical question, ad hominem argument, climax and antithesis. All are to be found in the Bible.

Simile and Metaphor. These are the two most common figures of speech both in the Bible and in secular writings. We find them frequently in prose and much more often in poetry. They are closely related, and metaphor may be regarded as simply a stronger form of simile. But there is an important difference between them. The simile expresses resemblance: the metaphor asserts or assumes identity. Both the similarity and the difference between the two figures are well-illustrated by the familiar words of Isaiah 40:6-8: "All flesh (is) grass, and all the goodliness thereof (is) as the flower of the field: the grass withereth the flower fadeth: because the spirit of the Lord bloweth upon it: surely the people (is) grass. The grass withereth, the flower fadeth: but the word of our God shall stand for ever."[7] The strong figure here is the metaphor and it is repeated twice: "all flesh (is) *grass* . . . surely the people (is) *grass*." The *identification* of "all flesh" with "grass" is then made the basis of a *comparison* expressed in terms of the simile "and all the goodliness thereof (is) as the flower of the field." Then the reason for the double figure is explained by the twice repeated assertion: "the grass withereth, the flower fadeth." The grass and the flower fade; and man, whose goodliness is *like* grass, who *is* grass, will likewise fade away. One thing only is enduring, "the word of the Lord," it shall *stand forever.* Or we might express it this way: the Easter flowers testify to man that he is mortal; the Easter sermon tells him that death is abolished by the resurrection victory.

The similes of the Bible are often very striking. But the metaphors are even more so. The italics in the AV and ARV often give the reader an indication of the boldness of the identifications used and which the translators have felt obliged to paraphrase. "I (am) prayer" (Ps. 109:4) says the psalmist, which is far more impressive than "I *give myself to* prayer." "Myrrh and aloes, cassia (are) all thy garments" (Ps. 45:8) is the description of the fragrant garments of the Messianic king. So fragrant are they, it is as if they were made of them. "I (am) peace" (Ps. 120:7) is stronger than "I *am for* peace." "The season (is) showers" (Ezra 10:13) "for we (are) yesterday" (Job 8:9), "The vines (are) blossoms" (Cant. 2:13, cf. 15), "the whole earth (was) one lip" (Gen. 11:1); "and lyre and harp, tabret and pipe and wine (are) their feasts" (Isa. 5:12) — they are not merely in them, they are all there is to them; for God and his works they have no thought.

The use of a noun instead of a descriptive adjective is at times a stronger form of expression, although such use is sometimes due to the fact that the Hebrew did not have as many adjectives or at least did not use them as freely as we do. But the preference is noteworthy in itself. "God (is) truth," "thy commandments (are) truth," "God (is) love," — the use of the noun is much more impressive and vigorous than the adjective would be. The Lord's word to Ezekiel concerning the children of Israel is "for they (are) rebellion" (2:7, AV marg). Isaiah's denunciation of Israel's watchmen leaves nothing to be de-

sired for vivid definiteness: "His watchmen are blind: they are all ignorant, they are all dumb dogs, they cannot bark; sleeping, lying down,
loving to slumber. Yea, they are greedy dogs, which can never have
enough . . ." (56:10). David says of the water from the well of Bethlehem which the three mighty men brought to him, "the blood of the
men that went in jeopardy of their lives" (2 Sam. 23:17). Such figures
are vivid and impressive and in most cases we have no difficulty in
recognizing that the language is figurative. Yet the last illustration
serves to remind us that the question whether the words "This is my
body . . . this is the new testament in my blood" are literal or figurative
has divided Christendom for centuries and has, in the Romish sacrifice
of the Mass, led to as grievous a perversion of the solemn rite which
the Lord gave to his church to be kept until He come, as was ever connected with the bloody sacrifices of the Old Dispensation.

Comparison, as in the case of the simile, and *identification*, as in the
metaphor, readily pass over into *substitution*. The comparison of
Jerusalem with Sodom and Gomorrah (Isa. 1:9) prepares the way for
the addressing of her rulers as "rulers of Sodom" and her people as
"people of Gomorrah" (vs. 10). "Thine eyes (are) doves" (Cant. 1:15)
prepares us for "O my dove, that art in the clefts of the rock" (2:14).
Psalm 22 contains striking metaphors. The Psalmist says, "I (am) a
worm" and he describes his enemies as lions, dogs, bulls, unicorns.

The fact that simile always states a comparison, while metaphor
asserts or assumes identification or substitution naturally makes a great
difference in the interpretation of the two figures. In the case of simile
it is clear that we are dealing with a figure. In the case of a metaphor
this is not always so. The metaphor to be appropriate must represent
something that is truly applicable to that with which it is compared. But
the exact nature of this connection may not be entirely obvious. Is the
word "hornet" as used of the conquest of Canaan (Exod. 23:28; Deut.
7:20; Josh. 24:12) to be taken literally or figuratively? In Isaiah 7:18,
"the fly which is in the uttermost part of the rivers of Egypt and the
bee that is in the land of Assyria" apparently stand for the armies of
Egypt and Assyria. The "razor" (vs. 20) is declared to be the king of
Assyria, as are also "the waters of the strong and mighty river" (8:7).
Does the "hornet" have a similar figurative meaning?[28]

Personification is one of the beautiful figures used in Scripture.
Again and again natural objects are referred to as serving God and
obeying his laws. They are called upon to rejoice in the goodness of
God and to praise him, and also described as suffering with man the
grievous tokens of his displeasure. The trees of the field are commanded to "clap their hands." The sun, moon and stars are called upon to
"praise the Lord." Isaiah tells us: "The wilderness and the solitary

place shall be glad for them; and the desert shall rejoice and blossom as the rose." In the rustle of the leaves of the trees, in the murmur of the watercourse, in the waving grain, in the flowers, in the fruits, the men of God of old saw all nature obeying the command of God by performing the duties assigned to it in creation.

Sometimes this figure is transferred to things of the spirit. "Mercy and truth are met together; righteousness and peace have kissed each other" (Ps. 85:10) are beautiful figures, which say much with few words. It is important to remember this for some would not hesitate to maintain that when Joshua set up the stone at Shechem and said to the people, "Behold, this stone shall be a witness unto us; for it hath heard all the words of the Lord which he spake unto us: it shall be therefore a witness unto you, lest ye deny your God" (Josh. 24:27), he was speaking in terms of primitive animism as if he believed the stone to be alive or to be indwelt by a *numen* and not simply using a striking rhetorical figure of speech for the purpose of making this stone an impressive reminder of the solemn covenant which the people had renewed in this memorable ceremony at Shechem.[9]

Anthropomorphism. This may be regarded as a special form of personification. It is the use of human characteristics to describe that which is not human, and more particularly the attributing of such characteristics to God. That "God is a Spirit and has not a body like men" is one of the clearest teachings of the Bible, of the Old Testament as well as of the New. Idolatry is a particularly heinous sin against Israel's God. Yet the biblical writers constantly use anthropomorphic language in speaking of God. They speak of his hands, his fingers, his eyes, his feet, his ears. They speak of him as seeing, hearing, touching, smelling, walking. They call on him to "awake" from sleep (Ps. 44:23), not to "forget" his people (Ps. 74:19), but to "remember" them (Ps. 20:3, *et pass.*). He is likened to "a man of war" (Isa. 42:13). His relation to Israel is that of a "husband" (Isa. 54:7) and the chosen people are his "children," and he is their father. "The clouds are the dust of his feet" (Nahum 1:3) and "rising up early and sending" (Jer. 7:13) are beautiful figures which graphically express the readiness and promptness, even the haste, with which the Lord carries out his purposes in human affairs. The warrant for this lies in the fact that man was created in the image and likeness of God (Gen. 1:27) and therefore can and must of necessity think of God as being like himself. But this natural and essential right, as we may call it, is strictly limited in two ways: by the law of *eminence* — man may ascribe to God only that which is worthy in himself and ascribe it to God in an infinite degree; and by the law of *negation* — he must deny to God everything that is sinful, unworthy, imperfect and finite in himself.[10] Thus Paul speaking to the philosophers in the Areopagus said to them: "Being then the offspring of God, we ought not to think that the Godhead is like unto gold, or silver, or stone, graven by art and device of man." Anthropomorphic language is found in all parts of the Bible; and some of the most precious passages in it are expressed in such terms. Psalm 23, for example, uses the figure of the shepherd and his sheep to illustrate the attitude of constant love and care and protection which characterizes the relationship in which God has placed himself to his children. The anthropomorphisms of Scripture do not represent, as some have held, a low and primitive conception of God. They express in most intimate terms the closeness of the tie which God has established between himself and his creatures, a tie which finds its fullest expression in the incarnation of the Son of God.

Irony and Sarcasm. Isaiah can be extremely ironical and sarcastic. He repeatedly calls Pekah, the "son of Remaliah" (7:4, 5, 9; 8:6), i.e., son of a nobody, speaks of "both of her kings" (vs. 16) implying that Rezin was really co-king of Samaria with Pekah, describes them as "two tails of these smoking firebrands" (vs. 4), implying that, however menacing they may seem, both will soon sputter out. Isaiah also rebukes Ahaz by calling him "house of David" (7:2, 13), a title which Ahaz did not deserve. Note the cutting sarcasm of the words of Jeremiah: "Behold, I proclaim a liberty for you, saith the Lord, to the sword, to the pestilence, and to the famine" (34:17b). The rich Jews of Jeremiah's day had made the "liberty" of the fiftieth year (Lev. 25:10) a farce and a by-word. So it shall take on a terrible meaning for themselves. We note the irony of 5:19. Those who have served strange gods in their own land shall serve strangers in a strange land.

Note the sarcasm bordering on ridicule in the words of Michal: "How glorious was the king of Israel today!" (2 Sam. 6:20), and in Joab's message to David, "and thy servant Uriah the Hittite is dead also" — *thy servant*, the man whom David had ruthlessly slain (2 Sam. 11:24); the golden calf, made by Jeroboam for the people to worship "shall be also carried unto Assyria for a present to king Jareb" (Hos. 10:6); "thou [disobedient Israel] thoughtest that I was altogether such a one as thyself" (Ps. 50:21); "Is my hand shortened at all that it cannot save?" (Isa. 50:2); "no doubt but ye are the people, and wisdom shall die with you" (Job 12:2); "a goodly price that I was prized at of them" (Zech. 11:13).

Micaiah's words to Ahab, "Go and prosper: for the Lord shall deliver it into the hand of the king" (1 Kings 22:15) are ironical as Ahab seems to have recognized clearly, and the true answer to the solemn yet obviously hypocritical adjuration by Ahab to speak the truth is given in Micaiah's answer, "I saw all Israel scattered" (cf. Amos 4:4f.).

More familiar are Elijah's taunting words to the prophets of Baal, "Cry aloud [literally, with a great voice] for he is a god: either he is musing, or he has gone aside or he is on a journey, or peradventure, he is sleeping and must be awaked" (1 Kings 18:27 ARV). It has been much debated whether Jeremiah's words in reply to Hananiah, "Amen, may the Lord do so" (28:6) express the pious wish of the prophet that Hananiah's favorable prediction might be fulfilled or are intended to be understood ironically.

Popular Terminology of Scripture. In reading the Bible it is important to remember that it is not a scientific treatise. It uses the language of human experience to describe the world as it is known to man. To speak of the sun rising and setting is to speak in terms of the daily observation of those who live on the earth. The astronomer would use very different language, which to the average man would be quite unintelligible. Similarly, to speak of "the heaven above and the earth beneath and of the waters under the earth" is to use the same language of human experience. It does not justify the modern critic in speaking of the biblical view of the world as a "three structured universe" and to ridicule it as absurdly unscientific. Scripture has relatively little to say about the location of heaven and hell. It is no more absurd to speak of heaven as above and hell as beneath — it is under the ground that the dead are buried, so it is naturally called the place of the dead — than it is to speak of east and west. East and west are terms which everyone understands. The language is accurate for all ordinary purposes, despite the fact that the rotation of the earth brings it about that an arrow pointing east at noon would be pointing west at midnight, that is in the exactly opposite direction. But when the Bible tells us that God has removed our transgressions from us "as far as the east is from the west," the meaning is perfectly clear and the statement most impressive.

Symbolic Actions. Closely related to the subject of literal interpretation is the question of the actuality or reality of some of the situations described in the Old Testament. By this we mean whether or to what extent they actually took place. A good illustration of the problem is furnished by comparing Chapters 27 and 25 in Jeremiah. In the former passage we are told that Jeremiah was commanded to prepare yokes and send them to the kings of Edom, Moab, Ammon, Tyre and Sidon, "by the hands of the messengers which came to Jerusalem unto Zedekiah king of Judah." The kings of these neighboring nations had sent messengers to Zedekiah probably for the purpose of urging him to unite in a concerted revolt against Nebuchadnezzar; and the sending of the yokes by the prophet would serve as a salutary warning as to what would be the outcome of such an enterprise. The yokes would speak more plainly perhaps than any message which the prophet could send. There is no sufficient reason for anything but a literal and factual interpretation here.

In Chapter 25 the whole situation is quite different. Jeremiah is commanded to take "the cup of wine, even this fury" (vs. 15) from the hand of the Lord and to cause all the nations of the earth to drink of it. More than twenty such nations are named and the comprehensiveness of the command is indicated by the words "and all the kingdoms of the earth, which are upon the face of the ground"; and to cap it all "the king of Sheshach," which probably means the king of Babylon, namely Nebuchadnezzar himself, is mentioned last. Jeremiah is to offer this cup of fury to the kings of all the nations of the earth. He is to do it personally: "and it shall be, if they refuse to take the cup at thine hand to drink, then shalt thou say unto them, Thus saith the Lord of hosts; Ye shall certainly drink." And Jeremiah is to pronounce a curse upon them. In this case it seems quite plain that the command was not intended to be carried out literally or actually. This is indicated first by the words "wine cup, this fury" (cf. Isa. 51:21-23). What is it? It must be a cup which represents or symbolizes the wrath of God, by the drinking of which the nations are to be made drunk that in their drunken fury they may destroy one another. The cup may be a real cup and it may have real wine in it. But it symbolizes the wrath of God. Furthermore Jeremiah is to take this cup and compel the kings of all the nations of the earth to drink of it. Taken literally, such a task would have been humanly impossible. Had Jeremiah devoted the remainder of his life to journeying like Herodotus from nation to nation and kingdom to kingdom, he could not have carried out such a world-embracing commission completely; and there is nothing in the Book of Jeremiah which even suggests such an undertaking. He seems to have spent most of his ministry at Jerusalem, until compelled to go to Egypt. It hardly seems necessary to argue that, as the whole description indicates, what is here described is a symbolic action. To what extent it was acted out, we cannot say. Jeremiah may have taken an actual cup, filled it with wine, called it the cup of the Lord's fury, and offered it to some of his auditors, giving each a royal name. He may merely have spoken it and allowed his hearers to visualize for themselves the action which he placed before their eyes. In a word it may have been a parable so vividly told by word and gesture that it impressed Jeremiah's hearers as if it were actually taking place before their very eyes. There are other similar symbolic actions which might also be discussed; and there is much difference of opinion among commentators as to the measure of actuality, as we may call it, in each of them. But these two passages will serve to illustrate the problem involved.[11]

The command given the Israelites to place the blood of the passover lamb upon the side posts and lintels of their doors before the tenth plague took place in Egypt was clearly to be carried out literally (Exod. 12:7, 13). Whether, or to what extent, the similar command to bind the "words" of the Lord as a "sign" upon their hands, that they might be "frontlets" between their eyes, and to write them upon door-posts and gates, was intended to be carried out with similar literalness is not an easy question to answer (Deut. 6:8f.).[12] The command regarding the fringe and ribbon of blue which the Israelites are to make in their garments "throughout their generations" and the reason given for it, "that they may look upon it, and remember all the commandments of the Lord to do them" (Num. 15:38f.) is clearly literal and favors the taking of the similar command regarding the phylacteries literally.[13] An objective and visible reminder or symbol is helpful and may even be necessary for peoples of every degree of culture. The fact that the Pharisees of our Lord's time took these commandments literally does not prove that their interpretation was incorrect as such. *Abusus non tollit usum* is an axiom which is widely applicable. Many a good thing has been perverted and made a positive evil. But it should be remembered that such outward, material signs or symbols were solely intended to point to a spiritual reality. Otherwise they could easily degenerate into fetishes, which is what they became to unspiritual Israel. And in the clearer light of the gospel, the symbols and ceremonies of the Old Covenant lose their significance and value.[14]

Visions and Dreams. Revelations which are made in dreams or visions may likewise be simple and plain or they may be figurative or symbolic and require interpretation. We read in 1 Kings 3 that "in Gibeon the Lord appeared to Solomon in a dream by night" (vs. 5, cf. vs. 15), and we are told what he said to him. There is nothing mysterious or obscure about the words of promise spoken by the Lord to Solomon. On the other hand the seven fat and the seven lean kine of Pharaoh's dream (Gen. 41) were merely prophetic symbols representing seven years of plenty and seven years of famine, and Joseph so interpreted them. Such a dream, if interpreted, causes us no difficulty. But when we turn to such a passage as Ezekiel 8-11 and read the detailed account of all that the prophet saw in Jerusalem, we are tempted to forget the express declarations at the beginning (8:3), and at the end (11:24), that we are reading a vision, that it was in vision that Ezekiel went to Jerusalem and saw the abominations which were practiced even in the very temple itself. That this vision was a true picture of what was going on in Jerusalem we must, of course, believe. But the fact that it is a vision justifies us, for example, in assuming that the man with the writer's inkhorn is not to be taken literally and that none of the devout persons in Jerusalem had actual inkmarks placed on their foreheads. A great spiritual truth is here set forth in a very striking way. But we are dealing with a vision and must not take it with entire literalness. This is true of the Jerusalem which Ezekiel then saw in vision. We may, we must, infer that it is equally true of the vision of the future of Jerusalem and of the Holy Land which forms the conclusion of that wonderful book (chaps. 40-48). These and other visions in the Bible set forth great spiritual realities. But we must always remember that we are dealing with visions, with dreams, which may or may not correspond exactly to the realities of earthly life and experience.[15] In this respect the visions of the Old Testament may be compared with the parables of the New.

Allegory. This figure of speech has been described as "a prolonged metaphor." It is the using of an incident or story told in the language of ordinary mundane affairs to set forth a moral or spiritual truth or situation. Such accounts as Isaiah's description of the finery of the women of Jerusalem, Ezekiel's minute description of Tyre as a great ship to the construction and outfitting of which a host of nations have made their contributions, are in a sense allegory, since they are told to convey a moral and spiritual lesson. Hosea's marriage to Gomer, Ezekiel's account of the birth, upbringing and later conduct of Judah (chap. 16), the Song of Songs which is Solomon's, are all told and intended to convey a moral lesson, a spiritual truth. This is obvious. But the question as to the exact amount of factuality has been a matter of debate for centuries. Thus the Song of Songs is interpreted by some as a story of romantic love, by others as an allegory of the relationship between Christ and the church. That conjugal affection, which is the highest form of human love, is a type of divine love, is shown by Paul's completing his discussion of Christian marriage by describing it as a type of the relation of Christ to his church (Eph. 5:32f.). But does this typical use of this human relationship justify the treating of Canticles as merely an allegory? It would hardly seem so, especially since there are no quotations from this book in the New Testament. Whether Hosea was actually directed to marry an unchaste woman has been affirmed and denied by scholars of eminence on equally cogent grounds.[16]

Puns. There are a good many passages in the Old Testament where there is a play upon words, which usually is lost in the translation. In Jeremiah 50 the expression: "a sword (*chereb*) is upon" occurs five times in verses 35-37. It is followed by "a drought (*choreb*) is upon her waters." In Isaiah 5:7 we read "and he looked for judgment (*mishpat*), but behold oppression (*mispach*); for righteousness (*tsedaqa*), but behold a cry (*tse 'aqa*)"; 24:17, "fear (*pachad*) and pit *(pachath)* and snare *(pach)*"; also cf. "summer fruit" *(qayits)* and "end" *(qets)* (Amos 8:2). In Micah 1 there are several word plays, e.g., "In the house of Aphrah roll thyself in dust *('aphar)*." Samson apparently was a good deal of a punster: "with the jaw-bone of an ass *(chamor)*, a heap *(chamor)*, two heaps *(chamoraim)*, with the jaw-bone of an ass, have I slain a thousand men" (Judg. 15:16). There is also a word-play in "and he took their spoil *(chalitsotham)* and gave the changes of garments *(chaliphoth)* unto them which expounded the riddle" (14:19). In Ecclesiastes 7:6 we read that the laughter of fools is like the "crackling of thorns *(sirim)* under a pot" *(sir)*. In 2 Kings 18:4 there is a word-play in the word *nehushtan* on the words *nehosheth* (bronze) and *nachash* (serpent), since the serpent-symbol was made of bronze.

Emphasis

An important feature in rhetoric is emphasis. This is the reason Hamlet says to the players "suit the action to the word, the word to the action." For the mere stress of voice or the gesture which accompanies it may make or mar the true sense. In so simple a sentence as "I will go today," the stressing of any one of the four words would give a special meaning to the whole. One of the major difficulties in translation is to indicate the emphasis correctly. The Bible is a very emphatic book. It deals with matters of the utmost importance and it states them at times very emphatically. This is done in various ways:

(1) By the use of colorful and striking words: "vanities," "unclean," "abominations," "dung" (or logs), "detestable things" used to describe the idols of the heathen; "a worm and no man" (Ps. 22:6), "thou worm Jacob" (Isa. 41:14), "a dead dog" (2 Sam. 9:8), "one little ewe lamb" (2 Sam. 12:3; cf. 1 Sam. 25:41). The expression "who pant after the dust of the earth on the head of the poor" (Amos 2:7) is a most scathing indictment of the land-grabbing rich in Israel;[17] "cleanness of teeth" (4:6) an ironical description of famine; "thy father was an Amorite, and thy mother a Hittite" (Ezek. 16:3) indicates how utterly pagan Israel has become; "rulers of Sodom . . . people of Gomorrah" is Isaiah's scornful epithet for the chosen people (1:10). "Hew" and "slay" are used of the prophetic word as being the sword of the Lord in the hands of his prophets. In Psalm 23:6 the word rendered "follow" is more frequently "pursue." In Isaiah 53:10 "pleased" is represented by a strong word usually rendered by "delighted."

(2) By the *position* of words: "a leper" is the terrible anticlimax to the glowing description of Naaman (2 Kings 5:1). Compare 1 Kings 1:25f. where the AV brings out the emphasis well by ending Nathan's

complaint to king David, as does the Hebrew, with the words "hath he not called." Note the "and Asahel" of 2 Samuel 2:30. The words "in peace" with which three verses in 2 Samuel 3 end (vss. 21, 22, 23) are made doubly emphatic by the words "in battle" of verse 30 as well as by the account of Asahel's death which has been given in the preceding chapter. In Isaiah 7:17 AV brings out the emphasis on the words "the king of Assyria," by inserting (in italics) the word "*even*."

(3) By the *repetition* (double or triple) of the same word or phrase. This is especially noticeable in Isaiah: e.g., "I, I" (43:11, 25; 51:12), "peace, peace" (26:3; 57:19), "Ariel, Ariel" (29:1), "Comfort ye, comfort ye" (40:1), cf. 21:11; 28:10, 13; 38:19; 51:9, 17; 52:1; 57:14. Also Psalm 115:1, 16; 124:1f; 135:1; 150:1-6; Jeremiah 6:14; 8:11; Ezekiel 21:9, 28. Triple: "holy, holy, holy" (Isa. 6:3), "earth, earth, earth" (Jer. 22:29); cf. Jeremiah 7:4; Isaiah 24:19; Ezekiel 21:27. Very striking is the three-fold "betroth" in Hosea 2:19f. Note Psalm 129:1, 2; 130:6.

(4) By grouping similar words: "God *(El)*, God *(Elohim)*, Lord *(Yahweh)*, (Josh. 22:21f; Ps. 50:1).

(5) By the recurrent use of the same or similar words:

(a) "Rebellion" or "rebellious" is used in Ezekiel 2 (5 times), 3 (3 times), 12 (5 times) a total of twenty-four in Ezekiel.

(b) "Vanity" (c. 30 times) in Ecclesiastes, the first two and the last being emphatic "vanity of vanities, all is vanity" (1:2; 12:8).

(c) "I am the Lord (your God)" occurs about 40 times in Leviticus 17-26. "Jeroboam the son of Nebat who made Israel to sin" occurs about 20 times in Kings.

(d) The use of the word *sword* as the symbol of judgment goes back to Leviticus 26 and Deuteronomy 32. It appears in the prophets to describe one of the sore judgments which will be visited upon impenitent Israel. Jeremiah uses it about seventy times, joining it thirteen times with "famine" and sixteen times with "famine and pestilence." In 15:2-4 he speaks of four kinds of judgment: sword, dogs, birds, beasts, to devour and destroy (cf. Ezek. 14:21). Ezekiel refers to the *sword* even oftener than Jeremiah does. In 21:9-17 we have what might be called "the song of the sword," the word occurring fifteen times in the chapter (cf. chap. 32, "slain by [or, of] the sword" [8 times], "slain, fallen by the sword" [3 times]). "Day" occurs eleven times in Obadiah (vss. 8-14) and leads up to the emphatic "the day of the Lord" in verse 15. The phrase "under the sun," which occurs more than a score of times in Ecclesiastes, emphasizes the mundane and secular philosophy which pervades the book and leads up to the moral, "Fear God and keep his commandments; for this is the whole (duty) of man" (12:13).

(e) Refrain-like recurrence of words and phrases is met with frequently in the impassioned language of psalmist and prophet: "For his mercy endureth forever" (Ps. 136, 26 times); "Oh that men would praise the Lord for his goodness" (Ps. 107:8, 15, 21, 31); "then they cried unto the Lord in their trouble" (vss. 6, 13, 19, 28; cf. Ps. 46:7, 11 and 57:5, 11); "And it shall be forgiven him" (8 times in Lev. 4-5); "and when thou hearest, forgive" (5 times in Solomon's prayer in 1 Kings 8); "no God beside me" or "none else" (6 times in Isa. 45, cf. 47:8-10). Isaiah uses "in that day" (44 times in chaps. 1-30), Zechariah (20 times); Jeremiah uses "behold the days come" (14 times), "rising up early and sending" (14 times). Ezekiel uses "shall know that I am the Lord" (60 times), "son of man" (90 times), "as I live saith the Lord God" (15 times), "that I (the Lord) have spoken it" (15 times). "Yet is his anger not turned away" is a striking emphasis in Isaiah (5:25; 9:12, 17, 21; 10:4). "Who" appears six times in Proverbs 23:29. This form of emphasis is very marked in Amos: "For three transgressions and for four," etc. (8 times in chapters 1 and 2); "yet have ye not returned unto me" (4:6, 8, 9, 10, 11). We note also the twelve "cursed be"s and the twelve "amen"s in Deut. 27:15-26; and the emphatic contrasts in Deut. 30:15-20 between life and death, blessing and cursing.

(f) "For mine own name's sake" (Isa. 48:9, 11; cf. 37:35; 42:21; 43:25; cf. Jer. 14:7, 21; also Ezekiel 20:9, 14, 22, 44; 36:22, 32). That God's deliverance of Israel was pure grace and not a reward of merit is repeatedly stressed by the prophets. But it goes back to Exodus 32:11-14 and to Deuteronomy 7:7; 9:28. The deliverance from Egypt freed God from the reproach brought by the Egyptians against him (Josh. 5:9). Joshua 7:9; 1 Samuel 12:22; 2 Kings 19:34; 20:6 all indicate that God's honor (name) is involved and unjustly impugned because he has seemingly been unable to deliver his people from their enemies. Appeals to God's name are frequent in the Psalms (23:3; 25:11; 31:3; 54:1; 79:9; 106:8; 109:21; 143:11; cf. Isa. 63:11-14).

(g) By the heaping up of words or phrases: "And the children of Israel were fruitful and increased abundantly, and multiplied and waxed exceeding mighty; and the land was full of them" (Exod. 1:7). Elisha's words: "Is it a time to receive money and to receive garments [which Gehazi had already received] and olive yards and vineyards, and sheep, and oxen, and menservants and maidservants [which Naaman's money would enable Gehazi to acquire] (2 Kings 5:26) serve to expose the avarice which was the servant's motive in his deceitful conduct. Isaiah uses more than a score of words which describe the finery of the women of Jerusalem, simply to show how utterly worldly and carnal-minded were these "daughters of Zion" (3:16-23).

(h) Isaiah is fond of the rhetorical question. It occurs more than fifty times in his prophecies. In Chapter 40 we meet it six times.

Similar emphatic repetitions occur for example in Isaiah 24:16-19; 28:9f.; 33:22. In Daniel 3 the musical summons is described in detail (cornet, flute, harp, sackbut, psaltery and all kinds of music) in verse 5 and repeated in detail in verses 7, 10, and 15.

Usually these repetitions are significant, impressive and helpful. They place the emphasis where the writer clearly intended it to fall. But sometimes they are somewhat confusing. Thus in Jacob's dispute with Laban (Gen. 31:38, 41), where we read "These twenty years. . . . This is to me twenty years . . . fourteen years . . . and six years" some scholars hold that two different periods of twenty years are referred to and not the same one twice over. In Malachi 3:1, if the words which follow the statement, "and the Lord, whom ye seek, shall suddenly come to his temple" are in synonymous parallelism, which seems to be the case, we should render, "even the angel of the covenant, whom ye delight in." For the "messenger" is a man (John the Baptist) while the "angel" is the Lord, the promised Messiah.

The biblical writers often repeat the same word or phrase where we would perhaps prefer some variety of expression: e.g., "sing praises" (4 times in Ps. 47:6), "how long" (4 times in Ps. 13:1-3). The Psalter ends with five Hallelujah Psalms. "Praise" occurs 13 times in Psalm 150. "Answered and said" introduces most of the speeches in Job (21 out of 24) and the connective is uniformly the simple conjunction "and," which *AV* renders variously ("and," "then," "but," "furthermore," "more over"). On this wise a variety of rendering is introduced into the translation which is not justified by the Hebrew. *RSV* usually renders by 'then.' On the other hand *RSV* reduces the "answered and said" to "answered," treating the "and said" as tautological and sufficiently indicated by the quotation marks which it has introduced into the translation.

Especially interesting is the itinerary given in Numbers 33, which lists the journeyings and the encampings of Israel. Each is mentioned 42 times; and only two Hebrew words are used. The *AV*, following the *Vulgate* renders each of these verbs in several different ways: the one by "journeyed, took their journey, departed, removed, went," the other by "encamped, pitched."

The question may be raised whether or how closely a good and faithful rendering should follow the Hebrew style. For example in Psalm 121 the *AV* renders the same Hebrew expression by "keep" (3 times) and by "preserve" (3 times), while *ARV* and *RSV* use "keep" throughout. *BV* has "keep" (4 times), "preserve" (once) and "shield" (once). The words "and also" which occur five times in

Joshua 7:11 are not uniformly rendered in *AV*, a fact which weakens the emphasis. A literal rendering would be: "Israel hath sinned, and also they have transgressed my covenant which I commanded them, and also they have taken of the accursed thing, and also they have stolen, and also they have dissembled, and also they have put (it) among their own stuff" — stroke after stroke like the tolling of the bell of doom! In Deuteronomy 10:20 the Hebrew makes the object of the verb emphatic by placing it first in each of the four brief sentences: "Jehovah, thy God shalt thou fear, him shalt thou serve, to him shalt thou cleave, and by his name shalt thou swear." *AV* and *ARV* weaken the emphasis by changing the word-order arbitrarily and beginning with "thou."

The tragic story of Absalom (2 Sam. 13-18) tells of the seduction of his sister Tamar by Amnon, the revenge taken by Absalom, and its consequences: "fled ... fled ... fled ... fled" (13:29-38). It is not the death of Amnon, but the flight of Absalom which especially concerns the writer. This seems to justify us in interpreting the words: "and he [David] mourned for his son every day" (vs. 37) as referring not to Amnon but to Absalom. This emphasis must be taken into consideration also in dealing with verse 39. At least it makes it probable that the rendering "to go forth unto Absalom," i.e., to bring him back from exile, is to be preferred to "to go forth against Absalom" i.e., to punish him. Yet against such an interpretation is the fact that it was only when tricked by Joab that David consented to Absalom's return and then he refused to see him for "two full years."

Sentence Structure. It is difficult to reproduce in a translation the finer shades of meaning and the emphasis which is indicated in the original. This is true especially of the sentence structure in Hebrew. There are two broad classes of sentence, the nominal and the verbal. The one as we have already noted, has no verb expressed; the other has a finite verb which usually stands at the beginning. The one "represents something fixed, a state or in short, *a being* so and so" the other "something *moveable* and *in progress*, an *event* or *action*." This distinction has been well described as "indispensable to the more delicate appreciation of Hebrew syntax."[18] In Hebrew, unlike English, in the nominal sentence, subject and predicate are placed together without a copula (the verb "to be"); English requires the use of the copula. Thus in Psalm 23:1 the Hebrew says simply, "The Lord my shepherd." This expresses a "something fixed," a "being so and so." We might almost represent it by the equation "The Lord = my shepherd." The *AV* inserts the copula *is*. But it puts the "is" in italics to indicate that it is supplied to bring out the meaning, despite the fact that the "is" may suggest present *time* rather than *state* or *condition*. The emphasis is on a fixed relationship, not on a present situation which may be ephemeral and transitory, changeable as time. Compare for example, "The Lord (is) my light" (Ps. 27:1).

In the case of the nominal sentence there is a usage which is especially interesting. It is the compound nominal sentence, with the *casus pendens.* Thus, "Man, his days as grass" (Ps. 103:15) appears in AV as *"As for* man, his days *are* as grass." Here the Psalmist instead of saying "the days of man (are) as grass," which would place the emphasis on "days," takes the word "man" out of its natural position, places it at the beginning and replaces it in the sentence by a retrospective pronoun. Note also "(As for) God, his way (is) perfect" (Ps. 18:30). A more literal rendering of Psalm 125:2 would be "Jerusalem, mountains are round about her; and (or, but) the Lord is round about his people"; "and (as for) the stork, the fir trees (are) her house" (Ps. 104:17).

POETRY

The emphatic repetition of which we have been speaking, while occurring frequently in prose, finds its fullest and most characteristic expression in poetry, in the Psalms and in Proverbs. In fact parallelism or balance is its basic and most essential characteristic. This parallelism may take various forms.

As regards its form, the metrical unit (stich, or colon) usually consists of three or four word-groups, each group (indicated by hyphens) having a single accent or stress (Hebrew poetry, unlike Greek and Latin is accentual, not quantitative). These units may be independent of one another or be joined together in twos or threes to form couplets (distichs) or triplets (tristichs). But the Hebrew poet allowed himself considerable freedom in applying the basic principle of balance and parallelism in outward form and subject matter. That such was the case is illustrated for example by the beautiful 103rd Psalm.

Bless the-Lord, O-my-soul; and all-that-is-within-me, his-holy name.
Bless the-Lord, O-my-soul; and forget-not all his-benefits.

Here two units are joined together to form a couplet; and the first couplet stands in parallelism with the second, the first unit of each line being strictly synonymous, the second unit of the second being adversative. Then the Psalmist proceeds

Who-forgiveth all thine-iniquities;
Who-healeth all thy-diseases;
Who-redeemeth thy-life from-destruction;
Who-crowneth-thee with-mercy and-compassions;
Who-satisfieth thy-desire with-good-things

No one of these lines is joined with the one which immediately precedes it, although the first four could be regarded as forming two pairs (distichs). But the last is followed and expanded by the words

(So that) thy-youth is-renewed like-the-eagle's

forming a double line. Then the Psalmist proceeds with units which naturally form couplets

The-Lord executeth righteousness and-judgments for-all oppressed.
He-made-known his-ways unto-Moses, to-the-children of-Israel his-doings.

Here in each line the second unit completes the first; and the two lines stand in general parallelism in thought and structure.

Sometimes the units are separate, oftener they are joined together, very often in pairs (distichs) sometimes as triplets (tristichs). Thus in Judges 5:28 we have two pairs or couplets:

Through the-window she-looked-forth and-cried,
The mother of Sisera (cried) through the lattice
Why delays his-chariot in-coming?
Why tarry the hoof-beats of-his-chariots.

Here the second line requires a verb. In other respects the second and fourth are in synonymous parallelism with the first and third.

The song has already given us in verse 27 a good example of a triplet in

At-her-feet, he-bowed, he-fell, he-lay;
At-her-feet, he-bowed, he-fell:
Where he bowed, there he-fell-down dead.

Here the parallelism is synonymous.

We often find that the last unit of a metrical line is shorter than the preceding. Thus it may have the 3 + 2 form. This is the case in Psalm 27:1.

The-Lord (is) my-light and-my-salvation; whom shall-I-fear?
The-Lord (is) the-strength of-my-life; of-whom shall-I-be-afraid?

This form is called the Qinah or dirge metre. But it is not restricted to dirges as the above example very clearly indicates.

As regards content, the parallelism may be synonymous, the second unit, or line, repeating the thought of the first in practically identical terms, as in the example just cited. Or the parallelism may be adversative or antithetic. This is especially true of the first part of the central section of the Book of Proverbs, Chapters 10 to 15, for in this group of chapters the fact that the parallelism is antithetic is indicated only by the subject-matter since the Hebrew uses the ordinary conjunction, "and". A striking example of this is Ps. 103:17 where the psalmist after likening the brevity of man's life on earth to that of a flower of the field, goes on to say, "and the mercy of the Lord is from everlasting to everlasting." Our English versions express the antithesis by "but".

> Whoso-despiseth the word shall-be-destroyed;
> But-he-that-feareth the-commandment shall-be-rewarded (Prov. 13:13).

The parallelism may involve what may be called a split metaphor:

> A-wise son maketh-glad (his) father;
> But-a-foolish son (is)-the heaviness-of his-mother (Prov. 10:1)

Here each half of the verse expresses half of the entire meaning. The wise son delights both father and mother. The foolish son brings sorrow to both alike. So we may say that the parallelism is both antithetic and cumulative or supplementary. What concerns both parents is divided between them.

Aside from its beauty and artistry, the parallelism has at times an important bearing on the interpretation. Thus in the verse

> He-made-known his-ways unto-Moses,
> His-acts unto-the-children of-Israel.

the question arises whether the parallelism is synonymous, or antithetic. Does "ways" suggest the more intimate and personal relation in which Moses stood with the Lord as shown in the Theophany of Exodus 34:6f. (cf. Num. 7:89), while "acts" refers only to the tokens, the visible signs and wonders by which God forced an often times disobedient and rebellious people to recognize his sovereign control over them? The AV rendering suggests this.

Sometimes the parallelism gives welcome light on the meaning of an unusual word or phrase, as in Psalm 68:4 where we read:

> Sing unto God, sing praises to his name.
> Extol him that rideth in the deserts.
> His name is Jah, and rejoice before him.

The word rendered "extol" means "lift up or raise up." In Isaiah 57:14 it is used of the making of a highway (AV, "cast up"). Here the parallelism indicates rather clearly that it is used of raising up the voice in song. But aside from questions of interpretation, all will agree that this basic feature of parallelism adds greatly to the beauty of Hebrew poetry.

One of the most beautiful of the Psalms, considered as an example of poetical parallelism, is the 19th. It begins by celebrating the wonders of the universe as created by God:

> The heavens declare the glory of God
> And the firmament showeth his handiwork.

Then with the words

> The law of the Lord is perfect, converting the soul:
> The testimony of the Lord is sure, making wise the simple,

it sings the praises of that Word which God has given to man, who is the crown and masterpiece of his creation, to be his guide in ruling over it.

It is to be noted, however, that this feature of Hebrew poetry is neither unique nor distinctive. We find it in the Pyramid Texts of the Ancient Egyptians, in the hymns of the Babylonians and Assyrians, and it is not rare in modern poetry. Consequently there was nothing really surprising in the discovery of this feature in the Ugaritic mythological poetry. However, these newly discovered texts have made it clearer that it is the parallelism which is the basic and essential feature.

The regular use of parallelism in Hebrew poetry may be regarded as an illustration of the fact that repetition, or elaboration is a very natural form of expression. Consequently, we often find in prose narratives a kind of balance or parallelism which resembles formal poetry to a considerable degree. For example, the blessing pronounced on Rebekah by her family as she departed to become the wife of Isaac (Gen. 24:60) is treated by some as poetry:

> Our sister (art) thou; become thousands of myriads
> And may thy seed possess the gate of its haters.

But in this same chapter which is a splendid example of Hebrew narrative prose there are a number of verses which could be treated in the same way since there are a number of sentences of about equal length in which a certain element of balance is quite as obvious; e.g.:

> The thing proceedeth from the Lord,
> We cannot speak unto thee bad or good.
> Lo Rebekah is before thee.
> Take (her) and go
> And let her be thy master's son's wife,
> As the Lord hath spoken.

This tendency to rhythm and balance which appears even in simple prose makes it difficult at times to draw the line between prose and poetry. The beautiful language in which Ruth expresses her devotion to Naomi might be cast in poetic form as follows:

> Intreat me not to leave thee,
> To turn back from after thee,
> For whither thou goest, I will go,
> And where thou lodgest, I will lodge,
> Thy people, my people, and thy God, my God.
> Where thou diest, I will die,
> And there will l be buried.
> The Lord do so to me, and so may he add
> If death should part between thee and me.

Yet recent translators seem to regard it as simple prose and print it as such.

The balance and parallelism in Rehoboam's words to the people when they came for his answer on the third day:

> My father made your yoke heavy,
>   And I will add to your yoke.
> My father chastised you with whips,
>   And I will chastise you with scorpions   (I Kings 12:14),

is certainly more marked than in the words of the people:

> What portion have we in David?
>   We have no inheritance in the son of Jesse.
> To your tents, O Israel!
>   Look now to your own house, David (vs. 16).

Yet *RSV* treats the former as prose, despite its carefully balanced phrasing, and the latter as poetry.

It is especially in the case of the Prophetical Books that this tendency to "metricize" is most apparent. *RSV* treats most of Isaiah as poetry But the attempt to do this often changes elevated speech or impassioned oratory into what is very lame poetry to say the least. What is gained, for example, by printing Isaiah 2:5 as

> O house of Jacob,
>   come, let us walk
>   in the light of the Lord *(RSV)*.

If this is poetry, we see no reason why the words of the women in 4:1 should not be treated in the same way:

> We will eat our own bread
>   and wear our own clothes,
> Only let us be called by your name;
>   take away our reproach

instead of being printed in *RSV* as simple prose. If Jeremiah 3:1 is poetry and should be treated as such:

> If a man divorce his wife
>   and she goes from him
> And becomes another man's wife,
>   Will he return to her?
> Would not that land be greatly polluted?
> You have played the harlot with many lovers
>   and would you return to me?
>   says the Lord *(RSV)*

where is the dividing line between poetry and prose?

Isaiah 24:2 contains twelve nouns each of which is preceded by the preposition "like." It begins "like the people, like the priest" and ends with "like the creditor, like the one against whom (there is) a creditor." Since these twelve units represent pairs which are more or less antithetic, the *AV* has rendered each pair by "as with . . . so with," and it has been followed in this by *ARV* and *RSV;* but with this difference: *AV* and *ARV* print this series as simple prose. *RSV* prints them as poetic couplets. It may be admitted that this makes many biblical passages resemble the free verse (*vers libre*) which passes as poetry today. But it tends to abolish the distinction, a proper and even necessary one, between poetry and prose, with the result that the picturesque and even impassioned prose of the prophets becomes anything but impressive poetry.

Parallelism and rhythm do not in themselves constitute poetry.[19] The attempt to treat the at times highly rhetorical utterances of the prophets as formal poetry, an attempt which goes back two centuries to Bishop Lowth, has been carried to such an extreme in recent years as to make the theory that the prophets were poets rather ridiculous.[20]

Alphabet Poems. A special feature of Hebrew poetry is the tendency to arrange the verses according to the 22 letters of the Hebrew alphabet. The most familiar example is Psalm 119. It has 176 verses because 8 consecutive verses begin with the same letter of the alphabet. The only other example of such a multiple alphabetic poem, as we may call it, is Lamentations 3 which has 66 verses because 3 consecutive verses each begin with the same letter of the alphabet. In Lamentations 1, 2 and 4, the verses are of varying length (two or three lines), but only the first word of the first line follows the alphabetic order. Other examples of alphabetic poetry are: Psalm 25; 34; 37; 111; 112; 145; also Proverbs 31:10-31.

Anacoluthon. A noteworthy feature of poetry and hortatory address is the frequent and sometimes sudden change in person and number from singular to plural, from objective to direct address. A good example of such changes is Psalm 18. In verse 1 the Psalmist speaks to the Lord: "I will love thee." Then at once he passes to a description in the third person (vss. 2-24) using "Lord" (9 times) and "God" (3 times), "Highest" (once). "Thy" appears in verse 15. In verses 25-29 he uses "thou" (8 times) with "my God" (twice). In verses 30-34 he returns to the third person, using "God," "Lord," and "he." With verses 35-40 he again uses "thou," but in verse 41 "Lord." And so on: "thou" (vs. 43), "Lord" or "God" or "he" (vss. 46-48), "thee, O Lord" (vs. 49), "he" and "his" (vs. 50).

It is interesting to compare Psalms 103 and 104. In some respects they are quite similar. Both celebrate the greatness of the Lord and both begin with the words: "Bless the Lord, O my soul." The one is a hymn of redemption, the other of creation. Psalm 103 uses the third person throughout, with Lord as subject eleven times. Psalm 104 on the other hand passes frequently from the third person to the second and back again: e.g., in verses 1-10 we have "thou . . . thou . . . his . . . his . . .

his . . . thou . . . thy . . . thy . . . thou . . . thou . . . he." "Lord" appears ten times in this psalm and "God" or "my God" three times.

Psalm 145 refers to the Lord eight times; and it uses "he," "him," and "his," about a dozen times in speaking of him. On the other hand the Psalmist addresses God directly nearly twenty-five times using "thou," "thee," and "thy." Thus we read: "The Lord is good to all: and his tender mercies are over all his works" (vs. 9), followed immediately by "All thy works shall praise thee and thy saints shall bless thee." Such shifts are not infrequent in poetry and occur also in prose. In Psalm 34:17, the Hebrew reads "they cried." The *AV* inserts (in italics) *"the righteous"* to make it clear that the nexus is with verse 15 and not with verse 16.

The most familiar example, so familiar that we scarcely notice it, occurs in the 23rd Psalm. Beginning with the words, "The Lord (is) my shepherd," it speaks *of* God and of his gracious dealings with David. Then with verse 4 it changes and speaks *to* God: "thou . . . thou. . . ." Finally with the words "and I shall dwell in the house of the Lord unto length of days," it reverts again to the third person.

Such examples as the above make it easy for us to understand the shifts from the singular to the plural of the second person in the hortatory addresses of Moses in Deuteronomy, e.g., "What thing soever I command you, observe to do it: thou shalt not add thereto, nor diminish from it" (12:32), and "Ye . . . ye . . . your . . . thou . . . thy . . . thee" (14:1f.).

It also sheds welcome light upon the words "as many were astonished at thee" (Isa. 52:15) in a context in which the Servant is repeatedly spoken of objectively in the third person. This passage has been much debated. The Targum and Syriac read "at him." But the MT is supported by the Qumran Scroll (1 QIsaᵃ), and by LXX and Vulg. Similarly we read "their arm" (Isa. 33:2) in an "us . . . our" context; note also "my mouth . . . his spirit" (34:16). In Ezekiel 37:25 "wherein your fathers have dwelt" appears in a long "they-them" passage (vss. 24-28).

The sudden shifts in Micah 7:14-20 are striking and somewhat confusing. The prayer begins with the words, "Feed thy people," addressing God directly. In verse 15 the Lord answers: the "thy" is Israel, the "I" is Jehovah, the "him" or "it" is Israel. The reference to the nations in verses 16f. ends with "they shall be afraid of the Lord our God and shall fear because of thee [the Lord]," which prepares for the question, "Who is a God like unto thee?" and the description which follows in the third person ends with another shift: "He [God] will subdue our [Israel's] iniquities; and thou [God, reverting to direct address] wilt cast all their [Israel's] sins into the depths of the sea."

Such shifts occur repeatedly in Hezekiah's prayer (Isa. 38:10-20), indicating perhaps the highly emotional state of the speaker. Compare also Psalm 33:22 with Psalm 34:22.

In Zechariah 12:10 we have a somewhat similar example: "and they shall look on me whom they pierced, and they shall mourn for him. . . ." God is speaking; and he is speaking of himself as pierced in the person of his Son. So the transition from the "me" to the "him," while seemingly abrupt, is both natural and significant, since it suggests what the New Testament makes fully clear, the oneness of the Father and the Son.[21]

This usage helps us to understand such an expression as "they bless with their mouth, but they curse inwardly" (Ps. 62:4b) which is literally, "they bless [each] with his mouth, but they curse with [or in] their heart [inwardly]"; or the more familiar; "I will bless them that bless thee and curse him that curseth thee" (Gen. 12:3). We note also Psalm 73:28 "I have put my trust in the Lord God, that I may declare all thy works" and Psalm 104:13 "who watereth the mountains from his upper chambers; the earth is satisfied with the fruit of thy works." In Psalm 24:6, "This is the generation of them that seek him, that seek thy face, O Jacob," the "him" and "thy" both refer to God; and the "Jacob" which follows is as Delitzsch points out "a summarizing predicate," describing the God-seekers. It is to be noted, however, that in some cases, as for example Psalm 91, the change in person may indicate a change in speaker. Thus the "my" of verses 2 and 9a is the Psalmist addressing God; the "me" and "my" of verses 14-16 is God himself speaking.

The Conjunction "And" in Hebrew. We have seen that in Hebrew poetry the parallelism may be adversative instead of synonymous and often warrants or necessitates the rendering "but" in English. It is also to be noted that there are cases where the synonymous parallel introduced by "and" may be simply explanatory, concomitant, or emphatic. In such cases the English equivalent is better expressed by "even" than by "and." We have seen that parallelism while characteristic of poetry is often met with in simple prose. To render it by "and" may be decidedly confusing. Thus, "And the God of Israel stirred up the spirit of Pul king of Assyria, even the spirit of Tilgath-pilneser king of Assyria" (1 Chron. 5:26) may be both explanatory and emphatic.[22] In Daniel 6:28 the statement "So this Daniel prospered in the reign of Darius, and in the reign of Cyrus the Persian" is confusing and misleading, since it suggests that the reign of Cyrus followed that of Darius. If, as seems now to be established by archaeological research,[23] Darius the Mede was sub-king or governor over "Babylon and the Region Beyond the River" under Cyrus the Persian, the "and in the reign of Cyrus the Persian" does not imply sequence in time but concomitance. The "and" is then to be taken in the sense of "even" or "that is." The dating of Hosea's prophecies: "The word of the Lord that came unto Hosea, the son of Beeri in the days of Uzziah, Jotham, Ahaz, Hezekiah, kings of Judah, and in the days of Jeroboam the son of Joash, king of Israel" (1:1) is to be similarly understood. Here as in Amos 1:1, the "and" does not express temporal sequence. The reigns of Uzziah of Judah and of Jeroboam of Israel ran parallel for many years. Similarly in 2 Samuel 23:1 "David the son of Jesse said, and the man *who was* raised up on high . . . and the sweet psalmist of Israel said" — the "ands" might indicate that two or even three persons are referred to. But it is quite clear that all refer to David.

METRICS

That parallelism or balance in thought and form is a basic feature of Hebrew poetry is obvious to everyone who reads the Bible with any attention to its literary form. But it was not until about seventy-five years ago that a serious attempt was made to determine the metrical patterns of the poetry of the Bible. As a result of the pioneer work of Ley, Bickell, Sievers, and others, it is now generally recognized that Hebrew poetry is accentual and not quantitative, that a metrical line contains a definite number of accented syllables. Various forms have been recognized, the most familiar being the so-called *Qinah* or lamentation verse, which has three accents in the first part of the line and two in the second. Hence it had been called inaccurately "pentameter." It was not long after this study had gotten under way that the claim began to be made that there was or should be a strict symmetry in the length of the metrical lines, and that lack of such uniformity was therefore to be regarded as indicating corruption of the text. Many of the changes in the text of the Old Testament, especially the Prophets, proposed by critical scholars were based largely or solely on metrical considerations. It is now being recognized, as a result of the discovery of the Ras Shamra mythological poems, that the metres need not be uniform, but may vary considerably even in the course of the same poem. Consequently it is now admitted that the test of uniformity which Alexander a century earlier had called a rhetorical chimera had been carried too far, and that metrics does not furnish the support to conjectural textual emendation, which the critics were hoping that it would.[24]

A great deal is now being made of the claim that the Israelites borrowed their metrical forms from the Canaanites.

Since the great feature which both Hebrew and Ugaritic poems have in common is the parallelism (*parallelismus membrorum*), it is important to recognize that this is a feature common to Semitic poetry in general; and it is found among other peoples as well. Fifty years ago Breasted wrote as follows regarding the hymns in the Pyramid Texts of Ancient Egypt:

> Among the oldest literary fragments in the collection are the religious hymns, and these exhibit an early poetic form, that of couplets displaying parallelism in arrangement of words and thought — the form which is familiar to all in the Hebrew psalms as "parallelism of members." It is carried back by its employment in the Pyramid Texts into the fourth millennium B.C., by far earlier than its appearance anywhere else. It is indeed the oldest of all literary forms known to us.[25]

Without pausing to compare the Babylonian hymns, which furnish us with as close if not closer parallels, it will suffice to point out in this connection that, if the Israelites were in Egypt for several centuries as the Old Testament declares that they were, and if Moses "was learned in all the wisdom of the Egyptians, and was mighty in words and in deeds," as the New Testament tells us that he was, and if Moses and the children of Israel "sang this song unto the Lord," which is recorded in Exodus 15, and if Moses "spake" the song recorded in Deuteronomy 32, as the narrative declares that he did, and if he wrote the 90th Psalm as the heading tells us he did, then it would be quite natural to conclude that it was Moses who gave to the poetical literature of the Israelites its definite literary form and style, and that he formed this style in Egypt, insofar as it was new and not familiar to the Israelites for generations, even to Abram in the religious poems of Babylonia when he dwelt in Ur of the Chaldees. The claim that, because of certain resemblances between the poetry of the Canaanites and Israelites, the latter must have borrowed them from the former will not appeal to anyone who is willing to allow to the Hebrews even a modicum of originality. If the Israelites knew and had used the parallel couplet (bi-colon as we may call it) for generations, does the fact that there are examples of the parallel triplet (tri-colon) in both Canaanite and Israelite poetry prove that the Israelites borrowed from the Canaanites? The claim would hardly deserve mention were it not advanced so seriously by the pro-Canaanite scholars of today.[26]

POETRY AND ITS INTERPRETATION

The question of the degree of literalness and factuality with which biblical poetry is to be taken is an important one. It is one of the problems in the interpretation of the Book of Job. Is it history, poetry, or drama? According to William Henry Green, for many years professor of Old Testament at Princeton Seminary:

It is related not as a parable, but as a history, instructive throughout, as all Bible histories are, but still an actual, veritable occurrence. And Job is spoken of in other parts of Scripture as a real person, and in connection with other real persons like Noah and Daniel, and the events of his life are referred to in a manner which implies that they had actually occurred. We can have no doubt, therefore, that, with all the poetic embellishment of the narrative, Job did actually live, and the history took place substantially as it is here related.[27]

Similarly Matthew Henry in his still widely used *Commentary* declares that the narrative "no doubt is exactly true, though the inspired penman is allowed the usual liberty of putting the matter of which Job and his friends discoursed into his own words."[28]

Both of these conservative writers insist on the historical truth of the story. Both allow for a poetical treatment. But neither defines the exact extent of "the poetic embellishment" which has taken place. We may well leave the matter where they leave it. The trend in recent years has been to stress the poetic and minimize or deny the historical. This we must regard as tending in the wrong direction. To Genung, for example, the Book of Job is "The greatest production of the Hebrew Wisdom literature and one of the supreme literary creations of the world." But he shows little interest in the question of the historical truth of the book.[29]

We naturally turn also to the Book of Joel. Whether or to what extent the locusts so vividly described in it are literal locusts has been a matter of discussion for centuries. Some scholars find only locusts here. Others see back of the locusts a human scourge of which the locusts were the symbol and type. According to still others, the transition from the literal to the figurative appears first clearly at 2:16ff. with the mention of the "northern *army*," by which the Assyrians are to be understood.

Ezekiel 16 is an elaborate parable or allegory which pictures in vivid language the terrible corruption of the chosen people. It describes this as inherited guilt: "Thy father was an Amorite and thy mother a Hittite" (vss. 3, 45). That the language is figurative is indicated with especial clearness by the reference to Sodom (vs. 46; cf. Isa. 1:9f.). Thus Fairbairn remarks: "To connect the chosen people with such a parentage was one of the most impressive ways that could be taken to mark their inveterately depraved and sinful character."[30]

Isaiah 10:24-34 pictures vividly the seemingly invincible advance of the Assyrians. But the downfall is expressed in definitely figurative language in verses 33f. Is it not then probable that the advance of the invader is also described in figurative or ideal terms? The path taken by their army seems to lie through the mountainous country as if this mighty enemy were treading upon the high places of the earth like the

Almighty himself (cf. Micah 1:3; Amos 4:13; Job 9:8). But while the Assyrian may think of himself as a mighty tree, a sudden change of figure, he is only a rod in the hand of the God of Israel, to be used and cast aside when it has served its purpose.

REPETITION AND ELABORATION

A form of emphasis which appears frequently in the Old Testament consists in the repetition of the same facts and narratives elsewhere and in the elaboration of detail in the narration itself.

We have three separate accounts of the struggle with Assyria in the days of Hezekiah (Kings, Chronicles, Isaiah); also three accounts of the destruction of Jerusalem by Nebuchadnezzar (Kings, Chronicles, Jeremiah). Ezra gives a list of the Jews who returned with Zerubbabel (chap. 2), Nehemiah gives a very similar list (chap. 7). One, quite obvious reason for these repetitions may be the desire to make each account sufficiently complete in itself; another, to emphasize the importance of what is described; a third, to add some details or to view the events from a different angle. Sometimes these more or less parallel records clarify matters for us considerably. At other times their differences in detail, especially when the accounts are short may seem contradictory and cause the Bible student no little difficulty.

The Flood. In the account of the Flood three great themes are emphasized by repetition and elaboration. They are, the sinfulness of man as the reason for the Flood (6:5, 11-13), the object of the Flood which was to destroy all flesh (6:7, 13, 17; 7:4, 21-23; 8:21), and the saving of a representative remnant of man and beast (6:8, 19-20; cf. 7:1-3, 7-9, 13-15; 8:16-19). These three major themes are so repeatedly stressed that the narrative can easily be divided into two or three accounts of the same event and this has been regarded by critical scholars as a clear proof that the Pentateuch is composite.[31]

A Wife for Isaac. There is much repetition in the story of the securing of a wife for Isaac (Gen. 24). We read in detail of the servant's prayer (vss. 12-14), of the answer to his prayer (vss. 17-22); and then the whole story is repeated to Laban and Bethuel (vss. 34-48). The camels are mentioned seventeen times. Much repetition! Yet this is one of the most beautiful prose narratives in the Pentateuch.

The Plagues. The account of the Plagues in Exodus 7-11 follows a definite pattern, which in the case of three of them (frogs, hail, and locusts) has the following form which is illustrated by the Frogs as follows: threat (8:1-4), command (vs. 5), execution (vss. 6-7), petition (vss. 8-11), removal (vss. 12-14) and result (vs. 15). Since this form of statement is quite elaborate, even unnecessarily so, it is abridged in the accounts of most of the other plagues. Thus murrain is restricted to three items (threat, execution, and result), boils likewise to three (command, execution, and result).[32]

The Sons of Jacob. An example of this method is the elaborate way in which the Pentateuch deals with the sons of Jacob. Genesis 29-30 gives an account of the births of all but one of Jacob's sons, which took place while he was serving his father-in-law Laban in Padanaram. In 32:22 we read that Jacob crossed the Jabbok with his "eleven sons." In 35:16-20 Benjamin's birth is recorded, as taking place near Ephrath (Bethlehem) after Jacob's arrival back in Canaan. Chapter 46 records the names of all the sons and descendants who went with Jacob to join Joseph in Egypt. Jacob's blessing of his twelve sons (Gen. 49) is further described as a blessing of "the twelve tribes of Israel" (vs. 28). Exodus begins with a summary statement (1:1-5), reminding the reader that all the tribes were in Egypt, and so gives definite meaning to the words "children of Israel" which occur frequently in the story of the oppression and of the exodus. At Sinai in connection with the giving of the law, Moses set up "twelve pillars according to the twelve tribes of Israel" (Exod. 24:4). The breastplate worn by the highpriest was to contain twelve stones, with the names of the twelve children of Israel engraved on them (28:21; 39:14). Obviously this is the reason that twelve loaves were placed on the table of shewbread (Lev. 24:5). The first four chapters of Numbers give a detailed account of the census taken at Sinai, both of the twelve tribes and of the Levites separately. It includes the regulations for the encamping of the twelve tribes around the tabernacle, and the order of the tribes when on the march. Furthermore, the total of the adult males which is given in Numbers 2:32 (603,550) corresponds exactly with the silver levy of a half-shekel which produced the 100 talents and 1775 shekels which were used chiefly for the silver sockets for the boards of the tabernacle (Exod. 38:25-28). In Numbers 7 the list of identical offerings for the dedication of the altar presented by the twelve princes as representing the twelve tribes of Israel is repeated in full twelve times (a total of 71 verses); the name of the prince is given at the beginning of the list of his offerings and repeated at the end; and a concluding summary or total is added, obviously to show that each of the twelve tribes had an equal right of access to the altar of the Lord. The "spies" sent out to search out the land number twelve, one "head" to represent each of the tribes (Num. 13). Finally the census taken at Shittim, shortly before the conquest, is of the same twelve tribes as were numbered at Sinai (Num. 26). The two and a half tribes (Reuben, Gad and half of Manasseh) were permitted to settle east of Jordan, on the condition that they assist their brethren of the nine and a half tribes in the conquest of the land (Num. 32; cf. Josh. 1:12-18; 4:12f.; 22:1-34). Consequently, when we read in Joshua 1:2 the command to Joshua, "arise, go over this Jordan, thou and all this people," it is perfectly obvious that *all* the Israelites are included in this command.

That Jacob and all his descendants were in Egypt, that all of them came out of Egypt, and that all of them took part in the conquest of Canaan is made perfectly plain by the oft-repeated and detailed statements of the Bible. Paul is simply referring to this unforgettable fact when in 1 Corinthians 10:1-4 he reminds his readers that "all" their fathers were under the cloud and "all" passed through the sea. Five times he uses this word "all" in referring to the experiences of the exodus. No facts connected with Israel are more repeatedly and emphatically stated than this, that the great events connected with the deliverance from Egypt concerned *all* Israel.

The Censuses at Sinai and in Moab. The Book of Numbers owes its title to the Septuagint Version; and this was due to the fact that the opening chapters of the book deal in such detail with the statistics of the children of Israel at the time of the exodus. Four chapters, as we have pointed out, are devoted to these largely statistical data. Chapter 1 gives first the date when the numbering is to take place and then the names of the renowned princes of the twelve tribes who are to assist Aaron in taking the sum of the children of Israel. Then the total for each tribe is given in accordance with the following specifications, which are repeated for each of the twelve tribes: "by their generations, after their families, by the house of their fathers, according to the number of the names (by their polls), every male from twenty years old and upward, all that were able to go forth to war, those that were numbered of them." This is followed by the grand total for all the tribes, 603,550 (vs. 46); and it is expressly stated that the Levites are not included in this numbering and total; but their duties are briefly summarized, and it is stated that they are to encamp around the tabernacle and that the other tribes are to camp around them according to their standards.

Chapter 2 gives the precise location of the standards of the four tribal groups with reference to the tabernacle, but "far off" from it (vs. 2), since it is to be immediately surrounded by the Levites and by Moses and Aaron. Then the total for each of the three tribes of each standard is given, followed by a total for each standard; and finally the grand total for all the tribes is repeated (2:32). Again it is stated that the Levites are not included in this total. In this listing the name of the prince over each tribe is given exactly as in 1:5-16. Chapter 10, in giving the account of the first journey from Sinai, gives, for the third time, the names of these twelve princes.

Chapter 3 is devoted to the Levites and their duties. They are "given unto Aaron and his sons" (3:9), it having been first recalled how Aaron's four sons were reduced to two (vs. 4). The numbering follows for each of these three sons of Levi, namely, Gershon, Kohath and Merari. They are to be taken instead of the first-born (vss. 12f.). In this numbering, which is to include all who are a month old and upward (vs. 15), the names of the heads of families of each of the three main divisions are included, the pitching place of each with reference to the tabernacle is designated, and the special duties assigned to each of these divisions are specified. It is further stated that Moses and Aaron are to encamp toward the east, where the entrance to the court was placed. The grand total (22,000) is then given (vs. 39). Finally, the details are given with regard to the taking of the Levites in place of the first-born (22,273) of the twelve tribes and as to the disposition to be made of the redemption money (1,365 shekels, i.e., 5 shekels per head) which was paid to Aaron and his sons because of the excess of first-born over the Levites.

Chapter 4 provides for a special census of the Levites for the service of the tabernacle. Unlike that in Chapter 3, it includes only those who are between the ages of thirty and fifty years of age, that is, who are in the prime of physical vigor. The duties of each of the three main divisions are carefully defined, those of Kohath being given first, because of the specially important duties assigned to them, the carrying of the ark and the vessels of the Sanctuary. The pre-eminence assigned to Kohath is obviously because Moses and Aaron were Kohathites. The peril attendant upon the carrying out of their tasks is clearly stated and the means of averting it (vss. 5-20). Then the special duties of Gershon and Merari are given in some detail including the numerical figures for each (vss. 36, 40, 44) followed (vs. 48) by the grand total (8,580).

Chapter 26. The census at the close of the forty years which was taken in Moab is much briefer. Like the earlier one it gives the total for each of the twelve tribes followed by a grand total for all of them, 601,730 (vs. 51), a figure which is slightly smaller than the earlier total (1:46). The period of the forty years was marked by stagnation, not by growth. This census has a markedly different form from that in Chapters 1-3. (1) The specification as to age, etc. is both much briefer, "from twenty years old and upward, throughout their fathers' house, all that are able to go to war in Israel," and it is stated only *once*. (2) It is constructed (vs. 5-50) after the pattern of the genealogies of the seventy sons of Jacob who went with him into Egypt, which makes it largely a repetition of Genesis 46. So it is pointed out that this census has special reference to the distribution of the land of Canaan among the tribes after the conquest (vss. 52-56). The statement closes with a brief enumeration. of the Levites, which includes some genealogical and historical data, but gives only one total, that for all the Levites (23,000), a total which differs only slightly from the figure given in the first census. The chapter closes with an impressive reference to the tragic difference between the two censuses. All who had been numbered at Sinai had perished except two, Caleb and Joshua.

The Feast of Tabernacles (Num. 29:12-34). The detailed enumeration of the sacrifices for the seven days of this feast shows the same repetitive method of statement. The number of bullocks is gradually reduced from 13 to 7. In other respects the sacrifices for the seven days are identical. But the specifications are given in full seven times (cf. chap. 7).

Pillar of Cloud. (Num. 9:15-23, cf. Exod. 40:36-38). A striking example of elaboration and detail in a single, relatively brief, narrative is the account of the role which the pillar of cloud and fire played in the journeyings of the children of Israel. The impressive fact that the restings and departings of the pillar determined these journeyings and sojournings could have been expressed in a single fairly brief sentence.[33] But it is given nine verses and the elaboration is impressive and serves to indicate how completely the daily life of Israel during the interval between Sinai and Canaan was controlled visibly and unmistakably by their God.

Reuben, Gad, and half Manasseh. Numbers 32:33-42 gives a summary description of the territory alloted to the two and a half tribes by Moses. In Joshua 13, apparently to make the account of the distribution to the tribes comprehensive, the account of the allotment to the nine and a half tribes (chaps. 14-17) is preceded by a much fuller account of the territory assigned to the two and a half tribes (chap. 13) than that already given in Numbers. Yet it is stated three times in Chapter 13 that Moses (not Joshua) gave these lands to the two and a half tribes (vss. 15, 24, 29).

Crossing the Jordan. The account of this memorable event, as it is given in Joshua 3-4, is an excellent example of elaboration and repetition. This is indicated by the following statements: "and the people passed over right against Jericho" (3:16): "until all the people were passed clean over the Jordan" (vs. 17); "and it came to pass when all the people were clean passed over Jordan" (4:1); "and the people hasted and passed over" (vs. 10); "and it came to pass, when all the people were clean passed over that the ark of the Lord passed over, and the priests, in the presence of the people" (vs. 11). We might think that this would end the account of the crossing. But it does not. Verse 12 adds the important detail that the children of Reuben, Gad, and half-Manasseh to the number of 40,000 were included among those who passed over. Then the narrative goes on to tell us that "On that day the Lord magnified Joshua in the sight of all Israel" (vs. 14); and the evidence of this is that "the Lord spake unto Joshua saying, Command the priests that bear the ark of the testimony, that they come up out of Jordan. Joshua therefore commanded the priests, Come ye up out of Jordan" (vss. 16f.). Their coming up out of Jordan has already been referred to (vs. 11). But here it is described as expressly ordered by the Lord through Joshua in order to magnify Joshua's authority, the proof of which is that after the priests obeyed the command of Joshua, "The waters of Jordan returned unto their place, and flowed over all his banks, as they did before" (vs. 18). We are then told the date when this momentous event occurred (vs. 19). And the narrative closes with an account of the "pitching" of the twelve stones at Gilgal and their significance for the generations to come. It almost seems as if the sacred historian is loath to leave this great historical event, this mighty work of God in behalf of Israel, and so he goes over it repeatedly and considers it from every angle.

Inherited Guilt. (Ezek. 18). Ezekiel is particularly fond of repetition and elaboration. This is illustrated by his discussion of inherited guilt. First the general proposition is stated: "Behold, all souls are mine; as the soul of the father, so also the soul of the son is mine: the soul that sinneth it shall die." Then specific examples are given: (a) the righteous father shall live (vss. 5-9), (b) the wicked son shall die (vss. 10-13), (c) the righteous grandson shall live (vss. 14-17), but (d) his father shall die (vs. 18). Then, on the basis of these examples, the whole subject is discussed in detail, returning to and reiterating the declaration of verse 4, "the soul that sinneth, it shall die" — righteousness and life, sin and death are thus stressed again and again. Thus it is made abundantly plain that the ways of the Lord are *equal*. And the final word is "Repent." We have a similar example in the great "Watchman Chapter" (33), which serves as a further disproof of the charge that "The way of the Lord is not equal." Seven times the word "equal" occurs in these two chapters. The same fondness for detailed elaboration appears in the description of the theophanies in 1:4-28.[34]

FIAT AND FULFILLMENT

A form of repetition which is not infrequent in Scripture consists in following the statement of a command or prediction with an account of its fulfillment or execution.

The Creation (Gen. 1). The account of the Creation is told in terms of a series of fiats, each of which is followed by a declaration of the fulfillment or execution of the fiat, which in most cases follows it very closely in phraseology; and in most cases the words "and it was so" are added to emphasize the fact that the commands of the Creator were fully carried out. There are many examples of this very natural way of emphasizing the importance of the divine commandments.

The Tabernacle. The most noteworthy example is the account of the construction and erection of the tabernacle, given in Exodus. We are given first a rather full account (chaps. 25-31) of the commands given to Moses for the construction of the tabernacle and its appointments, then an almost equally full account of the carrying out of these instructions (chaps. 35-39), and finally an account of the erection of the tabernacle and its acceptance by God (chap. 40). Thus, we have two practically identical descriptions of the ark: the one telling us the instructions given to Moses (25:10-21), the other the execution of those instructions by Bezaleel (37:1-9), the one account twelve verses long, the other nine. Then we are told that Moses was commanded to bring the ark into the tabernacle when it was erected (39:35), and that he did this (40:21). The object is clearly to stress the importance of the tabernacle and all of its sacred vessels, and also to stress the fact which runs like a refrain through the last two chapters that everything was done, "as the Lord commanded Moses."

Under this head we may consider also some examples which illustrate the wise pedagogical method which was used by the Lord and his servants in making known his will regarding coming events.

Spoiling the Egyptians (Exod. 3:21f.). Apparently the revelation which was made to Moses before he returned to Egypt declaring that the Lord would give the Israelites favor in the eyes of the Egyptians, and they should *ask* them for their *jewels* and *spoil* the Egyptians, was then given solely for Moses' own encouragement, and was not to be communicated to the people until the time of their departure had arrived (12:35f.).

Slaying of the First Born (Exod. 4:23). The same would appear to be true of the command which was given to Moses while he was returning to Egypt: "And thou shalt say unto Pharaoh, Thus saith the Lord, Israel is my son, even my firstborn: And I say unto thee, Let my son go, that he may serve me: and if thou refuse to let him go, behold I will slay thy son, (even) thy firstborn." This was to be the final threat; and it seems clear that it was not delivered until the nine plagues which preceded it had proved unavailing (11:4-8). But it was made known to Moses before he returned to Egypt.

The Passover (Exod. 12-13) is an even more remarkable illustration of this pedagogical method. In the first part of Chapter 12, very full instructions are given to Moses; they refer definitely to the passover and the seven day feast of unleavened bread; and it is stated that these regulations are to be kept throughout all their generations (12:14, 17; 13:9f.). In both chapters definite instruction is given Moses regarding the use of unleavened bread (12:8, 15-20; 13:6f.). But when we read the account of the instructions given by Moses to the people, we find that they are very brief (12:21-27). Nothing is said about using unleavened bread for seven days; and a few verses further on, we are told that "they baked unleavened cakes of the dough which they brought forth out of Egypt, for it was not leavened; because they were thrust out of Egypt, and could not tarry, neither had they prepared for themselves any victuals" (12:34, 39). Here a specific, circumstantial reason is given for their not using leaven: they had not had the time to leaven their bread, because they left in haste. This makes it quite clear that they had received no instructions regarding the eating of unleavened bread for seven days. It may look as if we have here two different accounts of the origin of the use of unleavened bread at the passover and during the days that followed it. And the literary critics find here two different sources, mainly J and P. But if we take the view that the instructions given to Moses in Chapters 12-13 were intended as a description of the feast as it was to be observed as a memorial in all coming generations, and that at the time of the exodus he gave the people only such instructions as were imperatively needed, the difficulty is largely removed. It then appears that the reason for the command that in the future they abstain from the use of leavened bread at the Passover and for the week that followed it, is to be found in the historical fact that for that period of time and perhaps even longer they were forced by circumstances to do this; and God made the eating of unleavened bread obligatory throughout their generations as a reminder and commemoration of this fact, a fact which showed how utterly dependent they had been upon their God for their deliverance from the bondage of Egypt.

The Manna (Exod. 16:12-36). The use of this method of communicating instructions is particularly clear in the case of the manna. The narrative in Exodus indicates quite plainly that the giving of the manna was intended both to prepare for and also to enforce the Sabbath law which was so soon to be given. In the first revelation regarding the manna which is made to Moses we read: "And it shall come to pass that on the sixth day they shall prepare that which they bring in; and it shall be twice as much as they gather daily" (Exod. 16:5). But when the manna first appears Moses simply tells the people that it is bread from heaven, that they are to prepare it, and that they are to leave nothing over for the next day (vss. 15-19); and failure to observe this command is severely rebuked (vs. 20). On the sixth day they discover that there is twice as much as on the preceding days (vs. 22). And Moses then tells them that the extra portion is for the sabbath day and that they are to prepare it for use on that day. An example of good pedagogy: he tells them what they need to know when they need to know it and not before.

The Coming Prophet (Deut. 18:15-22). In the great prophecy concerning the Prophet like unto Moses we have another instructive example of God's dealings with men. Moses makes this momentous promise known to the people in the course of the longest of the discourses delivered by him in the plains of Moab, shortly before his death. He has been their prophet in a unique sense (Num. 7:89; 12:7f.). He is about to be taken from them. So this is the proper time for such a comforting pronouncement. But in making it Moses points out to them that this revelation, so new to them, had already been made to him forty years before at Sinai. It had been a comforting assurance to Moses during all these years of desert wandering. God would not forsake his people. Israel would still be cared for when Moses' mission was ended. But the people di⌐ not need it as long as Moses was with them. Now the time has come for the full disclosure; and Moses makes it in a way which should bring double comfort and assurance to the people.

Elijah at Horeb (1 Kings 19:15f.). Such passages as the above help us to understand the three commands given to Elijah at Horeb: to anoint Hazael, Jehu, and Elisha. Elijah fulfilled the third command symbolically and it would seem immediately by casting his mantle over Elisha's shoulders (vs. 19). The first was fulfilled by Elisha when he said sorrowfully to Hazael "The Lord hath showed me [through Elijah?] that thou shalt be king over Syria" (2 Kings 8:13). The second was fulfilled by Elisha's sending a young man of the sons of the prophets to anoint Jehu (9:1-6). Why the long delay? No explanation is given except in the Lord's words to Elijah, when Ahab humbled himself: "Seest thou how Ahab humbleth himself before me, because he humbleth himself before me, I will not bring the evil in his days: but in his son's day will I bring the evil upon his house" (1 Kings 21:29). A suspended sentence! So Elisha takes over the unfinished tasks assigned to Elijah.

PROPHECY AND ITS FULFILLMENT

The Bible has much to say about the future, about things to come, promises of blessing, threatenings of punishment. Those predictions which concern events still future are of great moment and concern to Christians today as they face a prospect which is full of uncertainty and mystery. It is important to remember that the key to the understanding of unfulfilled prophecy is furnished us by the study of fulfilled prophecy. The record of God's dealings with his people in the past helps us to read aright the prophecies which deal with things to come. The principal difficulty in the interpreting of prophecy lies in the obscurity of the language and the conditional element which often attaches to its fulfillment. Prophecy is not pre-written history. Even the most explicit prophecy leaves ample room for diversity of fulfillment. The ominous prophecy of Jacob regarding his sons Simeon and Levi, "I will divide them in Jacob, and scatter them in Israel" (Gen. 49:7), was literally fulfilled to both tribes, but in strikingly different ways. In the case of Simeon, the implied curse remained a curse: Simeon practically disappeared from among the tribes. In the case of Levi the "dividing" and "scattering" was fulfilled in terms of blessings. Levi became the Levitical and priestly tribe; losing its equality with the other tribes, it became the representative of all of them in the service of God. Elisha's prophecy to the king's officer regarding the plenty which the starving people of Samaria were about to enjoy, "Behold thou shalt see it with thine eyes, but shalt not eat thereof" (2 Kings 7:2) was literally fulfilled (vs. 19f.), but the prophecy gave no hint as to the manner of fulfillment.

The history of the downfall of Israel's great enemies, Assyria and Babylon, as foretold by the prophets, illustrates this indefiniteness and obscurity very clearly. Nahum's prophecy of the destruction of Nineveh was fulfilled probably within a few years after its utterance. The assault is pictured with a vividness which almost makes the prophet an eyewitness of the scenes which he portrays; and apparently the overthrow was as complete as it was sudden. Nineveh has been a mass of ruins ever since. On the other hand the fulfillment of Isaiah's prophecy regarding Babylon was a very gradual one. Sargon and Sennacherib both sacked the city. But it was rebuilt by Esarhaddon; and Nebuchadnezzar, a century after Isaiah's time, raised it to its greatest prosperity and power. It was taken by Cyrus "without fighting," destroyed by Xerxes, weakened by the founding of Seleucia; and finally centuries after Isaiah passed away his words of doom (13:19-22) were completely fulfilled and Babylon became what it has been for centuries and is today, a desolation, an uninhabited waste.

As regards the time element the two predictions in Isaiah 7 are particularly instructive. The attempt of Rezin and Pekah to seize Jerusalem and overthrow the Davidic dynasty is treated with contempt; and it is foretold that "within three-score and five years shall Ephraim be broken that it be not a people"; and the overthrow of Samaria took place well within the designated period of time. On the other hand the great Immanuel prophecy which immediately follows it contains no specifications of time or place. It was fulfilled seven centuries later by the Incarnation at Bethlehem.[35]

Some interpreters, appealing to such an example as the woe pronounced by Jonah on Nineveh, "Yet forty days and Nineveh shall be destroyed," a sentence which was suspended because of the repentance of the people, claim that all prophecy is to be regarded as conditional, its fulfillment being dependent on the reaction to it of those to whom it is addressed. That this would be a decided overstatement of the case, has been well argued by Principal Fairbairn.[36] He points out that there are two classes of prophecies in the Old Testament which may be regarded as unconditional. The one is the group of prophecies which may be described as Messianic. They are referred to by Isaiah as "the sure mercies of David." The great promise of 2 Samuel 7 concerning the Davidic kingship concerned also the coming and reign of Christ and has been and is still being fulfilled in him. With regard to such prophecies, as Fairbairn points out, "there can be no room for the operation of any conditional element, except in regard to the subordinate relations of place and time."[37] Thus, the Immanuel prophecy of Isaiah 7 was, we may say, delayed in its fulfillment by the unbelief of King Ahaz to whom the great promise concerning "the house of David" (2 Sam. 7) meant nothing. But the fulfillment was only delayed; it was not, it could not be frustrated. The fulfillment of this great chain of prophecy, beginning in Genesis and running through Revelation, is as certain as is the being and existence of the God who uttered them. But the time and manner of fulfillment may be influenced by what we call "human affairs." The other example which Fairbairn cites is the prophecies concerning the heathen nations, of which we find so many in Isaiah, Jeremiah, and Ezekiel. Since no Hebrew prophet was sent to any one of these nations, Jonah alone excepted, the fulfillment was largely uninfluenced by their attitudes and reactions; the prophecy was rather simply a statement of the divine purpose concerning them.

But as regards the prophecies which directly concerned the children of Israel both collectively and individually, Fairbairn points out that the conditional element is present and prominent, whether expressly stated or not. Thus we find Moses, while foreseeing and plainly predicting the horrors which will inevitably follow upon disobedience to the law of God which it was given to him to proclaim, saying to the people, "I call heaven and earth to record this day against you, that I have set before you life and death, blessing and cursing: therefore choose life that both thou and thy seed may live" (Deut. 30:19). We find the same treatment in Isaiah's Great Arraignment (1:18-20);

and Ezekiel argues in detail the great question of inherited guilt (chap. 18). God has no pleasure in the death of the wicked but that the wicked turn from his wickedness and live (vss. 23, 32). There are, of course, cases where the sin is so grievous and the possibility of repentance and forgiveness so clearly absent that judgment is pronounced unconditionally and fulfilled as announced. Such for example is the case with the woe pronounced on Ahab and Jezebel. Elijah's words were fulfilled to the letter, although delayed in Ahab's case because he humbled himself. But the principle followed by the Lord in his dealings with his people is stated with utter plainness in the words in which the Lord proclaimed his Name to Moses at Mount Sinai: "And the Lord passed by before him, and proclaimed, The Lord, The Lord God, merciful and gracious, long-suffering, and abundant in goodness and truth, keeping mercy for thousands, forgiving iniquity and transgression and sin, and that will by no means clear *the guilty;* visiting the iniquity of the fathers upon the children, and upon the children's children, unto the third and to the fourth generation" (Exod. 34:6f.). So we may well infer that this principle should be kept constantly in mind in the interpreting of biblical prophecy.

THE LANGUAGE OF PROPHECY

In view of the fact that so much of Scripture consists of prophecy, it is important that the main features of the prophetic style and diction should be clearly understood. The subject of the conditional element in prophecy having been discussed, we pass on to the larger question of the intelligibility of prophecy, and we observe again that prophecy is not prewritten history. It is frequently expressed in obscure or figurative language, the full meaning of which is not made clear until the fulfillment has been reached.

One reason for this lies in that progressive element in prophecy which has already been referred to. Thus, the very first prophecy in the Old Testament, the Protevangel (Gen. 3:15), is couched in figurative language the full import of which requires the New Testament for its interpretation. The Shiloh prophecy (49:10) regarding the tribe of Judah is another familiar example. Even prophecies which may seem to be perfectly clear in their meaning may contain an element of obscurity or uncertainty. For example, Jeremiah's prophecy of the Babylonian captivity (25:11) foretold a seventy year servitude of the Jews to the king of Babylon. True, but when did the servitude begin? We read in Daniel 9:2 that Daniel having learned from Jeremiah's prophecy (25:12) that the desolation of Jerusalem was to last seventy years, made the expected restoration the subject of earnest prayer. Why did he do so? Two reasons suggest themselves. The one is that Daniel was uncertain as to the date at which the years of the servitude should end. Counting back 70 years from 539 B.C., the date of Cyrus' edict, brings us to 609 B.C., which was near the beginning of the reign of Jehoiakim and approximately the date of the carrying off of Daniel and his three friends to Babylon as hostages. But the capture of Jerusalem did not occur until 597 B.C., the destruction of the temple in 587 B.C., and the completion of the depopulation of the city in 582 B.C. From which date was the seventy year period to be reckoned? We might think, from 587 B.C., but the fulfillment places it about twenty years earlier. We have a similar problem in the case of the prophecy of the Seventy Weeks of Daniel 9, which is, furthermore, couched in highly figurative language. "From the going forth of a word to restore and build Jerusalem" admits of several different interpretations; and even today there is much difference of opinion not merely as to the date of the commencement, but as to many of the details of the prophecy. Consequently, Daniel may well have been uncertain as to the time when Jeremiah's prophecy was to be fulfilled. To this we may add the further fact that, as indicated by his prayer, Daniel may have been in doubt whether his people had really learned the lesson which the years of captivity were intended to teach and whether the Lord might prolong the days, the seventy years being regarded as a minimum penalty conditioned on good behavior and repentance. That the Lord might lengthen the period of captivity seems to be implied by the words of verse 19: "O Lord, hear; O Lord, forgive; O Lord, hearken and do; defer not, for thine own sake, O my God: for thy city and thy people are called by thy name."

The second reason for the obscurity of prophecy has been admirably stated by Fairbairn as follows: "It may be said, indeed, that the problem to be solved by prophecy was to speak of the future in such a way as to admit of the word being fulfilled, before its import was distinctly perceived by the persons taking part in the fulfilling of it, and yet to leave no proper room to doubt, that the things they did constituted the actual future pointed to in the prophecy."[38] And in concluding his lengthy discussion of the prophetic style and diction Fairbairn declares: "And in nothing, perhaps, more than in this wonderful combination of darkness and light observable in the prophetic word — in the clear foreknowledge it displays, on the one hand, of the greater things to come in Providence, coupled, on the other, with only such indications of time and place as might be sufficient to stimulate inquiry, and ultimately to dispel doubt, may we discern the directing agency of Him who knows our frame, and knows as well what is fit to be withheld as what to be imparted in supernatural communications."[39]

A further reason for the obscurity of prophecy lies in the fact, also stated by Fairbairn, that the indefiniteness of many prophecies constituted them a moral test to those whom they concerned. Nathan's parable of the ewe lamb was intended as a moral test of David's real character. The rich man was David, the poor man Uriah, the ewe lamb was Bathsheba. But David did not realize this until Nathan said, "Thou art the man!"

The Birth Oracle to Rebekah (Gen. 25:23) is a striking illustration of this feature of prophecy. "And the elder shall serve the younger" is the usual rendering of the concluding sentence; and it is generally assumed that the meaning is perfectly clear and consequently that Isaac deliberately and determinedly endeavored to frustrate the manifest intent of the oracle. Two things are to be noted in regard to such an interpretation. First, Isaac's unique experience on Mount Moriah (Gen. 22). That the terrible moment, when Abraham lifted up the knife to slay his son, left an indelible impression on the mind of Isaac is indicated by the name which Jacob used in referring to his father's God when he made the covenant with Laban: "Except the God of my father, the God of Abraham, and the Fear of Isaac had been with me" (Gen. 31:42).[40] Apparently Isaac at times must have referred to his God in a way that led Jacob to use this unique expression, "the Fear of Isaac" to describe him. That Isaac would deliberately defy the oracle of the One of whom he stood so in awe, seems psychologically impossible. Furthermore we read that when Isaac realized that he had been tricked by Rebekah and Jacob, "he trembled very exceedingly" (27:33). This may, of course, be taken to mean that Isaac was alarmed when he realized that he had failed in his attempt to transmit the blessing to his favorite son. It can also mean that he then for the first time realized that he had misunderstood the oracle. That Isaac may have done this is indicated by the language of the oracle itself. Let us examine it. We note first that up to the last clause, the oracle is racial and not individual. It speaks in terms of "nations" and "peoples"; and this meaning might be carried over to apply to the words "elder" and "younger." In other words it might be regarded as referring to the descendants of Esau and Jacob and not to the Patriarchs themselves. Secondly, we note that the phrasing of the oracle is peculiar. A literal rendering of the Hebrew would be: "Great shall serve little." It would be natural to assume that the order of words is: Subject — Verb — Object. But it is to be noted that it is possible to regard it as: Object — Verb — Subject. For an example of the latter order we turn to the theophany to Elijah at Horeb. The literal rendering of 1 Kings 19:17 is as follows: "And it shall be, the one escaping from the sword of Hazael shall slay Jehu; and the one escaping from the sword of Jehu shall slay Elisha." Here we have exactly the same order of words as in the Oracle to Rebekah; and it is clearly: Object — Verb — Subject. To treat it as Subject — Verb — Object would be absurd. The unusual order of words is clearly for the sake of emphasis.[41] Such being the case, it must be admitted that it is possible to find this same order in the Rebekah Oracle. We say possible, not probable. As the oracle reads, the meaning depends on the emphasis. Rebekah naturally placed the emphasis on the word "great" and regarded it as subject. Isaac because of his preference for Esau apparently succeeded in convincing himself that the proper meaning was the other way around, despite the fact that Esau had sold his birthright and had two Hittite wives. It is particularly to be noted that any possible misunderstanding of the oracle could have been avoided by the simple expedient of placing the sign of the accusative (the particle *'eth*) before one or the other of the two nouns. But in the form in which it is recorded there was enough possibility of diversity of interpretation to make the interpretation a moral test for the parents, to permit each to interpret it in the terms of individual inclination and preference.[42]

Ecstatic Prophecy. The claim has frequently been made that prophecy began in Israel in a form of ecstasy (mantic) which had orgiastic features and that it was only gradually that the stage of what may be called sober prophecy was attained. It is to be noted therefore that the true pattern of the prophet was Moses (Deut. 18:18), in whom there is not a trace of frenzy. It is true that it is definitely stated in Numbers 12:6-8 that the revelations made to the prophets would differ from those made to Moses, that the Lord would reveal his will to them in "dreams" or "visions" and in "dark sayings" and not by "face to face" speech (cf. Num. 7:89). But this does not imply that prophecy in Israel was originally ecstatic. In the encounter of Elijah and the prophets of Baal we have the difference set plainly before us. The brief and simple prayer of the one true prophet forms an amazing contrast to the orgiastic frenzy of the many false ones. That there were lower and cruder forms is made clear by the incident recorded in 1 Samuel 19:24, where the twice repeated "he also" indicates that both Saul and the prophets indulged in emotional excesses. But it is to be remembered that Saul had now been rejected by the Lord, which may mean that his own evil nature was responsible for the form of his reaction to the influence of the Holy Spirit. The attitude of the sons of the prophets toward the taking up of Elijah illustrates the fact that some, probably most, would-be prophets did not really understand the will of

God. They did not have a true call of God. The Old Testament points out very clearly that false and immature, as we may perhaps call it, prophecy was prevalent in Israel and was frequently, as in the case of Jezebel, introduced and fostered from foreign sources.

ISRAEL AND THE LAND OF PROMISE

The conclusion of the Book of Deuteronomy, beginning with Chapter 27, is largely taken up with the solemn enforcing of the law which was given at Sinai and had just been rehearsed and applied to the conditions which would face Israel in the land, whither they were going to possess it. The cursings and the blessings which will surely follow the breaking and the keeping of the covenant are emphasized. In Chapter 30 the promise is given of restoration to the land, after expulsion and dispersion because of unbelief; and it is definitely conditioned on repentance and obedience. "And it shall come to pass, when all those things are come upon thee, the blessing and the curse, which I have set before thee, and thou shalt call them to mind among all the nations, whither the Lord thy God hath driven thee, and shalt return unto the Lord thy God, and shalt obey his voice according to all that I command thee this day, thou and thy children, with all thine heart and with all thy soul; that then the Lord thy God will turn thy captivity . . . and will return and gather thee [i.e., gather thee again] from all the nations . . . and . . . bring thee into the land which thy fathers possessed, and thou shalt possess it . . . " (30:1-5). Here repentance and renewed obedience are clearly made the precondition to re-return and repossession of the land.

In Ezekiel 33:21-29, the claim of the apostate Jews to "possess the land" is summarily rejected; and it is further declared that the utter desolation of the land will prove to them that their punishment is the Lord's doing. Not a word is said here about repentance or restoration. In 36:8-15, restoration is promised and nothing is said about repentance. From 36:24-32, we might infer that the cleansing will follow the restoration. But verse 33 connects purification and restoration closely together: " . . . in the day of my cleansing you . . . I will cause you to dwell. . . ." Here the AV rendering, "in the day that I shall have cleansed," indicates that the cleansing is a precondition of the restoring. In Nehemiah 1:7-9, appeal is made to Deuteronomy 30:1-5 as making repentance a condition of restoration; and the whole course of God's dealings with his people, both in mercy and in judgment is set forth in the prayers recorded in Nehemiah 9 and in Daniel 9.

It is a sound principle of interpretation that the fuller statement should explain the less complete, that the conditional should be regarded as amplifying the unconditioned. Yet there are many students of prophecy who seem to regard those prophecies which do not specify repentance as a precondition of restoration as *annulling* the requirement of repentance so definitely presupposed in Deuteronomy 30.

This question has an important bearing on the present situation in Palestine. Thousands of Jews have returned to Palestine since World War II, and a Zionist State, The Republic of Israel, was established in 1948 and admitted to membership in the United Nations shortly thereafter. Many Bible students today see in this a fulfillment of prophecy and a significant step toward the promised return of Christ. Is this interpretation warranted by Scripture?

When we study the history of Israel as recorded in the Old Testament we find that possession of the land promised to the children of Abraham was always conditioned upon obedience. Failure to gain possession of the whole land was due to failure to keep the law. The oppressions in the days of the Judges were due to apostasy; and deliverance followed on repentance and renewed obedience. Solomon's lapses into idolatry were followed by the Great Schism; and the Kingdom of Israel which departed not from the sin of Jeroboam was finally destroyed and the Ten Tribes became the Lost Tribes. The sins of the Jews culminated in the apostasy of Manasseh and their city was destroyed by Nebuchadnezzar, whom the Lord called "my servant" three times (Jer. 25:9; 27:6; 43:10). The Babylonian Captivity followed and lasted for seventy years, and only a believing remnant returned to the land of their fathers. Five centuries later the promised Messiah of the Jews appeared; and they delivered him over to the Gentiles to be crucified and slain. Then the woe pronounced on them by their rejected Messiah (Matt. 24:2) took terrible effect: their city was destroyed and the people were scattered; Israel ceased to exist as a nation. This situation continued for the longest time of all, nearly nineteen hundred years. It ended with perhaps the most terrible of all the visitations of divine providence under which the chosen people have suffered in the course of their entire history, the genocide attempt of Hitler. We think with horror of this terrible scourge and of Hitler as a devil and a mad man. But, in the light of the Scriptures, can we deny that this, like the other visitations through which Israel passed, was a punishment for sin? During nineteen centuries of exile, of oppression, of persecution, the solemn warnings pronounced by Moses before his death and by all the prophets and last of all by Jesus in the Olivet discourse had sounded in their ears and had been disregarded. And finally this crushing blow fell upon them. Have they heeded it? Have they repented of their sin? Have they turned unto him whom they have pierced? The answer is No! They have returned in unbelief. Even this recent terrible demonstration of the wrath of God against the children of disobedience has not softened their stubborn hearts. And their defiant claim to possess the land promised to the seed of Abraham, while stubbornly refusing to follow in the faith of Abraham and refusing to accept him whose day Abraham saw and was glad, adds still further to the burden of guilt which they carry and for which they must suffer until it is repented of.

We must not forget, we need constantly to remind ourselves, that the Christian church to which we belong has failed sadly and sinfully to share the attitude of the Apostle Paul who had "great heaviness and continual sorrow" in his heart for Israel, a sorrow so great that he could wish, if it would avail for their salvation, to be himself "accursed from Christ" for their sake. Christians have ignored the Jew; they have despised him; they have persecuted him; they have failed to carry the gospel to him. If the sin of disobedience rests upon the Jew, it also rests heavily upon the Christian. For the Christian while professing with his lips to obey the gospel has often denied it by his works; and signs are not wanting that the Lord is using, and will use still more terribly, the scourge of atheistic and militant Communism to rebuke and punish an unfaithful church even as he used Nebuchadnezzar and Titus of old to punish disobedient Israel. The gathering storms will break over our heads unless we repent.

But to return to Israel. Can we in the light of prophecy and of God's providential dealings with Israel from the days of Abraham until now regard the return of the Jews to Palestine and the establishing of a Zionist State as a fulfillment of the promise regarding the land made to Abraham? The answer would seem to be plainly, No! The Zionists have not fulfilled the condition repeatedly imposed in Scripture for the possession of the land promised to their fathers. They have returned to the land in unbelief. They have taken violent possession of the portion which they occupy. They are maintaining themselves there by force of arms; and the State of Israel is a serious threat to the peace of the world. If the destruction of Samaria and the carrying away of the people of the Northern Kingdom was the punishment for their sins, especially that of the calves, if the destruction of Jerusalem and the Babylonian captivity were the punishment for the sins of Judah, if the siege of Jerusalem under Titus and the scattering of the Jews was, as foretold by Jesus himself, the punishment of the sin of the Jews in rejecting him as their Messiah, can it be denied that the recent genocide attempt of Hitler with its unutterable horrors was a further punishment for the age-long refusal of the Jews to recognize and receive their King? And what may the future have in store for them if they continue in unbelief? It is a solemnizing and terrifying thought! The Jews of today are demanding that the judgment of nineteen centuries, based on the New Testament record, which places on their race the guilt of the death of Jesus of Nazareth, be reversed. But this denial of inherited guilt does not carry with it any confession that the One whose death their ancestors demanded centuries ago is the Messiah promised to their race. Their continued rejection of Him is a judgment and condemnation from which no court of Christendom can free them.[43]

Summary Followed By Details

We often find that in describing an event, the biblical writer first makes a brief and comprehensive statement and then follows it with more or less elaborate details. This may involve some repetition and is at times confusing.

Creation of Man (Gen. 1:26-28). The account given here of the creation of man, generic man, male and female, is followed and expanded in Chapter 2 by an account of the creation of Adam (2:7) and of Eve (vs. 21-25) which leads up to the account of the fall.

Jacob and Laban (Gen. 31:36-42). When Laban overtakes the fleeing Jacob and charges him with ingratitude, Jacob defends himself vigorously and pouring out his bottled-up wrath he declares, "This twenty years have I been with thee" (vs. 38). Then a little later he says: "Thus have I been twenty years in thy house. I served thee fourteen years for thy two daughters and six years for thy cattle and thou hast changed my wages ten times" (vs. 41). Some very able scholars hold that Jacob is here speaking of two different periods of twenty years; and they believe that Jacob spent forty and not twenty years with Laban.[44] It must be admitted that this would solve some difficulties in connection with the chronology. But it seems more probable that Jacob is simply referring twice, in slightly different words to the same period of time. Twenty years was a long time to serve Laban, especially when it meant serving double time for his beloved Rachel!

Dwelling in Booths (Lev. 23:39-43). This chapter treats of the holy days and feast days which the Israelites are to observe. The sabbath is mentioned first. Then follow in order, passover and feast of unleavened bread, first fruits, feast of weeks, trumpet blowing, day of atonement, and feast of tabernacles (vss. 1-36). A summary statement follows (vss. 37-38) which begins with the words: "These are the feasts of the Lord" (cf. vs. 2). Then in verses 39-43 further instruction is given regarding the feast of tabernacles, *the dwelling in booths*. This direction is introduced by a word which may be rendered by "surely" or "only." AV renders it by "also," ARV changes it to "howbeit." The purpose is to call attention to a special and distinctive feature of the observance of this one feast. But the fact that it is mentioned after the regulations for all the feasts are concluded, instead of being included in the section dealing with this feast is noteworthy as an illustration of biblical usage.

The Order of March of the Tribes (Num. 10:11-28). Here a brief summary is given in verses 11-12, and then the details regarding the order of march are given rather fully. Then an account is given of Moses' invitation to Hobab to accompany them as guide (vss. 29-32). Then the account of their journeyings is resumed, the ark and the cloud are mentioned and the words of invocation used by Moses at the beginning and ending of each step of the journey are recorded (vss. 33-36).

Rahab and the Spies (Josh. 2:1-22). In this narrative the brief account of the agreement between Rahab and the spies seems to end with the words "Then she let them down by a cord through the window: for her house was upon the town wall and she dwelt upon the wall" (vs. 15). But there follows immediately a fuller account of the transaction which extends into verse 21. Then we read in verse 22 "and they went" which would seem to connect on directly with verse 15. It is absurd to think that, after Rahab had let the spies escape in the cautious and stealthy way which has just been described, she carried on a fuller conversation with them from her window, and did not until then, when they were out of her reach, demand solemn pledges which they were in a position to ignore. The solution is simply that the narrator here adds further details of the story, which while not essential seem to him sufficiently important to add.

The Battles with Benjamin, (Judg. 20:35-46). It seems proper (with Keil) to regard verses 36-46 as an expansion of what precedes, especially since the 25,100 mentioned in verse 35 are practically identical with the 18,000 + 5,000 + 2,000 = 25,000 enumerated in verses 45f.

The Murder of Ishbosheth (2 Sam. 4:5-7). Note the climactic repetition. Verse 6 tells us "and they smote him under the fifth *rib*"; verse 7 elaborates, "and they smote him, and slew him and beheaded him and took his head." This repetition as Keil points out prepares the way for the statement which follows and which makes clear the purpose of this dastardly act: "And they brought the head of Ishbosheth to David," clearly expecting a reward for having relieved him of a rival.

David and Hushai (2 Sam. 17:17-21). In this brief account of the way in which David was kept informed of the situation at Jerusalem after he fled from Absalom, the words "and they went and told king

David" (vs. 17) seem to conclude the statement. But it is followed by a brief account of the difficulties which Jonathan and Ahimaaz encountered in carrying out their dangerous commission and concludes with the words, "And they went and told king David . . ." (vs. 21) which occur already in verse 17.

Elijah at Carmel (1 Kings 18:30-32). Sometimes the brief statement passes so readily and easily into the more detailed one that we scarcely notice it. Thus the words "and he repaired the altar of the Lord that was broken down," is immediately followed by the account of the way in which it was restored, "using twelve stones according to the number of the tribes of the sons of Jacob," and digging the trench; then follows the preparation of the bullock, and the deluging everything with water, to show that there could be no fire there (cf. 2 Sam. 4:5-8).

Elisha's Death (2 Kings 13:14-21). The account given of the sixteen year reign of Jehoash, son of Jehoahaz, king of Israel is very brief (13:10-13). It is followed immediately by the account of the only event of his reign which the historian regards as important, his visit to the dying prophet. More than forty years have passed since his last mention of Elisha which was in connection with the anointing of Jehu. Yet the historian adds the account of Elisha's death to his summary of Joash's reign with a simple "and" (AV, ARV, "now"). He does not tell us in what year in Joash's reign Elisha died. He has given us all the information which he considers essential.

Jonah's Commission. We may note in this connection that the command first given to Jonah is stated in general terms: "Cry against her because [or, that] her wickedness has come up before me." The second statement is equally general: "Cry unto her the preaching which I speak [or am going to speak] unto thee" (3:2). Then we read what Jonah did: "he cried and said, yet forty days and Nineveh shall be overthrown" (3:4). Was this definite threat included in the message originally given Jonah? Or does his complaint merely mean that he felt from the start that his denunciation of the wickedness of Nineveh, however ineradicable and incorrigible it might be, would be followed by the merciful sparing of the city (4:2f.). As to this we cannot be certain.

Nahum and the Fall of Nineveh. This little book furnishes us with a striking example of emphatic repetition. The first chapter closes with the declaration of the Lord's purpose regarding Nineveh: "I will make thy grave for thou art vile"; and we are given a vivid word picture of the messenger bringing the "good tidings" to Judah of the fall of the bloody city: "the wicked shall no more pass through thee, he is utterly cut off." But then in Chapter 2 we read a vivid description of the siege of Nineveh and the summons to the enemy to take the spoil of the doomed city, ending with the prediction of its utter destruction. It would seem as if now all has been said that needs to be said. Yet Chapter 3 begins again almost as does Chapter 2 with the raging of the chariots and the fury of battle and ends as does Chapter 2 with the prediction of utter destruction and oblivion. The theme is a tremendous one and the prophet seeks to do full justice to it. For this is the Nineveh of Sennacherib, of the mighty Assyrian kings who "caused their terror in the land of the living" (Ezek. 32:23).

The Return to Jerusalem under Ezra. The statements with regard to this important event show the importance of collecting all the facts. 7:7 describes the "going up" as taking place in the seventh year of Artaxerxes. Verse 9 declares that the start was on the *first* day of the first month and goes on to say that Ezra's arrival at Jerusalem was four months later, "the first day of the fifth month." Then the writer inserts a copy of the royal letter authorizing the return and providing for gifts and offerings for the temple worship, which presupposes, of course, the rebuilding of the temple (6:15), following it with an ascription of praise to God. 8:1-14 deals briefly with the group who went back with Ezra. Verses 15-20 tell of the discovery, during the three day encampment by Ahava, of the absence of Levites from the company, and of the steps taken to meet that situation, which was followed by a fast (vss. 21-23), after which we read of the entrusting to the priests and Levites of the silver and gold vessels, donated by the king and his counsellors and by the Israelites of the company (vss. 24-30). Then we read of the departure from the river Ahava on the *twelfth* day of the first month (vs. 31), which apparently means that while the departure was planned for the first day (7:9), there was a delay of nearly two weeks for the reasons indicated above. We note also that here (8:31f.) while the date of departure is precisely stated, nothing further is said about the length of the journey, only of the divine protection which attended it. But we are told that after a three-day rest from their arduous journey, on the fourth day, the precious vessels were delivered to the authorities at Jerusalem; and we are to remember that this was the fourth day of the fifth month (7:9).

Chapter 9:1 begins with the rather indefinite statement, "Now when these things were done" and describes the ominous disclosure regarding mixed marriages as taking place at the time of "the evening oblation." Then we read of Ezra's prayer of confession, of the reaction of the people (9:5 — 10:4), and of the summoning of an assembly to be held three days later. We might think that this all took place during the fortnight after the arrival of Ezra and his company on the first day of the fifth month. But we are told (10:9) that the assembly took place in "the ninth month on the twentieth *day* of the month," nearly five months later, which fixes the date of the "three day" notice. Finally we read that Ezra and other heads of fathers' houses began an investigation on the first day of the tenth month and that the matter was finally disposed of by the first day of the first month of the next year (vs. 17). Thus we have all the important dates given us. But the method of stating them requires careful attention.

Samson's Riddle (Judg. 14:8-20). It is important to remember that a story may be told from more than one angle. This is illustrated by the account which is given us of Samson's riddle. The riddle was suggested by Samson's encounter with the lion and by the honey which he later discovered in its carcass. And he cast it into enigmatic form: "Out of the eater came forth meat, and out of the strong came forth sweetness" (vs. 14). Since Samson had kept the matter secret and apparently no one had heard about the lion and the honey, it is hardly surprising that the thirty companions were "stumped" by it. Samson fully intended this. And he seemed likely to succeed for "they could not in three days expound the riddle." So apparently they gave up trying. The reason was that they had another and what they believed to be a thoroughly effective way of solving the problem, without cudgelling their wits any longer. On the *seventh* day, the last day, they approached Samson's wife and threatened her with the direst consequences for herself and for her family, unless she secured by hook or by crook the answer from Samson. That is the men's story.

Now comes the woman's story. Note how it begins: "And Samson's wife wept before him, and said, Thou dost but hate me, and lovest me not: thou hast put forth a riddle unto the children of my people, and hast not told it to me. And he said unto her, Behold, I have not told it my father nor my mother, and shall I tell thee?" We might easily infer from this that the wife was simply pretending to be aggrieved and that her principal, perhaps her only reason for weeping was because of fear of what the Philistines would do to her if she failed them, that in fact it was only on the last day that the honeymoon became beclouded and Samson's wife became a veritable fountain of tears. But read a little further: "And she wept before him *the seven days*, while the feast lasted: and it came to pass on the *seventh day* that he told her." Now we get the whole story. The woman was not trumping up a plausible excuse for bringing up the question of the riddle on the last day of the feast when she said: "Thou hast put forth a riddle unto the children of my people, and hast not told it me." The riddle had beclouded the honeymoon from the very start. It had been an unforgettable and unforgivable grievance throughout all the seven days. Her feminine curiosity and her wifely pride had taken offense the instant Samson failed, and then refused, to confide to the wife of his bosom the answer to his riddle. And the dire threat of the Philistines now only served to increase the appeals and importunities and lamentations with which she had made her husband miserable for six days already. So he told her; and she told the Philistines; and they reported the answer to Samson; and he made the caustic remark: "If ye had not plowed with my heifer, ye had not found out my riddle." So he got even with the thirty *companions* by slaying thirty men of Askelon and giving them the spoil; and he got even with his *wife* by leaving her and going up to his father's house; and his father-in-law got even with *him* by giving his wife to one of the companions of the feast, which had had such an unhappy and even tragic ending.

Sun, Moon, and Stars. Three familiar statements such as the following are a good illustration of the fact that the form and content of a statement may be largely or wholly determined by the circumstances under which it is uttered: "And God made the two great lights . . . and the stars" (Gen. 1:16, literal rendering); "when I consider thy heavens, the work of thy fingers, the moon and the stars which thou hast ordained" (Ps. 8:3); and "in them hath he set a tabernacle for the sun, which is as a bridegroom coming out of his chamber" (Ps. 19:4f.). The first passage is concerned with the creation of the sun and the moon as the two great luminaries, the rulers of the day and of the night; and the stars are mentioned almost incidentally, as of relatively minor importance (AV in rendering, *"he made* the stars also" has seemingly sought to place more emphasis on this vastly significant fact). In the second passage, the Psalmist contemplates with awe and wonder the glories of the nightly heavens, the brilliant moon and the myriad stars. The sun is hidden from view and is ignored. In the third picture, the Psalmist is enthralled by the glory of the daybreak, the sight of the sun, which coming forth as a bridegroom from his chamber, rejoicing as a strong man to run his course, blots out the moon and the stars by its excess of light. Three statements, different in emphasis and content, yet each beautifully appropriate to the context in which it stands!

Jethro's Visit to Moses (Exod. 18) is a somewhat similar example of biblical narration. Verses 1-6 deal entirely with Jethro's attitude and actions. He heard of Moses' fame and decided to bring back Moses' wife and sons who had apparently been placed in his keeping. This brief statement ends with the words: "I thy father-in-law Jethro am come unto thee, and thy wife, and her sons with her." This states Jethro's side of the story. Then we read of Moses' side: "And Moses went out to meet his father-in-law and did obeisance, and kissed him."

Thus, verse 6 overlaps verse 7, which means that verse 7 must go back to verse 5 for the temporal sequence. This narrative consequently resembles Joshua 2:16, where as we have seen the "and she said" goes back of verse 15 in time and connects with verse 14. In both places the perfect tense is equivalent to a pluperfect, insofar as sequence of events is concerned, although it may be regarded simply as a supplement to the statement which precedes.[45] We note also that the Jethro narrative concludes with Jethro's advice to Moses about the appointing of judges. Verses 24-26 tell us that Moses heeded and carried out Jethro's advice, that he chose able men and made them heads over the people, "rulers of thousands, rulers of hundreds, rulers of fifties, rulers of tens" (a time consuming task which may not have been completed in the course of Jethro's visit). The record goes on to state that "they were wont to judge the people at all seasons" (the verbs in vs. 26 are frequentatives). Then verse 27 adds "And Moses let his father-in-law depart," a statement which may carry us back to verse 24 which may cover in summary all that is said in verses 25 and 26.

CONTRAST, CLIMAX, CATASTROPHE

As we read the Bible we are often struck by the abrupt, striking and even startling way in which the writer introduces a significant *contrast, climax* or *catastrophe*.

2 Samuel 12:1-14. Nathan's rebuke of David is a familiar example. Nathan tells the king the pathetic story of the poor man with his one ewe lamb; and his vivid picture of the callous avarice of the rich man arouses David's anger, a righteous indignation so intense that it leads the king to pronounce sentence of death on the offender. Then the prophet utters these terrible words, "Thou art the man!" And the righteously indignant judge becomes the culprit at the bar awaiting sentence from the spokesman of a higher Judge.

Esther 6:1-12. An even more striking example is the answer of king Ahasuerus to Haman's glowing description of the royal pomp which is befitting the one "whom the king delighteth to honor." Then the king said to Haman, "Make haste, take the apparel and the horse, as thou hast said and do even so. . . . " How Haman must have thrilled as he heard these words! His highest ambitions were to be realized; and he was about to "see his desire" on his enemy Mordecai. Then the king completes his sentence with the words: "to Mordecai the Jew, that sitteth at the king's gate," and Haman's overweening hopes are withered and blasted, his hope of revenge on Mordecai is destroyed, and he is made the instrument of the triumph of his hated foe. And finally, as if to drive home the barb, the king adds, "Let nothing fail of all that thou hast spoken." We can feel the irony, the menace, the dagger thrust, in these words. "Pride goeth before destruction and a haughty spirit before a fall."

1 Kings 13. The story of the mission of the unnamed prophet to Jeroboam is told in a striking way. Up to verse 11 the conduct of the prophet was most exemplary. He carried out his instructions to the letter; and we might think that with verse 10 we have the happy ending: "So he went another way, and returned not by the way that he came to Bethel." This might easily be taken to mean that he had completed his mission and returned safely. Then the tragic sequel is introduced, and we read how the old prophet of Bethel deceived the man of God and of the tragic consequences of disobedience, the death of the disobedient prophet and the perseverance of Jeroboam in his evil course.

Judges 5:27-31. The Song of Deborah ends in a most striking way. She described the death of Sisera at the hands of Jael:

> At her feet he bowed, he fell, he lay;
> At her feet he bowed, he fell:
> Where he bowed, there he fell down dead.

The three-fold repetition is for the sake of emphasis. The mighty enemy of Israel is dead! He lies dead; and at the feet of a woman! Then she pauses and with wonderful prophetic insight, she pictures the mother of Sisera at the window of the palace, eagerly awaiting the return of her warrior son. "Why is his chariot so long in coming? Why tarry the wheels of his chariot?" she cries. For her there can, of course, be only one answer. For is not Sisera invincible?

> Have they not found, have they not divided the spoil?
> A damsel, two damsels to every man;
> To Sisera a spoil of dyed garments,
> Of dyed garments embroidered on both sides, on the
>   necks of the spoil? *(ARV)*

How could utter contempt for the enemy, certainty of victory be better described? But it is only wishful thinking, the proud and contemptuous conceit of a vainglorious and infatuated woman, who does not know that her son lies dead with a tent-peg through his forehead. So Deborah draws the moral to adorn this tale of fancied triumph and terrible defeat.

> So let all thine enemies perish, O Lord:
> But let them that love him be as the sun
> When he goeth forth in his might.

What a climax for this triumph ode! Then we return to the prose of history and read, "And the land had rest forty years." But this is immediately followed by an even greater contrast; "And the children of Israel did that which was evil in the sight of the Lord: and the Lord sold them into the hand of Midian seven years." What a picture of victory and defeat, apostasy and punishment! But this is the constantly recurring theme of Judges; and indeed of all the historical books of the Old Testament!

Isaiah 10:33-34. We turn to another passage, that one in which the seemingly irresistible advance of the hosts of Assyria against Jerusalem is pictured so vividly, and which concludes with the words: "This very day shall he halt at Nob: He shaketh his hand at the mount of the daughter of Zion, the hill of Jerusalem." The Holy City is apparently doomed. But listen! "Behold the Lord, Jehovah of hosts, will lop the boughs with terror; and the high of stature shall be hewn down, and the lofty shall be brought low. And he will cut down the thickets of the forest with iron, and Lebanon shall fall by a mighty one" (ARV). Assyria is only one tree of the forest, a rod which the Lord will use to punish his people and then destroy it for its pride and self-esteem.

2 Kings 5:1. A literal translation of the Hebrew is particularly striking: "And Naaman, the chief of the hosts of the king of Aram was a great man before his lord, and lifted up of face [i.e., highly esteemed], for by him the Lord had given deliverence to Aram, and the man was a mighty man of valor" — a splendid tribute! And then the writer adds just one word, a terrible word, "leprous." Our English versions cushion the blow a little by rendering, *"But he was* a leper." The Hebrew says simply "leprous," as if to make the two sides of the picture stand side by side in the most glaring contrast. Just one word spells all the difference and shows the desperate situation in which this gallant warrior was placed.

While we are looking at this verse with its amazing conclusion, we may perhaps pause to ask ourselves, Why does the writer tell us regarding Naaman, that "by him the Lord had given deliverance to Aram?" Not Hadad or Rimmon, but Yahweh! One thing is quite obvious. We are to see in it one of the lofty flights of that prophetic insight, that world-view, which was characteristic of the great prophets, of Amos and Isaiah, for example, but which we can trace back to the time of the Exodus, when the Lord said to haughty Pharaoh by Moses, "For this cause have I raised thee up for to show in thee my power" (Exod. 9:16). But why is it referred to here? Speculation has been busy as to the meaning of these significant and yet enigmatic words. There is an old tradition that Naaman was the man "who drew a bow at a venture" (1 Kings 22:34) and shot the arrow which pierced the armor of Ahab, and resulted in victory for the Syrians. The writer does not tell us what the deliverance was. But he sees the hand of God in Naaman's victorious career, and in a single sentence commends him to our admiration and our pity and prepares us for the gracious act which is to make this servant of the king of Syria a servant of the God of Israel. For if by him the God of Israel could give deliverance to Syria, surely it must be but a little thing for him to give Naaman deliverance from his leprosy.

Amos 1 and 2. The way in which the prophet leads up to his culminating and climactic woe on the Northern Kingdom (2:6-16) is very impressive. The first woe is against Damascus, a distant city lying to the northeast, the capital of a nation with which Israel had often been at war. The second is Gaza, lying to the southwest, the most distant of the Philistine cities, a city of the uncircumcised, Israel's inveterate enemy. The third is Tyre, the great commercial city to the far north, the symbol of worldly wealth and luxury. Three foreign enemies of Israel and of Israel's God! Then the prophet comes nearer home: Edom to the south, the home of the descendants of Esau, long the enemies of Israel and Judah; Ammon to the east; and finally Moab next to Ammon. Three nations related to Israel: Edom, descended from Esau, who sold his birthright for a mess of pottage, Ammon and Moab, the incestuous descendants of Lot, who left Abraham to dwell in Sodom. Six nations, three pagan, three apostate, all enemies of Israel, in whose humiliation Israel will rejoice. Then comes the seventh, seven being the sacred number. The seventh is Judah, and the woe on Judah is surprisingly brief. Surely the prophet will stop with Judah! But does he? Far otherwise! An eighth woe is added, and it is the most terrible of all. Two or three verses at most suffice for each of the seven woes which precede. The woe on Israel is eleven verses long; and its severity and terror are greatly heightened by the way in which the prophet has prepared for it, lulling the people into a sense of false security that he may make the judgment pronounced on them the more terrible because it was so sudden and unexpected.

Ezekiel 31. This prophecy of the eleventh year of the captivity of Jehoiachin (586 B.C.) was uttered shortly before the fall of Jerusalem. It is addressed to Pharaoh, king of Egypt, but it is expressed in terms of a parable concerning Assyria, which is likened to a mighty cedar, whose majestic greatness is comparable only to the vastness of its fall. We naturally think of Daniel's prophecy concerning Nebuchadnezzar. Since Egypt and Assyria had been rivals for centuries, we might expect that the Pharaoh is being reminded of the utter downfall of his one-time dangerous rival, which had taken place some twenty years earlier, perhaps as a suggestion that Pharaoh's present rival, the king of Babylon, will suffer a similar fate. Since Babylon had succeeded Nineveh in the struggle for supremacy, it might be inferred that Babylon will share Nineveh's fate. This would be a natural inference. And since the prophet broadens the scope of this prophecy toward the end to include "all the trees of Eden" (vs. 16), Pharaoh might well find a salutary warning in the fate of Assyria. Yet Fairbairn is right in saying that "the whole of the present chapter with the exception of the last verse has immediate respect only to Assyria."[46] So the prophet does not leave anything to inference. He states it bluntly and impressively: "This is Pharaoh and all his multitude, saith the Lord." Assyria means Egypt! This is the startling climax and conclusion of this strikingly beautiful and yet ironically ominous prophecy.

Leviticus 10. The first seven chapters of Leviticus deal with the ritual of sacrifice, the performance of which was a priestly function. Chapters 8 and 9 describe in impressive detail the solemn and we may even say spectacular ordination and investiture of Aaron and his four sons. It concludes with the mention of the divine fire which consumed the offering and certified its acceptance by God. Then, like lightning out of a cloudless sky, comes the sacrilege of two of Aaron's four sons, the two who had been with Moses and Aaron and the 70 elders in the Mount before God (Exod. 24:1). No explanation is given. Their offering of "strange fire" must have been an act of defiance since the heavenly fire has just been described. The instructions, immediately given (vss. 9-11), may be intended to indicate that these two were not of sober mind when they were guilty of this act of sacrilege. Whatever the explanation the story, especially in its context, is amazing and most tragic, incredible but true!

Numbers 11:1. And the people were like murmurers. According to 9:1-5 the passover was celebrated on the fourteenth day of the first month and a special passover held a month later (vss. 9-14). The divine guidance by the pillar of cloud and fire is described. The date of departure is stated (10:11) and the order of march set forth in detail. Verses 33-36 speak of the supernatural guidance which Israel received and record the words of invocation which Moses spoke at the departure and encamping of the hosts of Israel. Everything is in order for a prosperous and successful journey to the land of promise. Then we read, "And the people were like murmurers." Shocking, because in a sense so unexpected and inexcusable! And the punishment was Taberah, "the fire of the Lord burnt among them."

2 Samuel 7. The way in which the great Messianic prophecy regarding David's house is told is both striking and startling. It serves to illustrate with amazing clearness the difference between the planning of man and the purposes of God. David's desire to build a house for the Lord is commendable. It appeals favorably to Nathan and courtier-like he approves it heartily. Then the Lord gives him a message to David which flatly rejects David's plan, while at the same time substituting a far grander one, but one in which David can have at best a minor role, a plan the achieving of which he must leave to another. It must have been humiliating to Nathan to have his wordly wisdom set aside; and we may think it strange that Nathan's blunder as we may call it is recorded. We might deem it wise to omit the introduction lest it seem to discredit the Lord's messenger. Not so does the inspired writer regard it. He tells the whole story, because it serves so strikingly to show the difference between Nathan the man and Nathan the man of God, between Nathan's personal opinion and Nathan's "Thus saith the Lord."

Psalm 89 is a striking example of sudden contrast. Verses 1-37 are a song celebrating the mercies of God which ends with an appeal to the promise of 2 Samuel 7. Then suddenly (vs. 38) with a simple "and" (AV "but") the Psalmist contrasts the actual situation with the promised good: "But thou has cast off and abhorred, thou hast been wroth with thine anointed." The plaint covers eight verses (38-45) and ends with the terrible charge: "Thou has covered him with shame." The plaint is then followed by the plea (vs. 46-51), which begins with the words "How long, Lord? Wilt thou hide thyself for ever?" — the "for ever" recalling the emphatic words of the promise as quoted in verses 36f. — and twice (vss. 47, 50) calling on the Lord to *remember*: to remember the brevity of human life and the reproaches of unbelievers which imply that God has been unmindful of his promise.

Isaiah 29 describes strikingly contrasted situations: first the desperate straits to which Israel is reduced (vss. 1-4), then the utter overthrow of her enemies (vss. 5-8); then the blindness and stupidity of the people (vss. 9-16), and finally the assurance of a blessed fulfillment of the promises made to Israel of old (especially to Abraham), promises which the people will be able to read in the book and understand (vss. 17-24).

Jeremiah 32:27, "Behold, I am the Lord, the God of all flesh: is there anything too hard for me?" These words are the Lord's reply to Jeremiah's words, "There is nothing too hard for thee" (vs. 17). Both seem to recall the Lord's words to Abraham, "Is anything too hard for the Lord?" (Gen. 18:14). The answer expected by Jeremiah seems to be clearly that the Lord will display his omnipotence by saving Jerusalem from her enemies, despite her desperate plight. But instead the answer which is given, "Behold, I will give this city unto the hands of the Chaldeans . . . and they shall burn it with fire . . . and I will bring them again unto this place . . . and I will make an everlasting covenant with them," plainly illustrates the fact that God's ways are beyond human foreknowing. For what we have here is an amazing combination of impending judgment and of mercy to follow, far different from the assurance of blessing given to Abraham in the promise of Isaac's birth and the promise given to Isaiah regarding Jerusalem (Isa. 37:21-35). Destruction must precede deliverance!

In *Zephaniah 3:1* the prophet turns abruptly from Nineveh whose pride and downfall is described vividly in 2:13-15 to speak of the sin of Jerusalem. Yet he begins with words which suggest that Nineveh is still the theme. The three words used of the city now to be described, "rebellious," "polluted," "oppressing," are all applicable to Nineveh. Yet each word is ambiguous and may be given a good meaning which would be appropriate to Jerusalem as the city of God, "reverend," "redeemed," "the dove" (i.e., dove-like). It is not until the words "she has not trusted in the Lord" are reached that it becomes plain that Jerusalem is intended and that the three descriptive words are to be taken in an evil sense.

Perhaps the greatest example of contrast and catastrophe in Scripture is the life of David. There is no character in the Bible whose life so amazingly illustrates the heights and the depths of human nature, its possibilities for good and for evil. It is hard to believe that the man who fought against Goliath and who wrote Psalms 23, 103 and 139, could be the man who compounded adultery with murder, in a deliberate, cowardly and heartless attempt to cover up a sudden yielding to the lust of the flesh. "We may not be all aware," Trench reminds us, "of the many and malignant assaults which were made on the Christian faith, and on the morality of the Bible, through the character of David, by the blind and self-righteous deists of a century ago." So he uses David to illustrate the proverb: "Better a diamond with a flaw than a pebble without one."[47] The flaw is there and it is relentlessly exposed to view, and not a few critical scholars since Trench's day have taken great pains to point it out to us. But it is a flaw in a diamond, and in the beauty of the jewel we forget that it is not perfect.

In *Daniel* the narrative passes abruptly at Chapter 5:1, without even an "and," from Nebuchadnezzar to Belshazzar, an interval of probably at least 25 years. The only connecting link, but an obvious and striking one, is in the last clause of 4:37, "and those that walk in pride he is able to abase." The account of Belshazzar's downfall is a striking commentary on Nebuchadnezzar's words and a singularly appropriate illustration of their truth. In the blasphemy of Belshazzar the cup of iniquity of the kings of Babylon is filled to overflowing.

Equally striking is the sudden transition in Isaiah 31:4. The chapter begins with a denunciation of those who seek help from Egypt. It describes the impotence of Egypt to help and declares that helped and helper shall fail and fall together. Using the figure of the lion and lioness, it pictures the coming of the Lord to battle: "So shall the Lord of hosts come down to fight. . . ." Then follow the words "for [or against, or upon] Mount Zion and for [or against, or upon] the hill thereof." The preposition is ambiguous. AV renders by "for"; ARV does the same, giving "against" as an alternative rendering; RSV gives the neutral or colorless rendering "upon." It seems clear that the prophet uses this ambiguous word in order to prepare the way for the promise of deliverance given in verse 6, while at the same time making the transition from menace to mercy all the more striking. This is confirmed by the use of the word "pass over," which is from the same root as the word passover (*pesach*) and suggests that the deliverance for Israel in this time of peril will be like the deliverance at the time of the Exodus, when the Lord slew the first-born of Egypt — a suggestion perhaps that the Egyptians of Isaiah's day to whom Israel was turning for help were as much their enemies as in the time of their, now perhaps forgotten, bondage to them.

A less startling but rather surprising conclusion is the closing verse of Psalm 119. After affirming scores of times in the course of the psalm his love for the law of God and his zeal in the keeping of it, the Psalmist concludes with the words: "I have gone astray like a lost sheep; seek thy servant; for I do not forget thy commandments." This may seem a feeble ending, an anticlimax. But should we not rather think of it as a most fitting conclusion for this great poem in praise of the law of God? For it shows us how deeply conscious the writer was of the perfection of the law and of his utter inability to fulfill its demands in his own strength. Only God the giver of the law can enable his servant to keep it.

Commenting on this verse Delitzsch follows the Massoretic accentuation and renders: "If I have gone [or should go] astray — like a lost sheep seek thy servant," on the ground that "it may seem strange that he can say of himself, 'I have gone astray like a lost sheep.'" But strange or not, such is the natural rendering. To tone it down is to weaken the climactic emphasis which the writer clearly intended to produce. We are reminded of the beautiful hymn by Anne Steele which begins with the words "Father of Mercies, in Thy word, what endless glory shines" and is full from beginning to end of the beauty and glory of the Holy Scriptures. Yet it ends with the words: "Teach me to love Thy sacred word, And view my Saviour there." These words may sound superfluous on the lips of such a lover of the Word. Yet they express most feelingly the writer's sense of the "endless glory" of that Word.

Isaiah 66:24. Perhaps the most impressive example of contrast in the Old Testament is presented by the closing verse of the Book of Isaiah: "And they shall go forth, and look upon the carcasses of the men that have transgressed against me: for their worm shall not die, neither shall their fire be quenched; and they shall be an abhorring unto all flesh." This conclusion is prepared for, it is true, by several threatening statements in this very chapter, especially verses 3-4, 15-17. But that the prophecies of this great prophet of consolation and salvation should end as they do seems most remarkable. It is a singular illustration of the truth stated in Isaiah 55:8, that God's thoughts are not our thoughts. If men had written the Bible according to their ideas and wishes it would be quite a different book from what it is. Man seeks to condone evil. God sees it in all its hideousness and abhors it. It is because it describes God's people as looking with horror (cf. Dan. 12:2) on the punishment of the wicked that Alexander can speak of this verse as the "sublime conclusion of this wonderful book ... because directly and primarily it is an integral part of the 'great argument' with which the whole book has been occupied, and which the Prophet never loses sight of to the end of his last sentence."[48] It is not to be forgotten that it is these very words of Isaiah, which Alexander describes as "an integral part of the 'great argument,' with which the entire book has been occupied," which our Lord himself uses in Mark 9:48.

The Book of Judges ends with the words: "every man did that which was right in his own eyes," a fitting conclusion to this story of Israel's iron age. Hosea ends with the solemn warning, "but the transgressors shall fall therein." The Book of Psalms, on the other hand, ends in a burst of Hallelujahs, in which "everything that hath breath" is exhorted to join.

"And much cattle" (Jonah 4:11) seems like an anticlimax as a *last* word. But is it? Compare on the one hand Psalm 104:11-31 and Deuteronomy 25:4, on the other hand 1 Corinthians 9:9. Especially noteworthy is Mark 5:43 (Luke 8:55) "and he commanded that something should be given her to eat." To some this may seem like a rather commonplace ending of a wonderful story of healing power. But it is, on the contrary, a beautiful illustration of that Divine love by which no need of man goes unnoticed.

In concluding the reading of the four books, Isaiah, Malachi, Lamentations and Ecclesiastes, the Jews are accustomed to repeat the next to the last verse of the book for the reason that it makes the ending of the book less sad. It is not a little significant that the last words of the last of the Old Testament prophets, Malachi, are a solemn warning: "lest I come and smite the earth with a curse."

UNITY AND COMPLETENESS

One of the noteworthy features of Biblical narration — a feature which is by no means limited to sacred literature — is the tendency to complete a topic or subject, carrying it forward to its conclusion or a logical stopping-place and then to return to the point of departure and resume the main thread of the narrative.

Genesis and Its "Generations." We have in the ten "generations" of Genesis, as they are called, a striking illustration of this method of writing. The first is "the generations of the heaven and the earth." The last is the "generations of Jacob." This involves a gradual process of elimination.

The First Generation (2:4 — 4:26) tells of the birth of Adam's three sons. It tells of Abel's death. It traces the line of Cain for seven generations, perhaps bringing it down to about the time of the Flood. Then with an "and" (4:25) it returns to Adam and tells of the birth of Seth, which probably took place soon after the death of Abel, many centuries, perhaps, before the birth of the three sons of Lamech who have just been referred to.

The Second Generation (5:1 — 6:8) traces Adam's descendants from Seth to Noah. Then it describes the state of the world at that time resulting from the corruption of the "sons of God" (the Sethites), by the "children of men" (the Cainites). This corruption certainly did not begin in the days of Noah. Men probably began to "multiply" long before the corruption reached such a height as to necessitate the judgment of the Flood.

The Third Generation, that of Noah, (6-9 — 9:28) gives the account of the Flood and of the Covenant which followed.

The Fourth Generation (10:1 — 11:9) is largely racial. It deals first with Japheth, then Ham, then with Shem, going only as far as Peleg and his brother Jaktan, who has thirteen descendants. Then it describes the Confusion of Tongues which probably took place in the days of Peleg, when the "earth was divided" (10:25).[49]

The Fifth Generation (11:10-26) is individual. It starts again with Shem and traces the line of Shem to Terah and his sons.

The Sixth Generation (11:27 — 25:11) deals with the life of Abraham. The precise dates in the life of Abraham follow one another in chronological order (12:4; 16:16; 17:1, 17; 21:5; 23:1; 25:7). But the dates of four important events are not clearly stated. The date of Abram's departure for Canaan is stated as in his seventy-fifth year (12:4). But it is only the apparently close connection between 11:32 and 12:1 which justifies the statement that this was after Terah's death (Acts 7:4). The dates of the invasion of Amraphel and his allies (14:1-24) and of the destruction of Sodom (18-19) are not given, but we may assume that they belong where they appear in the chronological framework. However the account of the destruction of Sodom (18:16 — 19:38) is carried forward to tell of the births of Moab and Ammon; and it refers to their descendants "unto this day." Similarly the story of Hagar and Ishmael is carried forward for some years. Consequently it must be regarded as doubtful whether the account of Abraham's marriage with Keturah (25:1-11) belongs chronologically after the death of Sarah. It may have taken place much earlier. Certainly the grandsons of Keturah may have been born after Abraham's death.

The Seventh Generation (25:12-18) gives a list of Ishmael's descendants, twelve princes. It does this in a way which implies that they have already become a numerous people.

The Eighth Generation (25:19 — 35:29) deals with the lives of Isaac's sons Esau and Jacob up to the time of Isaac's death.

The Ninth Generation (36:1 — 37:1) traces the line of Esau for many generations, certainly down to the time of Moses. It ends with a brief reference to Jacob.

The Tenth Generation (37:2 — 50:26) deals primarily with the career of Joseph. Beginning when he was seventeen years old, it tells of the events which led up to his being sold as a slave in Egypt. At that point the shameful story of Judah's family life is introduced (chap. 38). It apparently runs parallel with the story of Joseph's life as told in Chapter 37 and carries it forward to the time of the descent of Jacob into Egypt. Then with a simple "and" the narrative returns to Joseph in Egypt as the servant of Potiphar. It tells first of the period before Jacob came to Egypt (chaps. 39-45) and then of Israel in Egypt with Joseph. It has much to say about the close of Jacob's life and his imposing burial at Machpelah. The latter half of Joseph's life — he survived his father fifty-four years — is very briefly referred to and told in purely personal terms. Half of the twelve remaining verses are devoted to the quieting of the fears of his conscience-stricken brethren, the rest to his confident hope for Israel's future and his direction that he be buried in Canaan. Not a word is said about his public life. Whether he remained in favor and in office we do not know. The sacred historian has told us all that we need to know about Joseph, except that his dying wish was carried out (Exod. 13:19; Josh. 24:32). The words "and they embalmed him, and he was put in a coffin in Egypt," stand in striking contrast to the lengthy account of Jacob's imposing funeral. Are we to infer that before, perhaps long before his death Joseph lost the favor of his royal master?

A careful study of the framework of the Book of Genesis as it has been outlined above will help the Bible student to understand some of the problems and difficulties which appear elsewhere in the Historical Books of the Old Testament. This is shown by the following examples.

Manna. The account of the giving of the manna (Exod. 16) is completed by the command to lay up a pot before the Testimony (vs. 34) — i.e., before the ark which contained the Ten Commandments inscribed on the tables of stone which were not given until Israel was encamped at Sinai; and the statement is added in the next verse that the Israelites "did eat manna forty years until they came to the borders of the land of Canaan," which brings the story down to the close of Moses' life. This is anticipatory history, but it is told to complete or round out the important topic which is here introduced.

Rahab Spared (Josh. 6). After the destruction of Jericho is described in 6:12-21, which includes a brief reference to the sparing of Rahab and her family (vs. 17), and ends with the declaration that the total destruction commanded was fully carried out (vs. 21), then with verse 22 the writer reverts to the subject of Rahab and we read: "And Joshua said [AV, "But Joshua had said" is justified by the context] to the two men who had spied out the land, Go to the house of the woman, the harlot and bring forth. . . ." This was done. Rahab and her family were saved (vs. 23). Verse 24 returns to the theme of Jericho's destruction. Then verse 25 refers again to Rahab and tells us that she became a member of the Israelite community.

David's Sin and Its Consequences. This might be made the title of 2 Samuel 11-20. These ten chapters are almost wholly devoted to this subject. They might well be regarded as a homily on the words: "Now therefore the sword shall never depart from thine house; because thou hast despised me, and hast taken the wife of Uriah the Hittite to be thy wife" (12:10). A period of perhaps ten years is required for the events here recorded. But most of it is simply the story of Absalom's unfilial and treasonable conduct and its tragic ending. Since it is so fully told here, it is completely ignored in Chronicles, which merely records the names of Bathsheba (called Bathshua) and of Absalom, but has nothing to say about them.

The failure of the Chronicler to mention the sin with Bathsheba or the tragic career of Absalom has often been pointed to as an example of bias and prejudice; and his history has been described as partisan. In answer, it may be said that the account in Samuel is so full and so complete that there was no need of a second account; and the theme was not a pleasant one for a patriotic historian to dwell upon. It must also be recognized that the Chronicler did not hesitate to expose David's mistakes. This is made clear by the incident of the bringing up of the ark. The first attempt and the reason for its failure is much more fully described (13:1-14; 15:1-15) than in Samuel, which only hints at the reason for the first failure by the words "when they that bare the ark" (2 Sam. 6:13). In the matter of the census, the account in 1 Chronicles 21:1-30 is quite as severe on David as is that in 2 Samuel 24:1-25.[50]

David and the Temple. To his great sorrow David was not allowed to build the temple. Second Samuel records this fact (7:12f.) as made known to David; and Solomon refers to it (1 Kings 5:3; 8:19). But it is only in 1 Chronicles 22 — 29 that we read of the elaborate preparations which David made for the building of the temple and for the organization of the priests and Levites for the services of sacrifice and song. This the Chronicler adds to his account of the building of the altar on the field of Ornan the Jebusite, which has been already given in 2 Samuel where nothing is said about this important subject.

Solomon's Other Buildings (1 Kings 7:1-12). Having given an account of the construction of the temple, the writer passes on to speak of the other buildings which Solomon built: the house of the Forest of Lebanon, the porch for the throne, the palace for Pharaoh's daughter. Then he returns to the temple and its equipment and describes the two pillars, the chapiters, the molten sea, the bases for the lavers and the lavers themselves, and all the vessels which Hiram made for king Solomon (vss. 13-51).

Elijah and Elisha. The last five chapters of 1 Kings and the first nine of 2 Kings are largely devoted to the deeds and words of these two great prophets.[51] Chronicles does not even mention Elisha by name; and its only reference to Elijah is to an incident unmentioned in Kings, Elijah's message to Jehoram king of Judah (21:12),[52] which is especially interesting since it shows the concern of Elijah for the future of the Davidic house; for Elijah's personal ministry was in the Northern Kingdom.

The Fate of Hoshea (2 Kings 17:1-6). Keil has pointed out that many commentators have held the view that "it was not till the conquest of his capital city Samaria, that Hoshea fell into the hands of the Assyrians and was cast into prison." If this view is correct, it gives us another example of the method of narration under discussion. The narrator finishes with Hoshea before describing the fate of his capital. It seems improbable that Hoshea would have placed himself voluntarily in the hands of Shalmaneser or have risked a battle with his mighty enemy, instead of shutting himself up in his well-nigh impregnable city, which held out for three years against the Assyrian hosts. Yet if Hoshea was in Samaria throughout the siege and then fell into the hands of the conqueror, we might expect that Hoshea's fate would be mentioned in immediate connection with the fall of the city. Neither one of the solutions of the problem is without difficulty.

After the Fall of Samaria (2 Kings 17:24-41). After recording the fall of their capital city, the writer gives a brief summary of the subsequent history of the Northern Tribes. He begins with the statement that "the king of Assyria" having carried Israel into captivity brought in foreigners and pagans to replace them. When we turn to Ezra we read (4:2) that it was Esarhaddon (680-669 B.C.) who sent many of these colonists and that the "great and noble Asnapper," probably Ashurbanipal (668-626 B.C.) continued and perhaps completed this task. This would mean that the repopulating of Samaria occupied a considerable period of time, and if the words "since the days of Esarhaddon" are intended to mark the beginning of this undertaking, or at least the first major step in it, then there is an interval of about forty years between verses 23 and 24 of 2 Kings 17; and the words quoted mean either that the policy was introduced by Esarhaddon or "king of Assyria" is to be understood as referring to the Assyrian kings in general who as conquerors imposed their will upon Samaria. After sketching the course of subsequent events in broad outline, the writer returns to describe the course of events in Judah going back to the accession of Hezekiah which took place in the third year of Hoshea, six years before the fall of Samaria.

Sennacherib. The story of the attempt or attempts of this mighty Assyrian monarch to conquer Judah and Jerusalem is told in a single continuous narrative in each of the three biblical accounts, all of which end with his death which occurred in 681 B.C.,[53] many years after the death of Hezekiah. Then all three narratives turn back to record two important events in the life of Hezekiah; his illness which took place fifteen years before his death (2 Kings 20:6) and which may have been occasioned by the terrible strain of the Sennacherib invasion; and also the embassage of Merodach-baladan, which being ostensibly to congratulate him on his recovery from his illness probably took place rather soon after it. Yet the reader might readily suppose that both followed the death of Sennacherib, which was certainly not the case.

Jehoiachin, the captive (2 Kings 25:27-30). The final destruction of Jerusalem and the burning of the temple took place in the nineteenth year of Nebuchadnezzar (2 Kings 25:8ff.). It was followed by the flight of a remnant of the people to Egypt. This carries the history down to 586 B.C. Then with verse 27 an event is described which took place twenty-six years later, the freeing and honoring of Jehoiachin by Evil-merodach. How long this notable change continued we are not told. Evil-merodach reigned less than three years. Jehoiachin was about fifty-five when thus honored. Whether he long survived Evil-merodach or not is nowhere stated.

The Synchronous History. This simple way of describing events is very naturally followed in the history of the reigns of the kings of Judah and Israel as it is given in the Books of Kings. For example, the announcement of the death of Rehoboam is followed by the statement that Abijam succeeded him in the eighteenth year of Jeroboam, king of Israel (1 Kings 15:1). Then follows a brief account of Abijam's brief reign of three years (vss. 2-8) and of Asa's long reign of forty-one years which followed it (vss. 9-23), a considerable part of which is devoted to Asa's struggles with Baasha, the king of Israel who slew Jeroboam's son Nadab; and it concludes with the statement that Asa was succeeded by Jehoshaphat (vs. 24). Then with verse 25 the historian turns to the Northern Kingdom to bring things up to date. He tells us that Nadab succeeded Jeroboam in the second year of Asa (vs. 25), that Baasha overthrew Nadab in the third year of Asa (vss. 27f.), that Elah succeeded Baasha in the twenty-sixth year of Asa (16:8), that Zimri killed Elah in the twenty-seventh year of Asa (vss. 10, 15), that Omri began to reign in the thirty-first year of Asa (vs. 23), that Ahab succeeded Omri in the thirty-eighth year of Asa (vs. 28). More than five chapters are then devoted to the reign of Ahab, which is terminated by his death in battle with the king of Syria (22:40). The account of this battle requires the mention of Jehoshaphat's part in it. Jehoshaphat has thus far been mentioned only in 15:24. Now with 22:41 the historian resumes his account of the kings of Judah and tells us that Jehoshaphat began to reign in the fourth year of Ahab (some eighteen years before Ahab's death), that he reigned twenty-five years, and he gives a brief summary of his reign (vss. 42-50) which makes no mention of Ahab. The method used by the historian is an admirable one. But we need to keep it carefully in mind or we may become confused as to the sequence of events.

Ezra 4. The Books of Ezra and Nehemiah are closely related. But each has its special theme and interest. In Ezra it is the restoration of the *house of God* and the proper maintenance of its worship. In Nehemiah it is the rebuilding of the *walls* of Jerusalem. If we disregard for the moment verses 6-23 of this chapter, we observe that it tells of the hindrance put in the way of the Jews by their adversaries, which finally resulted in an interruption of the work of building the temple which continued until the second year of Darius (vs. 24). Then under the exhortations of Haggai and Zechariah (Ezra 5:1f.; Hag. 1:1; Zech. 1:16; 4:9), the building was resumed. A letter of protest to Darius (5:7-17) asking that the work be stopped was answered by instructions to promote it in every way (6:1-12). Four years later the house was finished and dedicated (vs. 15), and the passover and feast of unleavened bread were kept at the usual time (vs. 19-22). Then with the words, "And after these things," chapter 7 tells of the coming of Ezra to Jerusalem in the seventh year of Artaxerxes — more than fifty years later — and records his letter of instructions from the king regarding maintaining the temple ritual and also a list of the gifts which were given by the king. Chapter 8 gives an account of those who went up to Jerusalem with Ezra, of their journey, and their arrival. Chapters 9-10 are concerned with the foreign-wife question and its solution. Nothing is said in this narrative about rebuilding the walls of Jerusalem. In 5:3, 8, 9 the reference is clearly to the walls of the temple and in 9:9 the words "to give us a wall in Judah and Jerusalem" apparently are used of the temple as a wall of protection. Judah had no wall around it. The language is clearly figurative.

Nehemiah has a quite different task. He is concerned about the rebuilding of the walls of Jerusalem. Learning in the twentieth year of Artaxerxes that the walls and gates are destroyed (1:3), which of course means still unrestored after Nebuchadnezzar destroyed them, he secured permission to rebuild them (2:8). This he proceeded to do immediately after his arrival at Jerusalem; and "the wall was finished in the twenty and fifth day of Elul in fifty and two days" (6:15). This was Nehemiah's great achievement. When he refers to the house of God, which he does occasionally, it is always to a sanctuary already in existence and in use.

We turn back now to consider Ezra 4:6-23. We have seen that verses 1-5 have described the frustration of the plan to build the house of God, and we have traced the course of this opposition "even until the reign of Darius king of Persia." Verse 6 states that this opposition showed itself in the reign of Ahasuerus (Xerxes) in the writing of an accusation. Without stating the result, the writer passes on to the reign of Artaxerxes, when a similar accusation was made. Just when this occurred is not stated. It would seem probable that it was early in the reign of the new monarch. In this case both the accusation and the royal reply or edict are recorded. On examining them we find that they make no mention of the house of God, but refer only to "the bad and rebellious city" (vss. 12, 15, 19) and the rebuilding of its walls (vss. 12, 13, 16). Instruction is given that the "city" be not built, "until commandment be given" by the king. Armed with this edict Rehum the chancellor and his companions compelled the Jews "to cease by force and power" (vs. 23). The work which was stopped was, according to the accusation and the edict, the building of the *city* and *walls.*

Passing on to verse 24 we read, "Then ceased the work of the house of God which is in Jerusalem. So it ceased unto the second year of the reign of Darius king of Persia." Two things attract our attention at once: the mention of "the house of God" and of "Darius." The accusation and the edict of verses 7-23 concern the city and walls; and the king is Artaxerxes. Neither is referred to in this verse; and Chapter 5 goes on to speak of the rebuilding of the *house of God* as a result of Darius' discovery of Cyrus' edict. What is the explanation? Various solutions of the difficulty have been offered. The simplest and most likely one is, that, in giving a summary account of the opposition which the Jews encountered almost immediately in their efforts to rebuild the house of God and the walls of Jerusalem, Ezra has extended his brief narrative to include the greatest hindrance of all, Artaxerxes' command that the rebuilding of the walls of Jerusalem be abandoned. This was the *status quo* when Ezra returned to Jerusalem in the seventh year of Artaxerxes. Then, by a sudden transition which he apparently feels to be sufficiently indicated by the mention of the house of God which was completed, as he tells us later, in the sixth year of Darius, and by the further mention of Darius himself, he returns to the situation of verse 6 and proceeds to tell of the rebuilding of the house of God as a result of the favorable action of Darius. It is to be noted that there was probably ample time between the seventh year of Artaxerxes and his twentieth year for the king to change his mind as to the advisability of permitting the rebuilding of the walls of Jerusalem, all the more since the granting of Nehemiah's request is clearly due to the king's high regard for his cup-bearer.

Nehemiah 7:73f. We meet another somewhat similar example of abrupt transition in Nehemiah. Chapter 6:15 tells us that Nehemiah's great task, the building of the wall, was completed on the twenty-fifth of Elul, which was the sixth month, and that it took fifty-two days. But Nehemiah was not merely concerned to build the walls of the city. He was also determined that its citizens should be true Israelites, both in blood and in belief. So he made a register of the people, using as the basis for it a record made nearly eighty years previously in the days of Zerubbabel. This record which is given in Ezra 2 is reproduced in Nehemiah 7 and it concludes with the words: "and when the seventh month was come, the children of Israel were in their cities" (Neh. 7:73; cf. Ezra 3:1). Then we note a startling difference. In Ezra the narrative proceeds at once to speak of Joshua and Zerubbabel, while in Nehemiah it speaks of Ezra. This is confusing because both narratives refer to the seventh month; and both describe the celebration of the feast of tabernacles which took place in the course of that month. But the persons involved are quite different. So apparently with a view to guarding against confusion we are told that it was on the first day of the seventh month (Neh. 8:2) that Ezra began the reading of the law. Here the seventh month clearly means the seventh month of the twentieth year of the reign of Artaxerxes, while in 7:73 it apparently means the seventh month of the second year of Cyrus as king of Babylon.[54] For the modern reader the narrative in Nehemiah 8:1f. would be less open to misunderstanding if the recital of the document given in Ezra 2 had not included the mention of the seventh month. But apparently the writer was interested in the fact that these two memorable events, the setting up of the altar and the dedication of the walls, though separated by nearly eighty years, took place in the same month and were connected with the celebration of the same feast. The parallel is rendered more complete by the fact that on both occasions the religious ceremonies began on the first day of the month (Ezra 3:6; Neh. 8:2).

SEQUENCE NOT NECESSARILY CHRONOLOGICAL

It follows from what has been said above that the sequence in which events are recorded may not be strictly chronological. Ezekiel inserts a prediction of the twenty-seventh year (29:17-30:19) between one of the tenth year and another of the eleventh year, probably because all three concern Egypt. These three prophecies are all dated. But there are other cases where no date is given and the sequence may not be chronological.

In Deuteronomy 9:22-24, Moses digresses to add to his allusion to the sin of the golden calf at Sinai four other examples of Israel's sinfulness: Taberah, Massah, Kibroth-hattaavah, Kadesh. Taberah was after the departure from Sinai (Num. 11:3), Massah was before Israel came to Sinai (Exod. 17:7), Kibroth-hattaavah followed Taberah (Num. 11:34; 33:16), and was followed by the great refusal at Kadesh (Num. 14). And Moses adds, as if to complete the record of disobedience and rebellion, "Ye have been rebellious against the Lord from the day that I knew you." Then he returns to the starting point, the golden calf, and tells of his intercession for Israel for forty days and forty nights and repeats the prayer which he then offered on their behalf.

The two appendices to the Book of Judges (chaps. 17-21) are joined to what precedes by a simple "and there was" (17:1) and to one another by "and it was in those days" (19:1). The date of the first series of events (Micah and the Danites) cannot be definitely determined. But since the young Levite (17:7) who was installed as their priest was a grandson of Moses (18:30, *ARV*), the events described must have taken place long before Samson's death which is recorded in 16:30f. The fratricidal strife between Benjamin and the other tribes (chap. 19-21) must also have taken place long before Samson's time. This is clearly indicated by the fact that "Phineas, the son of Eleazar, the son of Aaron" was officiating as priest at the time (20:28). For Phineas had already distinguished himself during the lifetime of Moses (Num. 25:7-13); and he had been Joshua's representative when the question of the memorial altar arose (Josh. 22). The Book of Ruth was probably originally a third appendix to Judges, as the introductory sentence indicates: "And it came to pass in the days when the judges ruled...." But the date of the events which it describes is uncertain.

Elijah's Commission at Horeb (1 Kings 19:15f.). We have noted that three commands were given Elijah by the Lord. He was to anoint Hazael to be king of Syria, Jehu to be king of Israel, Elisha to be prophet in his room. The last of the three he apparently carried out at once (vss. 19-21). The other two were not carried out until a decade or more later, not by Elijah but by Elisha, and apparently in rather close succession. Yet in the case of these two the chronological sequence was observed. It is also of interest to note that the command to "anoint" was apparently carried out literally only in the case of Jehu. There is no evidence that prophets were anointed with oil. The sign or token given in Elisha's call was the casting of Elijah's mantle upon him (cf. 2 Kings 2:8, 14; Zech. 13:4). Kings of Israel were anointed. Hence Jehu, who had a divine commission to execute judgment on the house of Ahab, was anointed king. But Hazael was a foreigner; and for him the intimation that he was to be king, coming from the lips of the prophet, was sufficient to lead him to do what his evil heart considered a "great thing," to murder a helpless master and seize upon his throne.

The Sickness of Hezekiah. A striking example of the failure to indicate clearly the chronological sequence is the account of the sickness of Hezekiah. In each of the three accounts of it (Kings, Chronicles, and Isaiah) it is introduced by the indefinite statement, "In those days was Hezekiah sick unto death." In all three it is placed *after* the final deliverance from Sennacherib, an account which in all three narratives ends with Sennacherib's death. But even if Hezekiah's sole reign did not begin until 715 B.C., his twenty-nine years would only extend to about 686 B.C., which was five years before the death of his mighty enemy. Consequently the words "in those days" (2 Kings 20:1; 2 Chron. 32:24; Isa. 38:1) carry us back many years before the event which has just been recorded. The date of Hezekiah's sickness can only be determined in connection with the larger question of the period of his reign. News of his recovery was made by Merodach-baladan the occasion for a message of congratulation, which probably had the ulterior motive of inducing Hezekiah to join a confederacy against the Assyrians. But whether this was in Sargon's time or in that of Sennacherib is not stated.[55] The fact that this incident is placed in Isaiah after the account of Sennacherib's invasion which concludes with the mention of his death is apparently due to the close connection in Isaiah between this incident which occasioned the ominous prediction which Isaiah uttered at that time and the wonderful prophecy of deliverance and comfort which immediately follows in the Book of Consolation, this close connection being indicated by immediate juxtaposition. Comfort in view of, in spite of calamity!

The question has been much discussed whether in Isaiah 6 we have the inaugural call of the prophet which would belong chronologically before the "Great Arraignment" of Chapter 1, or whether the arrangement is chronological. While recognizing that the majority of commentators in his day, as apparently also today, took the former view, Alexander argued that the presumption is in favor of chronological sequence.

The *Historical Psalms* do not always follow the sequence of the historical narratives. The Plagues of Egypt are referred to in Psalm 105:28-36 in a different order from that given in Exodus. In Psalm 78, verses 12-41 deal with the exodus and the wandering; verses 42-51 go back to the plagues which led up to the exodus; then verses 54-72 deal with the conquest and the oppressions down to the time of David. In Psalm 106, the punishment of Dathan and Abiram (vss. 16f.) which took place during the wilderness wanderings (Num. 16) is immediately followed (vss. 19f.) by a reference to the golden calf at Horeb (Exod. 32). In verses 28-31 the sin of Baal-peor (Num. 25) is referred to and brought into relation with a previous incident, "the waters of strife" (Num. 20:2-13) by means of a simple "and." Then after mentioning the sad consequences for Moses which resulted from this incident at Meribah, the Psalmist passes on immediately to bring forward the further charge that "they did not destroy the nations concerning whom the Lord commanded them" (vs. 34), which presupposes the conquest of the land by Joshua. Similarly in Psalm 78:70, after speaking of the building of the temple, which was accomplished by Solomon, the Psalmist immediately proceeds to speak of the choosing of David, which preceded it by a generation.

Psalm 114, already referred to in another connection, is a beautiful illustration of this artistic grouping of historical events. It begins with the exodus: "When Israel went out of Egypt, Judah became [AV "was"] his sanctuary, Israel his dominion," a situation not fully realized until long after the conquest. Then it returns to the exodus period to link together two similar but widely separated events: the crossing of the Red Sea and the crossing of the Jordan. Then it describes a conspicuous event which took place between these two crossings: the tremendous theophany at Mt. Sinai. Then with beautiful poetic license it interrogates sea, mountains, river Jordan as to the reason for their remarkable conduct; and it calls on the earth to tremble at the presence of the Lord who has wrought these wonders. It concludes by coupling together two further and equally striking illustrations of omnipotence: turning the "rock" at Horeb into a pool of water, and nearly forty years later at Kadesh, the "flinty rock" (granite) into a fountain of water.

The Great Woman of Shunem (2 Kings 4:8-37). This episode in the career of Elisha throws a very pleasing light on the life of that great man of God who succeeded Elijah. It is one of numerous illustrations of the ways in which the prophets influenced the lives of the people among whom they dwelt and who looked to them for guidance and help. We mention it here because of the period of time which it covered. It tells of an undated action which apparently became a habit. How often the prophet stopped at the woman's home before it occurred to her to provide him a lodging place we are not told. The events which followed, including the birth, childhood, death, and restoration to life of the child, must have covered at least five years, perhaps ten. Then we read, "And Elisha came again to Gilgal" (vs. 38; cf. 2:1).

Gehazi's Testimony. The story is resumed in a striking way in 8:1-6. After a number of important events have been recorded: the healing of Naaman, the enlarging of the dwellings of the sons of the prophets, the invasions of the king of Syria, the surrounding of Dothan with its amazing sequel, and the siege of Samaria, we return suddenly to the woman of Shunem. When she appears, after seven years absence, to make her request to the king for the restoration of her property, her husband being apparently dead, she finds Gehazi in audience with the king. That Gehazi has been healed of his leprosy is contradicted by the words of the curse: "The leprosy therefore of Naaman shall cleave unto thee and unto thy seed forever" (5:27). That the king would be talking with a leper about "all the great things that Elisha hath done" (8:4), seems highly improbable especially when we remember Gehazi's leprosy was a punishment for disloyalty to his master who had discharged him from his service. Apparently we must assume that the healing of Naaman took place subsequent to the event recorded in Chapter 8:3-6.[56]

The Close of David's Reign. The last chapters of 2 Samuel contain certain memorabilia, as we may call them, which are clearly not arranged in chronological sequence. The last event mentioned is the sending of the plague as a punishment for David's sin in numbering the people, a punishment which was stayed, when David offered sacrifice on the altar which he had erected on the field which he had purchased from Ornan the Jebusite (2 Sam. 24). The narrative which follows in 1 Kings 1 proceeds at once to describe an event which took place when David "was old and stricken in years," viz., the attempt of Adonijah to gain the throne. The narrative in 1 Chronicles 21 runs parallel to that in 2 Samuel 24 and likewise describes the scene at the threshing floor of Ornan. But then it passes immediately to the subject of the building of the temple, a matter so dear to David's heart, the nexus lying in the fact that it was to be on the threshing floor of Ornan that the temple was to be built. Solomon is then referred to and addressed directly as the one who is to build the house of the Lord. Then the words "So when David was old and full of years, he made Solomon his son king over Israel" (23:1) indicate the feebleness of the king which is so fully described in 1 Kings 1, and this is apparently the reason that 1 Chronicles 28:2 records the fact that "David the king stood up upon his feet" to deliver his farewell address to the people. It was the last effort of a dying man, a solemn act of exhortation to the people in behalf of Solomon. Thus it appears that the Adonijah story, which assumes that David had not yet announced that Solomon was to succeed him is to be placed somewhere between 21:30 and 22:6 in 1 Chronicles. But how long the interval was between the Ornan incident and the accession of Solomon is uncertain.[57]

Joshua. The Book of Joshua concludes with his death and burial. The historian then goes on to mention the burial of Joseph's bones at Shechem and those of Eleazar, the son of Aaron, in the family property in the hill country of Ephraim. We may assume that the connection between these three burials is simply topical. It is very unlikely that Joshua left to his successors the solemn duty of carrying out Joseph's dying request. Quite probably it was carried out in connection with the solemn renewal of the Covenant at Shechem (Josh. 8:30-35).

Ahab and Jezebel. It would be natural to infer from the statement in 1 Kings 16:31 that Ahab married Jezebel after he became king. But when we note that Ahaziah of Judah who was the son of Athaliah was 22 years old when he became king (2 Kings 8:26), which was only about thirty-two years after the succession of Ahab, it would seem probable that Ahaziah's grandmother Jezebel was married to his grandfather Ahab several years before he became king. The fact that the historian represents Ahab's marriage to Jezebel as his greatest or crowning sin may be intended to make it clear to us that this international marriage was planned and carried out by Ahab himself while his father was still alive and was the greatest sin of Ahab's wicked career. Ahab not only did everything Omri did to provoke the Lord to anger; he went still further: he married the pagan princess Jezebel and he did this before he became king.

THE INDIVIDUAL STRESSED

A valid principle of law is expressed in the old saying *Qui facit per alium facit per se,* which means that a man is responsible (is entitled to the credit and must bear the blame) for the acts of his agents. "Thou hast killed Uriah the Hittite with the sword ... thou hast slain him with the sword of the children of Ammon" (2 Sam. 12:9) is an impressive example.[58] This principle is so generally accepted that we often fail to notice it.[59]

We read that Cain "builded a city" (Gen. 4:17), that Noah was commanded to build an ark which was to be 450 feet long (6:15). This certainly does not mean that these two men had no helpers. It rather indicates that they must have had many of them. The statement "And Terah took Abram ... Lot ... Sarai ... unto Haran" (11:31) does not limit the size of the caravan to three persons. We read later that Abram had 318 servants "born in his house" who were capable of bearing arms (14:14). The omission of the name of Nahor may mean that Nahor was already in Syria and perhaps justify the inference that Syria was the ancestral home of Terah and his family and that his sojourn in Ur was temporary and perhaps brief. Such examples as these are too obvious to require explanation. But there are cases where this principle is not so generally recognized.

Moses and the Ark (Deut. 10:3). The words "and I made an ark of shittim wood" need not mean that Moses made it himself. According to Exodus 31:1-11 the making of the ark was assigned to Bezaleel and his helpers. They made it according to the instructions given to Moses (25:10-22; 37:1-9). However, the question does arise whether the ark here referred to is the one made by Bezaleel or a temporary receptacle made by (or for) Moses to hold the Tables of Testimony until the permanent one was constructed. The order of words in the Deuteronomy passage: "And I made an ark of shittim wood and hewed two tables of stone ..." certainly suggests this latter interpretation which is favored by Exod. 35:12 where the ark is included in the list of objects to be built.

The Massacre at Shechem (Gen. 34:25f.) Here we read that Simeon and Levi, the brothers of Dinah, "took each man his sword, and came upon the city boldly and slew all the males." It seems scarcely warranted to take the statement as meaning literally that these two young men, without any assistance from their father's herdsmen, some of whom were probably directly under their authority, or from their brothers, slew all the males of Shechem. We are not concerned with the question whether under the circumstances these two men could have accomplished this dastardly feat, but whether we should understand the narrative to mean this. Since the Shechem of Jacob's day was as we now know a strongly fortified city, it seems highly probable that while Simeon and Levi were the ringleaders they had active assistance from the herdsmen under their direct control and perhaps from others, as verse 27 clearly implies.[60]

Jacob's Seventy Sons (Gen. 46:27). When we read the account of the descent into Egypt, we might easily infer that Jacob's entire household consisted of about seventy souls, and many calculations of the increase of Israel in Egypt have been based on such an assumption. It is of course recognized that counting wives, daughters, sons' wives, and granddaughters (46:5-7) would more than double this figure. But there are other matters to be noted. Abraham was "very rich in cattle" (Gen. 12:16; 13:2). He had many herdsmen (13:6f.). He had 318 trained servants, born in his own house (Gen. 14:14). All of them received the sign of the covenant (circumcision) as did also the slaves whom he had purchased (17:27). Isaac's herdsmen got into difficulties with Abimelech's herdsmen; and they were so numerous that Abimelech said to Isaac, "Go from us; for thou art much mightier than we" (26:16). Joseph told Pharaoh that his brethren were herdsmen, and had brought their flocks and herds with them to Egypt. It seems highly probable that Jacob's caravan numbered several thousand souls, who would all be classed as "children of Israel." But the tribal relationships of what we might call the "blue bloods" are given according to the male line in the list of the seventy given in Genesis 46.

Jacob's Ten Sons (Gen. 42:3). What has just been said about the seventy souls of Jacob throws light upon the account of the mission of the ten sons to buy grain. Unless the household of Abraham had been greatly reduced in size, a fact of which we have no direct evidence, ten ass-loads of corn, some of which would have been consumed on the return journey itself, would have been but a mouthful for so extensive a household as Jacob apparently had. When we compare this starvation ration with the ample supplies which Joseph gave his brethren for themselves and for their father merely as provision for their journey (45:21-23), we seem justified in inferring that on both of their journeys the ten brothers were accompanied by servants who bore away on their asses not a few ass-loads of corn in addition to the ones for which the ten sons were directly responsible.

The Blood-bath at Nob (1 Sam. 22:18f.). Doeg the Edomite "slew fourscore and five persons that did wear a linen ephod" and also destroyed all the inhabitants of Nob, the city of the priests, "both men and women, children and sucklings, and oxen, and asses, and sheep, with the edge of the sword." That Doeg was the leader in this ruthless butchery is clear. But we are hardly expected to believe that this was all the act of one individual. Doeg had an immediate following, directly responsible to him (vs. 9), who are apparently to be distinguished from Saul's personal bodyguard (vs. 17), and they probably took part in the dastardly deed.

The Slaying of Abner (2 Sam. 3:27). Here we read first that Joab slew Abner: he "smote him there under the fifth *rib,* that he died." Then in verse 30 we read "So Joab and Abishai his brother slew Abner." In both verses the same reason for the deed is given, revenge for the death of Asahel. Joab was clearly the instigator and principal actor while Abishai had some part in the deed. This is indicated by the curse pronounced by David. The words "all his father's house" include Abishai with Joab. But the detailed and grievous curse is pronounced on "the house of Joab."

Ishbosheth's Murderers (2 Sam. 4). When two of Ishbosheth's captains brought his head to David expecting a reward, David had them slain and he justified this act by appealing to his similar conduct in the case of the Amalekite who claimed to have killed Saul. Here David says of that action: "I took hold of him and slew him." Yet the earlier statement is "And David called one of the young men, and said, Go near and fall upon him. And he smote him, so that he died" (1:15). No contradiction! Simply two ways of saying the same thing.

And (David) Sacrificed Oxen and Fatlings (2 Sam. 6:13). It is not at all necessary to assume or infer that David himself acted as priest and actually performed the sacrifices. What he as king commanded to be done was his act!

Mephibosheth's Excuse (2 Sam. 19:27). Keil argues quite properly that there is no reason for changing the reading "for thy servant said, I will saddle me the ass" to read "for thy servant said to him [Ziba], saddle for me the ass," as is done by *LXX, Syr. Vulg.* The fact that Mephibosheth was lame and refers to this fact indicates that he had told Ziba or a servant to perform a service which any master might require of his servant. This explanation is supported by the description of the state of mourning in which Mephibosheth remained until king David returned. Mephibosheth placed the blame entirely on Ziba. But David's decision certainly implies that David thought his explanation inadequate, and that Mephibosheth could have joined him in his flight if he had really wanted to.

Solomon and the Temple. Solomon says of the temple: "I have built the house for the name of the Lord God of Israel" (1 Kings 8:20) although the actual building was done by a vast *corvée* of workmen. Similarly Nebuchadnezzar exclaims, "Is not this great Babylon, which I have built . . . ?" (Dan. 4:30). Yes, he built it, but thousands of captives and slaves did the work. 1 Kings 9:25, "And three times a year did Solomon offer burnt offerings and peace offerings upon the altar which he built unto the Lord . . ." (cf. 8:63). As in the case of David these words do not imply that Solomon personally acted as priest any more than that he himself built the altar. Yet some critics find in such statements as these regarding David and Solomon evidence that these kings performed priestly acts. Yet the tragic lesson of Uzziah's leprosy should show the fallacy of such a claim.[61]

OBJECTIVITY

It is not proposed to discuss here the large and important subject of Old Testament ethics, but to call attention to a single aspect of the problem as it relates to biblical rhetoric. The objectivity with which the Old Testament recites many of the events of history and the actions of individuals is at times very striking.

The serpent's words, "Ye shall not surely die" (Gen. 3:4), are not directly contradicted in the narrative. But their falsity is indicated by the words of the woman, "the serpent beguiled me" (vs. 13), by the punishment at once pronounced on the serpent (vs. 14), by the suffering pronounced on Eve, by the curse inflicted on Adam, "until thou return unto the dust" (vs. 19), by the mournful, oft repeated "and he died" of Chapter 5, and by the awful judgment of the flood.

The lies or half-lies told by *Abraham* regarding Sarah are not censured or condemned, except indirectly by the protestations of innocency made by Pharaoh and by Abimelech. The same is true of Isaac's similar conduct regarding Rebekah. In both cases the honorable conduct of the heathen king is sufficient condemnation of the unworthy conduct of the Hebrew Patriarch. They show that the conduct of the Patriarchs was not always up to the ethical standards of their heathen neighbors.

The deceit and trickery by which *Rebekah* and *Jacob* defrauded Esau of his blessing are described; and we cannot but sympathize with Esau's complaint (Gen. 27:36) and recognize that when Isaac used the words "with subtilty" in describing Jacob's conduct, he was using a term which always describes that which is unethical. But the aim of the writer is not to expose or reprove the unworthy conduct of this patriarchal family, but to show how the God of Abraham accomplished his sovereign purpose, making even the wrath of men to praise him.

We are not told whether *Jacob* actually went to Seir (33:14) or was merely inventing an excuse to get rid of Esau. In 36:6 we are given the reason why Esau went to live permanently in Mount Seir. We are not told when Jacob returned to his father Isaac (35:27). It may have been shortly before Isaac's death, mention of which immediately follows. The servility with which Jacob greeted Esau suggests that he placed little confidence in the blessing which he had secured by fraud; and it is noteworthy that when Isaac died, "his sons Esau and Jacob buried him" (35:29). These words suggest that Jacob did not venture to claim precedence over Esau until after his father was dead. The fact that no mention is made of the death of Rebekah suggests that Jacob never saw his mother again, that she was punished for her duplicity by the extending of the "few days" absence (27:44) which she thought sufficient for the cooling of Esau's anger, to cover all the rest of her earthly life.

Joseph is one of the most beautiful characters in the Bible. Paul might have used him as an Old Testament example when he said, "Be ye kind one to another, tenderhearted, forgiving one another." But Joseph's treatment of his brethren was high-handed to say the least. He accused them of lying. But he himself resorted to false accusation, trickery, deceit and coercion. The trumped-up charge of stealing the silver cup was highly unethical. He played the role of the despot and acted on the Jesuitical principle that the end justifies the means. His unethical acts are described and according to the Egyptian ethics of his day they were morally wrong. But they are not condemned. They are allowed to speak for themselves.[62]

Rahab's Lie (Josh. 2:4-6). Rahab's lie to the messengers of the king of Jericho is followed immediately by the expression of her conviction that Jericho will be captured by Israel and by her appeal for protection when this takes place. It is her faith which is praised in the great Faith Chapter of the Bible (Heb. 11:31). The words "when she had received the spies with peace" may be intended to indicate an extenuating circumstance. Having shown hospitality to these enemies of her city, she felt obliged to protect them. But she is not commended for her actions in detail.

Caleb. One of the finest characters in the Old Testament is Caleb the son of Jephunneh, the faithful spy, whose fidelity to the Lord is referred to in Numbers 14:24; Deuteronomy 1:36; Joshua 14:8, 9, 14. Of him the rare expression "wholly followed" (*AV*; literally "filled up after" i.e., followed closely) is used, which he shared only with Joshua (Num. 32:12) and David (1 Kings 11:6) with whom Solomon is contrasted as Caleb and Joshua are contrasted with the whole apostate generation (Num. 32:11f.). To Caleb the difficulty of the conquest, even the supreme task of dispossessing the sons of Anak who were a terror to the unbelieving (Num. 13:22-33), was a challenge to his indomitable faith (Josh. 14:12) and led to victory (15:14). He might well be called the Sir Galahad of the Old Testament. Yet he is not listed among the heroes of Hebrews 11, which suggests that many names are omitted which might be included there (vs. 32). The words which Bunyan puts on the lips of Mr. Steadfast: "I have loved to hear my Lord spoken of; and wherever I have seen the print of his shoe in the earth, there I have coveted to set my foot too," suggest that he was thinking of Caleb, who "wholly followed" after the Lord.

Jonathan. Of unselfish, self-forgetting love Jonathan is a shining example. His love for David was so deep and true that he was willing to recognize the fact that David was the Lord's choice to succeed Saul. When we think of the rivalries and jealousies which later arose between the sons of David, the loyalty of Jonathan shines out conspicuously. The only thing that can be laid to his discredit is his failure to accept the challenge of Goliath during all of the forty days before David appeared on the scene. That this was not due to cowardice is made clear by his almost single-handed attack on the Philistine garrison, which is told so fully in 1 Samuel 14, a story which exhibits both his courage and his faith and which is told apparently for that very purpose. It also suggests the reason Jonathan did not dare to fight Goliath. The terms of that combat were not personal but national. Jonathan was ready to face death for himself. But he lacked David's sublime confidence of victory; and he was not willing to engage in a conflict the outcome of which would, he believed, bring disaster on his own people. It was not courage which was lacking, but faith; and it was probably David's invincible faith which won him the admiration and love of Jonathan. In the light of Saul's conduct after Jonathan made his almost single-handed attack on Geba (1 Sam. 14:5, ARV), it is not at all unlikely that Saul forbade Jonathan to accept the challenge of Goliath lest his first-born and favorite son go to certain death. Apparently Saul was impressed by David's bearing and words and he probably had no more intention of abiding by the terms of the conflict, in case the outcome went against him, than had the Philistines who had fixed the terms because they felt sure of the outcome. Jonathan well deserved the praise which David expressed in his Lament!

Jephthah's Vow (Judg. 11). The story of Jephthah is one of the most terrible of the illustrations of the state of religion in the days of the Judges. It seems reasonably clear that Jephthah intended to offer a human sacrifice to the Lord if he were given victory over Ammon. His vow and his subsequent conduct must be judged in the light of the widespread ignorance of the Law of Moses and the no less general apostasy from it, of which the Book of Judges speaks so often and of which it gives so many terrible examples, and by the upbringing, or lack of it, which had made Jephthah what he was. The writer seems to shrink from telling us that Jephthah actually sacrificed his daughter and there are many scholars who hold that he did not.

Michal (1 Sam. 19:12-17). It is pleasant to read of the loyalty of Saul's daughter to her husband, when David's life was in danger. We read of the fraud which she practiced on the messengers who were sent by Saul to slay him, and of the lie which she told her father, even accusing David of threatening her life. It was the desperate game of a terrified woman. Perhaps the story is recorded because of the bitterness which darkened her life, when the husband whose life she had saved succeeded to her father's throne.

David and Achish (1 Sam. 27-29). The close of Saul's reign was a time of trial and great peril for David; and the narrative tells us of the trickery and treachery which David practiced on Achish during a sojourn of a year and four months in his land, by means of which he convinced Achish that "he hath made his people Israel utterly to abhor him; therefore he shall be my servant forever." We are told of the means by which David brought this about, the desperate game of a desperate man. But his conduct is not judged or condemned and we are left to draw our own conclusions as to what David would have done had the Philistines allowed him and his men to go out with them to battle against Saul. It was the lords of the Philistines who settled the question not David.

Saul's Death. We have two accounts of the death of Saul. One is the story told by the historian of the Book of Samuel (1 Sam. 31), the other the story told by the Amalekite lad who was seeking a reward from David (2 Sam. 1:1-16). No wonder they do not agree! The biblical history tells us first what actually happened and then gives the slanted version of the reward-seeking Amalekite, leaving it to the reader to compare the two and draw his own inferences as to the element of truth in the second.

Absalom. The revolt of Absalom furnishes many problems: Absalom's treachery toward his father, David's instructions to Hushai to pretend to be a supporter of Absalom, Hushai's weasel words of loyalty to Absalom and his insincere counsel, the use of Jonathan and Ahimaaz as undercover messengers, which led to the lie of the woman of Bahurim, all represent a tangle of trickery and falsehood which lends an almost Machiavellian touch to this tragic episode in David's reign. It is not easy to assess how much of this can be regarded as covered by the words: "For the Lord had appointed [commanded] to defeat the good counsel of Ahithophel, to the intent that the Lord might bring evil upon Absalom" (2 Sam. 17:14).

Elisha at Dothan (2 Kings 6:19). Elisha's lie when he said to the army of the Syrians which had come out to seize him: "This is not the way, neither is this the city: follow me, and I will bring you to the man whom ye seek" may be quite easily explained as a *ruse de guerre* (so Keil). But the fact remains that the Bible passes no immediate judgment on Elisha's conduct.

Esther's ruthless vengeance on her people's enemies (8:11; 9:5-16) is described with severe objectivity without any indication of approval or disapproval.

In view of these examples, it is significant that this non-committal attitude as we may call it does not appear in connection with those acts which are most often alleged to be morally reprehensible. The command to destroy the Canaanites is justified on two grounds: their long continued iniquity (Gen. 15:16) and the necessity of preventing their corrupting Israel by their evil practices (Exod. 34:11-16; Deut. 12:2f.). The Midianites were smitten because they seduced Israel to idolatry (Num. 25 and 31). The curse of extermination was pronounced upon Amalek (Exod. 17:16) because their enmity against Israel was both cruel, dastardly and in defiance of God (Deut. 25:17f.).

In discussing such passages Hodge remarks: "Some of them are simply recorded facts, without anything to indicate how they were regarded in the sight of God; but others . . . receive either directly or by implication the divine sanction." He argues that falsehood involves "an intention to deceive when we are expected and bound to speak the truth. That is, there are circumstances in which a man is not bound to speak the truth, and therefore there are cases in which speaking or intimating what is not true is not a lie."[63] He applies this principle especially to warfare. The least that can be said, which is also perhaps the most that can be said, is that all such passages must be examined and interpreted in the light of the clear and emphatic teaching of Scripture as a whole, that God is a God of truth; and the Decalogue makes it obligatory on man alike in relation to God and to his fellowmen (Exod. 20:7, 16; cf. Lev. 19:11f.).

Such examples as the above illustrate at least four important points. (1) The Bible guards against hero worship; it tells both the bad and the good about its great characters. (2) Its commendation of the good need not and does not imply the approval of the bad. (3) By ignoring second causes, the Bible often makes God directly responsible for events and actions which we might assign to natural causes. Consequently, "That must not be regarded as immoral in the direct revelation of the Old Testament which would not be so regarded in the indirect but equally divine revelation of providence."[64] (4) The incompleteness of Old Testament ethical teaching. It was preparatory and disciplinary, intended for a people under age; and while lower than that of the New Testament it was so high that the Old Testament is from beginning to end a continuous indictment of the failure of Israel to attain to the standard of conduct which it demanded.

In judging of such examples as have been cited, it is important to bear in mind the widely different attitudes which conservatives and critical scholars take to the Old Testament. Those who accept the Pentateuch as Mosaic and hold that the Decalogue was uttered by God at Sinai will see in the Jephthah story, for example, a terrible illustration of the widespread ignorance of the law in the time of the Judges. On the other hand, according to the critical view which regards most of the Pentateuch as post-Davidic and denies that the Decalogue was given at Sinai, Jephthah is an illustration of the low state of morality to which Israel had *attained* when he judged Israel. The difference between these two viewpoints is obviously very great.

Second Causes Stated or Ignored. In dealing with the subject "Of God's Eternal Decree," the *Westminster Confession of Faith* declares that God has ordained "whatsoever comes to pass," yet it also asserts that thereby "the liberty or contingency of second causes" is not "taken away but rather established." This states a mystery which we cannot fully understand. Yet it is clearly taught in Scripture. According to the Prologue of Job, Satan could do Job no injury until God gave him permission to do so. In 1 Chronicles 21:1 we read "And Satan stood up against Israel and provoked David to number Israel." In 2 Samuel 24:1 we read that the Lord "moved David against them, saying, Go number Israel and Judah." In the one case the second cause is made the sole cause; in the other the second cause is ignored. Two ways of dealing with the same mysterious problem! and a particularly striking example of the fact that "The divine method, as the popular method of declaring the whole truth, is by giving at one time an unqualified statement of one element of it and at another time an equally unqualified statement of the antithetic element."[65] We note how naturally the "Thus saith the Lord God" of Isaiah 7:7 passes over into "and the Lord spake again unto Ahaz" (vs. 10). The prophet's "Thus saith the Lord" was equivalent to "the Lord saith."

TELESCOPING HISTORY

A familiar type of Biblical narration may perhaps be best described by the word telescopic. For just as a telescope having a number of sliding tubes or joints can be so contracted that all but one of them disappear, or extended to the full length of each tube to give the maximum scope of the instrument, so by omission or inclusion of details, a narrative may be condensed or expanded as may best suit the aim of the writer. This practice is so general and so familiar to every one that it may seem superfluous to do more than mention it. But since it is a prominent feature in biblical narration, and since failure to recognize it may at times lead to confusion and even to serious misunderstanding it may be well to discuss it in some detail.

Genesis 1 and 2. We meet with an example of this method of narration in the opening chapters of Genesis. The "first account" of Creation is cosmic and comprehensive. It begins with formless matter and ends with man, created in the image of God, generic man, male and female, commanded to be fruitful, and given dominion over the creatures. It is a summary record of a series of divine fiats. The account which follows is an expansion, a "close-up," of the concluding verses of the first account. It speaks, not of mankind in general, but of the forming of a single pair, the first man from the dust of the ground and the first woman from the rib of the man, and of that union of the two, which is the basis for the command to be fruitful and multiply, which is the conclusion of the first account. Thus, the second narrative provides the details which the first omits; and in doing so it leads up to the account of the temptation and fall of this first pair of human beings, who were to be the parents of all mankind. Here we have contraction and expansion in close connection.

Exodus 2:1, "And there went a man of the house of Levi, and took to wife a daughter of Levi. And the woman conceived and bare a son: and when she saw that he was a goodly child, she hid him three months." So begins the story of the birth of Moses. From it we might easily infer that Moses was the first child born to Amram and Jochebed. We read on a few verses and discover that Moses had a sister who was old enough to stand guard over the little ark in which her baby brother was cradled and to give sensible advice to Pharaoh's daughter when the ark was brought to her and the baby discovered. We read on further and discover that Moses had a brother, Aaron the Levite, who was gifted with fluency of speech and was therefore to be Moses' helper (4:14). We read on still further and find that this brother was three years older than Moses, for "Moses was fourscore years old and Aaron fourscore and three years old, when they spake unto Pharaoh" (7:7). Now we have all the facts; and it is made clear that some eight or ten years are passed over in silence between verses 1 and 2 of Exodus 2. This illustrates what scientists call the *law of parsimony.* In the opening verses of this chapter, the aim of the writer is to bring Moses before us as quickly as possible, to describe the wonderful way in which this child of a Hebrew slave-mother became the son of Pharaoh's daughter. All other facts are subordinated to that primary purpose.[66] They are added only when needed or when occasion offers. And this method of narration is clearly designed among other things to press home to the reader the importance of collecting all the relevant information which the Bible furnishes on any subject before drawing conclusions regarding it. The natural first impression that Moses was the first-born of Amram and Jochebed is shown by the adducing of further evidence to be unwarranted.

Moses in Midian (Exod. 2:21 – 4:26). The forty years spent by Moses in Midian are dealt with very briefly in the biblical narrative. The few details that are given are only the necessary preliminary to the account of the Call which came to him at their close. We might infer from 2:21f. that the marriage with Zipporah took place soon after Moses' arrival at Jethro's home and that the birth of Gershom followed shortly, which would make Gershom a man in his late thirties when his father returned to Egypt. This is favored by the words which follow: "And it came to pass in process of time [AV; literally, "after those many days"] that the king of Egypt died." On the other hand the statement that "Moses took his wife and his sons and caused them to ride upon the ass" (4:20, a more exact rendering than AV) and the incident "in the inn" (vss. 24f.) would seem to indicate that both children were quite small, the younger still a baby. Does this mean that Moses served Jethro many years before he married Zipporah? Or was Zipporah barren for many years before the birth of Gershom? In a word, where are we to place the bulk of this forty year period? These are questions which naturally suggest themselves and which the writer leaves unanswered. They are irrelevant to the main interest of his story.

David at Hebron. That David reigned for seven years in Hebron over Judah is repeatedly stated (2 Sam. 5:5; 1 Kings 2:11). In 2 Samuel, about four chapters are devoted to the events of this period. Yet the narrative in Chronicles ignores it and passes directly from the account of Saul's death (chap. 10) to the story of David's anointing to be king over all Israel (chap. 11). This is all the more noticeable because in other respects the account in Chronicles of the events of this period follows the one in Samuel quite closely and also because elsewhere in Chronicles David's reign in Hebron and its duration are definitely mentioned (1 Chron. 3:4; 29:27).

David and Bathsheba. The most familiar, as it is also perhaps the most striking example of this elliptical method of narration, is the treatment of David's great sin. The first few verses of 1 Chronicles 20 tell us briefly of Joab's successful siege of Rabbah. We learn that

David "tarried at Jerusalem," that Joab "smote Rabbah and destroyed it," and that David reaped the results of the victory, taking the crown of the king of Rabbah and placing it on his head. Of the length of the siege nothing is said. We turn to 2 Samuel 11 and there we read that David sent Joab and his servants with him, and all Israel; and they destroyed the children of Ammon and besieged Rabbah, ending with the words: "and David tarried still [literally, was abiding] at Jerusalem." Then the writer proceeds to tell us what David did while he "tarried at Jerusalem" and of the tragic consequences. Fifty-one verses of what we may call the personal history of David are at this point introduced into the brief objective record of the siege. Then we return abruptly (2 Sam. 12:26; cf. 1 Chron. 20:1) to the siege of Rabbah, after reading of a course of events which, if they all took place while the siege was in progress, would indicate that the siege was a very protracted one. Then we are told how Joab saw to it that David should reap the fruit of victory and of the severity with which David dealt with the captured city, a rigor which was probably largely due to the length of the siege. Then the narrative in Samuel goes on to describe in some detail (nearly eight chapters) the consequences of David's sin, a narrative which we might regard as an historical sermon on the text: "Now therefore the sword shall never depart from thine house; because thou hast despised me, and hast taken the wife of Uriah the Hittite to be thy wife," and which covered a period of many years. Of this historical sequel also, Chronicles says not a word.

Genesis 5 and 11. The question whether the genealogies in Genesis 5 and 11 are intended to furnish the material for a chronology of the period from Adam to Abraham has been much debated. Until somewhat more than a century ago it was almost universally answered in the affirmative. The well-known Ussher Chronology is an example of this. But archaeological research has seriously challenged the correctness of this claim. When we study these lists, we notice two things especially:

(1) These lists follow a uniform pattern. Both give the names of ten Patriarchs,[67] the age of each at parenthood, the length of life after attaining that age, and add that he "begat sons and daughters." The first gives also the total length of life and adds the further words "and he died." Enoch is the only exception. Of him it is twice stated that "he walked with God." The fact that both lists are so obviously schematized suggests that as in the case of the genealogy in Matthew 1, where the 3 x 14 list is secured by omitting six kings and counting one twice (Jechoniah), the number 10 is intended as a symmetrical number, not a complete list, and that links are omitted. Many examples could be given of condensed genealogies.[68]

(2) A significant feature of both of these lists is the conclusion. Of the last member of each list we read that he "begat" three sons. The age of the father is given in each case: Noah was 500 years old, Terah 70. This apparently means that the first-born son of each was born when the father reached the specified age. The statement in 11:10 may indicate that Shem was the oldest of Noah's sons. That Abram was Terah's oldest son is suggested by the order, Abram, Nahor and Haran. Yet this is not stated as is done in 22:21, where we read that Huz was the "first-born" of Nahor. On the basis of Acts 7:4, "when his father was dead," it has been claimed that there must have been an interval of sixty years between the birth of Terah's oldest son and the birth of Abram (Gen. 11:26, 32; 12:4).[69] This would mean that Terah was 130 when Abram was born. A serious objection to this inference is that if his father was 130 years old when he was born, it would be hard to account for the incredulity with which Abram receives the assurance that he, a centenarian, will have a son (17:17). The problem is a difficult one. What we are here concerned to point out is the brevity and consequent ambiguity of the concluding statements of these genealogies. It might even seem that this was intended to guard against the taking of these lists as complete statements and therefore as furnishing the basis for a chronology. It is at least significant that nowhere in the Bible are they made the basis for such calculations as we find for example in Josephus.

"The first month" (Num. 20:1). It is generally assumed that this means the first month of the fortieth year. The only years which are mentioned in Numbers are the second (1:1; 9:1; 10:11) and the fortieth (33:38). But it is stated that forty years of wandering would be the punishment for the refusal of the people to go up to possess the land (14:33f.; 32:13). Since the death of Aaron on Mt. Hor, which took place in the fortieth year (33:38f.), is described in 20:22-28, it seems highly probable that the events of Chapters 20-36 belong to that year. If this is true, the only events recorded of thirty-seven years of wandering are those referred to in Chapters 15-19, the most significant being the rebellion of Korah, Dathan and Abiram, which was followed by a special divine certification of the high priesthood of Aaron. This period has been called "the 37 year chasm." Some scholars are of the opinion that the "first month" (20:1) was the beginning of the third year. This is possible but seems less probable. In either case a long period of time is passed over almost in silence. It is perhaps worthy of mention that apparently no attempts were made by Jewish or Christian copyists or translators to insert the number of the year into the text.

Eli's Judgeship. In connection with his tragic death, we are told that he was an old man and heavy, and that he had judged Israel forty years (1 Sam. 4:18). His age and his incompetence have already been mentioned (2:22f.), also his increasing blindness (3:2). We are also told of Samuel's growing up and of his establishing to be a prophet of the Lord (vs. 19f.). The question arises whether the forty years of Eli's judgment extended to his death. Was he fifty-eight years old when he began to judge Israel? Or did his judgeship begin somewhat or considerably earlier and was Samuel really judge for sometime before Eli died? It is an interesting question. That Eli's eyesight did not become seriously inpaired until after the incident recorded in 1:9-18 is indicated by the statement that Eli marked her mouth (vss. 12f.).

Jezebel's Death. Elijah's terrible woe on Ahab and Jezebel (1 Kings 21:17-24) was pronounced about three years before Ahab's death in battle against Syria which is dramatically described in 1 Kings 22. But not a word is said there about Jezebel. That she was active, the power behind the throne, during the reigns of Ahaziah and Jehoram is highly probable. But she is mentioned again, only to tell of her horrible death (2 Kings 9:30-37) which Elijah had foretold some fifteen years before it took place: a long delay, but an ignominious death.

Elisha's Prophetic Career. One of the last recorded acts of Elijah was apparently to predict the death of Ahaziah the son of Ahab (2 Kings 1). Elisha seems to have been quite active during the reign of Jehoram and he was responsible for the revolt of Jehu. We hear nothing of him during the reigns of Jehu and Jehoahaz; and he is on his death-bed when Joash visits him (2 Kings 13:14f.). Nearly forty years passed in silence.

The Coming of Ezra. The first part of the Book of Ezra is concerned primarily with the rebuilding of the house of God in Jerusalem. It was "finished" (6:15) in the sixth year of Darius Hystaspis (515 B.C.). With Chapter 7 we pass to the seventh year of Artaxerxes I (458 B.C.) an interval of more than fifty years. With Nehemiah 1, we pass on to the twentieth year of this monarch.

The Ancestry of Moses and Aaron (Exod. 6:16-27) raises a number of difficult problems. It would be natural to infer from this passage that the Amram, Izhar, and Uzziel, who are mentioned in verse 18 are the fathers respectively of Aaron and Moses (sons of Amram), Mishael and Elzaphan (sons of Uzziel), and Korah (son of Izhar) who are listed in verses 20-21, which would make them all to be grandsons of Kohath, the son of Levi. Yet all five are mentioned as living in the time of the exodus. Moses and Aaron are the two most prominent figures of that period; Mishael and Elzaphan play a sorrowful role in connection with the sacrilege committed by Nadab and Abihu (Lev. 10:4) and are there stated to be the sons of Uzziel, the uncle of Aaron; and Korah, son of Izhar, son of Kohath, son of Levi, takes a prominent part in the rebellion against the authority of Moses and Aaron during the period of the wandering (Num. 16). From this it has often been inferred that the period of sojourn in Egypt must have been comparatively short. But when we note that Amram and his brothers had 8600 male descendants at the time of the first census (Num. 3:27f.) and that the genealogies of two of their contemporaries, Bezaleel (seventh from Jacob, 1 Chron. 2:3-20) and Joshua (apparently eleventh, 7:20-27), contain many more names, it seems clear that here as in some other genealogies links are omitted. So Davis claims that "The language of Exodus 6:20 does not necessarily, nor even evidently, mean that Amram and Jochebed were the immediate parents of Moses and Aaron."[70] The closing words of 6:19, "These are the families of the Levites according to their generations" may be regarded as implying that there is an interval of time between the Amram of verse 18 and the Amram of verse 20.

Solomon, Bathsheba's Fourth Son. The narrative in 2 Samuel 12:1-25 which tells of Nathan's rebuke of David for his sin with Bathsheba, might easily be regarded as covering a comparatively brief period of time: as indicating that the child of sin was already born when Nathan rebuked David, that it lived only a short time, that shortly after the death of this child David "comforted Bathsheba," and that the child who received the name Solomon was the *next* child born by Bathsheba. Yet in the three lists of the sons born to David in Jerusalem (2 Sam. 5:14; 1 Chron. 3:5; 14:4) the first four names are Shammua (or Shimea), Shobab, Nathan, Solomon, Solomon being mentioned last; and in 1 Chronicles 3:5 the words are added "four, of Bathshua the daughter of Ammiel." Bathshua is clearly Bathsheba, with a slight difference of pronunciation; and it is natural to assume that Solomon was the youngest of the four sons.[71] This will then mean that a period of several years is involved in this account (perhaps to be found at 12:24) and that, as in the story of the birth of Moses, the writer ignores unimportant matters, the three inconspicuous children who were born to David by Bathsheba after the death of the child of sin, and passes on at once to refer briefly to the birth of Solomon. Then, after giving this condensed record of David's family, the writer reverts abruptly (with a simple "and") to the siege of Rabbah (12:26), which may have been terminated long before the chain of events described in the verses which immediately precede, was ended.

Daniel. A comparison of the Book of Daniel is instructive in this connection. Chapters 1 to 4 deal with events which occurred about the beginning of Nebuchadnezzar's reign, and mention only the second year specifically (2:1). With Chapter 5 the narrative passes to Belshazzar, and relates only the closing tragedy of his reign. Similarly Chapter 6 deals with a single event which occurred probably early in the rule of Darius the Mede. These datings are interesting in the light of archaeological research. Nebuchadnezzar reigned forty-three years. But Daniel mentions the second year only (2:1). In passing from Nebuchadnezzar to Belshazzar, Evil-merodach, Neriglissar, and Nabunaid are ignored; and while Belshazzar was probably associated with Nabunaid as king for a decade or more, the riotous revel which ended in his death is all that is told about him. Darius the Mede (6:1) is probably the Gubaru whom Cyrus made governor or sub-king (6:28) over "Babylon and the Region beyond" and who continued in office for at least fifteen years. The visions and prophecies occurred: in the first year of Belshazzar (chap. 7), in his third year (chap. 8), in the first year of Darius the Mede (chap. 9), in the third year of Cyrus (chap. 10). Why the last is dated in the third year of Cyrus instead of the third year of Darius the Mede (cf. 9:1 with 6:28) is not clear. But it is remarkable how archaeology has confirmed the accuracy of the statements of Daniel and at the same time thrown welcome light on the method used by the biblical writer.

While we are dealing primarily with the Old Testament it is of interest to note that we find in the New Testament striking examples of the telescopic method of which we are speaking. The most striking is the omission in the Synoptic Gospels of any mention of the early Judean ministry of Jesus which is recorded so fully in John (1:19 – 4:54). The only intimation in the Synoptics that there may have been a significant interval between the temptation of Jesus and the beginning of his Galilean ministry is the mention in two of them of John's imprisonment (Matt. 4:12; Mark 1:14) to which both Gospels refer later on (Matt. 14:3-5; Mark 6:17-20). Luke does not mention it at 4:14, but refers to it proleptically in 3:19f. before relating the baptism of Jesus which, of course, took place before it, how long before he does not tell us. Similarly with regard to the post-resurrection appearances we might easily assume that all of Luke 24:1-49 describes events of the resurrection day and that with verse 50 the narrative skips forward to the ascension, forty days later (Acts 1:3). Whether this is the correct interpretation or we should regard verses 44-49 as belonging to the period of forty days referred to in Acts 1:3, is not easy, perhaps impossible, to decide. It is singular that Luke, who is the only one who states the interval between the resurrection and the ascension to be "forty days" (Acts 1:3), should show so little concern to tell us of the sequence of events during that period.

RESULTS OF CONDENSATION
FACTS STATED WITHOUT EXPLANATION

In some cases the biblical writers state the extra-biblical sources upon which they have drawn (e.g., Josh. 10:13; 2 Sam. 1:18). In Kings and Chronicles we are often told (some 50 times) regarding "the rest of the acts" of a king, "Behold they are written in . . .," or "Are they not written . . .?" giving the source of the further information. There are similar statements in Ezra and Nehemiah.[72] They usually indicate that the information given is only part of what the writer might have supplied, had he desired to do so. On the other hand, there are many things in the Bible that are stated without explanation or proof. This is an illustration of the authority with which it speaks.

Creation, the Fall, the Flood. The question naturally arises as to the source of the account of these very ancient events which are described in the early chapters of Genesis. No documentation is given. How much of this information was given to Moses by revelation, how much he derived from tradition, and how the traditions were transmitted, whether orally or in writing, we do not know. There were no human eyewitnesses of the creation of the heavens and the earth, or of the creation of Adam; and Adam was in "a deep sleep" when Eve was formed. Josephus refers to "all the writers of barbarian history" as confirming the Genesis account of the Flood and mentions several by name, Berosus first of all. It is perhaps significant that he makes no mention of the breaking up of the fountains of the great deep (Gen. 7:11). This is, as far as the writer is aware, a unique feature of Flood stories. It must have been a matter of revelation.

Balaam. Numbers 22-24 gives what reads like an eye-witness account of how Balaam attempted to curse Israel and how the Lord forced him to bless them. We are told of Balaam's personal experiences, of his dreams and of the amazing circumstances attending his journey to Moab; we are told of his public appearances, that "all the princes of Moab" (Num. 23:6, 17) were with Balak when Balaam uttered several of his prophecies in the high places of Baal and in the heights of Pisgah. Whether they heard all of the prophecies of Balaam we are not told. Whether any Midianite or Moabite scribe recorded Balaam's utterances we do not know. We would hardly expect Balak to send his enemies a record of prophecies so favorable to them and so damaging to himself and his people; or that Balaam whose heart was filled with hate of Israel and who perished in the effort to falsify the prophecies which he had himself uttered (31:8) would do anything of the kind. How did this account of the efforts of Israel's enemies to destroy her reach the ears of Moses? No explanation is given. We are simply told what Balak and Balaam did and said. Whether it was by natural or by supernatural means or by both that this information reached Moses, we are not told. All that we can say is that this amazing story is recorded in the Book of Numbers as actual fact, and is referred to as such several times in Scripture both in the Old Testament and in the New Testament.[73]

The clue to the understanding of the Balaam narrative is given us in the words of one of the servants of the king of Syria, who sought to account to their master for the intimate knowledge of his military plans possessed by the king of Israel and to show that it was not due to the disloyalty of any of his own servants: "Nay, my lord the king, but Elisha, the prophet that is in Israel, telleth the king of Israel the words that thou speakest in thy bedchamber" (2 Kings 6:12). This was the explanation of a superstitious pagan. But his words were factually correct as is indicated by the context (vss. 8-10); and they enable us to understand that amazing story and such an incident as the Balaam story, and perhaps many other narratives, especially speeches, which many critical scholars regard as largely, if not wholly, artificial and imaginary. Such narratives as the above form an important part of that Scripture which our Lord declared "cannot be broken," to which he definitely appealed as a record of historical fact, and which the Apostle had in mind when he declared that "All Scripture is given by inspiration of God."

ALLUSIONS TO UNRECORDED EVENTS

Since it is as we have just seen important to ascertain all the facts recorded in Scripture before reaching a conclusion on any matter, it may be well to observe that we sometimes meet references to events the occurrence of which has not been previously recorded.

"After he had sent her back" (Exod. 18:2). Nothing has been said about this action of Moses or the reason for it. It is unlikely that the incident recorded in 4:24-26 led to a permanent estrangement between Moses and Zipporah, since Moses apparently sent back his two sons along with their mother. The result of Jethro's action is neither stated nor hinted at. But the silence probably means that Moses welcomed the return of his wife and sons. Refusal to do so would have been an affront to Jethro; and there is no suggestion of this.

"For he had married an Ethiopian woman" (Num. 12:1). When this took place we are not told. This woman cannot have been Zipporah, who was a daughter of the priest of Midian. Furthermore the mention of this marriage seems clearly to refer to a recent event, while the marriage with Zipporah had occurred before, perhaps long before

Moses' call to deliver Israel, at which time Aaron was fully aware of Moses' marriage to Zipporah as is indicated by the obviously close connection between Exodus 4:24-26 and verses 27-31. Why Moses married this Ethiopian woman is as much a mystery as Abraham's marrying Keturah (Gen. 25:1).

"Because I have given mount Seir unto Esau for a possession" (Deut. 2:5). The promise which is mentioned here is referred to again in Joshua 24:4. But it is nowhere recorded in Genesis, unless it is to be inferred from the blessing of Isaac (Gen. 27:39f.) which is couched in broad and even ambiguous language.

"I will raise them up a prophet" (Deut. 18:18). Here it is made clear that the revelation regarding the coming prophet which Moses makes known to the people in Moab, just before his death, had already been revealed to him at Sinai nearly forty years earlier.

Shiloh. Jeremiah's references to Shiloh (7:12, 14; 26:6, 9; cf. Ps. 78:60) imply that a divine judgment was visited upon Shiloh of which there is no mention in the account in 1 Samuel 4, or elsewhere in the Historical Books.

Saul and the Witch of Endor (1 Sam. 28:3, 9). The fact that Saul had "put away" those with familiar spirits and wizards from the land has not been previously mentioned. It is mentioned here partly to explain Saul's difficulty in finding such a woman, but more especially to show how utterly Saul had forsaken the Lord. In his despair he had recourse to a woman of a class which he had previously expelled from the land.

"And I gave thee . . . thy master's wives into thy bosom" (2 Sam. 12:8, cf. 16:20-22). This horrible practice which is alluded to so briefly here appears to have been customary in ancient times (cf. 1 Kings 20:3f.). To the victor belong the spoils! We have no record of Saul's having more than one wife, Ahinoam (1 Sam. 14:50), and a concubine Rizpah (2 Sam. 3:7; 21:8). Apparently these words are not to be taken with exact literalness. The language of the verse is intended simply to prove the enormity of David's sin. They throw light, however, on three tragic events in Bible history. Abner's seduction of Saul's concubine Rizpah may have led Ishbosheth to suspect that Abner planned to supplant him as king, and hence have led Abner to ally himself with David. Ahithophel's advice to Absalom regarding David's concubines (2 Sam. 16:21) and the serious view which Solomon took of Adonijah's request that he might marry Abishag (1 Kings 2:22) may acquire added meaning in view of this terrible practice.

The Three Years Famine (2 Sam. 21:1-14) which took place in David's reign is attributed to Saul's "zeal" in slaying the Gibeonites, whose right to a place in Israel had been established in the days of

Joshua (Josh. 9). We read elsewhere in the Books of Samuel of Saul's warfare with the Philistines, but nothing is said of an attempt on his part to exterminate the Gibeonites. The narrative in 2 Samuel 21 merely refers to this as the event which accounts for the famine.

David's Promise Regarding Solomon (1 Kings 1:13, 17). The attempt of Adonijah to secure the throne for himself as David's oldest surviving son was frustrated by Bathsheba who on the advice of Nathan reminded David of his oath to her that Solomon should be his successor. Here we have the only mention of David's oath to Bathsheba. The record in 2 Samuel 7:12f. is quite indefinite and might refer to any one of David's sons (cf. 1 Chron. 17:11). Yet in his charge to Solomon (22:9), as also in his charge to the princes of Israel (28:5f.), David makes it plain that he had been told the name of the son who should succeed him, which must have been before or at the time of Solomon's birth (2 Sam. 12:24). This revelation seems to have been a carefully guarded secret, which was not divulged until Adonijah forced the king to recall and fulfill it.[74]

And Moab rebelled against Israel after the death of Ahab (2 Kings 1:1). According to the Mesha inscription, "Omri king of Israel afflicted Moab many days," and he and his sons possessed Medeba for forty years. Omri's conquest of Moab was apparently one of the great events of his reign. It brought great wealth to the Northern Kingdom. For we are told that Mesha king of Moab rendered to Jehoram king of Israel 100,000 lambs and 100,000 rams with the wool (3:4).[75] But no mention of this is made in the brief account which is given us of the reign of Omri, though it is hinted at in the words, "and his might that he showed" (1 Kings 16:27). We learn of it in the account of the punitive expedition which the three kings, Jehoram of Israel, Jehoshaphat of Judah, and the king of Edom, undertook against Mesha, who had rebelled against Jehoram of Israel, and of its results, a story in which the prophet Elisha plays a conspicuous role (2 Kings 3).

The Great Earthquake (Amos 1:1). Amos' appearance as a prophet in the days of Uzziah and Jeroboam is more precisely dated as "two years before the earthquake." This earthquake must have been a very severe one. More than two centuries later Zechariah likens the terror which will be caused by the future "cleaving" of the Mount of Olives to the earthquake in the days of Uzziah (14:5). Yet neither in Kings nor in Chronicles is any mention made of this tremendous and awe-inspiring event.

Asa's Pit (Jer. 41:9). Here it is stated that Ishmael the son of Nethaniah cast the corpses of seventy men into the pit (a well or cistern, Hebrew *bor*) made by Asa for fear of Baasha. No mention is made of this in Kings or Chronicles in describing Asa's achievements.

Zacharias Son of Barachias (Matt. 23:35). In view of the examples which have been given, it must be admitted that the failure of the Old Testament to record the death of the prophet Zechariah, son of Barachiah (Zech. 1:1) is not an insuperable objection to the interpretation of our Lord's words as referring to him. The fact that Zechariah was one of the last of the canonical prophets favors such an interpretation and it finds general support in the immediate context (vss. 29-37; compare 21:35; also Acts 7:52; Rom. 11:3). The New Testament does not expressly refer to the violent death of any of the Old Testament prophets except Zacharias son of Barachias. But it does declare definitely that martyrdom was the fate of many, even of most of them.[76] Thus, it is quite possible that the tradition is true that the words "they were sawn asunder" (Heb. 11:37), refer particularly to the death of Isaiah, under Hezekiah's wicked son Manasseh.

Allusions to Events of Distant Past

The Dividing of the Sacrifice (Gen. 15:10). Here we read that the solemn ratification of the covenant with Abram was signalized by the dividing of the sacrificial animals in the midst and by the passing of the burning lamp, representing the presence of the Lord, between the pieces. The only other instance of such a ceremony is the one described in Jeremiah 34:18-20 where a solemn covenant is ratified in similar fashion and vengeance is pronounced upon the people and their leaders for their failure to keep the covenant. The exact meaning of this ritual act in these two cases is not perfectly clear.

The Cities of the Plain (Gen. 19:29) were Sodom, Gomorrah, Admah, Zeboiim and Bela, which was later called Zoar (Gen. 14:2, 8). That Sodom and Gomorrah were destroyed is made plain in Genesis 18-19 although it was Sodom which figured prominently because Lot was living there. The sparing of Zoar is definitely mentioned and the reason for it (19:19-22); Admah and Zeboiim are not mentioned. In Deuteronomy 29:23 they are mentioned together with Sodom and Gomorrah as destroyed with them. Isaiah refers to Sodom and Gomorrah (1:9, 10; 13:19) and calls Jerusalem Sodom. Jeremiah refers to the destruction of Sodom and Gomorrah (23:14) and elsewhere adds the words "and the neighbor cities thereof" (49:18; 50:40), thus showing that he knew that other cities were included with Sodom and Gomorrah. Especially noteworthy is Hosea 11:8 where not Sodom and Gomorrah, but Admah and Zeboiim only are mentioned.

Living in Booths (Lev. 23:42f.). This requirement is a special feature of the Feast of Tabernacles. It is surprising to read in Nehemiah 8:14-17 that this requirement had not been obeyed since the days of

Joshua the son of Nun, doubly so since it is pointed out that this regulation was laid down in the law of Moses (Neh. 8:1, 14). *The Brazen Serpent* (Num. 21:4-9). The historical incident is very briefly described. From 2 Kings 18:4 we learn that centuries later, in the reign of Hezekiah, this symbol of deliverance was still preserved as a sacred relic; and this fact is mentioned simply because the veneration accorded the image by the Israelites of his day was regarded by Hezekiah as idolatrous. So he destroyed it, calling it *nehushtan* (a thing of bronze). The only further mention of it is in John 3:14 where the historical incident is recalled and its typical significance pointed out, but no mention is made of the abuse of the symbol in Hezekiah's day.

These instances are noteworthy as illustrations of the fact that rites or practices which may, should, or should not have been repeated many times in the course of Israel's history, may be referred to, if at all, very rarely with intervals of many years or even centuries between them.

INEXACT OR INCOMPLETE STATEMENTS

It is important to remember that the Bible contains not only statements which are exact and precise but also statements that are broad, general and even, in themselves, misleadingly inexact. Some years ago a widely-known evangelist made a statement to this effect, "Never say 'Matthew's Gospel.' Say 'The Gospel according to Matthew.'" He went on to point out that "Matthew's Gospel" would convey the false impression that Matthew had discovered or invented it. Such a rule sounds logical and the reason given is impressive; but it is easily proved to be a mistaken one, unless its limitations are clearly recognized. In writing to the Galatians, Paul affirms emphatically that the gospel which he had preached to them was "not after man." He calls it "the gospel of Christ." He declares that he received it by "revelation." Yet we find him, in writing to the Thessalonian Christians, using the words "our gospel," and in writing to Timothy he says "my gospel." "Our" and "my" are ambiguous. They might imply that Paul was the founder of a new religion. But no one who has read the New Testament would dream of making such a claim. Paul could write thus loosely at times, because he knew that his meaning could not be misunderstood, unless willfully misrepresented.

We read in Luke 2 that Mary said to the child Jesus when she found him in the temple: "Thy father and I have sought thee sorrowing." According to the birth narrative in the preceding chapter, a full and exact statement would have been, "Thy father by adoption (or, thy foster father) and I have sought thee sorrowing." But such a full and precise statement would, of course, have defeated the very purpose of the manner of the Incarnation, which was twofold: to insure the perfect Deity and the full humanity of Mary's child and to safeguard the virgin mother from malicious and slanderous rumor, before the time for the full disclosure had arrived. According to recognized usage, then as now, an adopted son was recognized as a son and called such.

When Paul writing to the Galatians declares, "For all the law is fulfilled in one word (even) in this: Thou shalt love thy neighbor as thyself" (5:14), it is perfectly clear that he is speaking only of the second table of the Decalogue, that he is dealing with human relations. Yet such a statement taken by itself would reduce the Old Testament religion to mere philanthropy.[77]

The Bible often contains broad general statements, the scope of which is modified by other statements dealing with the same or similar matters. This is especially true of the Book of Proverbs. "Train up a child in the way he should go: and when he is old, he will not depart from it" (22:6) states a most important pedagogical principle and gives to parents and teachers the encouragement and incentive which they often sorely need. But we should not forget that the Book of Proverbs has much to say about the "fool" and the "disobedient son." Home training can accomplish much, but not everything, as is abundantly evidenced in Scripture (e.g., Deut. 21:18-21, cf. Ezek. 18).

1 Chronicles 6:33-38 traces the genealogy of *Heman* through twenty links back to Levi the son of Israel. It is followed (vss. 39-43) by the genealogy of *Asaph,* which consists of thirteen names, all different from those in Heman's list. Heman traces his descent from Kohath, Asaph traces his from Gershom, heads respectively of two of the three tribal families of the Levites. Heman and Asaph may have been twentieth cousins. Yet Asaph is called Heman's "brother" in verse 39.

In Acts 7:15f. the words, "So Jacob went down into Egypt; and he died there, himself and our fathers; and they were carried over unto Shechem and laid in the tomb that Abraham bought for a price in silver of the sons of Hamor in Shechem" are ambiguous. The "they" might include Jacob with his sons. But we know and may assume that Stephen, and his auditors also, knew that Jacob was buried at Hebron (Gen. 49:29f.; 50:12f.). Consequently the *ARV* is justified in changing the comma of the *AV* to a semi-colon in order to indicate that the "they" need not include Jacob.[78] The inexact statements are to be interpreted by those that speak more fully. Jehu is usually called the "son of Nimshi." But his full name was Jehu, the son of Jehoshaphat, the son of Nimshi (2 Kings 9:2, 14). Zechariah the prophet was the son of Berechiah the son of Iddo (Zech. 1:1, 7), but in Ezra 5:1; 6:14, he is called the son of Iddo. Whether this Iddo is to be identified with the priest mentioned in Nehemiah 12:4, 16, as returning with Zerubbabel is uncertain.

Sennacherib, king of Assyria. The question as to the date of Sennacherib's campaign against Hezekiah is, we must admit, a very difficult one. But we may well hesitate to insist that the use of the titles "king of Assyria" and "king of Ethiopia" must mean that Sennacherib and Tirhakah were already kings at the date referred to. The title king may be used proleptically of men who later became king, especially if they exercised royal prerogatives for a considerable time before they became so. To question the accuracy of the Book of Daniel because in referring to the invasion of Nebuchadnezzar in the third year of Jehoiakim, Nebuchadnezzar is called "king of Babylon," a few months before his father's death, is petty and captious.[79] We must treat the Bible fairly and not expect in it a meticulous accuracy of statement which would be pedantic and boring. When we read in Matthew 1, "And Jesse begat David the king" we recognize that this means Jesse begat as his youngest son an infant whom he called David, who at the age of thirty became *king* of Judah in Hebron, and at thirty-seven was anointed *king* of all Israel. "Begat David the king" gives the essential facts in the fewest possible words.

Inexact statements frequently appear in connection with the mention of numbers. The promise of the Lord to Abraham that his seed should be as the stars in heaven and as the sand on the seashore (Gen. 22:17) was hyperbole. We read of the phenomenal increase of the Israelites in Egypt, that they "were fruitful, and increased abundantly, and multiplied, and waxed exceeding mighty; and the land was filled with them" (Exod. 1:7). In his farewell addresses to Israel Moses reminds the people that this promise has already been fulfilled (Deut. 1:10; 10:22; 28:62). Such statements graphically describe the amazing growth of Israel in Egypt under the blessing of God. Similarly, we read regarding the Midianites in the time of the Judges that "they came up as grasshoppers for multitude; for both they and their camels were without number" (Judg. 6:5). Such statements are clearly not intended to be taken with absolute literalness. Yet they must be carefully tested. Thus when we read that Zerah the Ethiopian came out against Asa with "a host of a thousand thousand" (2 Chron. 14:9), we are tempted to regard a million as an impossible figure. But when we note that Asa had 300,000 fighting men of Judah and 280,000 from Benjamin, the "thousand thousand" of Zerah if taken literally would mean that Asa was outnumbered nearly two to one. No wonder then that he cried unto the Lord for help. The statement that Zerah had three hundred chariots, while Asa apparently had none is a further indication of the substantial accuracy of the figures.

One of the most remarkable examples of the looseness or ambiguity of language of which we are speaking is the applying of the name "gods" to the judges in Exodus 21:6; 22:8f. (perhaps also in 22:28). But this understanding of these difficult passages is supported by the words "I said ye are gods" (Ps. 82:6), which clearly refer to the judges of Israel; and it is raised to certainty by the use which the Lord makes of the latter passage in John 10:34f. where he takes the Hebrew word *Elohim* as plural and renders it by "gods."

Three days and three nights. Whether this period of time is to be regarded as precise in the case of Jonah (1:17) we do not know. When used by Jesus of the time he was to spend under the power of death (Matt. 12:40), we learn from the specific statements of 27:46 and 28:1 that this period was actually only about a day and a half, from the ninth hour on Friday to about sunrise on Sunday. Yet the three Synoptists all describe the resurrection as to take place or as having taken place, on "the third day" (Matt. 20:19; Mark 9:31; Luke 18:33: cf. Matt. 27; 63 and Luke 24:21); and Peter (Acts 10:40) and Paul (1 Cor. 15:4) declare that it did so take place. We know that the Jews regarded a fraction of a day as a legal day for matters of business, which indicates that the expression "three days and three nights" was currently regarded as a round number. That this remarkable shortening of the period by nearly one-half of its full extent was intended to be significant and was so regarded is indicated, it would seem, by Peter's words "because it was not possible that he should be holden of it" (Acts 2:24). This may mean that this period was shortened in the fulfilment because of the superior dignity of the person of the Antitype.

Totals. The forty years of wandering (Deut. 1:3) which corresponded to the forty days of spying (Num. 13:25; 14:34) included the year and a half which preceded the apostasy. Yet it is called forty years, since during this entire period they were out of the land of promise. The "forty years" of David's reign (2 Sam. 5:4) are defined in the next verse as seven years and six months plus thirty and three, which makes the total forty years and a half, while 1 Kings 2:11 gives the same total, ignoring the six months. According to 1 Kings 6:1 Solomon began to build the house of the Lord in the month Zif of his fourth year. Chronicles is more precise, stating that it was "the second day of the second month" (3:2).

Ruth the Moabitess. Twelve times in this short narrative Ruth is mentioned by name. In five of them, "the Moabitess" is added (e.g., 1:22). This is the main interest in the story: a Moabitess becomes an ancestress of king David. Who was Ruth's husband? Elimelech had two sons Mahlon and Chilion (1:2), who "took them wives of the women of Moab" and "the name of the one was Orpah, and the name of the other Ruth" (vs. 4). This does not tell us which married which. The order would suggest that Mahlon, the elder, married Orpah, and Chilion married Ruth. But the younger brother might have been the first to marry and the names of the wives might be given in that order. So the statements are ambiguous. Orpah disappears shortly (vs. 14) and Ruth is usually called "the Moabitess." She is the widow of one of Elimelech's sons, of which of them it does not concern the reader to know until the climax of the story is reached in the marriage of Ruth to Boaz, when Boaz plays the kinsman's part "to raise up the name of the dead upon his inheritance" (4:10); and in that context Ruth is called for the first and only time, "the wife of Mahlon," and the doubtful question is settled and is shown to be the less probable of the alternatives.[80]

Nabal's Wife. In 1 Samuel 27:3 we are told that David took with him his two wives, the second being "Abigail the Carmelitess, Nabal's wife." "Widow" would have been more exact and the Hebrew word for widow (*almanah*) is not an infrequent word in the Old Testament. But apparently having already described the circumstances adequately the writer preferred to call her the wife of Nabal, as a reminder of that instructive episode. In 30:5 and 2 Samuel 2:2; 3:3 the similar statement occurs, "Abigail, the wife of Nabal, the Carmelite"; 2 Samuel 3:3 is especially noteworthy since it is there stated that David's second son was born to "Abigail, the wife of Nabal the Carmelite." Apparently to have married the widow of as prominent a Judean as Nabal (1 Sam. 25:2; cf. vs. 36) was quite a distinction for David the son of Jesse, who does not seem to have been a man of prominence or of wealth (cf. Jesse's gift as described in 1 Sam. 16:20; 17:17f. with the much more elaborate gift made by Abigail without Nabal's knowledge 25:18). Possibly also the words "wife of Nabal" are used to distinguish this Abigail from David's sister or step-sister who had the same name.

Athaliah is called "the daughter of Ahab" (2 Kings 8:18) and "the daughter of Omri," Ahab's father (vs. 26; cf. 2 Chron. 21:6; 22:2).

Mephibosheth is called "the son of Jonathan, the son of Saul" (2 Sam. 9:6), and "the son of Saul" (19:24). Has the omission of Jonathan's name in the latter passage any significance? Does it imply that the writer regarded Mephibosheth as ungrateful and disloyal to David, that he accepted Ziba's charge (16:3) and so did not wish any longer to think of Mephibosheth as Jonathan's son? We do not know.

Ezra was probably a grandson or even a great grandson of Seraiah (Ezra 7:1; cf. 1 Chron. 6:14f.).

In commenting on such passages as the above John Murray re-marks: "The Scripture abounds in illustrations of the absence of the type of meticulous and pedantic precision which we might arbitrarily seek to impose as the criterion of infallibility. Everyone should recognize that in accord with accepted forms of speech and custom a statement can be perfectly authentic and yet not pedantically precise. Scripture does not make itself absurd by furnishing us with pedantry."[81]

ALL THE FACTS NEEDED

Reuben, Gad, Half-Manasseh and the Conquest. In Joshua 4 we read that "the children of Reuben, and the children of Gad, and half the tribe of Manasseh, passed over armed before the children of Israel, as Moses spake unto them" (vss. 12f.). This was in fulfillment of the solemn pledge which they had given Moses, that they would carry out the condition which he had imposed before granting them permission to settle in the territory east of the Jordan, which had been already conquered by all Israel under Moses (Num. 21:21-35). Moses had seen in this request a serious threat to the solidarity of Israel and also the suggestion of a desire of these tribes to evade their share in the onerous task involved in the conquest of Canaan (32:6-15). So the words "passed over armed" indicate that they not only fulfilled their promise but apparently that they "spearheaded" the invasion. It also seems probable that they were the "armed men" who made the circuit around Jericho.[82] This does not mean, of course, that they alone of all the tribes were armed. For the punitive expedition against Midian, which concerned all the tribes, an equal number — one thousand — was taken from each tribe (Num. 31:3f.). But for the first step in the conquest of the land, yet to be possessed by their brethren, it was especially appropriate that the task should be assigned to the tribes which already possessed their possessions. This relieves us of the necessity of assuming that all the men of all the tribes — more than half a million — took part in the encircling of the city.

The statement that "about forty thousand prepared for war passed over" (Josh. 4:13) has been misunderstood by some readers. It has been inferred from it that these were all the men of the two and a half tribes, that they left their wives and little ones unprotected in the recently conquered regions east of the Jordan while they took part in the conquest of Canaan; and it has even been claimed that the Lord must have protected these defenseless women and children in a supernatural way, or they might have been massacred by the warlike tribes east of the Jordan. Such inferences are quite unwarranted. According to Numbers 26 the families of the Reubenites totalled 43,700, of the Gadites 40,500, of Manasseh 52,700. Counting only half of Manasseh, the total is 110,550. This means that only about a third of the adult males of these tribes actually took part in the invasion. Furthermore we read that they (those left behind) built sheepfolds and fortified cities (Num. 32:16f.). The women and children were not left defenseless; they were amply protected. That Joshua regarded the 40,000 as fulfilling the promise is an illustration of that sanity, as we may call it, which is characteristic of Bible history.

From Dan to Beersheba. This expression occurs nine times in the Old Testament. We meet it first in Judges 20:1 which would indicate that the conquest of Laish by the Danites took place, as the order of the two narratives would also indicate, before the fratricidal strife with Benjamin, and while the grandson of Moses[83] was still a "young man" (18:30). Since the phrase is clearly used to describe the extreme limits of the land of Israel, it necessarily presupposes the migration of Danites to the north, since the territory assigned them by Joshua was somewhat south of its center. Consequently this expression would be confusing and meaningless to us were it not for the account given in Judges 17-18 and briefly summarized in Joshua 19:47f. It may seem somewhat surprising that such importance should be attached to this rather insignificant event. Dan was the second largest of the tribes when the census was taken at Sinai (62,700). It was one of the seven tribes which increased in numbers during the wilderness period (to 64,400). Yet when the five Danite spies reported favorably with regard to Laish only six hundred men with their families are said to have migrated to the north — barely one per cent of the tribe. That there were other and larger migrations seems certain. For so small a migration would not accomplish much in solving the over-population problem of the Danites. Nor would it justify the transferring of the name Dan from the territory originally assigned by Joshua to the new territory conquered by the sword. But the Old Testament is silent regarding the further migrations. Laish appears to have been in or very near the extreme north of the territory assigned to but not fully occupied by Naphtali. It would seem that there must have been special reasons which are not stated in the Bible for the significance attached to this relatively minor incident in the turbulent period of the Judges. It marked the beginning of an important population shift in Israel.

Saul the Benjamite. In the narrative of the events which led up to the accession of Saul to the kingship, we read that when Samuel said to Saul, "And on whom is all the desire of Israel? Is it not on thee, and on all thy father's house?" (1 Sam. 9:20), Saul replied, "Am not

I a Benjamite, of the smallest of the tribes of Israel? and my family the least of all the families of the tribe of Benjamin?" Was this a statement of fact, or an exaggeration, due to Saul's sense of his own unworthiness of such a tribute as Samuel had just paid him? According to the historical record Benjamin had 35,400 males of twenty years old and upward at Sinai (Num. 1:37), which made it the ninth among the tribes, and at the end of the forty years it had grown to 45,600 (26:41) which made it the seventh, a notable increase. To be the seventh among twelve is certainly not to be the least! But turning to the second appendix of the Book of Judges, we read that in the fraternal strife which resulted from the sin at Gibeah, the tribe of Benjamin was reduced to six hundred warriors (20:47) for whom wives had to be provided from among the inhabitants of Jabesh Gilead and of Shiloh. Saul's words were not modesty. They were simple and terrible fact. Besides this, Saul may have felt that a certain ignominy still attached to the fact that he came from Gibeah, the very city, as it appears, which was rendered infamous by the horrible event which had proved so disastrous to the entire tribe to which he belonged.[84]

Ahijah's New Garment (1 Kings 11:29). Ahijah's prophecy to Jeroboam is referred to several times. But the symbolic action which he used to impress it on Jeroboam is mentioned only once. Consequently, it is to be noted that the words, "and he had clad himself with a new garment," are ambiguous. We naturally ask, does the "he" refer to Jeroboam or to Ahijah? A moment's thought should convince the reader that the garment belonged to Ahijah, that he had put it on for the express purpose of performing the symbolic action which is here described. Had the mantle belonged to Jeroboam, the prophet would have been seizing Jeroboam's own robe, taking it from his shoulders, rendering it worthless by rending it into twelve pieces, adding insult to injury, as it were, by restoring him only part of what belonged to him by right and keeping so substantial a part of the mantle that it could not be pieced together again, even if Jeroboam should want to make the attempt. The whole action would have been discourteous, insulting and inexcusable. But, if the mantle belonged to the prophet, then it was perfectly right and proper for him to do as he would with his own. And in handing Jeroboam ten pieces of his own garment, he was making Jeroboam a present of something which did not belong to him, on which he had no possible claim, and which he could accept or reject, retain or cast away, as he saw fit. So interpreted, the appropriateness of the symbolic action could hardly be greater; and it was calculated to impress upon Jeroboam the significance of the words with which the prophet accompanied and explained this remarkable performance.

In the somewhat similar case (1 Sam. 15:27f.), it seems clear that Saul laid hold of the tip or hem of Samuel's robe with a view to detaining him, in the hope of obtaining if possible a more favorable verdict from the prophet. Whether the rending was due to Saul's impetuosity or to the prophet's firm resistance is not stated. But the prophet saw in it the confirmation of the rejection which he had just announced.

Morning-cloud Righteousness. The importance of considering the context in interpreting a difficult passage is illustrated by the familiar words of Hosea 6:1-3. The words themselves read like an expression of sincere repentance, placed in the mouth of the sinful people by the Lord's prophet. Some commentators have even seen in the mention of the "two days" and the "third day" a prophecy of the resurrection of Christ. There are two serious objections to this interpretation. The one is that the words of the people sound flippant and irreverent. The confident way in which the two and three days are mentioned sounds as if the speakers had no real sense of the greatness of their sin and ill-desert. The other reason is that these words are at once followed, not by a promise of that mercy and restoration which the speakers so confidently expect but by vigorous though sorrowful denunciation. Their goodness is likened to the beauty of the sunrise (the "morning cloud") and to the dew which vanishes soon after the sun has risen (cf. 13:3 for a similar use of these figures). The context seems to make it quite clear that the words of verses 1-3 do not represent a sincere and abiding repentance, but a turning to God in the face of calamity and misfortune which is merely a passing mood and will be followed, as soon as the danger is over, by further wilful and stubborn disobedience, as was so often the case in Israel's history.[85]

Jonah and the Great Fish. Another of the frequent misrepresentations which we meet with is the case of Jonah and the whale (i.e., "great fish"). A well-known Bible story book for children which the writer remembers from his own childhood, contains a picture of a ship in an angry sea. Beside the ship is a whale or great fish with its mouth yawning wide. Jonah is in mid-air. The seamen have cast him into the air (not into the sea). The fish is ready to swallow him and Jonah is in transit from the ship through the air to the fish's belly. He will never be in the sea at all. It is a thrilling picture. But it is not at all the picture which the biblical narrative sets before us. Chapter 1:15 tells us expressly "So they took up Jonah, and cast him forth into the sea; and the sea ceased from her raging." The narrative does not state or suggest that the sailors saw the fish or had the slightest suspicion that any other fate than that of drowning befell their late and luckless passenger. But according to the story-book picture they not only saw the "whale" and saw Jonah disappear in its cavernous mouth, but they might almost have expected that they and their ship would share his fate.[86]

When we read on in the biblical account we learn that "the Lord had prepared a great fish to swallow Jonah" and we are told further that Jonah was in the belly of the fish three days and three nights. We are also told that "Jonah prayed unto the Lord his God out of the fish's belly," and the very words of the prayer which Jonah uttered are told us. This is important. What was Jonah's mental state, what were his feelings, in view of all that had befallen him? Had he seen the great fish? Did he know that he was in its belly? Was he afraid he would never get out alive? Was he in mortal terror of being digested by the great monster that had swallowed him up? We turn to the prayer for the answer; and what do we find? It is, as we have seen, a prayer "from the belly of the fish." But it says not a word about the fish. It tells of falling into the raging sea, of sinking down, down, down, into its depths, of being suffocated and losing consciousness, of deliverance from death by drowning, of praying to God, and of vows expressing gratitude, which Jonah expects to perform, apparently at Jerusalem, and it closes with the words, "Salvation is of the Lord." In short, it says not a word about the great fish. But it does describe very vividly the gratitude of a man who has passed through the terrible experience of being cast into the sea and almost drowned and then been delivered from death and brought back to life. And since we are told that Jonah uttered this prayer from the belly of the fish and that after he had uttered it "the Lord spake unto the fish, and it vomited out Jonah upon the dry land," the inference is natural that when Jonah uttered his prayer he was in entire ignorance as to where he was. He had been marvelously delivered from drowning. That was sufficient reason for gratitude and for hope. When he was fully delivered by being cast forth onto the dry land, then the command came a second time and he obeyed it.

The popular misconception of the story of Jonah is a dangerous one, because it gives plausibility to the claim that we have here two inconsistent and contradictory accounts of Jonah's experience on the voyage to Tarshish, the one an account of deliverance from drowning which says nothing about the fish, the other a "fish story," which has little or nothing to say about drowning. If the story book picture gave us a correct idea of what happened, it would be hard to understand the prayer of Jonah with its vivid picture of the agonies of a drowning man. But when we take the whole account as it stands in the Bible, there is no conflict or contradiction. The narrative and the prayer are in entire harmony.

Boaz's Generosity and Considerateness. The Book of Ruth tells us that Ruth at the close of the first day of her labors in Boaz's field carried home to her mother-in-law an ephah of threshed barley. An ephah was about three-fifths of a bushel; so an ephah of barley would weigh some thirty pounds, a staggering load for a woman, accustomed as many oriental women are to the bearing of heavy burdens. Its size indicated both the eagerness of Ruth to provide for the home, and the lavishness with which the reapers carried out Boaz's command as to gleaning. Boaz let her carry it, because he was trying her out. But after she has come to him in the night with her request and he has promised to marry her if the way be clear, we read that he poured six (measures of) barley into her cloak saying, "go not empty unto thy mother-in-law." The six measures were probably six-tenths of an ephah. Boaz may have noted that the ephah load had taxed her strength to the utmost; and he will not overburden the woman he has learned to respect and to love. So he gives her a generous portion, but one which she can easily carry, as a present to her mother-in-law. For there must be no want in Naomi's home while he is concluding the business in hand. We are tempted to infer from Naomi's words, "the man will not be in rest until he have finished the thing this day," that Naomi rightly interpreted the size of the gift.

Ishmael (Gen. 21:15). "And she cast the child under one of the shrubs," may suggest that Ishmael was a babe in arms or a small child when Hagar was finally expelled from Abraham's household. But it is clear from 16:16 and 21:5 that Ishmael was fourteen years older than Isaac. Since in the Orient the weaning of a child often does not take place until it is two or even three years old, Ishmael was probably at least sixteen when he incurred the wrath of Sarah. Consequently, "cast" probably has the sense of "dumped." Ishmael was fainting from exhaustion and thirst. Hagar staggered along, half-supporting, half-carrying him and succeeded in getting him to the shade of a bush, where she let him slip to the earth from her nerveless arms, unable to go a step further with him.

Benjamin (Gen. 44:20) "child of his old age, a little one." When Benjamin went down into Egypt with his brothers in response to the insistent demand of Joseph, Joseph had been in Egypt twenty-two years. If Benjamin was only three years old when Joseph was sold, he was now a man of twenty-five; and according to Genesis 46:21, the father of a number of sons. Yet Joseph speaks of him as if he were the little lad that he had kissed goodbye when he went to greet his brothers expecting to return in a few days time. Jacob had no sons after Benjamin. This may account for Judah's words, "child of his old age." It was now many years since Jacob had had a son, and he was now about one hundred thirty years old (47:9).

Vengeance on Amalek (Exod. 17:14). The vengeance pronounced on Amalek is so utter and the punishment pronounced on Saul for his failure to carry out fully the command regarding them which came to him through Samuel (1 Sam. 15:2f.) was so severe — his rejection from the kingship — that we are inclined to ask why the sin of Amalek was so grievous; "set himself in the way" is a rather mild statement. The answer is given elsewhere as follows: "Remember what Amalek did unto thee by the way, when ye were come forth out of Egypt; how he met thee by the way, and smote the hindmost of thee, even all that were feeble behind thee, when thou wast faint and weary; and he feared not God" (Deut. 25:17f.). This attack, when Israel was en route to Sinai, was particularly cruel, dastardly, and God-defying. The words "and he feared not God" seem to indicate that it had been made clear to Amalek that they should not oppose and attack Israel, either by a special warning (Gen. 31:29) or by the way in which "the Lord fought for Israel" (Exod. 17:11f.).

Moses' Prayer for Aaron. Aaron plays such a sorry role in the incident of the golden calf (Exod. 32:1-6) and his attempt to excuse his great sin is so weak and even contemptible that we are disposed to wonder why he was spared when about three thousand were slain at the command of Moses (vss. 26-29). In Deuteronomy 9:19f. we read: "and the Lord was very angry with Aaron to have destroyed him: and I prayed for Aaron also the same time." It was the intercession of the angry Moses which appeased the anger of an outraged Deity.

Korah, the Rebel (Num. 16). The challenging of the authority of Moses and Aaron and the vindication of it by the condign punishment of the rebels and by the sign of the rod that budded (chap. 17) is the only important event which is recorded of the long period (the 37 year chasm) covered by Chapters 15-19. The statement in 16:32 might seem to imply that the family of Korah was involved in his fate, as was the case with those of Dathan and Abiram (vs. 27) or that they perished in the plague which took the lives of 14,700. But this is not expressly stated, and such an inference is guarded against by the statement made elsewhere in this book: "notwithstanding the children of Korah died not" (26:11). Later in this history we find the sons of Korah occupying honorable positions and as the authors of nine of the Psalms.

Elijah at the brook Cherith (1 Kings 17:1-7). We read in verse 4, "And it shall be, that thou shalt drink of the brook, and I have commanded the ravens to feed thee there": two sources of supply, the one ordinary, the other extraordinary. Then we are told that "the ravens were bringing him bread and flesh in the morning and bread and flesh in the evening and he was wont to drink [frequentative imperfects] of the brook." Then we read, "And it came to pass at the end of days, that the brook was [or became] dry." This was the final result of a long period of drought. For days the supply of water had become less and less. Finally it ceased entirely. What a test of Elijah's faith! The drying up of the brook was the fulfillment of his own prophecy to Ahab. But was this fulfillment to cost him his life? It is perhaps significant that we are not told that the supply of bread and flesh ceased or that it stopped when the water supply came to an end. It would seem that we are intended to infer that the food supply continued unabated. It was this which sustained the faith of Elijah. The drying up of the brook was in answer to Elijah's own prayer (James 5:17). The continuing supply of food was the proof that the Lord was watching over his servant and would supply his needs. The narrator tells us all we need to know and expects us to read between the lines.

Naboth's Sons (2 Kings 9:26). The calculated ruthlessness of Jezebel in ordering the judicial murder of Naboth (1 Kings 21) is made still clearer by the words of Elijah as quoted by Jehu: "Surely I have seen yesterday the blood of Naboth, and the blood of his sons, saith the Lord, and I will requite thee in this plat, saith the Lord." Naboth's heirs shared his fate!

The Burial of Elisha (2 Kings 13:20) is mentioned partly perhaps to indicate that he was not translated as Elijah had been, partly because of the miracle performed by his bones (vs. 21). Elisha's *ministry* lasted about fifty years (Jehoram to Joash). Nothing is said about him between 2 Kings 9:1 (the anointing of Jehu) and his last illness in the days of Joash, some forty years later.

Shebna and Eliakim. Comparing Isaiah 22:15-25 with 36:3 (2 Kings 18:18) it appears that the prophecy of the degradation of Shebna must have been uttered prior to the appearance of Sennacherib's Rabshakeh before Jerusalem. It appears also that there was a gradual fulfillment of the prophecy: first the superseding of Shebna by Eliakim as major domo ("over the household") and the demoting of Shebna to the status of scribe, which is clearly indicated in both Kings and Isaiah, and then the final disgrace, death in exile, which is not recorded in Scripture.

THE SILENCES OF SCRIPTURE

There are many things that the Bible does not tell us. And these silences have given rise to questions which have often "stumped" the reader. Sometimes they have received rather curious answers.

One of the stock questions asked by sceptics for centuries has been, "Where did Cain get his wife?" The only answer given in Scripture is the statement in Genesis 5:4 to the effect that during the eight hundred years which Adam lived after the birth of Seth, he "begat sons and daughters." Since no other human beings are mentioned, it is clearly to be inferred that Cain married one of these daughters. The biblical record does not give the names of the wives of any of the antediluvians of the line of Seth. But it does state, as it does of Adam, that each of them "begat sons and daughters." In the line of Cain, only the wives of Lamech are mentioned by name, the reason being that Lamech had two wives: he was the first polygamist. Similarly in the case of Jacob, only one of his daughters is named (30:21; 46:15) and that for special reasons which are given in Chapter 34. One grand-daughter is named (46:17).[87] But 37:35 tells us that "all his sons and all his daughters" rose up to comfort Jacob for the loss of Joseph. According to Jewish tradition the sons of Jacob, except, of course, Judah and Joseph, married half-sisters. Whether or to what extent this may have been the case, we do not know. We may note in this connection that the New Testament does not name the wives of any one of the Apostles, although it is made clear that some or most of them were married.[88] When we study Scripture as a whole, many difficulties become of minor importance.

It has often been pointed out that the rest of the Old Testament has little or nothing to say about the observance of many of the requirements to which great importance is attached in the Pentateuch. Examples of this are the following:

Circumcision. This sign of the covenant was given to Abraham and observed by him (Gen. 17; 21:4). It was made a condition in the negotiation regarding Dinah (34:15). It is required by the Mosaic Law (Exod. 12:44-48; Lev. 12:3). It was not observed during the years of wandering (Josh. 5:5). After its solemn reinstitution by Joshua (vss. 2-9) it is only referred to inferentially through the mention of Israel's enemy neighbors as uncircumcised (e.g., 1 Sam. 14:6; Ezek. 32:21-32) and as a rite which should be regarded as spiritual rather than merely as physical and external (Jer. 4:4; 6:10). Yet that it was strictly observed as a national rite is indicated by the fact that neither Ezra nor Nehemiah in their reforms make any mention of it. In the time of the Maccabees and in the New Testament it became vastly important.

The Sabbath. The sanctifying of the seventh day is referred to in Genesis 2:3. But while the number seven appears rather frequently in the Book of Genesis, there is no mention of the sanctifying of the seventh day by the patriarchs. In Exodus it is first referred to in connection with the giving of the manna (16:23), where the words "the rest of the holy sabbath unto the Lord" seem to imply that a seventh day of rest was already known to Israel at the time of the exodus.[89] The sabbath law is proclaimed in the Decalogue (Exod. 20:8-11) and referred to repeatedly in the rest of the Pentateuch. Yet in the historical books (Joshua to 2 Kings) it is mentioned only on three occasions (2 Kings 4:23; 11:5-9; 16:18).[90]

The Annual Feasts. The three annual feasts at which all the adult males were to appear before the Lord are described in Exodus 23:14-17; 34:23; Leviticus 23. Elsewhere these three solemn feasts are referred to only in 2 Chronicles 8:13 as observed by Solomon according to the Law of Moses. Of the passover only four celebrations are recorded: in the time of Joshua (5:10), of Hezekiah (2 Chron. 30), of Josiah (2 Kings 23:21-23; 2 Chron. 35:1-18), of Ezra (6:19). Ezekiel requires its future observance (45:21). The observance of the feast of weeks is nowhere else mentioned outside of the Pentateuch; of the feast of tabernacles only in Ezra 3:4, Nehemiah 8:13-18, Hosea 12:9; Zechariah 14:16-19.

The Day of Atonement may rightly be called the most important day in the entire year, since on it the high priest made atonement "for the priests and for all the people of the congregation" (Lev. 16:33; cf. 23:27; 25:9). Its first observance is clearly referred to by the words "and he did as the Lord commanded Moses" (16:34). But nowhere else is it expressly mentioned. Numbers 29:7-11 speaks of the sacrifices for the tenth day of the seventh month which is the day of atonement. But it makes no mention of the special duties of the high priest which were its unique feature, his entrance into the holy of holies, or of the scapegoat (Azazel). It apparently views the day from the standpoint of the people. Zechariah 3:9 can hardly be regarded as containing more than an allusion, if even that.[91]

The Drink-offering. The laws governing the animal sacrifices are given in detail in Leviticus 1-7. The meal-offering which is to accompany them is referred to twenty-five times in these chapters, but no mention is made of the drink-offering. That the drink-offering was known to the Patriarchs is indicated by Genesis 35:14. In Exodus 29:40f. it is mentioned as accompanying the daily morning and evening sacrifices; 30:9 states that it is not to be poured out on the altar of incense. It is mentioned nearly thirty times in Numbers 28-29 along with the meal-offering. Why then is it not once mentioned in Leviticus 1-7? The only answer is, we do not know.

The Sabbatical Year. The sabbath rest of the seventh year is prescribed in Exodus 23:10f and Leviticus 25:1-7. Leviticus 26:34f., 2 Chronicles 36:21 and Jeremiah 34:14 deal with the consequences of failure to obey it.

The Year of Jubilee. This culmination of the sabbatical principle is described in Leviticus 25:8-17. It required the return of the land, if alienated, to its original owners in the fiftieth year. There is no clear reference to its observance in the Old Testament. Whether 2 Kings 19:29 refers to a Jubilee as well as to a sabbatical year is at least doubtful. Ezekiel 7:12 and Jeremiah 34:8-10 are even more uncertain as references. But Ezekiel 46:17 refers definitely to "the year of liberty" as a feature of the future administration of the land; and Isaiah 61:1 uses language which suggests it.[92]

The data given above are significant in themselves and also as illustrating the way in which the inspired authors of the Old Testament dealt with the subjects which they treated. At the best we must describe the treatment of these important institutions as meagre. In extreme cases there is complete or almost complete silence. How is it to be explained? Three explanations naturally suggest themselves. (1) We are expected to assume that since these institutions were expressly required by the law, they were performed as required unless we are informed to the contrary. (2) We are to assume that the many and terrible apostasies of the people from the law of their God and the disorganization which resulted from them are to be regarded as accounting for the practical nullification of the law which is referred to on numerous occasions. These two explanations taken together have been generally accepted as accounting for the phenomena which we have been discussing. (3) The explanation which is widely held today and which is largely responsible for the critical reconstruction of the Old Testament advocated by Wellhausen and others is that these institutions which are described as Mosaic were not really Mosaic but belong to later times, that silence with regard to them in the history of the post-Mosaic period must mean that they were of later date and that occasional references or allusions to them in what are admitted to be early documents are to be treated as later interpolations. This solution of the problem while popular today is irreconcilable with the definite claims of the Pentateuch that the legislation which it contains is Mosaic.

It should also be noted that there are many other silences in Scripture which may seem to us remarkable and even improbable, but which would doubtless be explained if we had all the facts.

Joseph's Later Years. When we add up the data given in Genesis (37:2; 41:46; 45:6; 47:9; 47:28) we discover that Joseph was in the prime of life, fifty-six years old, when Jacob died. Joseph himself lived to a ripe old age, one hundred ten (50:22, 26). As regards this long period, more than half a century, the narrative is almost completely silent. It leaves us in doubt whether Joseph continued in power with the Pharaohs until he died or not. The words "and there arose up a new king over Egypt, which knew not Joseph" (Exod. 1:8) might be interpreted either way. Joseph's later years apparently contain nothing of vital interest and do not concern us.

Zipporah and Her Sons. We are told in Exodus 4:20 that Moses "took his wife and his sons" and "returned to the land of Egypt." In 18:6 we read that Jethro "took Zipporah, Moses' wife after he had sent her away, and her two sons" and brought them to Moses, into the wilderness where he was encamped. When Moses sent them back and why, we are not told. The fact that he had done so, is all the information we need and all that is given us.

Rehoboam, His Son (1 Kings 11:43). When we think of the very prominent role which David's sons and kinsmen played, for good or for ill, in his reign, it is surprising that the account of Solomon's reign is almost completely silent about Solomon's children.[93] It tells us that he had 700 wives and 300 concubines and that "he clave unto these in love" (1 Kings 11:1-3) — a statement which implies that these were not merely political alliances. Two daughters are mentioned as the wives of two of the twelve officers who were appointed to provide supplies for Solomon's household (1 Kings 4:11, 15). "Rehoboam his son" is never mentioned until he became king (11:43). That Solomon had only three children seems incredible. But only three are mentioned. Why this is so we do not know.

Naamah the Ammonitess. "Rehoboam was forty and one years old when he began to reign ... and his mother's name was Naamah the Ammonitess" (1 Kings 14:21; cf. vs. 31).[94] The silence of the Book of Kings regarding Rehoboam until his accession to power is paralleled by the fact that the name of his mother is not mentioned until near the end of his reign. Yet these brief statements are of great significance. They inform us that Solomon some two years before he became king, and while his father David was still alive, married an Ammonitess. Since Solomon can hardly have been more than twenty, probably considerably younger, when he became king, this probably means that Naamah was his first wife and Rehoboam his first-born son. But no mention is made of his marriage to her. We are told that Solomon married Pharaoh's daughter and built a special palace for her (1 Kings 7:8). We read about the visit of the queen of Sheba (10:1-14) and are told that "king Solomon loved many foreign women and the daughter of Pharaoh" (11:1). Ammonitesses are among those specified; and it is further stated that these women belonged to nations with which marriage was prohibited and that these women led Solomon astray "after other gods." Ashtoreth and Milkom, "the detested thing of the Ammonites," are specifically mentioned (vs. 5) and it is stated that Solomon built a high place for Chemosh, "the detested thing of Moab" (vs. 7). Yet Naamah is never mentioned in connection with Solomon. It is only in the account of Rehoboam's reign, and in what might be called the final summary which includes the invasion of Shishak, that Naamah is mentioned (14:21) and there the two important facts are clearly stated: Rehoboam was forty-one years old when he began to reign, which means that he was born before Solomon became king, and his mother was "Naamah the Ammonitess"; and this latter fact is repeated as the last word regarding Rehoboam: "And his mother's name was Naamah the Ammonitess" (vs. 31).[95] Little is told, but much is implied in this brief statement. The writer seems concerned to account for the apostasies of Solomon and of Rehoboam as partly, perhaps largely, due to the evil influence, probably extending over a long period of time, of an ardent idolatress on her husband and on her son. Naamah the Ammonitess may have been the chief of the pagan influences which had such baleful results in the lives of both Solomon and Rehoboam. Yet we are told almost nothing about her. How strikingly different is the case of Jezebel!

Elijah and the Calf-worship. The fact that Elijah made, it would seem, no attempt to overthrow the calf-worship has been appealed to as proof that he did not regard it as unlawful and that therefore idolatry was permissible in his day. At least three things are to be noted: (1) Elijah's great conflict was with the Baal-worship which was fostered by Jezebel. This appears to have been the task especially assigned to him. It was a tremendous task and it nearly cost him his life. (2) Elijah compared the doom which he pronounced on Ahab with the fate of Jeroboam, whose house had been cut off by Baasha, because of "the provocation wherewith thou hast provoked (me) to anger and made Israel to sin" (1 Kings 21:22). Jeroboam's provocation was the calves and by instituting their worship he had "made Israel to sin." The reference to and denunciation of this idolatry is unmistakable. (3) It seems proper to conclude, therefore, that it was the intention of the Lord to allow the calf-worship to continue as a test or "provocation" in Israel until its destruction (2 Kings 17:16), while denouncing it through his prophets (1 Kings 13:1-10; Hos. 8:5f.; 10:5).

King Jeroboam's Altar at Bethel (2 Kings 23:15). The express mention of the altar and high place erected by Jeroboam at Bethel, as being destroyed by Josiah in his reforming zeal, makes the omission of any reference to the calf which was placed there by Jeroboam remarkable and significant. A century or more before Josiah's time Hosea in denouncing the sinfulness of Samaria and Beth-aven (Bethel?) had declared regarding the calf: "It also shall be carried unto Assyria for a present to king Jareb (Sennacherib?)." When or how the calf was brought to this ignominious end is nowhere stated. But Josiah's failure to mention it shows that the prophecy had been fulfilled. The shrine at Bethel was empty. The calf was missing. Bethel had lost its distinction as a center of this idolatrous worship!

The Sojourn in Egypt. To the student of Egyptian history, the account in Genesis and Exodus is inadequate and tantalizing. He wants to know the name of the Pharaoh who exalted a Hebrew slave to be governor of Egypt. He thinks it strange that the name of Joseph's jailor, the name given Joseph by Pharaoh, the name of his wife, of her father the priest of On, of the two midwives, should be mentioned, but not the name of Pharaoh. But if we read the narrative carefully, we find that one reason is very clearly indicated. The passage which is probably of the greatest interest to the secular historian is 47:13-26, which tells us that when the Egyptians were reduced to desperation by the famine, they sold themselves and all their possessions to Pharaoh, a fact which is confirmed by the monuments. So fourteen verses are given to this important item of general history, because it was so entirely relevant to the career of Joseph as governor of Egypt. But seventeen verses are devoted to Judah's plea for Benjamin, and twenty verses to the imposing funeral rites accorded Jacob.

These things may seem very suspicious to the students of secular history; and it is charged that they indicate that the documents of which this account is alleged to be composed are late and fragmentary and that the "omissions" are due to the ignorance of the compiler. But that is because those who say this are looking at the record from a widely different viewpoint than that of the author. He is interested in history and he records facts of history. But the facts which he records are the ones that are important for the story which it is his aim to tell. He is not telling of a relatively brief episode in the age-long history of Egypt and fitting it carefully into its place in the framework of the history of that ancient people; he is telling the story of *Israel* in Egypt, of the wonderful way in which God preserved his people from famine; and this is only the prelude to the far greater story, that story which is one of the major themes of the Old Testament, the deliverance from Egyptian bondage, which is the type and foretaste of that greater deliverance from bondage, which is the supreme theme of the Bible and which was wrought for the seed of Abraham on the cross of Calvary.

This relative indifference, as we may call it, to the world situation both simplifies and complicates matters for the Bible student. It simplifies by relieving him of the necessity of correlating and harmonizing many details which a fuller account would involve. It justifies him, for example, in showing the same indifference to the names of the Pharaohs of the exodus period as the writer of the narrative has shown. The important thing is that these events actually *took place,* and not the exact dates and reigns at which or during which they took place. The writer's concern is to tell us salient facts and to trace the hand of God in all of them. It complicates the situation for us when we attempt to corroborate the events from Egyptian records and to prove from Egyptian history just when they took place. For the records of the Pharoahs show, as we are well aware, even more indifference to the presence of Israel in Egypt, than the biblical historian shows to the details of Egyptian history.

Shechem. In view of the importance of this city in Israelite history it is remarkable that nothing is said in Joshua or Judges about its capture by Joshua. It is not among the thirty-one royal cities listed in Joshua 12 as smitten by the Israelites. Yet the solemn rite which was performed at Mt. Ebal in fulfilment of Moses' command, would hardly have taken place under the walls of a hostile city (Josh. 8:30-35). Shechem was made a city of refuge (20:7) and assigned to the Kohathites (21:21). It was there that Joshua delivered his farewell to all Israel (24:1). That Shechem became Israelite in the days of Joshua seems perfectly clear. How this came about we are not told.

Daniel's Three Friends. Sometimes the silences of Scripture are particularly significant. In Daniel 2 we read of the honors conferred by King Nebuchadnezzar on Daniel and his friends. In the next chapter we are told of the refusal of these friends to worship the golden image which the king set up in the plain of Dura in the province of Babylon. We read of the wrath of the king, of the heroism of the three young men, of their miraculous deliverance from the fiery furnace, of the astonishment of the king, and of his edict in behalf of all who worshipped the God of Shadrach, Meshach and Abednego. Where was Daniel? How did he escape the fiery trial which his friends so triumphantly endured? We are not told. We are allowed to assume that for some reason which is not given, Daniel was either not there or was not summoned by the king. The writer clearly does not consider it necessary to tell us that Daniel could not and would not have worshipped the golden image. Daniel's integrity and fortitude needed no defense.

The Future Life. Especially noteworthy is the reticence of the Old Testament on the subject of the future life. That the Patriarchs believed in a life beyond the grave cannot be doubted for several reasons. There is the evidence that early man believed in a future life as shown by the implements and utensils found in ancient tombs. There is more specifically the evidence of the extreme emphasis on the future life in Egypt. It is, of course, true that pyramids, mastabas, and other elaborate burials were the prerogative of the rich and noble. But this must have given the people as a whole a sense of the reality of such a future existence. The mass burials at Ur and elsewhere indicate the feeling that a king or great man must be properly attended in the other world. Such facts as these indicate that, as has often been pointed out, the reason so little is said in the Old Testament about the life after death is twofold: on the one hand because the universality of the belief made it unnecessary and on the other as a reaction and protest against the extremes to which the belief was carried in Egypt.

That the Patriarchs and Moses and David believed in a future existence is indicated by such an expression as Jacob's regarding Joseph's supposed death, "I shall go down into the grave unto my son mourning," since Jacob believed regarding Joseph, "an evil beast hath devoured him; Joseph is without doubt rent in pieces" (Gen. 37:33ff.). Also to be noted is the expression "to go to one's fathers," as used of Abraham who was the first of his line to be buried at Machpelah; of Moses (Deut. 31:16) who was buried in the land of Moab in a place known only to God. We have also David's words when he learned of the death of Bathsheba's child: "I shall go to him, but he shall not return to me" (2 Sam. 12:23). The ironical description of the arrival of the king of Babylon in the realm of the dead (Isa. 14:15-20) is not intended as a proof of a future life, but simply as a scathing rebuke of the overweening pride of a pagan world ruler (cf. Ezek. 32:17-32). Most important of all is the fact that "the communion instituted by revelation between the living God and man imparts to human personality an eternal importance."[96] This great truth is brought out with special clearness in Jesus' appeal to Exodus 3:6: first by his general comment, "Do ye not therefore err, because ye know not the Scriptures, neither the power of God?" and then with special reference to this verse he adds, "Ye therefore do greatly err" (Mark 12:24-27), clearly implying that the meaning of the revelation to Moses at the bush was so clear, "God is not the God of the dead, but of the living," that they should not have failed to understand it. It is impossible to explain adequately the faith shown by Abraham when he was commanded to sacrifice Isaac without recognizing that Abraham's faith was an other-world faith, that he believed in a union and communion with God which not even death itself could terminate. It is so interpreted in Hebrews 11:19.

Reticence and Restraint. The reticence of Scripture is sometimes quite striking. Perhaps the most striking example is the story of the sacrifice of Isaac (Gen. 22). How terrible was this trial of Abraham's faith is indicated by the words of the command: "Take now thy son, thine only son, whom thou lovest, (even) Isaac . . . and offer him there for a burnt offering." Every word a stab! Yet not a word is said about the anguish which this command occasioned Abraham. All that we read about is his obedience and the reward of it. As to Isaac's re-action to this terrible experience we are given only a hint in the words of Jacob's oath: "And Jacob sware by the fear of his father Isaac" (Gen. 31:53).

The death of Aaron is described with similar brevity: "And Moses stripped Aaron of his garments and put them on Eleazar his son; and Aaron died there on the top of the mount: and Moses and Eleazar came down from the mount" (Num. 20:28). We may assume that Aaron was buried where he died, on the mountaintop. But that is not stated. It is the succession of Eleazar, as indicated by his investiture with the highpriestly garments which is the important thing in this connection. Moses' grief over Aaron's death is also passed over in silence.

The death of Ezekiel's wife is described in similar fashion. He is commanded to show no outward signs of grief and we read: "So I spake unto the people in the morning; and at even my wife died; and I did in the morning as I was commanded" (24:18).[97]

Of the testing of Elijah's faith by the drying up of the brook we read nothing in 1 Kings 17. It must have been a heart-searching ex-perience. But James tells us that both the drought and the rain came in answer to Elijah's prayer (5:17f.).

Such examples stand in sharp contrast to what we are told of David's terrible anguish over the sickness of the child of sin and over the death of Absalom which are described so poignantly, a grief which was in-tensified by his sense of his own guilt (2 Sam. 12:10-12). And Jere-miah does not hesitate to bewail his own sufferings on a number of occasions.

In the biblical treatment of such incidents we note the difference be-tween the Bible and the Apocryphal literature of the Jews. The latter has sought to supply what the Bible leaves untold. In Daniel we read of the wisdom and understanding of Daniel and his three friends; and we are told of the heroic stand taken by the latter when called upon to bow before the golden image (chap. 3). The Apocrypha inserts sixty-seven verses after 3:23: the Songs of the Three Children, and the books of Susanna and Bel and the Dragon which are intended to il-lustrate the wisdom of Daniel. We read in 2 Chronicles 33:12f. of Manasseh's repentance and prayer. The Apocrypha records such a prayer. The additions to Esther run to 107 verses, which are added at 4:17 or 10:3. Among the first scrolls discovered in the Dead Sea caves is an apocryphal story dealing with incidents recorded in the Book of

Genesis. It illustrates the tendency of the Midrashic literature of the Jews to expand the biblical narratives with data which may or may not have any foundation in fact.

The Historians and the Prophets. The close connection between prophecy and history in the Bible is made especially clear by the occasional references in Chronicles to the prophets as writers of history: to Samuel, Nathan, and Gad (1 Chron. 29:29), to Nathan, Ahijah, and Iddo (2 Chron. 9:29), to Isaiah (26:22; 32:32). That the downfall of the Northern Kingdom was due to the failure of Israel to obey the word of the Lord as spoken by his prophets is definitely stated in the great indictment in 2 Kings 17:13, 23. A considerable portion of the Books of Kings is devoted to an account of the prominent role which Elijah and Elisha played in the history of the Northern Kingdom when the conflict with Baal became a duel between the man of God and Jezebel of Tyre. The fact that the God of Israel is the God of history, of the past, the present, and the future, is made abundantly clear in the Historical Books of the Old Testament. Consequently, it may seem a little remarkable that so few of the prophets whose writings appear in the Prophetical Books, a collection which constitutes about one fourth of the entire Old Testament, are mentioned by name in the Historical Books. Isaiah is mentioned because of the prominent part which he played in the struggle with Sennacherib. Jeremiah is never mentioned in Kings and rarely in Chronicles. Ezekiel is nowhere mentioned. Daniel is not mentioned in Ezra or Nehemiah. Of the twelve Minor Prophets only four are mentioned: Jonah (2 Kings 14:25), Micah (Jer. 26:18f.), Haggai and Zechariah (Ezra 5:1; 6:14).[98]

These facts are interesting and some readers will find them surprising. But when we consider the brevity of the Historical Books as compared with the extended periods of time which they cover, it is not remarkable that they have so little to say about these heroes of the faith.[99] Their own writings speak for themselves and need no express confirmation or commendation by the historians. We are, of course, inclined to wonder why Josiah consulted the otherwise unknown Huldah about the Book of the Law discovered in the temple instead of Jeremiah or Zephaniah. There may have been several reasons. None is given. Perhaps she was the most available prophet, since we are expressly told that she dwelt in Jerusalem in the second or lower quarter of the city. The king's command required haste.

A somewhat similar question is, Why does Daniel 9:2 refer only to Jeremiah's prophecy of the 70 years (Jer. 25:12) and say nothing about Isaiah's prophecy regarding Cyrus (Isa. 44:28)? It may of course have been due to the fact that Jeremiah's prophecy was precise, as to time, seventy years (2 Chron. 36:21). But Cyrus' proclamation referred expressly to the (re-) building of the temple, which is specifically mentioned by Isaiah, but not by Jeremiah. Apparently the writer regarded a single reference as sufficient.

SILENCES IN SECULAR HISTORY

Such silences as we find in biblical history can easily be matched in secular history, both ancient and modern.

Lachish. The excavations at *Tell-ed-Duweir,* which many scholars now identify with Lachish, have raised an interesting historical question. Kraeling tells us that "The siege of Lachish must have been a particularly satisfying memory to Sennacherib, for he had it portrayed on the walls of the great palace which he built for himself at Nineveh, with an inscription reading: 'Sennacherib king of the world sat upon a throne, whereupon the captives of Lachish passed by.'"[100] This fine alabaster relief has often been reproduced and is one of the best known. So, it is remarkable that nowhere in his inscriptions does Sennacherib make any mention of the *capture* of Lachish. In fact we might call the mural "The Siege of Lachish" rather than the "capture," since it is evident that the city is still stoutly resisting. If it had actually been captured we would certainly expect Sennacherib to have recorded the fact. The biblical narratives also make no definite mention of the fall of Lachish but only state that Sennacherib laid siege to the city and was present there. That he actually took the city may be inferred from the general statement that "Sennacherib came up against all the fortified cities of Judah and took them" (2 Kings 18:13). But since the narrative goes on to tell of his signal failure to take Jerusalem, it is at least possible that Lachish was also an exception.[101]

The Death of Belshazzar (Dan. 5). In both the *Nabunaid Chronicle* and the *Cylinder Inscription* of Cyrus it is stated that the armies of Cyrus entered Babylon "without battle." Cyrus declares that he "entered Babylon as a friend" and that he "established the seat of the government in the palace of the ruler under jubilation and rejoicing." This may be true in general. But it does not necessarily conflict with the statement that "in that night Belshazzar the Chaldean king was slain" (Dan. 5:30). Both statements are equally possible. The people of Babylon may have received Cyrus gladly, while and despite the fact that Belshazzar was holding a drunken revel in the palace and thus became an easy victim of the conquering Persians. Cyrus may have deemed it politic to ignore this vice-king whom he so easily got rid of.[102]

DATA BOTH SCANTY AND SCATTERED

The fact that the Bible not seldom gives us only quite brief accounts of many periods and events makes it very important that we endeavor to learn and understand all that is told us about them. The problem is quite often complicated by the fact that the relevant and even necessary information is not all given in the same place. This is made especially clear when we compare the accounts of events given us in Samuel-Kings and in Chronicles.

Ishbosheth. In dealing with David's reign in Hebron, which he describes as lasting seven years and six months (2 Sam. 2:11), the historian simply tells us that Ishbosheth "reigned two years" (vs. 10). He does not consider it necessary to explain how it came about that Ishbosheth "reigned" only two years over Israel while David reigned seven years and six months in Hebron, although he seems to imply that the death of Ishbosheth was speedily followed by the crowning of David to be king over all Israel. His main interest is in David; and it might seem that his principal reason for telling about Ishbosheth and Abner is to exhibit the magnanimous and chivalrous conduct of David. That he sees no conflict or contradiction in the statements that Ishbosheth reigned two years over all Israel and that David reigned seven years and six months in Hebron and then was made king of all Israel on the death of Ishbosheth is obvious. But he leaves it to the reader to figure out, if he wishes to do so, just how this can be, on the basis of the facts which he has given him. Chronicles mentions the fact that David reigned seven years in Hebron (1 Chron. 29:26f.) and lists Eshbaal (Ishbosheth) as a son of Saul (1 Chron. 8:33; 9:39) but ignores his reign completely.

The Ark. The first attempt by David to bring up the ark to Jerusalem is described briefly in 2 Samuel 6:1-11. It does not explain why "the anger of the Lord was kindled against Uzzah." The only hint given there as to the reason for the failure of the first attempt and the success of the second is in the words "when they that bare the ark of the Lord" (vs. 13) which indicate that the second attempt was successful because the ark was *carried* by the Levites as the law required. 1 Chronicles 15:2, 14f. makes it clear that David after the failure of his first attempt discovered the reason for it and complied with the requirements laid down in Numbers 4:5, 15-20. Chronicles, as we have seen, makes no mention of David's great sin or of its terrible consequences which form such a large part of the narrative in 2 Samuel 11-20. Absalom's name appears in Chronicles only as a genealogical link.

Abijah. Kings tells us that Abijah continued the state of war with

Jeroboam which his father had maintained (1 Kings 15:6f.). It makes no mention of the tremendous victory won by Abijah which is the principal theme of the account given in 2 Chronicles 13, a victory which effectually crippled Jeroboam during the brief remainder of his reign. Yet both Kings and Chronicles record the invasion of Shishak, in the days of Rehoboam. Abijah's occupancy of Bethel (2 Chron. 13:19) was probably brief and nominal since the calf worship which was distinctive of the Northern Kingdom was apparently not interfered with.

Benjamin. According to 2 Chronicles 14:8 there were 280,000 warriors in Benjamin in the days of Asa, which was nearly as large a total as the 300,000 of Judah. According to 2 Chronicles 17:17f., Jehoshaphat had an army of 780,000 men of Judah and 380,000 of Benjamin. Only in this way is attention directed in Scripture to the phenomenal "comeback" of Benjamin after its nearly utter annihilation early in the period of the Judges.

Zimri, Tibni, and Omri. The reign of Zimri was very brief, "seven days in Tirzah" (1 Kings 16:15). The army made Omri, its captain, king. Omri besieged Zimri in Tirzah; and Zimri burned down the palace over his own head and died. Nearly twelve verses are devoted to Zimri. Then we read that the people were divided, half following Tibni and half Omri, and that those who followed Omri prevailed. The result is stated briefly: "so Tibni died, and Omri reigned." Since it has just been stated that Zimri reigned seven days, we might infer from the fact that no mention is made of the length of Tibni's reign that it was even shorter than Zimri's. But such was apparently not the case. For the historian tells us that Zimri began to reign in the twenty-seventh year of Asa (vs. 15), that Omri began to reign in Asa's thirty-first year and reigned twelve years, during six of which his capital city was Tirzah (vs. 23), and that Omri's son Ahab began to reign in Asa's thirty-eighth year (vs. 29). This apparently must mean that while Omri's twelve-year reign is to be dated from Asa's twenty-seventh year, his title to the throne was contested by Tibni until Asa's thirty-first year, when Omri finally eliminated Tibni and became the unchallenged ruler over the entire Northern Kingdom. This period of some four years is summed up succinctly with the words, "so Tibni died, and Omri reigned." Two years later Omri was able to move from Tirzah to his new capital at Samaria.

Jehoash. In 2 Kings 12:2 we read the ominous sounding words "and Jehoash did right in the sight of the Lord all his days wherein Jehoiada the priest instructed him." The only lapse which is recorded is his taking "all the hallowed things" (vs. 18) and sending them to Hazael to save Jerusalem from assault by the Syrian king. No reason is given for the conspiracy against him which resulted in his death (vss. 20-21). It is in 2 Chronicles 24:17-27 that we read of his lapse into idolatry, of Zechariah's futile protest and martyr death, and of the judgments which the Lord executed upon the king at the hands of the Syrians, of the "great diseases" with which he was afflicted and of the conspiracy which brought about his death, because of "the blood of the sons of Jehoiada."

Amaziah. According to the biblical data, Amaziah became king of Judah at the age of twenty-five in the second year of Joash of Israel and reigned for twenty-nine years (2 Kings 14:1f.; 2 Chron. 25:1). Both Kings and Chronicles tell us of his avenging his father's murder, of his campaign against Edom, and of his foolish challenging of Joash to battle, and of his crushing defeat. Both tell us that he survived Joash fifteen years. Chronicles adds a few further details. Yet both conclude with a noticeably brief mention of the conspiracy which was formed against him, his flight to Lachish, his assassination, and the bringing of his body to Jerusalem for burial, a brief statement, which as will appear later is of great importance for the chronology of this period.

Azariah. Another striking example of this condensation of history is the story of the reign of Azariah as told in 2 Kings (15:1-7), when compared with the fuller account given us in 2 Chronicles (26:1-23). Kings tells us merely that "the Lord smote the king, so that he was a leper unto the day of his death, and dwelt in a separate house. And Jotham the king's son was over the house, judging the people of the land." It seems strange that no explanation is given of this terrible visitation. The writer evidently expects his readers to infer from the statement, "the Lord smote the king," that this visitation which resulted in practical deposition was well deserved and punitive. We may also infer that he assumed that his readers were so familiar with this tragic event as not to require to be reminded of an act of sacrilege which apparently had few parallels in Israel's history, and even that he shrank from referring to it directly. Nonetheless his silence is decidedly remarkable. On the other hand Chronicles devotes about ten verses to the achievements of Azariah along secular lines, and then five verses to the grievous sacrilege which was the cause of the awful punishment which was inflicted upon him. Kings simply states the awful fact; Chronicles both the fact and the reason for it.

Jotham. We read nothing in 2 Kings 15:32-38 of Jotham's building of cities or of his successful war against the Ammonites and the tribute he received from them (2 Chron. 27:4-6).

Ahaz. Isaiah 7 tells of Ahaz' fear of Rezin and Pekah and of Isaiah's contemptuous reference to these foes of God's people as "the two tails of smoking firebrands," implying that their attack will soon fizzle out. 2 Kings 16:5 records that Rezin and Pekah "besieged Ahaz, but could not overcome *him*," (or "engage him in battle"). It is only from 2 Chronicles 28:1-15 that we learn of the frightful carnage wrought in Judah by the invasion of Rezin and Pekah and of the release of the captives taken by Pekah at the demand of the prophet Oded. Kings, on the other hand, tells of Ahaz' appeal to the king of Assyria for help, and of the altar which he saw at Damascus and had copied for the temple at Jerusalem.

Hezekiah. Kings gives ninety-five verses (18:1–20:21) to the reign of Hezekiah; Chronicles gives one hundred seventeen (29:1–32:33). Kings passes over Hezekiah's reforms very briefly and does not even mention the great passover which he and all Israel observed; it concentrates on the struggle with Sennacherib, Hezekiah's illness, his pride and its punishment. In Chronicles, more than two-thirds of the account of Hezekiah's reign deals with his reforms and the passover. About twenty verses deal with Sennacherib, and the last ten with Hezekiah's sickness, recovery, and the prosperity that followed it; his sin of pride with which both Kings and Isaiah conclude the account of his reign is hardly more than alluded to (32:31).

Manasseh. Kings devotes eighteen verses to the reign of Manasseh (21:1-18). It describes the enormity of his sin and its terrible consequences for Judah, but says not a word about his repentance and the occasion of it. In Chronicles half of the brief narrative (33:11-19) is devoted to a description of the way in which the Lord humbled Manasseh by sending him to Babylon as a prisoner, and of his repentance and good works after he was brought back to Jerusalem.

Jehoiakim. We have three statements regarding the death of Jehoiakim: (a) "So Jehoiakim slept with his fathers and Jehoiachin his son reigned in his stead" (2 Kings 24:6); (b) "Against him came up Nebuchadnezzar king of Babylon, and bound him in fetters to carry him to Babylon" (2 Chron. 36:6); (c) "He shall be buried with the burial of an ass, drawn and cast forth beyond the gates of Jerusalem" (Jer. 22:19; cf. 36:30). Furthermore we have the statements that "Jehoiachin his son reigned in his stead" (2 Kings 24:6; 2 Chron. 36:8) and that "he shall have none to sit upon his throne" (Jer. 36:30). How these statements are to be harmonized, we do not know. We are entitled to hold that it would be possible if we knew all the facts.[103] But it is noteworthy that the Old Testament writers make no attempt to harmonize them for us.

Zedekiah. The journey which Zedekiah made to Babylon in his fourth year is only mentioned incidentally by Jeremiah as furnishing the occasion for the sending by the hand of Seraiah, who accompanied him, of the "book" containing Jeremiah's prophecy against Babylon with instructions as to the symbolic action of casting it into the Euphrates (51:59-64). Ezekiel mentions no king of Israel by name except Jehoiachin, the beginning of whose captivity supplies the date for his prophecies (1:2). He mentions also the David of the future (34:23f.; 37:24f.). Nearly all of his allusions to them are in parabolic or figurative language. Consequently, it is noteworthy how definitely and yet enigmatically (12:6, 12) he refers to the blinding of Zedekiah; "he shall not see it [Babylon] though he shall die there" (vs. 13).[104] Jeremiah foretells that Zedekiah shall see the king of Babylon eye to eye and speak with him (32:4; 34:3; cf. 2 Kings 25:7); and he declares that Zedekiah's sons were slain before his eyes and that then his own eyes were put out (39:6f; 52:10). In doing this Jeremiah is clearly aiming to bring out the stark horror and cruelty of the treatment which Zedekiah received. The last pictures which this feeble and wicked king carried with him into the land of his captivity, a land which his blinding did not permit him to see, were the face of his implacable conqueror, Nebuchadnezzar, and the death agonies of his sons, slaughtered before his eyes. That a king of David's line should be blinded was a tragedy and a disgrace; and the circumstances made it tenfold more terrible. So it is natural that both in prophecy and in history the blinding of the king should be specially noted and emphasized. Yet it is Jeremiah's terribly and tragically plain statements which make clear the meaning of the enigmatical words of Ezekiel: "he shall not see it though he shall die there." The close of Zedekiah's life is also described in somewhat enigmatic language. He shall be carried to Babylon and "there shall he be until I visit him, saith the Lord" (Jer. 32:4f.); so he was put in prison "till the day of his death" (52:11). Yet he should die in peace and have a worthy funeral (34:4f.). This would indicate that when after a captivity, which may have been long (Nebuchadnezzar reigned twenty-five years after he captured Jerusalem in 586 B.C.), Zedekiah finally died, Nebuchadnezzar or one of his successors allowed him a funeral such as became a king of Judah. Compare Evil-merodach's treatment of Jehoiachin.[105]

Ahaziah. The two accounts of the death of Ahaziah of Judah (2 Kings 9:27f.; 2 Chron. 22:8f.) are much harder to reconcile. Keil believed it was possible to do so. But many critics have not hesitated to pronounce them "irreconcilable." The fact that both appear in the biblical record would indicate that Jewish scholars did not so regard them.

THE LAW OF FIRST OCCURRENCE

One of the most important rules for interpreting the Scripture is that
the exact meaning of a word must be determined by its usage, more
precisely, by its biblical usage, as determined by the contexts in which
it appears. This may be made clear by the immediate context or it may
require a study of many other or even all the occurrences of the word
in the Bible. Its extra-biblical usage may also at times be decidedly
helpful as the study of the Ras Shamra texts has proved to be for the
Old Testament and of the Greek Papyri for the New Testament.

A curious attempt has been made to simplify this rule. It is called
the law of first occurrence. It lays down the principle that the biblical
meaning of words is to be determined from the *first* passage in which
they occur. It is an attractive rule because it seems so simple and easy;
and it has acquired considerable popularity through its advocacy by
E. W. Bullinger.[106] Unfortunately it requires only a few simple examples to prove that it will not work.

In Genesis 1:2 we read "and the *ruach* of God was moving upon the
face of the waters." The word *ruach* in Hebrew is used in two main
senses: it may mean *wind* or *spirit*. Most exegetes take it here in the
sense of spirit and spell it with a capital, Spirit. Some take it in the
sense of wind, "a wind of God," i.e., a mighty wind. The former seems
preferable. But both are possible. The important thing is that both can
hardly be used here at the same time. We must choose between them.
If we choose "wind," there are 232 passages in the Old Testament
where the AV renders by "spirit" or "Spirit," in most of which "wind"
would make nonsense. If we choose "spirit," there are 90 passages in
the Old Testament where the AV renders by "wind" and in most, if
not all, of them "spirit" would be out of place (e.g., Exod. 14:21).

Another example in point is the word *malak* which occurs 213 times
in the Old Testament. The AV (following LXX and *Vulg.*) makes a
distinction between the cases where it refers to a superhuman and
those where it is used of a human agent. In the one case it renders by
"angel" (111 times) in the other usually by "messenger" (98 times).
The first occurrence is in Genesis 16:7 where it is used of the "angel"
who appeared to Hagar. But the persons sent to Esau by Jacob were
clearly human like himself; and the proper rendering is "messengers"
(32:3, 6).

Since many Bible students believe they can find special significance
in the use of numbers, it is to be noted that the law of first occurrence
is equally meaningless as applied to them. We meet in Genesis 14:4f.
the first occurrences of the numbers 12, 13 and 14: "Twelve years they
served Chedorlaomer, and in the thirteenth year they rebelled. And in

the fourteenth year. . . ." Is twelve the number of servitude? There is no number that figures more frequently in the Bible than twelve. We think of the twelve tribes of Israel, the twelve apostles, the twelve months. Is the idea of servitude to be traced out in each of them? Genesis 17:20, the second mention of twelve, tells us regarding Ishmael, "twelve princes shall he beget." The twelve can hardly imply servitude. For we have already been told in 16:12 that Ishmael will live the wild, free life of the bedouin; and his descendants have done so for uncounted generations.

"And in the thirteenth year they rebelled." The context here speaks of rebellion. The number 13 is relatively infrequent, occurring less than twenty-five times in the Old Testament. Ishmael was thirteen when he was circumcised (Gen. 17:25). The cities allotted the priests, the sons of Aaron, were thirteen (Josh. 21:19). Solomon was thirteen years building his house (1 Kings 7:1). Haman's edict and the day of vengeance of the Jews were on or included the thirteenth day (Esth. 3:12; 8:12). Jeremiah was called to be a prophet in the thirteenth year of Josiah. Are we to discover rebellion in all of these? If not, to which of them does the rule apply?

"And in the fourteenth year came Chedorlaomer . . . and smote." The number fourteen is also of relatively infrequent occurrence. It is used most frequently of the day before the passover, the day on which the paschal lamb was slain. But would anyone suggest a connection between the two?

Such examples as the above suffice to show that while the first occurrence of a word may give a general idea of its meaning and usage, the various senses in which it may be used must be determined from a study of the, at times, widely different contexts in which it appears.

Occasional and Casual Statements

Attention has been directed to the fact that one of the services which archaeology is rendering the Bible student is to supply him with information with which the writers of the biblical records were familiar and acquaintance with which they assumed on the part of their readers. We need constantly to remind ourselves that the Bible is not a handbook of general information. The fact that, in many editions of the Bible, tables of statistics, such as money values, weights and measures, and chronology, are added as "helps" is a reminder of the fact that the Bible itself does not supply such information in systematic form, if at all. This is illustrated, for example, by the business dealings of the Hebrews.

Business and Trade. Abraham's purchase of the cave and field at Machpelah indicates that in his day business was conducted in orderly fashion and on recognized business principles. We read that he "weighed" (Gen. 23:16) Ephron four hundred shekels of silver. "Weighing" the bullion was according to custom, since minted coins of definite value were not introduced until a millennium after Abraham's day. At that time silver was the usual money, but gold was also used. The basic unit of exchange was the shekel. This is indicated by the fact that its value is specified: it is two *bekahs* (Exod. 38:26) or twenty *gerahs* (Exod. 30:13; Lev. 27:25; Num. 3:47; 18:16). It is also described as "current with the merchant" (Gen. 23:15), "according to the shekel of the sanctuary" (Exod. 30:15), "after the king's weight" (2 Sam. 14:26). Shekels are mentioned eighty-eight times in the Old Testament. But the *maneh* is mentioned only five times (1 Kings 10:17; Ezra 2:69; Neh. 7:71, 72; Ezek. 45:12) and it is only in the last mentioned passage that it is made clear that there were sixty shekels in a maneh. From the total of the half-shekel levy for the tabernacle (100 talents, 1775 shekels, for 603,550 adult males, Exod. 38:25f.) we learn that there were three thousand shekels in the talent (mentioned forty-eight times). But whether in ordinary business, the talent consisted of fifty manehs valued at sixty shekels each or of sixty manehs of fifty shekels each is not made clear. We know that the Babylonians had a double standard for the shekel, a light shekel and a heavy shekel twice the value of the light. But we are dependent on the statements regarding Solomon's golden shields, which we are told weighed both "six hundred shekels" (1 Kings 10:17) and "three hundred shekels" (2 Chron. 9:16), for a hint as to the use of this double standard in Israel. The *qesitah* is mentioned three times (Gen. 33:19; Josh. 24:32; Job 42:11). But its value is not given and is still unknown. The *daric* or *drachma* is likewise mentioned six times. But its relation to the shekel is not stated.

Judah's signet is mentioned incidentally (Gen. 38:18, 25). Whether it was a stamp signet or a cylinder seal, we do not know. The ring which Pharaoh gave Joseph (41:42) was probably a seal-ring. At any rate these signets served for identification and authorization. They were in use centuries before the time of Abraham.

The Hiring of Israelite Mercenaries (2 Chron. 25:6). One hundred thousand warriors hired for one hundred talents of silver would be at the rate of three shekels per man. But how much of this sum actually went to the soldiers themselves we do not know. Probably the Israelite warriors expected vast plunder beside. So this statement does not give us any accurate information as to the value of a man's life in the days of Amaziah king of Judah.

Similar statements might be made with regard to measurements of length and of capacity. Some information is given. But much is assumed to be familiar to the reader. Thus the *log* as a measure for oil is referred to only in Leviticus 14 and the *lethek* as a measure for barley (Hos. 3:2), but neither term is defined. Both are mentioned on Ugaritic tablets.

The above statements and many others which might be added indicate the care with which business both sacred and secular was conducted and the importance attached to strict honesty in business dealings (Lev. 19:36). But the form of statement often serves to point out the fact that our knowledge of the daily life and business dealings of the Hebrews is meagre and sketchy.

The mention of "camels" in the time of Abraham (Gen. 12:16), of "horses" in Egypt in the days of Joseph (Gen. 47:17), of Joseph's shaving himself before appearing before Pharaoh (Gen. 41:14), of Rebekah's veiling herself before meeting Isaac (Gen. 24:65), of the loathing which the Egyptians felt for shepherds (Gen. 46:34) are items of interest which throw light on the life of the times. Adoption is clearly implied in the relationship between Abram and Eliezer (Gen. 15:2) and was a well-known custom in patriarchal times. Mirrors are referred to as donated by the women for the construction of the laver for the tabernacle (Exod. 38:8). Such metallic mirrors (bronze or silver) were used in Egypt centuries before Moses' time. The right of the first-born son to a "double portion" is stated in Deuteronomy 21:17, a passage which explains Elisha's request for a double portion of Elijah's spirit (2 Kings 2:9). That Saul was much above the average height is pointed out only in comparison to others (1 Sam. 9:2) and in the case of Goliath in precise terms (1 Sam. 17:4). That Hebrew men wore beards is referred to in several contexts in striking fashion (e.g., 2 Sam. 10:4; 20:9; Ps. 133:2), but nowhere described as a national custom. The use of flint knives in the days of Moses and Joshua (Exod. 4:25; Josh. 5:2f.) is mentioned, although bronze (*AV*, "brass") was widely used at that period. Lamps (*AV*, "candles") are chiefly mentioned in connection with the tabernacle service. They burned olive oil. The removal of shoes in a holy place is referred to in Exodus 3:5; Joshua 5:15. The ceremony connected with the shoe as the symbol of possession appears in Deuteronomy 25:9, is illustrated in Ruth 4:7f. and has its echo in Psalm 60:8; 108:9.

The Three R's in the days of the Judges. The statement that a young man "wrote down" (*ARV*, marg.) for Gideon the names of the seventy-seven princes and elders of Succoth (Judg. 8:14) is of great significance for the history of writing. The statement is quite indefinite. The youth may have been a scribe, although this is not stated. However explained, the incident is a striking evidence of the use of writing in the time of the Judges. The retention of the word "described" (*AV*) in the text of *ARV* as a rendering here of the Hebrew word for "write" which occurs about twenty-five times in the Pentateuch indicates how hesitant scholars were at the turn of the century to recognize the early use of writing.

Chronology. The Old Testament has many chronological statements; but they are mainly in relative terms, one event being dated in terms of its relation to another event or series of events. This at times confronts the modern reader with difficult problems, some of which have received widely different answers.

The Calendar. Like the Chronology, the Calendar of the Old Testament raises many problems because it speaks in terms of customary usage and gives no detailed explanation of terms with which the reader is assumed to be familiar.

That there were twelve months in the year is to be inferred from the fact that each of the twelve months is referred to at least once, that no mention is made of a thirteenth, and that the great nations of antiquity with which Israel came in contact all employed a twelve-month year. That the months were lunar is to be inferred from the fact that the words for month (*yerach* and *chodesh*) define it in terms of the moon and more precisely the new moon. We know that the new moon was an important day in Israel (Lev. 23:24). But the lunar year is about ten days shorter than the solar. Consequently, since the three great feasts of the year were of seasonal and agricultural as well as historical significance, it was necessary to insert (intercalate) an additional month every few years to restore the harmony between the lunar and solar years. That this was done in Babylonia as early as the time of Hammurabi is a matter of record and how much farther back it goes is unknown.[107] It was probably customary in Israel in some form. But it is not mentioned in the Bible.

The months of the year are usually referred to by number. Occasionally they are mentioned by name. The Canaanite names of four are given: Abib (Exod. 13:4; 23:15; 34:18; Deut. 16:1), Ziv (1 Kings 6:1, 37 described as second month), Ethanim (1 Kings 8:2, described as the seventh month), Bul (1 Kings 6:38, described as the eighth month). These explanations are apparently added because the old names were then unfamiliar and likely to be misunderstood. The Babylonian names of seven of the months are mentioned, all of them in late post-exilic books, which indicates that they came into use during the Babylonian Captivity: Nisan (Neh. 2:1; Esth. 3:7), Sivan (Esth. 8:9), Elul (Neh. 6:15), Chislev (Neh. 1:1; Zech. 7:1), Tebeth (Esth. 2:16), Shebat (Zech. 1:7), Adar (Ezra 6:15; Esth. eight times), and the fact that the number is sometimes added (e.g., Zech. 7:1 "ninth month, Chislev") seems to make it clear that usually the months were referred to simply by number.

That the year began in the Spring is clearly stated (Exod. 13:4; cf. 12:2). This is made especially clear by the calendar of feasts in Leviticus 23. In view of this it would be possible to understand the references in Exodus 23:16; 34:22 to the "end" of the year as meaning the end of the agricultural season, which was completed by the "ingathering." But according to Josephus (*Antiq.* I.3:3) the Jews also had a secular year which began with the seventh month, the first day of which is celebrated today as Rosh Hashshanah (the beginning of the year). The reason for this double dating is not known. It is especially interesting to the Bible student, because it may explain the seeming discrepancy in Nehemiah 1:1; 2:1. If Nehemiah was writing in terms of the civil year which began with the seventh month Tishri (this name appears nowhere in the Old Testament), Chislev, the third month of the civil year would be followed four months later by Nisan the seventh month of the same year.[108] It may be significant that while here the Babylonian names of the months are given, in the latter part of the book where the feast of tabernacles is referred to, the usual designation of that month as the seventh (of the ecclesiastical year) is used three times (7:73; 8:2, 14).

An important inference which may properly be drawn from such examples as have been mentioned is this. There is a vast amount of history which the Bible does not give us. What is told us is sometimes hard to understand simply because we do not have all the facts. It is not the aim of the biblical writers to explain and justify every statement which they make. They often simply state the fact and allow it to speak for itself. Thus as we have seen the account of the leprosy of Azariah given in Kings simply states that the Lord smote the king. That was the bare fact, briefly and abruptly stated. We are to assume that the Lord's act was fully justified; and in Chronicles the reason is stated. But there are many cases where the reason is not given and we are left to explain the facts as best we may.

ERRORS IN THE MASSORETIC TEXT

The presence of errors in the text of the Old Testament as it has been transmitted to us is often alleged as an argument against its trustworthiness and authority. That there are such errors is undeniable. There are, we are told, 1353 various readings in the margin of the Hebrew Massoretic Bible.[109] Most of these variations are of minor importance. Many simply represent a difference in spelling. Some are clearly better than the reading of the text. But they were all put in the margin and not introduced into the text. A few examples must suffice.

Especially noteworthy are those cases where the variations bring the Old Testament into conflict with itself. We know for example that the letters *d* and *r* were originally so different in form that they could hardly be confused, but that in later times they were often written so much alike that this was easily possible. Thus, Riphath (Gen. 10:3) appears as Diphath (1 Chron. 1:6); Dodanim (Gen. 10:4) as Rodanim (1 Chron. 1:7). Both spellings cannot be right. But neither is "corrected" in the *MT*. Similarly, the name of the king of Zobah is spelled with *d* (Hadadezer) in 2 Samuel 8:3, 7, with *r* (Hadarezer) in 2 Samuel 10:16; 1 Chronicles 18:9f. It is possible that "Syria" (i.e. Aram) should be read as "Edom" in 2 Samuel 8:13 in view of 1 Chronicles 18:11f.; Psalm 60 heading. In such cases we must seek light from the context, from parallel passages, from the versions, or from other sources.[110]

Sometimes the variation is easily explained. In 1 Chronicles 2:7 the name of the troubler of Israel is given as Achar. In Joshua 7:1, 18, 19, 20, 24 it appears as Achan. The meaning of Achan is unknown. But Achar comes from a root which means "to trouble." So Joshua treated Achan's name as suggestive of trouble (*achor*) and called him "the troubler of Israel." Hence the name given the place of execution was "valley of Achor" (7:24, 26), i.e., "valley of trouble"; and the allusions to it in Isaiah 65:10 and Hosea 2:15 indicate that this tragic incident was long remembered. Consequently, it is very probable that some copyist confused the two names and in this way the Achan of Joshua became the Achar of Chronicles.[111]

"The five sons of Michal" (2 Sam. 21:8) should apparently read, "the five sons of Merab." According to 1 Samuel 18:19, Merab, while promised to David was given to Adriel the Meholathite. There is no mention of Michal's having born any children to David or to Palti the son of Laish of Gallim (25:44) to whom she was given by Saul. The final word regarding Michal, after her scornful treatment of David after the bringing up of the ark, "And Michal the daughter of Saul had no child unto the day of her death" (2 Sam. 6:23) seems to mean that Michal never had any children, that the shame of barrenness was hers even before David's virtual repudiation of her. The rendering "whom she brought up for Adriel" (2 Sam. 21:8 AV) is a forced and unwarranted rendering instead of "bare." It is better to regard "Michal" as a copyist's mistake for "Merab," for which there is some support in the versions.[112]

The age of Jehoiachin at his accession is given both as "eighteen" (2 Kings 24:8) and as "eight" (2 Chron. 36:9). Eighteen seems the more probable figure; and it is possible that the eight is a transcriptional error suggested by the words "in the eighth year of his reign," which obviously refers to Nebuchadnezzar's reign and not to Jehoiachin's age. But while one or the other is clearly a mistake (Keil calls it "a lapse of the pen") no attempt was made to correct it.

The "forty years" of 2 Samuel 15:7 is probably an error for "four," since Absalom was not yet forty when he died. Perhaps the "four years" would best represent the years since his recall from Geshur which would include the two years after his reconciliation with his father David.

The reading "thirty of the thirty" (2 Sam. 23:13) is clearly a mistake for "three of the thirty" (1 Chron. 11:15). "Berodach" (2 Kings 20:12) is probably a mistake for "Merodach" (Isa. 39:1). How it is to be explained we do not know.

Jehu's Letters to the Rulers of Jezreel (2 Kings 10:1). The statement that Jehu sent these letters from Jezreel to Samaria, to the chief men of Jezreel who had custody and care of Ahab's children in Samaria has been a serious problem for centuries. There is some evidence in favor of reading, "and sent unto the rulers of the city and to the elders." This would remove the difficulty. The reading "rulers of Jezreel" is a very ancient one; and the significant thing is that it has been retained, uncorrected in the MT for so many centuries despite the difficulties connected with it.

The Beginning of the Reign of Jehoiakim (Jer. 27:1). The fact that in verses 3 and 12 of this chapter as well as in 28:1 which introduces another prophecy of the same year, the name of the king is given as Zedekiah, makes it highly probable that the Jehoiakim of 27:1 is a transcriptional error.

Especially noteworthy is the statement in 2 Chronicles 22:2 that Ahaziah the son of Jehoram of Judah was "forty-two years old" when he began to reign. It is twice stated in the context (21:5, 20) that his father was thirty-two years old when he began to reign and that he reigned eight years. This would make Ahaziah older than his father. We are also told twice that he was the youngest son of Jehoram (21:17; 22:1), which makes the figure forty-two still more impossible. To this we must add the further fact that the parallel passage (2 Kings 8:26) has twenty-two, a quite possible figure, while the Greek versions of Chronicles have twenty or twenty-two. How the impossible figure forty-two got into the Hebrew text of Chronicles we do not know.

What we are concerned to point out is that for centuries this error has been preserved in the Massoretic text of the Old Testament. That the Massoretes were quite as well aware centuries ago, as we are today, that the figure forty-two is discredited by the evidence of the narrative of Chronicles itself is self-evident. Yet they did not venture to correct it.

Since proper names, especially those of foreigners, would be most likely to be mispronounced and misread, R. D. Wilson is justified in calling the accuracy with which the names of twenty-four foreign kings are reproduced in the text of the Old Testament "a phenomenon unequalled in the history of literature."[113] Paradoxical as it may sound, it is yet a remarkable fact that the very errors which are found in the Massoretic Text of the Old Testament, are a striking witness to the care with which the Jewish scribes safeguarded the text of the Oracles of God which were entrusted to them. Even where it was perfectly obvious that the reading of the text was wrong, they did not venture to change it, but put the reading which they preferred in the margin.

This attitude toward the text of the Hebrew Bible is not only significant in itself. It becomes even more remarkable when we observe the very different attitude to these Scriptures which Jewish scholars have taken in their extra-canonical writings. In the Targums, the Talmud, and in the Apocryphal and Apocalyptical Books which form such an extensive part of Jewish literature, we find many additions to and interpretations of the Sacred Text. Thus the Targums and Midrash have greatly embellished, if we may use the word in such a connection, the story of Esther. They tell us for example that the throne on which the king sat (1:2) was one which he had made for himself, an inferior throne, because he found that he could not sit on Solomon's throne, which was of course too big for him. This throne, according to Jewish tradition, had had a truly marvelous history. After being carried away by Shishak, it was brought from Egypt by Sennacherib and captured from him by Hezekiah. Then it was brought by Nebuchadnezzar to Babylon and finally taken by Cyrus to Elam. What Ahasuerus did with it when he found he could not sit in it — this we are not told.[114] They tell us that Mordecai's ancestor Shimei was the man who cursed David, that Haman was descended from Agag the Amalekite, and that his evil plans for exterminating the Jews were a punishment for Saul's failure to exterminate Amalek. They tell us that the length of the royal sceptre which the king held out to Esther was two cubits, and that the king extended it, some say to twelve cubits, others sixteen, others twenty-six, the longest estimate being sixty cubits. Such and many similarly impossible, improbable, or absurd things are to be found in the extra-canonical literature of the Jews which has long been familiar to us. There is a beautiful legend regarding the death of Aaron. It tells of Moses grief when the Lord told him that Aaron was to die, and of the loving and beautiful way in which Moses made this known to Aaron. As to this, Scripture is completely silent.[115]

Among the first scrolls discovered in the Dead Sea Caves, there was one which was at first called The Lamech Scroll but is now known as *The Scroll of the Patriarchs*. It is a curious combination of a close following of the biblical narrative and an expansion and elaboration of it in the style of the Midrash. Thus the writer expands the history of Genesis 12:10-20 very greatly, dwelling, among other things, on Sarai's physical charms, but in dealing with Chapter 14 he follows the biblical account rather closely. This contrast, this at times unbridled use of the imagination, in these extra-biblical writings makes the scrupulous fidelity of Jewish scholars in preserving the text of the Holy Scriptures all the more significant and remarkable.

This difference is illustrated by the commentary on Habakkuk which was also one of the first of the Dead Sea Scrolls to be discovered. The commentary is comparatively brief, yet considerably longer than the two chapters of the biblical text which it covers. It applies the prophecy to the times in which the commentator lived. The Chaldaeans are explained to be the Chittim; and there has been animated discussion among scholars as to whether the Chittim are the Romans or Greeks. A "teacher of righteousness" and a "wicked priest" are also referred to and mention is made of "the house of Absalom." But none of the statements are sufficiently definite to make the date of the commentary entirely clear. The interpretation is figurative or alegorical and may at times be called "wild." But what interests us in this connection is that the biblical text is apparently quoted with strict fidelity to the original. By this we mean that there does not seem to be any indication that the commentator has deliberately changed the text with a view to favoring his interpretation of it.[116]

One of the chief values of the discoveries which have been made in the Dead Sea Caves in the course of the past decades has been the discovery of several manuscripts of books of the Old Testament and a vast collection of fragments of more than a hundred others. These come from Qumran, Murabbaat, and Mird, those from Qumran being the oldest. It has been pointed out that while the biblical material from Murrabbaat agrees closely with the *MT*, some at least of the Qumran material, e.g., the fragments of Joshua and Samuel agree with the Greek *LXX*; and the inference has been drawn that the text of the Hebrew Bible was stabilized in the interval between these two periods, i.e., about A.D. 100. The objection to such an inference is that we do not know why the Qumran community followed the *LXX* in some cases and not in others. Thus the second Isaiah Scroll (IQIs[b]) agrees with the *MT* more fully than does the St. Mark Scroll (IQIs[a]). As to the history of these two manuscripts we know nothing. But it is encouraging to read such a statement as the following from the pen of one of the most diligent students of the new material, F. M. Cross, Jr.: "Certainly it was true that the text of Isaiah preserved in the Masora was based on an extremely early textual type, already at home in Palestine in the late second century B.C." Why in the case of Joshua and Judges, the Qumran scribes followed the *LXX* rather than the Hebrew as given in the *MT* we do not know. Were their relations with the Jews of Alexandria closer than with the ecclesiastical authorities at Jerusalem?

God's Thoughts and Man's Thoughts

"For my thoughts are not your thoughts, neither are your ways my ways, saith the Lord" (Isa. 55:8) expresses a truth which every student of Scripture and especially every would-be "critic" of the Bible should bear constantly in mind. For he is tempted again and again to place his own constructions upon the Bible and to take exception to what it says, because what it says is not what he thinks it ought to say.

A striking example is furnished by the prophecies of Ezekiel. In 24:1f. we read that "in the ninth year in the tenth month, in the tenth *day* of the month" the prophet was commanded to make special record of that precise day, to write it down, because on it the king of Babylon "set himself against Jerusalem." That this event and the exact date of its occurrence should be supernaturally revealed to the prophet Ezekiel, a captive in distant Babylonia, indicates its importance. Consequently, we would naturally expect that the date of the fall of the city would be revealed to the prophet in a similarly extraordinary because supernatural way. Both in 2 Kings (25:1-4) and in Jeremiah (39:1f.; 52:5f.) the two events are closely connected, the one being the inevitable result of the other. But while in Ezekiel 24:25-27; (cf. 33:21f.) the interval between the beginning of the siege and the arrival of the "escaped" is defined as a period of silence for the prophet, we find in Ezekiel no mention of the date of the fall of Jerusalem. No revelation was given to him of the fall of the city at the time that tragic event took place. But the arrival of the "escaped" is precisely recorded as having taken place on the fifth day of the tenth month of the twelfth year, i.e., a year and six months after the fall of the city (33:21).[117] This seems strange and must have some special significance.

The probable explanation is that the opening of the prophet's mouth, which was to mark the beginning of a new series of prophecies, predictions which were to be characterized by consolation rather than rebuke and threatening, was not to begin until the people had received irrefutable evidence, through the *arrival* of the "escaped," i.e., of those deported from Jerusalem after the fall of the city, that the city upon which they had centered their hopes had been destroyed. They will believe, will be forced to believe, the testimony of the remnant that has escaped, even though they had refused to hearken to the warning of the prophet that the city would certainly fall; and now that their confidence in the impregnability of their sacred city has proved vain and the woes pronounced by the prophet have found complete fulfillment, they — or at least some of them — will be ready to listen to and welcome the words of comfort which the Lord is about to speak through his prophet. So it is not the mere fact of the fall of Jerusalem, but the arrival of the "escaped" which in this case requires careful documenting. This is a probable and a sufficient explanation. But even if it is the correct one, it does not explain why the prophet should be told the very day of the beginning of the siege but be left for months in ignorance of its outcome. The obvious fact still confronts us that there is only one answer to the question asked by Job: "Canst thou by searching find out God? Canst thou find out the Almighty unto perfection?" Reverent study of Scripture will make the Christian humble and teachable.[118]

CHAPTER III

THE OLD TESTAMENT FROM WITHOUT

Having considered "The Old Testament from Within," we now turn our attention to "The Old Testament from Without" and look at it in the light of its historical setting and background. When we affirm that the Bible is a self-sufficient and self-interpreting book, we do not mean to assert that it has no connection with secular history. Redemptive history is part of secular history. It is embedded in it; and the interrelations between them are very many and often very intricate. Sacred history is not isolated history. It is history within history; and the more we learn of world history, the better will we understand that redemptive history for which secular history furnishes the stage and provides the setting.

It is no exaggeration to say that the period in which we are living is the most Janus-headed of all those of which we have any knowledge. The discoveries in the field of the natural sciences have led us to look forward with an enthusiasm and expectancy, not entirely free from apprehension and fear, into a future of seemingly limitless achievement in the mastery of the physical and material world with its seemingly inexhaustible possibilities. On the other hand, the discoveries of the archaeologist in all parts of the world have been so amazing, have made the mysterious past so exciting and intriguing, that archaeology has become a major science. "Digging for history" as it has aptly been called is claiming ever increasing attention. The spade is filling our museums with the results of successful "digs." Colleges and scientific societies are sending out teams of eager excavators who are constantly reporting discoveries which attract world-wide interest because of the surprises which are the reward of their indefatigable labors. A Mithra temple unearthed in the heart of London, colossal stone heads discovered in Guatemala, Easter Island and its strange images, Ur of the Chaldees and the tomb of Queen Shub-ad, Tutankhamun and his amazing sepulture, Mari and the Amorites, the Code of Hammurabi, the Vassal Treaties of Esarhaddon, Harappa and the Indus valley cities — a vast collection of relics of the past: curious, crude, skillful, beautiful, useful, ornamental, religious, royal, domestic, a motley and intriguing array of memorabilia of men and women of a long forgotten past!

In view of the great interest which now centers in archaeology, an

172

interest which is steadily growing, it will be well to call to mind the situation about a sesquicentennial ago, when archaeological research in the modern sense began. Napoleon's expedition to Egypt in 1798 has been referred to as marking its beginning; and the discoveries made by the French savants who accompanied him filled a score of volumes with valuable and interesting information.[1] But excavation did not begin until about half a century later: with Botta (1842) and Layard (1845) in Mesopotamia, and with Mariette (1850) in Egypt. The situation prior to this time has been well described by Ira M. Price. In *The Monuments and the Old Testament* (1899), Price included a chapter entitled "A Lone Old Testament." In it he called attention to the fact that the "Old Testament one hundred years ago stood alone in an otherwise unknown age. It was the only known representative of the ten centuries preceding the rise of Greece and Rome. One hundred years ago there was not a single document contemporaneous with the Old Testament known to be in existence." Consequently, "Its statements had to stand on their own merits. If contradicted or challenged, they could make no reply. The friends of the Old Testament had no contemporary witnesses to subpoena to the trial through which it was passing." How different the situation is today, when archaeology is one of the weapons which are constantly used both by defenders of the Old Testament and by its critics!

In his lectures on the *Development of Palestine Exploration* (1907) F. J. Bliss devoted an entire lecture to Edward Robinson (1794-1863), who has been called "'the pioneer and father of biblical geography.'"[2] While giving full credit to Robinson for his careful, scientific researches, Bliss pointed out that Robinson was a geographer rather than an archaeologist: "The true nature of the Tells or Mounds, in which centers the interest of the modern Palestine excavator, was not appreciated by him." He cited, for example, Robinson's reference to Tell-el-Hesy, where Bliss was later to discover eight superimposed cities. Robinson said of this mound: "A finer position for a fortress or fortified city could hardly be imagined. Yet we could discover nothing whatever to mark the existence of any former town or structure."[3] It was there that in 1890 archaeological excavation in Palestine, except at Jerusalem, really began.

Before we attempt to survey and evaluate the results of archaeological research, with particular reference to the Old Testament, we will do well to ponder the words of a distinguished biblical scholar, uttered more than sixty years ago, but which are even more applicable to the present day. In an address entitled "Christian Faith and the Truthfulness of Bible History,"[4] Professor Geerhardus Vos of Princeton Seminary pointed out that "Our age prides itself upon being preeminently the age of historical research." He went on at once to say "Nor is this a vain boast. More than in any previous period the records of the past are made the object of thorough, painstaking investigation,"[5] He saw a decided advantage in this appeal from philosophical speculation to historical facts. But he also saw clearly the danger inherent in this changed situation, the tendency to desupernaturalize sacred history. He described the new situation in the following terms:

First of all, we are face to face with the fact that the immemorial conflict between naturalism and supernaturalism has, more than ever before, concentrated itself in the field of history. This could not be otherwise, because it is a conflict which always assumes the specific form of whatever mode of thinking is characteristic of the age. Formerly, when the historical spirit was comparatively dormant and the speculative spirit supreme, this fight was largely waged in the philosophical field. Then the question was: Is the supernatural conceivable on the general principles of reason? Now the question is: Is the supernatural necessary according to the empirical data of history? In other words, historical study has become a powerful instrument in the service of the anti-supernaturalistic spirit of the modern age. Professing to be strictly neutral and to seek nothing but the truth it has in point of fact directed its assault along the whole line against the outstanding miraculous events of Sacred History. It has rewritten this history so as to make the supernatural elements disappear from its record. It has called into question the historicity of one after the other of the great redemptive acts of God. We need not say here that the apologetic answer to these attacks has been able and fully satisfactory to every intelligent believer. But the Christian public at large is not always able to distinguish between well-authenticated facts as such and historical constructions in which the facts have been manipulated and their interpretation shaped by *a priori* philosophical principles. People are accustomed to look upon history as the realm of facts *par excellence*, second only to pure science in the absolute certainty of its concrete results. They do not as easily detect in historical argumentation as they would in philosophic reasoning the naturalistic premises which predetermine the conclusions. It is not difficult, therefore, to give the popular mind the impression that it is confronted with an irrefutable array of evidence discrediting the Bible facts, whereas in reality it is asked to accept a certain philosophy of the facts made to discredit the Bible. Hence there has arisen in many quarters a feeling of uneasiness and concern with regard to the historical basis of facts on which Christianity has hitherto been supposed to rest.[6]

Dr. Vos pointed out that the raising of this issue had had in many circles the result that: "For some time past the assertion has been made, and it is being made in our day with greater confidence than ever, that our Christian faith and historical facts have very little or nothing to do with each other."[7] Against this position he insisted that biblical history is a supernatural history, "an organism of a divine economy of grace" and he declared: "In every one of its parts, even those that might seem to us to have but the remotest connection with the centre in Christ, it is worthy of our defense and protection."[8] And he declared, "We, for our part, believe, and we say it deliberately, that it were a thousand times better for the Church to be torn and shaken for many years to come by the conflict with criticism than to buy a shameful peace at the stupendous doctrinal sacrifice which such a position involves."[9]

A further issue with which Dr. Vos did not deal in this lecture but which has resulted from the archaeological research of the past century has been the great importance which is now attached to comparative study. When the Old Testament was generally regarded as a unique survival of the ancient past, there were those who challenged its historicity because of this fact. Today with a wealth of material discovered in Egypt, Mesopotamia and elsewhere in the Near East, dating from periods and civilizations as ancient as or far more ancient than the Mosaic, comparative study has come to figure more and more prominently in the sphere of biblical archaeology; and the uniqueness of the religion of Israel is constantly challenged on the ground that Israel did not develop in a vacuum, that her institutions must have been related to and even originally derived from these ancient and advanced civilizations which have now been brought to light. Thus both the *supernaturalness* of the religion of the Old Testament and its *uniqueness* are constantly challenged on the ground that it must have been originally similar to if not identical with these ancient cults.

For the Christian then, the most significant result of archaeological research — an inevitable one — is the one pointed out by Dr. Vos that the Bible and especially the Old Testament is now being subjected to the test of historical accuracy as never before. Every discovery of the archaeologist which has a bearing on the Bible, no matter how remote, raises the question, Does this confirm or contradict the statements of the Bible? For this reason it is especially important that the Christian reader should understand clearly what archaeology has proved, what it has not proved, and what it cannot properly be expected to prove.

Since the Old Testament deals so largely with the history of Israel and since Israel was a relatively insignificant people among the peoples of the ancient world, we cannot expect Israel to figure prominently in the records of the great nations of the past. Archaeology may set the stage, so to speak. It may prove and has proved the existence of nations and peoples and places, even of many kings and officials, mentioned in the Old Testament. It may verify many events, customs and practices. It may correct many erroneous impressions. But there is very much that it cannot be expected to prove. It may confirm the setting and background of the life of Abraham. It has done so to a remarkable degree. But it is not likely that any personal records of his life beside those contained in the Bible will ever be discovered. This is unlikely for several reasons. One is the fact that the Bible tells us so little about the life of Abraham and this little is told largely in terms of Abraham's intimate, personal experience. The other is that Abraham's contacts with the great world, even his victory over Chedorlaomer and his fellow kings (Gen. 14), were hardly likely to find a place in the historical records of his contemporaries.

It is also to be remembered that there is a vast difference between the religion of Israel and the cults of the neighboring peoples. The religion of Israel was spiritual; her neighbors were all idol-worshippers. Consequently, while images of the heathen gods — especially Astarte plaques — abound, there are no images of Israel's God to be discovered and no temples except the one at Jerusalem. Material evidences of Israel's worship (wood, stone, or metal) will therefore indicate not the true worship of her people but its perversion.

From the very beginning of modern archaeological research in Bible lands, the biblical issue, as we may call it, has figured prominently. The decipherment of the Taylor cylinder of Sennacherib (*c.* 1860) at once raised the question of the bearing of its statements on the biblical accounts.[10] The discovery of the Babylonian account of the Deluge, announced by George Smith in 1872, aroused such widespread interest that two trips by the discoverer to Nineveh in search of further evidence were financed by the London *Daily Telegraph* and a third by the British Museum. Eberhard Schrader made his reputation largely through his work *Cuneiform Texts and the Old Testament* which appeared first in German in 1872; and his successor at the University of Berlin, Friedrich Delitzsch, precipitated a storm of controversy through the *Babel-Bible* Lectures which he delivered nearly thirty years later.

The fact is that none of our archaeologists, whether actual excavators or not, have been or are today, or for that matter can be, completely objective and without prejudice or preconceived opinions. This is shown by the wide difference of opinion which prevails in critical and scientific circles today on many matters of archaeological interest. The scientist who is an anti-supernaturalist will reject the biblical record, where the supernatural is involved. The Bible believer will cling to it tenaciously as showing the presence of the hand of God in human affairs. If either accuses the other of dogmatism, he should at least be willing to admit that the same charge can be brought against himself.

There appeared in *The Biblical Archaeologist* a few years ago a somewhat surprising article by G. Ernest Wright entitled, "Is Glueck's Aim to Prove That the Bible Is True?"[11] The occasion of the writing of this brief article is to be found in several statements made by Nelson Glueck in his volume *Rivers in the Desert* to which J. J. Finkelstein took exception in a lengthy review. The statement objected to was, "It may be stated categorically that no archaeological discovery has ever controverted a biblical reference." This was regarded by Finkelstein as indicating that Glueck cannot be regarded as a truly scientific archaeologist, who views the discoveries of the excavator with complete objectivity and is quite unconcerned as to the conclusions to which they lead. Wright defended Glueck, or we may rather say, apologized for him, by admitting that Glueck's statement was extreme but excusing it on the ground that Glueck is "a warmly emotional person who is deeply attached to the things that really matter to him. He is one who really loves and respects his Bible, not simply as a cultural treasure, but as a religious testimony to faith." Wright points out that "this personal involvement" shows itself in Glueck's popular lectures and writings more than in his scholarly articles. But apparently Wright is inclined to deplore the fact that this personal involvement appears at all. He claims that "Archaeological research *by and large* has been largely backed by the humanist opinion that anything having to do with historical research, with the investigation of our past, is an obvious 'good' which needs no justification." This is quite true. But it is not the whole truth and his claim that "The introduction of the theme, 'archaeology confirms biblical history,' into the discussion of *scientific* archaeological matters is a comparatively recent phenomenon," is misleading, to say the least. Would Dr. Wright deny the name scientific to the work of Sayce, Naville, Clay, R. D. Wilson, J. D. Davis, Orr, Kyle, Dougherty, Whitcomb, Wiseman, and many others whose names might be added, because they have made careful and effective use of the results of archaeology in their defense of the Old Testament? Would he claim that Winckler and Jensen and Delitzsch were unscientific because they used these same results to discredit the Old Testament? As a matter of fact, aside from such exact sciences as mathematics, scientific research never has been and cannot be entirely objective. Archaeology concerns ancient man. It consequently involves such important questions as his origin, nature, and development. The evolutionist will view this subject from a more or less thoroughly naturalistic viewpoint; the creationist will view the same evidence quite differently. Each should endeavor to gather all the evidence and to evaluate it as accurately as possible. This is especially necessary in this field, because it is so vast and the evidence so incomplete, and at times so ambiguous and misleading.

MAGNITUDE OF THE TASK

First of all we must note the vastness of the field which confronts the biblical archaeologist. This is illustrated by a few statistics which have been recently given by D. J. Wiseman.[12] He estimates the number of sites which have been located in Bible lands, that is, in the Fertile Crescent and neighboring countries, at more than 25,000 and the number of cuneiform documents already discovered there at about half a million, an estimate which does not include the thousands of documents discovered in Egypt. This gives us a general idea of the vastness of the field and of the extent of the finds which have been made in the course of little more than a century of excavation. When Wiseman goes on to tell us that "several hundred of these long-buried ruins have been sounded, but less than a hundred have been thoroughly explored" and when he adds the further qualification, "none exhaustively," we get some idea of the present situation in the field of archaeology, which is, that while much has been uncovered, there is vastly more that has not. In a survey of archaeological research and excavation he gives a listing of twenty-four cities of Babylonia, in which are included such great cities as Babylon, Erech, Nippur, Sippar and Ur, at some of which excavations were carried out, more or less continuously, for a decade or more.[13] The list for Palestine totals fifty-four;[14] and to it several further names might now be added: Ashdod, Beth-hakkerem, Caesarea, Succoth, Zarethan. Similar lists for Assyria, Egypt, Anatolia, Arabia, the Aegean, the Indus Valley and other places where excavations have been carried out would add up to a very impressive total. Accident has figured largely in the discoveries that have been made. Among the important "finds" due wholly or largely to accident we may list the Rosetta Stone, which furnished the key to the Hieroglyphs, the palace of Sargon at Khorsabad, the Tell-el-Amarna Letters, Boghazkeui and the Hittites, Tell-el-Obeid and its pre-historic culture, Nuzu and the Hurrians, Ras Shamra and the Ugaritic alphabet texts, the Amorite city of Mari, and the Dead Sea Scrolls. Such accidental discoveries have often led to prolonged and exhausting excavation.

Few excavators have been as successful as Sir Leonard Woolley. For years he carried on excavations at Ur (1922-1934) with a success which is described by Parrot as "dazzling." He proved Ur to have been a great center of Sumerian culture. The greatest of his discoveries there was the Royal Tombs, especially that of Queen Shub-Ad, which is now dated about 2500 B.C. Writing years later of his work there Woolley describes the mound as "immense," and while stating that the maximum number of men employed at one time "topped the four hundred," he adds, "only a minute fraction of the city's area was thoroughly explored."[15] Yet very much has been learned. We know that this great Sumerian city reached the height of its glory under its Third Dynasty of kings (*c.* 2124-2016 B.C.), which may indicate that Abram and his father Terah lived in Ur during its most flourishing period. It may even have been the waning of this period of prosperity which induced Terah to go (or return?) to Haran. Ur was conquered by Hammurabi of the First Dynasty of Babylon. Yet Ur still enjoyed great renown more than a thousand years later. For we know that both Nebuchadnezzar and Cyrus claim to have restored the great temple there.

How necessarily incomplete the results of excavations have been at most if not all the sites where extensive work has been carried on is illustrated by the work at Calah. This ancient capital of Assyria was first excavated by Layard in 1845-47; and very successfully. He discovered seven palaces, notably those of Ashurnasirpal II and Shalmaneser III, one of the most important single discoveries being the Black Obelisk of the latter king, which mentions the tribute paid to him by Iaua son of Humri. About a century elapsed before excavations were resumed there in 1949 by Mallowan and with equally remarkable results.[16] At the entrance of the palace of Ashurnasirpal, a stele was discovered with an inscription of 154 lines, which describes the royal feast given to celebrate the opening of his palace in 879 B.C., giving the full menu which he offered to 69,574 guests whom he entertained for ten days, an event which reminds us of the great feast given by Ahasuerus which is described in the book of Esther. The discovery of the palace or fort of Shalmaneser III produced an amazing collection of ivories, as to which Mallowan writes, "It is no exaggeration to suggest that originally these treasures may have contained some 10,000 pieces of which only a small but splendid fraction now survives." More than a thousand inscribed tablets were also discovered. Of especial interest is a collection of fragments of treaty documents.[17] These latter are described by Wiseman as parts of eight copies of a treaty imposed by Esarhaddon on Ramataia and other vassal kings who were summoned to Nineveh in 672 B.C. to acknowledge Ashurbanipal as his heir and invoking terrible curses on treaty breakers. A further interesting discovery is what is described as "the oldest book," a series of ivory writing boards, which an inscription on the ivory cover proves to have been "a sixteen leaved polyptich," with evidence of the use of wax, as the writing surface and probably having had gold hinges, and dating at 711 B.C.

Such discoveries as these, made recently at one of the first sites to be excavated in Mesopotamia, indicate very clearly how vastly much remains to be done if a clear picture of ancient history is to be obtained and how cautious archaeologists should be in attributing finality to their discoveries.

When we think of the thousands of cuneiform inscriptions, written on colossal winged bulls or great alabaster murals, of the six- and eight-sided prism inscriptions, and of the numberless tablets of all kinds — contract tablets, letters, religious texts, omen tablets, prayers, hymns, magical, mythological, mathematical and astronomical texts — which have been discovered in Babylonia, and of the no less amazing discoveries in Egypt, the results of excavation in Palestine seem pitifully meager.

Writing in 1925, some fifteen years after his lengthy excavations at Gezer, Macalister made this rather surprising statement: "The chief light shed by excavation upon Palestinian political history has come, not from Palestine itself, but from foreign countries which from time to time influenced it in one way or another."[18] The statement is largely true today.

The paucity of the results of Palestinian excavation, so far as literary remains are concerned, was strikingly illustrated, when in 1950, the Princeton University Press published a volume edited by J. B. Pritchard of Harvard, entitled *Ancient Near Eastern Texts Relating to the Old Testament*. It is a book of about five hundred quarto pages. It contains the translations of texts, usually with brief comments, made by eleven leading archaeologists. This material is of great variety; and it is translated from Egyptian, Sumerian, Accadian, Hittite, Ugaritic, Aramaic, and Hebrew. The section entitled "Palestinian Inscriptions" is by Albright. It covers three pages, three pages out of nearly five hundred, less than one per cent. A very meager result from more than half a century of exploration and research! Extremely so, when we note that nearly one-third of the space is devoted to the Mesha inscription discovered in Moab in 1868 and the Siloam inscription discovered at Jerusalem in 1880, both before the era of excavation began. The only results of recent excavation included are the Gezer calendar (1908), and several of the ostraca from Samaria (1910), and Lachish (1935). Many volumes could be filled with the translation of the vast material which has been discovered in Egypt and Babylonia. Only a very small part is reproduced in this volume. But three pages do not represent a selection; they contain about all of the literary remains discovered in Palestine up to the present time which are sufficiently extensive and intelligible to be worth publishing. So Albright's caution is needed as a warning against overoptimism. After listing some of the notable discoveries made outside of Palestine, he adds: "But again it must be emphasized that the really great contribution of ancient Eastern Archaeology has been in the total picture, which enables us to see the life of the Chosen People against the background of the surrounding world. This is a contribution before which everything else fades into insignificance."[19]

We observe further that these results are not only meager; they are also more or less uncertain. In *The Archaeology of Palestine*, Albright speaks quite frankly of the mistakes which archaeologists have made in the past. He cites as a striking example, the excavations conducted by Macalister at Gezer (1902-9) which were described in three splendid volumes in 1912.[20] Albright reminds us that they were hailed as "a monumental achievement." Then he goes on to say: "But almost everything in them has had to be redated and re-interpreted; for instance, a fragment of a cuneiform tablet from about 1400 B.C. was dated about the sixth century while the famous Gezer Calendar was dated several centuries too late because of the erroneous ceramic chronology."[21] Why was this? It was because, so Albright tells us, Macalister failed to recognize the "almost complete gap in the history of the occupation of Gezer between the tenth and the fifth centuries." Assuming "continuous occupation" of the site, Macalister reached conclusions which are now regarded as seriously mistaken.

In speaking of the very extensive excavations carried on by the University of Chicago at Megiddo, Albright tells us that the initial plan to "dig the great site systematically stratum after stratum fortunately had to be abandoned because of the prohibitive expense." It cost as it was nearly a million dollars. Then he adds: "Our use of the adverb 'fortunately' may seem strange, but it must be realized that the very best techniques of today will probably seem primitive a century hence, and it is a sad mistake to exhaust the possibilities of any important site like Megiddo."[22]

These statements from one who is widely regarded as our foremost American archaeologist, are quoted for the purpose of calling attention to the fact that the final word has not been said as to matters archaeological, that conclusions which were announced quite positively fifty, twenty-five, even ten years ago are today seriously questioned or positively denied. No one will assert that all the mistaken and unwarranted conclusions of the archaeologist are a thing of the past. The revolutionary discoveries at Mari, Ras Shamra, Calah and in the Dead Sea Caves are too recent to make it at all proper for scholars to assert that there will be and can be no further changes, even radical changes, in the situation tomorrow or ten years hence. Even as to matters regarding which we were thought to have quite a good deal of information there have been quite remarkable changes of viewpoint and estimate. The radical changes which have been made in the dating of Hammurabi are a conspicuous example of this. Writing in 1949 Rowley made the statement that "anything written before 1940 on the chronology of the first half of the second millennium B.C. is in need of revision."[23] Yet despite such statements and admissions as these, we often find archaeologists speaking with a positiveness with regard to what happened thousands of years ago which is not justified by our present knowledge and may require radical revision when or if more light is obtained. And, what is especially regrettable, we find them doing so in statements and assertions which challenge and contradict the evidence given in the Old Testament.

Limitations of space will not permit an adequate survey of the achievements of the archaeologist in Bible Lands.[24] By way of illustration we here confine ourselves to three of the many sites where extensive excavations have been carried on: *Tell-el-Hesi, Tell-ed-Duweir,* and *Tell-es-Sultan.*

TELL-EL-HESI

Notable as the first of the mounds to be excavated in Palestine is *Tell-el-Hesi, ca.* twenty-five miles west of Hebron. Petrie started the work there in 1890 and it was continued by Bliss for several years. A cuneiform tablet was found containing the name Zimrida. Since it was known from the Amarna Letters that a man of that name was governor of Lachish (in writing to the Pharaoh he calls himself "the man of Lachish")[25] and since a mound in the vicinity was called *Umm Lakis* it was inferred that this was the site of ancient Lachish; and for many years this identification was quite widely accepted as correct. In 1907, thirteen years after his three years of excavation at Tell-el-Hesi were ended, Bliss, in referring to the more than 700,000 cubic feet of earth which had been removed by the excavators, stated that it "represented the material out of which had been built successively eight mud-brick towns, all bearing the name of Lachish, and covering a period of over 1,200 years."[26] As a matter of fact not one of these eight mud-brick towns showed any clear evidence of its ever having borne the name Lachish. It is now widely held that *Tell-el-Hesi* is Eglon which like Lachish was one of the five cities which sought to punish Gibeon for making peace with Israel (Josh. 10:3). This change in identification was due to the excavation of a near-by site, *Tell-ed-Duweir.*

TELL-ED-DUWEIR

During 1932-38 excavations were conducted by the Wellcome-Marston Expedition, under the leadership of J. L. Starkey, at *Tell-*

ed-Duweir a few miles distant from *Tell-el-Hesi* to the northeast. It is one of the largest mounds in Palestine, covering about eighteen acres and excavation has proved it to have been a very strongly fortified city.[27] Its water supply was assured by a deep well or cistern "cut 144 feet down at the northwest corner requiring the excavation of more than half a million cubic yards of limestone." A pit containing fifteen hundred bodies is regarded as evidencing the intensity of the siege. But whether this siege was by Sennacherib or Nebuchadnezzar is a matter of dispute.[28] The most important discovery made there consisted of the ostraca (18 in number, later increased to 21) on which there was writing in black ink in the Phoenician alphabet script. Of these twenty-one letters only five or six are sufficiently long and legible to be of any value. In fact Professor Jirku of Bonn asserted in 1939 that the identification of Tell-ed-Duweir with Lachish depends on a single statement in one of these potsherd letters. It reads as follows: "And (my lord) will recognize (i.e., will please note) that as far as the signal station at Lachish is concerned, we are giving heed to all the signs, which my Lord has given." And he adds "for we cannot see Azekah." Jirku regarded this statement as obscure and denied that it proved Tell-ed-Duweir to be Lachish.[29]

In addition to the ostraca which date either from the time of Sennacherib or of Nebuchadnezzar, an inscribed dagger and fragments of a ewer were discovered in the Late Bronze Age temple. They contained very brief inscriptions in early alphabetic script. On the one fragment the inscription reads according to Albright, "A gift, a sheep and . . . as a favor." The other has the phrase "in return for three."[30] Another discovery consisted of a bowl which was broken into twenty-five fragments on which an Egyptian tax collector had written certain memoranda. From the fact that all twenty-five pieces were found together and that the script resembled that of the time of Merneptah it has been claimed that the shattering of the vase took place at the time of the conquest by Joshua.[31]

At present the identification with Lachish seems to be increasingly accepted. Albright declares that it "unquestionably represents biblical Lachish."[32] But it is significant that Kathleen Kenyon confines herself to the less confident statement, "which must be identified as Lachish, since there is no other site of sufficient importance in the neighborhood"[33]— a decidedly disappointing statement in view of the many years devoted to the excavation of the site.

A singular fact with regard to Lachish is that Sennacherib, so far as we know, never mentioned the *capture* of Lachish in his *Annals*. Yet one of the best-known bas-reliefs from his palace at Nineveh pictures the siege of Lachish in a very vivid way. Kraeling infers that this must have been "a particularly satisfying memory to Sennacherib."[34] If so, why did he fail to mention its capture in his *Annals?*

Thus Lachish, or perhaps we should still say Tell-ed-Duweir, illustrates the successes and the failures of archaeological research. It has notable achievements to its credit. But the evidence is so fragmentary that definite conclusions are hard to arrive at; and widely different views have been advanced by scholars on the basis of the very meager evidence.

TELL-ES-SULTAN (JERICHO)

The mound lying on the outskirts of modern Jericho naturally was one of the first to claim the attention of excavators. Warren excavated there for a short time about 1868 under the auspices of the Palestine Exploration Fund. In 1908-11 Sellin and Watzinger conducted extensive excavations there. Several years later they published an elaborate account of their findings. They distinguished seven strata, and identified the middle one as Israelite. But it is now claimed that, owing to their inadequate knowledge of sequence-dating, "the successive remains of buildings were entirely erroneously ascribed by the Austro-German Expedition."[35] The second major expedition was conducted by John Garstang of Liverpool University. It began in 1930 and continued over a period of six or seven years. After four years of excavation of Jericho, Garstang declared that he had examined "more than 100,000 specimens or fragments and had not discovered anything that showed a later date than that of Amenhotep III, whose scarabs were found in the tomb deposits."[36] So he dated the destruction of the Bronze Age City by Joshua at about 1400 B.C. This date was disputed in favor of a date more than a century later. Albright claimed that the reason scholars differed was because the site had not been adequately excavated.

In 1952 excavations were resumed under the leadership of Kathleen Kenyon. We shall discuss presently the astonishing discoveries as to the great age of prehistoric Jericho. Here we are concerned with the destruction at the time of the Conquest. The most important conclusion and, if true, a disappointing one, is, as stated by Miss Kenyon that the houses of Late Bronze Age Jericho have "almost entirely disappeared." If this is true then there is on the mound itself almost nothing left of the town which Joshua captured. Two things are, however, to be noted in this connection. Miss Kenyon tells us that "over most of the summit of the *tell* even the houses of the certainly populous Middle Bronze town have vanished, and only levels of the Early Bronze Age remain." With commendable caution, therefore, she adds:

"It must be admitted that it is not impossible that a yet later Bronze Age town may have been even more completely washed away than that which so meagerly survives." But she insists that this town (the one captured by Joshua) must have been very small. "Any difficulties of reconciling this date with evidence from elsewhere may well be accounted for," she tells us, "by the small scale of this actual invasion by Joshua, and the gradual spread of Israelite influence."[37]

These decidedly negative results of the excavations have unfortunately been extensively used to discredit the biblical account of the destruction of Jericho. In an article in the *National Geographic Magazine*, G. E. Wright reminds us that "Even those who know little about the Bible have heard how Joshua 'fit de Battle of Jericho' and won for his people the land of milk and honey promised by the Lord." Then he goes on to say "Investigations at the site of Jericho itself, however, have been inconclusive.... Perhaps in Joshua's time Jericho was already an uninhabited *tell,* or mound of ruins: or perhaps the centuries have merely eroded all signs of the Israelite victory."[38] Elsewhere he stated it as follows: "An inference would be that whatever there was at the time was hardly the imposing city envisaged from the earlier excavations.... The Jericho of Joshua's day may have been little more than a fort. It was the first victory in Western Palestine for the invaders, however, and the memory of the great city that once stood there undoubtedly influenced the manner in which the event was later described."[39] Thus it appears that while Dr. Wright regards the results of excavation as inconclusive, he is ready to admit that the Jericho of Joshua's time may have been an "uninhabited tell," which would reduce the biblical story to legend, or that it may have been "little more than a fort," evidence of which might be easily eroded in the course of centuries. Both of these alternatives mean that the account given in Joshua is not true to fact. Such a conclusion is doubly unfortunate since Dr. Wright himself points out how impressive is the account of the capture of Jericho as we meet it in the Book of Joshua, and how deep an impression it makes on even the casual reader of the Bible.

This attitude is unfortunately taken by many archaeologists today. The biblical record is either rejected outright, or treated as late and unreliable and accepted only insofar as it can be fitted into the conclusions of the archaeologists. Miss Kenyon feels obliged to discuss the biblical account because "the capture of Jericho plays such an important part in the entry of the Israelites into Palestine."[40] But her solution is "critical" not biblical. She tells us that "the earlier books of the Old Testament are true history, but it is a traditional history, a record of tribal events transmitted verbally," that the books of the Pentateuch (and presumably Joshua) are "quite late, perhaps not earlier than the seventh century B.C." Back of them lies the "traditional history" and "Traditional, verbal, history is incomplete. Ultimately," she assures us, "archaeology will be the decisive criterion," but she admits that this will be so "only when the archaeological time-scale has been firmly fixed, which is not yet the case." As to the size of the Israelite host which entered Palestine under Joshua she states that it is the general opinion among scholars that their number could not have exceeded six or seven thousand and that three to five thousand is "a more likely number."[41] In other words, the "true history" of the fall of Jericho as recorded in the Bible can be accepted as true only in so far as it fits into the still uncertain conclusions of the archaeologists. It is conceded that allowance must be made for centuries of erosion and pilfering. But this cannot justify the acceptance of the biblical account as fully dependable!

The statements which have been quoted are significant because they either minimize or reject the biblical record which states that special, supernatural resources were provided to sustain the Israelites during their wilderness journey and sojourn, and that the fall of Jericho was a mighty act of God. Yet the archaeologist is forced to admit that "the limitation of archaeology" is that "it can only concern itself with those material remains which have survived,"[42] while in the case of the Bible it is the immaterial, the supernatural and spiritual which is of supreme importance.

From such statements as the above two things clearly emerge. The one is that the confident statements made by some writers as to the wonderful way in which archaeology has confirmed the Bible and confounded the critics are in need of careful qualification. Archaeology has confirmed the Bible at many points. This is generally recognized and is very gratifying. But at others, as in this instance, it has raised serious difficulties. In the nature of the case, it must do so. The record of the past, especially of the remote past, is fragmentary at best and difficult to read. Jericho illustrates this clearly.

It is deplorable that statements are not seldom made on the basis of meager evidence even by eminent archaeologists which challenge or deny the correctness of biblical statements. Thus Wright entitles the second chapter of his valuable book, *Biblical Archaeology* (1957), "Giants in the Earth" using Genesis 6:4 as a proof-text. He asserts that this represents the view widely held in the past that ancient men were of gigantic size. He then proceeds to argue that archaeology has disproved this idea and that the giants of ancient times were giants in personality or ability and not in stature. Yet the word *nephilim* (rendered by "giants" in *AV* following the *LXX*) occurs only here in the description of that antediluvial civilization which was utterly destroyed by the Flood and in the report of the spies (Num. 13:33) which was clearly colored and distorted by their cowardly fears.

As compared with the legends to be found in rabbinical lore,[43] the Old Testament is remarkably conservative. In speaking of the Rephaim and of the sons of Anak, it makes it very clear that it is speaking of exceptional men, men of unusual stature, but not of monsters. Caleb was not afraid to match his strength against the sons of Anak (Josh. 14:12); and David's warriors mastered the sons of the giant (2 Sam. 21:15-22). Goliath is the *only* man whose exact height is stated in Scripture (6 cubits and a span, about 9¼ feet). This makes it clear that he was a man of very extraordinary stature, which was the reason the Philistines made him their champion. Two Greek texts (Codex B of the *LXX* and *Lucian*) reduce the 6 cubits to 4. This would make Saul a taller man than Goliath (1 Sam. 9:2). Would Dr. Wright use this method to make Goliath only a giant in personality or ability? We are told that Og's couch (sarcophagus?) was 9 cubits long. But this does not necessarily mean that Og was much taller than Goliath. The results of archaeological research are much too meager to warrant the challenging of the statements of the Bible in the field of anthropometry.

Miss Kenyon tells us that the skeletons recently unearthed at Jericho indicate that "the expectation of life at this period [that of the Patriarchs] was short. Many individuals seem to have died before they were thirty-five and few seem to have reached the age of fifty." So she concludes that "The biblical figures only reflect the veneration felt for the tribal ancestors to whom tradition came to ascribe great years and wisdom."[44]

The excavation of *Tell-el-Hesi* was specially significant because it was there that Petrie introduced the principle of sequence dating which has since then figured so prominently in archaeological research. It required the careful study of the strata in which artifacts, usually pottery fragments, were discovered in order to determine the relative temporal sequence of the various types (the ceramic sequence) where historical information in the form of inscriptions is entirely lacking.

When we examine the results of the excavations at these and other sites in Palestine in the perspective of the far-flung archaeological research in the Near East and in other distant lands, we are as already stated rather disappointed and dismayed at the paucity of the results which have been obtained.

It is quite true that the spade has discovered in the mounds in Palestine the remains of great fortified cities with gates and bars, with high walls, deep wells, elaborate water tunnels, cisterns, burial pits, strata representing layer after layer of occupation, going back in many cases to pre-historic times. By the study of pottery patterns it has determined a time-sequence which is of value where documentary evidence is wanting. But the paucity of such evidence is both remarkable and regrettable.

It is one of the ironies of human life that of all the things that the hand of man has made, one of the most fragile is also one of the most indestructible. Go to a famous museum and there you will find beautiful china, porcelain, pottery, glass, wonderful ceramic collections, preserved in glass cases and guarded with great care. But in many a refuse dump in this country or abroad, you will find pieces, broken pieces, of the same pottery or crockery or glass ware, ranging from the coarsest earthenware up to delicate Wedgwood china and Favrile glass. Broken, worthless, yet all but indestructible! And so it was in the long centuries of the ancient past. When Isaiah would describe the nothingness of mortal man in comparison with the God who has made him he exclaims: "Woe unto him that striveth with his Maker! A potsherd among the potsherds of the earth" (45:9, *ARV*). And when he would describe utter destruction he speaks of a break in a wall so utter that there will not be left a sherd big enough to "take fire from the hearth, or to dip up water out of the cistern" (30:14). And when another inspired writer would picture to us the utter poverty and abject misery of Job he tells us: "And he took him a potsherd to scrape himself therewith; and he sat among the ashes" (2:8). It is regarding this humble potsherd that Petrie declared two generations ago, that a knowledge of pottery is really the essential key to all archaeological research. And even today it is largely the progress which has been made in the study of "potsherd chronology," which is the greatest achievement of exploration and excavation in Palestine.

This achievement is not to be minimized or disparaged. It is indeed a great one; and the archaeologists who have dug down through stratum after stratum and pieced together fragments of broken pottery, and tried to determine their relative order and date by the often quite wide differences in pattern and in decoration, which they exhibit and to gauge the type and degree of culture which they represent are deserving of high praise for their indefatigable and sometimes ill-rewarded efforts. But the very fact that they have been forced to work so largely with broken crockery and similar artifacts, is a striking confirmation of the prophecy of our Lord concerning Jerusalem: "There shall not be left here one stone upon another that shall not be thrown down" (Matt. 24:2). And if Jesus said this about that wonderful temple, which wicked Herod had "adorned with goodly stones and gifts," ought we to be surprised, that throughout Palestine the potsherd should be an important witness to the achievements of a race, "which received the law of God by the disposition of angels and did not keep it" (Acts 7:53)?

In view of the great number of sites of buried cities which have been identified and the vast labor required to excavate them even partially — stubborn and even appalling facts which might seem to make the task of the archaeologist a hopeless one — it will be well to bear in mind these words of the eminent French archaeologist, Parrot: "Except for Akkad, all the great capital cities of the Ancient East have now been located. The hundreds of Tells as yet unexcavated cover sites of small provincial towns, and it may be doubted whether anything unearthed in them will do more than recall or implement finds already made."[45] This statement may be true in general. But unfortunately it may be difficult or impossible for us to decide in advance as to the relative importance of these provincial sites and some of them may conceal information which throws welcome and important light on the general picture as well as on the details of ancient history. Mari might have qualified as a provincial town until it was located and excavated by Parrot, as a result of which we know it now as an important Amorite city. Ugarit was scarcely more than mentioned in ancient records. But its discovery and excavation marked another important step in archaeological research. Alalakh has proved to be another important site.

PRE-HISTORY

The digging of a great stratification pit at Nineveh in 1932 was indicative of the fact that in recent years more and more attention has been given by archaeologists to the pre-historic period. Earlier excavators had at times discovered examples of crude or pictographic writing and crude objects of various kinds which they recognized as apparently dating from very ancient times. But at first they were mainly interested in the discovery of monuments of great historic and artistic interest and value.

In Egypt, prehistoric research began with Petrie's excavations at Naqada, near Thebes, in 1894; and subsequent excavations have led to the distinguishing of four or more prehistoric cultures in Egypt: Tasian, Badarian, Amratian, Gerzian, Semainean and Merindian. These are all described as pre-Dynastic. More or less extensive excavation of various sites has shown great differences in the antiquity, length of occupation and periods covered.

As in Egypt a number of different types of culture have been distinguished in Mesopotamia, named, as in the case of Egypt, after the sites where they were first discovered: Hassuna, Samarra, Halaf, Obeid, Early Uruk, Late Uruk, Jemdat Nasr. All of these come under the general classification of Neolithic and Chalcolithic, which preceded the Bronze Age. Thus about the time that Woolley was carrying on his eminently successful excavations at Ur, members of the same expedition carried on excavations at Tell-el-Obeid (1919, 1922-23), a small mound about four miles away. There they found a distinctive prehistoric culture marked by a characteristic type of pottery, no writing, no use of metals. They called it the Obeid period. At Erech where German expeditions had worked from 1928-39, a large number of tablets in pictographic writing were discovered and published by Falkenstein in 1941. Within about ten miles of Nineveh several mounds were investigated, Tepe Gawra (1927, 1931-38), Arpachiyah (1932), Tell Billa (1930-33). At Tepe Gawra not a single written document was discovered in the twenty-six occupation levels which were distinguished. Arpachiyah also proved to be a prehistoric site, as did Tell Billa. The excavations at Obeid have thrown light upon the question as to the early inhabitants of Ur, because the distinctive Obeid pottery has been found at Ur below the typical Sumerian levels. This raises the problem whether the Sumerians were the descendants of the Obeid people or their conquerors. This question has been much discussed and experts differ regarding its solution.

By Neolithic is usually meant that period which was marked by the making of polished stone implements, by settled life and agriculture, by the domestication of animals and by the making of pottery. Until recently its beginning was placed at *c.* 6000 B.C. and the beginning of the Chalcolithic, the first appearance of metal, about 4500 B.C. But recent excavations at Jericho have pushed the date for Neolithic considerably further back. As a result of her excavations there Kathleen Kenyon gives the following time sequence:

> Mesolithic (or Proto-Neolithic), 13 feet of structureless deposit;
> Neolithic, divided into
> > Pre-pottery A and Pre-pottery B
> > Pottery A and Pottery B.
> Proto-Urban (or Chalcolithic) A, B, C. (C not found at Jericho)

all of which precede the Early Bronze Age. She describes the Mesolithic as represented by "innumerable floors . . . of slight hut-like structures." Regarding the Neolithic period two statements are especially significant. The two Pottery sequences were found to represent "undoubtedly a retrogression as far as Palestine, represented by Jericho, is concerned"; and the differences between the two classes of Pre-pottery and Pottery appeared to be due to different peoples and probably violent overthrow. While the Pottery A people brought with them the use of pottery, "in every other respect they were much more primitive than their predecessors." She would date the tower built by the Pre-pottery A people "at least as early as 7000 B.C." As to this Pre-pottery period she tells us:

We may therefore envisage pre-pottery Neolithic Jericho as a culture with all the attributes of civilization, except that of a written language. The town must have been almost modern, or at least medieval in appearance and it must have been surrounded by fertile fields.[46]

She speaks of this as "the revolutionary picture that Jericho has given us of a period nine or ten thousand years ago." In view of what might be called extravagant claims for the early date of Neolithic Jericho, Miss Kenyon in making the statement "It is a literal fact that at the time of writing (March, 1960) Jericho stands by itself in these periods between the eighth and fifth Millennia B.C."[47] expresses the opinion that this uniqueness will be disproved by further excavations elsewhere. This qualifying statement has been promptly confirmed by the discoveries in 1961 at Catal Huyuk (*c.* 30 miles S.E. of Konya) of a pre-pottery town three to four times the size of Jericho.

In view of the fact that for these remote periods, the evidence is so meager — for the pottery period depending on material, shape, decoration, etc., and for the pre-pottery period on the artifacts which have been discovered — we take note of this word of caution as to the danger attending dependence on "sequence chronology." Dr. Kenyon tells us: "Now it is recognized that many cultures represent regional developments, and several may have existed side by side."[48] And she warns us that "The older sequence-method tended to produce very inflated chronologies, which have had to be considerably reduced now that the picture has become more coherent." Whether or not this word of warning will prove applicable to the early dates assigned to Jericho remains to be seen. However, the net result of these researches into the pre-historical has been to show that back of the literary period which begins at least a thousand years before the time of Abraham, there is to be found a pre-literary period of perhaps several millennia which represented a remarkably advanced type of culture. This has effectually disposed of the claim made so confidently only a few decades ago that the patriarchal age in Palestine belongs to the realm of myth and legend.

WRITING

The archaeological research which has been briefly described has led to the discovery of inscriptions written in a number of different

scripts. The story of the deciphering of these scripts, often quite difficult, is as thrilling as the discovery of the inscriptions themselves. The
accidental discovery of the Rosetta Stone in 1798, with its threefold
inscription (in Hieroglyphic and Hieratic Egyptian and in Greek) enabled Champollion and Young to decipher the ancient Egyptian with
the help of the Coptic. The trilingual inscriptions of Darius at Behistun
enabled Rawlinson to discover that two of the languages were Persian
and Babylonian. The discovery that Babylonian was a Semitic language
akin to Hebrew and Arabic, was followed by the finding in the
Babylonian inscriptions of the presence of another language, Sumerian,
from which the Babylonians had borrowed their script and many of
their customs. And the Sumerians are now regarded as one of the important peoples of the ancient world. At Boghazkeui Winckler discovered in 1906 cuneiform tablets written in Hittite, which led to the
rediscovery of the Hittites and their language. In 1925 excavations
were begun at Nuzu where cuneiform tablets were found which led
to the discovery of the Hurrians, with whose language we are still
very imperfectly acquainted. The more than 300 letters, discovered at
Tell-el-Amarna in Egypt about 1887 and addressed chiefly to the
Pharaohs Amenhotep III and his son Ikhnaton, by kings and governors
of the Near East, of Babylon, Mitanni, Byblos, Tyre, Jerusalem, Lachish, indicate clearly how extensively the Babylonian cuneiform script
was used in the Near East about the middle of the second millennium
B.C.

The date of the discovery of writing is not definitely known. Professor Gelb of the University of Chicago, distinguishes "seven original
and fully developed systems of writing" which he thinks "could *a
priori* claim independent origin."[49] Three of these, Sumerian, Proto-
Elamite, and Egyptian he dates at about 3000 B.C., giving Sumerian a
slight priority (3100 B.C.), the Babylonian being derived from the
Sumerian. These systems of writing had very crude beginnings, were
very cumbersome, and used many signs or symbols some of which had
several different values, representing an idea, a word, a syllable, or a
vowel. More than three hundred were used in the Sumero-Babylonian
system. But despite their complexity these systems were extensively
used and over long periods of time. The Sumerian system continued in
use among the Babylonians until about the Christian era. This long
history has made it possible to trace the development of writing in
Babylonia, for example, from crude pictographic forms to the beautiful "spencerian" writing, as we may call it, of the scribes of Ashurbanipal's library.

Alphabetic Writing. In 1904-5 Petrie discovered at Serabit-el-Qadim in the Sinaitic Peninsula graffiti written in an alphabet script which is widely regarded as the ancester of the Phoenician alphabet. Later, ancient alphabetic inscriptions were also found at Byblos. This script may date from 2000 B.C. or even earlier. Syllabic scripts have been found in Crete and Greece from before 1500 B.C.[50] The evidence serves to show that at quite an early date, centuries before the time of Moses, various attempts were made to discover simple means of written communication between the various peoples of antiquity. If the Canaanite (Phoenician) alphabet script goes back to 2000 B.C., the Amarna letters prove that for some 500 years after its invention the Babylonian cuneiform, despite its complexity, continued to be the usual script for correspondence in the Near East. It was used by the Assyrian, Chaldean, and Persian kings in their royal inscriptions. It was used on contract tablets of the 5th century B.C. some of which contain Aramaic dockets written in alphabetic script.

The extensive use of alphabetic writing, despite its simplicity, apparently came about only gradually. Breasted claimed that "true alphabet letters" were discovered in Egypt twenty-five hundred years before they were used elsewhere and "had the Egyptian been less a creature of habit" might have been put in use as early as 3500 B.C.[51] But they were not so used. The discovery in 1929 at Ras Shamra (Ugarit) of mythological tablets dating from c. 1500 B.C. and written in an alphabetic cuneiform script of about thirty letters is very significant for the light which it throws on the history of writing.[52] Especially interesting is the fact that tablets have been found on which the letters of the alphabet are given in the same order as they appear in Hebrew in the 119th Psalm.[53] The evidence though meager indicates, according to Wiseman, that "Throughout the Ancient Near East, from at least about 3100 B.C. onward, writing was a hallmark of civilization and progress" and that "by 1500 B.C. the *alphabet* came into general use in Syria-Palestine."[54] In Palestine the list of inscribed material is decidedly meager. For the Canaanite period it consists only of a few characters or a word or two written in alphabetic script chiefly on potsherds discovered at several different sites. The Gezer Calendar (discovered in 1908) is dated by Albright c. 925 B.C. The Moabite inscription of king Mesha (discovered in 1868) dates from c. 830 B.C. The Samaria ostraca (63 in number, discovered by Reisner in 1910) are now assigned to the reign of Jeroboam II. They are very brief and are of value chiefly for the script and the proper names on them. The Siloam inscription (discovered in 1880) dates from the reign of Hezekiah. The Lachish ostraca (18, later increased to 21) were discovered by Starkey in 1938. Only one-third are sufficiently legible to be of real value. But they are described by Albright as "the only known corpus of documents in classical Hebrew prose."[55]

The fact that very few clay tablets either with cuneiform or alphabetic script have been found in Palestine may be explained in more than one way. It may be due to the fact that the work of excavating the cities of Palestine has not been carried far enough. There are many sites which have scarcely been touched and none have been completely explored. Since a hundred or more of the Amarna Letters discovered in Egypt were written in Palestinian cities (Accho, Hazor, Megiddo, Jerusalem, Ashkelon, Lachish, Gezer) and by or for Canaanite chieftains, who recognized the authority of Pharaoh and sought his help, it is highly probable that in the pre-Israelite strata of many of these cities there are "nests" of cuneiform tablets which have not yet been reached. A few such tablets have been found at Taanach, Shechem, Tell-el-Hesi, Ain Shemesh, and Hazor.

Several other reasons may be given for the failure to find extensive literary remains in Palestine dating from Old Testament times. (1) Suitable clay for writing tablets was difficult to obtain in Palestine. (2) Many of the thousands of potsherds which have been examined for evidence of writing may have been used as ostraca centuries ago, and in process of time have lost all traces of writing, or these traces may have disappeared in the washing. If the ink used was lampblack mixed with a soluble gum, the disappearance of such traces would be easily accounted for. As we have seen in the case of the Lachish ostraca only six of the twenty-one contain enough writing to be decipherable. (3) The most probable explanation is that the inhabitants of Palestine early adopted the use of a perishable material for writing. We have seen that the story of Wenamon tells of the shipping of "500 [rolls of] finished papyrus and 500 cowhides" to Byblos.[56] This would imply that the use of such perishable writing material was widely known in the Eastern Mediterranean region as early as the times of the Judges. (4) It is also probable that while writing was known and extensively used at least as early as 3000 B.C., the number of persons using it was for centuries relatively small. According to Wiseman "the six scribes to a population of about 2,000 at Alalakh in Syria in *c.* 1800-1500 B.C. is probably indicative of the literacy in important towns."[57] These scribes wrote in cuneiform. It is probable that when alphabetic scripts became generally available, papyrus and skin largely replaced clay as writing material in Palestine.

As to the Israelites two things are to be noted: (1) They came out of Egypt after a sojourn there of centuries. In Egypt the usual material for writing was papyrus. It was in use there long before the Israelites entered Egypt. That its use would be adopted by them seems highly probable. (2) It is significant that "rolls" (*megilloth*) are referred to about twenty times in the later books of the Old Testament, sometimes in the expression "roll of a book." This is particularly interesting because the expression must refer to a roll of *skin* or *papyrus*. And it would be quite natural to infer that "book" (*sepher*) is or may often be meant as an abbreviation of "roll of a book." The word "book" occurs by itself frequently (*c.* 175 times) in the Old Testament. We meet it first in Genesis 5:1, "This is the book of the generations of Adam." Moses was commanded to write the curse pronounced upon Amalek "in a book" (Exod. 17:14).

The words of Psalm 40, which the heading assigns to David, "In the volume [i.e., roll, *megillah*] of the book it is written of me. I delight to do thy will, O my God" (vs. 7), indicate quite clearly that writing upon *rolls* of skin or *papyrus* goes back to at least the time of David, which would be quite in harmony with the meager archaeological evidence.[58]

Two passages in Jeremiah are especially noteworthy in this connection. The transaction described in 32:6-16 clearly represents regular business procedure. The deed of purchase was written twice and was witnessed by several persons there present, before whom the purchase money was weighed on the scales. The two copies of the deed were probably written on a single piece of papyrus or skin. This was then cut nearly in two, and the one half rolled up and sealed, the other half folded over and rolled around the sealed half, but left open so that it could be read, a practice similar to the custom of enclosing tablets in clay envelopes on which the contents of the tablet was repeated. If this is the correct interpretation of the words "closed" and "open" it indicates the use of papyrus or skin for the making out of the duplex deed. That such documents were frequently preserved in earthen jars is proved by the excavations at Assur by Andrae and by the discovery of broken jar containers centuries later in the Dead Sea Caves.

The other passage is Chapter 36. There the document which contained Jeremiah's indictment of Jehoiakim and the Jewish nation is repeatedly referred to as a scroll (*megillah*) and we read that after Jehudi read three or four leaves or columns (*delathoth*) the king cut it with the scribe's knife or razor and burned it. So this also must have been of papyrus or of skin.

The same may be said of the document recording the curse on Babylon which was entrusted by Jeremiah to Seraiah who was going on a mission to Babylon (51:59-64). He was to carry the book (*sepher*) to Babylon and read it there, probably before witnesses (cf. 19:1-15) and then tie a stone to it and throw it into the river. Had it been a clay or stone tablet, it would not have needed a stone to sink it.

These examples indicate that the use of perishable writing materials was common in Jeremiah's day;[59] and the discoveries in the Dead Sea Caves have shown this conclusively for the period a century or more before the Christian era, as to which there had been hitherto so little data available. There is nothing to suggest anything unusual in Jeremiah's dealings with Hanameel. He acted in a perfectly businesslike way. And this transaction reminds us of Abraham's purchase of the cave at Machpelah, although in it there is no mention of a deed. On the other hand the words of 17:1, "The sin of Judah is written with a pen of iron, with a nib of adamant" proves the acquaintance of the prophet with inscriptions like the Code of Hammurabi. The wish expressed in Job 19:24 is interesting especially if the book is relatively early in date. The comparatively recent discovery that "writing-boards" of several leaves, i.e., tablets of wood or ivory "with a recess to hold wax" were in use in Assyria, at the time of Sennacherib,[60] is another striking illustration of the use of writing in biblical times. Whether they were used in Palestine we do not know. It is possible that the writing (*sepharim*) sent by Sennacherib to Hezekiah was of this nature. Such a message could be easily and quickly indited. The statement that Hezekiah "spread" it before the Lord might perhaps apply to such a hinged writing tablet or to a scroll, but hardly to a clay tablet.

Writing is referred to about forty times in the Pentateuch (13 times in Exodus, 5 in Numbers, 23 in Deuteronomy).[61] The first mention is Exodus 17:14. It is noteworthy that it is nearly always important matters that are said to have been written down: the curse on Amalek, the Decalogue (Exod. 20; Deut. 5), the Book of the Covenant (Exod. 24:4; cf. 34:27), the book of the law (Deut. 28:58; 31:24), Moses' song (31:22). A most significant incident bearing on this subject is the command, given in Deuteronomy 27:1-8 and carried out in Joshua 8:30-35, regarding the great symbolic rite to be performed at Shechem after Israel entered the land. The law was to be written on stones which had been plastered over so as to secure a smooth surface as well as a soft surface for writing. This would have been a relatively simple process as compared, for example, with the carving of the Code of Hammurabi on a great stele of diorite. There are also important references in Joshua, besides the writing on the altar at Mt. Ebal of the Law as commanded by Moses (8:32): the describing of the land (18:4-9), the appeal to the written law (23:6), the writing of the Shechem Covenant "in the book of the law of God" (24:26). In Judges the mention of Kirjath Sepher, i.e., "book-city," or "scribe-city" is particularly interesting because this is described as the *old* name of Debir (1:11). The mention of "the pen of the writer" (5:14) would point to familiarity with writing. But "staff of the marshal" is perhaps a more correct rendering. The statement in 8:14 is specially important, since it shows that a young man of Succoth knew and could "write down" (*ARV* marg., *RSV*) the names of the princes and elders of that city, seventy-seven names. We read also that Samuel "wrote in a book" the manner of the kingdom (1 Sam. 10:25).

It is to be noted that the word *shôṭer* which occurs twenty-five times in the Old Testament, thirteen of which are in the Pentateuch, comes from the same root as the Accadian verb meaning "to write." In the *LXX* it is rendered by *grammateus* and in the *Vulgate* by *scriba. AV* and *ARV* render is by "officer," *RSV* "foreman." But there is no reason why it should not be rendered by "writer" or "scribe." The name is first applied to the Israelite tally-keepers, who kept the work-lists of the vast corvee of slave labor in Egypt (Exod. 5:6). If the names of the men of whom they were in charge were written down, as seems probable, this would indicate that these men could themselves both read and write.[62]

The discovery of Alphabet Scripts reminds us that palaeography is an important factor in archaeology. The recent discovery of manuscripts in the Dead Sea Caves brought that fact vividly to our attention, since at first it was largely the style of writing which was appealed to in determining the age of the documents. The subject is a complicated one. But a few examples will serve to indicate its importance. It has long been recognized that most of the letters of the Phoenician alphabet are, as indicated by their names, the first letter of the words which the symbols originally represented (acrophonetic). Thus *aleph* means ox; and the letter aleph was originally a crude picture of the head of that animal. The letter *ayin* (a guttural sound which has no equivalent in English) is the first letter of the word which in Hebrew means "eye." In the earliest inscriptions it is represented by a circle. This is still the case with the Moabite Stone and the Siloam Inscription. But the tendency gradually developed to leave the circle open at the top; and in the Elephantine Papyri of about 400 B.C. we find the opening at the top so large that the circle came to resemble a U. Apparently the tendency then developed to write this U with two strokes instead of one and to extend the stroke beginning in the upper right beyond the point where it joined the corresponding stroke from the upper left. The result was that the U acquired a tail which made it look somewhat like a Y. This form of letter, with the tail, appears in the Isaiah scroll (1QIsa).

It is by tracing such developments in the style of writing that the comparative age of documents is determined from the distinctive features of the script.[63] Such careful comparative study of scripts, together with other evidence, has led to the conclusion that the Dead Sea documents date from the period covered by the last two centuries B.C. and the first two centuries A.D.

The explorations and excavations near the Dead Sea, at Khirbet Qumran (1947–) have led to the discovery of what is regarded as a scriptorium in the ancient monastery and of literally thousands of fragments of ancient documents in the caves in the neighborhood, as well as in other localities. It has been estimated that fragments of over one hundred biblical manuscripts already have been discovered. While these manuscripts may not date from the Old Testament period they are especially important for two reasons. On the one hand, they show that a period from which no contemporary documents were in existence was really a time of very considerable literary activity. The discoveries at Khirbet Qumran and the nearby caves prove that the Essene Community like a mediaeval monastery was a beehive of scribal activity, and the discoveries in the Wadi Murabba'at and Khirbet Mird show that other groups and sects were to some extent similarly engaged. Especially interesting are the Bar Kokhba letters dating from the second Jewish revolt. These discoveries justify us in believing that similar documents existed in much earlier times and warrant the hope that they may be discovered at any time.

We are frequently told today that oral tradition figured prominently in Israel's history long after the period for which the extensive use of alphabet writing has been established by archaeological research. Some scholars even claim that for centuries it was regarded as more dependable than the written word. Such a claim is improbable in itself and is not in accord with the existing evidence.

The historians who wrote the Historical Books of the Old Testament appeal frequently to documentary sources: "Is it not written in————?" or "behold it is written ———." To show how grievous was the sin of Israel, the Lord said through Hosea, the prophet, "I wrote for him the ten thousand things of my law; but they are counted as a strange thing" (8:12 ARV). The word "wrote" (the form is frequentative or iterative and describes an action "which continued throughout a longer or shorter period" or which took place repeatedly) may well refer to the entire pentateuchal legislation.[64]

In the Code of Hammurabi we read this statement: "The oppressed man, who has a case, let him come before the statue of me (who am) king of righteousness; my inscribed monument let him read (or, have read to him), my precious words let him hear, may my stele make his case plain, may he find his right, may his heart be stimulated."[65] This illustrates the importance attached to codified and duly recorded law in the time of Hammurabi and much earlier. And the vast number of contract tablets and other business and legal documents from that period and earlier indicate how necessary the men of four millenniums ago regarded it to be to have important matters made a matter of record, put as we say "in black and white."

The place and date of the invention of the alphabet are not known. G. R. Driver attributes it to a Semitic people who were in contact with the Egyptians. He is inclined to accept the tradition recorded by Herodotus, that the Phoenicians came originally from the shores of the Indian Ocean. He would place the discovery at a date when these tribes were in contact with the Egyptians and he holds that "the invention was developed in Palestine and perfected on the Phoenician coast." He dates the Sinaitic inscriptions "at some time between 1850 and 1500 B.C. which makes it definitely pre-Mosaic, and may well mean that it was while in Egypt or in Midian that Moses became familiar with the alphabet and adopted it because of its simplicity.[66]

Spacing of Words. In the case of alphabetic inscriptions in which only the consonants were written, it was apparently early regarded as necessary to indicate the extent of the word-units in some way. This was usually done by means of a stroke or a dot. In the Ugaritic texts it is a small vertical wedge. But the practice varies greatly. In the Phoenician inscription of Yehaw-milk the words are simply spaced. In the Aramaic inscriptions of Panammu and Bar-rekub from Zenjirli they are separated by a dot. On the Moabite Stone a vertical stroke divides sentences and a dot is used to separate single words; on the Siloam inscription only the dot occurs. The Lachish letters sometimes have a dot between words. Such being the case it is worthy of note that in the Egypto-Aramaic inscriptions of *c.* 400 B.C., the words are simply spaced. The same is the case with the Dead Sea Scrolls (e.g., the Isaiah Scroll, IQIsa). Consequently it is somewhat remarkable that the great uncial manuscripts of the Greek Old Testament do not space the words and give no indication of the dividing of a word at the end of a line. Since the Greek, unlike the Semitic, writes the vowels as well as the consonants, such unspaced writing is much easier to read in Greek than consonantal Hebrew would be if so written. Still it seems strange that so simple a device as the spacing of words was not used in the Greek Codices to facilitate reading. This is especially remarkable since the Greek translators certainly found spacing in the Hebrew manuscripts, which they translated, as is indicated by the Dead Sea Scrolls. The reason can hardly have been an aesthetic one since the endings of lines are not strictly uniform. But from the standpoint of legibility it was a backward step. We need perhaps to remind ourselves that legibility has not always been regarded as a virtue. Ancient scholars apparently often aimed to conceal knowledge, to make learning hard rather than easy, cryptic and mysterious rather than simple and plain. Even today an almost or quite illegible signature seems to be regarded by some as the hallmark of greatness!

Dividing of Words. Another matter of interest is the practice of dividing or not dividing words at the end of a line. In the Massoretic Bible words are not divided, but the final letter or letters of the last word are stretched if necessary to fill out the space. When or how this custom originated may be hard to determine. But apparently it does not go back to Old Testament times. The Isaiah Scroll does not divide words at the end of the line to make the lines end evenly. In the Mesha Inscription, many of the lines end with divided words. Clearly usage varied in ancient times as it does even today.

LANGUAGE

The polyglot character of our modern world is both a prominent feature and a formidable problem. There are more than one hundred nations which are members of the United Nations; and there are reported to be about one hundred fifty languages, out of several thousand, each of which is spoken by at least one million persons.[67] The General Assembly of the United Nations recognizes at present only five official languages; and the search for a universal language, natural or artificial, has not been successful and may never be. The cause and origin of this multiplicity of languages has been much discussed. Is it the result of variation from one or several original tongues? The evolutionist regards these differences as largely due to dispersion and gradual differentiation resulting from dispersion, as illustrated by dialectical differences in closely related peoples. But back of these dialectal deviations lie great basic differences which the evolutionists can hardly account for.

The account of the confusion of tongues in Genesis 11:1-9 has been treated by many modern scholars as a myth, a legend, an aetiological story, which has little or no factual basis. But this does not do it the justice which it deserves. When we study it carefully, the following facts emerge. The biblical account makes the dispersion the result of the differences and not the cause of them. It represents the confusion as a sudden act and not a process, a summary act of judgment which had immediate and catastrophic results. The people all spoke the same language (vss. 1, 6); and they started to build a tower, lest they be separated. The Lord inspected their work, disapproved of it and confounded their tongue that "they might not understand one another's speech." This had the immediate result that "they left off to build the city and the Lord scattered them thence." The confusion was a sudden act, catastrophic and fatal to their plan to stay together. It caused and preceded the dispersion. And this great variety and diversity of language has continued to the present day.

The Confusion of Tongues resembles in striking fashion the Creation as described in Genesis 1. Just as God made the creatures *after their kind,* that is with basic differences which, however much the species and sub-species may have varied, nevertheless have continued to exist for uncounted generations, so he divided the tongues into great families which despite all their dialectic differences have maintained their basic and characteristic features since the Lord confounded man's speech at Babel. The earliest forms frequently show a complexity of structure and a nicety of expression which tends to weaken or to disappear; as for example the loss of case-endings in Babylonian and Hebrew, for which we may compare Anglo-Saxon and Modern English, the trend being to the less complex and complicated. This may be regarded as an application of the law of entropy in the mechanical universe, a breaking down of the structure of language. The archaeologist has confirmed this account in several striking ways. We now know more about the number of ancient languages and about the radical differences existing between them, that these differences go back to very ancient, even to prehistoric, times and that the languages were widely distributed geographically. These differences are in some cases so great that it seems impossible that one could be derived from another or that both could have a common source. Dead languages such as Sumerian and Babylonian, Elamite, Hurrian, and Kassite, still-spoken languages such as Eskimo, Chinese and Turkish are so different that it is difficult if not impossible to trace a genetic relationship between them.

THE SEMITIC LANGUAGES

Our concern, as was that of the writer of the Genesis narrative, is especially with the Semitic peoples, the ancestors and descendants of Abraham. The Semitic languages have certain basic characteristics which set them apart from all the other great language groups; they can also be divided into a number of sub-genera or dialects which differ considerably among themselves within the general pattern of the family or genus. We distinguish, for example the following broad sub-divisions on a geographical basis: East Semitic (Babylonian and Assyrian, classed together as Accadian); West Semitic (Aramaic, Amorite, Canaanite, Hebrew); Northwest Semitic (Phoenician, Ugaritic); South Semitic (Arabic, Ethiopic, Sabean). Egyptian also has many characteristics which are Semitic. These various languages are more or less closely related, they are distributed over a very extensive area and show resemblances and differences which are both interesting and perplexing.

Tri-Consonantalism. A distinctive feature of all Semitic languages, which is shared even by Egyptian, is the tri-consonantal root. Unlike the Indo-European group, the vowels do not form part of the root, but are used to modify it and distinguish its various forms, as are also certain consonants which can be used as formative elements. Thus *KTB* has the root idea of "write" (*KaTaB*, he wrote, *KoTeB*, writing or a writer, *KaTaBtiy*, I wrote, *yiKToB*, he will write, *miKTaB*, a writing, etc.). By the adding of formative elements and of prefixes and suffixes quite formidable combinations can be built up: e.g., *keDiBeReykem* "according-to-your-words" in which only three of the consonants (*DBR* to speak) give the root meaning of the combination. Other distinctive features might be mentioned. But this one will suffice for our purpose. It is distinctive of the Semitic family as a whole. We pass on to consider some of the characteristic resemblances and differences which distinguish the different members of the Semitic family.

The Alphabet. The Semitic alphabet distinguishes about thirty different consonants, which are not all recognized in the different scripts. The fullest are Ugaritic and Arabic. Aramaic and Hebrew distinguish orthographically only twenty-two and Accadian nineteen or twenty characters. Dentals (7) and sibillants (5) are richly represented, as are also the gutturals (laryngials). Egyptian distinguishes four *h* sounds, Arabic, Ethiopic and Ugaritic three, Hebrew and Aramaic two, Accadian only one. There are also shifts in pronunication of which an example is furnished by Judges 12:6 according to which the difference in pronunciation between *sibboleth* and *shibboleth* drew a fatal distinction between an Ephraimite and a Gileadite.

A quite noticeable distinction appears in the case of the two consonants *sh* and *h*. In Accadian the pronoun of the third masculine both singular and plural begins with *sh* while in the West Semitic languages it begins with *h*. The Causative Conjugation in Accadian begins likewise with *sh* (*shaphal*) but in most other Semitic languages it begins with *h* or ' (aleph). Yet Ugaritic has the *sh* form and perhaps also the *h* form. The *sh* form appears in Egyptian and in certain forms of the verb in other Semitic languages. Biblical Aramaic which does not use the *sh* form has adopted three such words from the Accadian.

Somewhat similar variations occur in the case of single words. A few examples will interest the reader. The pronoun "I" has two forms in the Semitic family: a short form and a long form which appear in Hebrew as *ani* and *anoki*. The short form appears in Aramaic and Arabic, the long form in Accadian, Phoenician and Moabite. Both forms occur in Hebrew. The critics claim that in the Bible the long form represents early usage, that the short is characteristic of late usage. Yet both forms occur in the Ugaritic texts which are somewhat earlier than the Mosaic age.[68]

The relative pronoun is another interesting example. In Accadian it is *sha*, a form which appears rather rarely in Hebrew and in Phoenician. In Phoenician the usual form is *ash* or *ashsha*. In Hebrew the usual form is *'asher* a form which occurs in no other Semitic language. Another form of the relative pronoun is *di* or *de* which appears in various combinations in Arabic, Aramaic and Ugaritic; but not in Accadian; in Hebrew only very rarely as *zeh* or *zu (zo)*.

For an example of vocabulary we may take the two familiar verbs which express the idea of "speak" or "say." They are *amar* and *dibber*. *Amar* occurs 5287 times as a verb, but nouns derived from it are of rare occurrence. *Dibber* occurs 1142 times as a verb, and the noun *dabar* occurs 1439 times. Neither of these roots occurs in the other Semitic languages as the usual verb to express this idea. We meet *amar* in Aramaic and Phoenician, but not in Accadian. In Arabic it means "command." *Dibber* is not found in this sense in any other Semitic language.[69]

Another interesting example consists of two of the words for "window." One is *arubbah*, which comes from a root meaning to lie in wait or ambush, and perhaps had originally the idea of peephole. The other is *challon*, which means a piercing or a hole. Both of them appear in the Flood account in Genesis (7:11; 8:2); and have long been regarded as evidence that the narrative is composite, the one word appearing in the late document (P), the other in the early document (J). So it is noteworthy that in Ugaritic these words appear several times in parallel lines of the same poem.[70]

The presence in the Semitic group of languages of marked evidences of both stability and change has made the problem of change in the Hebrew of the Old Testament an interesting and also a complicated one. The stability of the language is remarkable when we remember that the books which it contains cover a period of a thousand years — Moses to Malachi. There is no such marked difference as there is in English in less than half that time between Chaucer and Macaulay. But there are certain variations which need explanation; and the question of the relation of Biblical Hebrew to the other Semitic languages is of interest and importance. Two subjects are of special interest and may be briefly considered.

Definiteness. Apparently the Semitic languages originally had no definite article. Old Babylonian added a *mimmation* to the singular of a definite noun which was not determined by a genitive (e.g., *shar-*

rum dannum, the mighty king, but *sharru Babili*, king of Babylon). But this ending tended to disappear in later times. In Aramaic the definite or emphatic state is indicated by the addition of a final *a'* or *ah* (e.g., *malka'*, the king). In Hebrew, Phoenician and Arabic what appears to be the same demonstrative particle is prefixed instead of affixed to secure definiteness: e.g., in Hebrew *hammelek* (the king).[71] Ugaritic did not have the article, but retained the mimmation in certain forms.

Case Endings. That the Semitic languages originally or at least very early distinguished three cases, nominative, genitive, accusative, by means of the three basic vowels, *u, i, a*, is indicated by the Old Babylonian inscriptions of Sargon of Agade and of Hammurabi of Babylon. That this distinction was widespread and has a long history behind it is indicated by its occurrence many centuries later in the Classical Arabic of the Koran. But there is no uniformity as regards usage. In Accadian these endings gradually disappear. Aramaic does not distinguish the cases. Ugaritic does to some extent but just to what extent is uncertain; Phoenician does not except perhaps in proper names; Hebrew only in a few sporadic cases.[72] It is to be noticed, however, that in Hebrew the disappearance of the case endings is replaced by the use of a special word to introduce the direct object (*'eth*) which occurs frequently in the Hebrew of all periods. The use of such a particle appears in Phoenician, in the Mesha inscription, and has its cognates in Syriac and the Aramaic of the Targums. It has not been found in Ugaritic, which is perhaps the clearest indication that in it the cases were sufficiently distinguished to make the use of a special sign of the accusative unnecessary.

Our reason for singling out these two features for special consideration is the following. It was formerly held, on the basis of the Old Testament data, that the relative infrequency of the article and of the sign of the accusative in poetry was to be regarded as simply a characteristic of poetry, since poetry has a style of its own and often uses words and forms which are unusual or archaic. This was a natural explanation as long as the prose documents in which the poem is imbedded (e.g., Judg. 5) were regarded as being as old as the poetry itself, that is, as long as the Mosaic authorship of the Pentateuch was accepted. But the late dating of much or most of the Old Testament which has been favored by the critics has led to the claim that such poems as the Song of Deborah are older, much older, than the prose narratives in which they appear, and that the peculiarities of language which we find in them represent an earlier stage of the language. Hence it is argued that the absence of the article and of the sign of the accusative is a "Canaanitism" and represents an earlier stage of the language than does the ordinary prose of the Old Testament. The main objection to this view is that it presupposes and involves the late date of the prose of the Pentateuch. If, for example, the Song of Deborah is regarded as dating from the time of the Judges because of stylistic affinities to the Ugaritic poems, the inference to be drawn will be that the prose narrative of Judges will be still later since it contains these "late" elements which are wanting in this early poem.

Such being the case it is important to note that there is no such radical difference between the prose and the poetry of the Old Testament as this theory involves. When we turn to it we find that the definite article is used in every book of the Bible, and on practically every page. The first verse of the first chapter of Genesis has the article twice and the sign of the accusative twice. If Moses wrote the Pentateuch and it has come down to us as he wrote it, then it is obvious that Biblical Hebrew contained these distinguishing features from the beginning. The definite article appears seven times in the prophecy of Balaam in Numbers 24; and the *'eth* in 23:10 and 24:21. In the Song of Deborah, the definite article occurs eight times and the inseparable preposition has the pointing of the article about as frequently. The definite article appears in more than one hundred of the one hundred fifty Psalms, in some of them rather frequently. The sign of the accusative appears in about one-third of them, which serves to show that the difference in usage in poetry and in prose is only a matter of frequency of use. These two features occur in the Hebrew of every period.

The few examples which have been given will serve to indicate the fascination as well as the complexity of the problem of the relationships of the different members of the Semitic family of languages and the difficulty of tracing the course of their differentiation and development. The period is a long one covering some five thousand years of recorded history. But unfortunately for the student of comparative philology the material at his disposal, especially as regards the early period, is both inadequate and confusing. It is one thing to gather together the evidences of similarity and difference. It is quite a different thing to account for them.

The history of the Hebrew people is too varied and complex to justify any very positive statements with regard to the nature and development of their language. A brief survey will suffice to make this abundantly clear. Abram lived in Ur of the Chaldees, a center of Sumerian culture, which had probably already in his day become strongly Semitic. His name is not Babylonian but Aramaic or at least West Semitic; and it is quite possible that his father Terah or an ancestor had come originally from Northern Mesopotamia, the home of

Bethuel and Laban, who spoke Aramaic (Gen. 31:47). Abraham
dwelled in Canaan for a full century in a Canaanite environment, having contacts with Philistines and Egyptians. Jacob spent some years in
Padan-Aram with his Aramaic-speaking kinsmen; and his descendants
were instructed to refer to him as an Aramaean (Deut. 26:5). Later
Jacob and all his family went down into Egypt, where Joseph occupied a high position at the court of Pharaoh. After several centuries
of sojourn there, which became a bitter bondage, Moses was born. He
was brought up at the court of Pharaoh as the son of Pharaoh's daughter; and was trained in all the wisdom of the Egyptians (Acts 7:22).
In Egypt he, of course, learned Egyptian and perhaps observed its
points of resemblance with Hebrew. He may have learned of the
Alphabet Scripts which were in use in the nearby Sinaitic Peninsula,
in Ugarit, and in Phoenicia and of the syllabic scripts of Byblos and
Krete. He may have noted that the Egyptian of his day used a definite
article *pa'*, as does Coptic, and that also like Coptic, it did not use
case endings.

Moses spent forty years at the court of Pharaoh and became a man
of culture and education. But he was a Hebrew, who loved his kinsmen and was eager to help them. His endeavor to do so resulted in
flight and exile; and he spent forty years in the land of Midian, and
married the daughter of the priest of Midian (probably a Semitic
people). Then God called him and sent him to deliver his people from
bondage in Egypt. He led them first into the wilderness of Sinai; and
there he received that law which was to govern the life and faith of
his people for generations to come. Being a man of culture he may
have given to the colloquial patois of his people that literary form
which we know as Classical Hebrew, the language of the Pentateuch,
and thereby have given Biblical Hebrew its standard and permanent
form. What Luther did for Germany by his translation of the Bible,
certainly Moses the lawgiver could have done for ancient Israel.[73] It
is to be assumed, therefore, that the language in which this law was
written would become "standard Hebrew." After forty years in the
wilderness, the Israelites returned to the land where their forefathers
had sojourned and which was promised to Abraham and his seed forever. They were strictly commanded to drive out and exterminate the
inhabitants of the land and especially warned against social dealings
with them and against the worship of their gods. But they disobeyed
again and again: they forsook the God of Israel and worshipped the
gods of the peoples among which they dwelt. They took them foreign
wives, even as late as in the days of Ezra and Nehemiah. But the last
of the prophets summed up the great message of the Prophets with the
words: "Remember ye the law of Moses my servant, which I com-

manded unto him in Horeb for all Israel, *with* the statutes and judgments." That was the message with which the prophets "hewed" (Hos.
6:5) their disobedient people and kept alive the knowledge of the law
of the God of Israel among them, and also the language in which that
law had been written.

It is customary to argue that in the course of the thousand years between Moses and Malachi, the Hebrew language must have passed
through many changes and that therefore the language as written and
spoken in the days of Moses must have been radically different from
that used, for example, by Jeremiah. But it should not be forgotten
that an authoritative corpus such as the Pentateuch, accepted as a
revelation of the will of the God of Israel through Moses, would have
the double tendency to maintain itself unaltered and also to stabilize
the language of those who accepted it as authoritative. That the Jews
of the post-exilic period had some difficulty in understanding the language of the Pentateuch is indicated by Nehemiah 8:8. Some hold
that this implies the popular use of a translation, an Aramaic Targum.
But the thing to be noted is that the Law of Moses was first read in
the original and then expounded or translated that the people might
understand it. Conservatism in the use of language is a familiar fact.
The ancient Sumerian language was used in religious rites a thousand
years and more after it ceased to be the vernacular. The Roman Cath-
olic Church still clings to the use of Latin for its ritual. The Koran is
a striking illustration of this same tendency. Lawyers and doctors
cling to the use of Latin words and phrases. Every great writer has
his own peculiarities of literary style.

With such a history as we have sketched, and it is simply an abstract of the biblical record, it would seem to be obvious that we
should expect to find a considerable number of foreign words and
especially proper names in the Old Testament. And such is indeed the
case. This was pointed out in great detail some years ago by Professor
R. D. Wilson in a study entitled "Foreign Words in the Old Testament
as an Evidence of Historicity."[74] There are Egyptian words: e.g.,
tebah (ark), *min* (kind), Pharaoh (literally, great house), Potiphar,
Asenath, On; Sumerian words, e.g., E.GAL, literally "great house"
which appears in Accadian as *ekallu* and in Hebrew as *hekal*, palace
or temple; Accadian words: *shed* (demon), *maneh* (mina), *tartan*,
shoṭer (scribe), Tiglath-pileser, *sagan* (for *shaknu*. Ezek. 23:6);
pechah (abbrev. for *bel pechati*, governor of a district, Jer. 51:23);
Philistine: *seren*, lord or chief (perhaps from Accadian); Arabic:
qatsin (captain, Judg. 11:6); Aramaic words: *yegar sahadutha*, which
is in Hebrew *gal 'ed*, (heap of witness), *chesed* (disgrace); Persian,
satrap, *apadan* (colonnade), daric, Ahasuerus; several Greek words to

which some Hittite and Hurrian may probably be added. Many of these words can be recognized by the fact that they have no suitable etymology in Hebrew and are clearly the same as words native to these other languages. But Dr. Wilson's object in this study was not merely to identify these foreign words as such, but to show "*that these foreign terms came into the Hebrew literature at the time when we would have expected them to come, provided that the original historical documents of the Old Testament from Abraham to Ezra were contemporaneous with the events recorded.*"[75] One conclusion which he reached is especially important in view of the recent developments. It was that "the poetical books of Psalms, Proverbs, and Lamentations and, as a general thing, even the individual poems such as Genesis 49, Exodus 15, Balaam's Oracles, Deuteronomy 32, 33, Judges 5, 2 Samuel 21, Habbakuk 3 and others, have in them no foreign words to determine their time and provenance" and he declared, "This almost complete absence of foreign words is a characteristic of lyric poetry in general. . . ."[76] It is one thing to speak as Albright does of "the innumerable parallels in diction between Ugaritic and Hebrew."[77] This was to be expected since both are Semitic (W. or N. Semitic) languages. It is quite a different thing to say that some of the Old Testament psalms "swarm" with Canaanitisms, or Ugaritisms. We may admit the one while emphatically rejecting the other.

Aramaisms. The presence of Aramaisms in the Old Testament is a linguistic phenomenon which is particularly important in view of the role which it has played in the history of biblical criticism. We have seen that Aramaic is one of the important members of the Semitic family of languages. While basically and unmistakably Semitic it has certain features which distinguish it from the other members of the group. In view of the fact that in the late period of Israel's history Aramaic replaced Hebrew to a considerable extent as the vernacular of the people, the claim was quite naturally made that the presence of Aramaisms in a document is evidence of its late date. Since Aramaic words were alleged to occur frequently in the Old Testament, the word "Aramaism" became a powerful weapon in the hands of the critics in support of their claim that Moses did not write the Pentateuch and that it and other presumably early books were late. Consequently R. D. Wilson devoted much time and careful study to the subject of Aramaisms. In 1912 he published an article on "The Aramaic of Daniel,"[78] in which he answered the claim of Dr. Driver that "The Aramaic of Daniel (which is all but identical with that of Ezra) is a *Western* Aramaic dialect of the type spoken in and about *Palestine*"[79] and that "The *Persian* words presuppose a period after the Persian empire had been well established: the Greek words *demand*, the Hebrew *supports,* and the Aramaic *permits,* a date *after the Conquest of Palestine by Alexander the Great* (332 B.C.)."[80] Dr. Wilson pointed out that the specific differences between Eastern and Western Aramaic which Dr. Driver appealed to did not appear until long after the time of Daniel and that the foreign words used were appropriate to Daniel's time.[81] In 1925 Dr. Wilson published a detailed study of the whole subject of "Aramaisms in the Old Testament"[82] in which he challenged the claim that had been made by critics for a hundred years or more "that the presence of Aramaisms in a given document proves the lateness of that document" and that "some three or four hundred words, which they enumerate, are Aramaisms."[83] After thorough study of the subject Dr. Wilson reached the conclusion: that the number of real Aramaisms had been greatly overestimated, that of the 360 words which Professor Kautzsch regarded as actual or possible Aramaisms only fifty have any apparent ground for being considered as such:[84] and further that these words occurred in contexts which were in harmony with the biblical claims as to the date of the documents containing them. "The most noteworthy fact brought out by the evidence . . . is that the documents relating to, or purporting to come from, men living in the time when history says that the Hebrews and the Arameans were in the closest contact, are the documents that contain nearly all of these alleged Aramaisms."[85]

CURIOSITIES OF LANGUAGE

The study of languages counsels caution in asserting what is possible or impossible, good usage or bad.

It is a familiar fact that in English there are words which are used only as noun or as adjective or as adverb, while there are others which are used in two or even all three of these senses. Thus, the use of "bad" as an adverb for "badly" is accepted by some grammarians, regarded as "questionable" by others.

When we turn to foreign words, we observe similar inconsistency. A rather striking example concerns the two classical words for man, *homo* (Latin) and *anthropos* (Greek). *Homo* is more or less familiar to English readers in the expressions *genus homo* and *homo sapiens.* But so far as the writer is aware, it is never used in English in combination. *Anthropos* is frequently so used, e.g., anthropo-centric means centered in or about man. But the homo-, which is used in combination, is quite distinct from the Latin *homo.* It comes from the Greek *homos* meaning "one and the same"; and it occurs in a large number of combined forms. Consequently, *homo*-centric does not mean man-centered, but "having the same center"; and the word homonym is regularly used to describe words which have the same sound but different meanings, due in most cases to different origin. The failure to use *homo* (man) in combined forms in English may be for the purpose of avoiding confusion with *homo-* (same), since homicide, hominid, hominoid (from homo) are used as being unambiguous terms. But examples of such confusion are not at all rare in English as in other languages.

The comparative study of words also furnishes many interesting and curious phenomena. What look like homonyms may be quite different in meaning and quite confusing. *"Gift"* is poison in German, a *"rock"* is a garment (coat), *"mist"* is dung, *"bug"* means joint. *Brücke* may suggest brook, but means the "bridge" which goes over the brook. *Schnecke* is not snake (*Schlange* in German) but snail (*Swedish, snack*). Why does the American speak of a chest of drawers (things to *pull out*), cf. Swedish *Dragkiste,* while the German calls it a *Schublade* (a box to *push in*)? Would we not expect the German and the Swede to have the same idea of such a useful and familiar object? In some parts of America, the word "dresser" means, as in England, a kitchen sideboard with shelves, while in others it is a bureau with mirror attached, which belongs in the bedroom.

In America a screwdriver is an instrument to *force* the screw *in;* in Germany it is a *Schraubenzieher,* an instrument to *pull* the screw *out.* In England it is a *turnscrew,* which describes it as serving both purposes, as does the French *tournevis.* In England 12/5/65 would be 12th May 1965; in the States it would be December 5, 1965. In England a quotation is placed within single-quotes and a quotation within a quotation is placed within double-quotes. In America it is the other way round. A billion is a thousand million in America, a million million in England, where a billion is called a milliard. No wonder misunderstandings arise in international relations!

"If" in Hebrew has the force of "surely not" when it is used in a vow or curse. "May thè Lord do so to me, if I do this," means "I will certainly not do it." The usage is perfectly clear if the main clause is expressed (1 Sam. 3:17), but if it is omitted, the sentence may be obscure as in Genesis 14:23 where the "that nots" (which are "ifs" in the Hebrew) clearly mean "surely not." We may compare the use of *plus* (more) in French. *Plus du roi* does not mean, "more of the king," but is equivalent to "down with the king" (*a bas le roi*) because the full expression is "*Nous ne voulons plus du roi*" (we don't want more of the king).

It is easy to ask questions, but not always easy to answer them. And when we find such differences in usage and in meaning in modern living languages we may well hesitate to assert what *must* have been the situation with ancient tongues which are far less adequately known to us.

GEOGRAPHY

Our knowledge of ancient geography has been greatly increased by archaeological research. This has been brought about mainly in two ways. On the one hand, exploration and excavation have led to the identifying of many ancient sites. Some few ancient cities like Damascus have been in more or less continuing existence since prehistoric times. Others have been known for centuries, even if not clearly identified, because of the imposing ruins which at once attract the attention of the traveler, such as Persepolis, Palmyra, Baalbek, Thebes. Still others have been covered by the dust and sands of ages and have required laborious and lengthy excavation. Thus Taylor in the course of his brief excavations at Muqqayyar in 1854 succeeded in identifying the city as Ur. But it was not until 1922 that Woolley began a series of twelve campaigns, which led to the amazing discoveries which proved Ur to have been a great and flourishing center of Sumerian culture centuries before the time of Abraham. Some of these cities are like Ur especially interesting because of their connection with the Bible: e.g., Babylon, Nineveh, Erech, Ur, Harran, Carchemish, Megiddo, Hazor, Lachish, Gezer, Memphis (called *Moph* or *Noph*), Thebes (*No*). Others were quite forgotten centuries ago, such as Eridu and Fara (Shuruppak), famous in Babylonian literature as the city of Ut-Napishtim, the hero of the Babylonian Flood story.[86]

On the other hand we have learned the names and approximate locations of many cities and lands through the documents which have been discovered. Ancient kings of Egypt and Assyria have recorded the names, and even left us lists, of cities and peoples against whom they waged war: Thothmes III and Shishak in Egypt, Hammurabi of Babylon, Tiglath-Pileser I, Sargon II, Sennacherib in Assyria and many others. Most of the Tell-el-Amarna Letters were addressed to kings of Egypt by kings, rulers and officials of distant lands and peoples including the Hittite lands, Mitanni and Byblos to the north but mostly cities in Syria and Palestine. About two hundred names of places and peoples are mentioned, some of them many times, others only once or twice. Some of these are well-known. But there are many which are scarcely known, if at all.

Ugarit is an impressive example of the way in which light has been thrown on the history and geography of the ancient Near East. This city or locality is mentioned in several of the Amarna letters. In one of them, a letter from Amenophis III to Kadashman-Harbe the Kassite king of Babylon, Ugarit is referred to in a way which implies that a woman (princess) from Ugarit would be no worthy wife for a king of Egypt. For forty years the location of Ugarit was not definitely known. Then in 1927 as the result of a chance discovery at Ras Shamra in the vicinity of Latakia, this city was found and proved to have been a place of importance, a commercial link between Babylonia and the cities of the Aegean. It was there that the texts in alphabetic cuneiform were discovered which are regarded as one of the greatest finds of the first half of the present century.

Another example is Mari. On the Sumerian King List, published by Langdon in 1923, Mari is No. 10 in the list of the 14 dynasties which followed the Flood (it is preceded by Adab and followed by the 3rd dynasty of Kish).[87] It is assigned 6 kings and a duration of 136 years. Mari was then little more than a name. Ten years later, as a result of chance discovery, excavations at Tell Hariri on the Euphrates, north of Babylon, uncovered Mari and proved it to be an ancient and important Amorite (?) city of Babylonia which had enjoyed a period of great prosperity which came to an end when it was conquered by Hammurabi.[88] A palace with 138 rooms and courts was unearthed; and some 20,000 tablets were discovered which furnished data connecting Hammurabi of Babylon with Shamshi Adad I of Assyria, thus throwing light on the relative chronology of these two great nations of Mesopotamia.[89]

Thus one discovery has led to another and our knowledge of the geography of the countries bordering Palestine and of Palestine itself has been constantly increasing. Ugarit and Mari are not mentioned in the Bible. But a great many of the cities and countries which are referred to are mentioned on ancient and more or less contemporary documents and some have been located with more or less definiteness. All of this tends to confirm the accuracy of the historical background of the Old Testament.

History

In spite of all the work which has been done, the many sites which have been excavated to a greater or less extent, it must be admitted that our information is, to say the least, meager and inadequate. It might be described as spotty. There are some periods and places for which the sources for an historical sketch are somewhat extensive. For the First Dynasty of Babylon we have the Code of Hammurabi, many letters (royal and private), and business documents, which have given us much valuable information, and which are now supplemented by the tablets from Mari. But for the *Kassite* period which succeeded it and which was much longer we have very little information. In fact we hardly know enough about the language which was spoken by the Kassites to determine its linguistic affiliations. The Hurrian civilization discovered at Nuzu and at Alalakh, the Amorite at Mari, the Canaanite at Ugarit are opening up new vistas of the past. For the Sargonid kings of Assyria the material is fairly extensive. But there are many kings of Assur, Nineveh and Babylon regarding whom we know little more than the name.

Like the Kassite period in Babylonia the *Hyksos* period in Egypt is a dark age.[90] These foreign (Asiatic) peoples ruled Egypt for a considerable period.[91] Petrie in 1915 estimated it at more than a thousand years. In 1931 he had reduced his figure to about eight hundred years. Most Egyptologists today assign it only a century or at most two centuries.[92] The Hyksos period itself is practically a blank. According to Steindorff and Seele "The Hyksos left no literary evidence of their occupation of Egypt. Indeed they left practically no large monuments at all. What we know about them has been painfully gleaned from a host of scarabs . . . cylinder seals, and a few other isolated objects."[93] And they point out that the interpretation of these "meager sources" requires "extreme caution." We scarcely know the language which they spoke. "Even the scarabs have often only muddled hieroglyphs, showing that the wearers were not able to read them."[94]

In 1874 George Smith discovered at Nineveh a brick with the inscription "Palace of Shalmaneser, king of nations, son of Adad-Nirari, king of nations." He claimed that this Shalmaneser was the builder of the oldest palace of Nineveh. Fifty years later R. C. Thompson, resuming work at Nineveh, pointed out that this Shalmaneser might be "either the king of *c.* 1280 B.C. (i.e., Shalmaneser I.) or of *c.* 781 B.C. (Shalmaneser IV)."[95] He gave two reasons for deciding in favor of the earlier king. The first was the fact that a duplicate of this inscription had been found by the German excavators at Assur, the early capital of Assyria. The second reason is especially significant: "Moreover, I believe there are no texts of Shalmaneser IV in existence."[96]

As a reason for the fact that "a consistently illuminated picture of ancient Egyptian times and events" cannot be drawn, Steindorff and Seele point out that the stream of tradition may vary from a torrent to a trickle and may even dry up entirely. But they give a second reason which is no less important:

A great majority of the historical monuments were intended as official propaganda with the purpose of transmitting to posterity a "correct" impression of the glory and power of the pharaohs. Crises of revolution and that type of inner strife so common in the Orient, as well as military defeats in foreign wars, were either passed over completely or were interpreted so that the monuments conveyed impressions much distorted and duly colored to the credit of the Egyptians.[97]

The same is true of the Assyrian kings and the accounts which they give of their mighty deeds. Contenau tells us:

> Complete historical reliance cannot, in the last resort, be placed on these documents. Not only, as we have seen, were they certainly guilty of exaggerating certain victories, but it is remarkable further that they never mention an Assyrian defeat. Does the Assyrian monarch vainly pursue a defeated enemy? The latter "like a bird hath gained a retreat where he cannot be reached." Do the royal armies retreat in battle? They are making a planned withdrawal to the capital. If we want an earlier example, we can find one in the account of the battle of Kadesh between Rameses II and the Hittites, each of whose written records claim it as a victory.[98]

Oppenheim speaks even more strongly:

> In all instances, we have to keep foremost in our mind that even historiographic documents are literary works and that they manipulate the evidence, consciously or not, for specific political and artistic purposes. . . . In short, nearly all these texts are as wilfully unconcerned with the "truth" as any other "historical text" of the ancient Near East.[99]

Such statements as the above are doubly significant because we are frequently told today that the historical narratives of the Old Testament are a glorification of Israel's past and are consequently not dependable as history. It is instructive to glance over the history of Israel in the light of such a statement regarding the Annals and Display Inscriptions of the Assyrian kings as: "they never mention an Assyrian defeat." In the Old Testament we read of both victories and defeats. And if the victories at times sound exaggerated, we must remember that the defeats sound equally so. The Bible is the most truthful book of history known to us. It pictures the ups and downs of Israel's checkered history with equal candor. The lives of David and Solomon illustrate this very clearly. The total picture of David shows us a man who rose to the heights and sank to the depths; and in his Psalms the poet-king reveals his inmost heart to us. Where in the histories of ancient times will we find such a story as is given us in the eleven chapters of First Kings, where we read of the glory and the shame of Solomon, of the glorious temple which he built, of his wonderful prayer to the God of heaven, and of the idolatries into which his many wives beguiled him?

Ancient may not mean Accurate. We are tempted in dealing with ancient documents to assume that because a record is ancient, practically contemporaneous with the events described, it must therefore be dependable, far more so than records which come from a much later period, or have gone through a long period of transmission. It is important to remind ourselves constantly that the contemporary record, even if the account of an eyewitness, may be inaccurate, prejudiced, one-sided, and undependable.

This is illustrated by the accounts of the reign of Nabunaid which have come down to us. In the Istanbul stele, published by Scheil in 1896, Nabunaid represents himself as the pious worshipper of Marduk and the benefactor of the great temples of Esagila and Ezida, as the restorer after fifty-four years of desolation of the temple of Sin in Harran.[100] In the "Memorial" written for the mother or grandmother of Nabunaid published by Pognon in 1907 we have a similar account of the piety of Nabunaid.[101] In the so-called "Verse account" of Nabunaid first published by Sidney Smith in 1924, we have something quite different. In it Nabunaid is accused of oppression, of heresy, of neglecting his people and kingdom, and is made responsible for all their sufferings; while Cyrus is praised as the restorer of peace and prosperity, the rebuilder of Babylon and the patron of her gods.[102] In the Barrel Inscription of Cyrus, published by Rawlinson in 1884, Nabunaid is again made responsible for all the misfortunes of his people, which are attributed to the anger of the gods; and Cyrus is represented as the favorite of the gods, especially Marduk, as one who entered Babylon as a "friend" and received presents from "the kings of the whole world from the Upper to the Lower Sea."[103] The "Nabunaid Chronicle" published by Pinches in 1882 apparently aims to be objective. It represents Nabunaid as "staying" in Tema from the seventh year through the eleventh year and perhaps much longer (the tablet is damaged) and as responsible for the lapse of the proper worship of the gods. It describes Nabunaid as ruthless and ineffectual in opposing Cyrus, and refers to the return to Accad by Cyrus of the gods which Nabunaid had brought to Babylon.[104]

Here we have what are apparently approximately contemporaneous accounts of the events of the same period, which describe them from partisan and conflicting viewpoints. Which is correct? How far are any of them objective and dependable?

The Barrel Inscription of Cyrus reads like a skillfully prepared piece of politico-religious propaganda. Its aim is to win the favor of the citizens of Babylon by attributing all their woes to Nabunaid's impiety and misrule and presenting Cyrus to them as their friend and deliverer. It is especially designed to conciliate and win the favor of the powerful priestly party in Babylon. It may even have been prepared by them. It reveals aspects of the existing situation which Cyrus skillfully turned to his own advantage, just as the Rabshakeh of Hezekiah's day tried to make profit out of the reform instituted by the Jewish king (2 Kings 18:22). But it seems quite improbable that the devotion to Marduk expressed by Cyrus represented his own belief. Cyrus was a Persian. We have very few historical inscriptions from his reign or from that of Cambyses his son.

But Darius who came to the throne less than a score of years later never mentions Marduk or any of the Babylonian deities but again and again gives to the Persian god Ahuramazda the credit and glory for all his achievements. The meager information regarding his successors indicate that they followed the same course, although Xerxes speaks of "the gods" who were the associates of the great god Ahuramazda. Artaxerxes I does the same. Artaxerxes II couples Anahita and Mithra with Ahuramazda. Artaxerxes III names only Ahuramazda and Mithra. No one of them mentions a single Babylonian deity. Yet we know that there was no violent change and that these Persian monarchs not merely tolerated, but to some extent actively supported and promoted the worship at the ancient Babylonian and Sumerian shrines.[105] One thing is clear, that Cyrus introduced a policy of tolerance and conciliation, which reversed the system of deportations instituted by the great Assyrian conquerors and allowed the displaced peoples of conquered nations to return to their own lands, thus inaugurating the policy which is attributed to him in the Book of Ezra.[106]

It also needs to be remembered that these ancient records are often in poor condition with the result that the readings are more or less uncertain. We give here three examples:

(1) It is frequently asserted that contrary to the statement of 2 Kings 23:29, Pharaoh Necho was going up to aid the king of Assyria, not to oppose him. But the tablet is seriously damaged and this reconstruction is by no means certain.[107]

(2) The question whether the Benhadad who was a contemporary of Baasha and Asa, is the same as the king of like name who fought against Ahab is largely dependent upon whether the restoration of the text proposed by Albright is correct.[108]

(3) The question as to the identity of Darius the Mede with the Gubaru mentioned in the Nabonaid-Cyrus Chronicle has been a vexing one. Whitcomb has recently argued cogently that we must distinguish two men, a Gubaru whom Cyrus made "governor of Babylon and the Region beyond the River" and who retained that office for at least fourteen years; and an Ugbaru, governor of Gutium, who took possession of Babylon for Cyrus and died soon after. The former he would identify with Darius the Mede who "received the kingdom" after the death of Belshazzar. This is possible, even probable. But unfortunately the imperfect state of the tablet makes the readings somewhat uncertain.[109]

Such facts as those mentioned above should be borne in mind when we compare the statements of the Bible with the data found in the ancient contemporary documents. For unfortunately many scholars today attach an importance to the statements of these ancient inscriptions which they do not deserve and make them the final judge of the accuracy of the biblical statements.[110]

Perplexing Problems. When documentary evidence is wholly lacking and our conclusions must be based largely or entirely on the strata in which objects have been found, the situation may be quite perplexing. Among the statues discovered at Mari, there is one which is called *Ur-Nanshe,* "the great singer." It is heavy and clumsy and reminds us of the statues of Gudea which were found at Tello (Lagash) and date from about 2300 B.C. Parrot assigns this statue to the middle of the third millennium. Among the other statues found at Mari, one which Parrot assigns to the 18th century, is called "the Goddess of the flowing vase." It is a striking statue, graceful in form and the face might almost be called beautiful. The difference is quite remarkable and it would be easy to assert that it is the result of many centuries of development at Mari.[111]

Woolley, who excavated at Alalakh for several seasons, speaks of this *tell* as providing "a magnificent sequence for the whole 2nd Millennium B.C." It apparently had extensive trade with Cyprus and the West as well as with the countries of Mesopotamia. In the 5th Level at Alalakh which Woolley places in about the middle of the second millennium B.C. and which he described as "quite a sophisticated period" he discovered in a chamber adjoining the town gate two basalt statues, one male, the other female, evidently a god and a goddess, which were so crude that they might belong to the most primitive period, and which he describes as "grotesquely, almost obscenely bad." They seemed quite incongruous and out of place. The explanation which Woolley gives is that they were probably brought from Mitanni which was then "artistically inferior but politically preeminent" in that region.[112] He does this on the ground that similar monstrosities have been found at Diarbekr. Yet when we think of the vast number of valuable presents which Tushratta of Mitanni sent to the Egyptian Pharaoh when he sent him his daughter to be his wife, and which he fully enumerates in several of the Amarna Letters, it is difficult to believe that the culture and the religious ideas of the Hurrians of Mitanni could have been as crude as this explanation would indicate. According to Frankfort as early as about 3000 B.C. "the human figure was for the first time sculptured in the round in stone for a monumental purpose." And he declared that Tell Asmar and Khafajah had yielded more pre-Sargonic sculpture than all other sites taken together."[113] Yet we find such crudities and monstrosities as the ones referred to more than a thousand years later at Alalakh!

Gordon Childe in speaking of some of the peoples dwelling on the

Upper Nile, e.g., the Dinkas, remarks "it really looks as if among these tribes on the Upper Nile social development had been arrested at a stage that the Egyptians had traversed before their history began." He adds, "There we have a living museum whose exhibits supplement and vivify the prehistoric cases in our collections."[114] It is impossible to judge of the culture of a people as a whole from their outstanding achievements. Looking back over the centuries we marvel at the beauty of the Taj Mahal, the Alhambra, the great Christian cathedrals, the Colosseum, the Parthenon, the Pyramids, and we ask ourselves how many of the men who toiled upon these great cultural and religious monuments of mankind were able to read and write; and perhaps we would be obliged to answer concerning all of them, probably very few.

Excavations have recently been carried on at Hazor by Yigael Yadin with marked success. In the fourteenth century level of the temple he discovered "a strange onesided bronze leaf figurine of a woman." He called it "a Picasso of 3300 years ago."[115] The Tate Gallery in London has recently received as the gift of "Friends of the Tate" a colossal bronze by Henry Moore which is called "King and Queen." It is described as one of Mr. Moore's "most important works," by those who admire his art. If it had been dug up in an ancient ruin in Mesopotamia, the archaeologist might easily describe it as a striking example of the crudity and even grotesqueness of primitive art.[116] Were an archaeologist of the future to unearth statues by Praxiteles and by Jacob Epstein, he might, were he not a devotee of "modern art," claim that the latter belonged chronologically centuries earlier than the former.

LAWS AND CUSTOMS

That the Old Testament patriarchs lived in an age when human conduct was governed by established laws and customs is indicated by various hints which are given us in the biblical narratives. The purchase of the cave of Machpelah is a clear example of this. According to Hittite law the purchase of the entire field from Ephron the Hittite involved the assuming of certain obligations, "he shall render the services,"[117] which would not have been required had he purchased only part of it. Whether this is the reason for Ephron's insistence that Abraham buy all of his field is not clear.

We have now more or less complete copies of legal codes in Sumerian, Babylonian, Assyrian, and Hittite which are both interesting in themselves and especially so because of the light which they throw on Old Testament customs and laws. The best known, as it is also the longest and the best preserved, is the Code of Hammurabi

(*HC*) which dates probably from a couple of centuries later than the time of Abraham. In addition to these laws we have a large number of contract tablets and letters which illustrate the actual practice although none of them appeal directly to the Code. These laws serve to show how completely the life of men and women of ancient times was governed by law and custom. There are laws governing family relationships, marriage and divorce, concubinage, adoption, inheritance; laws regarding slavery, businesses of every kind, property rights; laws for the punishment of immorality, of theft, of lying, of slander, of sorcery and magic. The treatment of these subjects varies in the different codes. Some are dealt with in some detail, others are only summarily treated or entirely omitted. The omissions may, of course, be due to the fragmentary character of most of the codes or their brevity.[118]

A great deal has been written on this important subject.[119] A few examples must suffice. It is perhaps significant that the first four of the more than three hundred statutes of *HC* deal with false accusation. If the charge constitutes a capital offense, the false accuser is to be put to death. So in Deuteronomy 19 we read "then shall ye do unto him, as he had thought to have done unto his brother" (vs. 19). It is also significant that the second of the false charges referred to is that of sorcery, for it indicates the prevalence of the practice of "black magic" in ancient Babylonia. In this case if the accuser cannot prove his charge, the accused is to submit to the ordeal of the River God. He is to cast himself into the river. If he drowns, the accuser is to take his property. If he does not drown, the accuser is to be put to death and the accused then takes the accuser's property. An ancient example of the principle, not unknown even today in some countries, that a man is guilty until he is proved or can prove himself innocent!

The only example of the ordeal in the Bible is the case where a woman suspected by her husband of infidelity is required to drink the "water of jealousy" (Num. 5:11-31). This is to be regarded as a special exception to the law of Deuteronomy 17:6 which requires that there be two or three witnesses in every legal process. According to *HC* § 131, a wife accused of infidelity by her husband is to "make affirmation by god and return to her house" (apparently her husband's house). But if the charge is made by another, "if the finger was pointed" at her (§ 132), then "she shall throw herself into the river for the sake of her husband."[120] The mention of the taking of an oath as a proof of innocence in the case under discussion illustrates the fact that this practice was a common one in the ancient Near East, as the Old Testament indicates was the case.[121]

A notable feature of the *HC*, is the high position which it assigns to women. A married woman may not only own property, but she has the right to control the property which she brought with her to her husband's home. She may carry on business in her own name. She may leave her property to her children. If she is childless her husband may take a second wife or concubine. But this woman may not claim equality with the first wife. An interesting and significant provision of *HC* is that after marriage a husband and wife shall both be responsible for debts incurred by them jointly (§ 152).

In the Hittite Code we read: "If a man has a wife and then the man dies, his brother shall take his wife, then his father shall take her. If in turn also his father dies, one of his brother's sons shall take the wife whom he had." The words are added: "There shall be no punishment" (§ 193), which indicates that the law is dealing with an anomalous situation and justifying conduct which under other circumstances would be a capital offense. This law is noteworthy because it resembles the law of the Levirate in Deuteronmy 25:5-10 (cf. Gen. 38). Among the Assyrian laws dealing with marriage there is a provision that if a father secure a wife for one of his sons and the son dies "he may give (her) to whichever he wishes of his remaining sons from the eldest son to the youngest son who is at least ten years old" or in the case of the son's death a grandson who is "younger than ten years" may receive her (§ 43). This statement has a bearing on the question of the age of Hezekiah when he became king. Comparing 2 Kings 16:2 with 18:2 we find that Ahaz was about eleven years old when Hezekiah was born, a figure which many scholars consider impossible or at least improbable.

Among the Assyrian laws, there is a rather detailed law dealing with the veiling of women (§ 40). It requires that a lady (the wife of a seignior) must wear a veil in public. A slave may not do so, nor a harlot. If a man sees a harlot wearing a veil in public, it is his duty to denounce her. "However, if a seignior has seen a harlot veiled and has let (her) go without bringing her to the palace tribunal, they shall flog that seignior fifty (times) with staves; his prosecutor shall take his clothing; they shall pierce his ears, thread (them) with a cord, (and) tie it at his back, and he shall do the work of the king for a full month." It is further required that the veiling of a concubine must take place in the presence of five or six neighbors. The seignior must veil her and say, "She is my wife."

This very severe law does not appear in the Code of Hammurabi. Whether its enactment was due to some special situation or not we do not know. Nor do we know how widely it was observed. In Genesis 24:65 we read that when Rebekah learned that Isaac was approaching "she took a veil, and covered herself." This would be in accord with the law just cited. However Rebekah's veiling herself has often been explained as due to the fact that she was a bride about to meet her bridegroom. The account of the servant's meeting with Rebekah seems to indicate that she was not veiled. The words of the servant, "and I placed the ring on her nose" (vs. 47) indicate this or that she removed her veil for the purpose of receiving the ring. But this law clearly does not fit the sordid incident recorded in Genesis 38. For we read there that when Judah saw his daughter-in-law Tamar "he thought her to be a harlot (*zonah*); because she had covered her face" (vs. 15). Her reason for doing this was, of course, to prevent Judah from recognizing her. But he could not have mistaken her status if this law or custom was strictly enforced in Palestine at that time.

The *HC* contains laws which indicate how completely a child was the property of the father and the dire consequences which this might involve. Thus, if a man strikes a woman with child and causes her death, his daughter is to be killed (§ 210). If a contractor builds a house and it falls in and kills the owner's son, the contractor's son is to be killed (§ 230). This law conflicts with Deuteronomy 24:16, cf. 2 Kings 14:6, Jeremiah 31:29, Ezekiel 18. On the other hand, a father is not permitted to disinherit an unworthy son, unless or until the judges have investigated the son's record and then only when he has been found guilty a second time of a serious offense (§ § 168-9).

According to *HC* (§§ 23-4) a community is responsible for a crime committed in its territory by a criminal whose identity cannot be determined. Compare Deuteronomy 21:1-9.

These codes are characterized in general by the aim after exact requital or recompense. The principle "a tooth for a tooth" (Exod. 21:24) is not properly speaking a law of revenge, as some call it, but of strict, though merciless, justice. It is clearly illustrated in *HC* §§ 196-7. But, as in Exodus 21, the nature of the punishment is partly determined by the status of the injured party. Thus we read: "If a seignior has knocked out the tooth of a seignior of his own rank, they shall knock out his tooth" (§ 200), but "If he has knocked out a commoner's tooth, he shall pay one-third mina of silver" (§ 201). But some of the laws are very severe.

There are laws which seem strangely unfair. Yet they may have had their justification. For example, *HC* prescribes that when a tenant has rented a field and paid the rent in advance, if the field is inundated by storm or ravaged by flood, the tenant is to bear the entire loss. But if the tenant has not paid the rental, owner and tenant are "to divide proportionately the grain which is produced in the field" (§§ 45-46). This seems to be quite a one-sided arrangement.

Both the code of Eshnunna (§ 54) and that of Hammurabi (§ 251) have provisions for the punishment of the owner of an ox known to be a gorer (Exod. 21:28). The former also provides for the punishment of the owner of a vicious dog (§ 56). In the Hittite Code we find laws against cruelty to animals. "If anyone strikes an *ordinary* dog so that it dies, he shall give a shekel of silver" (§ 89). "If anyone hires an ox, applies to him the lash or the whip and its owner finds him out, he shall give one grain [of silver?] *per streak*" (§ 78).

Many of the laws, of course, reflect local conditions. The importance of keeping the irrigation canals in Babylonia in good repair is illustrated by *HC* §§ 53-56. Failure to do so was severely punished. "If a man without the owner's consent has cut down a tree in an orchard, he shall weigh out half a mina of silver" (§ 59).

A very severe punishment is inflicted on a man who has been placed in charge of a field and supplied with oxen, etc. (§ 256). If he is guilty of misconduct and cannot "pay the compensation," he is to be "torn in pieces in the field by the oxen" (Ungnad, Johns) or "they shall drag him through that field with the oxen" (Meek). If a woman causes her husband to be killed, for the sake of another man, she is to be impaled (§ 153).

Finally we observe that most of the laws with which we are dealing can be described as "casuistical," i.e., as dealing with special cases and fixing the penalty for each. They usually begin with "if" (*shumma*) and sometimes the situation dealt with is described in considerable detail. "If a seignior has stolen the young son of another seignior, he shall be put to death" is a brief and simple example. The specific crime is described and the punishment stated. Less frequently we find in these codes laws which may be described as "apodictic," that is as stating rules for conduct which must be observed but without specifying the penalty for their infraction. Thus in the Code of Eshnunna we read: "The wages of a hired man are a shekel of silver; his provender is one pan of barley. He shall work for one month" (§ 11). Here the law is simply stated and it is assumed that it will be obeyed. In *HC* such laws are rare, but their presence is not to be overlooked. Thus the law, "In no case is the field, orchard, or house belonging to a soldier, a commissary or a feudatory salable" (§ 36), does not deal with a specific case, but lays down the principle which is to govern such cases. This is further illustrated by the law regarding adoption; "The (adopted) son of a chamberlain, a palace servant, or the (adopted) son of a votary, may never be reclaimed" (§ 187). With these we may compare certain of the Hittite laws. Most of the Hittite laws are casuistical; they are if-laws. But there are among them a number of laws dealing with the price of commodities; and they may be called apodictic, in the sense that they simply state the law, without dealing with a special case or imposing a penalty. Thus we read such statutes as the following: "The price of a weaned colt and of a weaned filly is 4 shekels of silver" (§ 181). "The price of one acre of vineyard is one mina of silver" (§ 185). With such statutes we may compare the casuistical laws to be found in *HC*, e.g., "If a seignior hired a cattle-herder he shall pay him six *kur* of grain per year" (§ 258), or, "If a seignior hired an ox to thresh, 20 *qu* of grain shall be its hire" (§ 268). These are merely two different ways of stating the same thing.[122]

It has been claimed that in the case of *HC* — this would apply to the other codes also — "most clauses are permissive rather than positive."[123] It would be better to say "some." In the case of the laws governing hire and sale, it is probable that the figure stated might be raised or lowered by common consent. But in the case of heinous crimes, we are hardly justified in assuming this unless the modification is definitely stated. E.g., in the case of a guilty wife, it is provided that her husband may spare her life if he wishes to do so (*HC* § 129). But in that case the king may spare his servant, the guilty man.

As might be expected changes were made in the laws from time to time. This is expressly stated in some of the Hittite laws. In some of these instances the "fine," as we may call it, is considerably reduced. Thus the penalty for biting off the nose of a slave is reduced from thirty shekels of silver to fifteen.[124]

Legal codes, in the strict sense, have not been found in Egypt. But whether codified, or not, similar laws were certainly observed and enforced in that land. This is clear, for example from the judgment scene in the Book of the Dead with its so-called "negative confession" in which the dead man enumerates the sins which he has not committed. It also appears clearly in the maxims and moral teachings of which the Egyptians were so fond. Thus in the "instruction of Amen-em-Opet we read "do not carry off the landmark at the boundaries of the arable land, nor disturb the position of the measuring-cord; be not greedy after a cubit of land, nor encroach upon the boundaries of a widow."[125] This indicates that the Egyptians had the same regard for property rights as did the Babylonians and Assyrians. But this offense is not mentioned in the *HC*, despite the fact that the discovery of many boundary stones inscribed with elaborate curses on the one who dares to remove them indicate how serious an offense this was considered to be.[126]

There is considerable difference between the laws of the various nations. The Assyrian laws were more cruel and brutal than the Babylonian.[127] This is shown in the laws and also in the contracts.

Mutilations are often ordered: the cutting off of ears, lower lips, plucking out of eyes, castration. The man who breaks a contract must take poison, or he must burn his own child in the fire. Compensation for breach of contract is usually tenfold. One penalty in the Assyrian Code is "doing the work of the king" for a month or a similar period, e.g., forty days. In the Hittite laws it is frequently stated that a guilty person shall "pledge his estate as security" for any fine which may be imposed on him.

The ancient world does not seem to have recognized imprisonment as a punishment for crime or the protection of society. Death, mutilation, the ordeal, fine, stripes, and enslavement were the usual forms of punishment. Imprisonment by the king for political offenses was, of course, recognized and practiced. Pharaoh put his chief baker and his chief cup-bearer in prison for a time. Potiphar did the same with Joseph. Amaziah of Judah may have been a virtual prisoner for a dozen years or more before his assassination. Nebuchadnezzar kept Jehoiachin a prisoner for thirty-seven years. Imprisonment for debt, does not seem to have been recognized.

Attention has been called to the fact that the Code of Hammurabi, like the earlier codes, "does not show any direct relation to the legal practices of the time." The contract tablets, while dealing with all sorts of matters, do not make any appeal to the law codes which were in existence and enforceable. This is significant in view of the fact that the infrequency of the mention of the law of Moses in the Historical Books of the Old Testament has been used as an argument that the Mosaic law is largely post-Mosaic.[128]

RELIGION

When we survey the archaeological field, especially that of the Near East, we note that Paul's words to the Athenians might be applied to all the peoples upon which light has been thrown by excavation; "in all things I perceive that ye are very religious" *(ARV)*. They had so many known gods that Paul was struck by the sight of an altar to "an unknown god."

The inveterate polytheism of the great nations of the Ancient Near East is impressively illustrated by the treaty of peace between Rameses II and the Hittite king Hattusilish. In it "a thousand gods of the male gods and of the female gods of them of the land of Hatti together with a thousand gods of the male gods and of the female gods of the land of Egypt" are invoked as witnesses.[129] Among the Egyptian gods eleven Seths are named: e.g., "Seth of the town of Sarissa." The conclusion invokes "the male gods, the female gods; the mountains; and the rivers of the land of Egypt; the sky; the earth; the great sea; the winds; and the sea," thus aiming to include the entire universe in the sanction of the treaty. It was of course, the prerogative of the gods to have their images and their places of worship. Polytheism and idolatry are the common characteristics of the many and diverse cults of the ancient Near East. Together with these common features there are many differences some of which are striking. We can deal with only the most obvious.

Egypt. According to Erman, the one respect in which the Egyptians differed from every other people was in "the extreme cult of the dead."[130] According to Petrie their attitude to the future differed so radically that he distinguished at least four religions "all incompatible, and all believed in at once in varying degrees":[131] the departed wandered about in the cemetery and had to be fed; they went to the realm of Osiris to which only the good were admitted; they were joined to the immortal gods; they were carried off by Hathor to wait for a bodily resurrection.

That the religion of Egypt was a composite derived from various sources is indicated clearly by the character of their idolatry. Some of their gods and goddesses are represented in human form, others have the head of an animal or of a bird, still others are completely animal, like the Apis bull, which represented the tendency to deify everything in the animal world, the cat, the hippopotamus, the ibis, the beetle. It has been held, quite correctly we think, that this animal worship (theriolatry) was the original cult of the Nile dwellers and that the Osirian cult (Osiris was never represented in animal form) was a foreign importation, probably Semitic.[132] It is claimed that the forty-two judges of the nether world originally represented the gods of the forty nomes of Ancient Egypt.[133]

In the cult the gods are represented as exalted human beings. According to Erman the cultus was in fact "nothing else than the regular service which a gentleman receives in his home. His servants take care of his clothing and provide his food and his women amuse him with music and dancing."[134] The same earthly conceptions appear in the cult of the dead which reaches its highest form in the deification of the Pharaoh. The building of vast sepulchres (mastabas, pyramids, rock tombs) and the elaborate mummification of the dead and provision for his nourishment and enjoyment in the other world imposed an insupportable burden on the living, which was only lessened by the substitution of "dummies" for the real objects which the king was supposed to require, these objects being placed in the tomb or represented in picture on its walls. So much of the wealth of the

Egyptians was placed in its tombs that tomb-robbing became a profitable business!

The Egyptian mythology is extremely complicated and inconsistent, which indicates that it is derived from different sources. Thus we have the story of the rivalry between Horus and Set and the stealing of the Horus eye, the killing and dismembering of Osiris by Set and the recovery of his body by Isis, which is followed by the birth of the other, and younger, Horus.

The Egyptians apparently had no deep sense of sin or of the need of atonement. This was not involved in the presentation of offerings; and the burning of the sacrifices is late and probably a foreign innovation. The so-called "negative confession" which the dead man makes when he appears before the judges in the great trial scene is not a confession of guilt but an assertion of innocence. It is worthy of note that Breasted in the preface to his study of the *development* of religion mentions as one of the topics which he has omitted "the concept of sacrifice, which I have not discussed at all."[135] Such an omission would be inexcusable had the idea of atonement figured at all prominently in the Egyptian religion. That the religion of the Egyptians was basically magical is indicated by the language of the Book of the Dead.

How much of uncertainty and difference of opinion must result from the study of so complicated a subject is illustrated by the fact that H. R. Hall, in concluding his sketch of Egyptian religion in the *Encyclopaedia Britannica* with a brief bibliography, prefaces it with the statement that it "partly consists of works with which the present writer entirely disagrees but which he quotes in fairness to their authors and to those readers who see things in the same light as they do."[136] The authors referred to are Erman, Budge, Naville, Wiedemann, Breasted, Gardiner, and Maspero.

As to these differences it may be noted that Erman stated definitely that it was his aim "to present the Egyptian belief as it would appear to an unbiased observer who knows nothing of the theories of the modern science of religion."[137] On the other hand, it was the aim of Breasted to discover and trace "A religious development of three thousand years analogous in the main points to that of the Hebrews."[138] That scholars whose aims differed so widely might be expected to arrive at radically different conclusions would seem to be obvious. Thus Breasted described Ikhnaton as "the first individual in history," "a god-intoxicated man,"[139] the founder of "the earliest monotheism." Yet it is to be noted that Breasted with all his enthusiasm for the genius and originality of Ikhnaton traces it to the imperialism of the Empire in the days of Amenhotep III and tells us: "Monotheism is but imperialism in religion";[140] and he found it "remarkable that the hymns as an expression of religious aspiration contain so little reference to character and to ethical matters."[141] Breasted regarded the Ikhnaton cult as culmination of the religion of Egypt, but he was forced to admit that it had little or no effect. For, as Hall expressed it, "So abnormal was this monotheism that the Egyptians would have none of it: Ikhnaton was branded as a 'criminal,' and the Egyptians, who had, of course, in reality never abandoned it for a moment, returned joyfully to the cheerful polytheism of their ancestors, in which they continued to believe till the coming of Christianity."[142]

Babylonia. The religion of Babylon, with which that of Assyria was practically identical, was basically and essentially the same as the Egyptian. It was quite as strongly polytheistic and idolatrous. The pantheon was immense. Some of the gods were originally Sumerian, others clearly Semitic. Thus Ellil was the god of Nippur and Nannar of Ur; Shamash was the god of Sippar, Ishtar (Innana) the goddess of Erech. The way in which these deities and their careers reflected political situations is illustrated by the case of Marduk, the god of Babylon. The most popular of all Babylonian legends is that of Gilgamesh. Yet Marduk is not mentioned in it. It is with the kings of the First Dynasty of Babylon that Marduk first became prominent and this was due to the triumph of Hammurabi, whose influence spread even as far as to Nineveh. In what we may call the Babylonian form of the Creation Story, Marduk is accorded a pre-eminent place among the gods, due we may well assume to the powerful influence of the Babylonian priesthood. Consequently, Marduk becomes Bel-Marduk and assumes a position similar or equal to that of the Bel of the great and far earlier trio, Anu, Bel, and Ea. In such wise the Babylonian pantheon grew and became more and more complicated. For it could be said of this Mesopotamian region as Jeremiah said of apostate Judah "the number of thy cities are thy gods." These gods are represented in human form and they require the same service which a human master expected from his servants: to be clothed, fed, amused.

In addition to the gods, and in some respects quite as prominent and life-controlling were the demons or evil spirits, such as the "wicked seven" (*utukki limnuti*), who were regarded as directly responsible for the sufferings of human beings and must be exorcised.[143] We find them represented as fiendish beings, with horrible heads. They made life utterly miserable for the people and all sorts of magical means were resorted to in order to placate or expel them. This led to the extensive practice of sorcery, which was the attempt by sympathetic magic to cast spells on one's enemies.

Thus by making a waxen image and melting it in the fire, or sticking it with pins, while reciting incantations, the sorcerer hoped to injure the object of his hate. In Babylonian the *Maqlu* and *Shurpu* incantation texts are evidence of such practices. In Egypt the Execration Tablets served the same purpose.

It is significant, perhaps highly so, that in the Code of Hammurabi, the second of the more than three hundred laws deals with the crime of sorcery. It requires that the accused prove his innocence by submitting to the ordeal of the Sacred River. If he drowns, he is guilty; if he does not drown, his accuser is guilty and is to be put to death.[144] In the Hittite Code (§ 170) we read, "If a free man kills a snake while pronouncing another man's name, he will give a mina of silver. If he (the offender) is a slave, he shall die." This is apparently a law dealing with sorcery by sympathetic magic, as is indicated by the words "while pronouncing another man's name." It does not indicate that killing a snake was a heinous act *per se*.[145] Whether in this instance the snake is thought of as the protector of the boundary is not clear. Jastrow has discussed the symbol of the snake (*Sir*) on the Babylonian boundary stones and also the snake as an omen in the omen texts.[146]

An example of magical ritual among the Hittites is found in "The Soldier's Oath." We are told that "They bring the garments of a woman, a distaff and a mirror, they break an arrow and you speak as follows: 'Is not this that you see here garments of a woman? We have them here for the oath.' "[147] Whoever breaks the oath is to be turned into a woman.

According to Wardle, the religion of Babylonia is characterized "by a great preponderance of the magical element, which, though no doubt the lower forms of Hebrew religion found it congenial, was utterly abhorrent to the writers of the Old Testament."[148]

According to Jastrow, "In general men laid the more important happenings of life in the hands of the gods, while they attributed the lesser annoyances, such as accidents, illnesses, misfortune and so forth to the (evil) spirits."[149] And he pointed out that the gods were regarded as, generally speaking, well-disposed to mortals, while the spirits were regarded as generally hostile. Sorcerers and witches were a baleful influence. Sympathetic magic was resorted to for the healing of the afflicted and to bring evil upon others. The magical texts are quite numerous.

Like the Egyptians, the Babylonians were intensely concerned with the future, but with a vast difference. The Egyptian was concerned with the life beyond the grave, with a blessed future or the means of making it blessed. For the Babylonian the grave was a "land of no return"; it was a place of darkness and gloom, and little if anything could be done about it.[150] His concern was with the future in this life, how he could penetrate the mystery of coming events. The king wanted to know the outcome of a warlike expedition and counsels of state. The common man was concerned over the weal or woe which attended his every step in daily life. Consequently, for the Babylonian every occurrence in heaven or earth must be observed as to what it portended of good or ill in the course of his earthly life.

Of the portents which were studied, two were by far the more important: hepatoscopy, which involved the study of the liver of a sacrificial animal, and astrology, the study of the heavenly bodies. Another system of divination was lecanoscopy, the pouring of oil into water.[151] These we may call ritualistic or ceremonial practices; and they were probably resorted to on all important occasions. But the importance attached to what may be casual occurrences, meetings with or observation of the actions of snakes, birds, quadrupeds, insects, and anything abnormal connected with the births of animals or humans, indicates the tremendous influence exerted by superstitions of the most varied kinds on the daily life of the people. Still it is to be remembered that, as stated above, these attempts to determine and control the future had no reference to the life beyond, upon which they had no bearing, but upon well-being in man's earthly existence for which they were regarded as of extreme importance.

A feature of the Accadian religion of which we have now convincing evidence is the theory and practice of substitution. This probably had its origin in sympathetic magic, as pictured in the *Maqlu* and *Shurpu* texts. An example of the ritual of substitution taken from Ebeling's *Tod und Leben* is given in full by Hooke,[152] where the procedure for the substitution of a goat for a sick man is described in detail. The substitute for the king *(shar puchu)* is especially noteworthy. This practice is referred to in a letter of the Sargonid period. The substitute was supposed to suffer any misfortune which might impend for the king; and if the life of the king was regarded as threatened, the substitute was to be put to death in his stead.[153] This shows that the idea of substitution was well known to the Assyrians in the time of the Sargonid kings and probably much earlier.

In this connection it is to be noted that there was no such cult of the dead as we find in Egypt. The pyramids of the dead Pharaohs have no counterpart in Babylonia. Except for the Royal Tombs at Ur, which were Sumerian, we have no imposing tombs of king or commoner. Burial was of course of great importance. But the manner of interment apparently was not. It has even been suggested that one reason for the secure disposal of the bodies of the dead was to prevent their returning to prey as vampires on the living.

That the Babylonian had a sense of sin and ill-desert is indicated by the complaints and confessions which form so large a part of the hymns and psalms of the people. But apparently much of this was due to the feeling that every ill of whatever kind must be the result of having offended some god, rather than to any consciousness of sin as such. The most familiar example is the oft-quoted penitential psalm which contains such expressions as the following:

> The anger of the lord, may it be appeased.
> The god that I know not, be appeased.
> The goddess that I know not, be appeased.
>
>   *   *   *   *
>
> The transgression that I have committed, I know not,
> The sin that I have wrought, I know not.
>
>   *   *   *   *
>
> To the god, known or unknown, I turn, I utter my prayer.[154]

This impression is strengthened when we observe the nature of the sins which are confessed:

> The pure food of my god have I unwittingly eaten.
> The clear water of my goddess have I unwittingly drunken.
> The taboo of my god I have unwittingly eaten.
> To an offense against my goddess I have unwittingly walked.
> O lord, my transgressions are many, great is my sin.

Here we are dealing not with morality and guilt as such, but with cultic taboos and ritual requirements.

Contenau may perhaps overstate the difference when he describes the Babylonian religion as "surely one of the harshest religions ever practiced by man," and in comparing it with the "happy religion" of Egypt declares that "spiritually the two were poles apart."[155] But the difference is there; and it illustrates the danger of stressing correspondences and ignoring differences with a view to establishing a pattern common to both. Contenau explains the difference as mainly due to temperament: the Egyptian had "natural good humor," the Babylonian was "a stranger to laughter." This illustrates the fact that both religions were anthropomorphic and man-made and thus fundamentally different from the religion of revelation in the Old Testament.

PERSONAL NAMES

It is quite appropriate to follow the discussion of ancient religions with a brief consideration of personal names, for the reason that religion figures so prominently in them. Much can be learned as to the religious ideas of the Israelites and also of the beliefs of the neighboring peoples, Babylonians, Egyptians, and others from the names which they gave to their children.

Archaeology has thrown welcome light upon the interesting subject of proper names. Names are primarily labels, identifiers. The business documents of the Babylonians contain thousands of names. Usually, as in the Old Testament, identity is indicated or established by paternity: e.g., David the son of Jesse, Isaiah the son of Amoz. There were no surnames, although a gentilic name might be used for purposes of identification: Uriah the Hittite, Naamah the Ammonitess, or a title might be added: e.g., "Eliakim, the son of Hilkiah, who was over the household and Shebna the scribe."

Simple Names. As in Babylonian a child might bear a very simple name: Shaphan (badger), Hamor (ass), Caleb (dog), Leah (wild cow), Rachel (ewe), Deborah (bee). Compare for example Babylonian *Shellibi* (fox), *Muranu* (young lion), *Sinunu* (swallow), *Nubta* (bee).

Compound Names. Very many Semitic names are theophorous, i.e., compounded with the name of deity. Thus Nathan (he gave) appears as El-nathan, Jehonathan or Nathanael, Nethaniah, the divine name appearing either at the beginning or the end. Sometimes both orders appear: e.g., Abi-el (my father is God) also occurs as Eli-ab, Ammi-el as Eli-am, Abi-jah as Jo-ab, Ahaziah as Jehoahaz. Hebrew compound names regularly contain only two elements as in the examples given above. But Babylonian names sometimes contained three or four: e.g., Nebuchadnezzar, the Babylonian form of which is *Nabu-kudurri-usur* (Nebo protect the boundary, or the succession rights), Esarhaddon (i.e., *Ashur-ahi-iddin.* Ashur has given a brother), Nabu-zir-kitti-lishir (may Nebo cause a true seed to prosper).[156]

Abbreviated Names. As the occurrence of long names in Babylonian suggests, quite frequently simple names may represent the shortening of a compound name. Thus, Nathan may be the shorter form of any one of the compound names mentioned above. Ahaz may be shortened from Jehoahaz, which appears as *Jauhazi* in the Annals of Tiglath-pileser. Or a letter or syllable may be omitted: Jehonathan may appear as Jonathan, Jehoash as Joash; Abram and Abner may be shortened from Abiram and Abiner. Adoram may be a contraction of Adoniram.

An especially interesting type of abridged names consists of those which have an ending added. Such names may be regarded as diminutive or pet names (hypocoristic). They occur frequently in the Babylonian. Nebuzaradan appears in 2 Kings 25:8 as the name of the officer who was left by Nebuchadnezzar in command at Jerusalem after the fall of the city. This name appears on a number of Babylonian tablets of that period as *Nabu-zir-iddin* and means "Nebo has given seed (offspring)." It also occurs combined with the names of other Babylonian gods (Addu, Ea, Bel, Shamash). A few times the name of the god is omitted; and the name appears simply as *Zir-iddin*. More frequently it occurs as *Ziri-ia* which apparently represents the word *zir* (seed)with hypocoristic ending *-ia*[157] which like the *-y* in Betty or Johnny makes it a pet name (*Kosennamə*). Such names occur very frequently in Babylonian. Thus *Ziria* might be the abbreviation of Nabu-*zir-ukin* or of several other names. It might represent *Zir-Babili* (seed of Babylon) which is apparently the Babylonian form of Zerubbabel.

A difficult problem emerges where this ending *-ia* appears in Hebrew proper names. It is quite clear that in the Old Testament *-ia* is often the short form of *Yahu* (i.e., Yahweh). This is obscured by the fact that in our English Bibles the final vowel is regularly dropped. Thus Elijah, Isaiah, Jeremiah, Hezekiah all end in *yahu* (e.g., Eliyahu for Elijah). The warrant for this is to be found in the fact that such abbreviations occur in the Hebrew text. The name of Elijah the prophet is usually written *Eliyahu*; but four times in 2 Kings 1 it is written *Eliyah*, which makes it clear that in this and many similar names *-ya* stands for *-yahu*, and that the name is theophorous. This may be a proper inference in all cases where the same name appears in both forms; as in the case of Ahijah the prophet whose name is written both with and without the final vowel. But in view of the fact that the word *ah* (brother) occurs in a number of combinations (e.g., Ahihud, Ahilud, Ahitub, Ahimelech, Ahimaaz, Ahinadab, Ahinoam, and a dozen more), it seems proper to assume that in some instances the ending *'yah* is simply the hypocoristic ending and not the abbreviation of the divine name Yahweh.

Another frequently occurring hypocoristic ending is *-i*. We meet it in such names as Abi, Abdi, Amzi, Bukki, Karmi, Libni, Omri, Tibni, Zabdi, and Zimri. That in some cases it is a shortening of *-ia* is indicated by the fact that Hezekiah's mother is called both Abi (2 Kings 18:2) and Abijah (2 Chron. 29:1); and as we have seen Abijah may stand for the clearly theophorous name Abijahu. Thus the name Zabdiyahu is shortened to Zabdiyah and then to Zabdi, which may also be the shortened form of Zabdiel; and all may be still further shortened to Zabad.[158]

Names may also be shortened by dropping the initial syllable. The name of king Hezekiah is occasionally spelled Yehizkiya(hu), but usually the ye- is omitted. A probable example of such abridgement is Hiram which may be shortened from Ahiram (cf. Abiram).

Confusion in Names. As in English many names indicate the sex of the bearer. Thus Leah (wild cow), Rachel (ewe), Eglah (heifer), Deborah (bee), Zipporah (bird) are appropriate to a woman, while Oreb (raven), Zeeb (wolf), etc. are given to men. Ben (son) is often used in masculine names, e.g., Benjamin, Benhail, Benhanan; Bath (daughter) in names of women, Bathsheba. Consequently it is to be noted that there are a number of names in the Old Testament which are given to both men and women. Abijah is the name of Rehoboam's successor and of the mother of Hezekiah. Maacah is the name of five men and six women (cf. also Abihail, Abiah, Ahlai, Hodiah, Shelomoth). Athaliah, the name of the bloodthirsty daughter of Ahab and Jezebel, is given to two men. Mehetabel is also used of men and women. Whether Nahash (serpent) which is a man's name in 1 Samuel 11:1; 2 Samuel 10:2; 17:27 is given to a woman in 2 Samuel 17:25 has been much discussed because of its bearing on the relationship of Zeruiah to David.

Identification Uncertain. Where only the name is given it may be difficult or impossible to be sure of the identity of the bearer and caution should be exercised.

Esau and Amalek. We read in Genesis 36:12 that Esau had a grandson, Amalek. According to Genesis 14:7 Amraphel and his allies smote all the land of the Amalekites in the days of Abraham, Esau's grandfather. Unless this is regarded as "a later editorial description"[159] of which there is no indication in the context, it implies that the tribe or nation of Amalek dates from a much earlier period than that of Esau and that there is no connection between Amalek and Esau. Amalek is not listed in the Table of Nations (Gen. 10). But this does not necessarily mean that Amalek was a latecomer among the nations. Balaam describes Amalek as "the first (*rosh*) of the nations," but the meaning of "first" is uncertain: in antiquity, in size, in influence? The Table is not comprehensive. It lists no descendants of Peleg, not even Reu (11:18), but it gives his brother Joktan thirteen children. Furthermore the histories of Edom (Esau) and Amalek in the Old Testament are markedly different. They are never connected either in war or in peace. The racial identity of Amalek is unknown.

The Name Asaph appears in the headings of twelve of the Psalms. This is not surprising since Asaph was a prominent Levite who, together with Heman and Jeduthun, was appointed by David to organize the service of song for Solomon's temple (1 Chron. 25). But several other Asaphs are mentioned in the Old Testament. We read that "the sons of Asaph" took part in Josiah's passover (2 Chron. 35:15) and also that 148 of them returned from the captivity under Zerubbabel (Ezra 2:41). Consequently, it is quite possible that the Asaph who is named in the headings of Psalms 74 and 79, which seem clearly to presuppose the destruction of Jerusalem and the temple by Nebuchadnezzar, was a descendant of the great Asaph, who lived after this terrible calamity took place. The one who added the heading may have regarded it as unnecessary to make it clear that this Asaph was a *descendant* of the singer of David's time.[160]

The Children of Elam. Elam is the name of a country and people, its progenitor being the first-born of Shem. The Elamites lived in the mountainous regions east of the Tigris. For the most part their history is distinct from that of Israel until the eighth century B.C. Yet in Ezra 2:7; Nehemiah 7:12 we read that 1254 of the "children of Elam" returned to Jerusalem from the Captivity, and we also read of an additional 1254 who were "the children of the other Elam"[161] (Ezra 2:31; Neh. 7:34), and of Jeshaiah and seventy males, who were also "sons of Elam" (Ezra 8:7). An Elam signed the Covenant (Neh. 10:14). Who these sons of Elam were we do not know. That they were Elamites (Ezra 4:9) is highly improbable. That they were called "sons of Elam" because they were Israelites who had been settled in Elam by their conquerors is possible (Acts 2:9). It seems strange that the ancestry of these sizeable groups in post-captivity Judaism is nowhere stated.

Significant Names. A name is often more than a mere label. There may be a special reason for it; and a special meaning may attach to it. This is especially the case with biblical names. A reason is assigned for the names Eve, Cain, and Seth. Noah means "rest," and the word "comfort" (*nacham*) involves a word-play. Isaac, Ishmael, Jacob, and Israel are all significant names. Most of the names of the twelve sons of Jacob are explained. In the case of the name Joseph, a double reason is given which involves a word-play: "and she said God has taken away [*asaph*] my reproach: and she called his name Joseph, saying, The Lord shall add [*yoseph*] to me another son" (Gen. 30:23f.). Similarly in the case of the name Babel, which means "gate of God," there is a play on the verb *balàl* which means "to confound," because the gate of a city was the place of judgment and the sentence pronounced was the confounding of the tongues. Significant names are sometimes given by the Prophets. Lo-ammi and Ammi, Lo-ruchama and Ruchama, Jezreel are so used in Hosea 1. Jeremiah in 20:3 gives the name Magor-missabib (terror round about) to Pashur the priest; Shear-jashub (a remnant shall return) is the name given Isaiah's son. Ezekiel uses the names Aholah (her-tent) and Aholibah (my tent is in her) to indicate the difference between Samaria and Jerusalem (23:4). Micah 1 contains a number of word-plays: e.g., "At Beth-le-aphrah [house of dust] have I rolled myself in the dust [*aphar*]"; "The house of Achzib shall be a lie [*achzab*] to the kings of Israel." The most beautiful as it is also the most familiar of significant names in the Old Testament is "Immanuel" (God with us), with which we may compare "*Yahweh ṣidkenu*" (the Lord our righteousness) as given to the Messiah in Jeremiah 23:6 and to his people in 33:16.

It is clear that many names expressed the wishes and hopes of the parent. So the question naturally arises as to the extent to which the name given to the child may have influenced his future career. Hannah tells us that she asked her first-born son of the Lord; and the name Samuel may have been suggested by the verb to ask (*shaal*). But the meaning of Samuel is uncertain. Elijah's name (my God is Yahweh) might be called the epitome of his life. Isaiah (salvation of Yahweh, or Yahwah is salvation) expresses the main theme of this great prophet of salvation. Joel (Yahweh is God), Micaiah (Who is like Yahweh?), Ezekiel (God strengthens), Zechariah (Yahweh has remembered), Daniel (God is my judge) — these and many other names may have exerted a powerful influence upon the lives of the men who bore them. But we must remember that such significant names — and all theophorous names are or should be significant — were probably often given for purely secular reasons; and in some cases they belied the attitude and intent of the one who gave them.[162]

The reason for the giving of a name may be quite obvious. Tamar (palm-tree) may suggest a tall, slender, attractive figure and be an appropriate name for a girl. It was the name of an ancestress of David, so was appropriate for one of his daughters. Absalom probably gave it to one of his daughters because of his love for his greatly wronged sister. The fact that Athaliah, the daughter of Ahab and Jezebel, bore a significant theophorous name (Yahweh is exalted), and that Jehu and his successors did so also may have little or no significance. The name Manasseh (causing to forget) was given by Joseph to his first-born son as a significant name full of meaning to him (Gen. 41:51). Why Hezekiah gave it to his son, we are not told. What was it that Hezekiah wanted to forget? In Isaiah 62:4 Hephzibah (my delight is in her) is a name expressing the delight of Israel's God in his people. But whether as the name of Hezekiah's wife, it had any religious significance is quite uncertain.

Ambiguous Names. It may also be the case that names are at times intentionally ambiguous. Amon is the name given to wicked Manasseh's son. A Hebrew etymology may give the meaning "steadfast," "faithful," or "master workman." But it is quite possible that Manasseh intended the name to suggest Amon the Egyptian god. This would be in accord with the statements made in Kings as to the abominations and provocations of which he was guilty.

The Changing of Names. There are a number of examples of this. God changed Abram's name to Abraham, Sarai's to Sarah, Jacob's to

Israel. He gave Solomon a special name, Jedidiah (2 Sam. 12:25), which is never used elsewhere. One of the most familiar examples is Uzziah (my strength is Yahweh), the name used in Isaiah 6 and in 2 Chron. 26. It appears as Azariah (Yahweh has helped) in 2 Kings 14-15. The meaning of these names is somewhat similar. It has been suggested that Uzziah took the name Azariah when he began his sole reign on the death of his father. But if this were the case, it would be strange for Isaiah to say "in the year that king Uzziah died." Jehoahaz, the son of Josiah is also called Shallum (Jer. 22:11). Why, we do not know. It was natural that Nebuchadnezzar should change the names of Daniel and his three friends from Hebrew to Babylonian, since he intended them for service at court. A significant change is Azubah (forsaken) to Hephzibah (my delight is in her), names given to Jerusalem in Isaiah 62:4.[163]

Foreign Names. In studying biblical names it is important to determine if possible the nationality of the bearer of the name. It is proper to assume that the names of foreigners are foreign not Hebrew names. This appears clearly in the names of foreign kings. Chedorlaomer is clearly Elamite, Hadadezer is Aramaic, Pharaoh is Egyptian, Shalmaneser is Assyrian. Pharaoh gave Joseph an Egyptian name which is never used by the writer of Exodus. The names of Joseph's jailor, of his wife, and of her father are all Egyptian. On the other hand the names of the midwives, Shiphrah certainly, Puah probably, indicate that they were Hebrew women. The name Uriah is given to six biblical characters. It means "my light is Jah." But whether this explanation fits the case of Uriah the Hittite is far from certain. This Uriah is called "the Hittite," apparently to distinguish him from other Uriahs. He may have adopted the Hebrew name, when he became a warrior of David's. Or his name may be a Hebraized form of a Hittite name. Whether the Uriah who is called "the priest" who was used as a witness by Isaiah (8:3) is the same as the priest who acquiesced in the demand of Ahaz that he make a copy of a heathen altar is questionable. The witnesses are called "faithful" or dependable. Whether this would apply to the high priest of Ahaz's time is doubtful.

It has been claimed that Abram was a Babylonian because a name Abarama has been found on cuneiform tablets. If the name means "exalted father" the -*ram* comes from a West Semitic (Aramaic) root and indicates that Abram was not a Babylonian but only a sojourner in Ur, and that he came there from Haran and returned to Haran, en route to Canaan. Whether the names of the five cities of the Philistines (Ashdod, Ashkelon, Ekron, Gath and Gaza) are

Canaanite or Philistine is doubtful. Gath and Gaza sound Semitic, but this may only be apparent.

The fact that the name, Nahor, is borne both by Terah's father (or ancestor) and by one of his sons raises several interesting questions. Was "the city of Nahor" (Gen. 24:10) named after the former or after the latter? Or does "city of Nahor" mean simply the city (Haran?) where Nahor lived? Does the fact that Terah's son Nahor is not mentioned as accompanying his father when he departed from Ur of the Chaldees mean that Nahor had already gone to Haran to visit or to live with his grandfather? Or is he simply not mentioned because he did not go with Abram to Canaan? In the light of such passages as Genesis 25:20 (cf. 24:4) and Deuteronomy 26:5 it seems not unlikely that Abraham came of Hebraic-Aramaic stock and that the residence of the family in Ur was a relatively brief one.

It has often been pointed out that the name of the city Haran (Gen. 11:31, AV) is quite distinct from the name Haran which is given to Terah's son who died in Ur (11:27f.). The spelling Charran (Acts 7:4, AV) indicates this quite plainly. The name Charran apparently comes from the Accadian word meaning "road" or "highway" and indicates that the city was an important artery of traffic in ancient times.[164]

Difficult Names. These are of two kinds: meaning unknown and apparent meaning questionable. Among the names whose meaning is entirely unknown we may list, for example, Amalek, Enoch, (*Henokh*), Baasha, Hagar and many others. Arioch (Gen. 14:1) may be Hurrian. But is this the same name as the one which is found centuries later as the name of the captain of Nebuchadnezzar's bodyguard? Or do they simply sound alike?

Sometimes the obvious meaning is so improbable as to be decidedly questionable. "Fool" is the natural meaning of *Nabal* (1 Sam. 25:25). But it seems unlikely as a given name. The suggestion that such a name was a kind of talisman expressing "an implied prayer that the child would be kept from folly" implies pagan superstition rather than true faith in God. It seems more probable that Nabal was not the given name, but a nickname (called by the Arabs a *laqab*),[165] which was given him because of his folly and perhaps resembled his real name. It is also possible that the root had in Hebrew a good meaning as well as a bad one, being one of the polar words which occur occasionally in Hebrew.[166] He was called Nabal (honorable, the meaning in Arabic) but as applied to him it proved to be Nabal (fool), the usual meaning in Hebrew. *Ahitophel* seems to mean "brother of folly." This also is unnatural as a given name. But it may not be a true rendering of the Hebrew. Or it may be the name by which this wise counsellor and friend of David was known and remembered after he transferred his loyalty to Absalom. *Jonah* (dove) is a strange name for a man, although Zippor (bird) occurs in the Old Testament. *Cushan-rishat-haim* — What seems to be the literal rendering (Cushan of double wickedness) seems improbable. The meaning must be regarded as uncertain, as in the case of *Ahimoth* (brother of death), *Ahira* (brother of evil). That a strict Jew should have the name *Mordecai*, which certainly suggests, even if it is perhaps not actually derived from the Babylonian god Marduk, seems very remarkable, as also the name *Esther* which likewise suggests Ishtar, the Babylonian goddess of love and war. We are told that Daniel's Babylonian name Belteshazzar contained the name of Nebuchadnezzar's god (Dan. 4:8).[167] As to the use of these pagan names by Israelites, we will do well to remember that Christians of Anglo-Saxon ancestry have for centuries continued to use names for the days of the week, which they inherited from their pagan ancestors, e.g., Wednesday being Woden's day.

The desire to find a derivation for all biblical personal names has produced some strange etymologies. To cite a single example, Mary (Hebrew Miriam) has been explained as meaning "contentious," "bitter," "fat," "star of the sea." We will do well to bear in mind that the meanings of many biblical names are either quite uncertain or entirely unknown.[168]

CHAPTER IV

THE OLD TESTAMENT AND ITS CRITICS

Criticism of the Bible, even very drastic criticism, is not at all a new thing under the sun. Nor is it distinctive of this Modern Age. As has often been pointed out, one of the early critics of the Word was Jehoiakim who applied to it the penknife-and-fire method of criticism. When Paul went as a prisoner to Rome, the leaders of the Jews came to him with what seemed to be an open mind: "We desire to hear of thee what thou thinkest: for as concerning this sect, we know that everywhere it is spoken against" (Acts 28:22). And the result was that after listening to Paul, their open-mindedness was turned in most cases to open opposition. So it has often been in the past; and the situation is much the same today. The Bible has been from the beginning the most loved and the most hated of books. It will continue to be this, as long as there are sinners to be rebuked and saints to be edified by it.

This is a matter which needs to be carefully borne in mind. When we read many of the books which have been written in criticism of the Bible, it would seem that they proceed on the assumption that the ancient Israelite and the early Christian were the most gullible persons imaginable, that they were ready to "swallow" almost anything, however impossible or incredible. They accepted traditions which were conflicting, inaccurate and largely untrustworthy. They accepted a body of laws as coming through Moses which contained many with which Moses had nothing to do. This is improbable, to say the least. For example, in the days of Ezra, who is described as "a ready scribe in the law of Moses, which the Lord God of Israel had given" (Ezra 7:6), the Jews who had taken foreign wives agreed to give them up because Ezra demanded it, but with this proviso, "Let it be done according to the law" (10:3). Some at least of the men who were involved must have dearly loved the wives which they had married contrary to the law. Is it probable that they would have submitted tamely to such a requirement unless they were firmly persuaded that this act of renunciation was one which they dared not refuse to perform? This is only one of many examples which might be given. The Bible is a book which makes many demands upon men, some at least of which are as much opposed to their carnal desires as Jehoiakim found the contents of Jeremiah's scroll. Yet throughout Christendom the Bible holds a unique place in the hearts of multitudes today. "The

Bible says" is a word of authority which carries conviction for the Christian as does no other book. Would it, could it do this, if it were a merely human book, clumsily put together, in which an intelligent person can easily find a multitude of conflicting, contradictory and quite undependable statements?

Today when we speak of "criticism" or "higher criticism" we usually mean that movement which began two centuries ago, with the publication by Astruc in 1753 of his theory that the Book of Genesis is compiled from two main documents, the one characterized by the use of the name Jehovah, the other by the use of Elohim. He did not deny the Mosaic authorship; on the contrary, he maintained it, as did also Eichorn who advanced much the same theory independently about thirty years later. This was shortly followed (1805) by the claim of the youthful De Wette that Deuteronomy is not Mosaic, but that the book was written shortly before it was "found" in the temple in the days of Josiah. This and the extension of the documentary analysis throughout the rest of the Pentateuch and even into Joshua led to the abandonment by the critics of the Mosaic authorship of the Pentateuch. In 1853, just a century after the appearance of Astruc's book, Hupfeld came forward with the claim that the Elohistic document was composite; and he divided it into two sources which we now know as P and E. This meant that there were four sources of the Pentateuch, P, J, E and D and, the redactor. In the course of several decades, through the studies of Graf, Reuss, Kuenen and especially Wellhausen, the conclusion was reached that P was not the earliest but the latest of these sources and that the proper order is J, E, D, P. As to their relative date there was difference of opinion but it was quite widely held that, however much or little of earlier material they might contain, all of these documents were post-Davidic; that J dates from about the time of Elijah and Elisha, that E is perhaps a century later, dating from shortly before the reign of Hezekiah, that D dates from the time of Josiah, that P which contains the bulk of the legislation is exilic or post-exilic; and that the whole Pentateuch as we know it dates from the time of Ezra.

There were two fundamental principles at work. The one was the theory of *differences*, that differences in diction, in style, in viewpoint, must mean diversity of authorship; and by hairsplitting analyses the critics often succeeded in making out of a simple, self-consistent account, two or even more accounts which contradicted each other at many points. The other principle was that of *development*. On the assumption that the religion of Israel had its beginnings in very crude and primitive beliefs and practices, such as were to be found in the religions of neighboring peoples, the attempt was made to trace the development along more or less definitely avowed naturalistic lines, from a primitive animism to the lofty monotheism of the Prophets.[1]

Connected with these, and in a sense underlying them all, was the belief that a book like the Pentateuch could not have been written as early as the time of Moses, and that therefore the sources of which it was alleged to be composed must date from a much later time. This claim was supported by the more fundamental one that supernatural events, such as are recorded in the Bible are incredible and are to be regarded as myth, legend, folklore, and therefore as clear indications of the historical untrustworthiness and probably late date of the Pentateuch.

Now it is of the utmost importance that we should recognize clearly that the natural and inevitable result of the acceptance of a view of the Bible which denies the authenticity and trustworthiness of much of its contents is that for all who accept such conclusions large areas of biblical history, including practically the entire pre-Davidic period, become to a large extent as far as dependable history is concerned a *void* or *vacuum*,[2] what the philosophers call a *tabula rasa*, which the enterprising critic is at liberty to fill in as he sees fit, or, to change the figure, it becomes a kind of happy hunting-ground in which the ingenious critic can find the most remarkable trophies of his prowess as a hunter. Turn to almost any critical treatment of the religion of Israel, and you find that it commences not with Adam, not with Abraham, perhaps not even with Moses, but with an account of so called "primitive Semitic religion" as reconstructed from biblical and extra-biblical sources. The Book of Judges, for example, has been a favorite place to begin, because it pictures so vividly the evil state into which Israel *fell* through disobedience to God and his holy law as given by Moses. This state the Bible describes as a terrible apostasy: "... they forsook the Lord God of their fathers, which brought them out of the land of Egypt, and followed other gods, of the gods of the people that were round about them ... and provoked the Lord to anger" (Judg. 2:12). Yet it is this very situation and condition which the critics regard as giving a true picture of the normal life and practices of "primitive" Israel during the times of the Judges and even later, a picture which both assumes and seems to justify the claim that until the time of the monarchy or even later the religion of Israel did not differ essentially from that of the peoples amid which they dwelt.

It must be admitted that the discoveries of recent years have made it much more difficult than it was a century ago to maintain the claim that the Mosaic age was *pre-literary*, and that the Pentateuch could not date from the time of Moses. The discovery of several alphabetic scripts, one near Sinai, which is associated with the giving of the Law, others at Byblos and Ras Shamra, in the Canaanite territory to the north of Palestine, which were probably as early as the time of Moses, or even more ancient, has made it much harder to maintain the view that all of the literature of the Old Testament must be late, than it was when the only ancient systems of writing known to us were the cumbersome Egyptian hieroglyphs and the Babylonian cuneiform. Yet on the other hand the meagre results of excavation in Palestine, the relative fewness of the literary remains discovered there, has made it possible for the critics of the Old Testament to continue to insist that writing did not come into extensive use in Palestine until comparatively late. And however much they may insist on the trustworthiness of oral tradition, as equal or even superior to that of written documents, it is a very obvious fact that many scholars are willing to trust this oral tradition only insofar as it supports the conclusions which they have arrived at more or less independently of it. As a matter of fact, the *vacuum* produced by criticism has not been filled by any extensive *literary* findings of the archaeologists. The *vacuum* still remains.

Still in view of the highly speculative character of the higher critical reconstructions and especially their radical disagreement with the statements of the Old Testament itself, it is not surprising that there have been quite evident signs in the last few decades that the iron grip of Wellhausen is weakening. We shall discuss briefly seven of the more recent trends:

1. *The Literary Critical.* This carries on in general the Wellhausen tradition of documents and development. There is still great interest in sources and documents in certain circles; and the attempt has been made by some scholars to carry the literary analysis still further. Among these we may mention Eissfeldt, Mowinckel, Morgenstern, R. H. Pfeiffer, Rowley, Von Rad (two P's), Noth, C. A. Simpson. On the other hand there have been those who like Volz, Rudolph and Winnett have endeavored to reduce the number of Pentateuchal sources.[3] About forty years ago there was a rather vigorous challenging (e.g., by Hoelscher, Welch) of the Josian date of Deuteronomy, which has been called the "Archimedes point" of the higher critical reconstruction. But Eissfeldt has assured us that it is now more strongly established than ever.[4]

In recent years there has been a rather significant change in the field of literary criticism. The tendency to connect Joshua with the Pentateuch and to speak of a Hexateuch is a feature of the Wellhausen hypothesis which can be traced back to Geddes.[5] "Hexateuch" supplanted "Pentateuch" in critical circles for many years. In recent years the emphasis on the Deuteronomic elements in the Historical Books (Joshua — 2 Kings) has been leading scholars to call these books the

Deuteronomic history and to connect Deuteronomy with them. This would reduce the Pentateuch to a Tetrateuch.[6]

2. *The Form Critics.* Their main interest is in the pre-literary form of the biblical traditions, the various patterns (*Gattungen*) in which the traditions of Ancient Israel were supposedly handed down orally until they were finally reduced to written form. This type of criticism goes back to Gunkel,[7] whose great aim was to determine the situation which produced and shaped these traditions, their "*Sitz im Leben.*" Since it is the claim of the Form Critics that these ancient traditions, whether stories, legends, war songs, marriage songs, dirges, proverbs, odes, hymns or even laws must have been rather brief in order to be easily remembered, the tendency was at first to split up extended passages, e.g., the prophetic discourses, into quite brief utterances. In fact, Form Criticism has been described as a return to the Fragment Hypothesis. But it is now being recognized that many oral traditions were worked up into a unified and more or less consistent whole before being incorporated in such a document as J. It is to be noted that since the Form Critics are especially interested in the *pre*-literary form of the traditions, they can accept and build on the documentary hypothesis, their main objective being to reach the sources lying back of the documents generally recognized by the literary critics. Consequently, Gunkel, Eissfeldt, Mowinckel and Von Rad, for example, are both Literary and Form Critics.[8] It is to be noted that, just as in the case of the New Testament, the Gospel narratives are assumed to have derived their final form through the Christian community, so that stories of the Pentateuch are supposed to have been shaped (formed) to meet the needs of the various centers in which they arose. Consequently, neither the Old Testament narratives nor the New can be regarded as thoroughly dependable accounts of the events which they record.[9]

The defense of oral tradition is a rather difficult one for the Form Critics to make. If they claim that oral tradition was so accurate that these traditions did not need to be written down, but were so correctly transmitted for centuries that recording was unnecessary, then when they try to get back of the literary form to a quite different oral tradition, they virtually admit the importance and necessity of the written record. On the other hand if they insist that traditions were molded and altered in the course of oral tradition, they must admit that the desire for accuracy would make a written record desirable and necessary, provided such a record was possible. And archaeology has proved conclusively that it was both possible and probable in the time of Abraham and for centuries before his time. The importance of the written record — setting things down "in black and white" — has found expression in such proverbs as the Chinese adage, "The weakest ink is stronger than the strongest memory" and the Latin epigram, *Verba volant, scripta manent*. The reason Hammurabi had his laws engraved on a huge block of diorite was to make them a permanent record for his subjects for generations to come.

3. *The British Myth and Ritual School*. S. H. Hooke is the most prominent figure.[10] To the same school belong in general W. O. E. Oesterley, T. H. Robinson, E. O. James, A. H. Johnson, J. H. Gaster and also the Americans, Graham and May. All of these scholars have found in Frazer's *Golden Bough* an anthology of mythology and folk-lore which is a fruitful mine of information.

To understand the position of this school we need at the outset a clear definition of the two words *myth* and *ritual* from which it derives its name. According to Hooke, such a story as the slaying of Tiamat is a myth. It is not historical in the strict sense, because "it is not the record of a single event which took place at a particular date in a definite locality." As an example of "a single, unique event which can never be repeated," he mentions the battle of Waterloo. From this it follows, he tells us, that the myth "possesses a truth which is both broader and deeper than the narrow truth of history." For "the essential truth of the myth lies in the fact that it embodies a situation of profound emotional significance, a situation which is in its nature recurrent, and which calls for the repetition of the ritual which deals with the situation and satisfies the need invoked by it."[11] Hence the myth and the ritual which enacts it are of "equal potency." And the performance of the ritual and the telling of the story (the myth) which explains it, accomplish by sympathetic magic the result desired. The special interest of members of this school is in the ritual pattern which they claim prevailed extensively in the Near East and was originally followed by Israel in early times. This emphasis on myth and cult is not new. Not to go farther back, we find it in the Pan-Babylonists of half a century or more ago. But it has recently received great impetus through the discovery of the Ras Shamra tablets; and it looks very much as if the Pan-Babylonian era is to be succeeded by a Pan-Canaanite, which will be even more serious because the religion of the Canaanites was a cult which the Israelites were especially exhorted to shun and abhor.[12]

4. The *Traditio-historical*, or as it is also called, the *Scandinavian* or *Uppsala School*, because its members are largely Scandinavians and some of them are connected with Uppsala University, has been becoming increasingly influential in recent years. Among its prominent representatives are Pedersen, Birkeland, Mowinckel, Nyberg, Widen-

gren, Engnell, Bentzen, Haldar, and Nielsen. Its most important features are the following:

(a) A high regard for the Hebrew Massoretic Text as compared with the versions, especially the *LXX*,[13] and a protest against excessive emendations of it.[14] It is to be noted, however, that this does not mean that these scholars regard the *MT* as thoroughly dependable. Thus Nyberg holds as do the Form Critics that the written Old Testament "is a creation of the Jewish church after the Exile. What preceded it was only to a small extent established in written form (*schriftlich fixiert*)."[15] Hence all that the textual critic can do is to determine the earliest written text.

(b) A marked tendency to minimize or ignore the "documentary" analysis of the literary critics and its widely accepted results, to insist that all the material dealing with early times is late, and to place the emphasis on the pre-literary traditions, as preserved and molded by oral transmission,[16] a viewpoint which they share with the Form Critics.

(c) The acceptance of the view that religion did not have its beginnings in Animatism and Animism, but that primitive man believed in a high god, and that polytheism represented a deterioration of this earlier faith.[17] This involves the rejection or radical modification of the development theory.

(d) Like the Myth and Ritual School it claims that a single more or less uniform cultic pattern characterized the religions of all the ancient Near Eastern peoples known to us, and that this must have been originally shared by Israel. Martin Noth has called those who hold this view the "Divine-Kingship School" since the claim common to both is as stated by Hooke that the "pattern consists of a dramatic ritual representing the death and resurrection of the king who was also the god, performed by priests and by members of the royal family."[18]

5. *The Barthians.*[19] The distinction which Karl Barth and his followers draw between history as a record of a course of temporal events (*Historie*) and supra-history (*Geschichte*) which is more or less independent of chronological sequence and of the laws of historical evidence, enables these scholars to accept the negative conclusions of the critics as to the actual occurrence of biblical events or to treat them with more or less indifference. If Abraham (or Adam), for example, belongs to the suprahistorical sphere, and is to be regarded as our contemporary, regardless of when he lived, then it is a matter of no great importance whether Abraham (or Adam) actually existed or whether he is merely an ideal figure; and the date and composition of the Genesis narratives is of minor importance.[20] Brunner, for exam-

ple, while differing from Barth in some important respects, assures us that even the most radical criticism leaves the essentials of Christianity unharmed. When we think of the extremes to which radical criticism has gone in the denial of even the most essential facts recorded in the Bible, such a statement is significant. It shows how far Crisis or Dialectical Theology can go in dispensing with the facts of redemptive history.

The tragedy in Barthianism consists in the situation in which it has placed itself. On the one hand Barth insists on the utter transcendence of God. Man by searching cannot find God. If man is to know God, God must break through and reveal himself to man. God has done so in the Bible which is God's Word to man, utterly indispensable to man for any true knowledge of God. But the Bible is communicated to man through fallible men. It is a human and fallible book and contains human error as well as divine truth. It contains the Word of God, but it is not the Word of God. It only becomes the Word of God to the individual man when and insofar as the Spirit of God makes it to be the Word of God to him. The result is a dangerous subjectivism. The Bible ceases to be the objective norm and standard of truth; and the Spirit of God must accredit the divine truth in it and distinguish it from human error. But since the Devil may appear to man as an angel of light, how is the individual to know that it is the Holy Spirit who is guiding him? The more the human errancy of Scripture is emphasized as is done by Tillich, Bultmann and others, the clearer does it become that Christian faith based on the Scriptures as the infallible Word of God is being replaced by Mysticism or Rationalism, with the result that the "Thus saith the Lord" of divine revelation gives place to the "I think so" or "I feel so" of the fallible individual or of the fallible guides to whom the fallible individual turns for guidance and enlightenment.[21]

6. *Existentialism.* This doctrine has two main features which are somewhat closely related. The first is traced back to Kierkegaard.[22] "Utterly removed from the dispassionate, spectatorlike attitude of the normal philosopher or scientist, it is characterized by decision, isolation, and an absence of demonstrative certainty."[23] According to C. F. H. Henry, "Rebellion against any objective comprehension of reality, against any rational rules for conduct, against any definition of man and his tensions in general or universal terms, is existentialism's keynote. It orients the whole discussion to the particular man and to his own inner experiences."[24] If man is "absolutely autonomous" and "the creator of his own law," the Scriptures can have no inherent authority for him. His decisions are subjectively determined and they are the "warp and woof" of his life. He will accept the Bible and the

opinions of others regarding it only in so far as it appeals to him personally. It is intensely subjective, personal and practical. It is concerned with living, with human existence, the life of the individual man, his personal problems, difficulties and needs.

Closely related to this subjective and individualistic attitude toward knowledge is, as a second and even more significant reaction, the widely current view that the supernatural viewpoint of the Bible is outmoded because incompatible with that scientific view which regards the intrusion of any extraneous forces or factors into the world-order as impossible, and hence treats the miraculous element in Scripture as a hang-over from an unscientific or pre-scientific past and regards it as both meaningless for and irrelevant to the thinking of the modern man. Hence Bultmann attempts to demythologize the New Testament — his method is equally applicable to the Old — while at the same time interpreting its "myths" in such a manner as to retain the "essential" truth and make them relevant for our living today.[25] But it becomes increasingly evident that to demythologize means to desupernaturalize; and a desupernaturalized Christianity will in the end become mere morality.

7. *Biblical Theology*. One of the more recent developments in the field of Old Testament studies is the movement which has rather inconsistently taken the name of "Biblical Theology." Its claim is that the Bible is to be studied "from within." This would seem to indicate that it is or aims to be thoroughly biblical. Unfortunately, as has been already pointed out, it is hampered and even stultified by its determination to be both biblical and critical. On the one hand it claims to believe in the supernatural and to reject the naturalistic evolution which as a theory of development lay at the root of the Wellhausen theory. On the other hand it still clings to the Documentary Hypothesis along with the late date and consequent untrustworthiness of the documents of the Pentateuch and is not very friendly to the supernaturalism of the Bible. Its advocates claim that archaeology has proved the accuracy of many things in the Old Testament which Wellhausen and the earlier critics challenged or rejected outright. But they are little more prepared to accept the statements of the Old Testament on their own authority, because they are the word of God, than was the old Liberalism which they assure us is now dead. Archaeology and Comparative Religion are their great sources for the accrediting and interpreting of Scripture; and the great weakness lies in the fact that they are unwilling to accept the fact as Packer has pointed out that "The Christian revelation is a complete world-view, supernatural from first to last. It makes a connected and intelligible whole; but being supernatural, it does not at any point admit of

demonstrative proof."[26] Thus Albright has written an article entitled "Return to Biblical Theology" in which he has stated that "Any attempt to go back to the sources of Christianity without accepting the entire Bible as our guide is doomed to failure."[27] But he still holds to the Wellhausen Hypothesis to no small degree; and his reasons for accepting the historical data in the Bible are not that they are recorded in the Bible but that they are confirmed by archaeology or by comparative religion. Where they conflict with these pillars of "Biblical Theology" he does not hesitate to reject them. Thus he regards the censuses recorded in Numbers as taken by Moses, which certainly are part of the "entire Bible," as recensions of the census taken centuries later by David, because he regards them as historically incredible, despite the care and detail with which they are given and the emphasis on the supernatural in the biblical narrative.

One of the leaders in this movement, A. G. Hebert, published a book entitled, *The Bible from Within* (1950). The title is decidedly intriguing, because it suggests that the aim of the author is to let the Bible *speak for itself.* It is especially noteworthy because the title expresses what the author declares to be the great aim of this movement, which he has elsewhere stated as follows: "They endeavor to see the Bible 'from within'; not to impose on it standards of judgment derived from any modern belief in 'progress,' but to sit at their feet and learn from them what it was that they were 'seeking to express.' "[28] With this statement in mind we turn to Hebert's statement regarding the Book of Daniel.

In speaking of the great struggle for freedom from the yoke of Antiochus Epiphanes of which we read in 1 and 2 Maccabees and in Josephus, he tells us

The history of it is recorded in the Apocrypha. But one book of the Old Testament belongs to this period, and was written to sustain the faith of the martyrs in their conflict: the Book of Daniel. This book *purports* to be a story of events in the time of Nebuchadnezzar, four hundred years before: but its actual reference is to this persecution.[29]

Here we see quite clearly the fallacy of the claim that "Biblical Theologians" seek to find out "exactly what the biblical writers meant to say to the men of their own time" and believe that "what the Biblical writers were expressing was in fact true." For by using the word "purports" Hebert admits that the traditional interpretation of Daniel is the one that was *intended* by the author of the Book of Daniel. This example is especially pertinent and significant because as everyone knows, it is primarily the supernaturalism in the Book of Daniel, its miracles and prophecies, which since the days of Porphyry, has been the insuperable objection in the minds of critical and rationalistic scholars to the acceptance of Daniel as being what it purports to be.

Hebert describes the denial of the miraculous as one of the numerous errors of the Old Liberalism which he assures us is now dead and replaced by Biblical Theology. Yet he shows by his own statements that the Biblical Theologians hold to no small degree to the old methods and accept the presuppositions of the Old Liberalism which lead them to the same conclusions: namely that the Bible is not to be taken at its face value and in its obvious sense, that it is not to be studied "from within," but is still to be read with the aid of spectacles provided by the rationalistic critics of fifty and a hundred years ago. When Walter Eichrodt in his *Theology of the Old Testament* declares that the domain of Old Testament theology "is closely linked" to "the prolific variety of pagan religions", he seems strangely oblivious of the fact that the religion of the Old Testament is constantly represented there as quite distinct from the ethnic faiths and as utterly opposed to them; and that the constant tendencies to "link" it with them by the adoption of heathen practices are denounced as apostasy and grievous sin. We note also that Eichrodt commends Albright's *Archaeology and the Religion of Israel* because in it the author "has set the faith of the Old Testament in the vast perspective of the history of the Near East." Martin Buber is an example of a Jewish scholar who has made extensive use of comparative religion, as in his *Moses* which deals with the religion in the Mosaic period.

There are also certain more or less independent scholars whose work is especially significant because it represents in one form or another a challenge to the still widely influential Wellhausen School. One of the most outspoken of these is Dornseiff,[30] professor of Classics at the University of Greifswald. As a classicist he is convinced that great literary works such as the Iliad and the Pentateuch belong to a much earlier period than the critics are prepared to admit. He also emphatically rejects the idea that such a work as the Pentateuch could ever have been put together with "scissors and paste" out of several different documents as the critics have been insisting for a hundred years or more was the case. And he proposes that all such analyses be disregarded at the outset of the study.

Professor Edward Robertson of Manchester University, England, would explain the Pentateuch as the work of an ecclesiastical council called together by the prophet Samuel.[31] Unfortunately his tendency to favor the Samaritan tradition as against the Hebrew and his relatively low view of the authority of the Old Testament text prevent his reaction against Wellhausen from commending itself to Conservatives. Thus he says of the Book of Judges: "It is an amalgam of unrelated tales and legends."[32]

The work of several Jewish scholars is significant. Benno Jacobs in his elaborate commentary on *Genesis* rejects the documentary analysis in its entirety.[33] He finds a marked numerical structure in Chapters 1-11 which leads him to speak of them as "poetry," which means that they are not to be understood with the literalness of prose narrative. He holds that in Chapters 12-25 there are fourteen "scenes" (*Akte*). While he is not sure as to the date of composition of the book, he insists that it is the work of a single author; and he claims also that the record in Genesis nowhere requires a date lower than that of Moses.

Quite recently Yehezkel Kaufmann's massive *Religion of Israel* (1959) has appeared in abridged form in English translation. He calls it "a fundamental critique of Classical Criticism." He accepts some of the features of the Wellhausen Hypothesis, but changes it radically at certain points. He insists that D knows nothing of P and therefore that the order of documents is J, E, P, D. Yet he dates D in the reign of Josiah. He restores the order Law and Prophets as against the claim that the Prophets preceded the Law. Yet he holds that Law and Prophets developed separately. Like the majority of critics, he does not hesitate to reject biblical statements where they do not accord with his theories as to the history of Israel.[34]

In an attempted synthesis of the developments in Pentateuchal criticism in recent years, C. R. North directs attention to two significant tendencies.[35] The one is to treat Old Testament history as *Heilsgeschichte*, i.e., as "redemptive" rather than actual history, that is, to regard it as a "cultic glorification" of historical events rather than as an actual record of them, the aim of which is *edification* rather than *information*, with the result that they are more or less discredited as trustworthy history. In speaking of a critical situation which developed at Sinai, Buber tells us: "Behind the ingeniously constructed conversations with God which have had so great an effect on the view taken by later generations of Moses' relations with God, we feel a reality that has been lived through."[36] True! But the critic must determine what the "reality" is which is to be felt behind these "ingeniously constructed conversations." This illustrates the large subjective element which enters into the work of these critics. The other trend discussed by North is the tendency to reject the Wellhausen view that the documents of the Pentateuch form a succession which reflects the course of Israel's religious history during a period of many centuries, and to hold instead that the written documents are all post-exilic and that they should be regarded as "parallel, contemporary and more or less co-terminous strata." He feels that "no one reading Pedersen can escape the feeling that he presents things on a flat surface, without dimensional depth."[37] In other words, if all these documents date from the same general period, the post-exilic, none of them can be expected to reflect any special period in the development of Israel's religion; and it must be the task of the critic to sort over the material and arrange it in the form of an historical development. This North feels would be very difficult: "The history of any one of these documents may well be as complicated as the history of the whole Pentateuch was conceived to be only thirty years ago."[38]

A comparatively recent development in the theological world is the God-is-Dead school of which Altitzer, Hamilton, and Buchanan are leading representatives. The emergence of this school, if it is to be called a school, came as a great surprise and shock to many. It should not have done so. It can be traced back to Comte, Nietzsche and other radical thinkers of the past century. As a movement which claims to be in any sense biblical, it has its rootage in the Higher Criticism, which has always been unfriendly, if not positively hostile to the supernaturalism of the Bible. Equally significant is the attempt which has been made to secure approval by the courts of the study of Bible History in state-supported colleges on the ground that the Bible is not a religious book, and that the question of State and Church is not involved. A desupernaturalized or demythologized Bible might be regarded as a secular book. But then it would not be the Holy Bible! For the Bible is from cover to cover a supernatural book.

To discuss all these different viewpoints in detail and the varying opinions of the scholars who may be regarded as holding more or less definitely to them would be an arduous undertaking. There are quite noticeable differences and equally obvious agreements. Thus the tendency to lay less stress on literary analysis and to emphasize the pre-literary stage is quite strong, with all except what we may call the strict Wellhausenians. The rejection of the evolutionary view of the development of the religion of Israel by the Scandinavian School is another significant development. The emphasis placed upon Comparative Religion, the insistence on the "pattern" may be regarded as merely the broadening of the tendency which has been evident for many years and in which Max Mueller and Sir James Frazer have played such prominent roles.

The one feature which is characteristic of all of these trends and which is of especial importance for the Bible student is the tendency to insist that the Old Testament books which avowedly belong to and describe the early period, are all relatively late, post-Davidic and even post-exilic, and therefore undependable. However strongly it may be emphasized by them that oral tradition is accurate and dependable, the fact remains that it is not so treated by the scholars who affirm this of it. On the contrary they often treat the sources with the same freedom which has been characteristic of the literary critics. That is, they accept the (oral) tradition as finally stabilized in the Masoretic Text insofar as it supports what they believe to have been the course of Old Testament history, but they do not hesitate to modify or reject it when it does not.

In the essay on "The Present Position of Old Testament Criticism" which he contributed to the first volume of essays published by the Society for Old Testament Study (1925), Professor J. E. McFadyen made the following rather striking confession:

> It is because the facts are so few that they are capable of such diverse interpretation; they have to be co-ordinated by necessarily imaginative synthesis: if they were more numerous there would be proportionately less scope for the play of imagination in their co-ordination, and more unanimity in their interpretation. Yet however numerous the facts, the personal equation inevitably remains.[39]

This is an important statement for the two reasons which we have pointed out: the comparative meagreness of the results of archaeological research bearing directly on the Old Testament period and the treatment of the data furnished in the Old Testament itself as relatively late and undependable by "critical" scholarship today. For if the biblical narratives are late and undependable and the critics are at liberty to decide for themselves what statements they will accept as true and work into their syntheses and what data they will either reject in toto or interpret in a way which will fit into them, then it is not at all remarkable that very wide differences of opinion prevail even among those who in general hold the same position as to the course of Old Testament history. Obviously the field for imaginative synthesis must be very great.

It is now forty years since McFadyen penned this statement and a number of important discoveries have since been made and welcome light has been thrown on some knotty problems. But when we consider the immensity of the field and the meagreness of our knowledge of it, Professor McFadyen's caution is quite as necessary as it was when he first gave it. Much of what follows in this and in the final chapter may be regarded as illustrative of the significance of his words. It will also serve to show how tragic it is that much of what we do know, much of what the Bible, which is our principal source of information, tells us, ceases to be of real value for the critics because they regard it as relatively late and therefore unreliable. In other words, it will serve to show that a conspicuous feature in all of the following examples is what we may call the screening of the evidence. By this we mean that the biblical data opposed to the theory proposed is screened or sifted out and only that residuum retained which is regarded as supporting it.

Conservatives. The critical theories which have been briefly considered all represent a more or less definite break with the past. Consequently the scholars who hold them largely ignore the past and those who today hold to the old views; they are obscurantists as to both past and present. Conservative is a good name for those who hold to the old views as to the authority and trustworthiness of Scripture. For it is their aim to conserve and preserve all that is true and valuable in the biblical scholarship of past generations, especially since the time of the Reformation. Hence they value the writings of Luther and Calvin, of the Puritan divines and of more recent writers such as Hengstenberg, Haevernick, Keil, Pusey, Patrick Fairbairn, Addison Alexander, Jamieson, Fausset, and David Brown. All of these held what may be described as the biblical view of the Old Testament: the Pentateuch Mosaic, the Prophets later than the Law, the majority of the Psalms Davidic. Some others, like Franz Delitzsch and von Orelli, were supernaturalists but accepted many of the critical views regarding the Old Testament. All of these works of the past are of value today.

Coming now to those who have defended the Old Testament against the critics we have the writings of W. H. Green, James Orr, Wilhelm Moeller, R. D. Wilson, A. H. Finn, J. H. Raven, M. G. Kyle, R. L. Dabney, Edward Mack, A. T. Clay, H. M. Wiener, Geerhardus Vos, W. J. Beecher, J. D. Davis, A. H. Sayce, J. Urquhart, G. F. Oehler, most of the contributors to the *International Standard Bible Encyclopaedia*, and more recently E. J. Young, J. P. Free, Wick Broomall, S. J. Schultz, M. F. Unger, J. S. Wright, J. C. Whitcomb, Jr., H. M. Morris, J. I. Packer, A. R. Short, H. C. Leupold, C. F. Pfeiffer, M. G. Kline, M. C. Tenney, G. T. Manley, D. J. Wiseman, A. A. MacRae, and many others, few of whom are even mentioned in books written by critical scholars.[40] Especially worthy of mention are the numerous publications of the Inter-Varsity Christian Fellowship, which has recently published two elaborate works which indicate a definite turning of the tide. They are *The New Bible Commentary* (1953) and its companion volume, *The New Bible Dictionary* (1962). Also to be mentioned are the *Pictorial Bible Dictionary* (Zondervan), Holman's *Biblical Expositor*, and the *Wycliffe Bible Commentary*.

We shall now pass in review a number of the solutions of Old Testament problems proposed by the critics and consider them in the light of McFadyen's statement.

CREATION

"When God began to create heaven and earth" (Gen. 1:1). This

rendering of the first verse of the Bible has become increasingly popular in recent years. We find it in the *Moffatt*[41] and the *American*[42] translations; and it has been placed in the margin of the *RSV*. Albright has declared that "it is practically certain"[43] that it should be adopted. He gives two reasons. The first is based on the JP analysis which is generally accepted in "critical" circles today. If Genesis 2:4 is split in two and the second half, "in the day that the Lord God made earth and heaven," which then has no finite verb of its own, is joined to the following verse or verses as a temporal clause, and made the beginning of the J account, then it can be claimed that the two accounts begin in much the same way. This assumes, of course, that the critical analysis is correct.[44] This we do not admit.[45] But what here concerns us is Albright's second reason: "Most Sumerian and Babylonian cosmogonies begin in the same way, so stylistic influence seems likely." We are prepared to admit the fact stated in the first part of this statement. But we challenge the correctness of the inference which is drawn from it.

No unbiased person can read the account of creation in Genesis 1 and compare it with the Sumerian and Babylonian accounts without being impressed with the vast difference between them. The one breathes the spirit of lofty and sublime monotheism. The others are pervaded and marred by a grotesque polytheism. W. L. Wardle, after a thorough comparison reached the following conclusion: "Above all, though it is quite probable that the writers of the early chapters of Genesis were acquainted with the Babylonian stories, their attitude is rather one of revulsion from than dependence upon Babylonian models."[46] More recently Heidel has reached somewhat similar conclusions. He opposes the view that "In the beginning" can be regarded as introducing a temporal clause. He tells us: "The Babylonian creation stories are permeated with a crude polytheism"; and further: "In the entire Old Testament, there is not a trace of a theogony, such as we find, for example, in *Enuma elish* and in Hesiod."[47] Albright would probably agree with E. A. W. Budge that the monotheism of the Babylonians and Assyrians "entirely lacked the sublime, spiritual conception of God that the Israelites possessed, and was wholly different from the monotheism of Christian nations."[48] Why then should he insist on interpreting the greater by the lesser? The words, "In the beginning God created the heaven and the earth" are the language of monotheism and of monergism. They are the natural rendering of the Hebrew, which has been so rendered for centuries. "When God began to create the heaven and the earth, the earth was waste and void," can then easily be interpreted as suggesting primordial dualism, God and matter co-existent eternally. If the Hebrew writer, if Moses had a unique revelation of God, why must he have made use of pagan language to express it?

"And the Spirit of God moved upon the face of the waters" (Gen. 1:2). In the Ugaritic Myth of Aqhat, the vultures are represented as "soaring" over Aqhat in order to dart down upon him and destroy him because he has refused to give his bow to the goddess Anath. In Deuteronomy 32:11 the figure is quite different. The eagle is represented as "fluttering" (*AV, ARV, RSV*) over its young clearly with the idea of protective nearness and helpfulness. Yet Albright tells us that in view of the Ugaritic evidence: "it thus becomes certain that we must render Gen. 1:2 'and the Spirit of God was soaring over the surface of the water.'"[49] Albright secures his meaning for the verb from the context of the Ugaritic legend. Why should we not derive its meaning in Hebrew from its biblical context?

THE CREATIVE WORD

And God said, Let there be light: and there was light (Gen. 1:3). Here at the beginning of the account of creation we meet the statement that the creation took place by divine fiat. This doctrine is summarized in the *Westminster Shorter Catechism* in the words: "The work of creation is God's making all things of nothing by the word of his power, in the space of six days and all very good." S. N. Kramer in *From the Tablets of Sumer* (1956) has gathered together twenty-five "firsts," which he attributes to the Sumerians. Regarding "Man's first cosmogony and cosmology" he tells us: "As for the creating technique attributed to these deities, Sumerian philosophers developed a doctrine which became dogma throughout the Near East — the doctrine of the creative power of divine word." This is interesting because in the Bible this doctrine is plainly stated in the first chapter of Genesis, a narrative which for more than a century most critics of the Bible have assigned to the latest of the documents of the Pentateuch (P) and regarded as post-exilic. We are not prepared to admit that Moses learned of this doctrine from the Sumerians. It may have been a matter of direct revelation. But it is noteworthy that in this case the archaeologist places first what the higher critic places last in his reconstruction of his biblical sources.

In this connection it may be well to remind ourselves that the radical difference between the biblical and the critical attitude to the Old Testament appears nowhere more plainly than in the treatment of this chapter. According to the one view, the Old Testament record begins with an affirmation of unqualified monotheism. According to the other, that viewpoint was not arrived at until after the Babylonian

Captivity and is the result of a long process of development.

CAIN AND ABEL

To the ordinary reader the story of the killing of Abel by his brother (Gen. 4:1-15) shows every indication of being a historical incident which is related to show how speedily the terrible effect of the Fall showed itself in the human race: the oldest son of Adam became a fratricide, venting his anger over the rejection of his sacrifice by God upon his innocent brother. As such it is a most instructive story with lessons that should never be lost sight of. None of the seed of Adam are free from the taint of Adam's sin; and the consequences of that outbreaking evil may be as terrible as they are inexplicable. There is no reason for treating it as other than factual; and as factual it has its terrible and salutary lessons.

Professor Hooke of the Myth and Ritual School claims that originally this "saga" described a fertility ritual, "not an impulsive murder instigated by jealousy, but a ceremonial killing intended to fertilize the soil".[50] This setting aside of what may be called the obvious or surface meaning for a hidden and recondite one he justifies on the ground that such practices were a part of the framework of religion of the ancient Near East and so must have formed part of the pagan heritage of Israel. He suggests that we have here "the survival in Hebrew literature of the tradition, worked over by a later hand in the interest of an entirely different religious point of view, of a fertility ritual of the Tammuz type, where a shepherd was ritually slain at the time of the summer drought, and his official slayer was obliged to flee in order to remove the ceremonial guilt of the slaying from the community."[51] The reader will note the words: "worked over by a later hand in the interests of an entirely different religious point of view." This is a very plain admission that, in the interest of folk-lore, Professor Hooke has rewritten this biblical narrative to make it accord with a preconceived theory which he is concerned to prove correct.[52]

ABRAM, THE HEBREW

Ever since the discovery of the Amarna Letters in 1887, the question has been debated, whether the word *habiru* which occurs several times in the letters of Abdu-Heba of Jerusalem is to be understood as referring to the Hebrews and to the conquest of Canaan by them. Subsequent discoveries at Boghazkeui, Mari, and elsewhere have made it at least probable that the word was used in a broad sense which might refer to the Hebrews but might also apply to other foreigners, or mercenaries. A further problem is the possible connection between the word *habiru* and the similar word *apiru* which had already been found on Egyptian inscriptions.[53] If these two words are identical, we should then read *hapiru* instead of *habiru,* which would make the identity of *hapiru* with Hebrew more doubtful than ever. The whole question is still very much *sub judice.* Those who favor the early date of the Exodus are naturally inclined to regard the Habiru of the Amarna Letters as the Hebrews.

Under such circumstances we should be very careful in our interpretation of the use of the word Hebrew in the Bible. As compared with the name Israel its occurrence is extremely rare. It is used about thirty-five times of the people themselves, and about ten times of their language. Several explanations of the name have been given: (1) that it is derived from the name Eber (Gen. 11:16); (2) that it describes Abraham and his descendants as men who came from "beyond" (*'eber*) the Euphrates: or (3) from "beyond" the Jordan.

The word appears usually on the lips of non-Israelites: Egyptians (Gen. 39:14, 17; Exod. 1:15, 16, 19; 2:6) and Philistines (1 Sam. 4:6, 9; 14:11; 29:3). That there is sometimes a note of contempt in the word Hebrew, especially as used by them seems rather probable. But in the reference to Abram as "the Hebrew" (Gen. 14:13), and in Joseph's words, "I was stolen from the land of the Hebrews" (40:15), we may note on the contrary an element of pride. Its use in the title "(Lord) God of the Hebrews" (Exod. 3:18; 5:3; 7:16; 9:1, 13; 10:3) may be regarded as lending dignity to the name. Certainly in the law regarding slavery the words, "If thou buy a Hebrew servant," draw a sharp and favorable distinction between Hebrew and non-Hebrew. A man who is a Hebrew has certain rights which must be respected (cf. Jer. 34:9, 14). When Jonah declares his nationality with the words, "I am a Hebrew," he is not speaking in self-deprecatory terms, for he adds, "and I fear the Lord, the God of heaven, which hath made the sea and the dry land." There is rather here the same note of racial and national pride which we meet in Paul's words, "Are they Hebrews? so am I," (2 Cor. 11:22; cf. Phil 3:5). Consequently to say as Rowley does that the word is "generally used in a pejoristic sense"[54] is not warranted by the biblical use of the word.

No less questionable is the statement that "there is no evidence that it was ever associated with Israelite nationalism."[55] On the assumption that the word is used originally of foreign mercenaries, marauders, "free companions," who were both feared and despised, it is easy to read contempt into the use of the word, where none may have been intended. On the other hand, if any one of the three explanations given above is accepted, the word acquires dignity and distinction. Rowley in his insistence on the "pejoristic" sense, is clearly influenced by the use of the word *habiru* in the ancient inscriptions. Yet he warns his readers to beware of supposing that the extra-biblical evidence in favor of the equation *habiru* = hebrew is "more than speculative and disputable."

<h3 style="text-align:center">ABRAM AND MELCHIZEDEK</h3>

Eduard Nielsen assures us that Genesis contains "at least one definitely *Jerusalemite* tradition" (Gen. 14:17-24).[56] He explains this incident in Abram's life as follows:

> Passing *Shalem* he is blessed by the priest of *El 'Eljon*. Abram identifies this god with the Lord, and gives him "a tenth of all." Who is Abram, and what does this tribute mean? Nyberg has given the final answer: [57] Abram is David. *Shalem* is Jerusalem. *El 'Eljon* is the real master of Canaanite soil, he is moreover the God who was especially worshipped at Jerusalem. The story reflects the Davidian conquest of Jerusalem, and the inauguration of the great symbiosis between the Lord and the Canaanite "Landesgott." The payment of the tithes reflects the Israelite acknowledgment of the primacy of *El 'Eljon*.

We note: (1) Nielsen is correct in claiming that Abram identifies Jehovah with the "most high God" (*El 'Eljon*).[58] But it is nowhere stated that this God is a Canaanite deity ("the real master of Canaanite soil"). On the contrary, *El 'Eljon* is described by both Abram and Melchizedek as "maker (or "possessor") of heaven and earth" and Abram identifies him with Jehovah. In other words they both recognized *El 'Eljon* as the one true God. This is the interpretation placed on the incident in Psalm 110:4 and Hebrews 5-7. And the Christian church has always regarded it as an example of the appearance or survival of a primitive monotheism in a heathen environment. (2) Nielsen allegorizes the story. He tells us that there can be no doubt that "Abram is David" and that the story "reflects the Davidian conquest of Jerusalem, and the inauguration of the great symbiosis between the Lord and the Canaanite 'Landesgott.'"

This is a startling example of the way in which a member of the Traditio-historical school can deal with and manipulate a biblical narrative in the interest of a theoretical reconstruction. The claim that Abram is David is not supported by any statement in the narrative itself. The story describes an event which happened centuries before the time of David. But if the story can be assumed to be late and unreliable, then the Form Critic can claim that the tradition which lies back of the narrative really was quite different from what the prima facie evidence would imply and that it really is a legend or folk-tale recording one of the exploits of David. How it came to be connected with Abram and to be recorded very early in the patriarchal history becomes a mystery which the critics will find it hard to explain. If a tradition which concerns David and Zadok and the bringing up of the ark to Jerusalem after the conquest of Jebus is really the basis for the story which is told in Genesis 14 about Abram, what confidence can we place in the Biblical narratives?

THE COVENANT

Professor G. H. Davies, in dealing with the eighth century prophets finds a problem in "the virtual non-use of the term 'berith' (covenant) by these prophets in speaking of Israel's election."[59] He asks how this is to be explained "in view of the use of this term in certain of the traditions now incorporated in the J and E documents." His answer is: "This evidence from the tradition in the prophets strongly suggests that the relationship created by Yahweh's election of Israel came to be expounded through the medium of the 'term' covenant late in the history of that tradition."[60] He offers the following explanation: "It is possible that we may have to look for a Canaanite source for this term, and in view of the figure of El-Berith at Shechem, we have probably not far to look."[61]

We turn to the Book of Judges and read regarding Baal-berith: "And it came to pass, as soon as Gideon was dead, that the children of Israel turned again and played the harlot after the Baalim and made Baal-berith their god. And the children of Israel remembered not Jehovah their God, who had delivered them out of the hand of their enemies on every side" (8:33f.).[62] This statement can only mean that any connection of Israel with Baal-berith was an act of apostasy. The Book of Judges tells us further that Abimelech the son of Gideon burned the stronghold of the tower of El-berith with fire, so that about one thousand men and women perished in the overthrow. This is all we are told in the Bible about Baal-berith or El-berith of Shechem. Yet Professor Davies does not hesitate to tell us that we "have probably not far to look" to find this word in the Canaanite deity of ancient Shechem. This ignores the fact that the covenant with Noah is referred to in Genesis 6 and in Genesis 9, and that the covenant with Abraham is referred to in Genesis 15 and 17; Exodus 2:24; Leviticus 26:42; and the covenant with his descendants in Exodus 6:4f.; 19:5; 24:7f.; 34:10, 27f.; Leviticus 26:9, 15f.; Deuteronomy 4:13; and frequently elsewhere in Deuteronomy. The body of laws in Exodus 21-23 is called the "book of the covenant" (24:7); "ark of the covenant" is one of the frequent designations of the ark (e.g., Num. 10:33). We read of the covenant of the Sabbath (Exod. 31:16; cf. Lev. 24:8), of a covenant with Phineas (Num. 25:13).

Covenant is certainly a common word in the Pentateuch. Yet apparently none of this evidence is to be regarded as dependable. So we are referred to the allegedly Canaanite god, Baal-berith, of Shechem; and we are told that we are to find in his name (covenant-lord) the source of the covenant idea despite the fact that Judges so definitely represents worship of Baal-berith as an act of apostasy which was inexcusable because of all that Jehovah Israel's God had done for them. Could negative criticism of the Bible be carried further?

The Sacrifice of Isaac

That the Canaanites of Abraham's day practiced Moloch worship seems probable. Consequently it has been inferred by many scholars that the command to Abraham to sacrifice Isaac seemed justifiable and proper to the Patriarch because in doing so he was following the pagan custom of offering his best to his God. Others have simply taken the purely naturalistic view that the idea was Abraham's own and that it was inspired by pagan ideas. These interpretations fail to do justice to the biblical narrative (Gen. 22). Such a religious rite as was practiced by the Canaanites would probably have been performed at the temple of the god, as a public act of worship, by an officiating priest; and the victim would usually have been an infant. Abraham was commanded to make a three days' journey to an unknown destination. He took with him only two of his many servants; and they were finally left behind, probably lest they might interfere with the carrying out of Abraham's purpose, as is further indicated by his words, "I and the lad ... will come again to you." There were to be no witnesses of this terrible scene! Furthermore, Isaac was not an infant. He was at least a well-grown lad. We are expressly told that the wood for the sacrifice, which must have been a very considerable burden, was placed on his shoulders, while his aged father carried only the fire and the knife. Josephus' statement that Isaac was twenty-five years old may be an exaggeration. But his representation of Isaac as a willing victim seems to be born out by the biblical account. It seems to be implied that this strong and vigorous son could have resisted and even defeated his father's purpose had he wished to do so. The only hint which is given us as to Isaac's attitude is in Jacob's words, "the fear of his father Isaac" (Gen. 31:42).[63] It was a uniquely personal transaction, the supreme test of Abraham's faith and obedience. It is not stated or implied that the two servants were told what had happened or that Sarah ever learned of it. It seems to have been a closely guarded family secret. Hence, while it may be possible that his acquaintance with a heathen custom may have made it easier for Abraham to accept and obey the command of God, on the other hand it is to be noted that the narrative seems to be told with a view to make it impossible to connect Abraham in any way with such a horrible practice. The entire setting and tenor of the narrative is so unique that great caution should be exercised in any attempt to explain or justify it by an appeal to archaeology. Oehler pointed out many years ago that while many have seen in the story a proof that human sacrifice was originally a characteristic of Old Testament religion, "on the contrary the tendency of the story leads directly to the exclusion of human sacrifice from Jehovah-worship."[64]

BETHUEL, THE SYRIAN, (Genesis 25:20)

According to the narratives in Genesis, Abraham was closely related to Arameans. He sent his servant to "my country and to my kindred" to secure a wife for Isaac (Gen. 24:4). The servant went to Aram-Naharaim (Mesopotamia) to the city of Nahor (Gen. 24:10) which is in Padan-Aram (25:20). Rebekah is described as the daughter of Bethuel and the sister of Laban (24:24, 29), both of whom are repeatedly referred to as "the Aramean."[65] It was to Padan-Aram that Jacob was sent by Isaac to secure a wife (28:5). He came to "the land of the people of the east" (29:1), and to the well outside the gate of the city where Nahor lived which was apparently Haran.[66] There he served Laban for his wives and children and for his cattle. When Laban and Jacob made their covenant, Laban called the "heap of witness" *yegar sahadutha* using the Aramaic words, while Jacob called it *Galeed,* the Hebrew equivalent. In Deuteronomy 26:5 we read the formula for the dedication of the first fruits. The offerer is to describe himself by a formula which begins with the words: "A Syrian (Aramean) ready to perish was my father; and he went down into Egypt, and sojourned there with a few, and became there a nation, great, mighty and populous." It might be inferred from these passages that we should regard Abraham and Jacob as Arameans in the strict sense of the word.[67] But since the genealogies in Genesis 10 and 11 make Abram a descendant of Arphaxad and not of Aram it may be that Jacob is called an Aramean simply because he spent many years among them, and Laban and Bethuel *a fortiori* for the same reason. But in any case to those who accept the plain statements of Scripture, this means that there were Aramean settlements in Northern Mesopotamia, Aram-Naharaim, as early as about 2000 B.C.

In his book *Les Araméens* (1949), Dupont-Sommer refers to the

Genesis passages cited above and tells us that "unfortunately" (*malheureusement*) they are legends which were not committed to writing until the ninth and eighth century B.C.[68] Consequently they can only reflect a late and therefore undependable tradition. He apparently considers it unnecessary to state that he accepts the Josian date of Deuteronomy. Such being the case it is to be noted that the earliest reference to the Arameans in extra-biblical sources is according to Dupont-Sommer in a small and badly mutilated Tell Amarna letter dating from the fourteenth century.[69] It is so badly preserved that all we can ascertain from it is that the senders wish to tell the Pharaoh something which concerns the Akhlamu and the king of Karaduniash (Babylon). From the fact that later, especially in the inscriptions of Tiglath-pileser I, the double name *Akhlamu-Aramu* is used and later still *Aramu* alone, Dupont-Sommer argues that the Arameans were closely related to the *Akhlamu* and finally became so dominant that the name *Akhlamu* was dropped entirely. Thus it appears that by refusing to accept the statements of Genesis regarding the Arameans many archaeologists deprive themselves of evidence going five or more centuries back of the earliest, dependable evidence provided by archaeological research — a striking illustration of the result of negative criticism.[70]

The Fear of Isaac

This remarkable name (Gen. 31:42, 53) is naturally to be explained as due to the terrible experience through which Isaac passed on Mount Moriah (22:1-19). That such an experience would make an indelible impression on the mind of a young man is only to be expected; and while in that event mercy triumphed over judgment, it would not be surprising if the severity of God rather than his compassion made the strongest and most lasting impression on the mind of Isaac. The noun that is rendered "fear" (*pachad*) occurs forty-nine times in the Old Testament and always has this general meaning. The verb from the same root occurs twenty-five times and in a similar sense. So the meaning "fear" is favored both by the biblical usage of the word and by the circumstances of Isaac's life. It seems to be largely restricted to the Hebrew.

Consequently, it is interesting to note that another word which is written exactly the same way in the Bible occurs once (Job 40:17), apparently in the sense of "thigh."[71] This rendering is favored by the context and supported by the usage of the Arabic. Whether the roots of these words were originally the same is uncertain, since the word does not occur in the Arabic in the sense of "fear." It is to be noted, however, that the Arabic word is also used in the sense of "sub-tribe," a meaning which finds support in Palmyrene and also in Ugaritic in the sense of "flock."[72] On the basis of this decidedly tenuous line of argument, it is now claimed that the rendering in Genesis 31 should be "kinsman of Isaac."[73] The aim of this definition is to find in this name the evidence for a primitive belief in a blood relationship between the worshipper and his god. This is another example of the quest of the inobvious in the interest of evolutionary theory. It will commend itself only to those who are concerned to fit the biblical narratives into an evolutionary framework.

THE TWELVE TRIBES OF ISRAEL

The fact that there were twelve tribes of Israel, which claimed descent from the twelve sons of Jacob, is referred to again and again in the biblical records. We are told of the birth of each one (Gen. 29:31 − 30:24; 35:16-18). We are told that they were twelve in number and are given a brief summary (35:22-26). The reference to "ten" is explained (42:3, 13), Benjamin is produced (43:15) and Joseph reveals himself (45:3). A detailed list of the twelve sons and their sons, making with Jacob and Joseph a total of seventy, is given (46:5-27) and we are told how Joseph's two sons were raised to a position of tribal leadership (48:5-22). Then Jacob blesses each of his sons individually (49:3-27) and they are called "the twelve tribes of Israel" (vs. 28). Then the Book of Exodus begins with a list of "the names of the children of Israel which came into Egypt" — eleven "for Joseph was already in Egypt." But, if according to many critical scholars, as we have seen, a sojourn of all the tribes in Egypt and a covenant with all the tribes at Sinai is to be regarded as improbable and even as impossible, how then did the idea of twelve tribes arise and acquire such importance?

Professor Martin Noth has endeavored, according to the principles of Form Criticism, to get back of the simple statements of the Bible to the source of the oral tradition which embodied them. His study of Genesis 49, Numbers 26 and Numbers 1 leads him to the conclusion that the tradition of an early amphictyony goes back to the time of the Judges. But he does not regard the biblical explanation of the number twelve as historical. Instead he appeals to 1 Kings 4:7, according to which "Solomon had twelve officers over all Israel, who provided victuals for the king and his household: each man his month in a year made provision."[74] It may be regarded as somewhat uncertain just to what extent this apportionment followed tribal lines. Only five or six of the tribes are expressly mentioned. But Noth regards the fact that twelve is the number of the months of the year as the simplest and most natural explanation of the number twelve as used of the Tribes of Israel.[75] This is a striking illustration of the way in which the critics fill in the void which results from their refusal to accept the statements of the Old Testament as dependable. The explanation given by the learned professor is a somewhat plausible conjecture, but it is not at all the reason given in the Bible. Noth accepts and makes use of a single verse which suits his theory. But he rejects or ignores the many other verses which give a totally different explanation.

<h3 align="center">ISRAEL IN EGYPT</h3>

That Jacob, when he went to Egypt at the invitation of Joseph who had become viceroy of Pharaoh, took all of his other sons with him is plainly stated in Genesis 46 which gives the names of sons and descendants to the number of sixty-six, which with Joseph, his two sons, and Jacob himself added, raises the total to seventy. We are also told that when Jacob was on his deathbed, he called his sons to him and gave a parting word to each (chap. 49) — each of the twelve is addressed individually and we are expressly told: "These are the twelve tribes of Israel: and this is it that their father spake unto them" (vs. 28). We are also told that his request to be buried at Machpelah was granted by Pharaoh, that he was given an imposing funeral and that then "Joseph returned into Egypt, he and his brethren, and all that went up with him to bury his father." These statements are supported by Exodus 1:1-5 which gives the names of the twelve sons of Jacob and declares that his descendants "were seventy souls," including Joseph who was there already — a condensed repetition of Genesis 46. The "children of Israel" who are referred to frequently in the Book of Exodus are clearly represented as the descendants of the sons of Jacob. And the census at Sinai which is given in such detail in Numbers 1-3 makes this unmistakably clear. Consequently Orelli could summarize the situation by saying simply: "During a long period of famine the sons of Jacob, through divine providence, which made use of Joseph as an instrument, found refuge in Egypt. . . ."[76]

In view of these clear and explicit statements in the Bible regarding the presence of the Israelites in Egypt, the almost complete silence of the Egyptian records regarding them is remarkable, to say the least. The boast of Merneptah in his victory stele: "Israel is laid waste and has no seed" is still in spite of many years of exploration and excavation "the only mention of the name of Israel in any Egyptian inscription";[77] and that reference is to Israel not in Egypt but apparently in Palestine. The claim that the tribe of Asher is referred to on an inscription of Seti I is now regarded as unwarranted.[78]

It may surprise some readers to be reminded by Unger that as far as archaeology is concerned "perhaps the most unanswerable bit of testimony that part of Israel (the tribe of Levi at least) resided in Egypt for a long time is the surprising number of Egyptian personal names in the Levitical genealogies."[79] Yet Unger assures us that "all scholars agree" that the words "house of thy father" (1 Sam. 2:27) refer to the Levites "and indicate that the tribe of Levi actually had been in Egypt."

As to the Egyptian names, we may well raise the question whether the number is really so surprising. Unger lists only seven names: "Moses, Assir, Pashhur, Hophni, Phineas, Merari, and Puti-el in its first element" as all "unquestionably Egyptian."

That the word "unquestionably" is applicable to all these names is doubtful. Assir may come from a good Hebrew root. Hophni appears only as the name of a son of Eli, long after the Egyptian sojourn and has been claimed as Sabean. Merari may also come from a Hebrew root. The same may be said of several other names which are claimed as Egyptian: Levi, which is referred to a Hebrew root in Genesis 29:34, Korah, Kohath, and Aaron. Pashhur is the name of several men of the line of Levi who were prominent in the days of Jeremiah and later. Whether the name can be traced back to the Exodus period is another question.[80] The number of *unquestionably* Egyptian names which can be cited as proof of an Egyptian sojourn is really quite small. While admitting that Egyptian names are "apparently confined to Levites," Unger rejects as unwarranted the inference which is drawn by some scholars that only Levites were in Egypt. He argues that "the persistent tradition that all the tribes had been there must have had some solid basis in fact, and other lines of evidence support it." Unless the historicity of these narratives is to be entirely rejected, we would expect the critics to admit that at least the Joseph tribes were in Egypt.

The appeal to 1 Samuel 2:27 for proof of the correctness of the claim regarding Levi is one of many examples of the "pick and choose" method which is so characteristic of critical scholarship. The many passages which state definitely that all the tribes were in Egypt are simply set aside or ignored, while this one statement that Levi was there, a statement which in its context deals simply with Eli and his house and has no broader application, is interpreted to mean that the other tribes were not there, an inference which is wholly unwarranted.

All this practically amounts to a confession that the only proof which we have that the Israelites ever were in Egypt in patriarchal times is supplied by the Bible. The reason there is so much difference of opinion as to Israel in Egypt is because there is so much difference

of opinion as to the meaning and dependability of the biblical statements. In view of the negative attitude of many scholars toward the
biblical narratives it is remarkable that many of them believe that
Israelites really were in Egypt at all. But this can hardly be denied in
view of the many references to the sojourn in the subsequent records
and to the wonderful deliverance from oppression there.

The God of Abraham, the God of Isaac, and the God of Jacob

Some thirty years ago, Albrecht Alt, of the University of Leipzig,
published a monograph entitled *The God of the Fathers*,[81] which is
still often quoted and referred to. Briefly stated Alt's argument is this.
In the narratives of the Old Testament dealing with the early period
we find various instances where a god or *numen* is connected with a
person. Thus we read in Genesis of "the God of Abraham," of "the
Fear of Isaac," and of the "Mighty One of Jacob." Alt points out at
considerable length that there are analogies in other nations for calling
a god or *numen*, the god of a specific person. It is to be noted, however, that the examples which he cites are taken from inscriptions of
the third century A.D. or later.[82] From them he draws the interesting
conclusion that since we find the "God of Abraham" referred to in the
Old Testament, we are entitled to conclude that Abraham was a historical person. So far so good. But he does not stop there. He argues
that, following the analogy of other religions, the "God of Abraham"
and the "Fear of Isaac" and the "Mighty One of Jacob" are *three* different gods or *numina*, all distinct but belonging to the same general
class of divine or superhuman beings. He argues that the worship of
these *numina* goes back to the time before the Israelites entered
Palestine; and further that the worship of Jehovah (Jahweh) has no
direct connection with these three *numina* who were worshipped by
the patriarchs, but that Jahweh was a similar *numen* who became the
god of the nation and gradually replaced these other lesser gods or we
may rather say, absorbed them.[83] Yet if the words of the Lord recorded
in Exodus 3:6 as spoken to Moses are taken in their obvious sense,
Jehovah then at the time of Moses' call declared himself to be "the
God of Abraham, the God of Isaac, the God of Jacob" and he instructed Moses to so speak of him to the children of Israel (vs. 15).

It may be noted in this connection that Lods regarded it as possible
that "Abraham, Isaac, Jacob, and Joseph, before being presented as
founders of certain holy places, had been their gods or 'baals':
Abraham at Hebron, Isaac at Beersheba, Jacob at Bethel, and perhaps
Joseph at Shechem."[84] Alt and Lods differ because neither of them
accepts the statements of the Old Testament as they stand. Each fills

in the vacuum as he sees fit. Each accepts as much as he can use to support his theory of the development of the religion of Israel, and rejects the rest.

THE EXODUS

The deliverance from Egyptian bondage is the most important, as it is the most spectacular, redemptive event in the history of Israel. Together with the events leading up to it, it is described in detail in Exodus 3-15 and referred to a hundred or more times in the rest of the Old Testament. To eliminate it from the Bible would be well-nigh impossible. It is clearly stated, as we have seen, that all of the tribes went down into Egypt and that all of them came out of Egypt. Paul in reminding the Corinthian Christians that all their ancestors shared in these unforgettable experiences (1 Cor. 10:1-5) is simply recalling facts so emphatically and repeatedly stated in Scripture that it might seem that no one would think of denying them. Yet we are confidently assured by a prominent critic, H. H. Rowley, that "any simple view of a fifteenth century Exodus of all the tribes under Moses and Joshua is out of the question." And he quotes with approval the words of O'Callaghan to the effect that "The story of the Exodus has become, more than ever before, one of the most vexing historico-Biblical problems that confront us today,"[85] which means that having rejected the biblical view, the critics have found no substitute on which they can agree.

Since critical scholars are uncertain which or how many of the tribes went down into Egypt, they are naturally no less uncertain as to which tribes took part in the exodus and as to when the different tribes finally arrived in Palestine. Wellhausen distinguished two invasions of Palestine proper: the first made by Judah, Simeon and Levi, the second by the rest of the tribes, except Reuben and Gad, under the leadership of Joshua.[86]

We may take Rowley's theory as a recent example of the explanations proposed. It is quite complicated, but may be summarized as follows.[87] Abram's migration from Haran is placed at *c.* 1650 B.C. Two centuries later Hebrew groups (including Kenites and Habiru) were located at Kadesh (*c.* 1440 B.C.) and after thirty-eight years[88] began to press northward, Simeon and Levi reaching Shechem but failing to hold it, while kindred groups (including Asher, Zebulon, Dan and other Israelite tribes, called SA GAZ in the Amarna letters)[89] pressed in from the north. Between 1400 and 1200 Judah and the other Southern tribes became established in the South; and the Northern tribes became settled in their locations. Joseph was taken to Egypt *c.* 1370; and *c.* 1360, some other Hebrews, "particularly some of those who had failed to hold Shechem" went down into Egypt. Oppression under Rameses II *c.* 1300, was followed by an exodus *c.* 1230 under Moses whose mother was a Kenite. This exodus was in the name of the Kenite God, Yahweh; and the Covenant and the Ethical Decalogue were introduced at Sinai. Two years later Joshua led this Covenant people into Central Palestine.[90] This gives us four "invasions" if we may call them that, spread over a long period of time: two centuries between Abram's coming and the invasions from the South (Judah and other) and the North (Northern tribes), two more centuries before the beginning of the conquest under Joshua. It reduces the sojourn to a small part of Israel and the period in Egypt of the few who were there from four hundred thirty years to about one hundred forty years.

We may call this a complicated theory for several reasons. The following may be noted. The late date assigned Abram is based partly on the view that the sojourn in Palestine was less than three hundred years. Kadesh, which is associated rather with the exodus than with Abraham, is made the point of departure, after a thirty-eight year sojourn, for an invasion of Palestine from the South (Num. 14:39-45) which the narrative plainly describes as an utter failure.[91] These thirty-eight years for the sojourn at Kadesh are arrived at by deducting two years from the forty years of wandering inflicted as a punishment for disobedience (Num. 14:35; Deut. 2:14), the two years being assigned to the trek of the "Egyptian" group via Sinai and Moab to the Jordan. Apparently there is little or no connection between these tribes and the tribes which entered from the North and settled there. It may be assumed that Joseph was joined in Egypt by some members of his tribe. Why men of Simeon and Levi should have gone there is not clear. Nor is there any indication that this was due to an alleged failure to hold Shechem. The mention of Levi is probably due to the meagre facts mentioned above. The claim that Rameses II was the Pharaoh of the oppression has already been discussed. The Kenite god and the ethical decalogue will be discussed shortly.

When we examine the evidence which is presented in support of this theory of multiple invasion, we are surprised to find how meagre it is; and we are not surprised to discover how little agreement there is with regard to its complicated details. Rowley points out that the advocates of two or more invasions of Canaan differ as to the relative order of these invasions, some placing the invasion from the South earlier than the one from the East, while others place it later. The question whether the *Habiru* who are mentioned in the letters of Abdu-hiba of Jerusalem are to be regarded as Hebrews is still by no means settled. The date of the destruction of Jericho is a matter of lively discussion. If Jericho fell 1400 B.C. and the Habiru of the Amarna Letters are Hebrews, this supports the early date of the entrance of Israelites into Canaan. But the advocates of the late date of the exodus regard these data as supporting their claim that this invasion must be quite distinct from the one led by Moses, and that the latter was made from the South. Two facts appear quite clearly as a result of this debate. The one is that the evidence produced by archaeology is meager and its interpretation uncertain, the critics themselves being the judges. The other is that it is only when the plain, emphatic, and oft-repeated statements of the Bible are treated as late and undependable, so that the critic may accept what he pleases and reject what he pleases, that this modern theory of two or more invasions becomes at all plausible. For the biblical narratives make it as definite as could be that all of the tribes were in Egypt, that all left Egypt under Moses, and that all entered the land under Joshua.

THE PILLAR OF CLOUD AND OF FIRE

This manifestation of the divine presence is first referred to in Exodus 13:21f. It appears as the guide and protector of the Israelites as they start on their exodus journey and throughout its course. It is more frequently referred to simply as "the cloud" (Num. 9:15-22); and it was undoubtedly the same "cloud" which filled the tabernacle (Exod. 40:34-38) and the temple (1 Kings 8:10f.; 2 Chron. 5:13f.) at their dedication. It is there described as the "glory" of the Lord; and sometimes this word alone is used of this visible manifestation of the divine presence. No mention is made of it in Joshua or in Samuel, and we should probably infer that like the manna (Josh. 5:12) this special token of the Lord's care and presence ceased, after its main function, that of guidance, had been accomplished. It is perhaps significant that at the crossing of Jordan it is the ark and not the cloud which is spoken of as leading the people into the land of promise. And it is the ark which is mentioned frequently in certain of the incidents described in Joshua — 2 Samuel. Consequently, while the statement in 1 Kings 8:10 might be regarded as strictly parallel to Exodus 40:34-38, it is quite possible that it refers to a return to the Exodus-situation after a long period of intermission. Yet in 2 Samuel 7:6f. the words "dwelt" and "walked" and "to this day" may seem to suggest the continuance of the same situation as in the exodus period. It is significant that no mention of the presence of the cloud is made in the description of the dedication of the second temple. Ezekiel sees an impressive vision of the removal of the "glory" from the temple about the time of the destruction of the temple. This is probably the source of the Jewish tradition that the shekinah, as they called the cloud as the manifestation of the "dwelling" of God among his people, was not present in that temple. Here again we have a significant silence in the biblical record. Both Isaiah (4:5f.) and Ezekiel (43:4f.) refer to the shekinah as a future glory of obedient Israel. But that time lies still in the future; and it is fulfilled in him who by his incarnation "tabernacled" (John 1:14) among men and manifested forth his glory and the glory of the Father.

We naturally ask the question whether the shekinah was present in the first temple up to the time of the captivity. Three passages in Isaiah are of special interest in this connection. In 29:1-8 we have a prophecy regarding Jerusalem, called Ariel, which probably means God's hearth or altar, as the place where the fire of God burns. So understood the passage refers to an attack on Jerusalem by her enemies which is brought to naught by the presence of the God of Israel among his people. This explanation is favored by 31:9 which declares that the Lord's "fire is in Zion and his furnace in Jerusalem." In 33:14 the words "Who among us shall dwell with the devouring fire? Who among us shall dwell with everlasting burnings?" describe the terror of the "sinners in Zion." It may be that these passages refer only to the altar fire which had been kindled by God himself and was never to be allowed to go out, and which consequently symbolized the presence of God as a God of both holiness, righteousness, and mercy, the hope of the pious and the penitent, and also as the terror of the ungodly and sinner. But it at least raises the question whether there may be in these passages rather a reference to the pillar of cloud and fire which manifested the presence of Israel's God. The Lord appeared to Moses in the burning bush (Exod. 3:1-6) and when Moses came down from the mount where he had been in communion with God, his face shone with the reflected light of the divine radiance. Apparently the "glory of the Lord" which the Israelites saw at Sinai was a theophany in fire (Exod. 24:15-18). Whether the vision of Ezekiel when he saw the "glory of the Lord" depart from the temple (8:4; 10:4; 11:23) justifies us in assuming that the Lord was really manifest in fire in the temple up to the time of the captivity is far from certain. But it would seem to be at least a possible inference. This is apparently the view of Franz Delitzsch who explains Isaiah 31:9 as referring to "the resident (heimische) light of the divine presence in the Sanctuary on Zion."[92]

The critical view is stated as follows: "It has been very generally held that the idea of a pillar of cloud preceding the people in the wilderness had its origin in the custom of carrying braziers containing burning wood at the head of an army or a caravan, the smoke by day, the fire by night serving to indicate to all the line of march."[93] The aim of such a statement is obviously to give this symbol of the divine presence a purely natural origin and explanation.

THE GOD OF THE KENITES

That all of the tribes of Israel traced their ancestry to Abraham, that all of them were in Egypt, that all of them came out of Egypt together, that all of them accepted the Covenant at Sinai and that all of them entered Canaan together, is the consistent and repeated claim of the biblical writers. Consequently, they were bound together by ties of race, religion, and close association. For example, in the call of Moses we read that the Lord said to him, "I am the God of thy father, the God of Abraham, the God of Isaac, and the God of Jacob" (Exod. 3:6). In the context we have already been told that Moses' father-in-law was the priest of Midian and that Moses kept his flocks. The narrative suggests that Moses was an utter stranger to Jethro. We are not told the name of the god whom Jethro worshipped. We are told that Moses "led the flock of Jethro to the back side of the desert, and came to the mountain of God, to Horeb." This may have been a journey of a hundred miles or more, which took a considerable time, perhaps several months. So it is significant that it was when he was far removed from his Midianite environment, that the God of his fathers, not of his father-in-law, spoke to Moses. The object of this revelation was to send Moses back, not to Midian and his father-in-law, except temporarily, but to Egypt to deliver his brethren from Egyptian bondage, and he was to say unto the elders of Israel: "The Lord God of your fathers, the God of Abraham, of Isaac, and of Jacob appeared unto me." He was to deliver to them the promise of the God of their fathers, to deliver them from their bondage and to bring them into the land promised to Abraham their father.

This is what the biblical record tells us. Yet for nearly a century, prominent critics have been insisting that Yahweh was the God of the Kenites and that it was through Jethro, the priest of Midian, his father-in-law, that Moses became a worshipper of Yahweh.[94]

How little confidence can be placed in the narrative in Exodus 2 and 3, by those who hold this view, is too obvious to require proof.[95] It is claimed that the account of the visit made by Jethro to Moses after he had brought the Israelites out of Egypt (Exod. 18) makes it probable that Jethro was a worshipper of Yahweh. It is even claimed that the feast of which Jethro partook with Aaron and all the elders of Israel was one in which he initiated them into the worship of Jehovah. Yet this is not stated. His words in response to Moses' account of the wonders of the deliverance, "Now I know that Yahweh is greater than all gods: for in the thing wherein they dealt proudly he was above them," make it clear that he regarded the deliverance from Egypt as wrought by Israel's God; and his words sound rather noncommittal and more like a polite comment or assent, than as the tribute which a worshipper of Jehovah would pay to his own God. He does not say "Jehovah, my God." The fact that Jethro offered sacrifice to "God" (it does not say "to Jehovah") and took part in a communal meal does not suffice to prove that Jethro was a worshipper of Jehovah; far less does it prove that the Israelites were *not*. We know nothing about the god or gods of the Midianites in the days of Jethro; and when we meet the Midianites a little later in the history, they are certainly the enemies of Israel (Num. 22-24; 25:16-18; 31:1-54). The Kenites were among the ten nations of Canaan which Israel was to dispossess (Gen. 15:19). That the Kenites had some connection with the Midianites is clear from the fact that Jethro, "the priest of Midian," is called a Kenite (Judg. 1:16); and we find that in later times there were Kenites who were friendly with the Israelites, notably Heber the Kenite, whose wife slew Sisera (Judg. 4). Later we read that Saul desired to spare the Kenites when he was warring against Amalek (1 Sam. 15:6). On the other hand, David fought against them, or claimed to have done so, when he was in the service of Achish of Gath (1 Sam. 27:10).

Rowley has defended this Kenite theory vigorously. The reason is that he is convinced that it supplies the nexus which will serve to bring the tribes of Israel together as worshippers of Jehovah, it being assumed that only a part of the tribes were in Egypt and that there were several invasions of Palestine, separated by wide intervals of time. It illustrates that arbitrary and inconsistent use of the biblical evidence to which the critics so often resort. The Old Testament declares again and again that Jehovah was the God of Abraham and that Abraham was the ancestor of the twelve tribes. The Bible tells us very little about the Kenites. They played a very inconspicuous role in Israel's history. Archaeology apparently has added nothing. We do not know whom the Kenites worshipped. It has frequently been claimed that the Kenites were a tribe of smiths (iron workers), because *qayin* means "smith" in Arabic. But this is certainly a very dubious warrant for connecting them with the mines of the Sinaitic peninsula, and holding as some do that as smiths they were worshippers of the god of the smoking mountain, i.e., of an active volcano, with which they would identify the Mount of God. Jehovah is never called "the God of the Kenites." We do not know what the connection between Kenites and Midianites was, nor how Jethro the priest of Midian came to be a Kenite. We do know that Jethro refused Moses' offer to join forces with Israel, and that while Moses was still alive, the Midianites and Moabites endeavored to corrupt the Israelites and that as a result of the sin of Baal-peor, Israel was commanded to wage a war of extermination against Midian (Num. 31). Later, in the times of the Judges, the Midianites grievously oppressed the Israelites. In view of the close connection between Midian and Moab it seems probable that the Midianites were worshippers of Chemosh. But this is not certain. Yet Professor Rowley would have us believe that Jehovah was in the days of Moses the god of the Midianites and that the Israelites were introduced to the worship of Jehovah through Jethro the priest of Midian who had some connection with the Kenites, and whose attitude toward Jehovah was, to say the least, uncertain. The obvious facts have to be ignored and inobvious ones made much of in order to make this theory sound at all plausible.

THE DECALOGUE

The Decalogue occupies a pre-eminent place in Old Testament religion. That it teaches an ethical monotheism cannot successfully be denied. If the words, "Thou shalt have no other gods before me," may seem to suggest the existence of such beings and consequently to demand no more than the exclusive worship by Israel of their God Jehovah, it is hardly necessary to go beyond the Second Commandment to realize that such an interpretation is unwarranted. For this commandment prohibits the making and worshipping of the image of any created thing; and idolatry was an inseparable feature of the religions of the peoples of which Israel had any knowledge. Furthermore in the Fourth Commandment it is stated that Jehovah made everything that is in heaven and earth and sea. That the Decalogue sets forth a lofty monotheism is in fact recognized by critical scholars.[96] For they have long maintained that this "ethical Decalogue" is late and was preceded by a "ritual Decalogue" which they find in Exodus 34 and which concludes with the commandment, "Thou shalt not seethe a kid in its mother's milk."[97] Wellhausen argued that "the entire series of religious personalities throughout the period of the judges and the kings . . . make it very difficult to believe that the religion of Israel was from the outset one of a specifically moral character." And he declared, "The true religion may be gathered much more truly from Judg. v than from Exod. xx."[98] So the tendency has been since the days of Wellhausen to determine the nature of the religion of Israel in the days of Moses, of the judges and even of the kings, not from what the Pentateuch declares it to have been, but from the conduct and practices of the people and their leaders not only in Moses' day but for half a millennium or more thereafter; and, in spite of the fact that such departures from the law as given through Moses are again and again denounced and condemned as acts of wilful disobedience and apostasy or are clearly to be regarded as due to that ignorance which was the result of the failure of the leaders to instruct the people and parents to instruct their children in the law which had been given to them at Sinai.

It cannot be too strongly emphasized that we have here a fundamental difference between the biblical and the critical attitude toward the Mosaic law. The Bible places at the beginning of Israel's history as a nation what the critics treat as the product of a long development. Thus the Bible makes no concealment of the fact that Israel again and again turned away from the service of her God and worshipped the gods of the neighboring peoples. It states this definitely and repeatedly. But it also represents this conduct as due to ignorance of the law or to deliberate forsaking of it. The critical view is that the real religion of Israel was derived from and was for centuries largely the same as that of these other nations and that ethical monotheism developed in Israel first under the teachings of the great prophets of the eighth century. In other words, when we read in Judges 2:10-13 that the children of Israel "forsook the Lord, and served Baal and Ashtaroth" this is to be regarded as an attempt by a writer who lived centuries later in the days of these great prophets to represent the crude beginnings of the religion of Israel as an apostasy from a religious standard which was not actually reached until his own day centuries later. It must be obvious to the thoughtful reader of the Old Testament that it is only by dividing the Pentateuch into sources which are late and undependable and by placing them in the framework of naturalistic development that the theory that ethical monotheism begins with the eighth century prophets can be made at all plausible.

It is by dating the document late and denying its trustworthiness that the critics justify their claim that the Decalogue is not Mosaic. There are two reasons for this. The one is the undeniable *fact* of the pervasive idolatry and polytheism of all the nations by which Israel was surrounded; and the other is the *claim* that Israel derived her religious beliefs originally from them. The *fact* is as clearly taught in the Bible as it is confirmed by archaeological research. The *claim* is flatly denied in the Bible which treats the idolatry and polytheism repeatedly practiced in Israel for many centuries after the time of Moses, as an apostasy from the law revealed and imposed at Sinai.

THE BOOK OF THE COVENANT

Exodus 21:1 – 23:19 records "the ordinances" which the Lord gave Moses in the Mount (20:21f.) and which the people solemnly promised to observe (24:3). It has long been recognized that there are two types of laws in this code. Driver described them as the "words" (or commands) and the "judgments."[99] The former are categorical, the latter hypothetical. Various explanations were given of this difference, as due for example to the compiler and redactor. More recently Albrecht Alt has applied the principles of Form Criticism to the laws of the Pentateuch.[100] He has classified the laws as *apodictic* and *casuistic*. The apodictic laws which might also be called categorical are declarative and may be described as "shalt" or "shalt not" laws: e.g., "Three times a year thou shalt keep a feast unto me in the year" and "Thou shalt not revile the gods (judges) nor curse the ruler of thy people." Most of the laws in 22:18 – 23:19 are such laws. The casuistic laws may be described as "if laws." They deal with a hypothetical case: e.g., "If thou buy a Hebrew servant, six years he shall serve: and in the seventh he shall go out free for nothing." The main difference between these two classes of laws is that the one is absolute and takes compliance for granted, while the other states a hypothetical case or situation and affixes a definite course of action or a penalty. There is no reason why laws of both kinds should not appear in the same code. No Canaanite code has been discovered up to the present, but the Sumerian, Accadian, and Hittite codes which are known to us contain both types of laws although the "if laws" are much the more numerous. Yet despite these facts the claim is made that the Book of the Covenant is a composite made up of apodictic laws which are Israelite and casuistic laws which are Canaanite, a claim, which not only destroys the unity of the code but derives the greater part of it from pagan sources, despite the fact that the Bible asserts definitely that these laws were made known to Israel by God through Moses at Sinai, and expressly warns the people to shun the cults and customs of the Canaanites. The attempt to draw a distinction here between Israelite and Canaanite laws is unwarranted. But it illustrates the attempt which is constantly made to derive from pagan sources laws, practices and beliefs which the Bible declares to have been revealed to Israel by her God.

THE TABERNACLE

"And Moses reared up the tabernacle" (Exod. 40:18) is quite explicit. But by assigning the entire account in Exodus (13 chapters) to P, a document which he regarded as late and unreliable, Wellhausen was able according to John Bright, to treat it as "a completely idealistic backward projection of the later Temple into the distant past." How tenaciously this view, that the account is not historically correct, is still held by critical scholars, is illustrated by Bright's substitute: "More probably, however, the description rests on traditions of the tent-shrine erected by David (2 Sam. 6:17) which was, in turn, the successor of the amphictyonic shrine and presumably patterned upon it, albeit, no doubt, with elaborations."[101] This is a slight modification of the Wellhausen view according to which the tabernacle of the exodus period was the tent (Exod. 33:7-11), which as a punishment for rebellion and before the construction of the tabernacle and of the ark Moses pitched outside the camp. No description of it is given. Consequently it can be claimed that it was a very simple affair, quite different from the elaborate structure described in the P account. This has been the usual view we believe in critical circles. The tent which is mentioned in 2 Samuel 6:17 was erected by David to be only the temporary abode of the ark. Like the tent of Exodus 33, it is only mentioned, not described, and was probably also a rather simple structure. It is to be observed that both of these views treat the elaborate and detailed biblical account in Exodus 25-31; 35-40 as late and undependable.

The Ark

In the Mosaic legislation the ark is the sacred symbol of the presence of Jehovah. Note especially Numbers 7:89, which represents it as the throne of Jehovah (cf. Jer. 3:16f.) who sitteth (enthroned) between the cherubim (Exod. 25:22). That it was made at Sinai is definitely stated and it is mentioned thirty-six times in the Pentateuch and twenty-nine times in Joshua. It is more fully described as "the ark of the testimony" (e.g., Exod. 25:22) because the "testimony," i.e., the two tables containing the Ten Commandments, was placed in it (25:21). It is also frequently called "the ark of the covenant" (Num. 10:33; 14:44; Deut. 10:8; 31:9, 25, 26 – also 12 times in Joshua).

In view of this evidence which connects the ark with Moses and the Sinaitic legislation, the following statement by a member of the traditio-historical school is significant: "In the true historical traditions the ark does not appear until the Shiloh traditions of 1 Sam. 1-4."[102] This means that none of the statements recorded in the Pentateuch, in Joshua, and we may add Judges 20:27, give us true information regarding the ark. This is sufficiently destructive of the historical value of the "traditions" regarding the period of the exodus and conquest. But our author goes still further. He assures us that Shiloh was a

Canaanite "shrine" and that the account in 1 Samuel does not "at all try to conceal the Canaanite character of the cult there" (i.e., at Shiloh). Since most of what is said in 1 Samuel 1-4 about the worship at Shiloh concerns the perversion of the true worship of the Lord by the sons of Eli, the above statement must mean that the practices that are so severely denounced there are to be regarded as Canaanite rites which were lawfully practiced at Shiloh and prove Shiloh to have been a Canaanite shrine with the ark its principal object of worship. Yet according to Joshua 18:1, it was during the life of Joshua and for the purpose of completing the division of the land that "the whole congregation of Israel assembled together at Shiloh and set up the tabernacle of the congregation there," where it remained until the days of Samuel. The ark is not expressly mentioned. But it is to be assumed that it was placed in the tabernacle, where it continued to be till it was captured by the Philistines.[103]

THE SHOWBREAD

A striking example of the difference between the religion of Israel and the ethnic cults is the showbread (Exod. 25:30). It has been pointed out that at Erech, for example, bread is referred to in the daily sacrifices offered to the gods. Consequently it would be easy to argue that the showbread of the Mosaic tabernacle was directly connected with and derived from this ancient practice. To draw such an inference is to ignore the basic difference between the two rites as indicated by the conceptions which lie back of each.

In the case of the Sumero-Babylonian cultus the idea of feeding the god seems to be prominent. Thus, in the story of the flood as told in the Gilgamesh Epic we read that after the deluge had subsided and Utu-napishtim offered sacrifice to the gods, "the gods smelled the savor, the gods smelled the sweet savor, the gods crowded like flies about the sacrifices."[104] This reminds us of the statement in the biblical account: "and the Lord smelled a sweet aroma; and the Lord said in his heart, I will not again curse the ground any more for man's sake" (Gen. 8:21). But the Babylonian account definitely suggests that the gods gather about the offerer because they are hungry, since the flood and the destruction of man has deprived them of food. For the gods the supply of their physical needs was very important. This need of the gods for food is strikingly illustrated by an Accadian tablet which lists the "daily sacrifices to the Gods of the City of Uruk (Erech)."[105] The list is exceedingly elaborate and shows how completely earthly and human was the conception of the gods and of their life and activities. Similarly the Pyramid Texts give elaborate accounts of the offerings for the deified Pharaoh.[106]

The showbread in the Mosaic ritual was something quite different. This is made clear by the fact that during the entire period of the exodus, Israel was fed with manna by her God.[107] Psalm 50 which is ascribed to Asaph contains a most emphatic repudiation of the pagan idea: "If I were hungry, I would not tell thee; for the world is mine and the fulness thereof. Will I eat the flesh of bulls, or drink the blood of goats?" (vss. 12f.). The offering of the showbread was not intended to feed the Deity, but as "a memorial" (Lev. 24:7), a recognition of the fact that man received his daily bread from God — a vastly different conception! The twelve cakes (one for each of the twelve tribes) to remain a whole week (from sabbath to sabbath) would have been according to pagan standards a niggardly, a starvation, ration for a powerful divinity. But by its very smallness it witnessed to the fact that it was a symbolic and token offering, an acknowledgment that Israel owed the supply of her every need to him who was the bountiful giver of all good.

Furthermore we are told plainly, a fact which the heathen cults tend to conceal, that after it had served its purpose this food-offering was to be eaten by the priests in the holy place (Lev. 24:5-9). The apocryphal story of Bel and the Dragon tells how Daniel exposed the priestly fraud that the food offered by the people to the dead and to the gods and supposedly eaten by them was really eaten by the priests and their families.[108]

AARON AND HIS SONS, THE PRIESTS

That Aaron and his descendants constituted the lawful priesthood in Israel is made abundantly clear in the Old Testament. The name of Aaron occurs there 346 times, of which about 300 are in the Pentateuch. Only David and Moses are mentioned more frequently in the Old Testament. Nevertheless ever since the rise of the Wellhausen School of criticism there has been a strong tendency to minimize the importance of Aaron. The reason for this is not far to seek.

According to the widely accepted critical analysis, Aaron is mentioned fifteen times in J. In all but two of these occurrences, his name is coupled with that of Moses. So it is argued that Aaron was a kind of lay figure, who played an inconspicuous role; and his name is treated as a later gloss. This has made it possible for the members of the Wellhausen School to assert that "Aaron is missing from J."[109] It is further to be noted that in none of these passages is a priestly role assigned to Aaron.

Aaron appears twenty-three times in E, nine of which are in connection with the disgraceful story of the golden calf (Exod. 32) and five in the account of the challenging of Moses' supreme authority by Aaron and Miriam. As in the case of J, none of the passages in E assign divinely authorized priestly functions to Aaron. So we are told that Aaron is "only incidental in E."[110]

In Deuteronomy Aaron is only mentioned four times and in only one of these is the priesthood referred to (10:6). Of the remaining occurrences of the name of Aaron in the Pentateuch all (about 260) are assigned to P or to H. That is to say, they are treated as *exilic* or *postexilic*. In Joshua four of the six occurrences are given to P. In the Historical Books of Judges and Samuel, Aaron is scarcely mentioned. Most of the remaining occurrences are in Chronicles, Ezra and Nehemiah. The nine references in the Psalms would be assigned to various dates by the critics. The only mention in the Prophets is Micah 6:4.

With such manipulation of the sources it became easy for Wellhausen to claim that the hereditary character of the priesthood "really first arose in the later period of the Kings,"[111] and that David "exercised unfettered control over the sanctuary of the ark which stood in his citadel, as also over the appointment of the priests who were merely his officials." Hence it was also possible for him to speak of the sons of Zadok of Jerusalem "as at first parvenus" who "afterwards became the most legitimate of the legitimate." This amazing result is accomplished simply by treating as late and untrustworthy all the evidence to the contrary. For those who take this general position, the question as to the origin of the Aaronic priesthood becomes a debatable problem. Some would connect it with Bethel or Shechem, because Aaron figures to a slight extent as we have seen in the E document, or even with Mount Hor which is referred to in P.

THE CENSUSES OF THE TRIBES

Closely connected with the question whether all of the twelve tribes were in Egypt is that of their increase in Egypt and the size of the hosts of the Lord which left that land to go and possess the land promised to Abram. The fact that there is so slight evidence on the Egyptian monuments for the presence of the Israelites in Egypt, taken together with the obvious difficulties connected with the leading of a great body of ex-slaves through the wilderness to the land of Canaan, has led many scholars to challenge the figures given in the biblical narratives — 600,000 (Exod. 12:37; Num. 11:21), 603,550 (Exod. 38:26; Num. 1:46; 2:32), 601,730 (26:51) — and to regard them as the result of mistake or as due to the exaggerated notions of the men of a later age who sought to glorify their national history.[112] Petrie claimed

that the word for "thousand" (*eleph*) here means "family" and he reduced the total to 5,550 persons. But it is clear from the calculations
in Numbers 1-2 as checked by Exodus 38:25f. that *eleph* must mean
"thousand."[113] Consequently Albright argues that the totals given in
Numbers 1-3 and 26 represent two different recensions of the census
taken by David (2 Sam. 24).[114]

This is a serious charge whichever form of it is adopted; and it is
not to be lightly treated. Several matters are involved in dealing with
it:

(1) In the manuscripts of the Old Testament numbers were, so far
as we know, always written out in full, as in AV, ARV and RSV.[115]
They were not represented by figures, which is a novel feature of the
Berkeley Version. The writing out of the numbers would tend to safeguard the accuracy of the numbers given, since there would be less
danger of errors of copying. It is important to notice also that no question of text is involved. These large totals are recorded six times; and
there is no variant either in the Hebrew text or in the ancient versions
to indicate that there is any uncertainty as to their accuracy.[116]

(2) The large totals are represented again and again as due to the
Lord's special blessing and favor. Such passages as Exodus 1:7-12 (cf.
Gen. 47:27) definitely describe the increase as the fulfillment of the
promises to the fathers (Gen. 15:5; 22:17; 26:4; 46:3; compare also
Deut. 1:10; 10:22; 28:62). These totals are also in accord with the
fact that Thutmose III and Rameses II were great builders and required a vast number of slaves to perform the tasks involved in their
enterprises. Breasted refers to Thutmose's annual tours of inspection
in Egypt: "On these journeys, too, he had opportunity of observing
the progress on the noble temples which he was either erecting, restoring or adorning at over thirty different places of which we know,
and many more which have perished. He revived the long neglected
Delta, and from there to the third cataract his buildings were rising,
strung like gems, along the river."[117]

(3) These statements are supported by what we read of the opinions and fears of others. The words of Pharaoh, "Behold the people of
the children of Israel are more and mightier than we" (Exod. 1:9),
are echoed in the words of Balak (Num. 22:5) and in those of Rahab
(Josh. 2:8-11). Furthermore, archaeological research in Palestine has
confirmed the report of the spies: "the people be strong that dwell in
the land, and the cities are walled *and* very great" (Num. 13:28).
Excavations at Megiddo, Shechem, Hazor, Dothan, Gibeon and other
cities have fully confirmed the biblical statements. The conquest of
these powerful nations and their strongly fortified cities would imply

that the hosts of Israel were very numerous despite the fact that it is declared again and again that it will be the Lord who will cause Israel to triumph over her enemies.[118]

(4) Attention has already been called to the careful and precise way in which the Mosaic census is given in Numbers 1-3; and the reader is referred to that discussion for the details which need not be repeated here.[119] Suffice it to say that the statistics for the twelve tribes are first given by tribes and then by standards and in each case the grand total for all the tribes is given at the end of the enumeration. Furthermore the census recorded in Chapter 26 likewise gives a total for each tribe followed by a grand total which does not differ materially from the previous one. It is definitely stated that the one was taken by Moses "in the wilderness of Sinai . . . on the first day of the second month of the second year" (Num. 1:1) while the other was taken at Shittim (25:1) by Moses and Eleazar the son of Aaron the priest, after the death of Aaron in the fortieth year (33:38). Both of these censuses fully confirm the statement in Exodus 12:37, that the Israelites on leaving Egypt numbered "about six hundred thousand on foot *that were* men, besides children."[120]

(5) It is especially noteworthy that the detailed statistics which are given in Numbers 1-2 are elsewhere checked in a striking way and their accuracy established. The 603,550 total for the twelve tribes (Num. 1:46) is checked by the silver offering which every man is to pay when he is numbered (Exod. 30:13). Every male is to pay a half-shekel and the total is stated to be 100 talents and 1775 shekels of silver (Exod. 38:25). One hundred talents at 3000 shekels to the talent are 600,000 half-shekels; and the 1775 shekels make 3,550 half-shekels, which gives exactly the 603,550 of the census. This, it is to be noted, not merely serves as an exact check on the figures given in Numbers 1 and 2, but also illustrates the important fact that the tabernacle was constructed to be the place of worship for all Israel and that for this reason every Israelite was required to contribute to its construction. For the narrative states that the 100 talents were used to make the sockets for the 100 gilded boards which formed the framework of the sanctuary, while the 1775 shekels were used to make hooks for the pillars and to ornament them and join them together (Exod. 38:27f.).[121]

(6) These figures are supported by other data. According to Numbers 16:35, 49, the total of those who perished as a result of the uprising of Korah and his confederates was 250 plus 14,700. If only a few thousand came out of Egypt, Israel would have been more than totally exterminated by this divine judgment. Joshua 4:11f. states that the warriors of the two and one-half tribes which passed over armed

before the hosts of Israel numbered 40,000 (cf. Num. 32:29). According to 8:2f. Joshua chose 30,000 warriors out of Israel "to lie in wait" against Ai, and about 5000 "to lie in ambush" between Bethel and Ai (vs. 12).

(7) Finally, it is to be noted that these large figures stand in relation to and can only be accounted for when viewed in the light of the special supernatural dealings of the God of Israel with his people: the plagues culminating in the slaying of the firstborn of the Egyptians, the pillar of cloud and of fire, the crossing of the Red Sea, the manna, the water from the rock at Horeb and at Kadesh. Without these wonders, the numbers are incredible. This is stated very definitely in connection with the sending of the quail (Num. 11). Notice especially Moses' presentation of the problem of logistics, the feeding of 600,000 footmen, and the Lord's answer (vss. 21, 31-32).[122] It is only when full justice is done to the Supernatural in the record that they become credible and we can accept and rejoice in them as the biblical writer would have us do.

Vengeance on Midian. The detailed statement regarding the distribution of the spoil taken from the Midianites by the 12,000 Israelite warriors who were sent to avenge Israel (Num. 31) is especially significant in this connection. The totals which are given are immense, almost incredibly so: 675,000 sheep, 72,000 beeves, 61,000 asses, 32,000 virgins (vss. 32-35). But their accuracy is checked in the following way. The spoil is divided into two equal parts (vs. 27). One half is to be the portion of the men who went to war. The Lord's portion of this half is one five-hundreth (vs. 28), or one one-thousandth of the whole: namely 675 sheep, 72 beeves, 61 asses, 32 virgins (vss. 36-40). It is then stated that of the half which fell to the congregation Moses assigned one-fiftieth to the Levites. In this case the figures are not given, the details being superfluous. The story told here is an amazing one. That 32,000 female children not yet of marriageable age should have fallen into the hands of the Israelites implies that the number of the warriors who were slain was very great. Yet only 12,000 Israelites were sent against them and we are expressly told that not a single Israelite warrior was slain (vs. 49).[123] In this case the difficulties are quite different from those supplied by the two censuses. But it is noteworthy that in these two outstanding examples of what many would call impossible figures, the large totals are so thoroughly checked by the details that are given. This calculation of the spoil is especially noteworthy because it proves so conclusively that the Hebrew word *eleph* means thousand and not family, clan, or a small indefinite number, as was suggested by Petrie.[124]

The Census of Benjamin. In connection with the censuses which indicate the amazing increase of Israel in Egypt and the problems which they raise, it is well to compare the history of the tribe of Benjamin. The total given for this tribe at the first census was 35,400 adult males (Num. 1:37). At the time of the second census it had increased by nearly one-third to 45,600 (26:41), making it the seventh in size of the twelve tribes. At the time of the terrible fratricidal strife between Benjamin and the other tribes, 26,700 men (Judg. 20:15) were mustered by Benjamin to oppose the 400,000 of the rest of Israel. The outcome was that all but 600 men of Benjamin were slain (vs. 47); and these 600 were supplied with wives from Jabesh-Gilead (21:12) and from Shiloh (vss. 19-23). This was in the time of Phineas, the grandson of Aaron, and early in the period of the Judges. Yet the men of Benjamin figured prominently in the struggle between David and Saul who was a Benjamite; and in the days of Asa the muster of Benjamin (2 Chron. 14:8) was only slightly less (280,000) than that of Judah (300,000), a remarkable comeback of an almost annihilated tribe!

THE TWELVE SPIES

In discussing the list of the twelve tribal chieftains (Num. 13:4-16) who were sent to spy out the land, Albright takes issue with Martin Noth for treating it as "very late." He insists on the "consistent archaism of the names, where they are fully preserved." He says further: "I regard the list in question as very ancient and important, though I should not care to insist that it referred originally to the spies."[125] The reason for this mixed attitude as we may call it is not far to seek. Albright belongs to the numerous group of scholars who hold that the only feasible solution of the problem of the exodus and conquest is that some of the tribes were never in Egypt, that there were at least two invasions of Palestine, one from the East, the other from the South, and that these conquests were quite distinct and separated by a considerable interval of time, a century or more. Such being the case, the mention of twelve men as representing the twelve tribes of Israel in the spying out of the land must be regarded as a late tradition which developed after the establishment of the Israelitish Amphicytony in Palestine, when the number twelve had become significant. So while Albright is quite willing to break a lance with Noth over the question whether these names are early or late, he is not prepared to risk his reputation as a scholar by accepting the statement, which is the only reason for the mention of the twelve names, to wit, that they are the names of the twelve representatives of the twelve tribes which came out of Egypt with Moses and Joshua.

DEUTERONOMY

"THE LAW AND THE PROPHETS"

For a century and a half Old Testament criticism has quite generally accepted as basic to its reconstruction of the Old Testament,
the claim, first advanced by De Wette in 1805 that the Book of
Deuteronomy is not Mosaic but dates at least in so far as its influence is concerned from about the time of Josiah, when it was "discovered" in the temple and made the basis of his great reformation.[126]
This claim is not merely radical as regards the Book of Deuteronomy
itself, but its consequences for the whole course of Israel's religious
history are so drastic and revolutionary that it requires careful study
and testing. We begin by considering the evidence in favor of the
traditional view that Deuteronomy is Mosaic.

We note at once that Deuteronomy claims and purports to be
Mosaic. It begins with the words "These are the words which Moses
spake unto all Israel beyond Jordan in the wilderness." The situation
is Moab (1:5; 29:1; 34:1f.).[127] Moses appears as speaking or acting
twenty-seven times. In fact the book consists mainly of three or four
great discourses which Moses is said to have delivered (1:6 – 4:40;
5:1 – 26:19; 27:11 – 28:68; 29:1 – 30:20), and it concludes with the
Song (32:1-43) and the Blessing (33:1-29), both of which are described as Mosaic. The concluding chapter, which describes Moses'
death and pays tribute to his great service to Israel, is clearly not by
Moses. It is not cast in the form of prophecy. It is a tribute, a memorial
to the dead leader and may have been added many years after Moses'
death (vs. 10).

The contents of the book are in harmony with the time and situation.
The conquest of the lands east of the Jordan has been completed, a
great achievement which is described quite briefly in Numbers
21:21-35, as if to suggest that the conquest of Canaan might be as
simple and easy a matter, if only Israel trusted in the Lord for
victory. Moses is about to leave his people and place the leadership in
other hands. The conquest of the land of Canaan is the mighty task
which confronts them; and contamination with its heathen and idolatrous inhabitants threatens their future security in it. So there is an
earnestness and urgency in his words which suits the occasion. They
are hortatory and challenging, persuasive and pleading. It is Moses'
last chance to influence the people for their good; and he makes the
most of it. He rehearses the history of the years of wandering, which
he and they have experienced. They are alive and their fathers have
perished (4:4; 5:3), a solemnizing thought. The promise of the possession of the land is set before them, a glorious future. The whole future

hinges on obedience: life or death is the alternative (30:15-20). No man ever had such an opportunity to influence for their good an obstinate and wilful people. Moses makes the most of it, reminding them of God's dealings with them and striving to win their obedience. As a telling and for himself poignantly painful example of the consequences of disobedience, he cites his own recent tragic experience. Almost at the end of the forty years, on the eve of conquest he had failed to obey God perfectly; and for this reason he is not to be permitted to lead Israel into the Land of Promise. Five times he mentions it, partly as the expression of his own personal sorrow but also and especially, we may well believe, as a lesson and warning to them.

The historical situation accords with the Mosaic date. The overthrow of Sihon and Og is quite recent and strongly emphasized. The Conquest of Canaan is spoken of again and again, always as still future (4:1; 6:1, 11; 7:1; 8:1; 9:1; 11:8, 29; 12:1, 29; 17:14; 18:9; 19:1; 26:1; 27:1-4, 12; 29:1; cf. 16:1; 20:16f.). Of the six cities of refuge to be appointed (Num. 35:10-15), only the names of the three cities east of the Jordan, as in already conquered territory, are given (4:43); the others are not mentioned until after the conquest (Josh. 20:7).

The command regarding the extermination of the Canaanites (7:1-5, 16; 12:1-3, 30f.; 19:1; 20:16-18; 31:1-5) suits the situation when the conquest was about to take place as does also the curse on Amalek (25:17-19). Both would have been anachronisms for the age of Josiah. Especially significant is the statement that the conquest is to be gradual, together with the reason which is given, "lest the beasts of the field increase upon thee" (7:22). Similarly the command not to meddle with Edom (2:4f.) whom Moses calls "Your brethren the children of Esau" (v. 8), accords better with the time of Moses than that of Josiah, in whose days the mutual hatred and hostility of the two nations was intense and of long standing. Also the sharp distinction drawn between Edom (23:7f.) and Ammon and Moab (23:3), is better suited to the Mosaic period. The execution of apostate Israelites (13:6-18) would have been impossible in Josiah's day since the apostasy in the days of Manasseh and Amon had been so nationwide. The mention of the erection and dedication of an altar at Ebal (Shechem is not named), as ordered by Moses, which was to follow the entrance into the land, would have been quite out of harmony with Josiah's aim to enforce the law of the one sanctuary, as applying to Jerusalem, which had been fulfilled centuries earlier in the erection of the temple (27:4-6; cf. 2 Sam. 7:13; 1 Kings 8:29).

Great emphasis is placed on obedience as the precondition of successful conquest of the land and peaceful and prosperous possession of it. Two words of similar sound (*shama'* and *shamar*) occur about one hundred fifty times. The one is rendered by "hear, hearken, take heed, obey," the other by "keep, observe." Especially to be noted is the vivid rehearsal of the scene of the giving of the Decalogue at Sinai when they, the generation then living, heard the voice of the living God speaking to them out of the fire (4:36), an experience which was unique (4:33, 36) and terrible (5:23-27; 18:16f.; cf. Exod. 20:18-21), so terrible that they asked that God speak to them only through Moses (5:23-29). They are reminded of the fate of their fathers, how the generation of disobedience perished (2:14-16); and that they themselves had witnessed the mighty acts of God which their fathers had disregarded (11:2-9). Those less than twenty years old at the time of the great refusal — the men of war under sixty at the end of the forty years — probably made up the majority of those to whom Moses addressed himself in 29:1 (cf. 4:9; 7:19; 10:21; 11:7; 29:2).

The great challenge which came to the people at Sinai is expressed in the words of the Shema: "Hear (*shema'*) O Israel, the Lord our God is one Lord" is the reassertion of the monotheism of the Decalogue; and the requirements of the First Table are summed up in the command to love him with the whole heart fervently (6:5); and the love motive — God's love to Israel inspiring and requiring Israel's responding love — is the great theme of this book (cf. 10:12f.; 11:1). The promise of security and peace in the land given to their fathers is the promise of a loving God and it demands their love in return. Some thirty times "love" is referred to in this book.

The worship of the one God is to be performed in the place which the Lord "will choose" to set his name there. That choice is yet to be indicated. It is referred to about twenty times and in eight different chapters. But Jerusalem is never mentioned. Furthermore the setting up of the central sanctuary is not to take place immediately. It is to depend on the state of the nation, "when he giveth you rest from all your enemies round about, so that ye dwell in safety" (12:10; cf. 2 Sam. 7:10-13).

Likewise the kingship; that Israel is to have a king is stated (17:14f.), but this is to be after Israel enters the land promised to their fathers and possesses it.

The appointment of judges (16:18-20) and their duties, of which several examples are given (17:8-13; 19:15-21; 21:1-9; 25:1-3) has its warrant in the situation at Sinai (1:9-18) which recalls Exodus 18:13-26, although Jethro is not mentioned.

Aaron's sin concerning the golden calf (Exod. 32) is referred to here and the pardoning of his transgression is stated to be due to

Moses' intercession (9:20); and Aaron's death on Mt. Hor (Num. 20:28) is referred to as the consequence of their trespass against the Lord at Meribah-Kadesh (32:50f.). Thus Deuteronomy is full of impressive reminiscences of the events of the exodus period which is still fresh in the minds of his hearers.

Deuteronomy powerfully influenced the *subsequent history*. The incident of the building of the Memorial Altar (*Ed*) at Jordan by the warriors of Reuben, Gad, and half-Manasseh and the tragic misunderstanding as to its purpose which nearly led to a terrible inter-tribal war, shows that the idea of the one sanctuary for all Israel was clearly recognized in the days of Joshua, by Phineas, and by the leaders of the Twelve Tribes (Josh. 22:10-34).

The frequent apostasies and the resulting breakdown and confusion which appears in the days of the Judges, accounts for the worship at pagan shrines (high places) and for the existence of altars where Israel's God was worshipped (1 Kings 18:30). Thus Gideon at the command of the Lord built an altar at the place where the angel of the Lord appeared to him (Judg. 6:26), as was the practice of the Patriarchs and as was provided for by Exodus 20:24. Likewise David built an altar on Ornan's threshing-floor, where the angel of the Lord appeared to him (2 Sam. 24:25). That Solomon's temple was built at the place chosen by God (1 Kings 8:44, 48) to be the center of worship for all Israel is made clear by Solomon's prayer (1 Kings 8:29, 33, 44) which declares that prayer is to be offered at or toward (e.g., vs. 44) the temple. The reason given by Jeroboam for instituting the worship of the calves at Dan and Bethel indicates how firmly the ideal of the central sanctuary for all Israel had entered into the worship of the Twelve Tribes (1 Kings 12:26-33). The reform of Asa (1 Kings 15) was not so thoroughgoing as it should have been and the same is true of Jehoshaphat's (22:43). But the high places where pious Israelites worshipped, like the altar of the Lord which Elijah repaired, find their explanation, if not their justification, in the abnormal conditions in both Israel and Judah as a result of the frequent apostasies of the people. The reform of Hezekiah (2 Kings 18:4-7) was thoroughgoing (cf. 2 Chron. 29-30); and that it was directed toward centralization of worship was sufficiently obvious to attract the attention of Sennacherib (2 Kings 18:22). In fact the law of the one sanctuary was certainly enforced by Hezekiah as strictly or more strictly than by Josiah. That it was recognized and observed by post-captivity Judaism needs no elaborate proof. The zeal for the rebuilding of the temple and the reason for it is clearly stated in Ezra 3:1-6. That it was to be the sanctuary for all Israel is indicated by 6:16; cf. 8:35.

The influence of Deuteronomy on the prophets is very marked.

Hosea's emphasis on the love of God for Israel is the echo and response to Deuteronomy 6:5. (See Isa. 5:1; 43:4; 56:6; Jer. 31:3; Dan. 9:4; Zeph. 3:17; Mal. 1:2; also 1 Kings 10:9.) Also in the Psalms and Proverbs we find the love motive expressed and emphasized.

The influence of Deuteronomy on the New Testament is indicated by the numerous quotations from it.[128] Especially significant is it that Jesus refuted Satan by three quotations from this book; and the summary of the First Table of the Decalogue, which appears in 6:4f. is quoted by Jesus and called by him "the first and great commandment" (Matt. 22:38).

This is in brief the witness of the Scriptures to Deuteronomy and its place and influence in the development of the religious history of Israel. But for a century and a half the theory has been increasingly influential, that Deuteronomy is not Mosaic but belongs, at least in so far as its influence is concerned, to about the time of Josiah, many centuries after Moses' time, when it was "discovered" in the temple at Jerusalem by Hilkiah the high priest (2 Kings 22:8). This theory was accepted by Wellhausen, S. R. Driver, Kautzsch and most of the leading critics and may be regarded as the keystone of the widely accepted critical theory.

As has been the case with many another, this theory has suffered more or less radical change in the course of its development. De Wette in assigning Deuteronomy to the time of Josiah argued that the earlier books of the Pentateuch [Exodus to Numbers] had nothing to say about the centralization of worship at the one sanctuary. Wellhausen in adopting this theory found himself obliged, in order to justify the claim that the Priest Code is later than Deuteronomy, to resort to the following remarkable explanation: "In that book the unity of the cultus is *commanded*; in the Priestly Code it is *presupposed*,"[129] which is a noteworthy admission that the late dating of Deuteronomy based on the centralization of worship finds no support elsewhere in the Pentateuch. This is the argument *ex silentio*. But apparently it has served the critics well. For it has been the great contention of the Wellhausen School, not only that Deuteronomy is late, but that the Priest Code to which the greater part of the three preceding books of the Pentateuch is assigned is still later than Deuteronomy.

But Deuteronomy is not mainly or even primarily concerned with the centralization of worship. It sets forth a philosophy of the religious history of Israel which does not accord with other and even more important claims of the critics. Of prime importance is the fact that the worship at the one sanctuary requires the sole worship of one God, the God who has chosen Israel; and Deuteronomy not merely demands the worship of this one God, but sets forth in considerable details the ethical demands of this unique Deity. In other words, Deuteronomy is the proclamation of ethical monotheism.

This fact presents the critics with a problem. The Historical Books (Joshua-2 Kings) have much to say about the failures of the Israelites to follow and observe the lofty teachings of Deuteronomy. They speak again and again of disobedience and apostasy, of idolatry and the worship of false gods, of worship at the high places, of doing the very things which Deuteronomy most earnestly and emphatically condemns and warns against. Now since the theory of naturalistic evolution was adopted by Wellhausen and those who shared his position, a theory which denies or ignores the depravity which is inherent in fallen human nature and insists on the principle of progress and perfectibility, which means that all that man needs is education not regeneration, it was of course necessary to eliminate from the Historical Books as from the Pentateuch all the evidence which conflicts with this theory of Development which the late dating of Deuteronomy presupposes.

For an example we turn again to Joshua 22. This chapter deals as we have seen with a very significant event in the history of Israel. After the conquest of the kingdoms of Sihon and Og, the representatives of the Two-and-a-Half Tribes requested that the conquered territory be assigned to them. If their request were granted, they agreed to play their full part in the conquest of the land of Canaan which the other tribes were to possess as their inheritance. Their request was granted; they fulfilled their pledge; and in this chapter we read of their dismissal by Joshua, that they may return to the land which the Lord has given them east of the Jordan. In dismissing them Joshua exhorts them as follows: "But take diligent heed to do the commandment and the law, which Moses the servant of the Lord charged you, to love the Lord your God, and to walk in all his ways, and to keep his commandments, and to cleave unto him, and to serve him with all your heart and with all your soul." What followed? On the way back, they stopped at Jordan and there they built an altar unto the Lord. The consequences of this act were momentous. The other tribes were so outraged by this apparent breach of the Covenant, that they were prepared to go to war with their brethren and recent brothers-in-arms. But cool heads prevailed and they sent Phineas, the son of Eleazar the priest, to investigate the situation. The result was that they were given the most positive assurance that the altar which they regarded as sacrilege was not intended for sacrifice, not at all a rival shrine to the tabernacle and its worship, but merely a memorial, a witness set up to testify to their right to the tabernacle and its worship, that it was really for all Israel, and that it belonged to them and to their children.

What greater proof could be given that in the days of Joshua the idea and law of the one central sanctuary was recognized by all Israel than this incident affords? How do the critics deal with this amazing and vitally important record? They assign it partly to the Deuteronomist and in the main to the still later priestly writer, which means that it does not represent the actual history of the times of Joshua, but that it is a story invented to justify Josiah's reformation and the developments of the post-captivity period. This strikingly illustrates the method employed, which must be employed, if the critical theory is to be made plausible.

As a further example, we turn to the account of the dedication of the temple by Solomon. Since it stresses the idea of centralization of worship, it must be regarded as largely Deuteronomistic. Thus Driver claimed the prayer recorded in 1 Kings 8:23-61 "in its present form is clearly the work of the compiler,"[130] i.e., of the Deuteronomist. It has to be, unless the theory is to make shipwreck on the facts.

We turn to the Prophets. We have seen that love to God is the great demand of Deuteronomy. Moses summarizes and restates the First Table in terms of love: "Hear, O Israel: The Lord our God is one Lord: And thou shalt love the Lord thy God with all thine heart, and with all thy soul, and with all thy might" (6:5). Again and again, the "love motive" as we may call it appears in Deuteronomy. Joshua, as we have seen, exhorts Reuben, Gad, and half-Manasseh to love the Lord and to walk in all his ways (Josh. 22:5). So the same method is resorted to in dealing with this doctrine as with the historical facts which we have just been considering. It is now more than half a century since Ryle pointed out that in Deuteronomy "The relation in which the God of the people stands to the people is represented primarily as one of love rather than law"; and he goes on to say that "Deuteronomy shares with Hosea (3:1; 11:1; 14:4) the distinction of first familiarizing Israel with the thought and teaching that underlies so much of New Testament theology." Later he says: "It has already been noticed that the emphasis laid upon the *love* of God is a feature almost unique (except for Exod. 20); and it is generally believed that the prophet Hosea is the first exponent of this teaching"; and he quotes Driver's statement that Deuteronomy "builds upon the foundation of the prophets."[131] Here again we have a striking illustration of the method of the critics. Ryle first tells us that Deuteronomy shares with Hosea this great doctrine. Then he proceeds to claim that Deuteronomy owes it to Hosea; and he claims that "this is generally believed." Yet for centuries it has been held on the ground of the express statements of Scripture that this great doctrine which appears first in the Decalogue (Exod. 20:6) was made the great theme of

Moses' farewell addresses as recorded in Deuteronomy, where he bases it on the love of God to Israel shown in the great redemption from Egyptian bondage which Israel has recently experienced. It would be hard to find a clearer example of *hysteron proteron*, or as it is popularly stated "putting the cart before the horse," the Prophets before the Law, instead of the Law before the Prophets. Yet this theory, beset as it is with difficulties which require drastic, even herculean efforts to make it plausible, is as confidently advanced today as it was in the days of Wellhausen, nearly a century ago.

Especially significant are the repeated references to Moses' exclusion from the land of promise (1:37; 3:23-27; 4:21f.; 31:2; 32:49-52; cf. 34:1-6 and Josh. 1:1), which have been already referred to. This tragic ending of the life of the great lawgiver is referred to elsewhere only in Numbers 20:12; 27:12-14. The rest of the Old Testament passes over it in almost utter silence. The allegedly "Deuteronomic" editor of Kings feels that candor requires that he qualify his brief eulogy of David with the words "save only in the matter of Uriah the Hittite" (1 Kings 15:5). But the only allusion (outside of the Pentateuch) to this fatal lapse in Moses' life of obedience is in Psalm 106 where in the words "it went ill with Moses for their sake" and "he spake unadvisedly with his lips" (vs. 32f.), the subject is dealt with, we may say, as tactfully as possible. Nowhere else is the sin of Moses and its sad consequences for Moses and for Israel alluded to. But here in Deuteronomy it is not merely referred to but so dealt with that the poignancy of Moses' disappointment and grief must impress itself on every thoughtful and sympathetic reader. As coming from Moses these expressions are natural, appropriate; they are tragic and pathetic. As the words of a writer of a largely imaginary history they are hard to understand. Why should the writer of such a "history" make so much of a long past and all but forgotten event? Was it simply to give verisimilitude or local color to a book which he wanted to be accepted as Mosaic?

If the repeated references to a probably all-but-forgotten event and one which chiefly concerned Moses are remarkable when found in a book which is alleged to date from long after Moses' time, even more so are the failures to mention matters of more recent occurrence and great national interest. For more than three centuries Jerusalem had been in the days of Josiah the Holy City, the site of the Temple. Yet Jerusalem is not even mentioned by name as the place which the Lord will choose to place his name there. Jerusalem had also been for centuries the royal city, where was the palace of the great king of David's line. Yet even the kingship itself is only mentioned as a possible future option of the tribes of Israel. Even more strange is it that while warning is given against a return to Egypt, there is no hint of the possibility of that great tragedy of Israel's kingship, the Schism which split the kingdom into two rival and often hostile parts. A prominent feature of the eighth and seventh centuries in Israel was prophetism, when Hosea and Amos, Isaiah and Jeremiah exerted such a powerful influence. Yet Deuteronomy speaks only of a great prophet yet to come, while clearly indicating that prophecy will in Israel take the place of heathen divination. All these things are entirely suited to Deuteronomy as Mosaic, but as the product of a far later age they are simply amazing. Remarkable also is the fact that no mention is made of Shechem. Shechem was an ancient city; in patriarchal times Abram built an altar there. It was eminently appropriate that it should be there in the center of the land that the solemn rite of ratification of the covenant should be performed. Yet Shechem is not mentioned in Deuteronomy, while Ebal and Gerizim at whose feet it nestled are expressly named. This may be due to the fact that from the high plateau of Moab, it was the mountains on the distant skyline and not the city at their feet which attracted the attention of Moses as Israel was about to enter the land of promise.

A striking example of the extent of the reconstruction required by the late dating of Deuteronomy is the critical treatment of the Ninetieth Psalm. According to the heading it is "A prayer of Moses, the man of God." Franz Delitzsch said of it in his *Commentary on the Psalms*: "There is hardly a literary monument of antiquity, which can so brilliantly justify the traditional testimony to its origin as this Psalm. Not only in respect of its contents, but also in respect of its literary form, it is thoroughly appropriate to Moses."[132] On the other hand Kirkpatrick tells us in arguing for the late date, "But if, as is now generally held, Deuteronomy in its present form is far later than the time of Moses, the Deuteronomic language of the Psalm points to a later date than the Mosaic age" and he assigned it "probably to the time of the Exile."[133]

This has recently been strikingly illustrated by a posthumous work of R. H. Pfeiffer.[134] There, after reference is made to a number of passages in Deuteronomy, we are told that they illustrate "how much the Jerusalem priest who composed the Deuteronomic Code had learned from the books of Amos, Hosea, Isaiah, and Micah."[135] Further, "The whole Hebrew Bible grew eventually around Deuteronomy . . .";[136] and "After 621 the history of Israel was rewritten from the Deuteronomic point of view. . . . First our Books of Kings were written about 600 by a man who had witnessed the reforms of Josiah twenty-one years earlier and was still filled with enthusiasm for them. . . . Fifty years later (about 550 B.C.) the Second Deuteronomist published the

Books of Kings in a new edition and edited Joshua and Judges likewise as religious histories. Thus Deuteronomy gave birth not only to the notion of inspired Scripture but also of sacred history — an idea which was brought to its culmination in the Priestly Code (about 450 B.C.) and in Chronicles (about 250 B.C.)...."[137]

Many other statements from this book as well as from a host of others which advocate the same general position might be cited. But the above quotations will suffice to show how absolutely indispensable the late dating of Deuteronomy is to the whole reconstruction of the Old Testament which is advocated by the critics. Two things are made especially clear. The late dating of this book is not an isolated phenomenon. It carries with it two inevitable consequences. One is the alleged rewriting or reediting of the Historical Books (Joshua to Second Kings) to bring them into accord with the late date of Deuteronomy. Everything in these books which indicates or presupposes the teachings of Deuteronomy must be treated as due to the Deuteronomic editors who wrote or edited these histories at or after the time of Josiah and under the influence of the recently discovered Lawbook. This means, of course, that everything in these books which is called "Deuteronomistic" represents the presenting of the earlier history in terms of the ideas and practices of the post-Deuteronomic, which means Josian or post-Josian age.[138]

No less significant is it that according to this view the Deuteronomic writers are to be regarded as dependent on the prophets of the eighth and seventh centuries B.C. for their religious concepts and ideas. Thus Pfeiffer claimed that "Deuteronomy 4 is a post-exilic addition based on the Second Isaiah (540 B.C.),"[139] the reason being that it is only here in Deuteronomy that the monotheism of Deutero-Isaiah is clearly taught. Here we have the reversal of the biblical order, law and prophets, illustrated in its most drastic form. The Deuteronomists lived after the Prophets and were largely dependent upon them!

In view of the claim that "the priest who composed the Deuteronomic Code" owed so much to the prophets, the following statement is very illuminating and significant. As to the prophets we are told: "The most important contribution of the prophets was in the field of religion but, curiously enough, they did not realize how revolutionary and epoch-making this contribution was. They did not know that they were preaching a new religion."[140] This statement is a further illustration of the difficult situation in which the advocates of the late date of Deuteronomy and its dependence upon the Prophets place themselves. The explanation of this attitude of the prophets, which is so surprising to this advocate of the critical theory, is that it is Deuteronomy which furnishes the connecting link between the Mosaic Law and the

Prophets of the eighth and seventh centuries in Israel. It was because they were conscious that they were merely stressing the great doctrines so forcibly presented in Deuteronomy which they accepted as Mosaic that the thought did not occur to these prophets that they were "preaching a new religion."

We note in this connection the explanation which is given of the fact that Deuteronomy so clearly claims to be Mosaic. "The author wrote the book and ascribed it to Moses with perfect sincerity and good faith. ... He had no idea of an evolution of religion and law, and if his book presented true law and true religion, which, like the multiplication table, are always the same, they must have been preached by Moses if, as all admitted, he was divinely inspired."[141] This statement illustrates how completely the theory of evolution still dominates the now widely discredited Development theory. It is equivalent to saying that unless an ancient writer accepted the modern theory of evolution, he could have had no true conception of history and no true knowledge of the past, a truly preposterous statement. But such an explanation must be given, if the critics are to avoid the necessity of admitting that the Book of Deuteronomy was a clever forgery. For if Deuteronomy is Mosaic, then it follows that the history of Israel was not a record of steady upward progress, but as is asserted again and again in Scripture, a story of frequent and tragic apostasy, of turnings away from the teachings of the Mosaic Law. The lofty ethical monotheism of Isaiah is shown to be essentially the same as the monotheism of Mount Sinai. And the closing exhortation of the last of the writing prophets, Malachi, "Remember the law of Moses my servant, which I commanded him in Horeb for all Israel" becomes a most fitting conclusion of Old Testament prophecy.

It is the attempt to fit the Old Testament into a scheme of evolutionary development which largely if not completely ignores the supernatural factors at work on the one hand and the persistent downward trend in Israel on the other, that is responsible for this perversion of history which is so widely accepted today. According to the author we have quoted, "Thus Deuteronomy gave birth not only to the notion (*sic!*) of inspired Scripture but also of sacred history,"[142] which according to this writer reached its culmination in the Books of Chronicles, where the hand of God in Israel's history is made exceedingly plain, yet no more plain than elsewhere in the Bible. So the conclusion is reached, "Until modern times, biblical history has remained sacred history." This means that by dating Deuteronomy in the time of Josiah and treating as "Deuteronomistic" additions everything in the Historical Books (Joshua to 2 Kings) which is "sacred", i.e., which describes that ethical monotheism which is so conspicuous a feature of

Deuteronomy, the history prior to 621 B.C. can be "secularized." But it has to be admitted that this "modern" task is still incomplete, since this secularization cannot be accomplished in the case of the Books of Chronicles; and this is, of course, the reason that Modern Criticism has regarded these books as largely unhistorical. So it appears that even in these modern times some at least of biblical history must be regarded as sacred even if unhistorical!

This discussion has been given the title "The Law and the Prophets" for the reason that this phrase which occurs about a dozen times in the New Testament on the lips of the Lord and his apostles indicates so clearly the true sequence of biblical revelation. It is this sequence which the critics have endeavored for a century and a half to reverse. The extremes to which they are obliged to go in order to make good their claim constitute the strongest evidence of the falsity of that claim.[143] The late dating of Deuteronomy does not stand alone. It is both foundation and keystone — either word is applicable — of the entire critical theory. For it practically requires the reconstruction of the entire history of the religion of Israel. And this fact makes it the most vulnerable while at the same time the most dangerous of all the theories of the critics.[144]

THE PERIOD OF THE JUDGES

And the people served the Lord all the days of Joshua, and all the days of the elders that outlived Joshua, who had seen all the great works of the Lord, that he did for Israel. . . . And the children of Israel did evil in the sight of the Lord and served Baalim. . . . And they forsook the Lord and served Baal and Ashtaroth (Judg. 2:7, 11, 13).

This is one of a number of statements in the Book of Judges which clearly and emphatically assert that the period which it covers was to a very large extent a time of apostasy from the lofty ethical monotheism to which the nation had committed itself at Mount Sinai.[145] It has long been the contention of critical scholars that these statements represent the estimate placed on the religious beliefs and practices of their fathers by a generation which had come to regard that faith and those practices as base and unworthy and therefore they represented them, that is to say *mis*represented them, as an apostasy from a loftier and worthier faith and cultus which as a matter of fact, so they tell us, was not at all the faith of that earlier generation, but represented the result of a long and painful process of evolution from a crudely polytheistic faith to the ethical monotheism of the eighth century prophets.

Not to go farther back, we may refer to Johannes Pedersen as an oft-quoted advocate of this position. He tells us:

The Israelites of exilic and post-exilic times, who considered the acknowledgment of anything divine other than Yahweh as a capital sin, regarded their history from the immigration into Canaan till the fall mainly as a chain of sins and apostasies, which must give them all the more reason to humble themselves before their God. This view of their history, which falls into line with the judgment of the prophets, is displayed in the great confessions of sin from post-exilic times and finds expression in the adaptation of the book of Judges and the Books of the Kings.[146]

Having summarized thus briefly the testimony of the Bible itself on this important subject, Pedersen draws the conclusion which he states as follows: "The strange thing, then, is that Israel in an essential degree came to deny her real history." Yes, this is the strange thing, and it is something which the critics have difficulty in explaining. According to this theory of Israel's history, the Israelites, instead of trying to forget and ignore their early history, carefully preserved the record of it, and instead of trying to excuse it pictured it in all its infamy as a gross and inexcusable departure from a lofty ethical and spiritual religion from which they represented it as a horrible apostasy. We often read stories of the "good old days" and are tempted to cherish the nostalgic feeling that they were better than the days in which we are living. But here we have those days denounced as a grievous departure from a situation, a manner of life which we are told never existed because the so-called Mosaic law, allegedly promulgated and accepted at Sinai, itself belonged to the later age and could not have been a standard for the conduct of the Israelites of the period of the Judges since they had never heard of it. This is a truly amazing situation. But it is the inevitable result of the application to the history of Israel of a claim regarding her development which is utterly contrary to the statements made in her own records, a development the nature of which is determined by applying a more or less thoroughgoing theory of naturalistic development to the Old Testament records, which speak in terms of redemptive supernaturalism.

Pedersen tells us further:

The greater part of the Israelite cult was determined by the influence of foreigners. . . . The adoption of a peasant life meant a psychic transformation, which was reinforced by the sanctification that bound together the Israelite soul and that of the Canaanite agricultural world.[147]

This "psychic transformation" is referred to again and again both in the Law and in the Prophets. But Moses and the Prophets called it by a quite different name. They called it "forsaking" their own God and serving the fertility gods of Canaan. They used a very strong and offensive word to describe it, to "go a whoring" after the gods of the neighboring peoples.[148] It represented the failure of Israel when they settled in the land of Canaan to recognize that they received the blessings of fruitful seasons, of abundant harvests, of increase of flocks and herds, not from "the Canaanite agricultural world," i.e., from Baal and Ashtoreth through the fertility rites practiced by the Canaanites, but from their own Covenant God who was the Creator of heaven and earth and the author and source of their every blessing.[149]

A number of years ago a German scholar, Johannes Hehn, described this phenomenon and the reasons for it as follows:

Just as the monotheism of Israel distinguishes itself from the religions of other peoples of Asia Minor, so also there runs through the entire religious history of Israel from the beginning to the time of the Exile, a peculiar antithesis, which is to be observed in no other religion of the ancient orient: it is the antagonism between the demands of the religion of Jahweh and the inclination of the people toward polytheism and nature worship. The religion of Jahweh is indeed, as has been clearly established, determined in its essence by this very fact, that Jahweh is the God of the people of Israel and addresses himself with his promises and demands to the people. But on the other hand it is also unquestionable that this religion does not correspond to the inclinations of the people and for this very reason is not the product of their instincts and moods. Far otherwise, the strict Jahwism has to wage a constant battle in order to establish itself in opposition to the strivings of the people and often to their rulers also.[150]

This is a striking testimony to the distinctive nature of the religion of Israel and to the fact that it owes its unique character not to human invention but to divine revelation.

The attempt has often been made to explain this inner conflict which we constantly observe in the religious history of Israel merely as one between the austere faith and life of the bedouin, the desert dweller, and the more luxurious and often licentious habits of the settled, agricultural community. But such an explanation is clearly inadequate. When T. H. Robinson tells us, "The story of Israel presents a phenomenon with few parallels, if any in human history," we expect an adequate explanation of so nearly unique a phenomenon; and we cannot but feel that there is a decided let-down when he goes on to say: "It is the record of the interaction of two distinct types of ideal in social life and in religion, each proper to a particular form of economic order"[151] as, the interaction between the "pastoral nomad" and "the farmer and the city dweller." Surely this is no sufficient explanation of what Robinson regards as a very rare if not unique phenomenon. Nomad peoples have again and again settled down peacefully amid and become absorbed by the settled community.[152] According to the Bible the conflict lies far deeper than this: it is a conflict between obedience to the revealed will of God as made known through patriarch and lawgiver, through priest and prophet, and the turning away to go after other gods, to serve and worship them.[153] What could be more definite than the words with which Moses concluded the "book of the law" which he entrusted to the Levites: "See I have set before thee this day life and good, and death and evil . . . therefore choose life that both thou and thy seed may live" (Deut. 30:15, 19). Yet Moses foretold solemnly and sadly the long and terrible record of Israel's failure which was yet to be enacted in the course of her history when he said: "For *I* know (the "I" is emphatic) that after my death ye will utterly corrupt yourselves and turn aside from the way which I commanded you; and evil will befall you in the latter days; because ye will do evil in the sight of the Lord to provoke him to anger through the work of your hands" (Deut. 31:29). In these frequent and grievous turnings away from their God which are so faithfully recorded in the biblical record we have the explanation of many of the difficulties which emerge in that record, the vast difference between what Israel should have been and what Israel actually was.

SAMUEL

And she called his name Samuel (1 Sam. 1:20). The three most prominent figures in the First Book of Samuel are Samuel, Saul, and David. Each of them is introduced to the reader in a different way.

In the case of Samuel, the story begins long before his birth. The proverb, "Hope deferred maketh the heart sick" is the story of Hannah's long years of longing and waiting until the son she asked for comes to her arms. She gives him a name which is appropriate; and sings a song of praise to celebrate the birth. Then with a truly amazing display of gratitude to God she gives back her first-born to him. He gave and she returns the gift; and the Lord rewards her five-fold for her act of self-denying love. This is the perfect setting for the life-story of this man who became the prophet, the judge, and the king-maker of Israel.

With Saul the situation is entirely different. The incident which first brings Saul to our attention is the straying of the asses of Saul's father Kish. We are told briefly who Kish was; and his son Saul is described as "a choice young man and goodly." Then we learn how Saul came to Samuel and was recognized by him as the Lord's anointed. How old Saul was when he became king, we do not know. His mother's name is not mentioned. No account of his birth is given.

David is introduced to us as the youngest of eight sons of Jesse the Bethlehemite, whom Samuel anoints to replace Saul. We do not know his mother's name; and it seems probable that Abigail and Zeruiah were his half-sisters. After the secret anointing by which the divine purpose regarding David is made clear, we read of the two ways in which that purpose began to be fulfilled: Saul's need of a minstrel introduces David, temporarily it would seem, into the royal presence and favor, then David by his own act of courage and faith makes a name for himself as a national hero through the slaying of Goliath.

Three men could hardly be brought on the stage of history in more strikingly different fashion than are Samuel, Saul, and David in the First Book of Samuel.

Various attempts have been made in the course of a century of criticism to divide the Books of Samuel into sources as has been done in the case of the Pentateuch.[154] According to the French critic Adolph Lods, there are two sources in the earliest of the documents. He calls them the "seer source" and the "Jabesh-source." The Jabesh-source, according to Lods, originally began with a legendary account of Saul's birth (1:1f.).[155] But, according to the present text, it tells the story of Samuel's birth. How is this remarkable change brought about? The explanation given is this. Hannah's great desire was to have a son. That was her petition, her "asking"; and the word "ask" occurs in verses 17, 20, 27. In the Hebrew the verb "ask" is *sha'al*. Saul (Hebrew *Sha'ul*) means "asked." "Asked" would be an appropriate name for this long asked-for son. *Sha'ul* is somewhat similar to Samuel (*Shemu'el*) in Hebrew (three consonants being the same in the two names). So it is claimed that "Samuel" is a corruption of "Saul" in the original text or of the tradition lying back of the text and that what we have here was originally a tradition regarding the birth of Saul. This explanation proceeds on the assumption that because Hannah "asked" a son of the Lord, she must have called him "asked" (*Sha'ul*). This ignores the fact that Hebrew names often involve a word-play or pun. The exact meaning of Samuel is not certain. A perfectly possible explanation would be "God has appointed him" (*Semoel*) which would give a very suitable meaning and involve no change in the consonantal text.[156]

This theory leaves unexplained the name which actually appears in the text, Samuel. It does not tell us how, if Saul was so obviously the correct name, the suitable name in the context, it came to be changed to Samuel, or why in view of the prominence of Samuel in the events which led up to the founding of the monarchy it is necessary to transfer the birth narrative from Samuel to Saul. It is simply a plausible theory which can carry weight only with those who regard the text of the Old Testament or the oral tradition lying back of it as quite unreliable.

ZADOK

The first important political event in the career of David after he was made king of all Israel was his capture of the Jebusite fortress and making it "the city of David"; the first religious ceremony was the bringing up of the ark to Jerusalem. The latter event is described briefly in 2 Samuel 6, where no mention is made of either Zadok or Abiathar. In the fuller account in 1 Chronicles 14-17 we read that after his first tragic failure David, having discovered that "none ought to bear the ark but the Levites" (15:2), called for "Zadok and Abiathar the priests" (vs. 11), and commanded them to sanctify themselves and their brethren in preparation for this important ceremony. This brings to our attention the striking and anomalous fact that during the reign of David over all Israel there were two high priests,[157] a fact which is not mentioned in 2 Samuel until 8:17; and also the question which here immediately concerns us, Who was Zadok?

We have seen that according to Wellhausen there was no hereditary priesthood in the time of David and that he treated Zadok and his successors as "parvenus" who in the course of time came to be regarded as "the most legitimate of the legitimate." This he accomplished by treating all the evidence to the contrary as late and untrustworthy. He says of Zadok: "Obviously he does not figure as an intermediate link in the line of Aaron, but as the beginner of an entirely new genealogy,"[158] adding in a footnote: "To satisfy the Pentateuch it is shown in the Book of Chronicles, by means of artificial genealogies, how the sons of Zadok derived their origin in an unbroken line from Aaron and Eleazar." This led to the conclusion, which has been stated bluntly by Addis: "We know nothing of his real origin; nor can we say when or how he became priest in the royal sanctuary at Jerusalem."[159] Such a negative result was of course decidedly unsatisfactory.

About fifty years ago a theory was proposed by Mowinckel regarding the origin of Zadok which has become rather influential in view of the increased emphasis now placed on Canaanite influence as a result of the discoveries at Ras Shamra. It is that Zadok was the last priest or priest-king of the Jebusite fortress which was captured by David, and that David made him priest in his new sanctuary at Jerusalem.[160] Since Rowley has discussed it at considerable length, we may use his treatment as a basis for its evaluation.[161]

Rowley starts out with the statement that the Old Testament gives us "no reliable information" as to whence Zadok came. To justify this statement he is of course obliged to reject as did Wellhausen the genealogies which the Old Testament gives us. The first of these (2 Sam. 8:17) in which Zadok is called "the son of Ahitub," he rejects because he thinks this would make Zadok belong to the line of Ithamar, since Eli's grandson Ichabod had a brother Ahitub, as if it were quite unlikely if not impossible that these Ahitubs were, as the record clearly indicates, two different men of the same name.[162] The other genealogies, those in 1 Chronicles 6 and Ezra 7, which trace Zadok's ancestry through Ahitub back to Aaron, Rowley brushes aside, attributing them to "the pious fabrications of a later age."[163] Having thus disposed of the evidence to the contrary, he is then in a position to say of Zadok that he appears "suddenly" and that the Old Testament gives us "no reliable information as to whence he came," which means that Rowley has now cleared the ground for any theory which can be regarded as plausible. Coming then to his claim that Zadok was the last priest or priest-king of Jebus, we ask for proof of this claim.

1. *Zadok and Abiathar.* Rowley points out that the first mention of Zadok in Samuel occurs after the bringing up of the ark to Jerusalem (2 Sam. 8:17). From this he infers that Zadok was the priest or priest-king of the captured fort. As to this it is to be noted that this mention of Zadok occurs, not in the account of that event (6:12-23), but in a summary record of David's achievements and appointments (chap. 8) which makes no mention of Jebus or of Jerusalem or of the ark. In this summary of David's principal men "Zadok, the son of Ahitub and Ahimelech, the son of Abiathar" are listed as priests. To infer from this that Zadok was a Jebusite, that he was the priest-king of the captured fortress is an extreme illustration of the *post hoc, ergo propter hoc* argument which may be speciously plausible, but has no real validity.

According to the account in 1 Chronicles, which Rowley of course regards as late and untrustworthy, David after his initial failure (chap. 13) discovered that "none ought to carry the ark of God but the Levites; for them hath the Lord chosen to carry the ark of God and to minister unto him forever" (15:2). Then we read that "David gathered all Israel together to Jerusalem." No mention is made of the Jebusites. Then we learn that "David assembled the children of Aaron and the Levites" (vs. 4), a total of 762 being listed and "called for Zadok and Abiathar the priests" and for the six leaders of the groups of Levites just listed (vs. 11) and, addressing them as "the chief of the fathers of the Levites," commanded them to sanctify themselves and that "the priests and the Levites did so" (vs. 14). A list is given of the "Levites" who were appointed by the "chief of the Levites" to take part in the service of song. Then follows the account of this successful and joyful event, the bringing up and placing of the ark in the city of David. In this David took a prominent part and the psalm which he composed for the occasion is recorded (16:7-36). Then we read that David "left there before the ark of the covenant of the Lord, Asaph and his brethren . . . and Obed-edom . . . " (vss. 37-38). Finally we read the statement: "And Zadok, the priest, and his brethren the priests, before the tabernacle of the Lord in the high place that was at Gibeon. . . ."

Several things are to be noted regarding this account: (1) The ark was not placed in the ancient shrine of the Jebusite fortress, but in "the tent which David had placed for it." (2) No mention is made of Abiathar's assignment to minister at the tent before the ark. It is apparently to be assumed that such was the case. For (3) it is expressly stated that Zadok and his brethren were "left" (vs. 39) "before the tabernacle of the Lord in the high place that was at Gibeon."[164] No reason is given. It may be that Zadok was merely being continued as priest of the high place where the tabernacle and the great altar had been for a period of time the length of which we cannot determine. At least it is clear that his post was not Jerusalem and the ark but Gibeon and the tabernacle. And since some years later "Solomon and all the congregation" went to the high place that was at Gibeon to worship (2 Chron. 1:3) while the ark was still in the tent at Jerusalem (vs. 4), it is probable that Zadok continued to minister there until the temple was dedicated when the ark *and* the tabernacle and its furnishings were brought into it (5:5).

It is quite possible that the reason for Solomon's preference for the shrine at Gibeon is to be found in the fact that Zadok who had supported him against Adonijah was particularly associated with the worship there, while Abiathar was in charge of the ark at Jerusalem. We must not, of course, make too much of this distinction in office as it concerns Zadok and Abiathar. They both exhibit loyalty to David at the time of the rebellion of Absalom (2 Sam. 15). But it is noteworthy that Zadok is apparently the more conspicuous: he is mentioned alone in verses 24, 25, 27. Yet we read that Zadok and Abiathar "carried the ark of God again to Jerusalem and they tarried there." It is also noteworthy that here and elsewhere when they are mentioned together the order is always, Zadok and Abiathar, never Abiathar and Zadok. Is it likely that if Zadok had been priest of the Jebusite shrine he would be given the post of honor at Gibeon — not at Jerusalem as Rowley claims? Is it likely that the biblical writers would always give him the precedence over Abiathar who was an Israelite and a priest (1 Sam. 2:35; 23:9), if he was a Jebusite and had been a worshipper of "a strange god"?

2. *Jebus.* The theory that Zadok was a Jebusite becomes increasingly improbable when we examine the history of this people as it is set before us in Scripture. The Jebusites are listed among the descendants of Canaan in Genesis 10; and they are included about fifteen times,[165] in the lists of the nations dwelling in the land promised to Abraham's descendants, peoples which Israel was to exterminate, whose shrines

and idols Israel was to destroy, whose abominations Israel was to abhor. They are spoken of as dwelling " in the mountains" (Josh. 11:3), "in Jerusalem" (e.g., Josh. 15:63; Judg. 1:21). "Jebus" is mentioned only twice (Judg. 19:10f.; 1 Chron. 11:4f.). At the time of the conquest, Adoni-zedek, king of Jerusalem, was the leader of a confederacy of Israel's enemies (Josh. 10:1-3); and after the great victory at Gibeon he and his four confederate kings were slain by Joshua and their bodies hung on five trees or stakes until the evening. The "king of Jerusalem" is listed among the thirty-one kings of cities west of the Jordan (12:10) who were smitten by Joshua and the children of Israel. Yet we are also told expressly, "As for the Jebusites, the inhabitants of Jerusalem, the children of Israel could not drive them out: but the Jebusites dwell with the children of Judah at Jerusalem unto this day" (Josh. 15:63). That is, the king of Jerusalem was slain, apparently in battle, but the Jebusites were not driven out of Jerusalem. Elsewhere we read that the children of Judah captured Jerusalem and burned it (Judg. 1:8). Whether this refers to the original conquest under Joshua, or to a subsequent campaign of Judah alone is not clear. The AV by rendering "had fought" and "had taken" apparently refers it to Joshua, who may have assigned this special task to Judah. Likewise we read "and the children of Benjamin did not drive out the Jebusites that inhabited Jerusalem; but the Jebusites dwell with the children of Benjamin in Jerusalem unto this day" (vs. 21).

When we study these statements in the light of the allotment to Judah which is recorded in Joshua 15:8, "And the border went up by the valley of the son of Hinnom unto the south side of the Jebusite; the same is Jerusalem," etc., and of that to Benjamin which includes "the Jebusite, which is Jerusalem" (18:28; cf. vs. 16), it seems clear that Jebus and Jerusalem are not equivalent expressions. The one may be less comprehensive than the other. Jebus may mean the citadel or fortress which was never captured by the Israelites until David's time, while Jerusalem may decribe the town which was captured and burned in the days of Joshua but was later rebuilt by the Jebusites who, holding their seemingly impregnable fortress, dominated and ruled the entire city, except at rare intervals. That this situation became a snare to the Israelites is plainly stated (Judg. 2:10-13). But even in those days of apostasy it was recognized that the Jebusites were aliens and idolators. In the terrible story in Judges of the Levite and his concubine, we read that on the homeward journey, when his servant proposed that they spend the night at Jebus, the Levite refused on the ground that it was "the city of a stranger, that is not of the children of Israel" (19:12). And we read finally that when David "went to Jerusalem unto the Jebusites," they met him with contemptuous defiance, declaring that the "blind and the lame" would suffice for the defense of the city (2 Sam. 5:6). There is no suggestion of a negotiated surrender on favorable terms. David "took" the city and called it "the city of David." Not a word is said about its *king* or its *priest* or the *shrine* or *temple* at Jebus. Yet we are told by the proponents of this theory that it is probable that Zadok was either the king or the priest-king of this ancient Jebusite stronghold which had so long defied Israel, and that David "took him over" as high priest of his new capital.[166]

3. *Genesis 14.* This chapter describes an event in the life of Abraham which according to the biblical chronology took place four centuries or more before the conquest. It tells of Abram's meeting a mysterious person named Melchizedek, who is called "king of Salem" and further described as "priest of God Most High."

a. Granting that Salem is probably the abbreviated form of Jerusalem,[167] we note that no mention is made of Salem as then belonging to the Jebusites. It is certainly possible, even highly probable, that in the course of four hundred years the city of Melchizedek may have changed hands several times, or at least that Melchizedek was a distinct and unique figure among the kings of Jerusalem. The Epistle to the Hebrews describes him as "without father, without mother, without descent" (7:3), which probably means that he was not a hereditary king and not the founder of a dynasty.[168]

b. Two reasons are given by Rowley for the appeal to Melchizedek. (1) Zadok, Melchizedek[169] (Gen. 14:18) and Adoni-zedek[170] (Josh. 10:1) bore names which are derived from or contain the root *ṣadaq* which in Hebrew means "to be righteous." So it is argued that this is a Canaanite root, and that the Jebusite god was called Zedek. This inference is opposed by the following facts: (a) This root is quite rare in the Ugaritic. (b) It is used only once in the El Amarna letters, a letter of Abdu-heba, king of Jerusalem, and there the expression (*ṣaduq ana iashi*), may mean simply, "I am right" and have no ethical significance.[171] (c) This king of Jerusalem, six of whose letters appear in the El Amarna collection, is named Abdu-heba (a Hittite or Hurrian name)[172] which would indicate that names containing this element (*ṣadag*) were not characteristic of a Jebusite dynasty. (d) On the other hand the root *sdq* (verb, adjective and nouns) occurs frequently (cir. 500 times) in the Old Testament and is characteristically Hebraic, occurring in such Hebrew names as Jehozadak and Zedekiah. It is not necessary to regard the *sedek* in Melchizedek as the name of a god. It may mean "my king is righteous" or "king of righteousness."

c. El Elyon (most high God). This name of deity is used by Dr. Rowley as a support for the claim that David took over the Jebusite shrine and its priest-king Zadok. In the Ras Shamra mythological texts, the supreme god is *'El* (i.e., God). So it is argued that *'El 'Elyon* was a Canaanite deity. *'El* (*ilu*) is the common Semitic name for deity. But, *'El 'Elyon* does not occur in Accadian, Phoenician or Ugaritic. In Hebrew *'El* (God) frequently has a descriptive adjective or noun joined with it, as jealous God, gracious God, almighty God, God of glory, eternal God. *'Elyon* apparently comes from the very frequently occurring Hebrew verb meaning "to go up" or "ascend." It is used about fifty times in the Old Testament in a local or geographical sense, meaning "high" or "upper," as "Beth-horon, the upper" (Josh. 16:5), the "upper pool" (Isa. 7:3). It is used of God, either with or without the divine name: God (Most) High (*'El 'Elyon,* Gen. 14:18-22), "Lord Most High" (Ps. 47:2) or simply "Most High" (Ps. 78:17). Like "great" (*gadol*) it is a very appropriate epithet to be used of God. It occurs a number of times in the Psalms. There is good reason for regarding it as characteristically Hebrew.[173] The critics have long been skeptical regarding Genesis 14 and have questioned its value as history. Rowley is not willing to vouch for its entire credibility. But he is willing to appeal to it for proof that Zadok came from the line of Melchizedek and was the last priest of pre-Israelite Jebus-Jerusalem.

4. A further confirmation of this theory is sought by Rowley in the words of Psalm 110, "Thou art a priest forever after the order of Melchizedek." This psalm, as is well known, has been a storm center for many years. The heading assigns it to David. It is appealed to by our Lord as Davidic. But many critics have confidently affirmed that it is post-exilic. They have even claimed that it contains an acrostic on the name of the Maccabean priest-king Simon. Members of the Myth and Ritual and of the Uppsala Schools are now claiming with equal positiveness that its ascription to David or to his time is correct, that it was a kind of coronation ode, to accredit and acclaim David as the priest-king of the Jehovahized Canaanite city and shrine of the Jebusites. Such an inference depends entirely on the interpretation Rowley gives to Genesis 14. It adds nothing to it.

5. Finally Rowley appeals to Numbers 25:11-13 where the promise of an "everlasting priesthood" is given to Phineas. He applies this to David. But in this very chapter, Phineas is twice called "the son of Eleazar, the son of Aaron the priest" (vss. 7 and 11). Rowley would thus claim an "everlasting priesthood" for David as priest-king at Jerusalem through Phineas, Eleazar and Aaron. But it is to be remembered that he has rejected as untrustworthy the records which trace the priesthood in Israel to Aaron and has argued that Zadok was a Canaanite priest. So he cannot apply this passage to him without admitting that these genealogies are of some historical value after all.[174]

The Brazen Serpent. Professor Rowley goes still further. He not merely makes Zadok the high priest of the Jebusite shrine at Jerusalem, he also claims that the "brazen serpent," which the record tells us had been made by Moses (Num. 21:9) and which Hezekiah destroyed because in his day it had come to be treated as an idol (2 Kings 18:4), was originally "housed in the shrine kept by Zadok, and that it was the principal sacred object of that shrine until the ark was brought in to be beside it."[175] This means that the Jebusites worshipped a serpent god, and that after David captured Jerusalem and made Zadok high priest, this worship continued side by side with that of Yahweh until the time of Hezekiah. The account given in Numbers 21 of the fiery serpents as the reason for the making of the brazen serpent he, of course, disregards as merely a late story invented to account for this serpent worship in the temple at Jerusalem. The only evidence in support of such a theory is that serpent worship was practiced to some extent in ancient times in this general area, the inference being that the Jebusites practiced it. We know nothing about the worship of the Jebusites. But this theory is offered us as a substitute for the very different account recorded in the Bible simply because it harmonizes better with Rowley's theory as to the origin and development of the religion of Israel.

There are some minor details of this theory which need not further detain us. The important thing to observe is, how utterly it disregards and rejects the plain and oft-repeated injunctions of the Old Testament against any compromise or contamination with the idolatrous abominations of the Canaanites. According to this view David inaugurated and strengthened his rule over all Israel by what Albright calls a "symbiosis," the introducing of a syncretistic Baal-Jehovah worship at the central shrine of his capital city and by making the priest of the Canaanite shrine of the captured Jebusite fort a co-priest with the Israelite Abiathar and eventually the only legitimate head of the worship of Jehovah at Jerusalem. What could be more contrary to the spirit and the express teachings of the Bible than this?

On the other hand, if we accept the statements of Scripture the difficulties are largely removed. We have the two lines of Eleazar and Ithamar represented in the days of David by Zadok and Abiathar. Both function as priests. Zadok is the representative of the elder line. But Abiathar has a special claim on David because of the tragedy of Eli's house for which David considered himself responsible (1 Sam. 22:20-23). But David's debt to Abiathar is cancelled by Abiathar's support of Adonijah (1 Kings 1:19). He is removed from office by Solomon (2:26f.) and with his disgrace the house of Eli falls, in fulfillment of the prophecy of the man of God to Eli (1 Sam. 2:27-36).

HEMAN, ETHAN — EZRAHITES

The claim that Zadok was a Canaanite (Jebusite) priest, is rejected as we have seen by Albright as lacking sufficient evidence. But strange to say, Albright does not hesitate to advance another theory which from the standpoint of the Bible is equally improbable and even disastrous. He tells us: "'It is very significant that two Psalms both of which swarm with Canaanitisms, 88 and 89, are expressly attributed to the Canaanites, Heman and Ethan in their headings, which reflect post-exilic tradition."[176] What is the evidence that Heman and Ethan were Canaanites?

The genealogy of the famous Heman of David's time is traced back twenty generations through Kohath to Levi (I Chron. 6:33-38); and that of his colleague Ethan is carried back fourteen generations through Merari to Levi (vss. 44-47). Since these two men were leaders of the singers appointed by David (15:17, 19), it would be very natural to suppose that they are the ones to whom the titles assign these psalms. The difficulty lies in the fact that they are called Ezrahites. This raises a problem because a Heman and an Ethan are elsewhere described as sons of Zarah and grandsons of Judah (1 Chron. 2:6) and a Heman who is an Ezrahite and an Ethan who is perhaps also an Ezrahite are listed among the wise men with whom Solomon is compared (1 Kings 4:31). That these wise men were non-Israelites might be inferred from the fact that it is stated in the context that "his fame was in all nations round about."[177] But such an inference is not necessary. The fact that the names of these wise men are almost exactly identical with the names of the sons of Zerah mentioned in 1 Chronicles 2:6 makes it decidedly more probable that the same men are referred to in both passages.

The question then is whether the Levite singers can be identified with the Judean sons of Zerah. If so, the appellation Ezrahite as given to the Psalmists would be accounted for. The natural and probable explanation is that the name Ezrahite was given to these Levites because, while of Levitical descent, they had been adopted into the Judean clan of Zerah among which they lived, since the Levites had no tribal allotments. It is to be noted that the descendants of Zerah of the tribe of Judah are called Zarhites (Num. 26:20; Josh. 7:17; 1 Chron. 27:11, 13). There was also a family of Zarhites in Simeon (Num. 26:13). If this explanation is correct, "Ezrahite" (from the same root as Zarhite) might distinguish the Levites who had been adopted into the family of Zerah from his true descendants who were called Zarhites.[178] This is certainly a possible explanation of the appellation Ezrahite as given to these two distinguished Levites.

We come now to the explanation of Ezrahite which is the basis of Albright's startling claim. There is a Hebrew word *ezrahite* (*'ezrachi*), which means "native, native-born." It occurs seventeen times in the Old Testament, chiefly in the Pentateuch. That such a descriptive epithet would be given to two distinguished Levites of impeccable descent seems quite absurd. That it should be given to famous wise men of the time of Solomon seems almost equally improbable, especially if these men are to be identified with the sons of Zerah mentioned in 1 Chronicles 2:6. So it is not surprising that such a view has not gained favor in the past. But Albright's contention goes far beyond this. He claims that "native" is used in the sense of aboriginal and describes Heman and Ethan the Psalmists as Canaanites. From the standpoint of the Law of Moses this would not be a title of distinction but of opprobrium. The Israelites were commanded to have no dealings with the Canaanites, but to drive them out or destroy them utterly;[179] and while they failed to do this, it seems highly improbable that "native" in the sense of "Canaanite" was ever regarded as a title of distinction or would have been used in the headings of psalms intended for sacred use. Yet Albright declares that "There can be no reasonable doubt that the word *'ezrach* meant originally 'aborigine.' "[180] In support of this statement he appeals particularly to Numbers 9:14, which he renders "There shall be one statute for you and for the *gêr* and for the native (*'ezrach*) of the land." He insists that three classes are mentioned here and that the third refers to the Canaanites. But another rendering is possible: "There shall be one statute for you, both for the *gêr* and for the native of the land."[181] This would make only two classes, the sojourner and the native Israelite. It must be admitted that Albright's rendering is the more natural in itself. But even if it were adopted it would certainly be possible that *'ezrach* means a special type of sojourner, one who was born in the land and was a native in that sense, although not an Israelite, as *indigenous* but not *aboriginal*. Either of these possible interpretations would be in harmony with the general teachings of the Bible, with which Albright's interpretation definitely conflicts.

That, contrary to Albright's theory, *'ezrach* refers to the native-born Israelite and *gêr* to the sojourner in the land, is made clear by the way in which these words are used elsewhere. In the regulations for the observance of the day of atonement, we read the command: "Ye shall afflict your souls and do no work at all, whether it be one of your own country (Heb., the *'ezrach*) or a stranger (Heb., the *gêr*) that sojourneth with you" (Lev. 16:29). Here the word "ye" is expressly defined by the words *'ezrach* and *gêr*. If *'ezrach* means native-born Israelite and *gêr* means sojourner, the description is comprehensive.

But if *'ezrach* means Canaanite, then the command refers specifically only to two minor, non-Israelite groups and we are allowed to infer that it was also applicable to the Israelite nation itself. This seems extremely improbable, to say the least. The meaning is even clearer in Leviticus 19:34: "The sojourner (*gêr*) sojourning with you shall be to you as the native-born (*'ezrach*), and thou shalt love him as thyself." If here the word *'ezrach* means the Israelite, then the command simply requires that the sojourner be treated as if he were an Israelite, which may imply that he is to be encouraged to become an Israelite. This explanation is the usual one. It is favored by the reference in the immediate context to the fact that the Israelites had been sojourners (*gêrim*) in the land of Egypt. The Israelite is to remember how he was mistreated when he was a *gêr* in Egypt in order that his treatment of the *gêr* in his own midst may be entirely different. But if this command is taken to mean that the *gêr* is to be treated as if he were a Canaanite and that for that reason the Israelite is to treat him as if he were a fellow Israelite, the verse becomes nonsense and conflicts utterly with the severe condemnations referred to above of any dealings with the Canaanites whose idolatries are abominations in the sight of the God of Israel.

The claim that Psalms 88 and 89 "swarm with Canaanitism" will be discussed later. Albright claims also that the names Heman and Ethan are "hypocoristic and resemble scores of such names on Ugaritic tablets." It is to be noted that Albright does not state that these names have been *found* on Ugaritic tablets. He simply claims that they resemble such names. He does not state wherein the resemblance consists. It is true that both names end in *n*. But the ending -*n* is found in many words and names in Hebrew, Aramaic and other Semitic languages. It used to be claimed as an Aramaism. Besides this, it is not clear that in the case of either name the final *n* is an ending. Heman may come from the same root as the familiar word "Amen," and mean "steadfast or dependable." This root appears frequently in Hebrew in a number of different derivatives. It has not yet been identified in Ugaritic. The same may be said of the name Ethan, except that the root from which it probably comes is much rarer in Hebrew,[182] but yields an appropriate meaning for this name, "steadfast, unvarying" or the like, a somewhat similar meaning to Heman. The root has not been identified in Ugaritic.

How much of guesswork is involved when the attempt is made to prove a theory on the basis of meager and quite inadequate evidence is illustrated by the explanation which Albright gives of the name of the wise man Chalcol (1 Kings 4:31). On several ivories discovered at Megiddo the name of a person named *Krkr*,[183] supposedly an Egyptian priestess, has been discovered. Since Egyptian does not distinguish *l* from *r*, Albright declares that *Krkr* (the vowels are not indicated in Egyptian) represents Hebrew *Klkl*. This is, of course, possible. But possibility is not proof! The name *Krkr* is, as has been stated, the name of a woman. As to this Albright tells us, "Since names of men and of women constantly interchanged in Canaanite and Hebrew, the difference need arouse no surprise."[184] True, though a decided overstatement! But two rather remote possibilities do not add up to proof that the name *Krkr* as given to an Egyptian priestess in a temple in Megiddo, probably in the thirteenth century B.C., has any connection with the name Chalcol of the wise man of Solomon's day, nearly four centuries later. Albright is quite severe in his denunciation of those who suggested formerly that the names of Chalcol and his confreres proved that they were Edomites. He expresses the hope that "the alleged 'Edomite' origin of these names will disappear from scholarly literature."[185] It does not seem to occur to him that his attempt to prove a Canaanite origin rests on equally flimsy evidence. So we may venture to express the hope that this attempt to prove Heman and Ethan to have been Canaanites will also and speedily "disappear from scholarly literature."

We may notice in this connection that the claim has also been made that the prophet Nathan was a Canaanite, that like Zadok he was taken over by David from the Jebusite sanctuary when David captured it. There is not a scintilla of proof of this. As for the name, it is to be noted that it comes from one of the most common roots in Hebrew, the verb "to give," which occurs 2,007 times in the Old Testament. Furthermore, Nathan (meaning "he gave") is the Hebrew form of the name. Were it Accadian, it would be *Nadan*. In Ugaritic or Phoenician it would be *Yadan*. The name Nathan occurs forty-two times in the Old Testament, as the name of eight or more different persons. In combination it appears as Elnathan and Jonathan, as Nathaniel, Nathaniah, Nathan-melech. What appears to be its equivalent in Ugaritic (*Yathan*) is comparatively rare. Yet we are told that the name Nathan is Ugaritic. On this basis it could easily be shown that there is no such thing as a Hebrew word, that everything Hebraic should be renamed Canaanite.

SOLOMON AND THE TEMPLE

F. J. Hollis of the Myth and Ritual School has attempted to connect the temple at Jerusalem with the cult of the sun. This is done through the name Ben-oni. According to the brief account in Genesis 35:16-20 Rachel, when she was dying, named the son, whom she bore at the cost of her life, Ben-oni, which means "son of my trouble [or, sorrow]," a name which was quite natural in view of the situation. Then it is stated that Jacob changed the name to Ben-jamin, "son of the right hand" (child of good fortune, or favor), which also suits the context admirably. But this explanation of Ben-oni does not give the meaning which this writer is in search of. So he tells us:

. . . this tribe of "Ben-jamin" seems to have been earlier known as Ben-oni, and "On" was the ancient name of the city called by the Greeks "Heliopolis," i.e., the city of the Sun-god, the unchallenged center indeed of his worship, save for the brief interlude of Amenhotep IV's championship at Aten, through the many centuries of Egypt's long political and religious history.[186]

In this way a connection is suggested between one of the tribes of Israel and the Sun worship of Egypt. Turning again to the Genesis narrative, we note that the incident referred to, the naming of Benjamin by his dying mother, is said to have taken place perhaps thirty years before Jacob and his sons went down into Egypt, that is, before they had any extended contact with the land of Egypt or its gods.[187] This illustrates the way in which the critics often take a statement which they can use, lift it out of its context, give it a totally different meaning from the one which was obviously intended, and then make it the basis for a conclusion which suits the purpose which they have in view. If the *account* of the naming of Benjamin is not true, how do we know that the *name* Ben-oni is to be depended on, and how do we know that the recondite explanation given by the critic is any more dependable than the obviously appropriate one given in the narrative itself?

SOLOMON AND THE TEMPLE WORSHIP

And three times in a year did Solomon offer burnt offerings and peace offerings upon the altar which he built unto the Lord (1 Kings 9:25). We have seen in our study of biblical rhetoric that one of its characteristics is to speak in terms of the individual, even when it is quite clear that the acts attributed to him were shared in or performed by others. This method of writing is so general that it may have seemed to the reader that it was quite unnecessary even to allude to it. But its importance is strikingly illustrated by the incident here referred to. Every one who regards the Pentateuch as Mosaic and recalls the functions definitely assigned to the priests in connection with the worship at the tabernacle, and who recalls also the punishment of king Uzziah for presuming to burn incense in the temple, will feel that there is no reason to assume that on these or any other occasions, Solomon personally performed priestly functions. When such statements as the above are made with regard to the proper and legitimate worship of God, it is, of course, to be assumed that the ritual was performed according to the law of Moses.[188] But if the laws governing the duties of the priests which are recorded in the Pentateuch are regarded as late and as the product of a long course of development, then it is possible to argue that, in the days of Solomon, the king still was permitted to perform priestly duties, that Solomon did so in person, that his conduct was proper and lawful, that the punishment of Uzziah either marked a development in the temple code or was itself a fabrication of the Chronicler to increase the authority of the priestly caste.

The Molten Sea in the Temple (1 Kings 7:23-26). The first mention of the "laver" occurs in Exodus 30:18-21; and there it is stated that it is to contain water for the washings of the priests (cf. 40:12, 30). Since the priests were "holy" men whose duty it was to offer the bloody animal sacrifices, such washings were, of course, necessary. Its location is also stated; it is to stand between the tabernacle and the altar (40:7, 30), which indicates that it is for the use of the priests and not of the people. When Aaron and his sons were inducted into the office of priest, they were washed with water from the laver (40:12; cf. Lev. 8:11).

The arrangement in Solomon's temple was, in the nature of the case, much more elaborate. There was first the "molten sea" (1 Kings 7:23-26) which clearly corresponded to the "laver" in the tabernacle. There were also ten "lavers" which were placed on bases with wheels (vss. 27-39). The capacity of the laver in the tabernacle is not stated; we are told that the molten sea contained two thousand baths and the lavers forty baths each, which means that there was five times as much water in the sea as in the ten lavers.[189] Since the lavers may at times have required refilling several times in the course of the day, especially on the Sabbath and the feast days, so large a reservoir would not be at all excessive, but even necessary. It is to be noted that while in the account in Kings the description of the sea and the lavers is rather elaborate, not a word is said about the use to which they are to be put. Apparently we are to assume that this has been stated with sufficient plainness in Exodus. But 2 Chronicles 4:6 assigns different uses to the lavers and the sea: the lavers were for washing the sacrifices, the sea for the cleansing of the priests.

For those who accept the Mosaic authorship of the Pentateuch this explanation is natural, obvious, and sufficient. But those who regard the Pentateuch as late and unreliable and hold with Wellhausen that the Mosaic tabernacle is a "reflection backward" of Solomon's temple, will very probably seek another, a more erudite or recondite explanation of the molten sea. Professor Albright is greatly concerned to prove that the construction and furnishing of Solomon's temple had "cosmic" significance and were intended to exhibit "the universal character of Yahweh's domain." And he attempts to connect it with various mythological and pagan beliefs and practices. Thus, "The Sea (1 Kings 7:23-26) has been universally recognized as having cosmic significance of some kind. In function it cannot be separated from the Mesopotamian *apsû*, employed both as the name of the subterranean freshwater ocean from which all life and all fertility were derived and as the name of a basin of holy water erected in the temple."[190] This is an overstatement to say the least. This theory is neither new, nor is it almost universally recognized.[191] There is nothing in the description itself to justify a "mythological" interpretation of these vessels or of their ornamentation. In view of the size of the temple and the permanent nature of its appointments, it was perfectly natural that there should be a large reservoir (the sea) and a number of movable basins (the lavers) for the numerous priests to use for purification and for washing the sacrifices. To attribute them to Phoenician influence is decidedly questionable. Those who tell us that "Solomon went far beyond the chaste, divinely ordained simplicity of the tabernacle and its symbolic ritual and furniture" and speak of "the paganizing movement which may be said to have been inaugurated with the building of the temple" should remember two things: *negatively,* there is not a word of criticism expressed in Scripture of Solomon's so-called "innovations"; *positively,* both Kings (8:10f.) and Chronicles (5:13f.) inform us that the temple at its dedication received the same attestation of divine acceptance and approval as had the tabernacle: "the cloud filled the house of the Lord." The shekina-glory was so overwhelming on both occasions that mortal man could not endure it. We cannot but feel that Albright, in his desire to trace the characteristic features of the temple to pagan sources, is himself responsible for this paganizing movement which he discovers in it.[192]

It is quite proper to direct attention to the fact that by a singular providence Moses the Hebrew was brought up at the court of Pharoah, that he spent forty years there and that as Stephen declares "Moses was learned in all the wisdom of the Egyptians" (Acts 7:22). We may well believe that Moses was quite familiar with the general design of the magnificent temples of Egypt. If the daughter of Pharoah who adopted him as her son was the redoubtable Queen Hatshepsut who built the great temple of Der el Bahri, Moses may have watched its growth with interest and amazement and learned much in so doing. But we need to observe carefully that what especially prepared him to be the leader and law-giver of his people was his call by the God of his fathers (Exod. 3) and the special dealings of God with him. The Bible tells us that "Moses was in the mount forty days and forty nights" (Exod. 24:18); and there the command was given him to make the tabernacle and everything connected with it according to the pattern showed him in the mount (25:9, 40; 26:30; 27:8), which accounts for the words "as the Lord commanded Moses" which almost form a refrain (13 times) in the account of the setting up and dedicating of the tabernacle (Exod. 39-40). Here lies the biblical emphasis: the tabernacle and everything connected with it was a direct revelation to Moses. How much Moses' Egyptian training was a preparation which fitted him to receive it is a matter of secondary importance.

The same applies to the temple erected by Solomon. We are told expressly of the help which Solomon secured from Hiram king of Tyre, of the cedars of Lebanon which were sent him, of the skill of the Tyrians in the building arts, and of the sending of expert craftsmen to supervise the casting of the brazen vessels and other things for the sanctuary.[193] But it is not to be forgotten that what is especially emphasized in the record is the God-given wisdom of Solomon and his originality. Thus we are told regarding the throne which he made, "there was not the like made in any kingdom" (1 Kings 10:20).[194] Most important of course are the statements regarding the Lord's blessing upon Solomon's work (6:11f.) and its acceptance. Solomon's temple was dedicated and sanctified by the cloud which filled the house (8:10f.) just as the cloud had filled the tabernacle which Moses had made. There is not the slightest suggestion that there were any foreign and pagan inventions, least of all any Canaanite influences at work in it.

"*Under the sun.*" This phrase occurs about thirty times in Ecclesiastes and in nearly every chapter. There is nothing particularly remarkable in the expression itself. It is perhaps a little surprising that while the sun is referred to a number of times in the Old Testament and sometimes represented as an observer of the doings of men and as an object of idolatrous worship, this exact phrase is found only in this book. Albright has pointed out that the phrase occurs "in a sepulchral inscription of Eshmunazar, king of Sidon, about the beginning of the 3rd cent."; [195] and he says further "not long before the time of the Preacher," the implication being that the Preacher derived it from this late Phoenician inscription. It occurs also on the inscription of Tabnith, the father of this Eshmunazar. If as appears to be widely recognized, these kings of Sidon lived later than the time of Alexander the Great, this would indicate a very late date for the Preacher. But why must we assume that the Preacher borrowed this phrase from two late kings of Sidon, each of whom used it once on his sepulchral inscription? Is it not at least equally possible that they borrowed it from the Book of Ecclesiastes? Why must we suppose that the Israelites did all the borrowing? If, as many would say, they were the "discoverers" of ethical monotheism — we would say, were the recipients of a unique revelation from God — why is it necessary to make them always the borrowers? Why must a wise man in Israel, such an one as Solomon, be dependent for his ideas and his ways of expressing them on nations which were outside the sphere of that special revelation which the Israelites enjoyed?

JEROBOAM'S CALVES

The sins of the chosen people, their frequent apostasies, their failures to remember and appreciate the good hand of their God upon them are a constantly recurring theme with the writers of the Old Testament. This is especially true of the denunciation of the calf-worship introduced by Jeroboam the son of Nebat, which appears a score of times in the Books of Kings. The nature of this sin is plainly set forth in 1 Kings 12:28, where we read that "the king took counsel, and made two calves of gold and said unto them, It is too much for you to go up to Jerusalem: behold thy gods,[196] O Israel, which brought thee up out of the land of Egypt. And he set the one in Bethel, and the other he put in Dan." That this was idolatry seems perfectly obvious. It could hardly be stated more plainly. Ahijah definitely accused Jeroboam of polytheism and idolatry as the reason for the fatal outcome of the illness of his son Abijah (1 Kings 14:9). And, that it was so understood is made clear by 2 Kings 17:16 and other passages.[197] We are told expressly that "Jeroboam drave Israel from following the Lord and made them sin a great sin" (vs. 21). (See 2 Chron. 13:8 where Abijah says to Jeroboam and his followers: "and ye be a great multitude, and there are with you golden calves, which Jeroboam made you for gods.") Failure to depart from this sin of Jeroboam is the sin which is specifically denounced against nearly every king of the Northern Kingdom;[198] and it was regarded as a major cause for its downfall.

In spite of this evidence we are being told quite insistently today, even by some conservative scholars, that Jeroboam did not intend to introduce worship of other gods or even an idolatrous form of worship of Jehovah. From the fact that representations of the gods of the Canaanites, Aramaeans, and Hittites have been found with the god or goddess standing on an animal, or seated on a throne borne by animals, but not themselves in animal form, Albright has argued that Jeroboam merely intended these calves to be a kind of pedestal on which the invisible Jehovah was to be thought of as standing.[199] He has claimed further that this pedestal idea is in line with the Scriptural description of Jehovah as "sitting above the cherubim," which were symbolic figures placed on the mercy-seat of the ark.[200]

There are very serious objections to this explanation: (1) The first is that if the calves were simply intended to take the place of the cherubim of the ark, it is hard to see why so much attention should be paid to them. The Old Testament has very little to say about the cherubim. It never speaks of the worship of the cherubim. When it does speak of them it clearly distinguishes them from the Divine Being whose presence they symbolize.[201] If Jeroboam wanted to introduce into Northern Israel a spiritual and non-idolatrous worship of Jehovah which would be nearly identical with that of the temple, the very least that could possibly be said would be that he attributed an amount of spiritual discernment to his subjects which is almost incredible, in view of the proneness of the people to idolatry and apostasy of which we read so often in the course of their history.[202] Where is there the slightest intimation that Jeroboam distinguished or taught the people to discriminate between these calves and the invisible Jehovah, for whom they were to serve but as the footstool? That the calves were idols is clearly indicated again and again. The idea that they were anything but idols has to be read into the narratives on the basis of the assumption that because certain heathen nations at times represented their gods as standing on an animal, this must also have applied to the God of Israel.[203]

(2) The narratives which tell about this calf worship represent it as a most heinous and grievous sin.[204] It is pre-eminently the sin which led to the downfall of the Northern Kingdom. If in its primary intent it was a very venial sin, if indeed a sin at all, then the biblical narratives are most unjust to Jeroboam, who, according to this interpretation, was at worst an idealist, a spiritually minded worshipper of Jehovah, a religious conservative, who made the mistake of expecting the people to make a good use of a harmless symbolism, which they perverted to gross idolatry.[205]

(3) It is to be remembered that Jeroboam had fled to Egypt and only recently returned from there. In Egypt gods and goddesses were frequently represented with animal heads or as animals; and the cult of the bull (Apis) was popular. Furthermore the Israelites knew that their ancestors had been in Egypt; and the sin to which Jeroboam seduced them was the same as that into which their ancestors had fallen at Sinai, when they said to Aaron "make us gods" (Exod. 32:1) and Aaron fashioned and made a molten calf for them to worship, a sin for which they were severely punished. So a comparison with

Egypt is much more appropriate than with the "Canaanites, Aramaeans, and Hittites."

(4) The most serious objection to this theory is that it utterly stultifies the biblical writers in their condemnation of the calf worship. When Hosea says: "Thy calf, O Samaria, hath cast thee off" (8:5), it is perfectly obvious that he is speaking of the calf as an object of worship, a false god who has failed his worshippers. And when he goes on to say "For from Israel was it also: the workman made it; therefore it is not God: but the calf of Samaria shall be broken in pieces," it is undeniable that he is describing and denouncing the calf as a manmade idol. If this theory were correct, if the calves were and were intended to be only pedestals of the invisible Jehovah, the utterly devasting answer of the priests and people of the Northern kingdom to Hosea might have been and certainly would have been this: "You are an idiot. You have no spiritual discernment. The calf is not our god. It is only the pedestal under the feet of our God. He is invisible, just as invisible as is the God who dwells at Jerusalem, with whom he is in fact identical. You just don't know what you are talking about." But where is there the slightest intimation that these followers of Jeroboam and worshippers of his calves offered any such defense as this for their calf worship?[206]

(5) This attempt to tone down the offense of Jeroboam on the ground that he could not have intended or attempted so radical a departure from the worship of Jehovah as this cult of the calves would represent ignores two things which are clearly stated in the biblical narrative.

(a) Reference is frequently made to the tendency of the Israelites to apostasy, even an apostasy which involved gross idolatry and abominable rites. We have the record of Aaron's calf at Sinai, the sin of Baal-peor, the many apostasies in the time of the Judges, and Solomon's idolatries. The record shows only too plainly how deep-rooted was this evil tendency. Furthermore, the Books of Kings which condemn Jeroboam's calf-worship also give us a terrible picture of conditions in Judah under Rehoboam (14:21-24), whose mother was an Ammonitess; and Chronicles tells us that "he forsook the law of the Lord and all Israel with him" (12:1). If this was the condition in Judah at the time of the schism, would it not have been the most natural thing in the world for Jeroboam to capitalize on this evil tendency and to make legal for the Ten Tribes what the Law of Moses and the faithful prophets of the Lord declared to be apostasy? The flagrant and brazen idolatry of Jeroboam — to represent it as anything less than this is to go directly contrary to the record — is exactly what we might have expected in view of the conditions under which the schism took place.

(*b*) This tendency of Israel to lapse into idolatry is usually connected with and attributed to the pervasive idolatry of Israel's neighbors, which is also highlighted in the Old Testament. The Ras Shamra texts strongly favor the view that this calf worship was idolatry, pure and simple. One of the most disgusting features of the mythological texts from Ugarit is the breaking down of the distinction between gods, men, and animals. The supreme god 'El is often called Tor 'El, i.e., Bull-god. The Ugaritic deities who speak and act like human beings have sexual intercourse with animals and beget animals.[207] If anything were needed to show the utter difference between the lofty monotheism of the Old Testament and the ethnic religions — the vast gulf which separates it from the religions of the neighboring peoples — the need would be amply filled by these Ras Shamra texts. Consequently it would be quite natural for Jeroboam to introduce and promote idolatrous worship in Israel in the form of a calf-worship, especially since he had recently been in Egypt, where as we have pointed out some of the great gods were represented with animal heads or as animals, where the cult of the bull (Apis) flourished for centuries, and where Aaron doubtless became familiar with the idea of animal worship which he put in practice under the very shadow of the mountain of the law.

It is especially to be noted in this connection, that there was a fundamental difference between the God of Israel and the idols of the heathen. The idols were plainly visible. There are countless representations of them in ancient statues, on murals, and on seals. The God of Israel was not merely formless, he was also invisible. We are told that he sat enthroned upon the cherubim. But his earthly throne, the ark, was hidden behind a veil, and manifested in the shekinah glory.[208] Only the priests could enter the holy place. Only the high priest could enter the holy of holies; and that on only one day of the year and wrapped in a cloud of incense, lest even he see plainly the throne of God. The ark had to be covered with the veil by Aaron and his sons before it could be carried (Num. 4). Nothing like this is suggested by the calf worship of Jeroboam. He made two calves of gold and he said to the people "Behold thy gods, O Israel, which brought thee out of the land of Egypt." The language suggests a public ceremony; we are not only told that Jeroboam made two calves, but that he called them "gods," and that he placed one in Bethel and the other in Dan, a city notorious for its idolatry. It is only when such a passage as Numbers 4 is treated as late and unhistorical[209] that this fundamental difference between the God of Israel and the gods of the nations can be ignored.[210]

Two statements of Scripture are especially impressive in this connection. The one is Hosea's prophecy that the calf of Beth-aven (Bethel?) shall be carried to Assyria for a present to king Jareb (10:6), which reminds us of Isaiah's words regarding Bel and Nebo (46:1f.). Samaria's calf and Babylon's chief idols were impotent to deliver their worshippers and themselves passed into the enemy's hands. The other is the statement regarding Josiah (2 Kings 23:15) that a century after the fall of the Northern Kingdom he went to Bethel where Jeroboam had placed one of the golden calves and destroyed the altar and the high place "which Jeroboam the son of Nebat, who made Israel to sin, had made, both that altar and the high place he brake down and burned the high place and stamped it small to powder and burned the grove." Where was the golden calf, which had been the peculiar glory of the Northern Kingdom? It had gone to Assyria as a present to king Jareb, as Hosea had foretold!

Why should Old Testament scholars, even some conservatives, be so concerned to minimize, excuse, and even approve, what the Bible itself so emphatically and repeatedly denounces as a sin, a great sin, the sin which more than all others led to the overthrow of the Northern Kingdom (2 Kings 17:16)?

EZRA AND NEHEMIAH

That these two prominent figures of the post-exilic period were to some extent contemporary is clearly stated in the biblical narratives. Ezra came to Jerusalem in 458 B.C., the seventh year of Artaxerxes (Ezra 7:8), Nehemiah in 445 B.C., the twentieth year of the same monarch (Neh. 2:1); and Ezra and Nehemiah are mentioned as taking part in the ceremonies (Neh. 8:9; 12:26) of the latter year.

The Book of Ezra does not mention Nehemiah because the events described in it took place either long before (in the days of Zerubbabel) or soon after Ezra went to Jerusalem and hence a decade and more before Nehemiah came there.[211] Nehemiah 1-7 deals with Nehemiah's coming and the rebuilding of the walls of Jerusalem. This was Nehemiah's special task. It was completed in fifty-two days on the twenty-fifth day of the sixth month which was Elul (6:15). On the first day of the seventh month (Tishri) after a careful census had been taken in accordance with a register made nearly a century earlier by Zerubbabel (7:7-69; cf. Ezra 2),[212] the people assembled for a solemn reading of the law of Moses (8:1f.). This was a religious function; and

Ezra, the priest and scribe, is immediately introduced as being in charge of it. His name occurs seven times in Chapter 8; and we read there that Nehemiah, the Tirshatha, and Ezra, the scribe, were both active in instructing the people (vs. 9). The reading of the law led to a strict observance of the feast of tabernacles (vs. 17); and this was followed almost immediately (on the 24th day) by a solemn service of confession of sin in which Ezra probably took the principal part — the prayer in Chapter 9 was probably composed by him.[213] Then a solemn covenant was ratified (9:38);[214] and the dedication of the walls followed (12:27-42). In the ceremony of dedication Ezra shared the honors with Nehemiah (vss. 31 and 36), each leading one of the two companies of the celebrating Israelites. This should suffice to show that Ezra, the priestly leader, was not merely present but actively cooperated with Nehemiah, the governor, in celebrating the completion of the building of the walls. The usual view has consequently been that the same Artaxerxes is referred to both in Ezra and Nehemiah, that this was Artaxerxes I (465-424 B.C.), although in so far as the dates mentioned in these books are concerned, it might have been Artaxerxes II (404-358 B.C.).

In recent years the theory has gained considerable currency that Ezra was later than Nehemiah,[215] that he returned to Jerusalem in the seventh year of Artaxerxes II, that is in 397 B.C., some forty years after Nehemiah's rebuilding of the wall.[216] This made it necessary for Batten, an ardent follower of Hoonacker to assert that "Nehemiah entirely ignores Ezra."[217] In defending this view Snaith tells us: "Those who find it difficult to suppose that they were active at the same time (they persistently ignore each other; the three contexts where they are both mentioned, Neh. 8:9; 12:26; 12:36, are all suspect) must find an alternative date."[218] Snaith describes the date 397 B.C. for Ezra as "the most likely solution." This is a curious misstatement of the issue. The biblical narrative makes it perfectly clear that Ezra and Nehemiah did not "persistently ignore one another." Ezra was as we have seen the prominent figure in the religious ceremony. The "I" of verse 31 is clearly Nehemiah and this passage is assigned by many critics to the Memoirs of Nehemiah. Consequently, if the theory that Ezra belongs so long after his *contemporary* Nehemiah that they could not have had any contact or association is to be made good, it is necessary to treat the express references to Ezra in Nehemiah 8:9; 12:26; 12:36 as "suspect" and reject them as witnesses against this critical theory. We note further that Snaith makes no mention in this connection of the six other references to Ezra in Nehemiah 8.

It is, of course, to be recognized that there are a number of problems connected with this question of the relative dates of Ezra and Nehemiah. But to assert that Ezra and Nehemiah "persistently ignore each other" when the basic source makes it perfectly clear that they did not, and to claim that the passages which assert their cooperation are "suspect," without admitting that the only reason they are suspect is because they disprove the theory the critic is determined to prove, is to say the least a glaring example of petitio principii, of assuming what is to be proved.

The main argument given by G. E. Wright for placing Ezra after Nehemiah is the statement in Ezra 10:6 that Ezra went into the chamber of Johanan the son of Eliashib.[219] He claims that this must have been Eliashib the high priest and that it was from his chamber that the solemn proclamation was issued. Neither of these claims is established by the statements of the text. Eliashib, "the high priest," is mentioned in Nehemiah 3:1, 20f.; 13:28; (cf. also Neh. 12:22). The succession Eliashib-Jaddua occurs in Nehemiah 12:10f., 22 (cf. 13:28 where Eliashib is called "high priest"). In 13:4 an "Eliashib, the priest" is mentioned, who had treasonable dealings with Tobiah (cf. vs. 7). Whether this is the same man as Eliashib the "high priest" (13:28) is not clear. That, on the other hand, the Eliashib who is the father of Johanan (Ezra 10:6) is the same as the high priest Eliashib mentioned in Nehemiah is an assumption which cannot be established. He is not called high priest and his son is Johanan, not Joiada.[220]

According to Bright[221] the strongest objection to the view that Ezra preceded Nehemiah is that it represents Ezra's attempts at reform, the foreign wives situation (Ezra 9-10), as abortive, since Nehemiah had to deal with a similar problem (Neh. 13:1-3, 23-30). He tells us: "That Ezra was a failure is, to me, unbelievable." This argument is not at all convincing. Judged by the success which they met with in persuading the people to heed and obey their messages of warning and exhortation, most or all of the Old Testament prophets, including Moses himself, were failures. Jeremiah denounced the breaking of the Sabbath Day (chap. 17), promising blessing for obedience, disaster as the sure punishment of disobedience. The evil which he threatened came, the seventy years of captivity. Ezekiel in the captivity rebuked this sin (chap. 20). Yet Nehemiah had to deal with it (chap. 13) as if Jeremiah and Ezekiel had never denounced it. Furthermore, it was on his second return to Jerusalem after an undeterminate interval that Nehemiah apparently first dealt with the Sabbath question. He had previously been governor for twelve years (5:14). Had this situation only come about recently or had he failed to deal with it for these twelve years?

The same questions arise as to the foreign wives. The evil as described in Ezra 9-10 was apparently much more serious than in

Nehemiah's day. "The Canaanites, the Hittites, the Perizzites, the Jebusites, the Ammonites, the Moabites, the Egyptians and the Amorites" are listed (9:1) as nations with whom Israel had defiled herself, and the names of 113 guilty persons are given. The situation described in Nehemiah 13 is quite different. Only "Ammonites and Moabites" are listed at first (vs. 1), Ashdod is later referred to (vss. 23-27), and then finally a son of Joiada (vs. 28). This was more than a decade after the completion of the wall and the celebration in which Ezra took part with Nehemiah (12:36). If Ezra came to Jerusalem in the seventh year of Artaxerxes and Nehemiah's second arrival was after the thirty-second year, there is an interval of twenty-five years between the two, Ezra may have died sometime during Nehemiah's first term as governor and the conditions Nehemiah rebuked after his return may have been due to Ezra's death and Nehemiah's absence, the length of which is unknown.[222]

DORNSEIFF

Professor Dornseiff has rejected, as we have seen, the literary analysis of the critics with its hair-splitting partitionings and declared that no great literary work was ever put together by such a "scissors-and-paste" method.[223] He rejected also the theory of DeWette that Deuteronomy dates from the time of Josiah. Instead he assigned Genesis 1:1 — Numbers 24, except for portions of Numbers 20 (vss. 1-13, 22-29), to his Tetrateuchist (T) and Numbers 25 — Deuteronomy 34 to the Deuteronomist (D). His date for T was not later than 880 B.C. and for his D some fifty years later. He thus placed the completion of the Pentateuch about the time of Ahab (c. 850 B.C.).[224] As a protest and revolt against the so-long dominant Documentary Hypothesis, this is in some respects decidedly encouraging. But when we examine the reasons for the dating of Dornseiff's T and D we find little ground for satisfaction. We turn first to his treatment of Zimri.

The Two Zimris. In 1 Kings 16, we read of the brief reign of Elah the son of Baasha, king of Israel; and we are told that "his servant Zimri, captain of half his chariots" conspired against him and slew him, "when he was drinking himself drunk in the house of Arza who was over the household in Tirzah." This reads like a simple straightforward account, which tells us in few words of the shocking state of affairs in Northern Israel just before the dynasty of Omri came to the throne. Dornseiff directs our attention to Numbers 25, which describes conditions some centuries earlier when Israel was encamped at Shittim in the fortieth year after the exodus from Egypt. A terrible blot on the record of that year was the sin of Baal-peor, and that awful apostasy reached its height when a man of Israel brought a Midianitish woman into the camp "in the sight of Moses and in the sight of all the congregation of Israel, while they were weeping at the door of the tent of meeting" (vs. 6). It was an act of effrontery and defiance; and Phineas the son of Eleazar, the son of Aaron, slew both the man and the woman. The name of the man was Zimri, the son of Salu, a prince of a father's house among the Simeonites. Comparing these two stories carefully we find that there is only one thing which connects them, the *name* Zimri. Everything else is quite different, men, events, situation, time. Yet Dornseiff assigns Numbers 25 to his D and tells us that this story about the Zimri of the time of the exodus, was intended to be a satire on the seven-day reign of the Zimri who slew Elah. Phineas then represents Omri who overthrew Zimri; and the story illustrates the opposition to marriages with foreign women which found its climax in Elijah's conflict with Jezebel. Dornseiff assures us that "D is the Commentary (*Begleitliteratur*) of the events of that time."[225]

The Two Nadabs. Dornseiff's treatment of Nadab is equally illuminating. Jeroboam I had two sons. The elder was called Abijah. His tragic career is described in 1 Kings 14:1-18. He became sick and his mother disguised herself and went to Ahijah the prophet at Shiloh to inquire "what would become of the child." The verdict was unfavorable, doubly so: the prophet said the child would die, and the words, "for he only of Jeroboam shall come to the grave," seem to imply that he alone would die a natural and not a violent death. And the prophet adds the words, "because in him there is found some good thing toward the Lord God of Israel in the house of Jeroboam." Then a little later (15:25f.) we read of the brief reign of Nadab, the second son of Jeroboam, who was slain by Baasha after a reign of two years. This is the biblical account.

Another Nadab figures in the tragic and terrible event described in Leviticus 10. After the consecration of Aaron and his four sons to the priesthood by Moses, which took place immediately after the erection of the tabernacle at Sinai, two of these sons, Nadab and Abihu, were slain "because they offered strange fire before the Lord."

That the two Nadabs — the priest who was Aaron's son and the son who succeeded Jeroboam as king of Northern Israel — were quite different persons would seem to be perfectly plain. They are separated by centuries. Furthermore the accounts of their careers are quite dissimilar. The priesthood was a very important office in Israel, according to the Mosaic law, and its institution is described in Leviticus 8-9. We might have expected, in view of the great size of the "congregation of Israel," that many priests would have been ordained to minister to the needs of the people. Instead we are told that only five were ordained; Aaron to the high priesthood, and his four sons to the office of priest. Then we read in Chapter 10 that two of the four sons, Nadab and Abihu, the two elder, who had been with the seventy elders on the Mount, when they "saw God and did eat and drink," were almost at once cut off for disobedience. This story seems to bear the evidence of truth on its very face.[226] It is hard to see how any one would or could have imagined or invented such a story, a story so damaging to the credit of Aaron and his family, and to the priesthood as a whole. Yet Dornseiff is impressed by the fact that Aaron and Jeroboam each had a son named Nadab, and that Aaron had a son Abihu and Jeroboam a son Abijah.[227] He holds that if we assume that the difference between the names Abijah and Abihu is merely due to divergent traditions, it becomes clear that the story of Leviticus 10, which he regards as the sequel or immediate consequence of Aaron's idolatry described in Exodus 32, was intended to be a covert and bitter satire on Jeroboam and his calf-worship composed by some opponent of that worship, either in the Northern Kingdom or in Judah, and designed to represent the deaths of the two sons of Jeroboam as the punishment for the idolatry of their father. Dornseiff admits that as a satire on Jeroboam it is decidedly lame. So he regards it as short-lived and holds that it fixes the date of T at about sixty years after 911 B.C. The Aaron of Leviticus 10 does indeed make a poor Jeroboam. But this treatment of the story shows how little historical value the critics often attach to a biblical narrative, and what remarkable meanings they can read into it or read out of it.

Aaron's Golden Calf. Dornseiff of course treats the story of the golden calf in Exodus 32 in similar fashion. Despite the differences in time, situation, and events, he maintains that it too was intended to be a biting satire on the calf worship introduced by Jeroboam and described in 1 Kings 12:28.[228]

It is interesting to compare this satire theory regarding Jeroboam's calves with the explanation given a few years previously by T. H. Robinson. According to Robinson the Exodus narrative was in no sense a satire on Jeroboam's calf worship but what may be called a pious editing of the original story. The original story as told "at the great bull sanctuaries such as Bethel" would have made Moses, not Aaron, the chief actor "and the pouring of molten metal into water would be a method whereby men could ascertain the exact form under which Yahweh preferred to be worshipped." In other words the story originally justified image-worship. "A later generation, with the prohibition of images in minds, could not endure the slur on Moses, and while they could not eliminate the tradition, they transferred it to Aaron. . . ."[229] Why the later generation could not eliminate so offensive a tradition, we are not told. Nor are we told how the later editors hit upon the expedient of turning a story which approved and justified idolatry into one which condemned it.

A third view is that of Snaith,[230] who, following Kennett, would connect the Aaronic priesthood with Bethel and make Aaron the priest of its golden calf. Exodus 32 definitely connects Aaron and the calf which he made with Sinai and the Exodus. But according to this method of interpretation, Aaron is transferred from the exodus period to the time of Jeroboam, and the golden calf from Sinai to Bethel.

What is especially interesting in these three theories is that three so different solutions can be arrived at in interpreting the same historical narrative. The explanation is that each scholar deals with and manipulates the evidence to suit himself, accepting what suits his theory, rejecting what does not, and so drawing conclusions which have this much in common, that all three flatly contradict the statements and the obvious meaning of the narrative itself.

Ships from Kittim. Dornseiff attaches special importance to the words: "But ships shall come from the coast of Kittim" (Num. 24:24) as fixing the earliest date for his Tetrateuchist document (T) which includes most of Genesis-Numbers. He interprets this verse as referring to the "Cyprian maritime sovereignty" (*Seeherrschaft*) which he assigns to *c.* 880-47 B.C.[231] He argues that "the quips (*Anspielungen*) on the kings, Jeroboam, Nadab, Zimri would of themselves not even require the ninth century for their creation (*Abfassungszeit*), such figures could even after a long time be employed as examples." But he claims that "in the very dramatic ninth century, an event of so secondary importance as a temporary oppression by Cyprian ships," which is his interpretation of the Balaam-saying, "can have only been used soon after it,"[232] and that this sets an *a quo* date for T of 880 B.C.

This line of argument is very illuminating. It amounts to this. As a lampoon or pasquinade on Jeroboam and his sons, Leviticus 10 might be too long lived to permit of exact dating. But a relatively trivial historical event like the Cyprian "embargo," as we might call it, would soon be forgotten. Consequently the latter is a more accurate indication of the date of the document than the former. The most significant thing about this argument is that it completely ignores the fact that Balaam's words are prediction, long-range prediction, words which were uttered before Israelites entered Canaan and which are to have their fulfillment "in the latter days." But the treatment of prophecy, especially long-range prediction, as *post eventum* history is a natural and inevitable result of the naturalistic and rationalistic interpretation of the Bible.[233]

While Dornseiff's trenchant indictment of the Documentary Hypothesis is interesting and valuable as coming from a student of the classics,[234] it loses much of its value because its viewpoint is in general much the same as that of the theory which it criticizes. Rejecting the redemptive supernaturalism of the Bible his treatment of Scripture is quite as destructive of its historical credibility and trustworthiness.

ISRAEL AND THE CANAANITES

Ever since the discovery at Ras Shamra of the city of Ugarit, it has been claimed by a number of scholars that the Ugaritic dialect can properly be called Canaanite and that this culture exerted a powerful influence on the development of Israelite culture and religion. Rowley did not overstate matters when he pointed out (1951) that "One of the main trends of our time has been the emphasis on the links between Canaanite culture and Israelite."[235] One of the most extreme statements which the writer has noted is the following:

Happily much of the best in Canaanite literature was adopted by their Hebrew cousins and neighbors and thus preserved in sacred writings. This is especially true of the lyric pieces and wise sayings — borrowed in Proverbs, the Psalms and the Song of Songs — and the mythological compositions imbedded in Genesis and the Prophets — a fact not fully recognized until the discovery of a forgotten city, Ugarit.[236]

With hardly less restraint Dr. Albright tells us that "The wealth of new Canaanite evidence for rare and archaic words or phrases in biblical Hebrew is overwhelming."[237]

It is to be noted, of course, that such claims are not new. Whenever important discoveries have been made in Egypt or in Mesopotamia, efforts have at once been made to relate them to the Old Testament and to establish dependence of Israel upon them. Fifty years ago, as we have seen, this was Babylon. Now it is Ugarit.

We have already seen that the question of the affiliations of Ugaritic with the other Semitic languages is far from settled. That it is a West Semitic language which is related to Phoenician is clear. But it also has features which relate it to Aramaic and to Accadian.

Furthermore it is to be noted that while Ugarit was closely linked with Assyria, the Hittite-Hurrian nations, and apparently also with the Aegean peoples, it was quite remote from Palestine. It lay far to the north, even of Tyre and Sidon, which are the only Phoenician cities mentioned at all frequently in the Old Testament. Arvad, Gebal (Byblos) are little more than geographical names. Ugarit, lying much farther north is not even mentioned. Consequently the claims that Ugarit was Canaanite and that it strongly influenced Israel are by no means convincing to start with. So we shall proceed to examine as briefly as we may the evidence advanced by Dr. Albright in support of his claim that certain passages, particularly poetic passages, "swarm" with Canaanitisms, and that the evidence is "overwhelming."[238]

In the Song of Moses the phrase occurs "in the mountain of thine inheritance" (Exodus 15:17). This is not remarkable since the word rendered "inheritance" or "heritage" occurs more than two hundred times in the Old Testament, being used especially to designate the land of Canaan as the heritage of the Lord which he has given or will give to his people Israel to whom the same name is also applied. In the Ugaritic myth of Baal and Anath, the expression "mount of my portion ... hill I possess" occurs once, as does also the similar phrase, "the Mount of Possession."[239] The mountain apparently is Mount Zaphon which corresponds roughly to the Olympus of Greek mythology. Regarding the context of the latter passage the translator, H. L. Ginsberg remarks, "In lines 16-29, which are poorly preserved, there is again talk of a buffalo being born to Baal, it being still not absolutely clear that his bovine mother was Anath herself."[240] This illustrates the gross polytheism of the myth. Yet Albright discovers in the fact that this phrase is found in "the Canaanite epic, which was composed not later than 1400 B.C.," an argument that "there is no longer the slightest valid reason for dating the Song of Miriam after the thirteenth century B.C."[241] We doubt that this argument will carry much weight with those who reject the Mosaic authorship of the ode which is affirmed in verse 1, while those who are willing to accept the biblical statement at its face-value do not need the support of Ugaritic mythology.

Psalm 68:4. Dr. Albright tells us:

> In Psalm 68:4 we have a curious expression which has been commonly rendered literally as "rider on the evenings," or by a reasonable guess as "rider on the heavens": in Ugaritic the expression occurs frequently with only a very slight consonantal divergence from the transmitted Hebrew spelling as "rider on the clouds," referring to the storm-god Baal. In Hebrew poetry this beautiful appellation has been transferred to Yahweh, without carrying with it any mythological connotation.[242]

As to this two things are to be noted. *a.* The Hebrew has two similar sounding words: 'ereb and 'arabah. They have the same consonants in Hebrew. But in Arabic the one begins with the rough gutteral (*ghain*) while the other begins with the smooth guttural ('ayin). 'Ereb occurs 131 times and is usually rendered "evening." It is a masculine noun and occurs only in the singular or dual. Its plural would naturally be 'erabim and not 'eraboth, which is the form in the verse under discussion. The rendering "evening" is found in both *LXX* and *Vulgate*, but not in *AV, ARV,* or *RSV*. The word 'arabah occurs sixty-one times. It means "desert-plain or steppe." *AV* usually renders it by "wilderness." It is a feminine noun and its plural *'araboth,* the form under discussion, occurs twenty times. Consequently both *ARV* text and *RSV* margin render by "through the deserts." This rendering is a perfectly proper one.[243] The only question which can be properly raised is, Does it suit the context?

b. The context reads: "lift up (or cast up) to him that rideth through the desert." (1) The verb which is here rendered "cast-up" or "lift-up" (*salal*) is comparatively rare. It usually describes the raising up of a "highway" (*mesillah,* 27 times) and from the same root we have also the word for the "mound" (*solelah,* 11 times), which besiegers raised up against cities they were planning to assault. The closest parallel to our passage is Isaiah 62:10 — "Cast up, cast up the highway; gather out the stones." (Cf. Isa. 57:14; Mal. 3:1, where the same figure seems clearly to be employed.) The idea of casting up a highway in the desert is a natural one; and it is familiar to us through the words of Isaiah 40:3 — "Make straight in the desert a highway (*mesillah*) for our God." Consequently, the rendering of *ARV* can be regarded as thoroughly biblical.

(2) It is to be noted, however, that another figure is also used in Scripture. The Lord is represented as riding on the clouds. Elsewhere in this Psalm we read "to him that rideth upon the heaven of heavens"[244] (vs. 33) and "his strength is in the clouds" (vs. 34). Note also the expression, "riding on a swift cloud" (Isa. 19:1; cf. Ps. 18:10). So it is claimed that the parallelism "Sing unto God, sing praises to his name" requires that "lift up" (*sollu*) be taken in the sense of "lift up a song" (cf. AV "extol"). This is by no means certain. But it is to be noted that such a rendering would not affect the rest of the verse. "Lift up a song to him that rideth through the deserts" (vs. 4) would make excellent sense.

Dr. Albright claims that the passage should be rendered "lift up a song to him who rides upon the clouds" (so *RSV* text), because the expression "rider on the clouds" has been discovered in the Ugaritic texts as a frequent epithet of the god Baal.[245] The thought of the God of Israel as riding on the clouds is a natural one; and as we have pointed out above, it is closely paralleled by the figure used in verse 33 of this psalm. But this does not prove that the same figure must be found in verse 4, far less that it is derived from Ugaritic. Both figures are biblical and both might properly be used here. A conclusive objection to the rendering "rideth upon the clouds" in verse 4 is that it necessitates an emendation of the text, or as Dr. Albright phrases it "a very slight consonantal divergence from the transmitted Hebrew spelling."[246] The word for "desert" (*'arabah*) is written with a "b" and occurs many times in the Old Testament. The word for "cloud" in

Ugaritic is written with a "p"; it does not occur in the Old Testament. So the reading "rideth upon the clouds" is unwarranted, since it would require textual emendation where the MT makes excellent sense. Least of all should this emended text be appealed to as a proof that this psalm "swarms" with Canaanitisms.

Psalm 89:19. According to Dr. Albright, "Ugaritic evidence proves that we must translate 'I have placed a youth above the mighty man; I have raised a young man above the people.' The context shows that David is meant."[247] This is an overstatement. The word which Albright would render by "young man" (*'ezer*) appears in AV and ARV as "help." It comes from a root which occurs in the Old Testament as a verb about eighty times; and nouns from this same root occur about fifty times. It also occurs in a number of proper names, such as Ezra, Azariah, Azrikam. In all of its occurrences the general idea of "help" seems appropriate. Here the AV and ARV render by "I have laid help upon *one that is* mighty; I have exalted one chosen out of the people." The figure of "laying help upon" in the sense of "raising up as a helper," as if "help" were a gift or endowment which is bestowed on those who need it, is attractive and decidedly poetic. It corresponds well with the thought of the parallel line: "I have exalted one chosen out of the people." How then does Ugaritic evidence "prove" that we must translate "I have placed a youth above the mighty man"? The evidence is as follows. In Ugaritic a word occurs which has in Hebrew the same radicals as the word "help" except that the first letter is not *Ayin* but *Ghain,* two consonants which in Hebrew are both represented by the same letter, although we know that they were distinguished, at least to some extent, in pronunciation. In the Ras Shamra tablets a root beginning with the harsh *Ghain* has been identified. It occurs about a dozen times; and the parallelisms in which it appears indicate the meaning to be "boy, man, warrior, hero" or something of the kind. The exact meaning is uncertain because the root apparently is not found in other Semitic languages or not, as in the case of the Arabic, with any such meaning as this. The fact that a word *ghozer* (lad) occurs in Ugaritic does not prove that it *must* appear in Hebrew. Far less does it prove that "I have placed help upon one that is mighty" *must* be changed to "I have placed a youth above a mighty man." The rendering "help" is supported by LXX and *Vulgate.*[248] It must be recognized, of course, that rare words and rare meanings of words appear occasionally in the Old Testament. A striking example of this is the word *chesed,* which occurs 247 times in the Old Testament in a good sense, but twice (Lev. 20:17; Prov. 14:34) in a bad sense, as is made clear by the context in both cases.[249] So it is possible that in one or two passages the word *'ezer* might come from a different root and have a different meaning. But the burden of proof would clearly rest with the one who proposed the new and exceptional meaning; and it would only be acceptable if the context clearly required it. Such is not the case here. The RSV Old Testament Committee of which Dr. Albright was a member apparently disregarded the "must." For it preferred a rendering, "I have set the crown upon," despite the fact that "crown" involved a conjectural emendation (changing *'ezer* into *nezer*), to the one which Dr. Albright regarded as a "must." The only warrant for the "must" is the desire to discover a Ugaritic word in this psalm-verse.

In 1928 shortly before the discovery of Ugarit, R. D. Wilson published a detailed study of "Foreign Words in the Old Testament."[250] In it he pointed out that "scarcely a foreign word is to be found in any of the numerous poetical productions from first to last" and he declared "This almost complete absence of foreign words is a characteristic of lyric poetry in general."[251] Dr. Wilson died in 1930, before the Ugaritic texts were available. But it is doubtful whether he would modify these statements to any considerable degree, if at all, were he living today. Ugaritic is a Semitic language or dialect as are Accadian, Aramaic, Phoenician, Canaanite, Hebrew and Arabic. The discovery that a word or a meaning is found in Hebrew and in Ugaritic does not prove it to be a Ugaritism in Hebrew. To note correspondence in meaning is one thing.[252] To assert, not to say prove, derivation or dependence is quite another.

Proverbs 26:23 begins with two words which are pointed in the MT as *kesep sigim* which AV rendered "silver dross," a possible rendering. But the words could be read "like a *sap sigim*," which Albright following H. L. Ginsberg renders by "like glaze" "crusted over pottery," etc.[253] This does not change the consonantal text, and gives an excellent sense.

Proverbs 21:9. The expression "wide house" (*beth-heber*) according to Albright occurs in both Ugaritic and Assyrian in the sense of "storehouse."[254] Since the word *heber* is clearly used in Hebrew in the sense of "association" or "company," the rendering "joint' or "common" house seems more preferable (cf. the free rendering of RSV, "in a house shared with a contentious woman").

Isaiah 27:1 mentions "leviathan the swift serpent and leviathan the crooked serpent." In the Baal-Anat myth there is a reference to the destroying of "Lotan, the serpent slant . . . the serpent tortuous" and of "Shalyat, the seven-headed."[255] But it is to be remembered that here and probably also in Psalm 74:14 the immediate reference is to Egypt and the Nile. In Job 41:1 the reference is probably to the crocodile, in Psalm 104:26 to the whale or some other great marine animal. Only in

Job 3:8 where the language is highly figurative does there seem to be a reference to a mythical sea monster.

Several further examples of proposed changes based on Ugaritic may be mentioned in this connection.

2 Samuel 1:21. Decidedly objectionable is the reading "nor upsurgings of the deep" (RSV) for *"nor* fields of offerings."[256] It is based on a phrase in the Aqhat Legend. This not only involves textual changes in both nouns, but it also introduces a mythological significance which is quite foreign to the poem. "Fields of offerings" makes excellent sense. These fields were probably the especially fertile fields, from which the first fruits were gathered. Hence the fields may have been regarded as sacred, as especially honored by God and dedicated to his service. The curse would then be a mild one, not barrenness but loss of special fertility and of the honor or distinction which resulted from it.

Job 9:8. The expression "and treadeth upon the waves of the sea" (AV, ARV) is a forceful and beautiful one. ARV adds a marginal note to "waves," "Heb. high places." The figure is, of course, that of one striding or tramping upon the crests of the waves which lift themselves up as do the high places of the earth. Hence the parallel figure in Amos 4:13, Micah 1:3. It expresses the thought of the complete and absolute mastery and sovereignty of the God of Israel over all created things, even when they seem in their impotent wrath to exalt themselves against him and defy him. Habakkuk closes with a verse which expresses the dominion promised by God to his people and his messengers over the works of his hands: "The Lord God is my strength and he will make my feet like hind's *feet,* and he will make me to walk upon my high places." In both passages the meaning is perfectly clear and the thought is appropriate and beautiful.

The word rendered "high place" (*bamah*) occurs about one hundred times in the Old Testament and is nearly always so rendered in AV. Recently it has been discovered that there is a word in Ugaritic (*bmt*) which has the meaning "back." It is only found a few times. It is used of the "back" of a donkey.[257] It is also used of the "back" of the chief god El who flagellates himself, "front and back,"[258] in his passionate grief over the death of Aliyan Baal. On the basis of these two passages it is asserted that in Job 9:8 we have an allusion to the "back" of the sea-monster, who figures so prominently in the Babylonian Creation myth. So RSV gives as an alternative rendering for "the waves of the sea," "the back of the sea dragon," thus introducing pagan mythology into this passage in Job. Such being the case it is significant that in the Creation Myth where, if this interpretation were correct, we might expect to find this expression used, there is no reference to the *back* of Tiamat or to Marduk as trampling on her back. The reason for finding a reference to the sea dragon here, is simply because in some of the mythological poems of Ras Shamra, Sea (*Yam*) — somewhat like Old Man River in some Negro songs — plays a rather prominent role. But that is very scant warrant for the introducing of such a mythological figure into this passage in Job.

Jeremiah 9:21. "For death is come into our windows *and* is entered into our palaces." It has been proposed to change "palaces" (*'armenoth*) into "casements" (*'arubboth*) by replacing two consonants, "m" and "n," by "b." In support of this proposal it has been pointed out that the words "window" and "casement" occur repeatedly in poetic parallelism in the account of the building of a house for Aliyan Baal in the Ras Shamra tablets.[259] This is no sufficient argument for this change which has no support in the Versions. But it is interesting because these two words both occur in the biblical account of the Flood, the one in Genesis 8:6, the other in 7:11 and 8:2, and it will be recalled that for a century and more the occurrence of these two apparently nearly synonymous words in that narrative has been used as an argument for dividing it into two parallel accounts.

Psalm 68:6, "He bringeth out those which are bound with chains" (*AV*). In the Ugaritic a root has been discovered (*k-th-r*). It apparently occurs only in proper names: in the name of a god or demigod Kother, who is also called Kother-and-Hasis. It is perhaps also given to a fisherman. It may perhaps mean "skilful." In the Ugaritic legend of Aqhat it is used several times of certain beings who appear to Danel, the father of Aqhat, seemingly to rejoice with him in the promise he has received of the birth of a son. They are called the *kthrt bnt hll snnm*, which seems to mean "the skillful ones, daughters of praise, the swallows."[260] Whether the last word really means "swallows" is doubtful as is also the question whether, if correctly rendered, the word is to be taken literally or figuratively. "Daughters of praise" (or, "joyful maids," Ginsberg) also is a descriptive appellative, apparently intended to define more precisely the character of these *artistes,* as Ginsberg calls them; they are skillful as singers. Consequently Gordon calls them "female jubilantes." This may be correct, but it is to be noted that it reads the meaning of the epithet into the meaning of the word which it explains.

The Hebrew equivalent of *kthrt* might be *kosharoth.* This word occurs only this once in the Old Testament. But the root has several derivatives and justifies such a rendering as "in success" or "(in) to prosperity." (*ARV, RSV;* also *BV*). The ancient versions had difficulty with the word. R. D. Wilson pointed out some years ago that the renderings "prosperity" (*RV*) and "chains" (*AV*) could both be supported from the Babylonian.[261] Both renderings find support in the context. It is possible that the Ugaritic throws some light upon the meaning of the Hebrew root. But to render the passage in Psalm 68, "with songstresses" ("female jubilantes," as Gordon renders the word) is decidedly questionable to say the least. Yet Gordon says of these songstresses who appear in *Aqht*: "The songstresses were called the Kosharot, who appear also in Psalm 68:7 where they celebrate the happy occasion of prisoners being released by God." Then he adds: "Like so many passages in the Bible, this one was not understood until the discoveries at Ugarit."[262] It is to such dogmatic and sweeping assertions that vigorous exception must be taken. For this is one of the passages upon which the claim is based that the Psalter of the Old Testament "swarms with Canaanitisms."[263] We welcome any light which the cognate languages throw on the meaning of rare and obscure biblical words. But we take vigorous issue with the claim that because a word or a meaning is found in both Hebrew and Ugaritic (both of which are Semitic languages) therefore the Hebrew must have borrowed it from the Ugaritic.

PSALM 29

Of all the Psalms, this one appears to be the one most positively assigned to a Canaanite origin. This is decidedly surprising since the name of Jehovah, the God of Israel, appears eighteen times in its eleven verses, which would seem to be a serious obstacle in the way of Canaanite origin. But we are confidently assured that it was "only slightly modified for use in the cultus of Yahweh," the chief modification being the substituting of Yahweh for Baal in the eighteen occurrences. In fact it is even claimed that the change has at times been made at the expense of the metre of the poem.[264]

In view of this claim it is remarkable that this psalm contains features which are somewhat rare in Hebrew poetry, but are characteristic of Hebrew prose, while entirely lacking in Ugaritic.[265] The definite article occurs three times: "the waters" (vs. 3), "the glory" (*id.*), "the Lebanon" (vs. 5); and four times the inseparable preposition receives the pointing of the article: "with the strength" (vs. 4), "with the majesty" (*id.*), "at the flood" (vs. 10), "with the peace" (vs. 11). The sign of the accusative appears twice: before "the cedars of Lebanon" (vs. 5) and before "his people" (vs. 11). These features are said to be characteristic of Hebrew prose as distinct from Hebrew poetry. Yet we find them in this Hebrew poem which is supposed to be adapted from the Ugaritic. If so the adaptation introduced other changes than the eighteen changes in the divine name. Verse 5 indicates this very clearly. A literal rendering is:

The voice of Yahweh breaketh cedars;
And Yahweh has broken the cedars of Lebanon.

The second line is an example of climactic parallelism. The simple "Yahweh" is stronger than "the voice of Yahweh" and "the cedars of Lebanon" more definite than "cedars," since the former were proverbial for beauty and strength. But in the phrase rendered by "the cedars of Lebanon" we have in the Hebrew both the sign of the accusative before "cedars" and the definite article before "Lebanon," both of which are characteristics of Hebrew and which are entirely lacking in "Canaanite." Furthermore the word "break" (*shabar*) used in verse 5, as participle and as finite verb is written with *sh* and not with *t* as would be the case in Ugaritic, and in Aramaic. Is this also to be explained as simply the Hebraizing of an originally Canaanite expression?

The expression *bene elim* (vs. 1) has been variously rendered: "sons of the mighty," "sons of God," "sons of gods" (i.e., angels). *Elim* may be regarded as the natural plural of the word *El*, and it is the usual plural of the word *il* (god) in Ugaritic. Here the words *el* (vs. 3) and *elim* (vs. 1) occur once each along with Yahweh (18 times). *El* (in the singular) occurs nearly two hundred fifty times in the Old Testament, most frequently in the Psalms and in Job, which indicates that it is more common in poetry than in prose. It is frequently accompanied by a qualifying adjective or noun, as in "mighty God," "God of glory." It occurs occasionally in the Prophets. It occurs in all periods and cannot be claimed to be distinctive of any one. It corresponds to Accadian *ilu*. The claim that it is "Canaanite" cannot be established. It appears frequently in proper names of the First Dynasty of Babylon.[266] That in the Ugaritic mythology it should be given to the chief god of the pantheon is not surprising; nor is its use in Old Testament passages to designate the one God of Israel at all remarkable. The word is Semitic; it is not specifically Canaanite, Accadian or Hebrew. It is the most comprehensive word or name for deity. *El* has two plurals in Hebrew *Elim and Elohim*. The former, which we may call the normal plural, is very rare, occurring only four times in the Old Testament (Exod. 15:11; Ps. 29:1; 89:7; Dan. 11:36) and whether in any of the four it is used of God is not certain. The other (*Elohim*) is the usual plural form and is used both of heathen deities and, as a plural of majesty, of the God of Israel. In Ugaritic the situation is nearly reversed, the normal form being much the more frequent. Since *Elohim* is so frequently used as a plural of majesty in the Old Testament, it seems proper to assume that the same would be true of the rarely occurring form *Elim*.[267] This would justify the rendering "sons of God" in our passage (Ps. 29:1).[268] The chief interest of the occurrence of both forms in Ugaritic is that it may indicate that these two forms, *Elim* and *Elohim*, come from the same root.

It is also to be noted that the poetic and unusual word for "give" (*yahab*) occurs three times in the beginning of this psalm. This verb occurs thirty-five times in the Hebrew of the Old Testament. It also occurs in Aramaic (e.g., in Ezra and Daniel) and in Arabic. It does not occur in Ugaritic nor on the Amarna tablets. Consequently, it cannot be called a "Canaanitism." The usual verb for "give" (*nathan*) occurs once in this Psalm (vs. 11). But since the verb is in the imperfect tense (*ytn*), it might be derived from either *ntn* (the regular Hebrew form, cf. Accadian *nadanu*) or from *ytn* which is found in Phoenician and Ugaritic. In a Hebrew psalm we would of course derive it from the frequently occurring verb *nathan*.[269]

Two comments are in order with regard to this attempt to Canaanize Psalm 29.[270] Professor Albright who has described Psalm 29 as "swarming with Canaanitisms" has also said: "One thing is certain: the days when Duhm and his imitators could recklessly emend the Hebrew text of the poetic books of the Bible are gone forever. . . . We may rest assured that the consonantal text of the Hebrew Bible, though not infallible, has been preserved with an accuracy perhaps unparalleled in any other Near-Eastern literature."[271] Yet he has not hesitated to make at least eighteen changes in this psalm to get back to its allegedly original form. Such a statement would indicate extreme inconsistency on Dr. Albright's part were it not that he is referring to the pre-Massoretic form of the psalm as determined by oral tradition. The Hebraizing of a Canaanite psalm might be explained on the principles of Form Criticism. But Dr. Albright has described the methods of the Form Critic as "highly subjective and improbable"[272] in dealing with the New Testament; and they are certainly no less so in dealing with the Old.

In discussing this psalm under the caption "Notes on a Canaanite Psalm in the Old Testament," Frank M. Cross, Jr., has made the statement: "In 1936 H. L. Ginsberg drew up conclusive evidence that Psalm 29 is an ancient Canaanite Baal hymn only slightly modified for use in the cultus of Yahweh." So Cross tells us, "Accordingly Psalm 29 takes on a rare new importance for the analysis of Canaanite prosodic canons and their influence on Israelite psalmody. The Ugaritic literature is largely epic, and while refrains and lyric or odic passages appear, we do not have from Ugarit a clear cut example of the Canaanite cultic psalm. Thus Psalm 29 fills a real gap in the extant Canaanite literature."[273] Such a statement is amazing. Cross admits that no such psalm as Psalm 29 has been found in Ugaritic. But he points out that if the eighteen occurrences of Jehovah are changed to eighteen occurrences of Baal, a Ugaritic Baal hymn is secured which is lacking in Ugaritic. And this, he tells us, causes Psalm 29 to take on "a rare new importance." In other words what is attempted is not to derive a Hebrew psalm from the Ugaritic, but a Ugaritic from the Hebrew and then make this Ugaritic poem the source of the Hebrew psalm, a truly remarkable performance!

Now if this is the correct view to take with regard to this psalm, and as to many other biblical passages, then Elijah the Tishbite showed a very intolerant and non-cooperative spirit when he said to the people assembled at Mount Carmel, "How long halt ye between two opinions? if Jehovah be God, follow him: but if Baal, then follow him." He should have said to the prophets of Baal something like this: "Brethren, we are aware, even painfully so, that many people, perhaps the vast majority, are sadly lacking in discrimination. They think that Baal and Jehovah are utterly and entirely different. But we educated men, leaders and moulders of religious opinion, know that such is not the case. The cults of Tyrian Baal and of Jehovah of Israel are really in some respects only different forms of the old Canaanite worship of which Ugarit far to the north is an important center. We are quite aware that many of our most beautiful psalms are borrowed from the Baal cult of Ugarit and its elaborate cultus. So I suggest that instead of engaging in unseemly and unbrotherly controversy, we all join in singing an old cultic hymn. Our Jehovah worshippers are fond of it because they believe it was composed by king David. But the fact is that he got it from the Jebusite temple at Jerusalem, and that he adapted it to Israelite worship by simply substituting the word Jehovah for Baal. So I suggest that as a fine gesture of harmony and ecumenicity we should all sing this grand old hymn, as a kind of 'Faith of our fathers, living still.'" Such would be the logical inference from this attempt to Canaanize the religion of Israel!

In speaking of the passages we have been examining, Dr. Albright remarks, "As in the case of many other sensational archaeological finds, the historical bearing of this new material was at first exaggerated by some distinguished authorities."[274] He mentions the alleged discovery of the name of Abraham's father Terah on Ugaritic tablets as an example of this. He speaks of them as "premature" and deplores the probability that "it will be a long time before the last traces of such divagations are eliminated from modern handbooks dealing with biblical history." We are afraid that this will be true of the claim made so positively by Albright and others that many of the Old Testament psalms "swarm with Canaanitisms." It is to say the least an exaggeration if not a serious misrepresentation of the facts; but we are afraid it will be "a long time" before it disappears from modern books on the Old Testament.

The securing of an "original" Baal hymn by changing the eighteen occurrences of Yahweh into Baal recalls to mind the old story about two scholars who were discussing the question of the authorship of the Pentateuch. One of them remarked: "I can prove that the Pentateuch was not written by Moses but by Middleton." "How would you do that?" his friend asked. "Why," was the reply, "that is easy. Simply drop off the -oses and put on the -iddleton." In the case of Psalm 29, the task is more difficult, for the names Baal and Yahweh do not have even one consonant in common. Such treatment of the biblical text is to out-Duhm Duhm with a vengeance. Yet Dr. Albright who adopts this view has assured us positively that the era of radical reconstruction, represented by Duhm, is definitely ended. Biblical critics cannot have it both ways. They cannot insist on the integrity of the biblical text and at the same time introduce into it changes which give it a radically different meaning when it serves their purpose to do so.

––––––––––

In the above rather lengthy but far from adequate discussion of critical opinion, the writer has chosen examples from the writings of able and distinguished scholars, men of national and international reputation, men whose erudition far exceeds his own. The aim has been to show that in dealing with the Old Testament many of their opinions and conclusions are unsound and at times erratic and even absurd for the reason that in dealing with a book which is the principal source for the study of the periods or events with which they deal, they deprive themselves of the proper use of this invaluable source material by accepting the view so long and so persistently held in critical and scientific circles that the Old Testament is composed of documents which are relatively late (as regards the events, etc., which they describe), contradictory, and unreliable, and that the scholar who deals with the Old Testament period must sift the evidence in the light of data from other and, according to the claims of the Old Testament itself, *alien* and *hostile* sources and accept only so much as can be fitted into what he regards as the pattern which they require. Is it any wonder then that there is so much evidence of what McFadyen called "imaginative synthesis" in the arguments they use and the conclusions they reach?

Scholarly Objectivity

In the third series of "Studies" published by the Society for Old Testament Studies (1951), the editor, Professor Rowley of Manchester University, in describing what he called "the broad agreement amongst the scholars of the world on a large number of questions" concerning the Old Testament, which existed thirty-five years ago, and which he believes still exists, though to a lesser degree, tells us:

There were conservative writers who stood outside the general body of critical scholars and 'who rejected most of their conclusions, but they did not seriously affect the position. For while' many of them had considerable learning, they made little secret of the fact that they were employing their learning to defend positions which were dogmatically reached. Their work had little influence, therefore, among scientific scholars who were concerned only with the evidence, and the conclusions to which it might naturally lead.[275]

We would ask our readers to weigh this statement in the light of the evidence we have presented in this chapter. Granted that conservative biblical scholarship has been largely ignored in critical circles, what is the reason? It is certainly not because the Bible defender is a dogmatist, while the "scientific scholar" is open-minded and unbiased. The "scientific scholar" is, generally speaking, quite as dogmatic in rejecting the authority of the Old Testament, as the conservative is in accepting and defending it. He is just as insistent on fitting the Old Testament into a world view, which rejects the redemptive supernaturalism of the Bible and the uniqueness of its history, religion and cultus, as the Bible defender is in insisting on the uniqueness of Old Testament history and the supernaturalism which pervades it. Is it "dogmatic," for example, to insist, that Zadok was a priest of the line of Aaron, because the Old Testament plainly tells us this? Is it an evidence of "open-mindedness," of concern "only with the evidence and the conclusions to which it might naturally lead," to reject the evidence that Zadok was an Aaronite, and to assert, without any real evidence that he was the priest-king of Jebus, a pagan and an enemy, yet given a high place in the religious worship of Israel? Is it dogmatism to accept the explanation of the brazen serpent as given in Numbers 21, but evidence of an open mind to assert without a scintilla of proof, that the serpent was a cult object in the Jebusite shrine and that David incorporated it into the worship of Israel? To charge an opponent with bias, with dogmatism, is an easy way of avoiding the issue. Unless we are much mistaken Dr. Rowley and the scientific scholars for whom he speaks are quite as dogmatic as he claims their conservative opponents to be.

In dealing with the "critics" of the Bible, conservative scholars are both at an advantage and also at a disadvantage. On the one hand they have the plain and obvious statements and claims of the Bible itself to appeal to, as well as a host of expounders and defenders of the faith from the earliest apologetes to the present time. They have also the evidence which archaeology has produced in the course of a century of intensive research in support of the traditional view of the

Bible. This new light is considerable and not to be neglected or minimized. But its value to the conservative lies in the fact that it supports and illuminates what the Scriptures themselves affirm to be true. It is not revolutionary but corroborative. This means that the element of novelty and discovery which has such a strong appeal to the general reader is largely the asset of the members of the Critical School. Since they are committed to an estimate of the Bible which rejects its plenary inspiration and entire trustworthiness, they have a wide field for speculation and novelty of opinion. And this field has been explored and exploited very fully by them; and many and diverse have been the novel discoveries which they have made in it. And since the evidence derived from archaeology is incomplete to say the least they are in a position to exploit apparent differences and alleged contradictions to the full, while the Bible-believer, admitting the seeming conflict, will hold to his belief in the authority of the Bible and cherish the hope that further discoveries and fuller evidence will clear away many of the difficulties as they have often done in the past.

RADICAL CONSERVATIVES

It should be pointed out in fairness to the critics that sometimes professedly conservative writers take great liberties with the simple facts of Scripture and put forward conclusions which are quite as baseless as the conclusions of radical criticism.

The Golden Calf (Exod. 32:20). A popular radio speaker has given a truly surprising explanation of the way in which Moses punished the sin of the golden calf. The record states that "Moses took the calf which they had made, and burnt it in the fire, and ground it to powder, and strewed it upon the water, and made the children of Israel drink of it." This reduced the gold to a colloidal condition and "Scientific records state that 'colloidal' gold in water is a rose-red color when the particles are of 10 micron size in a dilution of 1 to 100,000 (10 microns equal .0003937 or 0.0004 inches.)"

From this the following inferences are drawn: (1) that "this calf of gold need not have been very large to color sufficient water blood-red to furnish drink to at least two or more million people"; (2) that "The resultant waters would be blood-red and possess purifying qualities"; (3) that "This blood-red solution was taken by Moses before the Lord and presented to him as an atonement for their sin"; (4) that "The Lord saw in the blood-red solution a fit type of the blood of the Lord Jesus Christ. His wrath was averted, his justice appeased, and his love again flowed forth"; (5) that "Although it is not explicitly stated, it is plainly suggested that the three thousand men who were slain by the swords of the Levites on that day were those who refused to stoop down and drink of the crimson brook that descended out of the Mount. Those who accepted God's provision through the molten golden calf were saved. Those who rejected it were lost." This explanation is offered as a proof that Moses had "a supernaturally-given knowledge of the science of chemistry."

It may suffice to call attention to the following points. (1) The colloidal gold solution was not blood. It only looked like it. Since the Old Testament ritual of sacrifice required blood atonement, such a colloidal solution would have been merely a visual counterfeit of the real thing. The record does not state that Moses offered this colloidal "blood" in the tabernacle to atone for this great sin. That is read into the narrative, which simply states that Moses made the people drink the water into which the pulverized idol had been cast. (2) That it was not blood and did not even represent it is made plain by the fact that the Mosaic law makes even the eating with the blood a heinous and a capital offense. Yet it is asserted that it was the drinking of this imitation "blood" made by grinding up an idol image, which saved the lives of the vast majority of the sinful people. (3) That it was probably those who refused to drink who were the special objects of divine wrath — it is not stated that there were any such.

The Outer Covering for the Tabernacle (Exodus 26:14). More recently the same radio speaker has given an equally wild explanation of the outer covering of "badgers' skin" (AV; ARV, seal or porpoise covering) which was made for the tabernacle. From the words in Ezekiel 16:10, "I shod thee with badgers' skin" the inference is drawn that in asking the Israelites encamped at Sinai to give badger skins for the construction of the tabernacle, the Lord was asking the people to give the very shoes off their feet and go barefoot in their journeyings through the wilderness. So he infers from the statement, "thy raiment waxed not old upon thee, neither did thy foot swell, these forty years" (Deut. 8:4; cf. Neh. 9:21), that as a reward for their obedience and willingness to face hardship for his sake, the Lord used supernatural means to preserve their feet from injury during the long and tedious journey. The application that is made of the incident thus interpreted is excellent. But unfortunately the basis for it is so slight as to be negligible. A little figuring will establish the fact that if the children of Israel contributed the equivalent of less than a square inch of porpoise leather for each of the 603,550 adult males, this would have been more than enough for the covering for the tabernacle.

These examples illustrate the fact that it is quite as important not to read anything into the biblical text which is not clearly implied in it as it is not to read anything out of it which is clearly there.

CHAPTER V

COMPARING THE INCOMPARABLE

The braggart speech of the Rabshakeh, who was sent by Sennacherib to demand the surrender of the city of Jerusalem, contained these challenging words: "Now on whom dost thou trust, that thou rebellest against me?" And again, "Who are they among all the gods of these countries, that have delivered their land out of my hand, that the Lord should deliver Jerusalem out of my hand?" (2 Kings 18:20, 35). Had Rabshakeh known it, he was merely echoing the words of Pharaoh, king of Egypt, who centuries before had said to Moses, "Who is the Lord, that I should obey his voice to let Israel go? I know not the Lord, neither will I let Israel go" (Exod. 5:2). And it had required the plagues of Egypt and the whelming flood of the Red Sea waters to give a sufficing answer to this question in so far as Pharaoh and the Egyptians were concerned. So to Rabshakeh, the prophet Isaiah sent the answer, "Whom has thou reproached and blasphemed? and against whom hast thou exalted *thy* voice, and lifted up thine eyes on high? *even* against the Holy One of Israel" (Isa. 37:23). And the destruction of the Assyrian army confirmed the word of Isaiah to Sennacherib, and the blasphemer departed to his own land and perished there.

In Chapters 36–39 of Isaiah which form the connecting link between the first part and the second, two events are recorded which are of the utmost importance: the threat of Sennacherib and his overthrow, and the terrible rebuke of Hezekiah's pride contained in the ominous threat that his sons should be eunuchs in the palace of the king of Babylon. We may well believe that as Isaiah, perhaps many years later, meditated on these two vastly different yet in a sense quite similar themes, the blasphemy of Sennacherib and its condign punishment and the pride of Hezekiah and the ominous woe still impending in consequence of it, and set them in the light of the sovereign majesty of the God of Israel, "the fire burned" (Ps. 39:3) and the words of comfort and confident trust in Israel's incomparable God which are the great theme of the last twenty-seven chapters gradually took shape in his mind.[1]

As we read the fortieth chapter, we are struck by the insistent, oft-repeated interrogative pronoun, "who?"[2]: "Who hath measured the waters in the hollow of his hand?" etc. Who? Who? Who? Six times in this chapter, more than a dozen times in Chapters 40-48 we meet

341

this insistent "Who?" a question which reaches its climax in 46:5, "To whom will ye liken me, and make me equal and compare me that we may be like?"[3] We seem to hear, echoing through these chapters, Sennacherib's blasphemy and Isaiah's reply. And it is stressed by the insistent and emphatic "I" which appears more than fifty times in these nine chapters.[4] Compare especially 43:11; 45:6f., 18, 19f.; 46:9. "I am the Lord and there is none else" is the emphatic answer to the "who?" And Babylon which has dared to claim this unique distinction for herself (47:7-11) shall perish: "none shall save thee" (vs. 15). And do we not have in the repeated exposés of the utter folly of idolatry which run through these chapters almost like a refrain, a further answer to the question asked through the Rabshakeh? The gods of Hamath, of Arvad, of Sepharvaim had not delivered their cities from Sennacherib; and the great gods of Assyria, whom he worshipped, were not to deliver this seemingly invincible conqueror from the dagger of the assassin, not even in his temple and in the act of worshipping his god. Why? Because these gods were all "the work of men's hands,"[5] things of naught, while, to use the words of another spokesman of the God of Israel, "The Lord is the true God, he is the living God, and an everlasting king" (Jer. 10:10). If it is true that "a living dog is mightier than a dead lion" (Eccl. 9:4), what must then be the difference between the *living* God who is the God of Israel and the idols of the heathen? We turn to Psalm 115 for the triumphant and devastating answer to the question, "Wherefore should the heathen say, Where is now their God?" "Their idols are silver and gold, the work of men's hands." They have mouths, eyes, noses, hands, feet, ears, throats. Yes! Quite so! *But* they can neither speak nor see nor hear nor smell nor touch nor walk. And "They that made them are like unto them." What wonder that the Psalmist cries out: "O Israel trust thou in the Lord: he is their help and shield."

The scorn and contempt with which the God of Israel views his mighty enemy is illustrated with singular aptness by the reference to "hook" and "bridle" in Isaiah 37:29. The bull was the symbol of strength and ferocity. Assyrian kings likened themselves to bulls. Bull-gods were common. The God of Israel will turn back this raging bull; and with hook in nose and bridle on jaws he will tamely follow his master to the fate which awaits him, slaughter in the temple of his god (37:38). It is the same attitude which is expressed in the words of the "man of God" to Ahab, "Thus saith the Lord, Because the Syrians have said, The Lord is God of the hills, but he is not God of the valleys, therefore will I deliver all this great multitude into thine hand, and ye shall know that I am the Lord" (1 Kings 20:28). Such a clever, face-saving, explanation of Ben-hadad's first defeat, merited and received a decisive rebuke, despite the fact that Ahab was a wicked king and his people were largely apostate. The God of Israel is "a jealous God" (Exod. 20:5; Deut. 4:24), who has a great zeal for his own honor and glory. The struggle with Babylon is in a sense only a repetition of that with Pharaoh and the Egyptians. In the one case he got himself honor (Exod. 14:17f.) and in the other he will do the same. "I am the Lord; that is my name: and my glory will I not give to another, neither my praise to graven images" (Isa. 42:8). It had been the "reproach of Egypt" — the reproach which Egypt cast on Israel (subjective genitive) in the days of Moses that the Israelites, the people of Jehovah, were bondsmen in their land (Josh. 5:9); and his honor was gloriously vindicated when he triumphed over the gods of Egypt, the armies of Egypt, and over Pharaoh himself in the plagues and the crossing of the Red Sea. The Babylonian captivity led to a terrible profaning of the name of the God of Israel. For it enabled the heathen to say, "These are the people of the Lord and they are gone forth out of his land" (Ezek. 36:20). In these deliverances the Lord wrought primarily for his own glory and honor and not because his people deserved his help: "Thus saith the Lord God; I do not this for your sakes, O house of Israel, but for my holy name's sake, which ye have profaned among the heathen, whither ye went" (Ezek. 36:22, 32).[6]

Who then is the God of Israel? He is the incomparable God. And it is to this theme that we address ourselves in this concluding chapter. The incomparable God! We are living in an age which is hostile to a belief in the *supernatural*. This, we need to remember, is a comparatively modern objection to the religion of the Bible. Belief in signs and wonders, in miracles and predictions, was common and general throughout the centuries of the past. "Call ye on the name of your gods and I will call on the name of Jehovah; and the God that answereth by fire, let him be God" was the test proposed by Elijah; and apparently it was accepted without demur by the prophets of Baal. Trial by ordeal was common in the Middle Ages. And in shipping regulations even today, responsibility is disclaimed for unpredictable events, which are called "an act of God." One does not need to be deeply read in the history of the religions of the past and even of the present, in so far as they have not been influenced by the modern trend, to realize that disbelief in the supernatural is a relatively rare and new thing. But there is an older objection which has always been raised against the claims of the Bible, and that is the denial of its *uniqueness*. We have just been considering an impressive example of this attitude. Sennacherib knew gods many and lords many. He knew something of the enormous pantheon of Assyrian gods, and he knew that it had its counterpart among other nations.[7] He compared them in his mind with the God of

Israel and he could see no essential difference. Not merely that: the God of Israel suffered decidedly by comparison. For Judah was a little, insignificant land; and its God must therefore be correspondingly insignificant. So reasoned Sennacherib, king of Assyria.

One of the chief characteristics of our modern thinking and of our educational systems is the dominance of the *Comparative Method*. We have a whole bevy of comparative sciences: Comparative Philology, Comparative Anthropology, Comparative Physiology, Comparative Psychology, Comparative Ethics, Comparative Mythology and Folklore, Comparative Religion. There is nothing really new in this. We learn by comparison. Consequently, it is highly important *what* and *how* we compare. The writer remembers from his student days in Berlin hearing his professor of Arabic, Eduard Sachau, remark to the class "Gentlemen, he who distinguishes little knows little." This *obiter dictum* was not original with the teacher. But it has stuck in the memory of the pupil for more than fifty years. It is well worth remembering. It is a simple and obvious truth; but one which we are very prone to forget. An expert on money will detect a counterfeit, which most men would accept as legal tender. An expert on stream pollution will detect bacteria in a brook which to the thirsty wayfarer looks clear as crystal. An expert on any subject will treat as of great importance differentia which a tyro would overlook entirely or treat as of little or no significance, as mere trivialities not to be bothered with.

It is important, therefore, to remind ourselves, that all comparative study if it is to be successful and to deserve the name "scientific," must include the careful and judicious consideration of *both* correspondences and differences. To ignore the one or the other, or to attach undue importance to the one as over against the other cannot fail to lead to unjust and unwarranted conclusions. A scientist who is a convinced evolutionist will tend to minimize or ignore the great law of Genesis 1, "after its kind," despite the fact that this law is constantly illustrating and approving itself before his very eyes and has centuries of historical evidence behind it. Or he will magnify the seeming exceptions until he forgets the fundamental law. He will catalogue the resemblances between man and monkey and disregard the far more characteristic differences between them.[8] A scholar with a materialistic bias will minimize or reject everything that savors of the supernatural in his study and interpretation of the world about him. A student of religion who believes that all religions are but the product and expression of the spiritual nature of man will be impatient of any attempt to maintain the oft repeated claims of the Bible to set forth a religion which is *sui generis* and unique, a religion which was not discovered by man, but revealed by God. Compare! Yes, but be careful to keep the balance true, and not to make a farce of comparative study by question-begging assumptions which make a just conclusion impossible.

Since we hear so much today about comparative religion, we need to remember that the Old Testament prophets were experts on this subject. To many of our religious philosophers of today, pagan idolatry and polytheism with all its "abominations" is more or less an academic subject. They have never come to grips with it. But to the prophets of old the subject was a vital one; they were engaged in a life and death struggle with these religions and their gods. No greater expert on the subject of comparative religion can be found than Isaiah. No one has ever demonstrated with more devastating logic, irony, and invective, the nothingness of idols than he does in Chapter 44, where he pictures to us the man who cuts down a tree of the forest, uses part of it to make a fire to warm himself and cook his food, "and the residue thereof he maketh a god, even his graven image: he falleth down unto it, and worshippeth it, and prayeth unto it, and saith, Deliver me; for thou art my god." Again, in a magnificent flight of prophetic insight, he pictures the images of the great gods of Babylon being carried, not in pomp and ceremony as on the feast days along the great procession street of Babylon,[9] but carried *away* into exile: "Bel boweth down, Nebo stoopeth, their idols were upon the beasts and upon the cattle: your carriages were heavy laden: they are a burden to the weary beast. They stoop, they bow down together; they could not deliver the burden, but themselves are gone into captivity" (46:1-2). What a picture of utter impotence! Then we read, "Hearken unto me, O house of Jacob, and all the remnant of the house of Israel, which are borne (by me) from the belly, which are carried from the womb: and even to your old age I (am) he; and *even* to hoar hairs will *I* carry (you): *I* have made, and *I* will bear; even *I* will carry, and will deliver (you)."[10] And this leads up to the challenging question, "To whom will ye liken me and make me equal, and compare me, that we may be like?" What a comparison! What a devastating contrast!

Reader, when you want to study comparative religion, go and sit at the feet of an expert on the subject. Study the words of Isaiah, learn from the great prophets. Take to heart Hosea's annihilating words: "The workman hath made it; and it is not God," and remember that these prophets are in a very real sense only the faithful successors of Moses the man of God who came down from the Mount of God with the two tables of the testimony in his hands, on which were written these words: "Thou shalt have no other gods ·before me. Thou shalt not make unto thee any graven image or any likeness of any thing that is in heaven above or that is in the earth beneath or that is in the water under the earth; Thou shalt not bow down thyself to them, nor serve them" — Moses, who in his beautiful "Song" warns the people solemnly against pagan idolatries and calls the gods of the heathen "strange (gods)," "abominations," "devils," "new gods that came up newly," "not-gods," "vanities" (Deut. 32:16-21)! Compare! By all means compare! Compare diligently! And if the Holy Spirit is your guide, he will lead you to bow humbly and thankfully before One who can both challenge and defy comparison, because he is himself and he alone, the Incomparable One. "The God of the whole earth shall he be called" (Isa. 54:5).

One of the most scathing indictments of that misuse of the comparative method in the sphere of religion which is so common today is found in Psalm 50. In it the psalmist, picturing a great judgment scene, represents the Lord as rejecting scornfully mere external worship, sacrifices offered in the heathen manner, as if he needed to be fed by the blood of bulls and goats. Then he denounces the wicked man who seeks to justify his wickedness because, so runs the indictment: "thou thoughtest that I was altogether such an one as thyself." Here we have the comparative argument in its most extreme form. Sinful, corrupt, ruthless, as he is, man yet thinks of God as altogether like himself and forms his god in his own image. This, the Lord tells him, is because "I kept silence." It is the revelation which God makes of himself which corrects man's false ideas which are formed by comparing God with himself. It is this fact which makes the Bible so necessary and indispensable to the Christian; and when the modern critic applies the comparative method to it in the same way, magnifying minor similarities and ignoring or minimizing the vast differences, he is guilty of the same sin as the wicked man of old and invites the same rebuke and condemnation.[11]

We are often told today that the life of ancient Israel was not lived in a vacuum; and one of the chief aims of the archaeologist is to fill in that vacuum and to discover not only the background or context but also the sources of the religious beliefs of Israel. But, as we have pointed out above, this aim of many archaeologists and students of comparative religion runs counter to the constant and emphatic teaching of the law and the prophets which is that Israel's safety lies in her separation from the idolatrous nations which surround her and which warns constantly against the contamination and corruption which are sure to follow association with them and adoption of their culture and cults.

Sixty odd years ago when the writer entered Princeton Seminary as a student, the Opening Address was delivered by Professor Robert Dick Wilson who had been recently called to occupy the William

Henry Green Chair of Semitic Philology and Old Testament Criticism. The subject of the address was: "Babylon and Israel: A Comparison of their Leading Ideas Based upon their Vocabularies."[12] The reason Dr. Wilson chose this decidedly academic-sounding subject, which introduced a discussion, which was far above the head of an unsophisticated Junior, and the significance of which some of the Seniors even may have failed to appreciate fully, was this. In January of that year Professor Friedrich Delitzsch had delivered in Berlin a lecture which he entitled, "Babel und Bibel". In it he aimed to show that very many of the beliefs and laws of Israel were derived from the Babylonian, that the law of Moses was largely dependent on the laws of Hammurabi.[13] So the subject was a most timely one; and Dr. Wilson handled it in masterly fashion, pointing out the marked differences between the two as indicated by their vocabularies. But there was already developing a Pan-Babylonian school, of which Winckler, Jeremias, Stücken, and Jensen were prominent members. And the astral-myth theory, according to which the heavens are the exact counterpart of the earth, so that earthly events can be read in the heavenly bodies, a "return" to medieval astrology, became very popular. And it became fashionable to treat Abraham, Isaac, and Jacob as astral myths.

Such is no longer the case. The discovery of the Code of Hammurabi, epoch-making as it seemed at the time, was only one of a series of discoveries which opened up unsuspected vistas in the life of the ancient Orient. We now know that Hammurabi was not the first great law-giver, that he had Sumerian and perhaps Hittite and Hurrian law codes to borrow from. Long forgotten peoples and empires were coming to light.

Many years ago, in discussing the "present position of Old Testament criticism," J. E. McFadyen described the question in debate between two German scholars, Cornill of Breslau and Sellin of Berlin, as largely due to the fact that the older critics, Wellhausen and Robertson Smith, for example, "for the most part illustrated the life and thought of Israel by analogies drawn from pre-Islamic Arabia."[14] So he found it only natural for the younger men "to interpret Israel and her literature in the light cast upon her by Assyrio-Babylonia and Egypt rather than by ancient Arabia." But now the situation has altered still further. Assyria and Babylonia are far away, and so is Egypt in a sense, despite the fact that at times they both made their influence keenly felt in Palestine. But the Ras Shamra tablets have opened up to us a language and literature more closely related to Israel than either of these. How close is a matter of dispute. According to Albright, "it remains certain that Ugarit formed an integral part of the domain of Canaanite culture stretching in the late Bronze Age from Gaza in the south to Ugarit in the north."[15] On the other hand, Gordon believes that from the standpoint of philology, it "has not yet been proved that Hebrew and Ugaritic belong to the same subdivision (often called Canaanite) of the Northwest branch of the Semitic languages."[16] If this culture can be called Canaanite, it is important for us to observe at the very beginning that through it we are now brought face to face with a culture which is described in the Bible as so utterly anti-Israelite, that everything connected with it was to be abhorred and eradicated from the land, lest it corrupt Israel to her destruction.[17] Yet notwithstanding this fact we are now faced with what threatens to become a Pan-Near-Easternism or a Pan-Canaanitism which as it affects the religion of the Bible is more dangerous even than the Pan-Babylonianism of fifty years ago.

THE PATTERN OF NEAR EASTERN RELIGION

While as we have seen the study of the ancient texts discovered in the Near East, notably in Egypt and Mesopotamia, very speedily led to comparative study and the attempt to connect the religion of Israel with the religious beliefs and practices of these ancient peoples,[18] it is only comparatively recently that the effort has been made to discover a "pattern" which may be applied to the main religions of this area. This has been especially the task of the British Myth and Ritual School under the leadership of Professor S. H. Hooke[19] and of the Scandinavian (Uppsala) school.[20] They have concentrated their attention largely on the cult as it found expression in the great annual feasts, notably the Babylonian New Year feast (*Akitu*), with which they have endeavored to connect the annual feasts of the Israelites.

Professor Hooke has described the religious rites which dramatized the great events of the feast and were supposed to act by sympathetic magic in bringing the blessing of the gods on the people, as follows:

(a) The dramatic representation of the death and resurrection of the god.

(b) The recital or symbolic representation of the myth of creation.

(c) The ritual combat, in which the triumph of the god over his enemies was depicted.

(d) The sacred marriage (*hieros gamos*).

(e) The triumphal procession, in which the king played the part of the god followed by a train of lesser gods or visiting deities.[21]

This is, in general, the ritual pattern which scholars of the Myth and Ritual school in Britain and of the Scandinavian school are concerned to discover in the Old Testament as characterizing more or less fully the pre-exilic cultus in Israel.

The position taken by Professor Hooke and the influential school of thought which he represents may be summed up in three brief propositions:

(1) Such a cultic pattern as has been described prevailed extensively among the nations of antiquity, expecially among those with which Israel came more or less closely into contact.

(2) Israel *must* originally have shared this pattern.

(3) Therefore, the scarcity of the evidence of this sharing to be found in the Old Testament books dealing with the pre-exilic period *must* be due to the efforts to eliminate this evidence made by the writers and editors of the Old Testament books, as these books have come down to us.

The inference to be drawn from these propositions is that every effort must be made to discover traces of the pattern, to undo the work of those who sought to eliminate the pattern, in order to make good the basic *assumption* that the pattern actually applied to the religion of Israel in its early stages. It is to these three propositions that we shall now address ourselves.

1. As to the first, there can be little doubt that there was a marked resemblance between the religions of the Near East in ancient times. Whether or to what extent these resemblances amounted to a pattern, and what features properly belong to that pattern, may be a matter for debate among the experts in these fields of research. Thus, Henri Frankfort, in discussing one important feature of the program, the marriage of the king with the goddess (*hieros gamos*) criticizes Engnell and other advocates of the pattern, for trying to force "one single pattern upon the extensive material which he has collected, thus destroying the rich variety of pre-Greek thought in the name of 'comparative religion.'"[22] He declares that they all, in varying degree "over-shoot the mark." But whether these scholars exaggerate the extent of these resemblances and whether the pattern is as definite as is claimed is not for us a matter of great importance. The fact is too well established to require extended proof that these ancient ethnic religions resembled one another in many striking ways and these resemblances may be called in general a pattern.

2. The second proposition is of supreme importance. It is the claim that Israel originally shared that pattern. Hooke has stated it tersely as follows: "The religion which the ancestors of the Hebrews brought with them (into Canaan) probably did not differ very widely from that of the environment into which they entered, and after their settlement such differences as did exist would tend to disappear."[23] Hooke finds the beginnings of Hebrew religion in the elaborate fertility cultus

of the Ras Shamra tablets rather than in animism or animatism as did the Wellhausen school.[24] Regarding the period of the monarchy he holds that the religion of Israel was "a religion where the god was the incarnation of the desires and material needs of the community, a god who annually died and rose again, a cult whose roots were in the earth and of the earth."[25] This cult he holds centered in the king as the head of the official ritual; and the eighth century prophets protested against it.

This is essentially the claim the higher critics have been making for many years. It is to be carefully noted in evaluating it, that it rests upon the assumption that the books of the Old Testament, notably the Pentateuch, are late and untrustworthy. Otherwise such a statement as this could not be credited for a moment. For these books make two things absolutely plain as we have already pointed out in some detail: (1) The religion of the Mosaic and pre-exilic periods was essentially different from the religions of the neighboring peoples, and (2) the inveterate tendency of the masses of Israel was to forsake the religion of their fathers, the covenant made by Jehovah with Abraham and solemnly ratified with his descendants at Sinai. That Israel was influenced and corrupted by these heathen religions and their sensuously attractive cults is made as plain as language can make it. But it is no less plainly stated that this adopting of foreign cults was an apostasy and it is most severely denounced and condemned by Moses and the prophets. It is only when practically all the available evidence to the contrary has been discredited, by treating it as late and undependable, as the pious theological romanticizing of the religious leaders of later times, that room can be found for these heathen cults as representing the proper and legitimate cultus of early Israel. The early period must be made a practical vacuum before the vacuum can be filled in with the pattern which Professor Hooke presents to us.

3. That such is the case, that "traces" of the pattern as representing the legitimate religion of Israel at any time in her history are exceedingly hard to find is illustrated by such statements as the following. Professor Snaith tells us:

The difficulty of forming any reliable estimate of the worship in preexilic Israel is due to the work of those editors, from the Deuteronomists down to the Massoretes, who sought diligently to remove from the Sacred Text everything which did not accord with the strictest and purest monotheism. The measure of their success would be the extent of our failure, were it not for the work of the archaeologist. Even then the balance is not redressed, because the actual material found is very rarely indeed from the period of the kingdoms.[26]

Engnell of the Uppsala school, an ardent believer in the pattern, quotes with evident approval the following from Hooke:

The task of attempting a description of the early religious system of Canaan is not an easy one. It somewhat resembles that of the palaeontologist who has to reconstruct the skeleton of an extinct mammal from a bone or two, and there is at least this in common between the two endeavors, that both are guided by the knowledge of an original pattern.[27]

The last clause of this statement is significant, "both are guided by the knowledge of an original pattern." This shows how thoroughly evolutionary this theory is. If evolutionary theory can tell us what an extinct mammal must have looked like, then it can be reconstructed theoretically. Similarly if it can be assumed that in Ugaritic and Babylonian and Egyptian we have the original pattern from which the religion of Israel *must* have been derived, then the pattern of the early religion of Israel can be determined from them with the help of the vestigial remains still allegedly present in the Old Testament books.

For a single example of the application of this principle we turn to Professor T. H. Robinson. Pointing to the fact, which has been known for many years, that there were living in Elephantine in Egypt about the time of Malachi Jews who worshipped a goddess Anath, he argues that Anath was earlier worshipped in Palestine. He tells us:

> From our Old Testament alone we should never have guessed that Israel associated a goddess with Jahweh, even popularly, but the conclusion is irresistible, and we are justified in assuming that she played her part in the mythology and ritual of Israel. It is difficult to avoid the conclusion that rites, similar to those found elsewhere, were observed in pre-exilic Israel, and that these included a recital or a representation of the annual marriage of Jahweh and Anath.[28]

You observe how the pattern works! Can you think of anything more offensive or abhorrent than this? Yet note what follows:

> Details are entirely lacking, and no useful purpose would be served here by endeavoring to supply them conjecturally; the bare fact is sufficient to suggest that the normal pattern was broadly followed.

Such a statement as the one just quoted is incorrect both in what it asserts and in what it implies. It is incorrect in claiming that the Old Testament nowhere asserts or implies that members of the Israelitish race never practiced gross polytheism. That they did so is stated again and again. At Sinai after they had heard the words of the Decalogue, we read that they said to Aaron, "Up make us gods which shall go before us" (Exod. 32:1) — a lapse into idolatry, a grievous violation of the first two commandments of the Decalogue. Again, in the plains of Moab, they were guilty of joining themselves to Baal-peor and twenty-four thousand perished by a plague which was sent to punish them (Num. 25:9). After the death of Joshua we read: "And they forsook the Lord and served Baal and Ashtaroth" (Judg. 2:13; cf. 10:6). These same tendencies are condemned in the demand of Samuel,

"Put away the strange gods and Ashtaroth from among you and prepare your hearts unto the Lord and serve him only" (1 Sam 7:3); in the damning indictment of Solomon's idolatries (1 Kings 11) which reaches a climax in the words "because they have forsaken me, and have worshipped Ashtaroth the goddess of the Zidonians . . ." (vs. 33); in Jeremiah's denunciation of the cults, notably that of the "queen of heaven" (Jer. 7:18; 44:17, 18, 19, 25). This did not necessarily mean an utter forsaking of Jehovah for the gods and goddesses of the heathen nations by which Israel was surrounded. It involved in some cases at least such an attempted syncretism as was practiced by the Samaritans who "feared the Lord and served their own gods" (2 Kings 17:33). Ezekiel's vision (chaps. 8 and 9) of the pollution of the temple by idolatry is an extreme example. (Cf. also Ezek. 16 and 23.) But there was always a remnant, a faithful few, like the seven thousand who refused to worship Baal in Elijah's day. To one who has read the biblical account of the frequent and terrible apostasies of the Israelites and places upon them the interpretation which they are clearly intended to carry, it is not at all strange that Israelites in distant Syene practiced polytheism of such a nature as ought to have been utterly repugnant to every Israelite who knew and endeavored to keep the law of Moses. The Old Testament does not ignore or try to cover up and condone such lapses. It speaks of them with great plainness of speech and denounces them as a forsaking of the God of Israel and a turning to idols. It denounces them as an apostasy which is utterly foreign to the religion of Israel. What Professor Robinson and Professor Hooke and all those who share their viewpoint are loath to admit is that this is *apostasy*. They are determined to treat it as a legitimate early stage of the religion of Israel and as one of the vestiges which can still be traced even in the lofty teachings of the prophets; and they use these vestiges to reconstruct the early religion of Israel, or rather, to prove that it *must* have resembled and been derived from the pattern which they have discovered elsewhere.

Referring especially to the Canaanite religion, which he thinks is now "familiar to us in considerable detail" G. W. Anderson tells us that

To reconstruct its main features is easier than to estimate the extent of its influence on pre-exilic Israel. That Canaanite beliefs and practices were widely adopted by the Hebrews is, of course, shown by the Old Testament itself. How far that borrowing went, and how much of it became part of the officially recognized religious system, is one of the most strenuously debated problems of Old Testament study today.[29]

This is a much more accurate statement than either of the others which we have quoted. It points out that the real issue is not whether the religious beliefs of the Canaanites and other neighboring peoples influenced, at times to an almost overwhelming degree, the religious beliefs and practices of the Israelites. That as Anderson tells us "is, of course, shown by the Old Testament itself." The real issue is as to "how much of it became part of the officially recognized religious system"; and we believe it is not too much to say that only those who reject the equally plain statements of the Old Testament as to the uniqueness of the religion of Israel and its divine origin and insist on reconstructing it in accordance with an evolutionary and derivative pattern will be able to find this pattern taught in the Old Testament itself.

THE DYING AND RISING GOD

In the longest of the Ugaritic myths, that of Baal and Anath, the death and resurrection of Baal is a prominent feature. Aliyan Baal (the meaning of *aliyan* is uncertain; it may be an honorific title) is a son of El and one of the most prominent of the gods. Baal has an enemy Mot. The word obviously means "death." They engage in mortal combat. Baal is slain. Baal's sister and consort Anath assembles the parts of Baal's body and buries them. Then she fights with Mot and slays him. Finally Baal is brought back to life. It is the same seasonal myth which we find in Adonis-Tammuz, in Telepinus, in Osiris and Isis, in Ishtar's descent into Hades, in Orpheus and Proserpina.[30]

The discovery of this myth in the Ras Shamra tablets has naturally given increased impulse to the attempt to find it in the Old Testament as a part of the pattern. T. H. Robinson feels that the idea of the death and resurrection of the god "was less open to objection" as regards Israel's faith and he thinks "it is possible that several biblical passages are best interpreted as references to this cult-myth."[31] Thus the words with which Psalm 68 begins, "Let God arise, let his enemies be scattered," are to be explained as originally referring to the return of the dead god from the nether world where he has been imprisoned. The same claim is made regarding Isaiah 33:10, "Now will I arise, saith the Lord; now will I be exalted; now will I lift up myself." And recently the thesis has been advanced that in Old Testament poetry and prophecy the "desert" means the nether world, that the languishing and misery of the earth (cf. Isa. 33:8-9) is due to the dying of the god, and that the glorious prophecies (e.g., vss. 13-24), which describe the blessings which God will give his people refer to the springtime of the year when the dead god returns to bless the world with plenty and with joy.[32] It is distressing to find even Isaiah 53 referred to as possibly alluding to this myth. Very much must be read into such passages which is not there and quite as much read out which is there, before such radical theories as these can be regarded as at all probable:

The word "arise" occurs 211 times in the AV as the rendering of a verb (*qum*) which occurs more than six hundred times in the Old Testament. In the simple (*Qal*) stem it is ordinarily used of an activity or action which is to follow inaction. Thus it is the opposite or the sequel of "sit (still)." It refers repeatedly to the putting into effect of a purpose which involves activity: *e.g.*, "and Deborah arose and went with Barak to Kadesh" (Judg. 4:9). It is occasionally used of arising (awaking) from sleep (Song 2:13; Prov. 6:9; Lam. 2:19; Jonah 1:6). It is rarely used of the dead (Ps. 88:10; Isa. 26:19). It is used occasionally in the Psalms in a prayer invoking the presence and help of God.[33] It is said by God of himself in describing his purpose to deliver (Ps. 12:5); and it appears in declarative form (Ps. 76:9) and in the description of a theophany (Isa. 2:19, 21; cf. 31:2). In view of the general usage of the verb it would seem evident that the burden of proof must rest with those who would find in any of these passages an allusion to this heathen myth.

It is quite true that strongly anthropomorphic expressions are used of God. He is said to "be silent" (Ps. 28:1; 35:22), and "to sleep" (Ps. 44:23) and urged to "awake" (Ps. 7:6; 35:23; 44:23; 59:4f.; 73:20; Job 8:6; Isa. 51:9; cf. Ps. 80:2). On the other hand Psalm 121:4 emphatically declares that the God of Israel "slumbers not nor sleeps." And in ridiculing Baal and his worshippers Elijah says with biting sarcasm, "Perhaps he is asleep and will wake" (1 Kings 18:27). And the instant response of Israel's God to the prayer of his servant coming after the persistent and impassioned prayers of the Baal worshippers had received no answer, is sufficient proof that such a claim regarding Jehovah would be too absurd for serious consideration. He is a God who is afar off, heaven is his dwelling place (1 Kings 8:27-30), and he must "humble" himself to behold what happens on the earth (Ps. 113:6), and he must "come" to the help of his people.[34] Yet he also dwells in their midst, seated on his throne (the ark) between the cherubim within the sanctuary (I Sam. 4:4). He may close his eyes, may shut his ears, may hide his face from Israel because of their sins. He may seem to forget and be urged to remember his people. Such language is intensely human (anthropomorphic) and may even sound irreverent. But where is there the slightest hint that he dies and needs to come to life, to come to life annually; that his death brings distress and misery to his people, that his reviving or resurrection will bring them prosperity and joy?

The answer to this question is obvious. In contrast with these allegedly cryptic allusions to a living-dying-rising god, the counterpart of Tammuz or Aliyan Baal, a vegetation god whose death is to be bewailed (Ezek. 8:14) and whose restoration to life is to be hailed with rejoicing, we have the many times repeated declaration of Scripture that the God of Israel is the "living God." This is pointed out especially in connection with certain great events in Israel's history: the giving of the law at Sinai (Deut. 5:26), the crossing of the Jordan (Josh. 3:10), the blasphemy of Goliath (1 Sam. 17:26, 36), the blasphemy of Sennacherib (2 Kings 19:4, 16), Daniel and the lions (Dan. 6:20, 26); also Psalm 42:2; Jeremiah 10:10; 23:36; Hosea 1:10. It is this aspect of Jehovah which is stressed in the self-attesting oath, "as I live" which occurs in Numbers 14:21, 28; Deuteronomy 32:40; Jeremiah 22:24, and fifteen times in Ezekiel (first in 5:11). The oath by the living God ("as the Lord liveth") occurs nearly fifty times (e.g., Judg. 8:19; Ruth 3:13; 1 Sam. 26:10; 2 Sam. 4:9). It is most impressive when we meet it on the lips of Elijah — "as the Lord God of Israel liveth before whom I stand" (1 Kings 17:1). In Psalm 90, this thought is beautifully dwelt on and elaborated, "even from everlasting to everlasting thou art God." It is this God who gives to David the promise of an everlasting kingship (2 Sam. 7:13, 16; cf. vss. 24, 25, 29). It is, in fact, involved in the very first verse of Genesis, "In the beginning God created the heaven and the earth." The idea of Jehovah as an annually dying and reviving God is so utterly foreign to the Old Testament that it is no wonder the critics have such difficulty in finding "traces" of it. For this is one of the marked differences between the religion of Israel and the ethnic faiths, which are such a stumbling block in the path of the present day student of comparative religion. Confronted with the insistent claim that the God of Israel is the living God from whom all living things derive their existence and well-being, these attempts to find the origin of this lofty conception in a vegetation god who dies and comes to life again annually are extremely feeble and unconvincing to say the least.

In connection with the claims that pious Jewish editors sought to eliminate everything which savored of this cult of the dying and rising god from the religion of Israel, note should be taken of the reference to the Tammuz-cult which we find in Ezekiel 8:14. There the prophet is carried in vision to Jerusalem and to the temple itself. In the court of the temple, "at the door of the gate of the Lord's house" — he is very precise! — he sees women "weeping for Tammuz." They are bewailing the dead god, and looking forward to his return to life. That is, we find women of Jerusalem practicing this pagan rite at the very temple of the God of Israel. If the later Jews were so concerned to achieve a "cover up," of the idolatrous and pagan practices of their fathers, that they eliminated all but the faintest traces of it from the literature which had come down to them, why did they leave this utterly damning indictment in this passage in Ezekiel, which refers to a rite which was popular with Israel's heathen neighbors, but so utterly foreign to the religion of Moses and the prophets, and which is described with such abhorrence by Ezekiel? There is only one answer. They knew that these rites were and had been practiced in Israel. But they knew them as representing a terrible apostasy from the true faith of their people. Furthermore they had such high regard for the words of the prophets that they did not dare to remove such a terrible indictment from the prophetic volume. They permitted the fact of the occurrences of these "abominations" and the prophetic denunciation of them to stand in the record side by side; and it is in the light of the prophetic teaching that the abomination appears the more exceedingly abominable. It finds no support in it. It is utterly condemned by it.

It should be noted in this connection that the fact that the Old Testament contains these candid records of the apostasies and vices of the ancestors of the chosen people is a notable evidence of the truthfulness of the record. The Jews were a proud people. How ready they were to ignore their own sins and the sins of their fathers and to forget the oft-repeated punishments visited on them for these sins is illustrated by the amazing words recorded in John 8:33, "We be Abraham's seed and were never in bondage to any man." To such a people the record of their own history must have been painful reading. For it tells of slavery in Egypt, of oppression by the Philistines, of the schism of the tribes and the destruction of ten of them, of the captivity of Judah in Babylon. These things are all in the record. They did not dare to delete them. But they clearly ignored them as much as possible. Had they not had an almost superstitious reverence for the Word of God they would have changed it to make it support their notions of their own greatness and goodness.

THE CREATION MYTH

The Babylonian Creation Myth *Enuma Elish* was discovered by George Smith who published portions of it in 1875. Through the work of Sayce, Delitzsch, Zimmern, King, and many others, most recently of Heidel and Speiser, it has become very familiar to students of history and religion.[35] It tells of the revolt of Tiamat against the gods, of their choice of Marduk to be their champion in the fight against this monster, of the rewards promised him, of the preparation for the conflict, of its successful outcome, of Marduk's ordering of the heavens and the earth, of the honors paid to him, and finally it records the fifty names given to him celebrating his pre-eminence. This battle between Marduk and Tiamat is a favorite theme in Accadian art and also apparently in its cult and ritual. And it is claimed that it formed a conspicuous part in the annual New Year celebration (*Akitu*).

Many studies have been made of the Accadian creation legends since the first publication by George Smith in 1875. Some scholars, notably Gunkel, Gressmann, and Jensen[36] found the relationship close and the borrowings extensive. Others have taken a much more conservative view. J. D. Davis argued that the only comparison which can be drawn is to be found in the opening lines of this epic, which give a mythical account of the origin of the cosmos.[37] Pinches held that "the Babylonian account, notwithstanding all that has been said to the contrary, differs so much from the biblical account, that they are, to all intents and purposes, two distinct narratives."[38] According to Wardle, "On the whole the evidence seems to warrant the conclusion that *Enuma elish* was known to the authors of the early chapters of Genesis, but that their position is not so much one of dependence upon it as of revulsion from it."[39] Much the same conclusion was arrived at more recently by Heidel in his cautious and judicious study of the Creation Myth: "In the entire Old Testament there is not a trace of a theogony, such as we find for example in *Enuma elish* and in Hesiod."[40] His conclusion is that Genesis 1:1 — 2:3 "might (as far as a true view of inspiration is concerned) in a measure be dependent on *Enuma elish*. But I reject the idea that the biblical account gradually *evolved* out of the Babylonian; for that the differences are far too great and the similarities far too insignificant. In the light of the differences, the resemblances fade away almost like the stars before the sun."[41] Whether this conclusion is accepted or not, it is at least to be recognized that the Ras Shamra tablets furnish no evidence that the Creation Myth with which the Ritual Combat is closely connected was a part of the religious pattern as it was known to the Canaanites and practiced by them. In view of the lofty monotheism of Genesis 1 and the crude polytheism of the Babylonian Creation Myth, it is far more natural to find as its author a monotheist who was perhaps acquainted with that myth and perhaps adopted or adapted one or more of its familiar words[42] than to suppose that the first chapter of Genesis is an expurgated, de-mythologized version of this popular pagan myth. Certainly there is nothing in the Old Testament to indicate that this pagan myth with its polytheistic crudities was an annual pageant in Israel.

THE RITUAL COMBAT

The third element in the pattern as outlined by Professor Hooke is the Ritual Combat. As to it he tells us:

No one has attempted to deny the existence of numerous passages in the poetic literature of the Old Testament which refer to Jahweh's conquest of a dragon, or of the Sea personified, often in language closely resembling that of the Ras Shamra texts. But these are all explained as literary survivals, and it is strenuously denied that there ever was at any time in the history of Israel as part of the New Year ceremonies, either in the spring or autumn, a ritual enactment of the slaying of the dragon.[43]

To what extent these are "literary survivals" and just what their relation is to the Ras Shamra texts, if any, does not immediately concern us. What does especially concern us is that Hooke goes on to say:

It is perfectly true, as Professor Frankfort and others have argued, that we have no account of, or reference to, any such rituals in the Old Testament, but that holds good for all the early cult activities of the early period of Hebrew religion. We do not know what the Hebrew immigrants did in the Canaanite temples which they took over, nor what elements of the local pattern they adopted to secure the success of their agricultural operations, with Jahveh taking the place of the local Baal and assuming his title. But if we admit that they did take over such elements, then it is reasonable to believe that they would have taken over those which were most essential. Of these the seasonal re-enactment of the triumph of the god over hostile powers was clearly one.

Here we are told on the one hand that we have no account of or reference to any such rituals in the Old Testament — a very damaging admission — and on the other hand that "we do not know what the Hebrew immigrants did in the Canaanite temples." But it is inferred that they must have taken over some of these rituals and especially the most essential among which would be the ritual combat. This sounds quite reasonable, except for the fact that it is directly contrary to all the biblical evidence. All of the four or five main sources in the Pentateuch as generally recognized by the critics — J (Exod. 34:13f.), E (Exod. 20:2-6; 23:13, 24, 32f.), D (Deut. 7:5; 12:2f.), H (Lev. 19:4; 26:1), P (Num. 33:52-56) — tell us very definitely what the Israelites were to do "in" or rather *with* "the Canaanite temples which they took over." They were to destroy them utterly. And Leviticus 26:3-13 makes it perfectly clear that they were to secure the "success of their agricultural operations," not by adopting Baalism, but by utterly rejecting it and obeying the law of their God. But when all the biblical sources for our knowledge of this early period are treated as late and untrustworthy it is possible to give a very different account of it.

It is to be recognized, of course, that there are many passages in the Old Testament which speak of God's sovereign control over the world and over the men that are in it (e.g., Ps. 104:5-18, 29; cf. Ps. 68 and

89; Isa. 24, 27 and 30, Ezek. 21).[44] But there is no evidence to show that such passages formed part of a ritual, an annual ritual, corresponding to the celebration of Marduk's triumph over Tiamat in the Babylonian New Year celebration.

THE SACRED MARRIAGE

In a polytheism which recognizes both gods and goddesses, which regards them as magnified human beings, and thinks of the earthly king as closely akin to the gods, it would be natural to expect that the idea would be developed of a sacred marriage (*hieros gamos*) which was enacted every year and in which the king as representing the god might play the prominent role. According to T. H. Robinson, "Of the two main elements in the myth, the marriage and the death of the god, the former is that which was the more repugnant to the normal Israelite moral sense"; and he goes on at once to say "If it ever existed — as we suppose it may have done — its traces have been carefully eliminated."[45] Oesterley, with whom Robinson often collaborated, finds a trace of it in the "booths" which the Israelites dwelt in during the Feast of Tabernacles. He considers it possible that we have in Psalm 18:11, "His pavilion round about him were dark waters and thick clouds of the sky" and in Isaiah 4:6, "And there shall be a tabernacle for a shadow in the day time from the heat, and for a place of refuge and for a covert from storm and from rain," references to a "booth" or tent set on a roof, which may have been derived from one feature of the festival.[46] He refers also to the Song of Solomon as interpreted by T. J. Meek and to Hosea's marriage. Haldar thinks that in the "tent" (*qubbah*) referred to in Numbers 25:8 there may be a reference to this "vaulted tent."[47] If so the act performed there, whether it be regarded as merely a sin of passion or as a cultic rite of some kind, was promptly and severely punished; and the "yoking" of themselves with the Midianites is represented as a most grievous apostasy of Israel which required and received condign punishment.

It is to be recognized, of course, that in the Old Testament the relation between God and Israel is sometimes described under the figure of the most intimate and personal relationship known to man, marriage. We meet it especially in Hosea 1-3, also Isaiah 50:1; 54:1-9; Jeremiah 2:2f.; Ezekiel 16:8, 20. Sin against this relationship is defined as "adultery" (Isa. 57:3; Jer. 3:9; Hos. 2:4) and "fornication" (Exod. 34:16; Lev. 17:7; Deut. 31:16) with especial reference to the worship of false gods, a worship which often led to and sometimes involved or required orgiastic rites. That in the Old Testament the figure of marriage is used of a spiritual and not a physical relationship, is made clear by the rigid prohibition of idolatry (the God of Israel is a spirit and has no bodily form), by the lofty standards of morality and the exclusion of anything sensual from Israel's worship.[48] It is especially to be noted that the New Testament used the same figure to describe the mystical and spiritual relationship between Christ and the Church (Eph. 5:25-33; Rev. 21:9; John 3:29f.). Naturally, then, the Bible used the word "son" to describe the relation between Israel and God (Exod. 4:22; Hos. 11:1).

THE DIVINE KINGSHIP

A further important feature in the pattern as outlined by Professor Hooke is the divine kingship. It is held that not only was the king deified after his death, but that he was regarded as a divine being, whose birth was the result of a sacred marriage, and whose enthronement was celebrated annually at the great *Akitu* feast in the spring of the year. We have long been familiar with the fact that it was regarded as the duty of the legitimate king of Babylon to "grasp the hand of Marduk" on this solemn occasion. Johnson points out that Gunkel more than fifty years ago contended that Psalms 47, 93, and 95-100 are "Enthronement Psalms,"[49] and gave them an eschatological significance. More recently Mowinckel and Widengren have developed this theory. Johnson points out that now by advocates of this theory "a grand total of over forty psalms" are explained as cultic psalms.[50]

The theory starts out, as Johnson tells us, with the phrase which appears in five of these psalms, "the Lord reigneth" (47:8; 93:1; 96:10; 97:1; 99:1). It is argued that the words YHWH *malak* should be rendered "The Lord has become king," and hence must refer to an annual enthronement of Jehovah as king of Israel.[51] There are several objections to this view.

(a) The Hebrew perfect tense primarily denotes completed action and may represent the action as completed in past, present, or future time. Hence, YHWH *malak* might be rendered "was king, or reigned," "has become and so *is* king, i.e., reigns," or "will (certainly) be king, i.e., will reign."

(b) The word in question (*mlk*) was pointed by the Massoretes as a verb. It might equally well be pointed as the noun "king" (*melek*). So pointed we have in YHWH *melek* a nominal sentence, which would most naturally be rendered "the Lord (is) king." (Cf. Psalm 47:2, 8; 98:6, where the word is pointed as a noun.) Consequently, the context must decide the meaning to be attached to the phrase.

(c) In Psalm 93:2 we read "thy throne is established of old (literally, from then), from everlasting art thou." Psalm 95:8-11 carries Jehovah's dealings with Israel back to the time of the exodus. Psalm 96:5 declares that "Jehovah made the heavens" and verse 13 speaks of a coming judgment of the nations. Eternity is a predicate of the divine nature (Gen. 21:33; Deut. 32:40), it is affirmed of God's covenant (Gen. 9:16), of his laws (Exod. 29:28), of his promises (2 Sam. 7:13, 16, 25), of his relations to his people, of the Messiah (Ps. 110:4; 45:6; Isa. 9:6). Where is there the slightest evidence that this kingship of the eternal God over Israel has to be renewed every year?

Support for the theory of a divine kingship in Israel is claimed in such expressions as, "But thou art he that took me out of the womb: thou didst make me hope when I was upon my mother's breasts. I was cast upon thee from the womb: thou art my God from my mother's belly" (Ps. 22:9f.; cf. Isa. 44:2; 49:1, 5), "of the fruit of thy body I will set upon thy throne" (Ps. 132:11).[52] But such passages as these are to be compared with Jeremiah 1:5, "Before I formed thee in the belly I knew thee; and before thou camest forth out of the womb I sanctified thee, a prophet unto the nations have I ordained thee." This latter passage does not claim divine sonship for the prophet Jeremiah. It does affirm God's sovereign control over his entire being, with a view to preparing him to be a spokesman for God. And the same applies to the other passages quoted or referred to. Except where they are Messianic, as in Isaiah 49:5ff.; Psalm 2:7; 110, they merely describe God's special providential control and fatherly relationship as it concerns Israel and her kings. All life comes from the Creator-God (Gen. 1:27; 2:7; 18:10, etc.).

The sonship of the king does not differ essentially from that of the commoner (Exod. 4:22f.; cf. vs. 11). In dealing with such passages as Ezekiel 28:11ff. and Isaiah 14:4ff., it is to be remembered that it is the arrogant pride, even amounting to self-deification, of the kings of Tyre and of Babylon which is satirized and rebuked in these passages, even as the plagues of the Exodus period were a rebuke to Pharaoh (Exod. 9:16). David, in his prayer of praise after Nathan brought him the great Messianic promise (2 Sam. 7), and Solomon, in his prayer at the dedication of the temple (1 Kings 8), show an entirely different spirit, a realizing sense of the vast difference between the God of Israel and their unworthy selves.

The claim of the divine kingship school that in Israel the king must have been regarded as divine has been vigorously attacked by Martin Noth. He directs special attention to the very significant fact that in the time of the patriarchs and for centuries thereafter Israel had no king.[53] If the king played such an important role in the religious and secular life of the people, it would be only natural to expect that the kingship would go back in Israel, as in other nations, even in many small city states, to a remote antiquity. But there is no hint of this in the Old Testament and furthermore we find that in the kingdom age, kings were rebuked for performing priestly functions, the conspicuous example of this being Uzziah.

In a paper which he read before the Oriental Society of the University of Manchester· (1954) entitled "Myth and Ritual Reconsidered" and published in his collection of essays entitled *The Siege Perilous* (1956), Hooke replied to criticisms of the Myth and Ritual school by Henri Frankfort. As against Frankfort he insists that the claim, "based on Frazer, that differences are specific and similarities generic," is justified from the point of view "both of logic and of scientific method"; and while admitting that the words "pattern" and "patternism" may be applied too rigidly and that there are marked differences between the course of development in Babylonia and in Egypt, he nevertheless defends in general his position that the features of the pattern indicated above were characteristic of the religion of the Canaanites and can be traced to some extent in the Old Testament. He is especially insistent on the importance of the "sacred marriage" (*hieros gamos*) as a magical ritual "intended to promote all the powers of fertility in man, in beast, and soil" and connects it with sacred prostitution which "is intended to extend and multiply the potency belonging to the sacred marriage." He admits that "it is naturally repugnant to most people to entertain the suggestion that Jahveh could ever have been thought of as possessing a female consort like all the Baals of Canaan." But he declares, "I am not afraid of the idea myself"; and he reaches this conclusion:

When the prophets of the eighth and succeeding centuries appeared on the scene, challenging the whole established order of the cult as unworthy of the God they had encountered, and transforming the elements of the ritual pattern, the ritual combat, the sacred marriage, and other familiar features of the cult into images of a divine reality, the triumph of Jahveh over the powers of evil, Jahveh's betrothal of Israel to himself, and the shining figure of a Messianic king, they rightly claimed to be, not innovators, but in the great tradition that went back to Moses and Abraham. I feel that I ought to apologize for being so personal, but what I have now said represents the "reconsidered element" in my title.[54]

Elsewhere he tells us:

It is noteworthy that in the only great New Testament Apocalyptic book all the vital images characteristic of this stage of religious development — creation, kingship, the sacrificial victim, the dragon-combat, the sacred marriage — appear transformed, glorious and eternal.[55]

To those who share with the present writer the "natural repugnance" to the finding of gross polytheism in the early religion of Israel, this attempt to sanctify and even glorify this abomination by making it the source of the mystical union of the Lamb and his Bride will be even more repugnant. The eighth century prophets did not represent themselves as innovators. That is true. But it is even more true that they represented themselves as calling the people back to the true religion of Israel, the faith of Abraham, the law of Moses, with which these Canaanite abominations had nothing in common, and from which the call of Abraham to depart from home and kindred was clearly intended to separate him and his descendants.

A significant and striking development in the recent study of the psalms is to be found in the tendency in certain critical circles, notably the Scandinavian school, to date the psalms early. Thus Engnell has made the following remarkable statement: "Speaking candidly, there is merely one psalm in the whole Psalter of which I am quite convinced that it is post-exilic: No. 137."[56] And he adds: "And as far as I can ascertain, no other psalm is comparable with it in contents and style. Should this be a mere coincidence?" This statement would probably be regarded as extreme by most critical scholars. But it is noteworthy in view of the fact that the dictum of Wellhausen has so long held sway, according to which the question is not whether there are any post-exilic psalms, but whether any are pre-exilic. And North points out that Gunkel, the father of form criticism, claimed that "with the obvious exception of the royal psalms and those which were thought to contain allusions to a reigning king," the contents of the Psalter was for the most part to be assigned "to the sixth and fifth centuries B.C."[57]

THE SACRED DANCE

To the features of the religious and cultic pattern which we have examined Professor Oesterley would add the sacred dance. He tells us that the feast of the passover was originally "a nomadic Moon-Festival," that the word passover, i.e., *pesach* means "to dance with a limp," and that one of the peculiarities of this feast was a "special ritual dance."[58] He passes over as unworthy of notice the explanation of the name "passover" which is given in Exodus.[59] He tells us further that the "earliest form" of this festival known to us contained the following features: the sacrifice of an animal of the flocks or herds, the smearing of its blood at the entrances of the tents, a sacrificial meal, and a sacred dance. He tells us that, according to "a large number of authorities," the sacrifice was a fertility rite to insure the "increase of the flocks and herds," that the smearing of the blood was a "prophylactic" against evil spirits, that the meal was one by which "union with the deity was effected," and that the dance was an "act of homage in honor of the deity."

This is an instructive example of the method which is often followed by students of comparative religion in dealing with the express and explicit statements of Scripture. It is so obvious that it reads out of the biblical narrative what is there and reads into it what is not there, that it does not deserve serious consideration. The account of the passover which is given in Exodus says not a word about a dance. The idea of a "limping dance" is taken from the fact that there is a Hebrew verb *pasach* meaning to "limp" which may or may not be identical with the word used in the account of the passover.[60] But the obvious fact is that according to the account in Exodus the word is used, not of a dance performed by the people but of the "passing over" of the tents of the Israelites by the Angel of Death. How this act of the Angel is to be made the basis of a ritual dance of the people, is hard to understand. Professor Oesterley holds that these rites go back to an "immemorial antiquity." This means that since they go back allegedly to prehistorical times, their origin is largely if not wholly a matter of speculation. But according to the Bible, the passover was connected with a definite historical event, the nature of which is clearly stated. But since the biblical explanation of the historical event does not fit into an evolutionary scheme, an explanation is sought in the dim vistas of prehistory.

An inevitable result of these attempts to find traces of the pattern in the Old Testament is that it becomes to a striking degree a quest of the inobvious and a misinterpretation of the obvious. To take a recent example, when we read in the account of Elijah's conflict with the prophets of Baal at Mount Carmel, that he ordered four jars to be filled with water three times and poured over the sacrifice, so that the trench was filled with water (1 Kings 18:33ff.), the obvious explanation is that Elijah wanted to make it unmistakably clear that there was no possibility of fraud, that the altar and everything on and about it was so completely water-soaked that by no natural means could it be set ablaze. Yet the explanation given by some modern scholars is that the pouring of water on the sacrifice was "a thaumaturgical action to compel the coming of rain."[61] This is not only an inobvious explanation. It faces two difficulties. If this was thaumaturgy or sympathetic magic, why had not the prophets of Baal who fully believed in the efficacy of such practices already resorted to it during the many hours of their fruitless, frantic supplications, and before Elijah did? It is also to be noted that the answer to Elijah's action and prayer was not the coming of rain, but of fire from heaven which consumed the offering and was accepted by the people as indisputable evidence that Jehovah the God of their fathers, had heard and answered the prayer of Elijah. The rain came later and it came in answer to Elijah's prayer after the victory and vindication of God's prophet was already complete.

COMPARISON BRINGS OUT CONTRAST

The mythological texts of Ugarit give the clearest illustrations of the nature of Canaanite religion. They throw a lurid light on its "abominations." They show us Oriental polytheism at its worst. In them we see clearly that the gods of the Canaanites were only magnified men. "They that make them are like unto them," the psalmist declares. But even this says too much. For a marked feature of this cult is that the dividing line between man and beast is largely broken down. Not merely is the supreme god called Tor-el, the "bull-god," but he is represented as having intercourse with a heifer and begetting a "son" of her.[62] In one of the texts "he-lamb gods," "ewe-lamb goddesses," "bull-gods" and "cow-goddesses," "throne-gods" and "chair-goddesses" are referred to.[63] The god, Aliyan Baal, has intercourse with his "sister" who is called "the virgin Anat."[64] Anat is represented as frightfully bloodthirsty:

> Much she fights and looks,
> Battles and views.
> 'Anat gluts her liver with laughter;
> Her heart is filled with joy.
> 'Anat's liver exults.
> Her knees she plunges in the blood of soldiery,
> thighs in the gore of troops.
> The Virgin . . . Anat washes her hands,
> The Sister-in-law of nations her fingers;
> She washes her hands in the blood of soldiery
> Her fingers in the gore of troops.[65]

One of the main themes of these religious texts is the need of a house or temple for Aliyan Baal, the vegetation god.[66] His sister Anat is very insistent. Anticipating that the High God, Tor-El, may not be ready to grant this, she says,

> "Tor-'Il, my father, will reconsider,
> Reconsider for my sake and his
> (Lest I) trample him like a lamb to the earth,
> (Make) his grey hair (run) with blood,
> The grey of his beard with gore,
> *Unless* a house be given to Baal like the gods
> (Yea a court) like the sons of Asherah."[67]

In *Baal and Anath*, El, the supreme god, is represented as mourning over the death of Baal with the same irrational, violent grief as would any pagan man or woman who sorrows "without hope." He sits on the earth, pours dust on his head, gashes his cheeks, chin, arms, chest, back, and cries "Baal's dead! — What becomes of the people? Dagon's son — What of the masses? After Baal I'll descend into earth."[68] This illustrates how thoroughly man-made the religion of Ugarit was.

These are samples of the religion and ethics of the Ras Shamra texts. There is so much that is nasty and disgusting in them that the subject becomes a painful one. As Paul, who knew the depravity of the Greco-Roman world and described it so clearly and yet so briefly in Romans 1 has reminded us, "Professing themselves to be wise, they became fools, and changed the glory of the uncorruptible God into an image made like to corruptible man, and to birds, and four-footed beasts, and creeping things." Since we are being told so insistently, that the religion of Israel stands in close genetic relation to the religion of the Canaanites, it is important for us to recognize clearly the tremendous differences, and also the fact that for Israel the result of contact with these religions was always corrupting and defiling. It meant the falling away from the worship of the God of Israel to the abominations of a degrading and sensual polytheism.

Archaeological research has thrown a lurid light upon the religion of the Canaanites. The mythological poems from Ras Shamra have shown us a polytheism which was, sensuous, licentious, and vile. The gods and goddesses of Ugarit, like the gods of Greece and Rome are magnified human beings who have all the parts and passions of men. Archaeology has given us a ghastly picture of Canaanite religion and fully confirmed the statements of the Old Testament regarding it. Archaeologists and students of comparative religion may strive to excuse these "abominations." But they do not succeed very well. To excuse the fact that in the Ugaritic myth of Baal and Anat Baal is described as copulating with a heifer, and that there are bull-gods and cow-goddesses, it is not sufficient to say that beastiality was not a crime in Ugarit, and consequently gave no offense to the people even when it appeared in their religious myths and legends. It is easy to shrug off evil practices by saying, "When in Rome, do as the Romans do," but that does not cancel out the fact that what the Romans do is a clear indication of the state and level of their culture and morals.[69] That fertility cults were very common in the ancient Orient is undoubtedly true. It may also be admitted that the orgiastic rites which were connected with the worship of Baal and Istar, while pandering to and expressive of the carnal appetites of man, also had a religious side and were regarded as religious acts. But this does not help matters. It makes it all the worse.

Zedeq. We have seen that personification is one of the beautiful figures of speech which we find in the Bible, especially in poetry. A striking example is Psalm 85 in which the "Christian virtues," as we might call them, are brought together and personified: mercy, truth, righteousness, peace (vss. 10-13). Yet Widengren finds in Zedeq (righteousness) "an old Canaanite deity" whom he further describes as "an independent deity, though belonging to Jahve's retinue and subordinate to him."[70] It is safe to say that were it not for the emphasis now placed on comparative religion and the quest of the primitive, such literal and prosaic treatment of beautiful literary tropes would be regarded as betraying a sad lack of appreciation of the poetry of the Bible.

In the Ras Shamra tablets mention is made of two deities, or as some hold a single deity with a double name; Shalem and Shahar, are (is) mentioned a few times. There is a word in Hebrew (*shachar*) which means "dawn." It occurs usually in the literal sense. *Shalem* appears twice (Gen. 14:18; Ps. 76:2) apparently as an abbreviation of Jerusalem. There is no real warrant for taking either name as the name of a god. Yet Engnell refers with apparent approval to the fact that Widengren in his elaborate study of Psalm 110 argues that "the Jerusalem king, a fruit of the *hieros gamos* of Shalem and Shahar, appears as *tal* 'the dew' which is evidently a personification of the 'vegetation deity,' "[71] such as Aliyan Baal or Tammuz, an amazing inference with no foundation in fact!

Isaiah 7:14, "Behold a virgin shall bear a son." In one of the Ugaritic poems, which has been called by Gordon, "The Wedding of Nikkal and the Moon," we read the following:

> A virg[in] will give birth
> [To the K]trt
> Daughters of *shouting*
> [swallows].
> Lo a maid will bear a s[on].[72]

The passage is difficult because the tablet is defective. The word rendered virgin is the Hebrew *bethulah*. The rendering "to the Ktrt, daughters of shouting [swallows]" is doubtful here but is supported by lines 15f. and 41f. where they are described as "goddesses, daughters of the *New Moon*."[73] The poem closes with a reference to some one (meaning uncertain) who is "the fairest, the youngest of the Ktrt." In the line rendered "Lo a maid will bear a son," the word maid (*glmt*) is apparently the same etymologically as the word rendered "virgin" (*'almah*) in Isaiah 7:14. Since the end of the line is mutilated, it is not clear whether we should read son or sons, daughter or daughters. The parallelism would suggest that the word would be plural. As to this passage Engnell says: "Virolleaud himself has already pointed out the parallel with the Immanuel prophecy. And I think Gaster hardly exaggerates when he says that Isaiah 7:14 is 'shown thus to be a quotation.' "[74] An amazing statement!

In this connection we call attention to a passage which Goetze has called "Peace on Earth."[75] It begins with the words: "Message of Aliyn Ba'al, Word of Aliy *qrdm*." The message follows.

Remove war from the earth.
Do away with passion.
Pour out peace over the earth,
Loving consideration over the fields.[76]

Goetze tells us: "It is illuminating to find in the Ugaritic epics (our texts were written about 1400 B.C.) a passage which seems to be related to the verse in Luke." He tells us further, "Its similarity with the Christmas message is striking. It is hardly accidental. Luke (or his source) drew on an old formula, which as far as I know, has not yet been found in Jewish literature, but which no doubt developed from the formula encountered in the epic literature of the Ugaritians."[77]

As to this claim we note first that the translation is by no means certain. Gordon's rendering, made five years later is:

Put *bread* in the earth
Place *mandrakes* in the dust
Pour a peace offering in the midst of the earth
A *libation* in the midst of the fields![78]

The words placed in italics Gordon regarded as of uncertain meaning. A comparison with Goetze's rendering will indicate how uncertain the rendering is. Then we note that the message is sent to the virgin Anath who is one of the most bloodthirsty of the members of the Ugaritic pantheon, as is shown in the quotations given above. Yet Goetze finds here the source of the Christmas message which he tells us "has not yet been found in Jewish literature." However we believe that our readers will have no difficulty in finding the source of Luke's Christmas message, not in the epic literature of the Ugaritians, but in the glorious Messianic promises in the Old Testament, so many of which are found in the Book of Isaiah (e.g., Isa. 7:14; 9:6f.; 11:1-9).

It is quite true that there are and must be certain resemblances between the language of adoration and supplication in all religions. We read that the prophets of Baal at Mount Carmel "called on the name of Baal from morning even until noon saying, "O Baal, hear us"; and we read that Elijah said, "Hear me, O Lord, hear me," — the same words. But in the one case no answer came, though they cried from morning until the time for the evening sacrifice. In the other case, there was an immediate answer. The fire of the Lord fell; and when the people saw it they cried, "The Lord, he is the God, the Lord, he is the God."

It is to be recognized that we find at times striking parallels between the Old Testament and the other religions of the ancient Near East. The myth of the descent of Ishtar into the lower world has been known for many years. Classical scholars know it as the story of Persephone. It is a familiar form of the seasonal myth of the dying and arising god. In it Ishtar apparently either swoons or dies and is restored to life and returns to the world of the living. Recently the

Sumerian form of the myth has been discovered. According to it Inanna, the Sumerian equivalent of Ishtar, is struck dead when the eyes of the seven Anunnaki are fastened on her, her dead body is impaled on a stake, and remains there for three days and three nights. Then she is restored to life and returned to the upper world. How is this brought about? After the three days and nights Inanna's messenger Ninshubar, as previously instructed by Inanna, makes frantic efforts to have her restored to life, and finally succeeds. Father Enki, the great god, we read, "brought forth dirt from his finger nails" (if the rendering of the parallel line *"red-painted* fingernails" is correct, it has quite a modern sound) and fashioned two creatures to which he entrusted the "food of life" and "the water of life" with instructions to proceed to the nether world and sprinkle them sixty times upon Inanna's impaled corpse.[79] This they did and Inanna revived and was returned to the upper world. We are naturally reminded of the three days and three nights spent by Jonah in the belly of the great fish and by Jesus in the tomb. But where is there the slightest connection between them? There is none, absolutely none.

Attention has been directed by Bentzen and others to this polytheistic blessing:

> Ea rejoice over thee,
> Damkina, the queen of the ocean, illumine thee by her face,
> Marduk, the prince of the gods, raise up thy head.[80]

It is the language of religious devotion. It resembles the Priestly Blessing of Numbers 6 rather closely in form. The difference, the all important difference, is that, like the cry, "O Baal, hear us," it was addressed to gods who were no gods and could neither hear nor answer.

Genesis 14:14: *Three hundred and eighteen trained men.* It is not difficult to find rather startling parallels or correspondences both in history and in literature. But we need to be on our guard against attaching any real significance to them. C. H. Gordon has pointed out that the number 318 used of Abram's trained servants is "strikingly paralleled" by the mention in the Amarna Letters of the 317 girls who accompanied Giluhepa, the Mitanni princess, on her journey to Egypt to marry Amenophis III. He points out that when Giluhepa herself is included the number becomes 318 and he draws the inference: "Thus 318 looks like a conventional number for a large group (be it a company of soldiers or a bevy of maidens) in a milieu whence the Mitanni princess and the Hebrew Patriarch hailed."[81] On the other hand Winckler in working out his astral myth theory explained the 318 as the days of the year when the moon is not visible.[82]

Daniel. In two passages in Ezekiel a Daniel is mentioned. In the one he is grouped with Noah and Job as a man conspicuous for righteousness (14:14, 20). In the other he is mentioned as one who is preeminent for wisdom, "Behold thou art wiser than Daniel; there is no secret that they can hide from thee" (28:3). While exception has been taken by some scholars, the most common view has been that the Daniel here referred to is the great statesman of the time of the captivity who was in high favor with Nebuchadnezzar and with Darius the Mede. One of the first tablets from Ras Shamra to be published (1932) tells the story or myth of a *Dn'il* (Daniel) who is childless and prays for a son.[83] His prayer is granted. But when his son *Aqht* grows up the goddess Anath destroys him because he refused to give her his bow. Daniel recovers his body from the craw of the vulture that has devoured it and buries it. He mourns for Aqhat seven years. Whether Aqhat is finally restored to him or replaced by another son can only be guessed, since the rest of the tablet is mutilated and it is uncertain whether this tablet is part of a series. The title of the poem seems to have been simply, "Pertaining to Aqhat"; and Ginsberg points out that "closer study reveals that the text really tells about Daniel only what concerns Aqhat."[84] Yet ever since the tablet was published the claim has been made, sometimes very positively, that it is this Daniel who is referred to by the prophet Ezekiel. This claim is based chiefly on the similarity of the name and on a single brief passage in the poem which reads as follows: "Straightway Daniel the Rapha-man, Forthwith *Ghazir* the Harnamiyy-man, is upright, sitting before the gate, beneath a mighty tree on the threshing floor, judging the cause of the widow, adjudicating the case of the fatherless."[85] This is certainly very meager evidence on which to base a theory that Ezekiel is here referring to this legendary figure of Ugaritic lore.

Woman at Window. The allegorizings of Origen, with his three senses of Scripture, are often held up to ridicule today; and we are told that the historico-grammatical method of interpretation is alone entitled to be called "scientific." But we are now confronted with a determined effort to mythologize and culticize the Old Testament which bids fair to outdo Origen and all the allegorizers of the past.

For example, we have in the Old Testament three instances of a woman looking out of a window: (1) In Judges 5:28, the mother of Sisera is pictured as looking out of the window, impatient for the return of her warrior son, and her words illustrate the utter confidence in victory with which Sisera met the tribal levies of Deborah and Barak. (2) In 2 Samuel 6:16, Michal looks out of the window as David is bringing up the ark to Jerusalem; and she despises him for his undignified conduct and tells him so. (3) 2 Kings 9:30ff. describes the death of Jezebel. That old tigress wife of Ahab, tracked to her lair, is determined to die like a queen, to die as becomes a daughter of the king of Tyre and a worshipper of the Tyrian Baal. So we read, "She painted her face, and tired her head, and looked out at a window," from the second floor of the palace where the state apartments would probably be; and from there her eunuchs threw her down to the pavement of the court and Jehu's horse-hoofs trampled her to death.

All three stories seem perfectly true to life and to the lives of the persons described; and there is nothing to suggest a legend or myth. Yet Haldar, of the Scandinavian school finds in all three stories examples of "the goddess at the window," thus assigning cultic or mythological significance to each of them.[86] There is not the slightest warrant for such allegorizings. It is far more probable that the woman at the window who is often represented in Assyrian art (e.g., on the recently discovered Nimrud ivories) is as Mallowan asserts simply a courtesan, not a goddess at all.[87]

Drunkenness. In Isaiah 51:17f. the prophet refers to Jerusalem as a woman in a drunken stupor from having drunk the cup of fury at the hand of the Lord. Then he says of her, "There is none to guide her among all the sons whom she hath brought forth; neither is there any that taketh her by the hand of all the sons that she hath brought up." But these words may suggest weakness rather than drunkenness. For it is not certain that the figure of verse 17 continues in verse 18. In the "Tale of Aqhat" which begins with Daniel's desire for a son, there is a description (Col. 1) of the many services which a son would normally render a father and of which Daniel is deprived because of his childless state. One of these is described in the words: "Who takes him by the hand when he is drunk, carries him when he is sated with wine." This is another of the parallels between the Old Testament and the Ras Shamra poems which are cited by scholars. There is a slight resemblance we must admit. But to appeal to such a correspondence as proof of dependence of Isaiah on the Ras Shamra mythological poetry would certainly be very forced to say the least.[88]

DISTINCTIVE FEATURES

We turn from a consideration of the resemblances which are sought so diligently and pointed to with such evident satisfaction by the students of comparative religion, to direct attention once more to the differences, the distinctive features which characterize the religion of the Old Testament. It is not necessary, we believe, in view of all that has been already said, to discuss this subject in further detail. It will suffice to direct attention to nine features of this religion which set it apart from the religions of the peoples with which Israel was more or less closely related or associated. They are these:

I. The religion of Israel is *historical* and *supernatural*. This is stated impressively in the Preface of the Decalogue in these majestic words: "I am the Lord your God, which have brought you out of the land of Egypt, out of the house of bondage" (Exod. 20:1; Deut. 5:6). The God who declares his will to Israel and requires their worship is the God of their fathers who has accredited himself to them by a mighty deliverance, a series of mighty acts which are described in the first fourteen chapters of the Book of Exodus. This deliverance is both historical and supernatural.. "For a thing is no less historical because it is supernatural; the supernatural is the highest history."[89] This history is unparalleled and amazing, seemingly incredible, and yet perfectly true. Two proofs of this are especially stressed. The people have heard the voice of the living God speaking to them out of the midst of the fire and lived; and they have experienced the taking of a nation from the midst of another nation by a mighty hand and by a stretched out arm and by great terrors (Deut. 4:33f.). This deliverance is the fulfilment of a covenant made with their fathers, with Abraham, Isaac, and Jacob (Exod. 6:4), and which has now been fulfilled; and it is now proposed by God to their descendants (Exod. 19:5f.) and which on being accepted by Israel (Exod. 19:5f.) will make them to be a peculiar people, the people of the God of Israel.

II. The religion of the Old Testament is *monotheistic* and *monergistic*. This is made clear in the first verse of Genesis: "In the beginning God created the heaven and the earth." It is stated in the First Commandment of the Decalogue (Exod. 20:3). It appears in the Shema (Deut. 6:4). It appears again and again in the Law and the Prophets and the Psalms. Jehovah is the only God, the only object of worship for Israel. Polytheism is a prominent feature of the worship of all of Israel's neighbors. The heathen nations had many gods. Israel is to know and worship only him who is the true God and the living God and an everlasting king (Jer. 10:10).

III. The religion of the Old Testament is *spiritual*. The Second Commandment forbids the making of any image or likeness of God. Moses carefully reminded the Israelites that in the great theophany at Sinai, they saw no image, they heard only a voice (Deut. 4:12, 15). The Old Testament scriptures not only denounce idolatry, they ridicule it (Isa. 44:10-20). The idols are man-made and so are man-like. They have eyes and ears and noses and hands and feet. But they are impotent. They can neither see nor hear nor smell nor walk. To worship them was idolatry, a turning away from the living God. Yet idolatry was the most prominent feature of the ethnic faiths. It usually assumed human form. They that made images were like unto them! These images were male and female, because the heathen worshiped gods and goddesses. Fertility rites were performed in their honor, which were both sensual and sexual, rites of which it is a shame even to speak. Such acts were forbidden and carefully guarded against in the religion of Israel.

IV. The religion of Israel is *reverential*. Its piety is a wonderful blending of fear and love. The God who manifests himself in such awful majesty on Mount Sinai that even Moses said, "I do exceedingly fear and quake" and who forbids the people even to touch the mountain lest they die (Exod. 19:13) is not to be maligned or lightly esteemed. His holy name is not to be misused. He is the One whose name is holy. He is infinitely exalted above his creatures. Yet he craves and claims their love. "Thou shalt love the Lord thy God with all thine heart and with all thy soul and with all thy might" is his demand (Deut. 5:6). The God who is "a consuming fire" (Deut. 4:24) desires and demands the filial love and devotion of his earthly children, of this people which he has so wonderfully blessed by delivering them from bitter bondage and made them free to serve him with their bodies and spirits which are his.

V. The religion of Israel had a holy day, a day of remembrance. Her week was patterned on the creative week of Genesis 1. Six days were for labor and the seventh was to be a holy resting from labor, a day on which the Israelite was to remember, to meditate upon the wonderful works of his Creator and all the blessings which he had received from his mighty and gracious hand. The man who thus kept the sabbath holy could not but be a supernaturalist, could not fail to see the hand of God in all the experiences of his daily walk. "Remember the sabbath day to keep it holy" was the great test and proof of Israel's piety. And this command is the fitting conclusion of those commands which make up the believer's duty to his God.[90]

VI. The six commandments which follow deal with the relation of the Israelite to his fellowmen, and especially to his fellow Israelite. It is more than the golden rule; it is the rule of love, "Thou shalt love thy neighbor as thyself" (Lev. 19:18). All the sinful practices of the Egyptians which they know through their bondage there, and all the abominations practiced by the Canaanites whose land they are to inherit are to be shunned and abhorred (Lev. 18:3). They are to be a holy nation (Lev. 19:2). So the religion is to be a religion of holiness. Its moral standards are high. The God of Israel is a holy God. He is a righteous God. His laws are right and just. He is the defender of the weak, the poor, the widow, the orphan. Dishonesty, extortion, cruelty are denounced as sins against this God who is both just and loving and merciful. He is "The Lord, the Lord God, merciful and gracious, longsuffering and abundant in goodness and truth, keeping mercy for thousands, forgiving iniquity and transgression and sin and that will by no means clear the guilty; visiting the iniquity of the fathers upon the children, unto the third and to the fourth generation" (Exod. 34:6f.). The gods of the nations are not only man-made; they have the characteristics of man, fallen man, both evil and good. So their worship was not elevating but corrupting. "Thou thoughtest that I was altogether such an one as thyself" (Ps. 50:21) is the Lord's condemnation of the wicked man. It is also the characterization and condemnation of the ethnic faiths. The myths of Ugarit show that the gods of the Canaanites were but magnified men with all the appetites, passions and lusts of men. They set their worshippers an unworthy and evil example of living.[91]

VII. The religion of the Old Testament is *miraculous* and *redemptive*. It records and rejoices in the mighty acts of God. The God of Israel showed his mighty power in his deliverance of his people from the bondage of Egypt. Nothing is too hard for Israel's God. The giving of a son to aged and barren Sarah (Gen. 18:14), the feeding of the famished hosts of Israel (Num. 11:22), the destroying of wicked and rebellious Jerusalem (Jer. 32:27f.), are all proofs of his sovereign power. The idol gods are powerless before him. This is shown most impressively in Elijah's contest with the prophets of Baal at Carmel (1 Kings 18). It is he who alone doeth great wonders (Ps. 136:4). Jesus' reply to the trick-question of the Sadducees regarding the resurrection is no less applicable to the modern skeptical critic: "Do ye not therefore err because ye know not the scriptures, neither the power of God?" (Mark 12:24). They did not really know the scriptures because they did not recognize in them that power of God which pervaded them and is illustrated by the record of the mighty acts of God which is their constant theme. As to the gods of the heathen, Jeremiah admonishes his people: "Be not afraid of them; for they cannot do evil, neither is it in them to do good" (10:5). But the God of Israel is the refuge and strength of his people, "a very present help in trouble" (Ps. 46:1). The mighty acts of God were a stumbling block to unbelieving Israelites as they are to modern skeptics (Ps. 78:18-20). But to the Bible believer this God "who alone doeth great wonders" is he "whose mercy endureth for ever" (Ps. 136:4).[92]

VIII. The religion of the Old Testament is *prophetic* and *messianic*. More than a quarter of the Old Testament is given to the utterances of the prophets. They were great preachers of righteousness and exerted a powerful influence on the people of their own day and age. But they often spoke of things to come; and the fulfilment of many of their predictions are recorded in the Scriptures. The most impressive examples come to us from the lips of Jesus himself. He began his public ministry by quoting from Isaiah 61:1f. and after his resurrection he rebuked the two disciples on the way to Emmaus for being "slow of heart to believe all that the prophets have spoken"; and "beginning at Moses and all the prophets he expounded unto them in all the scriptures the things concerning himself" (Luke 24:24-27). Prophecy and its fulfilment has always been regarded as a strong link binding the two Testaments together.[93] Yet an eminent Old Testament scholar, Walther Eichrodt, in dealing with the question of "prediction and fulfilment" has warned his readers that "Many well-trodden ways to an answer to this question have been shown to be no longer open to us; and the tendency is spreading to regard this point, which once provided men with an unshakable foundation, as the most brittle 'part of the relation between the Old and New Testaments."[94] It has become "brittle" in modern times only for those within the Christian Church who have accepted the teaching that biblical prophecy is not predictive, a theory which plays even greater havoc with the New Testament than it does with the Old. Eichrodt's own words are most significant. He calls attention to "the torso-like appearance of Judaism in separation from Christianity."[95] A torso is a mutilated body, headless, armless, legless. Such he tells us is Judaism, without its fulfilment in the Christ of the New Testament. The great and exceeding precious promises of the Old Testament have always been the joy and confidence of the Bible-believing Christian of every age, because they point forward to and have their fulfilment in the Christ of the New Testament.

IX. The religion of the Old Testament is a *special divine revelation*. This sets it apart from all the ethnic faiths. The psalmist praises the Lord because "he hath not dealt so with any nation: and as for his judgments they have not known them" (Ps. 147:20). Isaiah's counsel to Israel is this: "And when they shall say unto you, Seek unto them that have familiar spirits and unto wizards that peep and mutter: Should not a people seek unto their God: for the living to the dead? To the law and to the testimony: if they speak not according to this word, it is because there is no light in them" (8:19f.). Jeremiah brings this accusation against the people in the name of the Lord: "Be astonished, O ye heavens, at this, and be horribly afraid, be ye very desolate, saith the Lord. For my people have committed two evils; they have forsaken me, the fountain of living waters, and have hewed them out cisterns, broken cisterns, that can hold no water" (2:12f.). Hosea is very terse, but very impressive: "Ephraim is joined to idols: let him alone" (4:17); "The workman made it; therefore it is not God" (8:6). The idols are vanities: they can neither see nor hear, taste nor smell; they cannot talk nor walk. And they that make them are like unto them; so is everyone that trusteth in them (cf. Ps.. 115). Of the effect of idolatry on the image-worshipper Jeremiah tells us: "Every man is brutish in his knowledge: every founder is confounded by the graven image: for his molten image is falsehood, and there is no breath in them" (10:14). Such passages as these state clearly the attitude of Moses and the other inspired leaders of Israel toward the religions of their neighbors. Yet Eichrodt, speaking for many others and using italics for emphasis, tells us: "*No presentation of OT theology can properly be made without constant reference to its connection with the whole world of Near Eastern religion.*"[96] The best answer and the sufficient answer to this claim is this: one can search through the whole Bible only to find that there is no warrant for it in scripture, that on the contrary it runs counter to the clearest teachings of the Old Testament, as the above passages quoted from it are sufficient to prove. The teaching of the Bible from Genesis to Malachi is that Israel is to shun, to have no dealings with her heathen neighbors, particularly and especially in matters of religious worship, lest she be corrupted by them. An acceptance of or linkage with these "abominations", by which name the idolatry of these nations is described, is a sin against the Lord. And again and again, where it occurs it is visited with severe and condign punishment. The Old Testament emphasizes the utter difference between the religion of Israel and all the ethnic faiths, while the aim of many comparative religionists is to relate and link them by emphasizing and stressing superficial resemblances and minimizing or ignoring fundamental and essential differences. Eichrodt has himself given the needed rebuke to his own zeal for the study of comparative religion, when he tells his readers: "We cannot help being aware that the fact that Jesus and the whole New Testament make almost exclusive use of the Old Testament canon and thereby accord it a special significance for all their thinking is no superficial coincidence. The plain fact of the matter is that within these limits is to be found the major and most valuable part of those thoughts and ideas which gave the faith of Israel its character."[97] Surely the example of the New Testament writers and of Jesus himself should be normative for those who bear his name and follow his example! Of the danger in the appeal to comparative religion for the intrepreting of scripture it will suffice to give a single example. Eichrodt speaks of the "extravagant honorifics" heaped on the head of the king in Psalms 2, 45, 72, and 110, and says: "We are in fact confronted here with stylistic forms common to the East, associated with Babylon in particular, and belonging to the cult of the divinized monarch."[98] We need only to turn to Matt. 22:41-46 and to Hebrews 1 for a totally different interpretation of these "honorifics". There they are explained as referring to Israel's glorious Messianic king!

One of the clearest illustrations of the uniqueness and exclusiveness of the religion of Israel is given to us in the New Testament in the conduct of the apostle Peter. When in obedience to the thrice-repeated heavenly vision, he entered the house of Cornelius, where the friends of this believing Gentile were assembled to hear him, Peter at once said to his auditors, "Ye know how that it is an unlawful thing for a man that is a Jew to keep company, or come unto one of another nation, but God hath showed me that I should not call any man common or unclean" (Acts 10:28). Here Peter was speaking as a devout Jew, who had been taught to keep the law of Moses; and both the law and the prophets forbid and denounce such intercourse, especially in religious matters.

That there are such fundamental differences has been impressively stated by Dr. Warfield, when, after classifying all the "religions which men have made for themselves as corresponding to the three main varieties of the activities of the human mind, as prevailingly religions of the intellect, the emotions, or the active will," he goes on to say:

We say advisedly, all the religions which men have made for themselves. For there is an even more fundamental division among religions than that which is supplied by these varieties. This is the division between man-made and God-made religions. Beside the religions which man has made for himself, God has made a religion for man. We call this revealed religion; and the most fundamental division which separates between religions is that which divides revealed from unrevealed religions. [99]

Revealed religion is the religion which is set forth in the Bible. It is unique because it is "God-made," while all the ethnic religions are "man-made." And in the Old Testament these man-made religions only serve as a background, a foil which serves by contrast to exhibit and, if it were possible, to enhance its perfections. When the study of comparative religion is used for this purpose, it is of value because it serves to emphasize the desperate state of those who have only the light of nature to guide them into the truth, and to stress the vital importance of the missionary enterprise. But when the comparative religionist seeks to link up and associate the revealed religion of the Bible with the ethnic faiths and to make it one of them, he cuts the nerve of Christian missions by treating the religion of the Bible as if it were one of the many religions which man had made for himself.

These distinctive features of the Old Testament religion need to be recognized and emphasized by every student of the Bible for two reasons both of which are of great importance. The one is that they are under constant and vigorous attack today. The other and more basic reason is that it is only as they are recognized and stressed that the importance of the Old Testament for the New Testament Christian will be understood. For it was an Old Testament prophet who said, "The word of our God shall stand forever"; and a New Testament apostle who adds, "And this is the word which by the gospel is preached unto you."

CHAPTER VI

CHRONOLOGY

Attention has already been directed to the fact that the Bible is more concerned with genealogies and synchronisms than with era or period, datings.[1] For this reason the data which it supplies are, on the whole, meager and sometimes hard to interpret. It is, of course, true that chronology is the backbone of history. Without chronology history becomes decidedly invertebrate. But it is also true that within the limits of a broad outline of history there may be room for much indefiniteness as to detail.

A few examples will illustrate this rather obvious fact. There are very few long-period datings in the Old Testament: the 400 years of Genesis 15:13, the 430 years of Exodus 12:40, the 300 years of Judges 11:26, the 480 years of I Kings 6:1; cf. the 400 years of Acts 7:6, the 430 years of Galatians 3:17, the "about 450 years" of Acts 13:19. The fact that such period dates are so few makes them especially significant and important. It is also noteworthy that they all relate to some part of the period between the call of Abraham and the building of the Temple. Why this is so we do not know.

The dates in the life of Abraham are all simply biographical. He was 75 when he departed from Haran (Gen. 12:4), 86 when Ishmael was born, 100 when Isaac was born (21:5), 175 when he died (25:7). But how old he was when Amraphel invaded Palestine or in what year of Amraphel's reign in Shinar this took place or which king of what dynasty Amraphel was — as to these matters Scripture is silent. The biographical data given in 12:4; 21:5; 25:26; 47:9 enable us to estimate the length of the sojourn in Canaan as 215 years. But this total is nowhere to be found in the Bible.

The words "in the fourth generation" (Gen. 15:16) seem to indicate that a generation is to be reckoned as a hundred years (cf. Exod. 6:16-20). In Numbers 20:1 only the month is given, not the year. Hence it is a matter of some uncertainty whether the year is the third or the fortieth, i.e., whether "the thirty-seven years chasm," as it has been called, begins or ends with this verse. "And it came to pass in those days" (Judg. 19:1); "Now the days of David drew nigh that he should die" (I Kings 2:1); "in the year that king Uzziah died" (Isa. 6:1); "two years before the earthquake" (Amos 1:1) are decidedly indefinite. "In the reign of Artaxerxes, king of Persia"

(Ezra 7:7) is ambiguous to us because there were two kings of that name. The failure to give the name of his father may justify the inference that Ezra was written before there was a second Artaxerxes. But "Artaxerxes son of Ahasuerus [Xerxes]" would have removed all uncertainty.

Such facts as these indicate quite clearly that the Bible student should not as a rule concern himself overmuch with "times and seasons" (Acts 1:7). Yet in view of the importance frequently attached to such matters and especially because of the charges which are often made that the biblical chronology is at fault, it is necessary for us to study it carefully.

CREATION

Time as man knows it begins with Creation. The Creation of the universe had no human eyewitnesses. All our information regarding it must come, therefore, either from the correct reading of the Book of Nature or from Supernatural Revelation.

THE NATURAL ACCOUNT

We look first at the world of the astronomer. It is now three centuries and a half since the invention of the telescope. We have long been familiar with the fact that light travels at a speed of 186,000 miles a second and that it takes about eight minutes to cover the distance from sun to earth (c. 92,900,000 miles). This makes the speed of light a convenient unit in measuring time and distance. It is instructive to compare the discoveries made by means of the Mt. Wilson reflector telescope (100 inch), which was in 1928 the largest in the world, with the disclosures of the Mt. Palomar (200-inch) instrument which was completed in 1952.

In 1929 Eddington described the spiral nebula in Andromeda, as representing "more or less the limit of our exploration."[2] He stated that its light left the nebula "900,000 years ago." This meant that traveling at 186,000 miles a second or 5,800,000,000,000 miles a year, its light took nearly a million years to reach this planet. This is a truly enormous figure: and it was arrived at before the 200-inch Mt. Palomar instrument was available. We are now told that research has led "eventually to the great clusters of nebulae at the utmost limits of the 200-inch telescope — a span estimated at the almost inconceivable distance of 2,500,000,000 light-years, 600,000,000 times the distance to the nearest known star."[3] (the nearest star Proxima Centuri being 4.3 light-years or about 25,000,000 miles away.) This means that the 200-inch telescope, with double the diameter of the Mt. Wilson instrument has exceeded the range of the latter more than 2500 times, a perfectly fantastic figure. We are further told that it proves the Galactic nebula (Milky Way) in which our sun is only "an inconspicuous star" to be only one of a collection of perhaps 1,000,000,000 similar systems within the range of the Mt. Palomar instrument.[4] This would suggest that the extent of the discoverable universe is solely dependent upon the size of the instrument which the genius of man and his mechanical skill can produce.

As to the age of the universe, the three now widely held theories — the Steady State, the Big Bang, and the Oscillating — all require an immense or infinite amount of time. According to the first of them: the age of the universe is "infinite, but the age of each bit of matter in it is finite and is at any given time on the average just equal to 1/3 H, or 1,800,000,000 years,"[5] a statement which it requires an expert to interpret. The situation has recently been described as follows: "Thanks to astronomy, the enquiring spirit of man has at last discovered the true status of humanity in the Universe: a mere atom, but a thinking atom, situated on a microscopic planet, one of several revolving about a small and commonplace star, itself indistinguishable from a thousand others, in the heart of a galaxy which in turn is lost among the millions that populate the tiny corner of space that we have been able to explore."[5a]

The Sun. It is worthy of note that within the course of a decade, there has been a welcome change in the views of many astronomers. A generation ago the Tidal theory was widely held. According to it the earth was originally a part of the sun, the planetary system being formed from a mass of gaseous or liquid matter drawn forth and detached from the sun by a passing star. This theory which cannot be reconciled to the statements of the Bible, has now been replaced by the Protoplanet Theory of Kuiper according to which these planets "must have had the same chemical constitution as the original interstellar material . . . in the form of fine dust. The dust particles gradually settled toward the centre of the protoplanets forming solid spherical cores." The important point of Kuiper's theory is that "the formation of protoplanets took place in darkness, since the sun itself was not yet sufficiently condensed to emit any appreciable light. When, later on, the body of the sun contracted to almost its present size, and its surface temperature went up to several thousand degrees, it began to pour intensive radiation into the space around it."[5b] This closely resembles the biblical account in several important respects. If it were permissible to interpret the word "light" in Genesis 1:3 as referring to cosmic rays, the resemblance would be even more remarkable. The main difference would then be that between the fiat creation of Genesis which can dispense with time and the limitless time-claims of the evolutionary minded astronomer.

The Earth and Man. Having looked at the heavens we turn now to the earth and to man. About two centuries ago Buffon the celebrated French scientist estimated the age of the earth at 75,000 years. We are now told that it may be placed at 5,000,000,000.[6]

Man. The anthropologist has been competing with the geologist and the astronomer in making lavish claims as to the antiquity of the human race. Some years ago anthropologists dated Java-man 400,000 and Peking-man 1,000,000 years ago.[7] Now we are being told that the newly discovered Zinjanthropos (East Africa man) "has been in his rocky coffin for 1,750,000 years" and that thus "Genus Homo's history has been extended back about 1,200,000 years further than its previously known span."[8]

Space, time and process figure prominently in human affairs. But they have their limitations. Adding on ciphers to an already immense total does not really solve anything. The Mt. Palomar telescope has not succeeded any better than the Lick or the Mt. Wilson instrument in solving the riddle of the universe. It has, on the other hand, vastly complicated it. It has extended time and space both backward and forward to an inconceivable and almost infinite distance. But it has not discovered its boundaries, either the beginning or the ending. And the tragedy of it is that nowhere has it found God. Rather has it for many scientists removed him to such an infinite distance that he is tacitly and virtually even if not expressly excluded from the world which he has made. There are, of course, scientists like Cunningham Geikie who when speaking nearly a century ago of "the inconceivable remoteness of the creation of our earth" and of "periods vast beyond imagination" which must have elapsed since the first stages of the history of our earth was impelled to say of them that "they so vividly aid us to realize the greatness and glory of the Creator."[9] We are reminded of the words of Kepler, that in reading the book of the heavens, he was thinking God's thoughts after him. Surely the more vast the Creation the greater must be the Being who created it. Yet, apparently with very many students of Nature, the God of Nature is a negligible or even a minus quantity. Yet, while they can multiply ciphers in calculating the age of the cosmos, they cannot answer the question, however remote they may make it, how the cosmos came into being. They may describe the beginning of things as a "big bang," but what it was that banged or what caused the bang remains a mystery. Matter practically becomes eternal, unless its Creator is recognized.

The claims and conclusions of scientists which have been briefly stated are made on the basis of naturalistic uniformitarianism or evolution. This theory might not inaptly be called the "Cipher Hypothesis." For it places the emphasis on time-consuming process and not on the creative fiats of Almighty God. It is constantly adding on ciphers, increasing thousands to millions and millions to billions, now to trillions, as if it were in possession of an inexhaustible treasury of time over which it could claim unquestioned control.

It is important to remember when we read of the immense expansion of time and space which the astronomer, the geologist and the anthropologist are demanding for the production of the universe, of the earth, and of man, that this is only one side of the picture. On the other side is the almost equally amazing contraction of the same picture, which science is constantly bringing about. We read and speak about labor-saving devices. They are amazing. Modern machinery can turn out vastly complex gadgets, as we may call them, such as costume jewelry, artificial flowers, mechanical toys, in almost no time. We travel now by super-sonic jet planes. A New Yorker talks to a Californian by telephone as if both were in the same room. We use a satellite (Tel-Star) to enable us to witness a "live" panel discussion between Europe and America. We now have a mechanical computer which works at almost lightning speed and with an accuracy which makes it the terror of the income-tax evader. It has recently been reported that "at least 400 words can be transmitted on a laser pulse lasting only one thousandth of a second."[9a] In short, if we are living in an expanding world, we are also living in a contracting one in which mechanical robots can perform wonders that to a generation ago would have seemed as impossible for man as the dreams now come true of many a Jules Verne. Yet the scientists who have brought all this about, hesitate, with rare exceptions, to attribute to Almighty God that mastery over the powers of nature which they claim for themselves and so clearly possess. When we think of this inconsistency at all seriously we cannot but be amazed at it!

The Supernatural Account

We turn now to the biblical account. We are immediately struck by its simplicity. It is told in terms of Fiat and Fulfilment. "God said, Let there be light: ánd there was light" — Fiat Creation! — and so on to the completion of the Hexameron. The whole is summarized in the words of the psalmist, "By the word of the Lord were the heavens made, and all the host of them by the breath of his mouth" (33:6), and again, "For he spake and it was (done); he commanded and it stood fast" (vs. 9). Effortless creation, the work of Omnipotence!

This creation we are told took place in six days, each of which had an evening and a morning. This would seem to imply that the days were days of twenty-four hours each, like our own days. But we need to remember that the sun and the moon, as rulers of day and night, did not come into being until the fourth day and also that we are told in Scripture that one day is with the Lord as a thousand years, and a thousand years as one day (2 Peter 3:8; cf. Ps. 90:4). Consequently many scholars hold, as did Augustine, that the days of Genesis 1 were not like our days. So they either make the days into ages or insert ages between them. This seems like a plausible solution of the problem. But it is not without difficulties.

(1) It does not explain why the account is given so precisely and carefully in terms of six "days," which include eight creative periods, and why these days are so precisely defined as each having an "evening and a morning,"[10] words which are usually, perhaps always, used in the Bible in a literal sense.

(2) The Decalogue makes the six days of Creation, followed by the day of rest, the type and pattern for man's daily life. It is, of course, possible that it is only the number and sequence and not the time period which is to be regarded as relevant. But it is hard to be sure just at what point the analogy or comparison ceases to apply. Strict logic would suggest that the "days" are the same in both accounts, in Genesis 1 and Exodus 20.[11]

(3) It is especially important to note in this connection that immediate acts of God, such as the creative acts described in Genesis 1, are essentially timeless and independent of time. We read in Colossians 1:16 that it was by the pre-incarnate Son of God that "all things were created, that are in heaven, and that are on earth, visible and invisible." Of those acts of creation there were and could be no human witnesses. But of the creative acts or miracles performed by the incarnate Son during his earthly ministry we have many recorded examples: the turning of the water into wine, the feeding of the five thousand, and of the four thousand, the miracles of healing, of raising the dead, etc., all of them acts of immediate power with no appreciable element of time or process involved or implied. Of these acts as of the acts of the creative week we may say as did the psalmist: "He spake and it was (done), he commanded and it stood fast." The Roman centurion understood this when he sent the message to Jesus, "Say in a word, and my servant shall be healed" (Luke 7:7). Being a soldier he knew that authority meant power. And of this believing Gentile Jesus said, "I have not found so great faith, no not in Israel." And in Hebrews 11:3 we are told that it is "through faith we understand that the world was formed by the word of God so that things which are seen were not made of things which do appear."

These biblical data fully justify the claim of Morris and Whitcomb[12] that a distinction is to be made between the creative period as described in Genesis 1-2 and the period which followed the fall of man. Of the creative period we have no direct knowledge except what is given to us by revelation in that narrative. Its creative acts are assigned to six days and in the light of biblical teaching as a whole and especially of the miracles of Jesus referred to above, they were essentially timeless and could have taken place instantly, but are stated to have taken place in six days, each of which had an evening and a morning; and these six creative days with the following seventh day of rest are represented as the pattern for man's life on earth (Exod. 20:8-11), which clearly implies that God's creative plan was formed with express reference to the life of man, who is the culmination of that plan. For God made the earth and everything in it to be the abode and the kingdom of the man whom he purposed to create in his own image. The importance of the seven-day week is indicated by the fact that the *six* creative days include *eight* creative fiats which might easily have been made into eight days. With the fall were introduced those changes, gradual probably, except in the case of the flood, which are governed by the second law of thermodynamics, the principle of entropy, which the geologist and anthropologist can study and to which many of the principles of uniformitarianism may properly be applied.

Adam and Eve. As to the origin of man the Scriptural doctrine is "that man was originally created in a state of maturity and perfection."[13] This view which involved a "full grown" creation with "rapid, almost instantaneous attainment of maturity" was widely or universally accepted until about a century ago. Among its most recent defenders are Morris and Whitcomb. It is, of course, directly contrary to the modern doctrine of naturalistic and uniformitarian evolution according to which the development of man from lower forms of life covered a vast period of time and even the date when he arrived at human status lies in a remote past. But it is the natural and obvious sense of the biblical narrative. Furthermore it forms an important element in that supernaturalism which is so prominent, pervasive, and essential a feature in the entire biblical record. Thus, if it is denied that Adam could have been created full grown, with the apparent age of a mature man, it follows logically that Jesus could not have created *real* wine at the wedding feast and that he could not have fed the five thousand men with *real* bread and fish. Yet we are told that the master of the wedding feast declared the wine supplied by Jesus to be better than that which was provided by the host, and the bread is compared to the heavenly manna with which the Lord fed the children of Israel for forty years in the wilderness. The biblical history is consistently and sanely supernatural from beginning to end. The thoughtful Christian who recites the Apostles Creed with its majestic and awe-inspiring beginning, "I believe in God the Father Almighty" should hesitate to quibble over the meaning of the words "Maker of heaven and earth" as they are magnificently expounded in the Creation account which is given in Genesis.

The Fall of Man. There is no statement in the Bible on which we can base a conclusion as to length of the interval between the creation of Adam and his fall. Some scholars would make it very short; Ussher made it the same day. Legend has made it as much as five hundred years. But the sequence of events is clearly indicated. The Fall was followed by expulsion from the garden; and it was after this that Adam knew his wife, a statement which includes all of their descendants in the guilt of their transgression; and the terrible consequence of the Fall, the corruption of the entire human race, showed itself in the first-born child of the sinning pair: Cain became the first murderer! This teaching of Scripture is either ignored or denied by the evolutionist. For the biblical doctrine of the fall of man runs directly contrary to his doctrine of the rise of man. But the facts of life, the course of human history, argue strongly in its favor. The presence of sin in the human heart and the corruption and depravity which it produces — call it persistent abnormality, or whatever else you please — are stubborn facts, which only the biblical record adequately accounts for. The rosy image of the innate goodness and perfectibility of man which was so popular fifty years ago has been sadly tarnished by two World Wars with all their attendant and consequent horrors and atrocities.

The Fall of Man while clearly stated and described in Genesis 3 is rarely mentioned in the Old Testament (Hos. 6:7; Isa. 43:27; Job 31:33), although its tragic and terrible consequences (sin and death) are constantly referred to. But the doctrine is clearly set forth in the New Testament on the basis of the Genesis narrative. Barth and Neo-orthodoxy and the Demythologizers may treat the early chapters of Genesis as supra-history or as myth. But they cannot escape the admission that moral evil is in the world and has cast its dark shadow over human history from the beginning; and they must admit that Paul in Romans 5 places the sin of Adam in direct relation, antithetic relation, with the redemption provided by the Second Adam. Again and again he there contrasts the sin of the *one* man (Adam) with the obedience of the Second Adam (Christ); and elsewhere he tells us: "For as in Adam all died, even so in Christ shall all be made alive" (1 Cor. 15:22). Compare also the reference to Adam's transgression

(Rom. 5:14) and Paul's further words, "For Adam was first formed, then Eve" (1 Tim. 2:13) and "for the man is not of the woman, but the woman of the man" (1 Cor. 11:8), which clearly indicate that Paul took the statements in Genesis literally; and they are so treated in the great historic Creeds of Christendom.

It is especially because of this New Testament confirmation that these chapters of Genesis have become the battleground between the Orthodoxy and Neo-orthodoxy of the present day. As Jewett has so clearly pointed out, the aim of Neo-orthodoxy is to restore "to theology its proper foundation, namely revelation, without becoming involved in a view of the Bible which would implicate one in what appears to them to be a hopeless scientific obscurantism."[14] So Neo-orthodoxy, which includes Barth, Brunner, Tillich, Bonhoeffer and Bultmann, relegates these chapters to primal history (*Urgeschichte*) and makes a distinction between geschichte (i.e., suprahistory, a region to which the ordinary categories of time and space do not apply) and history (to which they do apply), or simply treats these chapters as myth, legend, folklore, which alike undermines their trustworthiness and authority. Consequently it is of the utmost importance to recognize that these chapters form an integral and essential part of the biblical revelation, that they are referred to in the New Testament as factual, and that their truthfulness is involved in and supported by that theistic view of the universe and of man, which is inherent in the biblical revelation and which, we maintain, is in entire harmony with the claims and conclusions of true science.

The Antediluvians. There are two genealogies: of Cain (4:16-24) and of Seth (5:1-32), who took the place of Abel, "for Cain slew him." They differ considerably. Cain's line is traced through six generations to Lamech, who has three sons, whose descendants are referred to but not named. We may infer that it is intended to cover the same period of time as the genealogy of Seth which follows. We note, however, that unlike Seth's genealogy, that of Cain gives no relative dates either for Cain or for any of his descendants. It mentions the technical skills acquired by Cain's descendants and concludes with a "hymn of hate," which signalizes the terrible effects of sin in the seed of the first-born of Adam. It is the prelude to Genesis 6:1-6, which seems to connect the awful situation before the Flood with the contamination of the Sethites by the Cainites.

In the genealogy of Seth, on the other hand, whose line is traced through nine generations to Noah, who has three sons, special importance apparently attaches to the numerical statements. The age of each of the Sethites at fatherhood, the years of his life which followed, and finally his total life-period is stated in each case. Apparently the longevity of these patriarchs is mentioned as being significant.[15] All except two lived more than 900 years. The total for this period, based on the age at parenthood of each of the patriarchs is 1656 years according to the *MT;* but the *LXX* gives the much larger figure of 2242. No total is given in the Bible itself. Accepting these lists as complete and the figures given in the *MT* as correct, Ussher dated the creation of Adam at 4004 B.C. But today most scholars who take these figures seriously assume that the lists are not intended to serve as the basis for an exact chronology, a use to which they are never put in the Bible itself. From the analogy of other genealogical lists in the Bible they feel justified in inferring that the genealogies in Genesis 5 and 11 are condensed, that links are omitted.[16] They see in the fact that the first list of ten names ends with a father who has three sons and is closely parallel to the similar list in Chapter 11,[17] an indication that both are schematized as is the case with the genealogy in Matthew 1,[18] and that the figure given by Ussher for this period, 1656 years, a total which is not given in the biblical account, may be much too short because of the omission of links in the genealogical chain.[19]

The Flood (Gen. 6:13–9:17). After the Fall of Man the next great tragedy or catastrophe was the Flood. Its importance is indicated by the elaborate description, the emphatic repetition, and the detail with which it is described. That it was a divine judgment upon the sinfulness of man, that it was of vast extent and destructiveness is made emphatically clear. The climactic statement is: "And every living substance was destroyed which was upon the face of the ground, both man, and cattle, and the creeping things, and the fowl of the heaven; and they were destroyed from the earth: and Noah only remained alive and they that were with him in the ark" (7:23).

That there was a vastly great flood (or floods) in ancient times is well established by geology. The vast "fossil graveyards" in widely scattered areas of the earth, notably those in northern Siberia where the frozen carcasses of prehistoric mammoths have been found in vast numbers, furnish irrefutable evidence both of sudden catastrophe and of great change of climatic conditions.[20] Furthermore the flood stories of ancient times[21] are too widespread to be ignored.[22] Whether these flood stories have any connection with the Genesis flood has been much debated.[23] Many scholars seek to minimize the biblical account; they insist that the flood was local, restricted to the Mesopotamian area;[24] others believe that it was sufficiently extensive to destroy the entire human race;[25] still others believe that it was universal both geographically and anthropologically, which is certainly the view which does the fullest justice to the biblical description.[26] When it took place, is also a matter of dispute. On the basis of the genealogy in Genesis 5, Ussher dated the Flood 2348 B.C., i.e., 1656 years after the Creation and 352 years before the birth of Abraham. This date is widely regarded as much too low. Seven to ten thousand years ago is a figure which commends itself to a number of conservative scholars.[27]

The Confusion of Tongues (Gen. 11:1-9). This third Catastrophe is recorded after the Table of Nations. But no date is given. Many scholars would place it in the days of Peleg, since "in his days was the earth divided" (Gen. 10:25), which they regard as referring to the scattering which followed the Confusion. The reason given for the building of the tower "lest we be scattered" implies that the human race had not yet spread at all widely after the Flood. Ussher dated it 100 years after the Flood (2247 B.C.)[28] and 250 years before the birth of Abraham. It is a curious fact that the standard Jewish Chronology places it 48 years *after* the birth of Abraham (1774 B.C.), which accords with the rabbinical tradition that Adam and Eve spoke Hebrew.[29] But since tablets in Sumerian have been discovered which date at least as early as 3000 B.C. such a date for the Confusion is out of the question. The statement that "the Lord did there confound the language of all the earth" that they might not understand one another seems to imply a sudden act of a very drastic character. The great differences between the known languages of mankind, together with the fact that at least some of them show marked evidence of deterioration in process of time favor such an explanation.[30] The fact that in the Table of Nations, the line of Seth ends with Peleg and his brother Joktan whose sons to the total of 11 are listed, while the line of Peleg is not resumed until 11:17 where it is then continued to the sons of Terah, makes it probable that the Confusion took place at that time.

The Postdiluvians (Gen. 11:10-26). This genealogy resembles that of Chapter 5 in a number of respects. There are ten names, if, following *LXX* and Luke 3:36, a Cainan is included, and the last named is the father of three sons. The age at parenthood is given in each case. On the other hand the total age of each patriarch is omitted, perhaps as being superfluous,.and instead the words are added, "and begat sons and daughters," a phrase which is perhaps added in view of the utter destructiveness of the Flood. Assuming that the list is complete, Ussher figured the total of years from the Flood to the birth of Abraham at 352 years. But, as in the case of the Antediluvians, it is now generally recognized that this figure is much too low and that the list of names in this genealogy has been much condensed.

With the eleventh chapter of Genesis that series of events is concluded, which are·recorded as simply history, but which Neo-orthodoxy refuses to accept as a record of historical facts, but insists on treating as suprahistorical or simply rejects as myth, legend or allegory.

The Patriarchs. The history of the Hebrew people begins with Abraham. Here, at the very beginning, we are faced with a problem. How old was Terah when Abraham was born? The statement in 11:26, "And Terah lived seventy years and begat Abram, Nahor, and Haran," is extremely brief. It suggests that at the age of seventy Terah became a father through the birth of the first of three sons, Abraham. But the statements that "after his father was dead" (Acts 7:4) and when he himself was seventy-five years old (Gen. 12:4), Abraham went to Canaan seems to indicate that Abraham was probably the youngest of the three sons, born sixty years after the birth of the oldest.[31] Numerous dates are given for the events of this period. But they are all given as we have seen in terms of the ages of the individual patriarch. E.g., "and Abram was seventy-five years old when he departed out of Haran" (12:4). By adding them up we find that the total of years between Abraham's arrival in Canaan and the descent of Jacob into Egypt was 215 years. No contacts with the outside world furnish conclusive evidence regarding this period. The king of Egypt of Abram's day is not named. The four foreign and five local kings of Genesis 14 have not been identified with any certainty although many attempts have been made to do so. It has been often claimed and as often denied that in Amraphel we are to recognize the famous Hammurabi of Babylon.[32] The Abimelech, king of Gerar, of Abraham's day has not been identified. But the language of the Philistine king of Isaac's day, "Go from us; for thou art much mightier than we" (26:16) indicates that at that time the Philistines played an insignificant role in Palestine. The "children of Heth" of Abraham's day may be Hattians rather than Hittites.[33] It is now widely recognized that the setting of the Patriarchal narratives accords well with the situation in Palestine in the Middle Bronze Age. But as far as archaeology is concerned no exact dates can be arrived at. Two thousand B.C. may be taken as an approximate date for the birth of Abraham.[34]

In view of the difficulties connected with the Chronology it will be well to make a brief survey of the views which are widely held today with regard to it. To do this we compare the figures given by Ussher and by four widely used Bible Dictionaries.

	Ussher	HDB	DDB	NBD	ZPBD
Abram's arrival in Canaan	1921	1870	1965	1915	2090
Jacob's descent into Egypt	1706	1655	1750	1700	1875
The Exodus	1491	1225	1320	1280	1445
Founding of the Temple	1012	965	967	967	966
Rehoboam's Accession	975	935	931	931	931
Athaliah's Usurpation	884	849	842	841	841
Fall of Samaria	721	722	722	722	722

Comparing these five chronological arrangements, we note three matters which are of importance: (1) The difference is greatest, as we might expect, at the beginning; (2) For the date of the Founding of the Temple it is reduced to less than fifty years; (3) It disappears with the date of the destruction of Samaria for which the date 722 or 721 B.C. is accepted by practically all scholars. We must now consider these differences and the reasons for them.

The Sojourn in Egypt. It is important to remember in dealing with the sojourn in Egypt that the only contemporary record of the presence of Israelities in Egypt is contained in the Old Testament. The only mention of Israel on Egyptian monuments of that period is on the Merneptah stele which describes Israel as having perished, outside of the land.[35] Furthermore, those scholars who reject the statements of the Old Testament as to the presence of all the Tribes in Egypt and regard the census figures as completely unreliable, must admit that it is from the Bible alone that they derive the evidence for the Egyptian sojourn. If this sojourn was such an insignificant factor in the history of Egypt as they claim, it is not at all strange that the Egyptian records do not refer to it. If on the other hand it was as significant as the Bible represents, then it is the Bible which must be our source of information regarding it. So we turn to the biblical account.

The biblical account of the sojourn begins at Genesis 37:28 "And they (the Ishmaelites) brought Joseph into Egypt." Nearly all the rest of Genesis (chaps. 39-50) deals with what we may call the preparation for the coming of Jacob and his other sons to Egypt and their sojourn there until Jacob's death. Similarly the first fifteen chapters of Exodus deal with the oppression of Israel in Egypt and their deliverance from bondage there. In short we have about twenty-five chapters dealing with this vastly important period of Israel's history, as to which the Egyptian monuments are practically silent. We say practically silent because there are, as we shall see, facts in Egypt's history which accord with the biblical record. There are none which expressly and specifically confirm it. We consider first the length of the sojourn.

This is stated in round numbers as "four hundred years" (Gen. 15:13) or "in the fourth generation" (vs. 16) and more precisely as "four hundred thirty years" (Exod. 12:40). It is particularly to be noted that these are the first period-dates in the Old Testament. Period chronology, as we may call it, begins with Abraham and his descendants and it concerns the formative period of Israel's existence, the sojourn in Canaan and Egypt to the founding of Solomon's Temple. A problem arises in connection with these figures. The *LXX* and the Samaritan-Hebrew text insert the words "in the land of Canaan" in the text of Exodus 12:40, which makes the total of 430 years include the prior sojourn of Abraham and his descendants in Canaan. Since these years total 215, to include them in the 430 reduces the sojourn in Egypt by exactly one-half: 215 years instead of 430. Those who accept this lower figure find it supported by Galatians 3:17, which seems to treat the entire period from the call of Abraham to the Exodus as 430 years. But it is possible that Paul is simply mentioning the 430 years of the sojourn because it is a figure which is given in Scripture and which is sufficiently indicative of the long interval of time between Abraham and Moses, without the inclusion of the additional 215 years which is, as we have seen, a calculated total based on the figures given in the Book of Genesis, but nowhere mentioned as a total for the period. It has also been suggested that Paul regarded the entire sojourn in Canaan as a period of promise and dated the 430 years from the renewal of the promise to Jacob (Gen. 46:3f.), instead of from the first announcement (Gen. 12:2f.).[36] Josephus included the 215 in the 430; and Ussher and many others have done likewise. But apparently that view has few advocates today.[37]

The difficulty in determining the period of Egyptian sojourn is illustrated by the statement, "Now there arose up a new king over Egypt, who knew not Joseph" (Exod. 1:8). This might refer to a natural succession, a son following his father in orderly fashion, to a change in dynasty, or to violent overthrow. Some scholars have seen in it a reference to the coming of the Hyksos. On the other hand if Hatshepsut was the "daughter of Pharaoh" mentioned in Exodus 2:5, it might equally well refer to their expulsion; and the new king would then have belonged to the Eighteenth Dynasty. Why the names of none of the Egyptian kings of this period are given is not known. If the writer of Genesis could give the names of four kings and their countries with whom Abram battled successfully nearly half a millennium before the Exodus,[38] it would be strange if the name of not a single king of this later period were remembered. Apparently the title "Pharaoh" (i.e., "great house") or the less frequent designation, "king of Egypt," was regarded as a sufficient identification. The fact that the writer gives the name of Joseph's jailor, of Joseph's wife and of her father, and the names of the two midwives makes such an inference highly probable. The omission of the names of the Pharaohs may be due to regard for the Egyptians' exalted conception of their monarch (Pharaoh being a recognized title), or it may have been used simply for convenience, since the kings of Egypt had several different names, a custom which would have been quite confusing to foreigners like the Israelites.[39] The first Pharaoh to be mentioned by name in the Bible is Shishak, the contemporary of Rehoboam.

The Date of the Exodus

The fact that there is now apparently a strong tendency to accept the 430 years of Exodus 12:40 as substantially correct makes the wide difference of opinion as to the supplementary period-date for its termination (480 years) a matter of especial importance. The question at issue is, briefly stated, whether accepting the 480 year figure as correct the Pharaoh of the oppression was Thutmose III of the Eighteenth Dynasty or Rameses II of the Nineteenth which reduces that figure by nearly 200 years.

The reason for this difference of opinion is to be found largely in the conflicting interpretations of the name Rameses, which is given to the city built by the Israelites for the unnamed Pharaoh or Pharaohs who oppressed them. The widely accepted explanation of the name, as held by the advocates of the later date, was stated for example by Breasted as follows: "It was familiar to the Hebrews as 'Raamses' (Exod. 1:11), and through this Pharaoh's other great enterprises here, this region became known as 'the land of Rameses,' a name so completely identified with it that Hebrew tradition read it back into the days of Joseph, before any Rameses had ever sat on the throne."[40] This statement assumes that the name Rameses in Genesis 47:11 is to be treated as an anachronism, while the same name[41] as it occurs in Exodus 1:11 is to be accepted as proof that Rameses II and not Thutmose III was the Pharaoh of the oppression. Consequently the advocates of the late date either ignore the evidence of Genesis 47:11, or reject it as an anachronism. This is important because it shows that the name Rameses is "notable as affording the mainstay of the current theory that King Rameses II was the Pharaoh of the oppression and his son Merneptah the Pharaoh of the exodus."[42] So it is to be noted, as to the name itself, that the title "son of Re" had been adopted by the Pharaohs of the Fifth Dynasty, nearly a thousand years before the sojourn. Furthermore those Pharaohs resided at Memphis in the

Delta. Consequently, as Conder has pointed out, "it seems possible that a town may have borne the name 'Ra created it' very early."[43] It is not necessary to assume that the name Rameses (Gen. 47:11) originated with the Pharaohs of the Nineteenth Dynasty. It is quite possible that when the kings of this Dynasty reestablished their royal residence in the Delta, they also revived the old name of the city or region of Rameses and adopted it to serve as a royal name. The presumption is that Rameses was the name of a district in Egypt in the time of Joseph.[44]

The location of the two "store cities" which the Israelites built for Pharaoh is still somewhat uncertain. Pithom is probably to be located in the Wadi Tumilat at Tell-er-Retabeh or at Tell-el-Maskhutah about eight miles to the east as formerly claimed by Naville. We are told that there are no monuments there of kings earlier than Rameses II who built a great temple. But it is to be remembered that Rameses was a great plagiarist and may have claimed credit for such buildings, as he did for those built by other monarchs. As to the city Rameses, G. E. Wright holds that the identification with Avaris-Tanis-Zoan (*San-el-Hagar*) is probable. But he admits that Qantir some nineteen miles to the south is a possibility.[45] If Zoan (the name which appears in the Bible) was a great Hyksos city, as Hazor in Palestine has recently been shown to have been, it is certainly possible that the city of Rameses which the Israelites built may go far back of the time of Rameses II. At the least it should be admitted that the evidence based on the name Rameses for the late date of the Exodus is by no means conclusive.

The prima facie evidence supplied by Genesis 47:11 that there was a place or district called Rameses in Goshen in the days of Joseph, should not be ignored or lightly dismissed as an anachronism. It is, of course, possible that the author or compiler of Genesis for the sake of intelligibility substituted a later name for the place where Jacob settled. If so, the original name would be unknown. But this is a supposition and not a fact.[46] The natural explanation would be that the name Rameses was the original name of the city or district, that the city built for Pharaoh by the Israelites received the old name of the district which happened to be the same as that later adopted by the first Rameses. This would do justice to the biblical narrative and it might also account for the name given to this line of kings of the Nineteenth Dynasty.

Exodus to Solomon's Temple

According to I Kings 6:1 the length of this period was 480 years.[47]

This statement refers us back to the similar one in Exodus 12:40 which defines the length of the sojourn as 43 years. The two data belong together as a chronological sequence.

1.) We have already pointed out that there are very few long-period dates in the Old Testament. This would certainly seem to attach special importance to those which are given. Furthermore the events to which this dating applies were two of the most important events in the history of the Covenant People. The Exodus from Egypt is the great redemptive event of Old Testament history, even greater than the Return from Babylon, and is referred to many times; and the building of the Temple is the fulfilment of the promise regarding the place which the Lord would "choose" to set his name there, referred to repeatedly by Moses in his farewell addresses to Israel (e.g., Deut. 12:5, 11, 14, 26) as a great event of the future. It was the fulfilment of David's great wish. Like 1776 in American history or 1066 in English history, it was a key event, the date of which might well be made a matter of careful record.

2.) We have seen that many scholars today accept the figure 430 years for the sojourn as at least substantially accurate. This should be regarded as a strong presumptive argument in favor of the correctness of this complementary date, as we might call it. Would one be likely to be nearly or quite exact and the other in error by more than a century?[48]

3.) The preciseness of the dating is significant. In Exodus 12:40ff. after the 430 years are twice mentioned, the words "in the selfsame day" are added;[49] and this day has just been defined as the day immediately following the first passover, which was celebrated on the fourteenth of Nisan in the evening (vss. 6-8) and was followed by the departure from Egypt. That day was a "memorial day" (vs. 14) which was to be observed by the Israelites in their generations "forever" (vs. 17). If any event in Israel's history could be regarded as dated and fixed in the minds and hearts of pious Israelites, this would be the date. Similarly we are told that it was "in the four hundred eightieth year after the children of Israel were come out of the land of Egypt, in the fourth year of Solomon's reign over Israel, in the month Zif, which is the second month, that he began to build the house of the Lord" (1 Kings 6:1) and that "in the fourth year was the foundation of the house of the Lord laid, in the month Zif" (vs. 37). Elsewhere we read still more precisely that it was "the second day of the month" (2 Chron. 3:2). Furthermore the date of its completion is stated with almost equal precision. It was finished "in the eleventh year, in the month Bul which was the eighth month, being seven years in building" (1 Kings 6:38).

4.) The 480 years have been treated in three different ways:

(a) They have been ignored. Josephus did so, probably because as Whiston pointed out, he could not harmonize his total of about 600 years with the figure given in Kings.

(b) The attempt has often been made, by Ussher, Whiston, Keil and many others, to harmonize the 480 years of 1 Kings 6:1 with the data furnished elsewhere in Scripture, mainly in the Book of Judges. They all accomplish the desired result, but differ more or less as to the way of attaining it. The most obvious solution is the acceptance of the view that some of the judgeships were contemporaneous or overlapping. In view of the method often employed, as we have seen, by the biblical writers in recording historical events, this explanation may be regarded as probable. Thus Keil regarded the eighteen years of Ammonite oppression (Judg. 10:8), the six year judgeship of Jephthah (12:7) and the seven years of Ibzan (12:9), all of which concerned the East as being contemporary with the forty-year Philistine oppression (13:1) in the West.[50] We are told the length of Eli's judgeship, forty years (4:18), and that he was very old (2:22), ninety-eight years at the time of his death (vs. 15), statements which make it doubtful whether his forty-year judgeship should be reckoned as continuing up to the time of his death, especially in view of the reputation which Samuel enjoyed while Eli was still alive (3:19–4:1).[51] How long Samuel judged Israel is not stated. Paul assigned Saul a reign of forty years (Acts 13:21) but many scholars (e.g., Ussher, Keil and Davis), regard this figure as including part or most of the judgeship of Samuel. That David reigned forty years is stated repeatedly (e.g., 1 Sam. 5:4f.). Solomon's forty years (1 Kings 11:41) included a co-reign with his father, which was apparently quite brief (2:1).[52] While no one of the proposals for reducing this period to 480 years can be regarded as entirely satisfactory in view of the inadequacy of the biblical data, it can hardly be denied that they furnish reasonable solutions of the problem and make it clear that so far as the biblical data are concerned the figure 480 may be accepted as correct.

(c) The difficulty connected with the figure "480 years" for this period has been greatly increased by the discoveries made in the field of archaeology. As has been pointed out above, the view is widely held today that the Pharaoh of the oppression was Rameses II. If this view is accepted it places the Exodus at c. 1280 B.C. instead of at c. 1445 B.C. and reduces the 480 years to about 320, i.e., by about one-third. This poses a very difficult problem for the advocates of this late date. They can hardly ignore or reject the figure 480 completely especially if they accept, as many of them do, the substantial accuracy of its companion date, the 430 years for the Sojourn. So they are obliged to find an explanation of the 480. According to Finegan the figure 480 "appears to be a late addition to the text" and it "may bear the marks of an artificial reckoning in that it amounts to twelve generations of forty years each."[53] As to the first statement, we note that there is no textual evidence in support of the claim that this statement is not an integral part of the biblical text. As to the second, which probably means that with Davis and many others, Finegan would reduce the suggested twelve generations of forty years each to twelve generations of thirty years each, this is a supposition which, however convenient for the advocates of the theory, has no real basis in fact. There is no sufficient reason for regarding 480 as an artificial number because it is 12 x 40. The figure 430 is not an artificial number. Why should this one be? There is no attempt in the biblical record to divide this period into twelve parts or units. Twelve, as the number of the tribes of Israel, figures prominently in Scripture. But it is nowhere used of periods of time. Furthermore the suggestion that 480 represents twelve generations of thirty years is far from convincing. It is nowhere stated that a generation was thirty years. But very clear evidence that a generation was and should be counted as forty years is furnished by the account given in Numbers 14:26-38 of the punishment to be visited on the Israelites for accepting the false report of the spies. This is further stressed in Deuteronomy 2:14 by the words "until all the generation of the men of war were wasted out from among the host, as the Lord sware unto them."[54] In view of the emphasis which the narrative places on the events of the Exodus period, we may well regard this forty year period as giving us the authoritative definition of the word "generation" at least for that period; and while it is natural to think of 480 as 12 x 40, in view of the prominence of the numbers 12 and 40 in the Old Testament, the number 480 is nowhere so treated or explained. On the other hand there is no satisfactory explanation of the 480 as a mistaken calculation if the actual total was less than two-thirds of that figure. Twelve generations of thirty years each would reduce the 480 to 360, but even this would be nearly fifty years too high if the Exodus is dated at *c.* 1280 B.C. But we have no proof for either the thirty or the twelve. So if the "480 years" total is regarded as quite inaccurate, the reason for such an egregious blunder on the part of the author of 1 Kings must be regarded as a mystery. Finegan in making the tentative estimate of 1290 B.C. for the Exodus, which reduces the 480 figure to approximately 328, admits that the 480 figure is "attractive" and that a good deal can be said in its favor.

Thutmose III would qualify admirably as the Pharaoh of the Oppression and Hatshepsut equally well as "the daughter of Pharaoh."[55]

In view of the fact that no clear evidence of the presence of Israelites in Egypt has yet been found outside of Scripture, that the theory of late date requires that the mention of Rameses in Genesis 47:11 be ignored or treated as an anachronism, that the figure 430 is accepted as substantially correct for the sojourn by influential advocates of the late date of the Exodus and the impossibility of finding a really satisfactory explanation of a mistake of more than 150 in the 480 years,[56] that the date of the fall of Jericho is still unsettled, that the connection between the Hebrews and the Habiru of the Amarna letters is still uncertain,[57] there is still good reason, we believe, for holding that the early date is even more "attractive" than Finegan admits it to be.[58]

THE KINGDOM PERIOD

The 480 years of 1 Kings 6:1 end with the fourth year of Solomon's reign. This carries us far into the kingdom period, since it includes the reigns of Saul and David and the beginning of Solomon's. Here the principal difficulty as we have seen concerns the reign of Saul. Its length is nowhere stated in the Old Testament. But Paul assigned it forty years (Acts 13:21), which as we have seen may be regarded as including as contemporaneous with it much or most of the judgeship of Samuel, the length of which is nowhere stated. We have noted that the Bible gives no period-dates or totals for the period or periods following the founding of the temple. Solomon's reign ended thirty-six years after that epoch-making event. It was followed by the Schism, which resulted in a divided kingdom, which continued until the fall of Samaria and the destruction of the Northern Kingdom. As to the length of this period we have no definite statement. But as to the date of its termination, there is happily no difference of opinion, 721 B.C., the date set by Ussher on the authority of the classical historians, being now generally accepted as accurate within a year. Consequently this date serves as a fixed point from which to calculate backward to the end of the 480 years and of the preceding 430 years, which we have been considering. Ussher dated the fourth year of Solomon 1012 B.C. *NBD* places it in 967 B.C., which makes a difference of more than forty years as to the date of the Schism (Ussher, 975; *NBD*, 931 B.C.). This difference, which affects the entire kingdom period, constitutes one of the major problems of biblical chronology.

THE DIVIDED KINGDOM (975-721, Ussher; 931-722, *NBD*)[59]

Among the early results of excavation in Assyria was the discovery and publication by Rawlinson a century ago of tablets containing the Eponym Canon. These tablets recorded the names of the kings and high officials who, like the archons at Athens and the consuls at Rome, gave their names in succession, each to a year, thereby establishing the chronological sequence. While the system of dating by eponyms began centuries earlier, these lists cover a period of about 250 years, beginning about 900 B.C. A gratifying result of the discovery of these lists lies in the fact that they connect with and overlap for about a century the Ptolemaic Canon, which had been known and used for centuries, but which only began with the Era of Nabonasser, 747 B.C. It was quickly discovered that the two canons were in agreement for the periods which they both covered; and thus the year 722 B.C. for the fall of Samaria, as given by Ussher on the basis of the Ptolemaic Canon, served to anchor the Eponym Canon for the Assyrian chronology.

The Eponym Canon was preserved in two forms; the one consisted merely of the names of the eponyms *(limmu)*, while the other of which several fragmentary duplicates were discovered, added to the name of the year a brief notation of some important event. Thus for the eponym of Pur-sagale, which was the ninth year of Ashur-Dan III, there was mention of an eclipse of the sun, which astronomers were able to verify as having occurred in 763 B.C., a further anchoring of the Canon. It was also discovered that, according to the Annals of Shalmaneser III, this king, in his sixth year fought a battle at Qarqar against an alliance of kings, among whom Ahabbu of Sir'ilaia was mentioned. This was in 854 B.C. So it was at once pointed out that if this Ahabbu was the Ahab of the Bible, as many assumed to be the case, this made a difference of more than forty years in the biblical chronology, which placed the death of Ahab, according to Ussher, in 897 B.C.

This difference between the biblical and the Assyrian chronologies led to a vigorous debate. Three main positions were taken regarding it. We may describe them as the *Gap Theory*, which sought to harmonize the Assyrian chronology with the biblical, the *Co-Reign Theory*, which sought to harmonize the biblical chronology with the Assyrian, and the *Objective Theory*, which sought to do justice to both. All three of these theories deserve careful consideration and at the risk of prolixity we shall proceed to do this.

THE GAP THEORY

It was claimed by some scholars, notably by Jules Oppert, one of the most distinguished of the pioneers in the Assyriological field,[60] that there was an unindicated break or interval of 47 years in the Canon. His principal arguments in support of this claim were: (1) An eclipse of the sun occurred in 809 B.C. just 47 years before the eclipse of 763. So he claimed that this eclipse was the one mentioned in the Canon. This involved an unindicated break in the Canon of 47 years, which he placed immediately before the reign of Tiglath-pileser III, i.e. between the years 745 and 744 of the Canon. (2) He claimed that Pul, who is not mentioned in the Canon, was a Chaldean king, who reigned in Nineveh before Tiglath-pileser during all or part of this 47 year interval, and this period did not appear in the Canon because the Babylonian kings did not list the years of their reigns by *limmus*. (3) He pointed out that this 47 year interval between the two eclipses was exactly the difference between the biblical and the Assyrian chronologies; and he raised the question whether this could be "a mere accident" *(pur hazard)*. Unfortunately for Oppert, his two main arguments have not stood the test of further discoveries. The Khorsabad and the Assur King List tablets make no allowance for any break in the sequence given in the Eponym Canon; and the claim made by Rawlinson, Schrader and others that Pul is another name for Tiglath-pileser has also been fully confirmed.[61]

The Co-Reign Theory

It was maintained by Rawlinson and Schrader that there was no evidence of any break in the sequence of names in the Eponym Canon and that the biblical chronology must be shortened to accord with the new data supplied by the Canon. This view has quite generally prevailed, even in conservative circles and the means used to accomplish the reduction has been, as we have seen, the postulating of a series of co-reigns. Both of these explanations of the difference between the biblical and the Assyrian chronologies have this in common. They proceed upon the assumption that the *Ahabbu* and *Iaua* mentioned by Shalmaneser are to be identified with the Ahab and Jehu, kings of Israel, referred to in Kings. So we now proceed to examine the way in which the advocates of this theory use it to solve the problem of the reduction of more than forty years in the chronology required as they believe by the Assyrian records.

This period, which begins with the revolt of the Ten Tribes and ends with the fall of Samaria, is divided into two parts by the revolt of Jehu who slew both Jehoram of Israel and Ahaziah of Judah, an event which furnishes an important synchronism for the two kingdoms.

Rehoboam–Ahaziah (975-884, Ussher; 931-841 *NBD*)

| | Judah | | | Israel | |
	Ussher	*NBD*		Ussher	*NBD*
Rehoboam	975-958	931-913	Jeroboam	975-954	931-910
Abijah	958-955	913-911	Nadab	954-953	910-909
Asa	955-914	911-870	Baasha	953-930	909-886
Jehoshaphat	914-889	873-848	Elah	930-929	886-885
Jehoram	889-885	853-841	Omri	929-917	885-874
Ahaziah	885-884	841	Ahab	917-896	874-853
			Ahaziah	896-895	853-852
			Jehoram	895-884	852-841

There were six kings in Judah between Solomon and the Schism and eight in Israel, if we disregard Zimri and Tibni as merely unsuccessful rivals of Omri. Only two series of datings are given above, those of Ussher and of the *New Bible Dictionary (NBD)*, since they are sufficiently representative. It is to be noted that according to both arrangements the total for this period is about ninety years and the dates for the ending as for the beginning differ by about forty years. This means that this considerable difference must be accounted for in the next period, which, for reasons which will appear later, we extend beyond the end of the Northern Kingdom to include the reign of Manasseh.

Athailiah–Manasseh (884-643, Ussher; 841-642 *NBD*)

| | Judah | | | Israel | |
	Ussher	*NBD*		Ussher	*NBD*
Athaliah	884-878	841-835	Jehu	884-856	841-814
Joash	878-839	835-796	Jehoahaz	856-839	814-798
Amaziah	839-810	796-767	Jehoash	839-825	798-782
Uzziah	810-758	791-740	Jeroboam II	825-784	793-753
Jotham	758-742	750-732	(Interreg)	784-773	
Ahaz	742-726	744-716	Zechariah	773	753
Hezekiah	726-698	729-687	Shallum	772	752
Manasseh	698-643	696-642	Menahem	772-761	752-742
			Pekahiah	761-759	742-740
			Pekah	759-739	740-732
			Hoshea	730-721	732-723

When we study these two chronological schemes in the course of which, namely with the fall of Samaria in 722 B.C., the forty-three year difference between Ussher and *NBD* disappears, we observe that this harmonization is brought about in *NBD* by means of co-reigns. Ussher found none in Judah in this period; *NBD* discovers five. They are the following:

Co-reigns according to NBD

Uzziah with Amaziah	792-761	24 years
Jotham with Uzziah	750-740	10 years
Ahaz with Uzziah and Jotham	744-732	12 years
Hezekiah with Ahaz	729-716	13 years
Manasseh with Hezekiah	696-687	9 years

Total 68 years

It is to be noted regarding this total that in this arrangement Jotham is given eighteen years instead of sixteen, Ahaz is given twenty-eight instead of sixteen. Another arrangement of co-reigns which is widely accepted today is that of Thiele.

Co-reigns according to Thiele

Uzziah with Amaziah	792-767	25 years
Jotham with Uzziah	750-740	10 years
Ahaz with Jotham	735-732	3 years
Hezekiah with Ahaz	none	
Manasseh with Hezekiah	697-687	9 years

47 years [62]

The difference between these two arrangements and totals is that here Ahaz is given only three years co-reign with Jotham instead of the twelve given him with Uzziah and Jotham; and Hezekiah is given none with Ahaz. If then we deduct nine plus thirteen years from the NBD total we arrive at nearly the same figure as Thiele's. In comparing these two systems of datings it is important to note that Thiele avoids giving Hezekiah a long coreign with Ahaz by rejecting as undependable the synchronisms in 2 Kings 18:1, 9 which place Hezekiah's reign as beginning in the third year of Hoshea, and lowering it to 716 B.C. Having stated his reasons for doing this in his article in *JNES*, Thiele apparently felt that he need not mention it in the brief Chronology in *ZPBD*. But this fact should not be overlooked since it is a major flaw in Thiele's chronological system.[63]

The Biblical Evidence of Co-reigns

In view of the extensive use of co-reigns as a means of solving the problems of the chronology of this period, we need to study carefully the biblical evidence with regard to them:

(1) Going back to the period of the Judges we have found that the chronological difficulties there are mainly due to the fact that several of the judgeships were more or less contemporaneous and local. Furthermore there is uncertainty as to certain details. We are told that Eli judged Israel for forty years (1 Sam. 4:18). But the fact

of his blindness and extreme age when he died (3:2; 4:15) and of Samuel's increasing reputation as a prophet (3:19-21) suggests that Eli's judgeship may have ended some years before his death or at least that Samuel may have shared his authority for a considerable time. It hardly seems necessary to follow Keil in dating Samuel's judgeship, as distinguished from his "prophetic labors," as beginning 20 years after Eli's death. *NBD* assigns Eli a judgeship of forty years (1115?-1075?), to Samuel a similar period (1075?-1035?), and in assigning a maximum of forty years to Saul (1050/45?-1011) it makes Samuel's judgeship overlap Saul's reign by ten or fifteen years.

(2) The accounts of David's last days (1 Kings 1:1 − 2:10; 1 Chron. 28:1 − 29:28) indicate that it was from his dying bed that David declared Solomon his successor and that he rose from that bed (1 Chron. 28:2) to give his final instructions to Solomon and to the people. The statement in 1 Chronicles 29:22, "and they made Solomon the son of David king the second time", is explained by the account in 1 Kings 1, which tells us plainly that the anointing there described was for the purpose of defeating Adonijah's bid for the throne. When David died Solomon was crowned a second time as confirmation of the first, irregular crowning.

(3) The only hint of a co-reign of Jehoshaphat with Asa is to be found in the statement that in his thirty-ninth year Asa became diseased in his feet (1 Kings 15:23; 2 Chron. 16:12). Whether this justifies the assumption of a three-year co-reign of Jehoshaphat with his father *(NBD)* must be regarded as uncertain. At least nothing is said about such a regency.

(4) A co-reign of Jehoram with Jehoshaphat is indicated by the statements, that Jehoram of Israel became king in the second year of Jehoram of Judah (2 Kings 1:17) and that Jehoram of Judah began to reign in the fifth year of Jehoram of Israel (2 Kings 8:16). This must mean that Jehoram of Judah was associated with his father Jehoshaphat for the last five years of his reign, which accounts for the statement "Jehoshaphat being then king of Judah," a statement which is the clearest recognition of a co-reign for this entire period. Ussher gave Asa his full 41 years (955-914) and Jehoshaphat his full 25 years (914-889) and included a co-reign of Jehoram in it (893-889), which he deducted from Jehoram's 8 years, reducing them to 4 or 5 (889-885). In *NBD*, Asa is given 41 years (911-870), Jehoshaphat 25 years (873-848) which include a 5 year co-reign with Asa, and Jehoram is given 8 years (848-841) with a co-regency with his father of 5 years (853-848) which are *not* a part of his 8 years of reign (848-841). This is certainly inconsistent.

(5) The usurpation of Athaliah. Athaliah is assigned six years (2

Kings 11:3, 21) and Joash is given forty years (12:1). Davis included Athaliah's reign in that of Joash, as a usurpation which is not to be counted in the schedule of reigns. But this method of shortening the chronology seems to be ruled out by the statements in the biblical text.[64]

(6) As to a co-reign of some two years of Amaziah with Joash (Davis), we have no information except the statement that his enemies, the Syrians, left him "very sick" (2 Chron. 24:25 ARV). But since this statement is immediately followed by the further information that "his own servants conspired against him . . . and slew him on his bed, and he died," and that "Amaziah his son reigned in his stead" (vs. 27), there seems to be no evidence of a co-reign, but rather a violent ending of one reign followed at once by the beginning of a new one.

(7) A very marked difference concerns the reign of Amaziah. He is assigned twenty-nine years (2 Kings 14:2); and we are also told that he survived Jehoash of Israel fifteen years (vs. 17). This must mean that his defeat by Joash took place within the first fourteen years of his reign, but how early in his reign we are not told. His great achievement was the conquest of Edom. But this victory had two tragic results: his apostasy in worshipping the gods of Edom, a sin the heinousness of which was aggravated by the fact that his victory over Edom had been foretold by a prophet of the Lord, and his arrogant challenge of Joash of Israel to battle, a piece of folly which led to a terrible defeat. The result was a conspiracy against him which the Chronicler tells us began "from the time that Amaziah did turn away from following the Lord" (2 Chron. 25:27). This refers apparently to his sacrificing to the gods of Edom and indicates that opposition to him began even before his defeat by Jehoash. If we accept the dates 798 for the accession of Joash of Israel and 796 for that of Amaziah, the two events of Amaziah's reign referred to above may both have taken place fairly early in his reign. So the conspiracy against him might have occurred as much as five to ten years before the death of Jehoash. This would make possible the dating of his virtual deposition as early as the fourth to sixth year of his reign (so Albright, van der Meer, NBD and Thiele). Davis places it as late as Amaziah's fourteenth year, and only a year before the death of Joash. On the basis of either calculation, Amaziah's actual reign was comparatively brief; and the greater part of it is covered by the seemingly simple but perhaps enigmatic words, "and he fled to Lachish; and they sent after him to Lachish and slew him there." Does this mean that after his deposition he remained in Jerusalem for many years and finally fled to Lachish, where he was promptly put to death; or are we to understand that his flight to Lachish took place soon after his deposition and that he was

a virtual prisoner there for a number of years before his assassination? We can only surmise.[65] But it is to be noted that, while these interpretations by reducing the actual reign of Amaziah from twenty-nine to as few as four or five are of great assistance in explaining the forty years difference between the two estimates for this period (Ussher and *NBD*), they read into the biblical account an interpretation which is not at all obvious. It may seem to be required by the Assyrian chronology and it is a possible explanation of the biblical account. But it is not a satisfactory one. Why, for example, are we expressly told both in Kings and Chronicles that Amaziah survived Joash fifteen years? If Amaziah had been a virtual prisoner in Jerusalem, his capital city, or in Lachish, for some years (a decade?) before Joash died, is it not strange that we should be told twice that this shadow king survived his conqueror fifteen years. This would make the statement look like irony or sarcasm of which there is no clear indication.

(8) A more serious difficulty emerges when we apply the above stated interpretation of 14:17f. to 15:1f. If the alleged deposition of Amaziah is placed as early as his fifth or sixth year (791 B.C.), then 15:1f. must be understood in the following way: "In the twenty-seventh year of Jeroboam [dated from the beginning of an 11 year co-reign with his father Jehoash], Azariah began to reign [after a 25 year co-reign with or regency for his father Amaziah, begun] when he was 16 years old, and reigned fifty-two years [of which 25 years as a co-reign with his father had already taken place and are included in the 52]." The bracketed words serve to show how complicated this co-reign theory becomes. For Uzziah is assigned fifty-two years; and synchronisms are recorded with the kings of Israel for the thirty-eighth, thirty-ninth, fiftieth and fifty-second years of his reign. Here two possible co-reigns or regencies are involved. The one, with or for Amaziah, has been discussed. Then the fact of his leprosy and the period during which Jotham was "over the house" (2 Kings 15:5) introduces a second rulership which unlike the first is clearly referred to in the record, although its length is not stated.[66]

(9) Jotham reigned sixteen years (2 Kings 15:33; 2 Chron. 27:1, 8). Yet it is stated in 2 Kings 15:30 that Hoshea of Israel began to reign in Israel in the twentieth year of Jotham. This seems to be a clear recognition of a four-year co-reign of Jotham with Uzziah. If so it indicates that a co-reign was not counted as part of a king's *actual* reign. Jotham *ruled* over Judah for twenty years, but he *reigned* only sixteen, i.e., the four years of *co-reign* are not counted as part of the *reign*.[67] This has an important bearing on the whole question of co-reigns. It appears to indicate that the years of co-reign of a king with his predecessor are not to be regarded as forming part of

the total reign as given in the formula "X was Y years old when he began to reign and he reigned Z years." Otherwise we would have to regard either "the twentieth year" of 2 Kings 15:30 or "the sixteen years" of verse 33 (cf. 2 Chron. 27:1, 8) as a scribal error. Yet it is by including the co-reigns which they discover in the totals for the reigns of this period, that *NBD* and Thiele bring the biblical chronology into accord with the Assyrian.[68] The extreme example of this modern method is Uzziah, his reign of fifty-two years being reduced to about twenty-seven years by *NBD* and Thiele, nearly cut in half by the deducting of co-reigns.

(10) Ahaz is assigned sixteen years (2 Kings 16:2). But *NBD* extends it to twenty-eight treating the first four years as a co-reign with both Uzziah and Jotham and the next eight as a co-reign with Jotham, followed by an independent reign of sixteen years. This means that from 744 to 739 there were three kings "reigning" in Jerusalem. On the other hand Thiele assigns Ahaz no co-reign but an independent reign of about twenty years beginning about 735 B.C. Biblical warrant for assigning him twenty years is found in the fact that Hezekiah is said to have been twenty-five when he became king, although his father Ahaz was only thirty-six when he died. This seems rather improbable.[69] So adding four years to Ahaz's reign removes this difficulty. But the main reason is to be found in the claim that Hezekiah did not begin to reign until 715 B.C.

(11) Hezekiah's reign of twenty-nine years (2 Kings 18:2) has recently been described as "one of the most difficult problems in the study of the entire Old Testament."[70] It is dated by Ussher 728-698 B.C. The date 728 for the beginning of his reign is required by the synchronisms which are given in 2 Kings 18:1, 9f., according to which Hezekiah became king in the third year of Hoshea, six years before the capture of Samaria in 722 B.C. *NBD* regards the years 729-716/15 as representing a co-reign of Hezekiah with Ahaz and reckons Hezekiah's sole-reign as beginning in 716 B.C. and ending 687. Such a co-reign is not in itself impossible. But it is to be noted that the years of the co-reign are not included in the total for the reign, as in the case of Uzziah, which would then be forty-three years instead of twenty-nine. Thiele rejects these synchronisms, extends the sole reign of Ahaz to twenty years ending in 715 or 716, and regards the "fourteenth year" of Hezekiah (2 Kings 18:13) as referring to the campaign of Sennacherib against Palestine in 701 B.C. These various solutions of what is a crucial problem in biblical chronology will be discussed a little later. Here we merely direct attention to the fact that the one solution adds another co-reign and a long one to the co-reigns of this period while the other involves the rejection of important biblical data.

(12) Manasseh's reign is assigned fifty-five years (2 Kings 21:1). No mention is made of a co-reign with Hezekiah, to which *NBD* assigns ten years, although the fact that he was only twelve years old when he became king might suggest it. Such an assumption is necessary if Hezekiah's reign is to be extended to 687 B.C. to allow for an invasion of Tirhakah as king after 690 B.C. and for Manasseh's reign to terminate in 642 B.C. He is mentioned among the twelve kings of the seacoast who paid tribute to Esarhaddon and to Ashurbanipal; but the dates are not known.[71]

Manasseh's co-reign with Hezekiah is the last of the co-reigns recognized by *NBD* and Thiele. It is remarkable, to say the least, that such an amount of co-reigning should be required to bring the biblical chronology of the period into accord with the Assyrian. It makes this method of solving the problem rather dubious to say the least.

(13) In the Northern Kingdom where Ussher assumed an interregnum of eleven years after the death of Jeroboam II, *NBD* finds no interrregnum; on the contrary it assigns Jeroboam II a co-reign with his father Jehoash of twelve years.

(14) Similarly in the case of Pekah Ussher assigns him twenty years (759-39) with an interval of nine years (739-30) before his murderer Hoshea established himself as king. *NBD* on the other hand assigns Pekah only eight years as king of all Israel and makes Hoshea's reign follow immediately.

The above brief survey indicates quite clearly that, while the biblical writers recognized the presence of several co-reigns, they differed from the modern writers by ignoring these co-reigns in determining the actual reign of a king. Thus they give Amaziah twenty-nine years and Uzziah fifty-two years of actual reign as against the modern theory which makes the one reign about five years and the other twenty-seven. It is the validity of this method of bringing the biblical chronology into harmony with the Assyrian which is the great question at issue regarding the chronology of this period.[72] But before passing on to consider the Objective Theory we need to study somewhat fully the knotty question of Sennacherib's invasion referred to above.

Hezekiah and Sennacherib

This is one of the most thrilling stories in the Bible. The blasphemous arrogance with which the captains of "the great king, the king of Assyria" demand that the king of David's line surrender his city to their master is the supreme test of Hezekiah's faith which is strengthened by the utter scorn and contempt with which the prophet Isaiah meets and answers this challenging of the might of the Holy One of

Israel, who Isaiah declares, will put his hook in the nose of this raging bull and his bridle on his lips and turn him back whence he came to die in a temple of the very gods in whose name he claims to be invincible. This great conflict was fought many centuries ago. It ended in an ignominious defeat for the aggressor. It has bequeathed to all subsequent generations an inspiring example of triumphant faith. But unfortunately the aftermath of the struggle, as we may call it, has now been waging for a century and is still going on.

The conflict, as we may call it, was suddenly renewed by the publication a century ago (1861) of a prism cylinder of Sennacherib.[73] In the lengthy account given there of the first eleven years of his reign Sennacherib states that in his third expedition (*girru*), he destroyed forty-six cities in Palestine, shut up Hezekiah like a bird in a cage, and exacted a very heavy tribute from him.[74] According to the Assyrian chronology, this took place in 701 B.C. According to the biblical account the date was the "fourteenth year" of Hezekiah, which the Ussher chronology places in 713 B.C. How was this difference to be explained?

1. A Single Invasion

a. In 714 B.C. According to the statements in 2 Kings 18: 1, 9, 10, Hezekiah began to reign in the third year of Hoshea king of Israel and in his sixth year which was the ninth of Hoshea, Samaria was captured by the Assyrians. The date 722 B.C. for the fall of Samaria has been accepted for centuries, as established by the classical historians. Ussher, whose Chronology was introduced into the margin of the A.V. in 1701 dated it 721 B.C. This date has not been challenged by modern scholars. If the fall of Samaria took place in Hezekiah's sixth year, the expedition of Sennacherib in his "fourteenth year" is to be dated 714 B.C., or thirteen years before the invasion of 701 B.C. described on the Taylor Cylinder.

The principal objections which have been raised against the year 714 B.C. for the invasion described in Chapter 18 are the following: (1) Sennacherib did not become king of Assyria until 705 B.C. (2) Sargon in his *Annals* refers to several expeditions to the West, subsequent to the Fall of Samaria, notably the campaign against Ashdod in 711 B.C., but he makes no mention of Jerusalem, or of Hezekiah, or of the tribute paid by him or of any such campaign as is described in the Taylor Cylinder, nor does he mention Sennacherib as representing him. (3) Sennacherib's account of his invasion resembles the account in Kings in several respects. (4) The mention of Tirhakah makes the date 714 B.C. questionable or impossible. In reply it may be said: (a) The proleptic use of the title king of Assyria in referring to Sennacherib would not be either unusual or improper, since Sennacherib later became king and was naturally from that time on thought of as such;[75] (b) According to Sargon's *Annals* Sargon himself waged war against Ashdod, while Isaiah refers to the Tartan or commander-in-chief as actually in command[76]. So Sennacherib, as representing his father Sargon, may have been in command of one of Sargon's armies in the West; and Sargon may not have wanted to attribute to his son such a successful campaign as Sennacherib describes in his Cylinder. So he may have hesitated to claim the large tribute received from Hezekiah because it was actually paid to Sennacherib. (c) On the other hand Sennacherib may have listed this tribute as an achievement of his own campaign in 701 B.C. to offset the disastrous ending of that campaign which must have been widely known, but of which, of course, he made no mention in his inscriptions.[77] (d) Tirhakah was a son of Pianchi who became Pharaoh *c.* 740 B.C. He may have been twenty in 701 B.C., old enough to be at least in nominal command of an Egyptian army.[78]

b. The Invasion of 701 B.C. The first impression produced by the study of 2 Kings 18-19 is that we are dealing with a connected story which describes events which took place in a relatively short period of time. This impression is modified when we learn that the last verse which describes the death of Sennacherib skips over an interval of nearly twenty years in order to tell thus briefly of the downfall of the tyrant. But in other respects the impression seems to be well founded that the period covered by the narrative is relatively brief. Consequently when the Taylor prism inscription indicated 701 B.C. as the correct date for the invasion, attempts were at once made to bring the biblical account into harmony with it.

(1) It was proposed to change the date "fourteenth year" (18:13) to make it read twenty-fourth, twenty-seventh, or twenty-ninth.[81] It is, of course, possible that fourteenth is a scribal error; and E. J. Young has recently reminded us that the difference between fourteenth and twenty-fourth in Hebrew involves only a minor change, which might easily be accounted for as a copyist's error, which inclines him to regard this as "a very simple expedient."[79]

(2) Instead of altering the text of 2 Kings 18:13, it is proposed that we postulate a lengthy co-reign of Hezekiah with Ahaz beginning in 729 B.C. and date the beginning of his sole reign in 715 B.C.[80] This would make the fourteenth year of his sole reign 701 B.C., the year of Sennacherib's invasion in agreement with the Assyrian chronology. If the occurrence of several co-reigns in this period is accepted, this is certainly a possible solution. It is, as we have seen, the solution given in *NBD*. But it is not free from difficulty. It is hard to believe that the devout Hezekiah would, as associate with or regent

for the apostate Ahaz, have been a silent partner in his father's sin for so long a period as this theory requires; and the radical reforms which he introduced are assigned in 2 Chronicles 29:2 to "the first year of his reign, in the first month." Furthermore, a serious objection to this solution is that it makes it necessary to recognize two systems of dating in the account of Kings: the dates of the synchronisms being in terms of Hezekiah's co-reign beginning 729 B.C., while the fourteenth year would be dated from 715, the beginning of the sole reign. This would certainly be confusing. But its merit is that it aims to do full justice to the biblical account.

(3) A slightly different view has been proposed by Auchincloss.[81] According to it we have in the mention of the fourteenth year a refer-ence to what may be called Hezekiah's "second term of office," the fourteenth year being the next to the last of the fifteen years which through the prophet Isaiah the Lord added to the reign of the seem-ingly fatally stricken monarch (20:6). The fourteenth year would then be 701 B.C. This would involve the same double dating which we have objected to in the preceding theory. But if the miraculous extension of Hezekiah's life was so widely known that Merodach Baladan sent to inquire about "the wonder that was done in the land" (2 Chron. 32:31), it would not be surprising if this "second term" rather than the entire reign came to figure prominently in the popular imagination and that the year of Sennacherib's invasion came to be called the four-teenth year. This significant double-dating might have been so familiar to the biblical historian that he did not consider it necessary to explain it.

(4) Far more drastic is the solution which was advocated by Well-hausen many years ago and which has been vigorously maintained in recent years by Thiele.[82] Thiele has made a very thorough study of the chronology of the kingdom period; and most of his conclusions appear to be well founded. But we cannot follow him when he rejects the synchronisms in 2 Kings 17 and 18 with the words, "we recognize that at some late date — long after the original records of the kings had been set in order and when the true arrangement of the reigns had been forgotten — certain synchronisms in 2 Kings 17 and 18 were in-troduced by some late hand strangely out of harmony with the original pattern of reigns." This means that if the carefully and precisely stated synchronisms in these chapters are rejected as late and unde-pendable, the difficulties in the chronology can be regarded as re-solved. This method of solving difficulties, the cutting of the Gordian knot, is very tempting and has often been resorted to. But it is well to remind ourselves that, as Rowley has pointed out, "Textual emenda-tion in the interest of a theory can never lend support to the theory in

the interest of which it is resorted to."[83] This theory cannot be regarded as satisfactory because it undermines the structure which it is designed to support. The words "strangely out of harmony with the original pattern" represent a subjective judgment arrived at in the endeavor to justify the treatment of these synchronisms as late and unreliable. But the reason for them seems to lie in the importance which the historian attaches to the fall of Samaria and the final destruction of the Northern Kingdom in its bearing on the continuing history of the Kingdom of Judah which he proceeds to relate. Since the entire record of the Books of Kings from the time of the Schism to the fall of Samaria is synchronous, it is not remarkable that the historian connects the reign of Hezekiah so definitely with the reign of Hoshea, and specifically with the tragic event which marked the close of his reign, the destruction of his royal city by the Assyrian king. In fact it is all the more appropriate because he clearly intends it to be a solemn warning to the people of the Southern Kingdom of the fate which awaits them if they follow a similar course, a fate which he proceeds to describe in the following chapters.

2. Two Invasions

a. 714 and 701 B.C. This has two forms. According to Davis an invasion in 714 B.C. is referred to in 2 Kings 18:13 (cf. 2 Chron. 32:1-8; Isa. 26:1), while the rest of the narrative describes the invasion of 701 B.C. In the narrative in Kings, Davis also found two accounts of the invasion of 701, a first stage (18:14-16) and a final stage (18:17 – 19:35).[84] Edward Mack on the other hand assigned 18:13-16 to the invasion of 714 B.C. with the words: "The necessary insertion of a paragraph indicator between vss. 16 and 17 satisfies every demand for harmony."[85] This difference between Davis and Mack is due to the fact that Mack assigned the payment of tribute (vss. 14f.) to the campaign of 714, while Davis assigned it to the campaign of 701, because of the close resemblance between the figures for this tribute as given in Kings and in the Taylor Cylinder. From the standpoint of the Assyrian account, Davis' arrangement is the more satisfactory since it makes it possible to assign the tribute-payment to the campaign of 701 which accords with the Assyrian account. But from the biblical viewpoint the analysis of Mack is much to be preferred. It does not seem probable that the biblical writer would devote only a single brief verse to this first campaign, despite the fact that the statement itself indicates the seriousness of the attack: "against all the fortified cities of Judah, and took them." And we have given what we regard as at least a possible reason why the tribute paid to Sennacherib in 714 B.C. was first claimed by him in 701 B.C. In favor of the view that a considerable interval of time elapsed between verses 16 and 17, or at least some unexpected event, such as a revolt of Hezekiah or his appeal to Egypt for help, is the improbability that Sennacherib, notwithstanding his reputation for ruthlessness and cruelty, would have followed the receipt of the huge tribute by almost immediately demanding the surrender of the city.[86]

b. The theory that Sennacherib made a campaign against Hezekiah in about 688 B.C. rests entirely upon Macadam claim, referred to above, that Tirhakah was only about ten years old in 701 B.C. Further study of the evidence has convinced careful scholars that Tirhakah may have been about twenty, and quite capable of being nominally in command of an Ethiopian army at that time. The fact that Tirhakah is called "king of Ethiopia" (Kush) is significant, since the name Kush is rare in the Historical Books of the Old Testament, while the name Egypt or Egyptian occurs many times. Its use shows the accuracy of the biblical historian since Tirhakah belonged to the Nubian dynasty.

It must be frankly admitted that not one of the various solutions of the problem regarding Sennacherib's invasion or invasions is entirely satisfactory. The "fourteenth year" is still "A thorn in the flesh of biblical students." We may hope that archaeological research will throw further light upon this difficult problem. But whether this hope is to be realized or not, we may continue to defend the accuracy of the biblical record, provided it is correctly interpreted.

The Objective Theory

This theory was proposed by George Smith in his book, *The Assyrian Eponym Canon*, which was published in 1875, a year before his tragic death at Aleppo, while on a mission to conduct further excavations at Niniveh.[87] We may call his solution objective because it consisted, he tells us, "of taking the Assyrian records to be correct as to Assyrian dates, and the Hebrew as to Hebrew dates"[88] and also of recognizing "the possibility of errors in the Assyrian accounts where they differ on Jewish matters from the Bible."[89] "Objective" is certainly a very suitable description of such a procedure. Rejecting the attempts to find a "gap" in the Canon or "to cut down the numbers in the biblical history" he tells us:

> I would suggest instead of these chronological alterations, that some of the biblical names in the Assyrian annals on which they are based, either do not refer to the kings supposed, or are errors on the part of the Assyrians. If we allow that the Ahab and Jehu mentioned in the Assyrian records may not be the Ahab and Jehu of the Bible, we are not under the necessity of altering the chronology of either nation in order to make the Assyrian notices fit the times of the Hebrew monarchs.[90]

Discussing the subject more in detail, he points out that the name of the country now usually read as Sir-'i-la-a-a is not certain but that

. . . even if the reading Ahab the Israelite has to be accepted, it would be possible that this was not the Ahab of Scripture. The time when this battle took place, B.C. 854, was, according to the Chronology here suggested, during the reign of Jehoahaz, king of Israel, B.C. 857 to 840; and at this time part of the territory of Israel had been conquered, and was held by the kingdom of Damascus: it is quite possible that in the part of the country under the dominion of Damascus a ruler named Ahab may have reigned, and that he may have assisted Ben-hadad with his forces against the Assyrians. It does not seem likely that the biblical Ahab, who was the foe of the king of Damascus, sent any troops to his aid, at least, such a circumstance is never hinted at in the Bible, and is contrary to the description of his conduct and reign. Under these circumstances I have given up the identification of the Ahab who assisted Ben-hadad at the battle of Qarqar B.C. 854 with the Ahab, king of Israel, who died, I believe forty-five years earlier in B.C. 899. [91]

This statement, which seems so fair and judicious, apparently attracted little attention; and the identification of the *Ahabbu* and *Iaua* of the inscriptions with the Ahab and Jehu of the Bible, which had been vigorously advocated by Schrader in 1872,[92] has been quite generally accepted as an established fact. It will be well, therefore, to reexamine carefully the evidence for these and other widely accepted identifications. In doing so it is to be carefully noted at the outset that the data, both biblical and extra-biblical, bearing on the chronology of this period, are meager and insufficient for a wholly satisfactory solution of the problems which are involved.

Israel and Assyria. First of all it is to be noted that there is no clear mention in the Bible of any Assyrian king[93] until the time of Menahem (772-61),[94] who sought the help of Pul king of Assyria "to confirm the kingdom in his hand" (2 Kings 15:19). This fact is important and deserves careful consideration. Egypt is frequently mentioned from the time of the Patriarchs onward. Solomon married a daughter of Pharaoh; and a few years after his death Shishak invaded Palestine and claimed to have captured many cities. Zerah the Ethiopian invaded Judah in Asa's time. Later on Isaiah and Jeremiah warned their peoples against looking to Egypt for help against Assyria. The Syrians were enemies of Israel for centuries from the time of David on; and several Benhadads and Hadadezers are mentioned. We read of wars with the Philistines and that, as late as the time of Jehoshaphat, they brought him presents. The Hittites are also frequently mentioned in the Pentateuch and in Joshua. Solomon traded with them (1 Kings 10:29; 2 Chron. 1:17); and in the days of Elisha they were regarded as a serious threat to Israel

(2 Kings 7:6). But not a word is said in the Historical Books about Assyria until the time of Menahem of Israel. If a century and more earlier Assyria had been regarded as so dangerous an enemy of Israel that Ahab felt obliged to fight against Shalmaneser at distant Qarqar, it is certainly remarkable that no mention of Assyria is made in Kings or Chronicles until so much later.

1. *Ahab and Qarqar*. According to his Monolith Inscription, Shalmaneser III, in his sixth year (854 B.C.) made an expedition to the West and at Qarqar defeated Irhuleni of Hamath and a confederacy of 12 kings, called by him "kings of Hatti and the seacoast." Qarqar is described as the royal residence of Irhuleni. It was there, not far from Hamath, that the battle took place. Irhuleni was the one most directly concerned. But in describing the allied forces, Shalmaneser lists them in the following order:

He brought along to help him 1,200 chariots, 1,200 cavalrymen, 20,000 foot-soldiers of Adad-'idri of Damascus, 700 chariots, 700 cavalrymen, 10,000 foot soldiers of Irhuleni from Hamath, 2,000 chariots, 10,000 foot soldiers of A-ha-ab-bu Sir-'i-la-a-a. [95]

These three are probably mentioned first as the most important. It is rather odd that Irhuleni's troops are mentioned only second in the list, inserted between Adad'idri's and Ahabbu's. Then follow in order the contingents of Que, Musri, Irqanata, Matinu-ba'lu of Arvad, Usanata, Adunu-ba'lu of Shian, Gindibu' of Arabia, Ba'sa of Ammon. Most of these countries were clearly in the distant north,[96] Syria and Ammon being the nearest to Israel, and both of them Israel's bitter enemies. Among the eleven listed (he speaks of twelve kings), only five brought chariots; and most of them brought fewer troops than the first three, though some of the figures cannot be accurately determined, because of the condition of the inscription.

In view of the make-up of this confederacy of kings, the question naturally arises whether Ahab, who had been recently at war with Ben-hadad and was soon to renew hostilities with him, would have joined a coalition of kings of countries, most of which were quite distant,[97] and the nearest of which were bitterly hostile, to go and fight against a king with whom he had never been at war, — an expedition which involved leaving his capital city and taking a considerable army to a distance of some 300 miles and through mountainous country, and, most questionable of all, leaving Damascus, the capital of his recent enemy Benhadad in his rear (thus exposing himself to attack), in order to oppose a distant foe whose coming was no immediate threat to his own land or people. Shalmaneser's father, the terrible Ashurnasirpal, had come as near to Palestine as Shalmaneser then was at Qarqar. But no king of Israel had felt it necessary to oppose his victorious advance to the West. Such an undertaking by Ahab, king of Israel, seems highly improbable to say the least.

The name Ahab (*Ahab̓bu*), while uncommon, is not unique. We meet it as the name of a false prophet, who was put to death by Nebuchadnezzar (Jer. 29:21). The name appears to mean "father's brother," i.e., "uncle." It may possibly be shortened from Ahabbiram (my uncle is exalted) or a similar name. But it is to be noted that the name *Ahabbu* might be read equally well as *Ahappu* and be an entirely different name than Ahab, quite probably Hurrian,[98] which would accord well with the make-up of the confederacy.

The name of Ahabbu's country is given as Sir'ila-a-a. The reading is somewhat uncertain, since the first character might also be read as *shud* or *shut*. Even if *sir* is correct, the name is a poor spelling of Israel; and it is doubly questionable because nowhere else on Assyrian tablets is Israel given this name. On the monuments it is called *mat Humri*, the land of Omri.[99] It is perhaps not without significance that although the battle of Qarqar is mentioned in several of Shalmaneser's inscriptions, Ahabbu is mentioned on only one of them.[100] The Assyrian kings were great braggarts. Israel was quite remote from Shalmaneser's sphere of influence. If Ahab of Israel were referred to, we might perhaps expect more than this one slight mention of him.

Adad-'idri was apparently Irhuleni's chief ally, being mentioned first. If this Syrian king was the enemy-friend of Ahab, we might expect him to be called Hadadezer which is the Hebrew equivalent of the name and is given to the king of Zobah of David's time. The name Adad-'idri may stand for *Bar* (Hebrew, *Ben*)-*Adad-'idri* (Heb., *ezer*) and so be shortened at either end, to Ben-hadad or Hadad-ezer. So it may be, that the Ben-hadad of the Bible and the Adad-'idri of Shalmaneser's *Annals* are the same king.[101] Ancient rulers often had the same name. We now know of three kings who bore the famous name Hammurabi. There were 5 Shamsi-Adads, 5 Shalmanesers, 5 Ashur-niraris among the Assyrian kings. Egypt has 4 Amenhoteps, 4 Amenemhets, 12 Rameses, 3 Shishaks, and 14 Ptolemies. Syria had apparently both Ben-hadads and Hadad-ezers. Israel had 2 Jeroboams; and both Judah and Israel had a Jehoash, a Jehoram, and an Ahaziah in common. It may be that Ba'sa king of Ammon who fought in Qarqar, had the same name as Baasha king of Israel. Names may be distinctive and definitive, they may also be confusing and misleading.

There is no mention of the battle of Qarqar in the Bible. It is generally assumed that it was fought several years before Ahab's death, though Thiele claims that the battle at Ramoth-gilead took place only a few months after Qarqar.[102]

In the account which Shalmaneser gives of this battle, he claims a glorious victory. On the Monolith Inscription, which gives the fullest account of it, we read: "The plain was too small to let (all) their (text, his) souls descend (into the nether world), the vast field gave out (when it came) to bury them. With their (text: sing.) corpses I spanned the Orontes before there was a bridge. Even during the battle I took from them their chariots, their horses, broken to the yoke."[103] We are accustomed to such bragging by an Assyrian king and to discount it. But this certainly does not read like a drawn battle or a victory for the allies; and if there is any considerable element of truth in the claim made by Shalmaneser, "even during the battle I took from them their chariots, their horses broken to the yoke," this loss would have fallen more heavily on Ahabbu than on any other of the confederates, since Shalmaneser attributes to him 2,000 chariots, as compared with Adad-'idri's 1200 and Irhuleni's 700. If Ahab had suffered so severely at Qarqar, would he have been likely to pick a quarrel with a recent ally and to do it so soon? The fact that Shalmaneser had to fight against this coalition again in the 10th, 11th, and 14th years of his reign does not prove this glorious victory to have been a real defeat for Shalmaneser. Yet, despite what would appear to have been very serious losses for the coalition (all their chariots and horses), we find according to the construction of the evidence generally accepted today, Ahab in a couple of years or, according to Thiele in the same year, picking a quarrel or renewing an old one with his recent comrade-in-arms, Ben-hadad, and fighting a disastrous battle against him (1 Kings 22); and a few years later we find Ben-hadad again fighting against Israel (2 Kings 6:8-18), and even besieging Samaria (vss. 24ff.). Is this really probable? Clearly Ben-hadad had no love for Israel!

The biblical historian describes the battle at Ramoth-gilead together with the preparations for it, in considerable detail (1 Kings 22), as he later describes the attack on Dothan (2 Kings 6:8-23) and the siege of Samaria which followed it. Of Qarqar he says not a single word. Why this should be the case if Ahab was actually at Qarqar is by no means clear. It was not because the Hebrew historian did not wish to mention a successful expedition of wicked king Ahab, for he has given a vivid account of Ahab's great victories over Ben-hadad (1 Kings 20:1-34) which led even to the capture of the king of Syria himself. And, if Qarqar had been a humiliating defeat for Ahab, we might expect that the biblical writer would have recorded it as a divine judgment on the wicked king of Israel, as he does the battle at Ramoth-gilead, in which Ahab perished.

It is of course true that the record of Ahab's reign is not complete (1 Kings 23:39). His oppression of Moab is mentioned only indirectly in connection with an event in the reign of Jehoahaz (2 Kings 3:4f.). It is the Mesha inscription which gives us certain details. Yet in view of its importance the omission of any reference to a battle with Shalmaneser in which Ahab took a prominent part would be strange, to say the least.

The problem of Ahab and Qarqar has been discussed here in some detail because for a century it has been so generally assumed that the Ahabbu there referred to is the Ahab of Israel and that this requires a radical reduction in the biblical chronology. Here two matters are to be carefully distinguished. The claim made by Van der Meer that the year 763 B.C., which is the year of the eclipse in the eponymat of Pur Sagale "is the sheet-anchor upon which depends not only the Assyrian chronology but also that of Western Asia"[104] may be accepted as correct. Smith held fully as high a view of the trustworthiness of the Canon[105] as does Van der Meer. But it is quite a different thing to assume or assert that it follows as a necessary corollary that the Ahabbu who fought at Qarqar nearly a century earlier (854 B.C.) must be the Ahab of Israel who according to the Ussher chronology had then been dead for more than forty years. It is quite possible to accept the one claim and to reject the other. This is what George Smith did a century ago. And it is safe to say that his reasons for doing so are no less valid than they were when he advanced them in opposition to Schrader in 1875. The identification of Ahabbu with Ahab has been a moot question for scholars. To treat it as an established fact is to beg the question, not to decide it.[106]

2. *Jehu.* The Black Obelisk of Shalmaneser contains, in addition to brief accounts of the first 32 years of his reign, "twenty small reliefs, with annotations, depicting the payment of the tribute of five conquered regions."[107] One of these annotations, which is placed over a relief picturing a prostrate king paying abject homage to Shalmaneser, contains the words "Tribute of Ia-u-a son of Hu-um-ri." No date is given; and Iaua is nowhere mentioned on the Obelisk, though he is elsewhere mentioned on a fragment of an annalistic list.[108] It has been widely assumed that this refers to Jehu of Israel, although as in the case of the battle of Qarqar there is no mention of this event in the Old Testament. Such being the case it will be well to examine these "annotations" carefully. The first is called

"Tribute of Sua, the Gilzanite." The only mention of such a tribute in the text of the inscription is in the record of the 30th year (a very recent event); and there we read, "The tribute of Upu the Gilzanite, . . . I received." Has Sua succeeded Upu in the course of a year? The fifth relief is described as "The tribute of Karparunda of Hattina." Yet the record of the 28th year (also comparatively recent) tells us that Shalmaneser made Sasi, son of the Uzzite, king over them and they sent him presents "without measure." How is this to be explained? Turning back to the mention of Iaua, we note that he is called "the son of Humri." This shows the inaccuracy of Shalmaneser's information. If Iaua is Jehu, then Jehu is called the son of Omri, whose grandson Jehoram was slain by Jehu. Jehu was not of royal descent; he was a usurper, what Shalmaneser called Hazael, "a son of nobody."

Furthermore, the identification of *Iaua* with Jehu is uncertain. Tiglath-pileser calls Ahaz *Iaua-hazi*,[109] which indicates that he knew of Ahaz as Jehoahaz. So *Iaua* might be shortened from Jehoahaz or from Jehoash, just as the name Hadad (1 Kings 11:14) given to an Edomite prince of the time of Solomon is shortened, perhaps, from the familiar Benhadad or Hadadezer.[110] If Shalmaneser knew so little about Jehu as to call him the son of Omri, he might easily have confused him with Jehoahaz or Jehoash. This would make the 18th year of Shalmaneser (840 B.C.) correspond to an event in the end of the reign of Jehoahaz or the beginning of that of Jehoash of Israel, according to the Ussher chronology. The biblical narrative makes no mention of Assyria, in describing the career of Jehu. Hazael of Damascus was Jehu's chief enemy (2 Kings 10:32f.), and this might not have been the case if Hazael was seriously threatened by Assyria at this time.

There is then good warrant for Smith's statement regarding Jehu:

Without advancing any theory for the identification of the monarch mentioned in the Assyrian inscriptions, I would urge that the identity of the Jehu of the Bible with the Jehu of the inscriptions is not proved, and that these notices are not enough to force us to alter all our Biblical dates. [111]

3. The statement that "the Lord gave Israel a saviour" (2 Kings 13:3) in response to the prayer of Jehoahaz (856-839) may refer to an invasion of the West by Shalmaneser III which "broke the power of that monarch for a time, and so gave a breathing time to the Israelites."[112] And we would again remind the reader that there is no mention of Assyria in the biblical accounts of the reigns of Ahab and Jehu. The argument from silence may often be weak and inconclusive. But in the case of events of such importance as these which are recorded in Chalmaneser's annals, if these kings of Israel

really figured in them, the silence of the biblical records regarding them must be regarded as significant.

4. *Hazael.* In the Bible Hazael is mentioned first in the command given to Elijah at Horeb to anoint him to be king over Syria (1 Kings 19:15). The wording of the command seems to imply that Hazael was then already a prominent figure at the court of Benhadad.[113] For some reason which is not stated, the commission was not carried out until about a dozen years later in the announcement made to Hazael by Elisha that he was to be king of Syria, which was followed immediately by Hazael's murder of Ben-hadad and seizure of the throne (2 Kings 8:7-15). This took place apparently shortly before the revolt of Jehu (884 B.C.), at which time Hazael was already established on the throne (8:28). It was in fighting against Hazael that Joram of Israel was wounded, an event which was speedily followed by the slaying of both Joram and Ahaziah by Jehu (884 B.C.). As a punishment for Jehu's disobedience, Israel was oppressed by Hazael all the days of Jehoahaz (10:3f., 13:3), a warfare which was continued by Hazael until his death, sometime in the reign of Joash of Israel (*c.* 838 B.C. or somewhat later, 13:3, 24f.). According to these data Hazael has been assigned a reign of more than forty years, which would not be extraordinary.

Here again the inscriptions of Shalmaneser raise serious problems in connection with the biblical dates. The Canon gives Shalmaneser a reign of 34 years (858-824), and his Annals state that he fought with a confederation of Western kings, among whom Adad-idri of Damascus is listed, in his 6th, 10th, 11th, and 14th years (853-844). We have noted that no mention is made of any of these campaigns in the Bible. In his 18th year (840), Shalmaneser's opponent was Hazael of Damascus. Two important facts emerge from these data: Adad-ezer reigned in Damascus for at least nine years, and Hazael was on the throne in 840, perhaps somewhat earlier.

Most scholars have held that the Adad-idri of the inscriptions and the Ben-hadad of 2 Kings 8:7 are the same king. But J. D. Davis claimed that they are to be distinguished[114], that Adad-idri (858-846) was succeeded by Ben-hadad (846-842), which would account for the name Ben-hadad as used in the Bible. He argued that the statement in the Asshur Inscription of Shalmaneser that Adad-idri "reached his mountain" means that he met a violent death[115] and that the statement which followed telling of the seizure of the throne by Hazael allowed for the brief reign of a Ben-hadad between Adad-idri and Hazael, although this is not referred to on the inscription. But apparently the general view is that Adad-idri is merely another name for the biblical Ben-hadad. Since Davis had adopted in his

Dictionary the theory of Schrader that the Ahabbu who fought at Qarqar was the Ahab of the Bible, he did not need to discuss in this article the major problem as to whether this lowering of the chronology by more than forty years was justified.

This major problem was answered by Smith by proposing the following schedule of reigns for this period:

Damascus		Israel	Assyria
Ben-hadad II	910-886	Ahab (1 Kings 20)	
Hazael I	886-857	Jehu (2 Kings 8:9)	
Ben-hadad III	857-844	Jehoahaz (2 Kings 13:3)	
Hazael II	844-830	Jehoahaz & Jehoash	Shalmaneser
		(2 Kings 12:17, 13:22)	
Ben-hadad IV	830-800	Jehoash & Jeroboam II	
		(2 Kings 13:24 f.)	

This schedule which aimed to do justice to both the biblical and the Syrian chronology as indicated in the Assyrian inscriptions, involved the distinguishing of two Hazaels. For Smith recognized that the Hazael of the time of Jehu and the Hazael of the time of Jehoahaz must be different persons, since an Adad-ezer called by Smith Benhadad III came between them. This solution encountered two difficulties. The one was the failure of the biblical narrative to make any distinction between the Hazael of 12:17 (cf. vs. 6) and the Hazael of 13:3. This might be accounted for by the fact that an interval of about a dozen years lay between the two Hazaels and they were sufficiently distinguished by the fact that they were separated by the intervening reign of Adad-ezer or, if Davis' theory is accepted, by two reigns, those of Adad-idri and Ben-hadad. It may be noted that no distinction is drawn in the Book of Kings between the Ben-hadad of the time of Asa (1 Kings 15:18) and the Ben-hadad of the time of Ahab (chap. 20-22); and there are scholars who are still not convinced that Albright's attempt to treat them as the same person is justified.[116] But it must be admitted that in this case the interval of time is much greater than in the case of the two Hazaels. Furthermore it is to be noted that in 2 Kings 13:3, which Smith uses as the proof-text for his Ben-hadad III, the Syrian king referred to is not called either Ben-hadad or Adad-idri but Hazael. As to this Smith made the comment: "The notices of the kings of Damascus in 2 Kings appear to me inconsistent in some places, and I suspect a slight error between 2 Kings 13:3 and 2 Kings 13:22." Just what this error was, he does not state specifically. But the fact that he has used 13:3 as a proof-text for his Ben-hadad III indicates that he would there change the "Hazael" of this text to "Ben-hadad." Such a transcriptional error might solve the problem. The data at our disposal for the solution of this problem are meager. We have no Syrian inscriptions which throw light on this problem. The Zakir inscription of a somewhat later date, mentions a Bar-hadad, the son of Hazael, who is the Ben-hadad of 13:3, 24 and may be the same as the Mari' who is mentioned on the inscriptions of Adad-nirari III.[117] This would support the theory that these kings of Damascus, like many others had more than one name. But it would not solve the problem of the identity of the one who is called Hazael in these verses.

It must be admitted that this is a weak point in Smith's argument; and also that we have here perhaps the strongest single argument for the Schrader chronology. For if the dates of Ahab and Jehu are lowered about forty years, the problem of Hazael disappears, since Hazael does not then appear on the scene until about 840 B.C. which is after the reign of Adad-idri as is indicated by the Assyrian inscriptions. But this advantage in the Schrader reconstruction is, as we shall soon see, more than offset by the congestion which it introduces into the reigns which follow.

5. *Menahem and Pul.* As has been already noted, the first mention of an Assyrian king in the Bible is in the reign of Menahem, the son of Gadi, a usurper who obtained the throne of Israel by violence and reigned for ten years (772-761 B.C.). Perhaps as an example of his ruthlessness and cruelty, we are told of his brutal treatment of Tiphsah, which was probably not far from Tirzah. That he was not firmly established as king is to be inferred from the present which he sent to Pul king of Assyria "that his hand might be with him to confirm the kingdom in his hand" (2 Kings 15:19). The further statement that he raised the money, a thousand talents of silver, by assessing all the men of substance in Israel fifty shekels each, sixty thousand of them, is an indication of the size and wealth of Israel at that time. it is further pointed out that Menahem continued in the sin of Jeroboam. His reign of ten years was followed by the brief reign of his son Pekahiah. A rather meager record (2 Kings 15:14-22)!

For the modern reader the most significant statement regarding Menahem's reign is the mention of Pul, king of Assyria. Who was this Pul? In the long lists of Assyrian kings which have come down to us, there is no mention of a Pul.[118] The name itself is an anomaly. Of the last fifty of the more than one hundred Assyrian kings whose names are known to us, all the names are theophorous, being combined with the name of a deity, Ashur, Shamash, Adad, the most frequent. Pulu, as used of an Assyrian king, was probably a nickname or pet-name. Why and how it came to be used, we do not know. A possibility would be that it was connected with the word *Aplâ* which was a well-known substitute or abridgement for sev-

eral theophorous names, such as Bel-apla-iddina.[119] Pulu might have
been a similar adaptation. We know that it was borne by Tiglath-
pileser as king of Babylon.[120]

That Pulu may be such an adaptation is rendered somewhat probable by the remarkable fact that Adad-nirari III (812-782) had four
sons, who followed him successively on the throne (Shalmaneser IV,
Ashur-dan III, Ashur-nirari V, Tiglath-pileser III[121]). He himself was
the son of the famous queen Samuramat, who ruled Assyria for five
years during his minority. It seems not improbable, to say the least,
that one or more of the sons of Adad-nirari might have been fa-
miliarly and popularly known as Pulu. We have reason to think that
these four sons of Adad-nirari had a strong brotherly feeling for one
another. Olmstead remarks "So clearly was it recognized that the
reigns of Shalmaneser IV and Ashur-dan III were one that the cursus
of eponyms was broken only to insert the new king and the old
turtan."[122] The years 773-2 B.C. or thereabout marked both the beginning of Menahem's reign at Samaria and two expeditions of an
Assyrian king to the West, to Damascus and Hadrach. Shalmaneser
IV (782-773) was succeeded by Ashur-dan III (772-755) at about
this time. But apparently the death of Shalmaneser did not affect
these campaigns materially. The Hebrew historian may only have
known that a king of Assyria popularly known as Pul was the invader, whether Shalmaneser or Ashur-dan was immaterial. The name
Pul might apply to more than one of the sons of Adad-nirari.[123]

That the name Pul was actually borne by Tiglath-pileser, is proved
by the Babylonian King List; and Ptolemy calls him Poros. But it
is to be noted that it was not as king of Assyria, but as king of
Babylon that he was known as Pul. So it may be significant that in
2 Kings 15:29 the Assyrian king who came against Pekah more than
fifteen years after the death of Menahem is called by his Assyrian
royal name Tiglath-pileser.[124] On the other hand it is to be noted
that, if Pul was a name used by or of one or more of the sons of
Adad-nirari, it would have an especial appropriateness to Tiglath-
pileser, whose name contained the element Apil (Tukulti-apil-eshar-
ra) which might easily be shortened to Pul. The suggested explanation of the name Pul is of course doubtful in view of the meager-
ness of our information. But it is worthy of consideration because it
would at least furnish a reasonable explanation[125] of the biblical data
in the light of the Assyrian inscriptions.[126]

6. *Tiglath-pileser III (744-727 B.C.) and his Contemporaries.* The
inscriptions of this monarch have come down to us in fragmentary
form. They contain long lists of names of conquered or dependent

rulers. Among them we find five names which have a bearing on biblical history.

(1) *Yauhazi* of Iaudaia is mentioned in a building inscription as paying tribute to Tiglath-pileser.[127] That this is a reference to Ahaz of Judah is highly probable. In 2 Kings 16 and 2 Chronicles 28 we read in considerable detail of Ahaz's dealings with the Assyrian king. The fact that he is called Jehoahaz *(Iauhazi)* instead of Ahaz indicates that he preferred to use the shorter, non-theophorous form of the name given him by his pious father whose faith in Jehovah he had forsaken. His dates (742-727) agree with this identification.

(2) The mention of Pekah and of his overthrow by Hoshea[128] also accords well with the biblical chronology. That Tiglath-pileser was entitled to credit for placing Hoshea on the throne is probably true as he claimed.

(3) The *Rasunu* of Damascus who paid tribute to Tiglath-pileser is likewise to be regarded as the Rezin who with Pekah endeavored to overthrow Ahaz.[129]

(4) *Menihimmu* of Samarinaia is mentioned in a list of 18 rulers who paid tribute to Tiglath-pileser.[130] In view of the length of the list and the fact that it is simply a list of names, the nature of the tribute not being stated, the possibility is not to be rejected that either a tribute paid some thirty years previously to an earlier king (Menahem) is here listed by mistake, or that the Assyrian scribe was unaware that Menahem was not still king of Israel. The only other mention of Menahem is in a questionable restoration of the name in the passage which goes on to refer to the overthrow of Pekah and the placing of Hoshea on the throne of Israel. If the restoration is correct and the scribe intended to bring Menahem, Pekah and Hoshea so closely together as to date, he must have been badly informed as to the actual course of events in Israel. For even according to the Assyrian chronology a considerable period of time, about a decade, lay between the death of Menahem in 742 and the accession of Hoshea in 732.[131] But the context of this passage does not seem to fit Menahem. It tells us:

[As for Menahem I ov]erwhelmed him [like a snowstorm] and he . . . fled like a bird alone [and bowed to my feet (?)]. I returned him to his place [and imposed tribute upon him to wit:] gold, silver, linen garments with multi-colored trimmings . . . great . . . [I re]ceived from him. Israel (lit: "Omri-land" *Bit Humria)* . . . all its inhabitants (and) their possessions I led to Assyria. They overthrew their king Pekah *(Pa-qa-ha)* and I placed Hoshea (A-u-si-') as king over them. I received from them 10 talents of gold, 1,000 (?) talents of silver as their [tri]bute and brought them to Assyria.

The two accounts are so different that we may well hesitate to accept the restoration. As to this Smith tells us, "In this case it is probable that the Assyrian writer did not know that the crowns had changed hands or that Ahaz and Pekah had more than one name."[132]

(5) A king *Azriau* is mentioned five times in a single passage in the Annals.[133] He is twice called the king of Ia-u-da-a-a. Whether he is to be identified with Azariah of Judah (810-758) has been much debated. The name suggests the identity. But the statement, "19 districts belonging to Hamath and the cities in their vicinity which are (situated) at the coast of the Western Sea and which they had (unlawfully) taken away for Azriau I restored to the territory of Assyria," certainly does not look like a reference to Azariah of Judah[134] and many scholars have accepted Winckler's claim that the reference is to a petty king of a principality in the neighborhood of Hamath.[135] If the further reading proposed by Oppenheim "Azriau . . . a royal palace of my own [I built in his city . . .]" is accepted as correct, this would render the identification of Azriau with Azariah still more improbable. It is natural that those who wish to bring down the date of the death of Azariah to about 740 B.C. should be disposed to accept this identification, despite the fact that it involves the acceptance of the view that all or nearly all of the reign of Jotham was a co-reign with his father.[136] But it must at least be admitted that the identification of Azariah with Azriau is questionable.

Looking back over these five references we note that it is only the last two which occasion the Bible student any difficulty, and that in the case of these two the evidence is decidedly inconclusive. As to the invasion of 738 B.C. Smith tells us:

This expedition fell within both the reign of Ahaz and that of Pekah of Israel, the predecessor of Hoshea, yet the Assyrian annals give the name of Azariah to the king of Judah and Menahem to the monarch of Israel. Menahem was the name of the king of Israel who had some years previously paid tribute to Pul, king of Assyria, and Azariah was his contemporary in Judah. In this case it is probable that the Assyrian writer did not know that the crowns had changed hands, or that Ahaz and Pekah had more than one name. [137]

He tells us further:

In the case of the expedition of Tiglath-pileser in B.C. 738, it appears to me far more reasonable to suppose that Ahaz and Pekah are intended, in preference to altering all the earlier Biblical chronology and bringing down the date of Azariah and Menahem to the middle of the reign of Tiglath-pileser. [138]

And again:

I am utterly unable to see how the Biblical chronology can be so far astray here as the inscriptions lead one to suppose. [139]

Again he tells us and even more emphatically:

The difficulty of crowding all the events, from the accession of Menahem, king of Israel, down to that of Hoshea, a period according to the Bible of three successive reigns, and forty-three years, into the seventeen years of Tiglath-pileser's annals, forms, I think, an insuperable objection to this view. [140]

Most biblical scholars of today apparently either have not paid much attention to this objection or do not regard it as "insuperable." We have seen that they overcome it by their theory of co-reigns. But they must admit that at this point their theory meets its supreme test, that it is stretched almost to the breaking point if not beyond it. Smith speaks of the difficulty which concerns the reigns of the kings of Israel. We have already discussed this theory in connection with the reigns of the kings of Judah. According to 2 Kings 15-16, Azariah reigned 52 years, Jotham 16, Ahaz 16. In the case of Jotham we are told that he "was over the house" (15:5), after his father was smitten with leprosy. As to this we have already noted that in this same chapter we are told that Hoshea secured the throne in Israel "in the twentieth year of Jotham, the son of Uzziah" (vs. 30), while in vs. 33 we are told that Jotham "reigned sixteen years in Jerusalem." These statements indicate that Jotham's co-reign with his father only lasted for four years and also that this co-reign is not to be counted as part of his own reign but as belonging to the reign of his father. In other words Uzziah's reign of 52 years included the four years of Jotham's co-reign; and while Jotham might be said to have ruled for 20 years, his official reign was only 16 years. This is very important. For here we have the only mention of a regency in this period of four reigns; and it is clearly implied also that the co-reign is to be ignored in calculating the reign of a monarch. [141] So Uzziah, Jotham, Ahaz, and Hezekiah are all to be given the number of years assigned to them. [142] This of course flatly contradicts the principle of the co-reign theory which according to many scholars practically eliminates Jotham, giving him scarcely any independent reign. In fact we are told that "for approximately 6 years the reigns of Uzziah, Jotham, and Ahaz were contemporaneous." [143] Yet the plain sense of the narrative of 2 Kings 15-17 especially when amplified by the parallel accounts in 2 Chronicles 26-27 indicates that they were not. [144] How hard put to it the advocates of the co-reign theory are to justify their theory at this point, is indicated by their readiness, we may even say eagerness, to accept the doubtful claim that Azariah of Judah is the Azriau of Tiglath-pileser's annals. More remarkable still is the attempt to fortify this theory at this its weakest point with the claim that "This practice of co-regencies in Judah must have contributed notably to the stability of that kingdom." [145] Such an argument loses all of its force when we remember who the kings were who are supposed to have so cooperated as to strengthen the throne in Judah. Uzziah was a good king. His act of sacrilege is the only misdeed recorded against him. Jotham followed in his father's footsteps. But Ahaz was an idolator, a Moloch-worshipper, and pro-Assyrian. He must have been a thorn in the flesh of his pious associates. Hezekiah proceeded at once to reverse the policies of Ahaz, as Ahaz had reversed those of Uzziah and Jotham. If there was any co-reign in which Ahaz was involved, it cannot have been harmonious and fortifying; if it occurred it must have strained the relations of the co-regents to the utmost. Furthermore, it is hard to see how David and Solomon set "a valuable precedent" in the matter of co-reigns. David did not have Solomon crowned until he was on his death-bed, and then only to counter the bid of Adonijah for the soon-to-be-vacant throne. As for Solomon, in the account of his reign, Rehoboam is ignored completely, not even mentioned by name until Solomon dies. There is not the slightest evidence of a co-reign before Solomon's death. It is noteworthy that Uzziah is not merely given his full 52 years in the Book of Kings, but the accessions of five kings of Israel are stated in terms of his reign (Zechariah, Shallum, Menahem, Pekahiah, and Pekah). Then we read that Jotham's 16 year reign began in Pekah's second year, and this is followed by the statement that Ahaz reigned for 16 years. It could hardly be stated more plainly that these three kings were not all contemporaneous, but followed one another in sequence.[146]

If the advocates of the Schrader chronology, as we may call it, ignore or reject the idea of two Hazaels, they are faced on their part with what may be called the "No Jotham" theory, which is, we think, even more difficult to justify on the basis of the biblical statements. For while it is not easy to explain why the biblical account does not clearly distinguish the "second" Hazael from the first, it is far more difficult to introduce three or four co-reigns into the Uzziah-Hezekiah period. We have seen that, according to the narrative in Kings, Jotham is assigned a four year regency with Uzziah, which is not to be regarded as part of his 16 year reign. Where is there the slightest evidence that his 16 years of reign was almost entirely a co-reign with his father which is to be nearly or entirely ignored in making up the chronology of this period? Such a situation as this makes it plain that for a century most biblical scholars have made the Assyrian chronology a kind of Procrustean bed into which the biblical chronology must be fitted at all costs. And one of the main casualties in the process is the practical elimination of Jotham from the list of the reigning monarchs of the Southern Kingdom.

7. *Sennacherib's invasion.* As regards the date of Sennacherib's invasion in the fourteenth year of Hezekiah, it may be noted that most of the solutions which have been proposed had already been proposed in Smith's life-time. As early as 1852 Hincks had suggested that the difficulty in 2 Kings 18:13 would be removed by reading "twenty-fourth" or "twenty-fifth" instead of "fourteenth." Smith was inclined to the view that "fourteenth" should be regarded as a [typographical] "error" for "twenty-fourth." But he mentioned Oppert's view that the "fourteenth year" was to be counted not from Hezekiah's accession, but from the date when he received the promise of fifteen years extension of life. He also mentioned the view of Sayce and of Bunsen that the expedition of the "fourteenth year" might refer to Sargon's expedition against Ashdod in 711 B.C. of which Sennacherib may have been in command. We have seen that according to E. J. Young probably the simplest explanation is to regard "fourteenth" as a typographical error for "twenty-fourth." Thiele's explanation, according to which the synchronisms in this chapter are to be regarded as a later insertion by a writer who was misinformed as to the actual course of events, is quite out of harmony with the high view of the authority of Scripture which he advocates in general. Smith on the other hand attached great importance to the synchronisms which Thiele is disposed to reject as late and undependable.

The special merit of George Smith's chronology of this period lies in the fact that he tried to do justice to both the biblical and the Assyrian data. In this lies the strength of his entire discussion. Why this has not been recognized by Christian scholars is hard to understand. Smith was not a theologian. He did not formulate his view as to the authority of Scripture. But he clearly held a high view as to its trustworthiness. It is hard to see how biblical scholars who share that high view as to the authority of the Bible can fail to look with favor upon the work of this early pioneer in Assyrian research, can fail to recognize that Smith followed the correct method in studying this complicated and intricate subject, and that in accepting the Assyrian chronology as an authoritative time check, to which the biblical data must be conformed they are assigning it an authority superior to that of the Bible itself. The true biblical attitude has been well expressed quite recently by J. W. Montgomery in the following words:

Extra-biblical linguistic and cultural considerations must be employed ministerially, never magisterially, in the interpretation of a text; and any use of extra-biblical material to arrive at an interpretation inconsistent with the veracity of the scriptural passage is to be regarded as magisterial and therefore illegitimate. Extra-biblical data can and should put questions to a text, but only Scripture itself can in the last analysis legitimately answer questions about itself. [147]

This means that in the case of Amaziah, for example, while the reduction of his actual reign from twenty-nine years to five or six, followed by a deposition or imprisonment of some twenty-five years, is a perfect god-send to the advocates of the short chronology, the basic question is whether the biblical record will admit of such an interpretation. If it is "inconsistent with the veracity of the scriptural passage," it is to be rejected as an illegitimate wresting of the Scripture by submitting it to the superior authority of "extra-biblical material."

As regards the accuracy of the Assyrian inscriptions a distinction is to be drawn between the Eponym Canon and the inscriptions of the kings. We have seen that Smith agreed with Schrader as to the accuracy of the Canon. But he called attention to the fact that this does not apply equally to the royal inscriptions.[148] He cites several examples of mistakes in these inscriptions. But he makes no mention in this connection of the boastings and exaggerations which are characteristic of them — amazing triumphs, no defeats.[149] A good example of this style of writing is supplied by the account given by Shalmaneser, in his Monolith Inscription of the battle of Qarqar, the only one, it is to be noted, of four inscriptions, in which *Ahabbu* (Ahab?) is mentioned.[150] There after ascribing his victory to the gods Ashur and Nergal, he speaks as follows: "I slew 14,000 of their soldiers with the sword, descending upon them like Adad when he makes a rainstorm pour down. I spread their corpses (everywhere), filling the entire plain with their widely scattered (fleeing) soldiers. During the battle I made their blood flow down the *hur-pa-lu* of the district. The plain was too small to let (all) their (text: his) souls descend (into the nether world), the vast field gave out (when it came) to bury them. With their (text:sing.) corpses I spanned the Orontes before there was a bridge. Even during the battle I took from them their chariots, their horses broken to the yoke." This is a characteristic example of such royal (Prunk) inscriptions. It is full of exaggeration and improbable statements.

A factual statement would seem to be this: "I slew 14,000 of their soldiers with the sword". Yet Unger points out that "The number of the slain increased with the passage of time from 14,000 (the conservative figure of the monolith which itself is doubtless exaggerated) to 20,500 Annals (66) to 25,000 of the Bull Inscription from Nimrud to 29,000 of a recent statue from Ashur."[151] And Unger quotes the rather sarcastic remark of the historian Eduard Meyer, "Man sieht was von diesen Zahlen zu halten ist." Yet Unger does not hesitate to identify *Ahabbu* with Ahab and Yaua with Jehu and he calls Winckler's identification of Azriau of Yaudi as a petty ruler of a principality north of Israel instead of with Azariah of Judah "an unhappy suggestion". We note further that despite Shalmaneser's boastful claim there are scholars who refuse to see in the battle of Qarqar a glorious victory but are inclined to regard it as indecisive since Shalmaneser did not return to the West for some years.

We will do well to recall the words of Edward Mack written half a century ago, "Surely the time has come, when all fair-minded men should recognize that a clear and straightforward declaration of the Sacred Scriptures is not to be summarily rejected because of its apparent contradiction by some unknown and irresponsible person, who could stamp clay or chisel stone."[152]

Conclusion. The data bearing on this period are not ample enough or sufficiently clear to amount to a demonstration. But one conclusion seems to the writer to be fully justified. It is that the method followed by George Smith in dealing with these intricate problems of chronology is the only proper one and that the attempt to force the Hebrew chronology to conform to the Assyrian makes the latter a Procrustean bed which is too short for the biblical data to rest comfortably on. If the writer has succeeded in adding to and strengthening the defense of what he agrees with Smith in regarding as the biblical chronology, he will feel that his labors have not been in vain. It is his hope that this discussion will at least result in new interest in and defense of that method of studying the problems of biblical chronology which George Smith advocated so ably a century ago.

Much more might be said on this interesting and important topic and on many other subjects which are discussed or not even mentioned in this chapter. The archaeological field as it relates to the Old Testament is so extensive, the period so protracted, the results so incomplete and fragmentary, that the subject would require volumes for an adequate treatment. The aim of this survey has been to stress two important matters. The one is the very valuable light which archaeology has thrown on the Old Testament period and on the Old Testament itself. This is very significant. It has produced contemporary evidence from ancient times which confirms the Scriptures in many and remarkable ways. It has proved that the patriarchal age was not legendary or mythical but historical in the full sense of the word. It has proved that this early period was a literary period, that writing was known centuries before the time of Abraham, that alphabetic scripts were used before the time of Moses, perhaps as early as that of Abraham, that languages and dialects closely resembling Hebrew were spoken in or near Palestine in Abraham's day, that legal codes were in existence then and that business and daily life had their rules and regulations. It has confirmed the background of Israel's history and thrown light on such nations as the Amorites, the Arameans, and the Hittites who figured in Israel's history; and it has furnished us with documents recording the deeds of many kings whose names figure for weal or woe, mostly woe, in the Bible. We are no longer dependent on the classical historians for our knowledge of these ancient times. The spade of the archaeologist has opened up many vistas of the past and confirmed the Bible in many ways. For this we owe a debt of gratitude to the toilers in this vast and often extremely difficult and demanding field of human effort. Their labors have not been in vain, but often richly rewarding.

On the other hand we need constantly to remind ourselves that the results of archaeological research are necessarily incomplete, fragmentary, and at times uncertain and even misleading, that they are often ambiguous, and that care and caution are greatly needed in interpreting them. If the spade has cleared away some difficulties and solved some problems, it must be frankly admitted that it has produced others to take their place. We may be thankful that in these days when the Bible is being so vigorously attacked, the Lord has given us many confirmations of its truthfulness through the findings of the archaeologist; and we may hope for further confirmation in days to come. But we need to bear constantly in mind that the biblical history is supernatural history and that only the eye of faith can read it aright. This applies no less to the findings of archaeology than to the Bible itself. The findings of the spade may confirm and strengthen our faith in the Bible, "our full persuasion and assurance of the infallible truth, and divine authority thereof, is from the inward work of the Holy Spirit, bearing witness by and with the Word to our hearts."[153]

NOTES

CHAPTER I

1 *The Westminster Confession of Faith,* Chap I, "Of the Holy Scripture" speaks as follows: "The whole counsel of God, concerning all things necessary for his own glory, man's salvation, faith, and life, is either expressly set down in Scripture, or by good and necessary consequence may be deduced from Scripture: unto which nothing at any time is to be added, whether by new revelations of the Spirit or traditions of men." This is what is known as the doctrine of the sufficiency of Scripture.

2 A few chapters and verses of the Old Testament are written in Aramaic, a Semitic language closely related to Hebrew.

3 A so-called, "modern speech" or "idiomatic" translation may be easier reading than the AV and ARV because it interprets difficult passages and assigns a meaning to them which is clear and seemingly obvious, despite the fact that the rendering itself may be questionable and even improbable. Translations which conceal the uncertainty of meaning may be at times dangerously misleading.

4 By "analytical" is meant a concordance which arranges or groups the English words according to the Hebrew or Greek words which they translate — giving these words in a phonetic transliteration — and so helps the reader to form some idea of the differences in diction which appear in the Bible and of their significance. The most widely used of such Concordances are those of Young and Strong. Thus, in Young, the main concordance tells us that "borrow" renders the Hebrew verb *shaal* six times. The "Index" at the back of the book shows that *shaal* is usually rendered by "ask" (87 times).This indicates that in Exodus 3:22; 11:2; 12:35, where there is clearly no intention of returning the objects obtained, "ask" (*ARV, RSV*) is a better rendering than "borrow." Readers who object to the changing of "charity" (AV) to "love" (ARV) in I Cor. 13, will perhaps be surprised to learn from the Index that the Greek noun *agape* is rendered in AV 86 times by "love" as against "charity" (27 times) and that the verb is rendered by "love" in nearly all of its 141 occurrences. Careful use of such Concordances can be of great assistance to Bible students who know little or no Hebrew or Greek.

5 Kitto's *Cyclopaedia of Biblical Literature,* edited by W. L. Alexander, 3rd edition, 1865, vol. 1, p. 551.

6 The plural form of the word for God (Elohim) may be intended to prepare for the doctrine of the Trinity. The same may be true of the "us" of Gen. 1:26. The clothing of Adam and Eve with coats of skin (3:2) may suggest the shedding of blood and be an intimation of Lev. 17:11. But great doctrines should be built on clear and explicit teaching. Gen. 3:15 may properly be called the protevangel, but the evangel is clearly set forth in Isa. 53 and John 3:16. This is said not to undervalue the intimations of these great truths but to put them in their proper place as intimations rather than proofs.

7 The earliest English translation is said to have been made by Lodge (1602). That of L'Estrange appeared in 1700 and five editions were published. Whiston's translation appeared in 1737 and is still widely used. An American edition of Maynard's translation was published in Philadelphia in 1795. The translation by Thackery and Marcus has appeared in the *Loeb Classical Library.*

8 H. A. W. Meyer, *Commentary on 1st Corinthians.* Among recent writers, Grosheide accepts the identification, F. F. Bruce regards it as uncertain.

9 In the book of Acts we read that Paul on two occasions appealed to his Roman citizenship; in the one case after submitting to scourging (16:37) in the other to escape this indignity and torture (22:25). It would be interesting to know why Paul acted differently on these two occasions and also how he established his claim to citizenship, when he did make it. We are not told. In the former case the command to scourge may have been given hastily to appease the mob, which was in danger of getting out of hand, by an act of summary punishment; and

Paul may not have been in a position to prove his claim to citizenship on the spot. In the other case, when he did make the appeal, Paul was in safe custody in the Castle at Jerusalem; and any claim made by him could easily be verified by correspondence with the Tarsus authorities. Hence Paul's claim was accepted, perhaps subject to verification and the scourging was omitted. Proof that Paul's claim was false would certainly have exposed him to a far more severe punishment than the scourging which his statement halted temporarily. Luke clearly did not think it necessary to explain the seeming inconsistency in Paul's conduct on those two occasions.

[10] Compare Joshua 22 where it is emphatically stated that the altar *Ed* (witness) is in no sense a rival of the tabernacle, that it is merely a memorial or reminder and is never to be used for the offering of sacrifices. A plainer recognition of "the exclusive legitimacy" of the Mosaic tabernacle and its worship could hardly be asked for.

[11] *Op. cit.*, p. 134.

[12] Having described Esther as "a brilliant hoax," R. H. Pfeiffer goes on to say: "Nor was such a successful deception unprecedented among the Jews. From the modern point of view, three of the most influential writings in the Old Testament — the Deuteronomic Code, the Priestly Code, and Daniel — were technically fraudulent — although their authors were sincere men, free from guile, and inspired by noble religious ideals" (*Introduction to the Old Testament*, p. 745).

[13] *Commentary on Isaiah*, Vol. 1, (1846), p. xxv.

[14] *Old Testament Prophecy*, p. 244.

[15] The great Old Testament type of the redemption wrought on Calvary is the deliverance from Egyptian bondage which is so fully described in the Pentateuch and referred to about one hundred times in the rest of the Old Testament. Contemporary Egyptian records tell us almost nothing about Israel in Egypt, and the lack of such data has led many students of ancient history to reject the biblical account as unreliable. Similarly, the classical historians have very little to tell us about the life of Jesus and what they do tell us adds nothing to what we learn from the Bible.

[16] J. I. Packer correctly describes it as "the central evangelical contention," that "Scripture has complete and final authority over the Church as a self-contained, self-interpreting revelation from God" (*"Fundamentalism" and the Word of God*, p. 73).

[17] This verse sounds what we may call the key-note of the biblical revelation, and it is significantly placed at the very beginning. The fact that Criticism has for a century assigned it to one of the latest of the Old Testament "documents" (P), thus making the sublime monotheism, which this chapter teaches the result of a long process of more or less exclusively naturalistic development, is one of the clearest evidences that can be cited of the radical difference between the critical and the biblical understanding of the religion of Israel, in its origin and development.

[18] Cf. a series of articles by the present writer, "Old Testament Emphases and Modern Thought," which appeared in *PTR* in 1923-24.

[19] *Biblical and Theological Studies*, 1952, p. 21. See also S. G. Craig, *Christianity Rightly So Called*, 1946, especially the chapters entitled, "Christianity and the Supernatural," and, "Christianity, Facts and Doctrines."

[20] B. B. Warfield, *The Inspiration and Authority of the Bible*, pp. 155f., "In the view of the Scriptures, the completely supernatural character of revelation is in no way lessened by the circumstance that it has been given through the instrumentality of men. They affirm, indeed, with the greatest possible emphasis that the Divine word delivered through men is the pure word of God, diluted with no human admixture whatever"(*Ibid.*, p. 86). "It is to be remembered that we are not defending a mechanical theory of inspiration. Every word of the Bible is the word of God according to the doctrine we are discussing; but also and just as truly, every word is the word of a man" (*Ibid.*, p. 437). Note especially Isa. 55:8-13, where God's thoughts and ways are set in sharp contrast with those of man and we read, "So shall my word be that goeth forth out of my mouth: it shall not return unto me void." How does God's word proceed out of his mouth? Usually from the lips of his servant the prophet, who is a man of God, and who introduces his words with the authoritative and impressive, "Thus saith the Lord," or an equivalent phrase.

21 Cf. Schaff's *History of the Christian Church* (3rd ed.), Vol. III, pp. 649f. Some years ago, the writer had occasion to refer to the treatment of a passage in Numbers in *BCBS*. The general editor of this widely used eight volume commentary was Bishop C. J. Ellicott. The commentator on the Book of Numbers was C. J. Elliott. The galley proof came back with a query, suggesting that C. J. Elliott should read C. J. Ellicott — a natural mistake of the proofreader, but a mistake just the same. On another occasion the writer, while serving as faculty editor of *PTR* in reading over the galley proof of the book reviews, discovered to his consternation that a book entitled *The Christian Doctrine of Immortality* was called *The Christian Doctrine of Immorality* — merely the omission of a single letter, one "t" instead of two, but a vast difference in the meaning!

22 *Westminster Shorter Catechism*, Answer to Question 13.

23 *Paradise Lost*, Book I, line 32.

24 When we read the careful instructions (Num. 4:1-20) regarding the covering of the ark and the sacred vessels before they could be carried by the Kohathite Levites, and the startling words, "Cut ye not off the tribe of the families of the Kohathites from among the Levites: but this do unto them, that they may live and not die when they approach unto the most holy things" (vss. 17f.), we realize the seriousness of Uzzah's offense when he took hold of the ark (2 Sam. 6:6). The story of the "new cart" illustrates amazingly the ignorance of the law on the part of David and especially of the priests.

25 If the reading of the *MT* is correct the ark was with Saul's army at Gibeah of Benjamin at the time of Jonathan's victory (1 Sam. 14:18). According to 2 Sam. 11:11, it would appear that it was in Joab's camp when he fought against Rabbah, perhaps for a considerable period of time.

26 This is indicated by 1 Kings 18:30 where we read that Elijah repaired the altar of the Lord that was broken down.

27 The reference in Ezekiel (8:11) to the Seventy Men who took part in the abominable rites performed in the Temple seems to be intended to point out that idolatry and obscenity had corrupted even the highest court of the nation. According to rabbinical tradition the Sanhedrin traced its origin to Moses.

28 Abraham took an oath of Eliezer (Gen. 24:3), Joseph of his brethren (50:25), Jehovah of Israel (Deut. 29:12). Questions of right or wrong might be determined by an oath (Exod. 22:11). The princes of Israel felt bound by their oath to the Gibeonites, even though it was secured by fraud. Wicked Ahab took an oath from neighboring kings that they were not harboring Elijah (1 Kings 18:10). "As the Lord liveth" was a most solemn oath.

29 Nearly thirty times the words "and the Lord spake unto Moses saying" appear in Leviticus. Only occasionally is Aaron named as recipient with Moses of these priestly laws e.g. Lev. 11:1; 13:1; 14:33; 15:1; Num. 2:1; 4:1, 17; 12:4; 14:26; 16:20; 19:1; 20:12, 23 and still more rarely is he addressed directly by God (Lev. 10:8; Num. 18:1, 8, 20).

30 It is significant that while sacrifice is referred to directly or indirectly a number of times before the giving of the law at Sinai, it was not until then that expiation for sin was clearly set forth as basic in it. It is noteworthy that the words used so often in Leviticus and Numbers "a sweet savour" (literally "an odor of satisfaction") occur already in Gen. 8:21. But it is only when with the law there came the knowledge of sin (Rom. 3:20) that the necessity of blood atonement was made clear (Lev. 17:11; Heb. 9:22). The Mosaic Law and the Aaronic priesthood are introduced together in the course of biblical revelation. The law of the altar follows immediately on the proclamation of the Decalogue, (cf. Oehler, *Old Testament Theology*, p. 263).

31 Whether "king" in Deut. 33:5 refers to God or to Moses has been much discussed. Probably the safest position to take is that while "king" does not here refer to Moses, "None the less, through his legislative function Moses typified the royal office of Christ" (G. Vos, *Biblical Theology*, 1948, p. 119).

32 It is said of Saul, "See ye him whom the Lord hath chosen" (10:24). But this choice was made at the insistent demand of the people, in spite of the solemn warning given by God through the prophet. This indicates a difference between the Lord's choice of Saul and his choice of David. He permitted them to have Saul; he gave them David.

33 This seems to be the meaning of the words used regarding Hoshea, "but not as the kings of Israel that were before him" (2 Kings 17:2), since nearly all of

them are denounced specifically for following in the footsteps of "Jeroboam the son of Nebat who made Israel to sin."

34 In his elaborate study of "The Headings of the Psalms" (*PTR*, 1926, pp. 1-37; 353-395), R. D. Wilson presented the evidence from the Headings, as well as from the Psalms themselves, in support of the traditional view that the majority of the Psalms are Davidic or belong to the time of David. He regarded it as significant that "there is not one proper name in all the Psalter that may not have been used already in the time of David, king of Israel. Even in the case of Ps. 137, it is not the use of Babylon, but the context, that shows us that the psalm was probably written in the generation after the captivity" (pp. 17f.).

35 We may compare the role which Isaac Watts has played in the psalmody and hymnody of the Presbyterian churches beginning in the early eighteenth century and continuing to the present time. Charles Wesley is another very prominent figure. He is said to have written about 6500 hymns. It may be noted that Heb. 4:7 attributes a quotation from the anonymous Ps. 95 to David, either because David wrote the psalm (cf. *LXX*) or because it belonged to a collection which was so predominantly Davidic that it could be referred to in this way.

36 Just as David's connection with the Psalter has been challenged by the critics for many years, so Solomon's connection with the Wisdom literature has been questioned or denied. The discovery of the Dead Sea scrolls has led to a reaction against the late datings proposed by radical scholars. R. D. Wilson, after a careful investigation of the claim that the diction of Ecclesiastes proves it to be late, reached the conclusion that "Ecclesiastes and the Song of Songs and most of the Book of Proverbs may, for all we know, have been written by Solomon" (*A Scientific Investigation of the Old Testament* (rev. ed. 1959, pp. 13, 91f., 111, 119ff., 123f.). It is certainly natural to render the titles of Psalms 72 and 127 "*by* Solomon" (the *lamedh auctoris*) as is done in the many cases where the name David occurs.

37 For a fuller treatment the reader is referred to Edward J. Young, *My Servants the Prophets*. Also of great value are the earlier works: Patrick Fairbairn, *Prophecy Viewed in Respect to its Distinctive Nature, its Special Function and Proper Interpretation;* Hengstenberg, *The Christology of the Old Testament.*

38 The ministries of Elisha, Gad, Nathan, Shemaiah, Jehu son of Hanani, Ahijah, Hosea, Isaiah, Jeremiah, and Ezekiel, extended over a considerable period of time. Prophets mentioned in connection with a single event are Azariah son of Oded, Hanani the seer, Micaiah son of Imla, Eliezer son of Dodavah. We also read of certain men upon whom the spirit of prophecy came on a special occasion: Isaac blessing Jacob and Esau, Jacob blessing his twelve sons, Eldad and Medad, Saul, Jahaziel son of Zechariah, Zechariah son of Jehoiada. (Balaam also belongs in this group, though he was not an Israelite, as does also the "old prophet" of 1 Kings 13:11-32.) Three prophetesses are mentioned: Miriam, Deborah, and Huldah; also a false prophetess, Noadiah. Several of the prophets were also historians: Gad, Nathan, Shemaiah, Jehu son of Hanani. Unnamed prophets are mentioned in Judg. 6:8; 1 Kings 13:1; 20:13, 22, 35; 2 Kings 21:10; 23:2; 2 Chron. 25:15). Though unnamed they exerted a powerful influence.

39 Cf. 2 Kings 2:16 which mentions "fifty strong men" as belonging to the prophetic community of Jericho. The great passage in Deuteronomy which speaks of the prophet like unto Moses (18:15-22) clearly is intended also to be a pattern and test for all prophecy (vss. 20-22). When considered in the light of its context (vss. 9-14), as the Lord's substitute for the practices of the heathen, it implies that the people were to go to their prophets for the satisfying of their desire to know future events, and to solve personal problems in so far as this desire was legitimate, even as the heathen went to their diviners, astrologers, necromancers. This is brought out clearly by Vos in his discussion of 1 Sam. 9:9 (*op. cit.*, pp. 245 f.).

40 See E. J. Young, *op. cit.* pp. 56-75 for a fuller discussion of these titles.

41 The prophet might even ask for an accrediting sign (1 Sam. 12:16-19) or it might be given in response to a demand of the one specially concerned (Isa. 38:4-8).

42 2 Kings 17:13, 23; 2 Chron. 24:19; 34:24; 36:16; Ezek. 38:17; Dan. 9:6, 10; Zech. 1:3-6. Ezekiel predicts his future vindication with the words: "Then shall they know that a prophet hath been among them" (33:33). The evils of oppression and exile are represented as the punishment for failure to hearken to

Moses and the prophets. Deut. 31-32 and Isa. 1 and Amos 2:4-16 — all the prophecies of woe and doom were finally fulfilled, even if the prophets did not live to see it.

⁴³ That the word which came to the prophet from God was at times confusing and amazing, even unwelcome and grievous, is proved by many examples. But it is equally clear that the prophet nevertheless recognized it as the word of God and felt constrained to obey it as such. This is illustrated by the incident of the purchase of the field by Jeremiah. The words "then I knew that this was the word of the Lord" (32:18, AV) implies that Jeremiah needed the arrival of Hanameel with his strange proposal, to confirm as the word of God the revelation which the prophet had already received. So it is important to note that in the Hebrew the conjunction is not "then", but the simple "and", "and I knew", which is simply corroborative and not definitive. This is made clear by the words of Jeremiah's prayer (vss. 17-25) which expresses both Jeremiah's amazement at the command and his assurance that it was the will of God.

⁴⁴ This incident serves to show in striking fashion that the state of inspiration was in the case of the prophets "an extraordinary one" (Oehler, *op. cit.* p. 472). The word of the Lord *came* to them, sometimes after a period of anxious waiting (Hab. 1:2; 2:1). Jeremiah waited ten days for the divine answer to a question of national importance (42:7).

⁴⁵ Oesterley and Robinson, *Introduction*, p. 100. Elisha apparently exercised the office of prophet for a full half century, perhaps longer. It would seem obvious that the deeds which are recorded concerning him are but a few of the many which he performed. The biblical narrative seems to justify the statement regarding his miraculous power, that "he used it largely, as did Christ, in simple deeds of kindness" (*DDB* art. "Elisha"). But such a statement as the following is both erroneous and misleading: "The great religious teachers whom we call the Prophets never pretended that they could perform miracles. The lives of Elijah and Elisha were full of miracles, but they departed without leaving posterity a single written word, even though Elijah lived only fifty years before Amos. And with Amos, the first literary Prophet, all miracles ceased" (Lissner, *The Living Past*, p. 132). This statement is also factually incorrect. The destruction of Sennacherib's army in the days of Isaiah, for example, was just as much a miracle as was the blinding of Benhadad's army in the days of Elisha. This attempt to draw a distinction between the age of miracle and the age of prophecy is obviously made with a view to the eliminating of the supernatural from both miracle and prophecy; to treat the miracles of Elijah and Elisha as mere folklore and to eliminate the predictive element from prophecy. It is largely because miracles and prophecy are a marked feature of the Book of Daniel that critical scholars are practically unanimous in holding that the book is Maccabean, its prophecies *post eventum* and its miracles spurious. The Gospels are full of the mighty works and words of him who was the supreme Prophet of whom Moses spake.

⁴⁶ Note also 2 Chron. 25:16; 36:16; Neh. 9:26; Jer. 2:30.

⁴⁷ "What things I wrought in Egypt" may perhaps be better rendered by "how I toyed with Egypt" (cf. *BDB* p. 759b).

⁴⁸ It is tempting to think that the figure of the "rod" (vs. 5) is carried over here and expanded in the reference to the forest of Lebanon which could furnish a vast number of mighty trees to serve as rods.

⁴⁹ The words of Ps. 86:9, "All nations which thou has made shall come and worship before thee, O Lord and shall glorify thy name," are an echo of the Abrahamic Covenant.

⁵⁰ In view of the importance which naturally attached to a prophecy, we might expect that the fulfilment would be carefully recorded when it took place. But such is not always the case. A remarkable example of this is Jeremiah's prophecy that Nebuchadnezzar would place his throne on the stones which the Lord commanded him to set up at Tahpanhes, in the land of Egypt whither the Jewish remnant had fled to escape from their great enemy the king of Babylon (Jer. 43:10). We might expect that the fulfillment of this remarkably specific prophecy would be recorded. It is not. We are clearly expected to assume that like the many other prophecies uttered by Jeremiah it was duly fulfilled.

⁵¹ The principal theme in Isa. 40-48 is predictive prophecy, as exhibiting the unique ability of the God of Israel both to predict and to bring to pass, and the utter impotence of heathen dieties to do either the one or the other (e.g., 41:4,

22-25; 44:6-8, 25f.; 45-21; 46:9-11; 48:3-8). In the light of such passages it is hard to understand the attempt of so many of the critics to deny that the prophets foretold the future, or to treat this aspect of their teaching as of minor importance. It can only be explained as due to their minimizing or rejecting the supernatural elements in the religion of Israel.

[52] *Lectures on Prophecy*, p. 445.

[53] See article "Isaiah" in *ZPBD*, p. 385, for a fuller discussion of these names of the Messiah.

[54] F. Delitzsch has beautifully described it: "A parable may be illustrative of the manner in which the Old Testament proclamation of salvation is gradually developed. In relation to the day of the New Testament the Old Testament is night. During this night there mount up two stars of promise in opposite directions. The one describes its path from above downwards: it is the promise of Jahve who is about to come. The other describes its path from below upwards: it is the hope which is reposed in the seed of David, the prophecy of the Son of David, which is at first altogether human and only earthly. These two stars meet at last, they blend together into one constellation; the night vanishes and it is day. This one constellation is Jesus Christ, Jahve and David's Son in one person, the king of Israel and at the same time the Redeemer of the world; in one word, the God-man" (*The Psalms*, vol. II, p. 343). Moeller points out that the "diadem" referred to in Ezekiel 21:26 is the high priest's mitre (Exod. 28:4, 39; 29:6; 39:28, 31) which thus connects the priestly and regal in the person of the "prince" (*ISBE*, p. 1080).

[55] *History of the Christian Church*, vol. II, p. 115.

[56] According to William Lee there are only two conceivable proofs of the divine nature of a revelation, prophecy and miracle. "Prophecy, from its embracing at once events of which living men might judge, and the history of the far distant future, performs the function of a witness to every age. Miracles, by virtue of the Creative and Revealing Presence, apparent in them, offer to all conscientious minds the clearest of proofs. The language of unprejudiced reason must ever be − 'We know that thou art a teacher come from God: for no man can do these miracles that thou doest except God be with him'" (*The Inspiration of Holy Scripture, Its Nature and Proof*, 1857, p. 212). In his lectures to the Senior Class at Princeton Seminary on *Prophets and Prophecy* (1881), Prof. Wm. Henry Green described their importance as fourfold: their authority as a divine revelation, their historical value, their messianic value, their apologetic value. As to the last he said: "They contain the most astonishing exhibitions of supernatural foresight in numerous predictions, and furnish us with a powerful argument for the truth and divinity of our religion" (p. 3).

[57] For an excellent popular treatment of this subject, see David J. Burrell, *The Teaching of Jesus Concerning the Scriptures*, 1904.

[58] *Westminster Confession* I, iv.

[59] Dr. Burrell was the pastor of the Marble Collegiate Church in New York City, in the course of which important pastorate he also served for several years as acting professor of Homiletics in Princeton Seminary. He declined to accept the position permanently.

CHAPTER II

[1] A. F. Kirkpatrick, *The Book of the Psalms*, 1902, p. 679.

[2] A helpful illustration of the important difference between literal and figurative language is furnished by the descriptions of the crossing of the Red Sea given in Exod. 14:21f.; 15:8; 19:4. The first is a literal, prose account. The others are just as obviously figurative. To take them literally would be absurd. The exodus from Egypt was no journey on a flying carpet, such as Arab legend ascribes to king Solomon. Compare also Isa. 59:21 and Jer. 1:8f. with Ezek. 2:8 − 3:4 and Rev. 10:8-11. When the prophet receives a word from God, it becomes as much a part of him as if he had eaten and digested it.

[3] After completing his eighth campaign (714 B.C.) Sargon wrote a rather lengthy account of it in the form of a letter which he addressed to the gods and the people of his kingdom. It begins with the words, "To Ashshur, the father of the gods, the great lord, who dwells in E-har-sag-gal-kur-kura, his great temple, the utmost well-beings (*adannish adannish lu shulmu*)." The message to the

Philistine cities (I Sam. 31:9) was probably sent orally. But the parallel is interesting. The gods were supposed not only to know but also to control the affairs of men. But it was only proper to inform them of and give them the credit for the triumphs which they brought about (Thureau-Dangin, *Sargon II, King of Assyria, Une Relation de la huitième campagne*).

4 When in 1917 the American Expeditionary Force arrived in France, General Pershing and his staff went to the grave of Lafayette. The famous words uttered there, "Lafayette we are here!" were, of course, a gross historical anachronism. Lafayette had been dead for four-score years! But the young Marquis who came to America in 1777 as a youth of nineteen to help in the struggle for freedom represented and symbolized in the eyes of American patriots liberty-loving France at her best. And this brief apostrophe packed more meaning than might have been expressed in the course of a lengthy oration (Cf. Gene Smith, *When the Cheering Stopped* (1964), p. 34).

5 The largest synagogue in New York City, said to be the largest in the world, is named Temple Beth Emanu El (Fifth Ave. at 65th St.).

6 Quoted from memory.

7 In Hebrew the nominal sentence does not ordinarily employ the copula. Such a sentence as "the house is large" would be expressed by simply placing the two words in juxtaposition, "the house large." Because of this the policy is here adopted of placing the copula in parenthesis in the translation.

8 Garstang understood it figuratively *(Joshua-Judges*, 1931), pointing out that the hornet was one of the emblems in the double crown of Pharaoh (cf. Isa. 14.29f.; Jer. 8:17). If the rendering "gadfly" (Jer. 46:20 *RV*) is correct, it would be a similar example. "Wall" in Exod. 14:22 and Ezra 9:9 is probably used in the figurative sense of "protection" as is clearly the case in 1 Sam. 25:16.

9 Such rhetorical use of personification and apostrophe is timeless. It is just as common today as it was in Joshua's day. The same principle applies to the heap and pillar erected by Jacob and Laban (Gen. 31:44-53). Laban was apparently an idolater and may have thought of the stone and heap as inhabited by a numen (Animism). But if Jacob was true to the faith of his grandfather Abraham he cannot have so regarded it. The same principle applies to apostrophe. In calling Jehu Zimri ("Is it peace, Zimri?") (*ARV*, 2 Kings 9:31) Jezebel shows her contempt for Jehu since Zimri reigned only seven days after slaying Elah.

10 Charles Hodge, *Systematic Theology*, Vol. 1, pp. 339-44. Note Exod. 20:4; Ps. 115; Isa. 44; Jer. 10, as a few of the many passages which denounce and ridicule that false anthropomorphism which shows itself in idolatry.

11 Cf. Fairbairn, *On Prophecy*, pp. 119-26 and 508-13.

12 Cf. article "Passover" in *ISBE*, p. 2256.

13 The words "and his sound shall be heard when he goeth in unto the holy place" (Exod. 28:35) show that the bells on the hem of Aaron's garment were real bells of gold and not merely embroidered bells like the cherubim on the veil.

14 Edward Mack (*ISBE*, pp. 2392f.) argues strongly for the figurative interpretation of Deut. 6:8f. and regards the use of phylacteries as a later concession to the carnal mind of the people.

15 The words, "and the Lord God caused a deep sleep to fall upon Adam and he slept" (Gen. 2:21) have led some commentators to infer that the account of the forming of Eve is to be regarded simply as a vision designed to convince Adam of the peculiar intimacy of the relationship in which Eve stood to him, that she was bone of his bone and flesh of his flesh and that this was because she was (according to the vision) "taken out of man." But Paul's words, "for Adam was first formed, then Eve" (1 Tim. 2:13) and still more specifically, "For the man is not of the woman but the woman of the man: for neither was the man created for the woman; but the woman for the man" (1 Cor. 11:8f.), indicate very clearly that, according to Apostolic teaching, there was something absolutely unique in the bringing into being of our first parents, and they warn us of the danger of attempting to tone down or mythologize the language of the Genesis account to make it fit into an evolutionary theory of the origin of man.

16 See articles, "Parables" in *DDB* and "Allegory," "Fable," and "Parable," in *ISBE*. It is true that the parable commonly illustrates truth "from the analogy of common experience." But it may also transcend it as in the parable of the Rich Man and Lazarus.

17 Cf. Isa. 5:8; Micah 2:2; also Amos 8:4.

[18] Gesenius-Kautzsch, *Hebrew Grammar* (Cowley, ed., 1910), p. 45.

[19] *BV* renders 2 Kings 19:3: "They said to him, 'Thus has Hezekiah said:

> A day of distress and reproach,
> And of dishonor is today,
> For children have come to birth
> But there is not strength to give birth.' "

This is singular because *BV* does not print a single verse of Isaiah in poetry, while *RSV* metricizes the greater part of it. Kittel, Moffat, *AT*, and *RSV* despite their proneness to metricize the Prophets, treat these words of Hezekiah as simple prose. This serves to illustrate the large amount of subjectivity which is involved in these attempts to make poetry out of what is commonly regarded as eloquent prose.

[20] E.g., in Amos 7:2f., 5f., 17 (*RSV*), where the judgment of the Lord on apostate Israel is stated in lines of similar content but unequal length, the parallelism or balance is obvious, but to treat them as poetry carries the theory to or beyond the breaking point.

[21] It is to be noted that in John 19:37 the "whom they pierced" might be understood as "(me) whom they pierced" or "(him) whom they pierced." There the emphasis is on the verb and not on the pronoun. In the English translation, the "him whom" might better be rendered "(him) whom" or "one whom." In the Old Testament the antecedent would be "me." The omission of the antecedent in the New Testament quotation is probably intentional; "me whom they pierced" would read awkwardly in the context in John and its presence is not essential to accuracy, since the person referred to is perfectly clear. For the construction, see A. T. Robertson, *Grammar of the Greek New Testament*, p. 705.

[22] Further examples are: Judg. 7:22 "even in all the camp" (*AV*); 1 Sam. 17:40 "even in a scrip" (*AV, ARV*); 1 Sam. 28:3 "even in his city" (*AV, ARV*); 2 Kings 13:17, "the arrow of the Lord's deliverance and the arrow of deliverance from Syria" (*AV; ARV* "even," *RSV* omits). In Isa. 27:1 the question is whether one, two or three enemies are referred to. Cf. Isa. 32:7 — "even when the needy speaketh right" (*AV, ARV*). In Isa. 1:1; 2:1 the "and Jerusalem" is included in the "Judah" which precedes and so is singled out for emphasis, as in Ps. 18 (heading) the "and from the hand of Saul." In Isa. 9:7 on the other hand the "and upon his kingdom" expands and emphasizes the "throne of David" which precedes.

[23] See R. D. Wilson, *Studies in the Book of Daniel*, chaps. V and IX; also J. C. Whitcomb, Jr., *Darius the Mede*, p. 48.

[24] It may be well to note that the Ras Shamra poetry gives no evidence of a metrical structure except the parallelism. It is written like simple prose. Furthermore the metre is far from uniform.

[25] J. H. Breasted, *The Development of Religion and Thought in Ancient Egypt*, p. 97.

[26] Albright prefers the terms colon and bi-colon to the more usual hemistich and stich (or stich and distich). Thus he describes the following as a tri-colon:

> Behold, thine enemies, O Baal,
> Behold thine enemies shalt thou crush,
> Behold, thou shalt smite thy foes!

Then he tells us: "In Psalm 92:9 this passage recurs with slight changes as follows:

> For behold, Thine enemies, O Lord,
> For behold Thine enemies shall perish,
> All doers of evil shall be scattered!

That there is a similarity here is quite obvious. But there is also a difference. The fact that there are three lines (colons) in both is purely accidental. We have seen that in Ps. 103:3-6 there are a half-dozen. It all depends on the content or subject matter. Compare, e.g., Ps. 115:5f., where there are four strictly parallel two-member lines beginning with the words, "A mouth have they, but they do not speak." There is absolutely no warrant for the statement that the Baal verses "recur" in Ps. 92, and that the change is only "slight." One change, we would prefer to say *difference*, is that the words are addressed in the one case to the Ugaritic God Baal, in the other to Yahweh, the God of Israel. A further and a characteristic difference is that the ethical element is absent from the one, which ends with the words, "Thou shalt smite thy foes," while the other concludes with "All doers of iniquity shall be scattered" (Cf. *The Archaeology of Palestine,* p. 231).

[27] *The Argument of the Book of Job Unfolded* (1873), p. 11.

[28] Franz Delitzsch called it a "drama" *(Biblical Commentary on the Book of Job* 1866), pp. 14f.

[29] *ISBE,* pp. 1680, 1687. He was inclined to regard it as "a prison-made book, like *Pilgrim's Progress* and *Don Quixote* and to attribute it to Jehoiachin.

[30] *Commentary on Ezekiel,* p. 341. That the genealogy is ethical and not racial seems perfectly clear. Yet some critical scholars find here a reference to the pre-Israelite history of Jerusalem. The historian, Jack Finegan, treats it as a statement of historical fact *(LAP,* p. 125) as does Gurney, *The Hittites,* p. 1.

[31] Cf. *FBM,* pp. 95-99, *PTR* (1925), pp. 603-606.

[32] *Ibid.,* pp. 99-101, and for a fuller discussion *PTR* (1925), pp. 606-636.

[33] Cf. Exod. 40:36-38.

[34] That repetition is a marked characteristic of Hebrew style is illustrated by a Hebrew letter discovered near Yabneh-yam in Judea and dating according to Frank M. Cross, Jr. from c. 625 B.C. His translation reads as follows:

"Let my lord the commander hear the word of his servant. As for thy servant, thy servant was harvesting in Hasar Asam; and thy servant harvested, and took measure and stored (the grain), according to regular practice. Before Sabbath when thy servant had measured his harvest and had stored (the grain) according to regular practice, Hoshaiah the son of Shobay came and took the garment of thy servant. When I had measured this harvest of mine, in the regular way, he took the garment of thy servant; and all my brethren will testify for me, those who were harvesting with me in the heat of the sun; all my brethren will testify for me. Truly I am innocent of (any) gu[ilt. Pray return] my garment. And if not, it is (still) incumbent on the commander to retu[rn the garment of thy servant; so let him gr]ant to him mer[cy . . .] thy [ser]vant, but do not drive him away" (BASOR, No. 165 1962, p. 43).

As Cross points out this letter "vividly recalls biblical law (Exod. 22:25-26; Deut. 10-13) and prophecy (Amos 2:8)."

[35] Regarding the Immanuel Prophecy, Fairbairn's words are especially noteworthy. "The sign, in which the nature and destiny of the kingdom were to be imaged, bursts upon the view as a prodigy from an unknown quarter; it is a child born, not to the *present* occupant of the throne, nor to any *future* occupant, but to a virgin; and even she marked out by no distinct specifications of place or time, — foreseen only by the omniscient eye of God. He it is alone, who charges Himself with the accomplishment of the result; in His own time He will bring forth the *almah* and her Son — as if Ahaz and his successors in the kingdom had no personal interest in the matter!" *(Hermeneutical Manual,* 1858, p. 423). This interpretation, as Fairbairn points out, does away with the necessity of assigning a double-sense and double fulfilment to the prophecy. Apparently Fairbairn regarded the times specified in vs. 16 as too vague to be significant for the fulfillment of the prophecy. The land was forsaken or desolated centuries *before* the Child attained to the age of accountability.

[36] *Lectures on Prophecy* (1865), pp. 58-82.

[37] *Ibid.,* p. 63.

[38] *Ibid.,* p. 102, cf. p. 140; also *PAC,* pp. 18-54.

[39] *Op. cit.,* pp. 180f.

[40] Cf. O. T. Allis, "The Fear of Isaac," in *PTR* (1918), pp. 299-304.

[41] A striking example of this word-order occurs in Isa. 40:19 where the word for word rendering would be "the image hath cast a workman." Here the usual (SVO) order makes the statement so absurd that the reader must understand that the order is reversed expressly for the purpose of driving home the absurdity of the thought that a man-made image could be a god. ARV treats the sentence as compound nominal and renders: "The image, a workman hath cast it," which is quite possible. But however construed it serves to illustrate and emphasize Isaiah's utter contempt for idolatry, which is a major theme in chapters 40-48 of his prophecy. (cf. Gesenius-Kautzsch, as cited, p. 456 and Driver, *Hebrew Tenses,* 1892, p. 279).

[42] Cf. O. T. Allis, "The Birth Oracle to Rebekah" *(EQ,* 1939, pp. 97-117).

[43] In dealing with Zionism, it is important to remember that the world-embrac-

ing nature of the Gospel is present already in the O.T. in the Abrahamic covenant: "In thee shall all the families of the earth be blessed" (Gen. 12:3). This
world-embracing promise is to be found elsewhere in the O.T.: Isa. 19:24f.; 55:1;
Joel 2:28-32; and in the Psalms: e.g., Psalm 72. The Psalter ends with the command, "Let everything that hath breath praise the Lord." The Great Commission
of Matthew 28:16f. is world-embracing. Peter quotes Joel on the day of Pentecost
(Acts 2) and he preaches the Gospel to the Gentile Cornelius and his household
(Acts 10). Paul declares most emphatically that the wall of partition between
Jew and Gentile has been broken down (Eph. 2:14; Gal. 3:9, 28f.; 6:15); both
are one in Christ Jesus. In Rom. 9-11 he declares his love for the Jews and his
hope for their salvation. But he says not a word about their return to Palestine.
The establishment of a Jewish state, regarded as the fulfilment of the Abrahamic
covenant, implies and even demands the rebuilding of the temple and the re-
instituting of the O.T. ritual of sacrifice, both of which are outlawed by the N.T.
(John 4:21f.; cf. Isa. 66:1 and Heb. 9:11-14). Hence Christians have generally
held that the promises to the Jews have their fulfilment in the Christian church,
that Jewish nationalism and particularism are abolished by the Gospel. This does
not necessarily mean that there cannot be a return of the Jews to Palestine. But
it certainly implies that such a return is not necessary to the fulfilment of the O.T.
prophecies concerning Israel.

⁴⁴ This view is ably defended by Payne Smith in *BCBS*, vol. I, pp. 184f.

⁴⁵ This may be the reason that S. R. Driver, in discussing this use of the perfect (i.e., waw consecutive with the imperfect), does not mention these passages
as examples of the perfect used with the force of the pluperfect. He regards the
"and they saw" of I Kings 13:12 as perhaps the strongest passage that can be
urged in favor of the pluperfect sense of the verb in this construction, but ignores these two passages completely (*Hebrew Tenses*, pp. 84-89). In the far
more important case of Gen. 2:12 Driver rejects the pluperfect sense. But
Delitzsch accepts it on the ground that in this chapter the narrative centers about
man, while in chapter I we have a course of development sketched of which man
is the culmination. He cites Isa. 37:5; Jonah 2:4; Zech. 7:2 as examples of the
pluperfect sense (*Neuer Commentar ueber die Genesis*, 1887, p. 92).

⁴⁶ *Commentary on Ezekiel, in loco*. Several emendations of verse 3 have been
proposed by those who regard the mention of Assyria (*Ashshur*) in this verse as
unsuited to the context: (a) Delete the word Assyria; (b) Read *te'ashshur* (box-
wood) instead of *'ashshur* and regard "a box-wood, a cedar" as equivalent to "a
mighty (or stately) cedar" (Toy, Moffatt, Gordon); (c) Change *Ashshur* into
ashweka and render "I will liken you to a cedar" (*RSV*). No evidence in Mss.
or versions is adduced for these proposed changes. They all overlook the fact
that the sudden shift from the "Assyria" of vs. 3 to the "Pharaoh and all his
multitude" of vs. 18 is intended, like the "Thou art the man" in Nathan's application of the parable of the Ewe-lamb, to introduce a startling and devastating
climax. Assyria suddenly becomes Egypt!

⁴⁷ Trench, *On the Lessons in Proverbs* (1853), p. 106.

⁴⁸ *Commentary on Isaiah*, vol. II, p. 500. Alexander points out that "The Hebrew phrase here used means to look with any strong emotion, that of pleasure
which is commonly suggested by the context being here excluded not by inference or implication merely but by positive assertion."

⁴⁹ The fact that this Generation ends, we might say breaks off with Peleg and
his brother would seem to indicate that the Confusion of Tongues took place in
their day (10:25), some generations before the time of Abraham. It seems strange
that the traditional Jewish chronology dates the Confusion in 1764 B.C., forty-
eight years *after* the birth of Abram which it places in 1812 B.C.

⁵⁰ There is a beautiful suggestiveness, however, in the Chronicler's omission of
any reference to David's great sin and its consequences. David prays in Ps. 51:1, 9
that his sins may be blotted out. In Ps. 32:1 he describes the blessedness of him
whose sin is "covered." In Ps. 103:12 he celebrates the love of God which removes our transgressions to an infinite distance. In Isa. 43:25 and 44:23 the for-
getting love of God is beautifully described. So, perhaps with all this in mind,
the Chronicler passes over this dark period of David's life as if it had never been.

⁵¹ The failure of 2 Kings to mention the name of the king of Israel in a large
part of the narrative in 3:7 – 8:15 may be due simply to the fact that he mentions Jehoram in 3:6 and 8:16 and expects his readers to understand that "the

king" (used 15 times) and "the king of Israel" (8 times) in the intervening narrative always means Jehoram. The twelve years of his reign (3:1) would allow time for all the events described in this group of chapters. To say that "the name of the king of Israel is apparently deliberately suppressed" (*NBD*, p. 698) seems an overstatement. Omitted as unnecessary, might be more correct. At least it seems clear that the writer's primary concern is with the doings of Elisha and not with the events of the reign of the king of Israel.

52 The reference in Elijah's letter to Jehoram's slaying of his brethren (21:4) indicates clearly that it was written after the death of Jehoshaphat. Consequently, the statement in 2 Kings 3:11 which describes Elisha, there present, as a servant of Elijah is not to be understood as meaning that Elijah was dead. He may well have been prevented by age from confronting Jehoram face to face. So he sent him a written message.

53 2 Kings 19:37; 2 Chron. 32:21; Isa. 37:38.

54 *ARV, RSV, BV* make the last sentence of Neh. 7:73, "and when the seventh month was come", the beginning of a new paragraph and thus make it refer to the feast in Ezra's day. This is probably correct but the fact that the phrasing of the following sentence is almost identical in both passages may indicate that a connection was recognized between the seventh month in both cases. And the statement in Neh. 7:73 that all Israel dwelt in their cities which is almost identical with Ezra 2:70 reads more like a quotation than a statement describing the situation in Nehemiah's day.

55 After the death of Shalmaneser V in 722 B.C. Merodach-Baladan became king of Babylon and reigned about eleven years. Then he took part in a conspiracy to overthrow Sargon and in 710 B.C. Sargon captured Babylon and made himself king. In 703 B.C. Merodach-Baladan again mastered Babylon but ruled there for only a year. So this incident might have taken place either before 710 or in 703 B.C.

56 Most readers will agree with Keil that this is "undoubtedly" the case. On the other hand it is less clear whether the Naaman story itself belongs chronologically before 6:8 or after 6:23. On the basis of Lev. 13:12f, J. S. Wright argues that Gehazi was "clean" and could continue in Elisha's service (*NBD*, p. 456). This would avoid the difficulty of assuming that the king conversed with a leper. But this explanation is entirely out of harmony with narrative in 2 Kings 5, according to which it was the leprosy of Naaman, from which Naaman was miraculously cured, which was to be upon Gehazi and upon his seed forever. And the words, "And he went out from his presence a leper *as white* as snow," certainly read like final dismissal.

57 2 Sam. 15:7 "at the end of forty years." Many scholars regard this as a scribal error for "four" (a reading supported by Syr. and some editions of *LXX*). Beecher (*Dated Events*, pp. 118ff) makes it refer to the fortieth year of David's reign and so places the census, the recognition of Solomon as king, Absalom's revolt, the Sheba affair, the physical breakdown of David, the preparation for building the temple and regulations of worship, etc. all at the very *end* of David's reign.

58 Compare 2 Sam. 4:10 where David says of the Amalekite who brought him tidings of Saul's death, "I took hold of him and slew him" with the earlier statement, "And David called one of the young men, and said, Go near, and fall upon him. And he smote him, that he died" (1:15). The statement that Jacob "made Joseph a coat or garment with long sleeves" (Gen. 57:3) certainly does not mean that Jacob wove or tailored the garment. He had it made for Joseph.

59 The ancient Babylonian kings recognized it. Hammurabi, for example, invoked the curses of the gods not only on anyone who removed, covered up or destroyed the stele on which his great code of laws was inscribed but also on the man who got some one else to do it for him (*ANET*, p. 179).

60 Note the further statements: "when they were sore" (34:25), and especially the words "and the sons of Jacob came upon the slain and spoiled the city" (vs. 27). Note also that, while Jacob reprobated this act of violence (vs. 30) he seems nevertheless to have claimed credit for it. For he says later on of the "portion" (*shechem*) which he gave to Joseph, "which I took from the Amorite with my sword and with my bow" (48:22). It also seems improbable that Jacob's sons would have been pasturing their flocks at Shechem (37:12) if the city had not been reduced to a state of practical impotence.

[61] On the other hand it is to be recognized that the exploits of such heroes as Shamgar (Judg. 3:31) and Samson (15:15f.) are recorded as proofs of personal prowess. To assume that they had helpers would detract from the obvious intent of the narrator. Jamieson thinks "that Shamgar was only the leader of a band of peasants who by means of such implements of labor as they could lay hold of at the moment, achieved the heroic exploit recorded" (*JFB, in loco*).

[62] Did Joseph's brothers lie when they informed him of Jacob's dying request that Joseph deal kindly with them after his death? Would not Jacob, if he had had any fear for the future of his sons, have made this a father's legacy, a dying request to Joseph? Is it not probable that it was the bad conscience of the brothers, which caused them to resort to such a device? We are not told. We are not even told whether Jacob ever learned of or suspected the perfidy of his sons (37:33-35). The curse pronounced on Simeon and Levi concerned their conduct at Shechem in avenging Dinah (Gen. 34). Neither of them was conspicuously involved in the selling of Joseph into slavery. Whether David lied regarding going to attend a feast at Bethlehem (1 Sam. 20:5f. cf. vs. 24, 35) is not perfectly clear. But the deceit he practiced on Ahimelech at Nob was lying pure and simple (21:1-9), although we need not infer that David realized in advance (vs. 22) what the terrible consequences of that deceit would be.

[63] *Systematic Theology*, vol. III, pp. 441, 443. A. H. Strong cites Rahab's conduct under the heading: "Where evil acts appear at first sight to be sanctioned, it is frequently some right intent or accompanying virtue, rather than the act itself, upon which commendation is bestowed" and he appeals to Heb. 11:31 and James 2:25 (*Systematic Theology*, 1907, p. 230). Hodge declares that despite its abuse by the Jesuits "the principle that a higher obligation absolves from a lower stands firm" (*Systematic Theology*, III, p. 442). Cf. James Orr, *Problems of the O.T.*, pp. 465-478; R. J. Rushdoony, *Intellectual Schizophrenia*, p. 79.

[64] Wm. Brenton Greene, Jr., "The Ethics of the Old Testament" in *PTR* (1929), pp. 153-192, 313-366, especially p. 172.

[65] *Ibid.*, p. 325.

[66] It is perhaps significant that the name of neither parent is given here: "a man from the house of Levi . . . a daughter of Levi." Their lineage, only, is important, both were descended from Levi. Later fuller data was supplied (6:14-27).

[67] That Gen. 11 counted ten generations is indicated by the listing of a Cainan after Arphaxed in the *LXX* and in Luke 3:36.

[68] The genealogy of David in Ruth 4:18-20 is significant because it also lists ten names: five belong to the Exodus period, five to the time of the Judges. Keil regarded the limitation to ten as for the sake of symmetry. The genealogy of Ezra (7:1-5) certainly omits some links, how many is uncertain.

[69] William Hales regarded it as Ussher's special contribution to the problem of the genealogies that he "happily rectified the vulgar error that Abraham was born in the seventieth year of his father's age" (*A New Analysis of Chronology* (1809), Vol. I, p. 23). For a fuller discussion see E. J. Young, *Thy Word is Truth*, pp. 175-9.

[70] *DDB*, p. 195.

[71] "David's youngest son, at least by Bathsheba" (*DDB*, p. 732). The elliptical statement "and she bare him after Absalom" (1 Kings 1:6) must mean that Haggith bore Adonijah after Maacah bore Absalom. According to seniority Adonijah was entitled to succeed, for all of Bathsheba's sons were born in Jerusalem. So Solomon could not have claimed seniority even had he been Bathsheba's oldest surviving son. According to Josephus (*Antiq.* VII, 14, 2) Solomon was David's youngest son.

[72] Ezra 262f.; 4:11, 23; 6:3-12; 7:11-26; Neh. 2:7-9; 7:64f. Note also 1 Kings 11:41; 1 Chron. 29:29f.; 2 Chron. 13:22; 26:22; 32:32.

[73] Num. 31:8, 16; Deut. 23:3-6; Josh. 13:22; 24:9; Neh. 13:2; Micah 6:5; 2 Peter 2:15; Jude 11; Rev. 2:14. Cf. Judg. 11:25.

[74] The only allusion in Chronicles to the anointing of Solomon as king during David's lifetime is in the words "the second time" which recall 1 Kings 1:34, 39.

[75] There is no "with" in the Hebrew. In the Hebrew the sentence ends with the word wool (e.g. fleece). Placed at the end of the sentence the word appears to be emphatic and to mean that Moab's annual tribute consisted only of fleeces.

[76] The only true prophet other than Zachariah whose martyrdom is referred to

in the Old Testament is Urijah, the son of Shemaiah (Jer. 26:20-23). Yet in the confession of sin in Neh. 9 we read "and they killed thy prophets" (vs. 26). Jeremiah mentions the terrible fate of two false prophets, Ahab and Zedekiah (29:20-23) and pronounces woes on two others, Shemaiah (29:31) and Hananiah (28:15-17).

77 In Heb. 7:27, "and this he did once" is ambiguous. It might be taken to include atonement for "his own sin." But as C. J. Vaughan has well said: "The question answers itself. To say so would be to contradict the whole language of the Epistle (as well as of Scripture throughout) as to the sinlessness of Christ" (*Commentary,* p. 139).

78 Cf. Plumptre in *BCBS, in loco.* H. W. A. Meyer thinks Stephen made mistakes. Addison Alexander defends the accuracy of his statements.

79 R. D. Wilson remarks: "We might dismiss the objection as puerile were it not apparently made in all seriousness." He made a thorough study of the use of the word "king" (*melech*) in *Studies in the Book of Daniel* (pp. 83-95) and also of the word "son" (pp. 117-22) with the conclusion that the biblical usage is entirely justified. Cf. also, E. J. Young, *The Prophecy of Daniel,* pp. 267-70.

80 In 4:11 we read the pious wish, "The Lord make the woman that is come into thine house like Rachel and like Leah, which two did build the house of Israel." Here Rachel is named before her older sister, and the concubines, Zilpah and Bilhah, who were the ancestresses of four of the tribes, are ignored.

81 In *Calvin on Scripture and Divine Sovereignty,* p. 30.

82 Josh. 6:9; cf. Num. 32:17, 20, 21, 27, 29, 30, 32; Deut. 3:18; Josh. 1:14; 4:12 with Josh. 6:7, 9, 13.

83 The reading "Moses" is apparently the original one. In the *MT* the *n* is a "suspended letter" i.e., written above the line to indicate it as an insertion. The reading Moses is supported to some extent by the ancient versions (*LXX,* Old Latin, *Vulgate*).

84 Yet it is significant that this confession made by Saul is the only allusion elsewhere in the Historical Books to the terrible events recorded in Judg. 19-21. On the other hand the loyalty of Benjamin to the house of David, partly shown even in the days of Saul, is referred to; and the fact that Benjamin remained faithful at the time of the Great Schism is one of the wonders of biblical history. The struggle between Saul the Benjamite and David of Judah must have left many scars. Shimei's conduct may illustrate this. Yet in his account of the Schism, the Chronicler summarizes Rehoboam's resources by saying "And Judah and Benjamin belonged to him" (2 Chron. 11:12). Hosea mentions Benjamin once (5:8) and Gibeah three times (5:8; 9:9; 10:9). But the sin of Gibeah is denounced as the sin of Israel (10:9). Pusey points out that the guilt of Israel must have been great since the Lord caused Israel to be twice smitten before Benjamin with a loss of 40,000 men as compared with the 25,000 of Benjamin (cf. Num. 31:49; Lev. 26:8; Josh. 23:10). Paul twice refers to himself as a Benjamite (Rom. 11:1; Phil. 3:5).

85 An even more serious objection to the Messianic interpretation is that this passage is nowhere quoted in the New Testament. If it were correct to say with Pusey, "The Resurrection of Christ and our resurrection in Him and in His Resurrection, could not be more plainly foretold," it would be strange indeed that Paul should refer only to Hos. 13:14 in 1 Cor. 15:55 and that elsewhere in the New Testament other passages in Hosea should be quoted, but this verse nowhere. The mention of "the third day" in Matt. 20:19 and Luke 21:22 is probably to be referred to Jesus' words regarding Jonah (cf. Matt. 12:40) and not to these words of Hosea.

86 *The Luebeck Bible* (1494), a copy of which is in the Speer Library at Princeton, has a double page, black and white illustration. On the right side Jonah is shown being shoved over the side of the ship into the fish's mouth; on the other he is kneeling in prayer as he is being landed by the fish on the shore near a castle, while the ship, in mid-picture, is still on the horizon, after the three days!

87 Sarah (Herah) is listed also in Num. 26:46 and in 1 Chron. 7:30: We may assume that there was a special reason for the inclusion although it is nowhere stated.

88 Mark 1:30; Luke 4:38 cf. 1 Cor. 9:5.

89 The expression is *shabbathon shabbath qodesh* (a rest, a rest of holiness).

It has been argued that the *AV* rendering ("the rest of the holy sabbath") is misleading, since it implies that the sabbath was already known, while the absence of the article in the Hebrew indicates the contrary. As to this it is to be noted that the word *shabbathon* which occurs only in the Pentateuch (11 times) and appears to be a technical expression, is never used with the definite article. If the sabbath was entirely new, we would naturally expect the first reference to it to be its solemn proclamation in the Decalogue. But if it goes back to the Creation (Gen. 2:3) and was observed by the patriarchs, as the word "remember" (Exod. 20:8) seems to imply, then its observance in connection with the giving of the manna would prepare for the proclamation of the Fourth Commandment and also indicate that, while the Decalogue was made binding on Israel at Sinai, all of its requirements were really applicable to all mankind as originally created by God. This is important because of the claim, which is sometimes made and based on Neh. 9:14 that the sabbath concerned the Jews only and has no connection except by contrast with the Christian Lord's day as is claimed in the *Scofield Reference Bible* (see Matt. 12:1). The exposition of the Decalogue is a substantial part of the great Catechisms of Protestantism (e.g., Luther's, Heidelberg, Westminster).

[90] Never in the Psalms (except the heading of Ps. 92), a few times in Chronicles (1 Chron. twice, 2 Chron. 7 times) and in a single context in Hosea, Amos, and Jeremiah; a few times in Isaiah, most often in Ezekiel. Its observance was rigidly enforced by Nehemiah.

[91] Yet it is referred to in Ecclus. 50:5 seq. and in 3 Macc. 1:11; also in the Dead Sea Commentary on Habakkuk discovered in 1947, which discovery has given rise to a lively discussion. (See the references in Millar Burrows *The Dead Sea Scrolls*, 1944, and *More Light on the Dead Sea Scrolls*, 1958). Cf. Wilhelm Moller, Art. "Day of Atonement" in *ISBE*, p. 327.

[92] Such being the case, it is rather remarkable that a number of historians from comparatively early times have endeavored to calculate the chronology of Israel from the time of the Conquest in terms of Jubilees. Whiston, in his lengthy discussion of Josephus' chronology (Dissertation V) described as his main design "the determination of the *years of jubilee*" (Sect. 55). He counted thirty-one jubilee years from 1493 B.C. to A.D. 27 (inclusive). Yet he admitted that he could find evidence in biblical and extra biblical sources for only ten of them.

[93] This is especially noteworthy since we read of David's "many sons" (1 Chron. 28:4f.) and are told that Rehoboam with eighteen wives and sixty concubines had twenty-eight sons and sixty daughters (2 Chron. 11:21) and that Abijah had fourteen wives, twenty-two sons, and sixteen daughters (13:21). The many wives and concubines may be mentioned as proof that Rehoboam and Abijah followed in the steps of Solomon in violating the Mosaic law (Deut. 17:17). But the mention of the number of the wives and children is unusual (Judg. 8:30; 10:4; 12:9, 14; 2 Kings 10:1) and especially noteworthy since nothing is said about Solomon's sons. That some of the other kings of Judah had large families is indicated but not expressly stated (2 Kings 11:1f.; 2 Chron. 21:2, 17; 22:1, 10; 24:3, 27).

[94] In the case of most of the kings of Judah, the name of the mother is given. One reason for this may be that the kings usually had several wives. Thus Jehoahaz and Zedekiah were sons of Josiah by Hamutal, while Jehoiakim's mother was Zabudah. The mothers of both good kings, Jehoshaphat and Hezekiah, and of bad kings, Manasseh and Amon, are mentioned. The king's mother apparently was, as was natural, a person of importance. Consequently it is the addition of the words "the Ammonitess" (*ARV*) and the mention of this damaging fact twice in Kings which makes the statement so significant.

[95] Cf. 2 Chron. 12:13. In all three occurrences the definite article is used, "the Ammonitess" (*ARV*). Various attempts have been made to avoid the implications of this statement. According to the *LXX* (Cod. B), which introduces a long insertion between 1 Kings 12:24 and vs. 25, Rehoboam was only sixteen when he became king and reigned twelve years. (Some *LXX* Mss. read 21). According to Josephus, Solomon reigned "eighty years and lived ninety-four" (*Antiq.* VIII. vii. 8). This would allow the apostasy described in chap. 11 to begin with his marriage to Naamah the Ammonitess at nearly the close of the first forty years of his reign and to extend during the forty years which followed. Apparently this remarkable doubling of Solomon's reign was due to the desire of Josephus and

probably of many Jews before his day to escape the damaging admission that the wise and good Solomon was already married to an Ammonitess before he became king. Whiston who accepted Josephus' statement as to the length of Solomon's reign gives this explanation in his Dissertation V, claiming that Solomon could not have married Naamah until "he had left his piety and was fallen in love with his foreign and idolatrous women" (Sections 20, 21). But Josephus himself says almost nothing about Naamah.

96 Oehler, as cited, p. 557.

97 Fairbairn (*Commentary on Ezekiel*, pp. 264f.) treats this as a vision and as an "acted lesson for the people." But the language used seems to imply that the reference is to the actual event.

98 Cf. 2 Chron. 36:15 on the fall of Jerusalem.

99 This does not justify the claim, "If literary prophecy goes entirely unnoticed in the historical books, it can only be that they were not its offspring" (Yehezkel Kaufmann, *The Religion of Israel*, p. 158).

100 *Rand McNally Bible Atlas*, p. 302, cf. *ANET*, p. 288.

101 2 Kings 18:13, 17; 19:8; 2 Chron. 32:1, 9.

102 *ANET*, p. 315.

103 "Sleep with fathers" is apparently a phrase of broad meaning. It is used of Moses, who was born in Egypt and was buried in a valley in Moab (Deut. 31:16). It is used of nearly forty kings of Judah and Israel, both good and bad. Thus Baasha of the house of Issachar (1 Kings 15:27), upon whose family terrible curses were pronounced, slept with his fathers and was buried in Tirzeh (16:6). Omri was buried in Samaria, a city which he had himself built and made his capital (16:28). Ahaz was not buried in the sepulchres of the kings (2 Chron. 28:27.) Yet all alike "slept with their fathers." We are even told that Jehoiakim did so in spite of the awful fate assigned him in Jer. 22:19 (cf. Keil, *Com. on Kings, in loco*).

104 The words, "my net also will I spread upon him and he shall be taken in my snare" (Ezek. 12:13) indicate that Ezekiel recognized as did Jeremiah that Nebuchadnezzar was the Lord's "servant" to punish his rebellious people.

105 2 Kings 25:27-30.

106 *How to Enjoy the Bible* (1910), pp. 304-319.

107 L. W. King, *Letters and Inscriptions of Hammurabi*, Vol. I, p. 24; Vol. III., pp. 12f.

108 Cf. *BCBS*, Vol. III, p. 485; also Batten in *ICC*, p. 182, who refers to Wellhausen.

109 This figure is given in Ginsburg, *Introduction to the Massoretico-Critical Edition of the Hebrew Bible* (1897). This monumental work has recently been republished with a *Prolegomenon* by H. M. Orlinsky.

110 E.g., the Rodanim of 1 Chron. 1:7 (*MT*, cf. *ARV*) is supported by *LXX* Rodioi; but in Gen. 10:4 it is Dodanim.

111 The word-play is obvious in the Hebrew, but not in the translation.

112 Only two Hebrew mss. are reported as reading "Merab" (Kittel *Biblia Hebraica*.

113 *SIOT*, p. 61.

114 See Batten, *Commentary on Esther* in *ICC*, pp. 125, 232.

115 S. Baring Gould, *Hebrew Myths*.

116 See *NBCR*, p. 768.

117 It is probable that the difference in datings "twelfth year" (Ezek. 33:21) and "eleventh year" (Jer. 39:2) is simply due to the fact that two different systems of dating were used, one beginning the year in the spring, the other in the fall. This would not only account for the difference but would also reduce the interval from eighteen months to six months, which seems a more likely figure (cf. *NBCR*, p. 680).

118 How misleading a single sentence may be when taken out of its context is strikingly illustrated by the sentence with which Millar Burrows begins the first chapter of his Second Volume on the Dead Sea Scrolls: "The Dead Sea Scrolls were discovered in America in the spring of 1955." Taken by itself this is an amazing statement. These famous scrolls were not "discovered in America," but in Palestine in caves near the Northwest boundary of the Dead Sea. They were not discovered in 1955, but "in 1947 or perhaps in 1945," and Dr. Albright of Johns Hopkins University was one of the first to recognize their importance and

to assign them to the period which is now generally accepted as the correct one. No one was better acquainted with these facts than Dr. Burrows. In his first volume on the Scrolls, published in the autumn of 1955 he includes a fifteen page Bibliography of books and articles on the Scrolls, many of them by American scholars. What Dr. Burrows is concerned to do and at once proceeds to do is to point out that it was the article published by Edmund Wilson in *The New Yorker* in May 1955, six months before Burrows' own first volume appeared, which first aroused in this country wide *popular* interest in this important discovery. But his first sentence is dangerously misleading. And taken in its natural and obvious sense it is entirely contrary to fact. The same might be said of meagre or fragmentary statements regarding events of ancient times, and especially of a vast number of simple statements when taken out of their context.

CHAPTER III

1 *Déscription de l'Égypte* (1809-1828).
2 *EB*[14], article Edward Robinson.
3 *Op. cit.*, p. 207.
4 *PTR*, 1906, pp. 289-305.
5 *Id.* p. 291.
6 *Id.* p. 293.
7 *Id.* p. 289.
8 *Id.* p. 302.
9 *Id.* p. 301.
10 F. Kenyon, *The Bible and Archaeology*, p. 19.
11 *BA*, XXII, pp. 101-108.
12 In *Revelation and the Bible*, ed. by Carl F. H. Henry, p. 301f.
13 *NBD*, article "Babylonia" (pp. 125-7).
14 *Ibid*, pp. 72-76.
15 *Excavations at Ur – A Record of Twelve Years' Work*, pp. 12f.
16 M. E. L. Mallowan, *Nimrud and Its Remains*, 1962.
17 *The Vassal-Treaties of Esarhaddon*, 1958, according to Wiseman, the more than three hundred and fifty fragments belong to eight or more large tablets which contained the treaty imposed by Esarhaddon on Ramataia and other vassal-kings in 672 B.C.
18 R.A.S. Macalister, *A Century of Excavation*, p. 143.
19 *OTMS* (1951), p. 28.
20 *The Excavations of Gezer* by R. A. S. Macalister.
21 *Archaeology of Palestine*, p. 31.
22 *Ibid*, p. 41.
23 Rowley, *The Servant of the Lord*, p. 278.
24 An extensive bibliography of books on Biblical Archaeology is given by D. J. Wiseman in his *Illustrations from Biblical Archaeology* (pp. 103-109) and to this the reader is referred.
25 El Amarna *Letter* 329 in Knudtzon.
26 *The Development of Palestine Exploration*, pp. 275f.
27 See article "Lachish" in *NBD* and appended Bibliography.
28 Olga Tufnell (*Lachish III*) favors the earlier date. But B. W. Buchanan in reviewing this important book expressed doubt as to the date of the Lachish letters based on the script employed. He further pointed out that only three levels were exposed "on somewhat less than a quarter of the mound" (*AJA*, 1954, pp. 335-39). It may be noted that the words, "for he (the Rabshakeh) had heard that he (Sennacherib) had departed from Lachish" (2 Kings 19:8) are decidedly colorless, if Lachish had fallen to the victorious Assyrian. They might mean that he had given up the siege as hopeless.
29 Jirku, A, in ZAW, 1939, pp. 152f.
30 *BASOR*, 58, p. 29; 63, p. 9.
31 *Ibid*, 74, p. 20.
32 *ANET*, p. 321.
33 *Archaeology in the Holy Land*, p. 276.
34 *RMBA*, p. 302.
35 Kathleen Kenyon, *Digging up Jericho*, (1957), p. 33.
36 Garstang.

[37] *Op. cit.*, pp. 261-63.

[38] *National Geographic Magazine*, Dec. 1957, p. 845.

[39] *Biblical Archaeology*, 1957, pp. 79f.

[40] *Op. cit.*, p.257.

[41] Approximately this figure is given by other archaeologists. That the Israelites who left Egypt were only a few thousands is and must be the conclusion of all scholars who are unwilling to accept the statements of Scripture as to the supernatural manner (water, manna, quail) by means of which the Lord provided for the needs of his people during the wilderness journey.

[42] *Archaeology in the Holy Land*, p. 188.

[43] See Baring Gould, *Legends of the Patriarchs and Prophets*, pp. 7-15.

[44] *Archaelogy in the Holy Land*, p. 194. She declares it to be certain that the dates given in Genesis for Abram's departure from Haran, the birth of Isaac, etc. cannot be regarded as "factual."

[45] Parrot indicates here his acceptance of Albright's rendering of "Calneh" (Gen. 10:14) as "all of them". It is noteworthy that *RSV* and *NEB* in adopting Albright's rendering omit the "and" which precedes.

[46] *Digging Up Jericho* (1957), p. 76, cf. in *Archaeology in the Holy Land*, p. 109.

[47] *Archaeology in the Holy Land*, p. 4.

[48] *Op. cit.*, p. 69. The writer remembers having seen many years ago in one of the great collections of Accadian discoveries (the British Museum) a great caldron, on the rim of which a long ladle was hanging, the end of the ladle being bent back to form a hook to hook it on the rim, and also perhaps to prevent it from slipping down into the caldron. He wondered then how often such a simple device had been discovered quite independently at wide intervals of time under varying circumstances and in widely separated localities.

[49] I. J. Gelb, *A Study in Writing*, 1952.

[50] Lissner, *The Living Past*, 1961, in his chapters on Crete (pp. 293-309), discusses these scripts in some detail. The Linear B script contained eighty symbols for writing a syllabic script. It is now generally recognized that Linear B has been proved by Chadwick and Ventris to be Greek. Nearly half of the symbols used in Linear B appear also in Linear A which indicates a close connection between them. But C. H. Gordon claims that the language of Linear A is Semitic. See also Joseph Alsop, *From the Silent Earth*. Gurney speaks of the Hittite hieroglyphs "as one of several new scripts (including that which gave rise to our own alphabet) of hieroglyphics or cuneiform type which were invented in the middle of the second millenium" (*The Hittites*, p. 127).

[51] Breasted, *HAE*, p. 47.

[52] The discovery of alphabet texts at Ugarit was made by Schaeffer in 1930 and the publication by Virolleaud in *Syria* followed promptly. A translation of the mythological texts by H. L. Ginsberg appears in *ANET*, pp. 129-155. C. H. Gordon has been one of the leaders in the study of these texts. The script may be a simplified form of Accadian cuneiform.

[53] First announced by Virolleaud in 1950, cf. Albright in *BASOR* No. 118, pp. 11-20; also No. 119, pp. 23f.

[54] *NBD*, pp. 1341, 1348. This article on "Writing" (pp. 1341-51) gives an admirable survey of the discoveries which have been made in this important field of research. G. R. Driver, in *Semitic Writing from Pictograph to Alphabet* (Schweich Lectures, 1944), placed the discovery of the Alphabet between 2500 B.C. and 1500 B.C. Albright in reviewing Driver's book dated the Semitic alphabet earlier than 1700 B.C. (*JNES*, x, p. 222).

[55] *ANET*, p. 322.

[56] *ANET*, p. 28. Gurney claims that the failure to discover administrative documents in hieroglyphic Hittite is due to their having been inscribed on tablets of wood (op. cit. p. 128).

[57] *Alalakh Tablets*, p. 13, also *NBD*, p. 1351.

[58] The word "table" or "tablet" (*luach*) is usually applied to the two tables of the Law which are repeatedly (a dozen times in Exodus and Deut., cf. 1 Kings 8:9) referred to as "tables of stone." This served to indicate and stress the permanence of the law recorded on them.

[59] From the Neo-Babylonian period we have the evidence of the clay seal of Gedaliah which carries on the reverse the fibre-marks indicating that it was af-

fixed to a document written on papyrus, (cf. Finegan, *LAP*, p. 161). We have also the fragmentary Aramaic letter of Adon, king of Ashkelon dating perhaps from the time of Nebuchadnezzar, and the *Elephantine Papyri* dating from the Persian period, which are written in Aramaic and on papyrus. The discoveries in the Dead Sea Caves have proved that papyrus and hides were extensively used in Palestine at least as early as the 2nd century B.C. and probably very much earlier; and the character of the writing indicates that writing was well known.

[60] Cf. *NBD*, p. 1343, also Plate XI.

[61] The usual word is *Katab*, but the Hebrews had several words to describe engraving on hard substances. Note especially Exod. 28:9, 11, 21, 36, where engraving (of names) is referred to. We know from the Lahun jewelry of the 12th Egyptian Dynasty to what perfection the engraver's art had been carried there centuries before the time of Moses. Whether Judah's signet (Gen. 38:18) was inscribed or not, we do not know. But it might well have been.

[62] The list of names of slaves (some Hebrew) on fragments of an Egyptian papyrus, of the time of Joseph (see *ZPBD*, p. 239, also *IBA*, p. 37), may resemble the tally-lists of Israelite slave labor in Egypt. Since those lists were kept by Hebrews (Exod. 5:14 should be rendered "and the scribes of the children of Israel, which the taskmasters of Pharaoh had placed over them were beaten"), many of the Israelites must have become familiar while in Egypt with the use of papyrus as writing material.

[63] See the Tables in the articles on "Writing" in *NBD* and *ZPDB;* also in Albright, *Arch. of Pal.*, pp. 191-193, and Wiseman *IBA*, pp. 11, 24, 49. It should be noted however that styles of writing varied from time to time. Thus some of Nebuchadnezzar's inscriptions are written in a script which closely resembles that used in the days of Hammurabi, a thousand years earlier. Some of the scrolls found at Qumran are written in a script which was either old fashioned (archaizing) at the time they were written, or it indicates an earlier date for the scrolls themselves.

[64] Even were the "wrote" to be taken as hypothetical, "were I to write" (*RSV*) the language clearly suggests a large collection or body of laws which have been or at least might be written down, if anything could be accomplished by doing this (cf. Oreilli, *Commentary*, in loco).

[65] *ANET*, p. 178.

[66] G. R. Driver, *Semitic Writing* (1954), pp. 194-7, cf. p. 79.

[67] Minzuo Pei.

[68] See *FBM*, pp. 43, 66, 78.

[69] Yet words which appear to have the same root, (e.g. *DBR*) appear in Hebrew with widely different meanings (*deber*, pestilence; *dober*, pasture; *deborah*, bee; *midbar*, wilderness; *debir*, the holy of holies in Solomon's temple). In Hebrew the word *qol* (voice or sound) occurs very frequently. But the verb from this root is never used. In Arabic the verb is frequent, but the noun occurs rarely if at all. Accadian does not use either. In it the usual verb is *qabû*.

[70] *FBM*, p. 78 and *ANET*, pp. 134f. (rendered by "window" and "casement").

[71] Modern German, Danish and Swedish furnish an interesting parallel. In Swedish and Danish the indefinite article is placed before the noun, the definite article after it; in German both precede the noun.

[72] In the Ugaritic script it is indicated only in words which end in Aleph.

[73] Of the popular German novelist, Fritz Reuther (1810-74) it has been justly said that he "made Plattdeutsch a literary language (*EB* 14).

[74] Wilson, *"Foreign Words,"* *PTR*, 1928, pp. 177-247.

[75] *Ibid*, pp. 245f.

[76] *Ibid*, p. 238.

[77] *OTMS*, p. 32.

[78] *Biblical and Theological Studies* by the Faculty of Princeton Theological Seminary, 1912, pp. 261-305.

[79] *LOT*, pp. 502f.

[80] *Ibid*, p. 508.

[81] Op. cit., pp. 270, 303. In 1929 H. H. Rowley published *The Aramaic of the Old Testament*, in which he defended Dr. Driver's view against Dr. Wilson. Dr. Wilson spent much of the last year of his life in preparing a reply to Dr. Rowley. Unfortunately his death prevented its completion and publication. But he told

the present writer and some others that he felt he could answer Rowley successfully. In 1930 H. H. Schaeder in his *Iranische Beiträge* arrived at the same conclusion as Dr. Wilson had done as to the Aramaic of Daniel. Cf. *NBD*, pp. 712.

[82] *PTR*, 1925, pp. 234-265.

[83] *Ibid*, p. 234.

[84] *Ibid*, p. 262f.

[85] *Ibid*, p. 264.

[86] Pritchard gives a list of 99 Asiatic cities and countries mentioned by one or more of seven of the Pharaohs (*ANET*, pp. 242f.) as under Egyption rule. The so-called Execration Tablets found in Egypt contain many names of countries and peoples regarded by the Egyptians as their enemies and deserving therefore to be cursed by their gods.

[87] *ANET*, p. 265. It is interesting to note that while the 1st Dynasty of Kish (the first after the Flood) is composed of 23 reigns, no one of which apparently was less than 100 years long, the total is given as "24,510 years, 3 months and 3½ days" — a strange combination of exact and inexact.

[88] More than fifty years ago Koldewey discovered at Babylon in the Nordburg some statues which had been carried away from Mari by Babylonian conquerors. But its location was then unknown.

[89] *ANET*, pp. 482f.

[90] Oppenheim adopts the name "Dark Age" for the period between the last kings of the Hammurapi Dynasty and about the midpoint of the Kassite. He speaks of the "long" and "short" chronologies for this period, "none of them based on more than circumstantial evidence" (*Ancient Mesopotamia*, pp. 392f.). Brinkman (in Oppenheim) dates Hammurapi 1792-1750, making his reign overlay that of Shamshi-Adad I (1813-1781) by about ten years. Neither Brinkman nor Oppenheim mentions the fact that Albright's date for Hammurapi is 1728-1686, a difference of 64 years, which represents the interval between two obscurations of Venus. But Brinkman refers to this difference in stating that "for dates before 1500 B.C., it is unlikely that they will ever be raised or lowered more than 64 years," which clearly makes Hammurabi's date depend on the astronomical data. (It is noteworthy that more than sixty years after the discovery of the Code it should be still uncertain whether his name should be spelled with a b or p).

[91] Fifty years ago Erman described our knowledge of Egyptian history as "very meagre." In the thirty dynasties of Manetho he described three periods as "little known intervals": Dynasties 7-10; 13-17; 21-25. He placed Menes *ca.* 3300 B.C., the 12th Dynasty at 2000 B.C., the 18th at 1580 B.C. Except for the tendency to lower the date of Menes by several centuries, the two other dates are widely accepted today as approximately correct. But the three periods must still be described as little known.

[92] According to Albright the Hyksos must be dated within the period *ca.* 1720 to *ca.* 1550 B.C. (*OTMS*, p. 44).

[93] Steindorff and Seele, *When Egypt Ruled the East* (rev. ed. 1957, pp. 25f.).

[94] M. A. Murray, *The Splendour that was Egypt* (1949, 1957), p. 29. Miss Murray was for many years closely associated with Petrie. It is significant that she gives both the 'long' and the 'short' chronologies without attempting to decide between them.

[95] *A Century of Excavation at Nineveh*, p. 118.

[96] See Oppenheim, *Ancient Mesopotamia*, p. 280.

[97] Steindorff and Seele, *op. cit.* p. 6.

[98] *Every Day Life in Babylonia and Assyria*, p. 214. Compare Gurney (*The Hittites*, 1954, pp. 35, 110) on the battle between Rameses II and Muwatallis at Kadesh.

[99] Oppenheim, *op. cit.*, pp. 148f.

[100] *ANET*, pp. 309-11. He mentions the Akitu festival in Babylon and the elaborate and costly gifts and offerings made by him at that time.

[101] *Ibid*, pp. 311f. It refers especially to the restoration of the temple at Harran.

[102] *Ibid*, pp. 312-5. While the name of Nabunaid appears only once on this tablet, and there in the form of a restoration, it seems clear from the contents that he is the culprit. Cyrus is only mentioned by name twice. It seems as if the

naming of contemporary rulers is avoided by the author or authors of this account, cf. Budge, *Babylonian Life and History*, pp. 52f.

[103] *Ibid*, pp. 315f.

[104] *Ibid*, pp. 305-7.

[105] See Weissbach, *Die Keilinschriften der Achaemeniden* (1911). Also Ghirshman's *Iran*, pp. 131ff., 152-163.

[106] It is not to be inferred from the edict of Cyrus which is recorded in Ezra 1:1-4 that Cyrus was a worshiper of the God of Israel. The words, "the house of the Lord God of Israel, (he is the God) which is in Jerusalem" (AV) may and probably should read "the house of the Lord God of Israel (he is the God, who is in Jerusalem)." The words "though thou hast not known me" which are used twice in Isa. 45:4f. may mean that Cyrus had no clear knowledge of God; and it is not unlikely that the words which follow, "I form the light and create darkness" (verse 7) are an allusion to that dualism which was a prominent feature of Vedic belief.

[107] See O. T. Allis, *The Fall of Nineveh* in PTR (1924), pp. 465-77.

[108] This identification is defended by M. F. Unger in *Israel and the Arameans of Damascus* (1957). But the fact that, following Albright, he lowers the date of Rehoboam's accession to c. 922 B.C. in order to avoid "any abnormally long reign for Benhadad" (p. 60) serves to illustrate the weakness of the one-Benhadad theory.

[109] John C. Whitcomb, Jr., *Darius the Mede: A Study in Historical Identification* (1959).

[110] Joseph Alsop (*From the Silent Earth*), 1964, pp. 155f. has reminded us that Mary Boykin Chestnut's *Diary from Dixie*, which he described as "one of the great Civil War documents' was first published in 1900 in a heavily edited edition from which everything unfavorable to the South was carefully removed and that the subsequently published "complete edition," restores omissions which are important enough "to change the whole picture as soon as they are restored" (pp. 155f.)

[111] Parrot, *Mari*, pp. 194f.; Pritchard, *Ancient Near East*, 1958, plate 143.

[112] *A Forgotten Kingdom*, pp. 97f.

[113] Frankfort, *Sculpture of the Third Millennium, B.C.* from Tell Asmar and Khafajeh, p. 1.

[114] Gordon Childe, *New Light on the Most Ancient East* (1953), p. 7.

[115] *ILN*.

[116] *Ibid*, Feb. 14, 1959, p. 272. In ILN (12/3/1960), a page is devoted to the London Exhibition of the sculptures of Henry Moore (born in 1894), who is described as "a great modern English sculptor" and also as "the man generally acknowledged to be the finest living sculptor in Great Britain, if not in the world." As an example of Moore's work his "Mother and Child, Maquette No. IV" of 1956, is reproduced and described as "an excellent example of the tender aspect of Moore's work." On the opposite page there is the reproduction of "an ivory figure of a child, perhaps playing with knucklebones: found at Palaikastro East Crete — late Minoan I," which would date from more than 3000 years before the time of Moore. Many readers of *ILN*, who are not enthusiastic admirers of "modern art" will find a marked resemblance between the two. The modern cult of the crude, ugly and grotesque relates itself, intentionally or otherwise, with what the archaeologist calls "primitive."

[117] *ANET*, p. 191, No. 47f. Except as otherwise stated, the laws referred to in the following discussion will all be found in *ANET*.

[118] The Lipit Ishtar (Sumerian) Code is very fragmentary, as is also the Ur-Nammu (Sumerian) Code which Kramer described in 1956 as the "oldest" (*From the Tablets of Sumar*, pp. 47-51). The Eshnunna Code (*ANET*, pp. 161-3) is apparently also older than that of Hammurabi. But none of them are of at all comparable length. The mid-Assyrian laws are recorded on several clay tablets.

[119] See the brief descriptive and bibliographical statements in *ANET*.

[120] According to § 129, the adulterer and adultress, who have been caught in the act are to be *bound* and thrown into the river, which means death by drowning. The words, "Then shall the man be guiltless from iniquity" (Num. 5:31) imply that if the ordeal proved the wife to be innocent, the husband was thereby proved guilty of slander and liable to severe punishment (Exod. 20:16; compare

Deut. 22:13-21). But some hold that the man was not blameworthy whatever the outcome (G. B. Gray, *Commentary on Numbers*, in *ICC*, p. 56).

[121] Gen. 24:8; 50:25; Exod. 22:11; Josh. 2:17, 20, etc. The Hittite law (§ 75) provides that in the case of the death of a draft animal, the one in charge of it (?) may contend, "It died by the hand of God" and take an oath.

[122] T. J. Meek in his translation of the Middle Assyrian Laws points out (*op. cit.*, p. 183, n. 24) that these laws are both casuistic and apodictic, which indicates that the sharp distinction drawn by Alt between Canaanite laws as casuistic and Hebrew laws as apodictic is invalid.

[123] See C. H. H. Johns, *Babylonian and Assyrian Laws*, p. 67.

[124] *ANET*, p. 189, § 14.

[125] *ANET*, p. 422.

[126] It is referred to in the Assyrian Laws (*ANET*, p. 186, § § 8, 9) and in the Hittite, p. 195, § § 168f.

[127] Kohler-Ungnad, *Assyrische Rechtsurkunden* (1913), pp. 455f. S. N. Kramer in reviewing Laessoe's *People of Ancient Assyria*, which he described as "a real treat" refers to Assyria as "one of the most powerful and most maligned people of the Ancient Near East" (*Archaeology*, Spring of 1965, p. 70). The evidence in support of the alleged "maligning" seems rather convincing to say the least!

[128] Cf. R. D. Wilson: "The code of Hammurabi is not mentioned in any known document except in the code itself." (*A Scientific Investigation*, Chap. 1, note 9); also Oppenheim, op. cit., p. 158.

[129] *ANET*, pp. 200f. Compare the elaborate lists of deities given on pp. 205f.

[130] Erman, *Die Aegyptische Religion*, p. 87; Breasted, *Development of Religion and Thought in Ancient Egypt*, p. 49; Steindorff and Seele, *When Egypt Ruled the East*, pp. 124-155.

[131] *ISBE*, pp. 914f.

[132] H. R. Hall, Art, "Egypt" (*EB* 14, vol. 8, p. 58).

[133] Breasted, *Development*, pp. 301f. The same may apply to the four Horuses (p. 9).

[134] Erman, *op. cit.*, pp. 74f.

[135] *Development*, p. x.

[136] *Op. cit.*, p. 61.

[137] Religion, *op cit.*, p. IV.

[138] *Development*, p. XIV.

[139] *History of the Ancient Egyptians*, pp. 265, 277, 286, 287, 288; *Development*, pp. 334, 339, 342.

[140] *Development*, p. 315.

[141] *Ibid.*, p. 336.

[142] *Op. cit.*, p. 58b. The estimate given by John A. Wilson, Breasted's successor as Professor of Egyptology at the University of Chicago is to be noted: "Because Akhen-Aton was devoted to this god (Aton) alone, the Amarna religion has been called monotheistic. This is a debatable question, and a reserved attitude would note that only Akh-en-Aton and his family worshipped the Aton, Akh-en-Aton's courtiers worshipped Akh-en-Aton himself and the great majority of Egyptians was ignorant of or hostile to the new faith" (*ANET*, 1955, p. 369). See also Erman's account of Ikhnaton and his cult (*op. cit.*, pp. 65-72), which Wilson's largely resembles.

[143] See R. C. Thompson, *The Devils and Evil Spirits of Babylonia* (1904).

[144] *ANET*, p. 166. The first law perhaps also deals with sorcery, the charge of laying a death-spell (*nêrtu*). If the accuser cannot prove his charge, he is to be put to death.

[145] Jastrow, *Die Religion Babyloniens und Assyriens* II, pp. 777, 779f.

[146] Jastrow has discussed the snake symbol (*Sir*), op. cit., I, pp. 166, 189, 195; II pp. 775-84.

[147] *ANET*, p. 354.

[148] *Israel and Babylon*, p. 332.

[149] *Op. cit.*, I, p. 284.

[150] In the myth of Ishtar's descent to the nether world, it is described as "the house where in the entrants are bereft of light, where dust is their fare and clay is their food, (where) they see no light, residing in darkness" (*ANET*, p. 107).

[151] Jastrow (*op. cit.*) devoted 202 pages to the liver, 333 pages to the stars,

25 pages to oil and water divination, — a total of 550 pages, or about a third of the entire treatise.

152 *The Siege Perilous*, p. 208. According to S. Moscati, *The Face of the Ancient Orient*, 1960, "One of the most significant of the Babylonian and Assyrian rites is that of substituting an animal for a sick man." (p. 71).

153 Contenau, *Everyday Life*, pp. 298. Hooke, following Labet, denies that the substitute was actually to be put to death (*Siege*, pp. 206-9).

154 Cf. Jastrow, *op. cit.*, II, pp. 102f.

155 *Op. cit.*, pp. 301f.

156 The fact that Nabu (Nebo) and Bel very frequently appear in names of the Neo-Babylonian period indicates the popularity of those gods at that time, as suggested by the name Nebuchadnezzar. Ashur, the chief god of the Assyrians, naturally appears very frequently in Assyrian proper names. Cf. Tallquist, *Neubabylonisches Namenbuch* (1905) pp. IX-XLII. In Egypt names are similarly compounded with those of gods and goddesses, e.g. Amon, Thoth, Re.

157 The ending -*ia* occurs with many Hurrian names at Alalakh where it certainly has no connection with the divine name Yahweh.

158 The same shortening of -*ia* to -*i* is found in both Accadian and Hurrian names.

159 *NBD*, p. 28.

160 This view was favored by J. A. Alexander in his commentary on *The Psalms* (1850), *in loco*.

161 To say with Batten, "This is a case of accidental repetition, and 'other' was added to cover up the error," (Commentary in *ICC*, p. 75) is an easy way out of the difficulty, but not at all an acceptable one. Batten takes Elam as referring to the country of Elam, but does not state whether "sons of Elam" means Elamites or how else it is to be explained. Elam occurs as the name of an individual in 1 Chron. 8:24; 26:3; Neh. 10:14; 12:42. The designation "sons of Elam" occurs in Ezra 8:7; 10:2, in connection with two different leaders, Jeshaiah the son of Athaliah and Shechaniah the son of Jehiel.

162 Does the fact that Joash called his son Gideon (hewer or smiter, Judg. 6:11) justify the inference that Joash hoped that his son might deliver his people from the hated oppressor? Joash's clever defense of Gideon after his son destroyed the altar of Baal might suggest that Joash was a crypto-Jehovah worshipper and patriot! But we must be cautious in drawing inferences from uncertainties.

163 Hengstenberg's statement that "Like all the names of the canonical prophets, that of Ezekiel is not that which he had borne from his youth, but an official title which he had received at the beginning of his calling," (*Commentary on Ezekiel* (p. 5) finds as little support in the case of Ezekiel as in the other O.T. prophets.

164 It is rather remarkable that the attempt is made to treat Haran, the name of Abraham's son as a slight modification of Charran, the name of the city. Philologically it is quite improbable.

165 See Wright, *Arabic Grammar*, I, p. 108 A.

166 Compare e.g. *Chesed* which means goodness, kindness, etc. (the usual meaning in Hebrew, occurring 247 times), but it also means shame or reproach (the meaning in Aramaic, found in Lev. 20:17; Prov. 14:34). The word *kesel* is used in the good sense of confidence (e.g. Prov. 3:26 and in the bad sense of folly in Job 31:24; Eccles. 7:25). Compare also *chanan* which nearly always means "to be gracious," but in Job 19:17 apparently means "loathsome" (*ARV* marg., *BV*, *RSV*).

167 In view of this statement, the best etymology of this name is the one proposed by R. D. Wilson, *Bel-lit-shar-user* (Bel protect the hostage of the king) in *Studies in the Book of Daniel*, 1917, pp. 30ff. Yet it is interesting that Nebuchadnezzar whose name and whose father's name is compounded with Nabu says of Daniel "whose name was Belteshazzar, according to the name of my god" (Dan. 4:8).

168 Cf. *FBM*, pp. 265-70.

CHAPTER IV

1 Cf. *FBM*[2] for a detailed discussion of this still widely accepted hypothesis; also E. J. Young *IOT;* James Orr, *POT*.

[2] Comp. F. Delitzsch's statement, "If history is critically annihilated, what is left but to fill the *tabula rasa* with myths" (quoted by James Orr, *POT*, p. 121).

[3] This has concerned especially the JE analysis, which has always been a weak point in the documentary theory.

[4] *Einleitung*, p. 190f. How essential the late dating of Deuteronomy is to the critical theory regarding the development of the religion of Israel is illustrated, as will appear later, by Pfeiffer's posthumus volume *Religion in the Old Testament* (1961).

[5] Young, *IOT*, p. 125.

[6] Noth, *Ueberlieferungsgeschichtliche Studien*, I (1943).

[7] *Die Sagen der Genesis* (1901) which was followed by his Commentary on Genesis (*3te Auflage*, 1910). Cf. E. J. Young, *IOT*, pp. 144f.

[8] Yet the form criticism must be regarded as undermining the foundations of literary criticism. For as C. R. North has well said: "Let the emphasis be laid upon oral tradition, and J, and with it the documentary hypothesis as a whole, is volatilized. We are obviously in sight of the position maintained from Uppsala" (*OTMS*, p. 59).

[9] Albright in referring to its application to the New Testament speaks of "the highly subjective and improbable view which form critics usually hold, that much of the content of the Gospels was adapted or invented to suit situations which arose in the life of the Church" (*AOP*, p. 242). The same criticism would apply to their treatment of the Old Testament.

[10] Hooke edited *Myth and Ritual* (1933) and *The Labyrinth* (1935), to both of which volumes a number of well-known scholars contributed articles. In 1938 he published his Schweich Lectures on *The Origins of Early Semitic Ritual*. He also brought together a number of his own articles, written in the course of a quarter century or more, in a volume entitled, *The Siege Perilous* (1956).

[11] *The Labyrinth* (1935), p. ix.

[12] Lev. 18:3, 24, 30; 20:23; Deut. 7:1-6; 20:16-18; Josh. 3:10; Ezra. 9:1.

[13] According to C. R. North (*OTMS*, p. 79), "It is the habit of Uppsala to depreciate the *LXX* in favor of the *MT*" (cf. also p. 64).

[14] Statements to much the same effect are made by Rowley (*OTMS*, pp. xv, xxv f.), by Albright (*ibid.*, p. 25), and by D. W. Thomas (*ibid.*, pp. 242-8). But all such statements must be taken *cum grano salis*. For these writers do not hesitate to emend the text whenever they feel justified in doing so.

[15] *Das textkritische Problem des A. T.'s am Hosea-buche demonstriert* (*ZAW*, 1934), pp. 241-54.

[16] North (*op. cit.*, p. 59f.) gives three main characteristics: enthusiasm for oral tradition, emphasis on divine kingship, and an anti-literary critical polemic. Kaufmann speaks very severely of the Scandinavian and the British schools: "The religio-historical views of this school are even more paganistic than those of the classical criticism" by which he means the Wellhausen School; and he adds, "the same may be said of the British School of Hooke and his adherents" (*The Religion of Israel*, p. 156).

[17] Cf. G. Widengren, *Hochglaube im Alten Iran*. He refers to the works of Andrew Lang and Wilhelm Schmid, also Pellazzoni. Cf. *OTMS*, pp. 286f.

[18] *The Labyrinth*, p. v.

[19] The rise of Barthianism may be dated from the appearance of Barth's *Commentary on Romans* (*Römerbrief*) in 1918. A *Short Commentary on Romans*, which Barth describes as "a smaller and younger brother" of the original work has recently been translated into English (1959). Cf. *Barth;* by A. D. R. Polman in the *Modern Thinkers* Series (1960).

[20] Cf. C. Van Til, *The New Modernism*, especially the chapter on "*Urgeschichte*" (pp. 80-106).

[21] In an article entitled, "The Quality of our Lives" in the *Christian Century* (May 11, 1960), Richard Niebuhr says of the development in Barth's thinking and the new scholasticism developed from it: "I record these developments without too much animus because Barth has long since ceased to have any effect on my thought: indeed he has become irrelevant to all Christians in the Western World who believe in accepting common and collective responsibilities without illusion and without despair."

[22] Cf. S. U. Zuidema, *Kierkegaard*, in *Modern Thinkers* series (1960).

[23] Article, "Existentialism" in *TCERK*.

[24] *Christian Personal Ethics*, p. 91. According to Van Til: "In the philosophy of *Existenz* we have the apotheosis of the would-be autonomous man" (*The New Modernism*, p. 124).

[25] See Herman Ridderbos', *Bultmann* in the *Modern Thinkers* series (1960).

[26] J. I. Packer, *Fundamentalism and the Word of God*, p. 162.

[27] *The Christian Century* for Nov. 19, 1958, pp. 1328-31. Dr. Albright has for many years described himself as an "orientalist." His great interest is in archaeology, more especially biblical archaeology; and he has made many important contributions to our knowledge in that field. He was for thirty-eight years, until his recent retirement, the editor of the *Bulletin of the American Society of Oriental Research* and many of the more than 800 articles which he has published have appeared in it and in the sister publication, *The Biblical Archaeologist*. But Dr. Albright is rather to be called a biblical archaeologist than a biblical theologian; and while he is clearly delighted when his discoveries support the Bible, he does not hesitate to defend them when they do not. *The Bible and the Ancient Near East* (1961), edited by G. E. Wright, a volume of essays presented to Dr. Albright on the occasion of his seventieth birthday, contains articles by two of his students, Bright and Mendenhall, which set forth his viewpoint and achievements with scholarly appreciation.

In *Recent Discoveries*, an article which has been appended to Young's *Concordance*, Dr. Albright writes as follows: "The reader may rest assured: nothing has been found to disturb a reasonable faith, and nothing has been discovered which can disprove a single theological doctrine — except that of verbal inspiration, which is not included in any Christian creed." Unfortunately, this claim of Dr. Albright is not true to fact; some of Dr. Albright's discoveries and claims are decidedly disturbing to many whose faith cannot justly be called unreasonable; the leaders of the Biblical Theology school may reject the doctrine of the plenary inspiration of the Bible, but they cannot truthfully assert that it is not included in any standard Christian creed. To cite a single example, this doctrine is stated very clearly and cogently in the first chapter of the *Westminster Confession of Faith* and serves as the basis of all the teaching of this historic confession.

[28] *Fundamentalism and the Church* (1957), p. 22. According to Hebert, the Biblical Theology movement is to be dated from the publication of *The Riddle of the New Testament* (1923) by Sir Edward Hoskyns, who is called "the great protagonist in England" (p. 21). According to Hebert "the characteristic of this Biblical Theology is that it is at once deeply orthodox in faith and thoroughly critical — more critical than the liberal critics, since it is also critical of the critics themselves." Hebert is impressed with "the manner in which the inadequacy of the doctrine of the inerrancy of Scripture has demonstrated itself" (p. 148).

[29] *Op. cit.*, p. 134.

[30] In *ZAW*, a series of articles beginning in 1934. His views will be more fully discussed later on. It is interesting to note the similarity between the work of Dornseiff and that of Noth (1943) and Engnell (1945). C. R. North in his article "Pentateuchal Criticism" (*OTMS*, pp. 67-73) deals with Engnell and Noth, but makes no mention of Dornseiff.

[31] See the articles published in *BJRL*.

[32] In the article, "The Period of the Judges" (*BJRL*, 1946, p. 91).

[33] Eissfeldt in his discussion of "Modern Criticism" in *RAR* (pp. 79f.) described the refusal of Pedersen, Benno Jacobs, Cassuto, J. H. Hertz and A. Bea, to accept the critical analysis as due to "a reverence for tradition coupled with earnest scholarship," which is a more generous treatment than most critics accord those who refuse to accept the conclusions of "modern criticism."

[34] More thoroughgoing in its rejection of the Wellhausen hypothesis is *This Is My God* by Herman Wouk (1957). While not an Old Testament scholar by profession, the writer, who is the grandson of a learned rabbi, has an intimate acquaintance with rabbinical literature. He rejects the Wellhausen hypothesis *in toto*. He is particularly severe in dealing with the "redactor." "With the discovery of the Interpolater, Wellhausen's difficulties were at an end. As a tool of controversial logic this figure is wonderful.... When all else fails Wellhausen — grammar, continuity, divine names or outright falsifying of the plain sense of the Hebrew — he works an interpolater." He declares that Engnell "dealt the death blow to the *Prolegomena* by analysing Wellhausen's villainous ghost, the interpolater, and driving it from the field with a polite scholarly horse laugh."

Bold words, indeed, but true ones all the same! The redactor is the *bête noir* of the documentary hypothesis.

35 *OTMS*, pp. 74-82. Since the word salvation-history (*Heilsgeschichte*) is now frequently used to describe a "cultic glorification" of history in which "the alleged 'bare facts' are transfigured by faith until they can be almost unrecognizable," which means usually that the miraculous element in the biblical narrative is to be relegated to the sphere of myth, legend, or folklore, it is to be noted that a century ago this same word was used in his lectures by Hofmann who drew from it exactly opposite conclusions. He used it of the miraculous content of the Bible which heads up and centers in the person and work of Christ; and he held that the entire truthfulness of this representation is guaranteed to the believer by the very fact of that connection. This redemptive, miraculous history he regarded as true history, in contrast with those events which took place in what may be called the natural course of history, which the writers of Scripture could ascertain through ordinary channels of information which being human might be of varying degrees of dependability. These lectures, which were delivered at the University of Erlangen in 1860 and published by a pupil of Hofmann in 1880, have recently appeared in an English translation by Christian Preus under the title, *Interpreting the Bible*, with a Foreword by Otto A. Piper, late of Princeton Theological Seminary. This book is particularly interesting because it shows two sharply contrasting attitudes toward the Bible. Hofmann agreed with the critics of today in rejecting the doctrine of plenary inspiration of the Bible, but for an exactly opposite reason from the one they adduce: in his case it was the "natural" events which it contains which are the stumblingblock, in their case it is the supernatural.

36 *Moses*, p. 154.

37 *OTMS*, p. 77.

38 *Ibid*, p. 81. The state of Old Testament criticism in the mid-century is well presented from the critical viewpoint in *OTMS* (1951).

39 In *The People and the Book*, 1925, ed. by A. S. Peake. Cf. H. H. Rowley, *From Joseph to Joshua*, p. 2. According to T. H. Robinson: "a sympathetic imagination, the *sine qua non* of a successful expositor, may easily go too far or take the wrong road, but this is a risk which has to be taken, and it is unlikely that every person who handles the Old Testament will make the same error" (*OTMS*, p. 351). To this statement we would add the qualifying words, *unless they proceed on the basis of the same presuppositions* and accept the conclusions which have been drawn from them without re-examination, an attitude which is responsible for not a little of the unanimity of opinion which is to be found among critical scholars.

40 As an illustration of this fact the reader would do well to compare two widely used *Introductions* to the Old Testament, those of S. R. Driver and E. J. Young. Young devotes much space to the discussion and refutation of the various critical theories which have been advanced. In fact, some readers may think that he has devoted too much attention to them. Driver's attitude is stated as follows: "Upon no occasion have I adopted what may be termed a critical as opposed to a conservative position, without weighing fully the arguments advanced in support of the latter and satisfying myself that they were untenable" (*LOT*, 1909, pp. vif.). This means that having satisfied himself that the conservative position was untenable, he felt justified in ignoring it. Hence the arguments for the Mosaic authorship of Deuteronomy and for the unity of Isaiah are ignored in *LOT*.

41 In the *Moffatt Translation* there is a rearrangement of the text and Gen. 2:4*a* is placed before 1:1.

42 Edited by J. M. Powis Smith and Edgar J. Goodspeed.

43 This illustrates Dr. Albright's interest in and zeal for archaeology as an interpreter of the biblical text. In Dummelow's *Commentary*, Gen. 1:1 is rendered "In the beginning when God created the heavens and the earth" and the statement is added: "On this rendering 'Creation' is not 'out of nothing,' but out of pre-existing chaos" (p. 3). Albright's rendering has the same result.

44 The problem then is, Where does the main clause begin? Since verses 5 and 6 read like a descriptive parenthesis, it would seem that the apodosis would most naturally begin with verse 7 "and the Lord God formed man." (In Hebrew the temporal clause may begin with "and" as, for example, in Isaiah 6:1 where the "also" of the AV should be omitted."

[45] For a discussion of this analysis see *FBM*[2], pp. 49-51.

[46] *Israel and Babylon,* p: 333.

[47] *The Babylonian Genesis,* pp. 96f.

[48] *Babylonian Life and History,* pp. 101f.

[49] *Archaeology of Palestine,* pp. 234f.

[50] *Siege Perilous,* p. 69 (paper read before British Association, 1937).

[51] *Ibid,* p. 71.

[52] Hooke does not restrict his search for folklore and myth to the antediluvian period. The extremes to which he is prepared to go are illustrated by another paper read before the Folk-Lore Society in 1934, entitled "Some Parallels with the Gilgamesh Story." In this paper, while admitting that "there can be no doubt that Elijah was an historical figure," he endeavors to link up the incidents in his life as recorded in I Kings 19 and 2 Kings 2 with incidents in the ancient Sumero-Babylonian legend and with legends current among the present inhabitants of certain small islands of the New Hebrides group. He lists about a dozen parallels between these stories as indicative of a widespread pattern. Here again he finds himself forced to admit that "The later trend of Hebrew religion under the direction of the prophetic movement was towards the complete obliteration of this early pattern." Nevertheless, he does not hesitate to add: "Hence the Elijah saga is particularly interesting, as showing that it is not only in the early myths of Genesis that clear traces of this older pattern are to be found." If the prophets of the eighth century aimed at "the complete obliteration" of the ancient pattern, yet left as many "clear traces" of it as Professor Hooke believes he has discovered, we can only say that they made "a poor fist" of the task which they had undertaken: either that, or they did not recognize any such pattern in the story as they recorded it!

[53] George Rawlinson in his *History of Ancient Egypt* (1882) pointed out that the possible identity of Hebrew and *Apiru* had already been much discussed (Vol. II, pp. 324f.), that is, before the discovery of the Amarna tablets.

[54] *From Joseph to Joshua,* p. 55.

[55] *Ibid,* p. 54.

[56] *Shechem: A Traditio-historical Study,* p. 318.

[57] Neilsen refers to Nyberg's statement in *Studien z. Rel. Kampf in A. M.,* 35, 1938, pp. 374ff.

[58] *'El Elyon* is a descriptive title "high god" and not a proper name as such. See *FSAC*[2], p. 261, where it is treated as an abridgement of "I will prevail."

[59] "The Yahwistic Tradition of the Eighth Century Prophets" (*Studies in OT Prophecy,* edited by H. H. Rowley), pp. 41f. Albright regards the word as "pre-Mosaic" (*FSAC*[2], p. 16; cf. p. 271.

[60] The word "covenant" *(berith)* is a good illustration of the way in which the critics deal with the data of Scripture. *Berith* is used nearly one hundred times in the Pentateuch. But only about a dozen of these occurrences appear in passages which they assign to documents of the pre-exile period. The twelve occurrences in Isaiah they do not assign to the eighth century prophet, although Hosea uses the word five times and Amos once; and they are certainly assigned by most critics to the eighth century. K. A. Kitchen in dealing with the Sinai covenant in his *Ancient Orient and Old Testament,* pp. 90-102, argues for its early date. For recent discussions see "Abram's Understanding of the Lord's Covenant" by J. Y. Mitchell (*WTJ,* November 1969, pp. 24-48); also "Canon and Covenant" by M. G. Kline (*Ibid,* pp. 49-58). Eichrodt, a leader among critical scholars today (*TOT,* Vol. 1, p. 36), emphatically rejects Kraetzschmar's theory that "the idea of the covenant first appeared as a result of the work of the major prophets." On the contrary he bases his study of biblical theology on the idea of the covenant relationship.

[61] The word *berith* has not yet been found on the Ras Shamra tablets, which would weigh against the view that it is of Canaanite origin. It is also not found in the Amarna Letters. The Babylonian has several roots from which it might be derived. Some scholars derive it from a root meaning "to bind," with the idea of a bond or tie, hence a contract. Zimmern derived it from a root meaning "to see or behold" and connected it with the word *baru,* the title of an important class of diviners in Babylonian temples. But there seems to be no proof that the word *berith* in the sense in which it is used in the Old Testament is found in any other Semitic language. Nielsen in a lengthy discussion of the word (*Shechem,* pp. 110-118), explains it as derived from the Accadian (*ina birit,* "in between").

He can cite no example of the occurrence of the word in Accadian but speaks of it "as adapted into Canaanite idiom perhaps centuries before the immigration of the Israelites." The importance of the word is now recognized by Albright (*FSAC²*, *Introd.* to 1957 edition, p. 16).

[62] It is quite possible that the worship of Baal-berith or El Berith is to be regarded as an illustration of that syncretistic tendency which appears so often in the Old Testament. From the days of the patriarchs Israel was the people of the Covenant (Gen. 17). It was quite natural then that in turning to the baals of Canaan they should give one of them the title Baal-berith, Lord of the Covenant.

[63] *PTR* (1918), pp. 299-304.

[64] Oehler, *TOT*, p. 63.

[65] Gen. 25:20; 28:5; 31:20, 24. The *AV* follows *LXX* and *Vulg.* by rendering Syrian instead of Aramaean. In Deut. 26:5, the words "an Armaean, ready to perish" must refer to Jacob.

[66] That the patriarchal names, Serug, Nahor, Terah should appear as names of cities in the Padan-Aram region is not surprising and lends support to the historicity of the biblical records. Cf. Albright, *FSAC*, pp. 236f. and Unger, *Archaeology and the Old Testament*, pp. 112f., 124f., also *Israel and the Aramaeans of Damascus*, pp. 8f. We note, however, that the "city of Nahor" (Gen. 24:10) was Haran (11:31f.; 28:2; 29:4). That there was a city named Nahor is not indicated in the Genesis narrative. That *Haran* (the name of Abram's brother) and *Haran* (more correctly *Charran*, Acts 7:4) the name of the city are quite distinct and should not be confused.

[67] The name Abram is, as we have seen, not Babylonian, but West Semitic. The root *rûm* (to be high) does not occur in Accadian, but is found in West and South Semitic languages. It is perhaps also significant that Nahor is not mentioned as accompanying his father to Harran (Gen. 11:31), but is dwelling there when the servant is sent to "my country, and to my kindred" (24:4) to secure a wife for Isaac. This favors the view that Harran may have been the ancestral home of Abram, and Ur the place of a lengthy sojourn (11:28). If this is correct the name ""Hebrew" given to Abram in Canaan (14:13) may describe him as one who had "come over" the river Euphrates.

[68] The adverb might be regarded as describing the state of mind of this eminent scholar rather than the date of the biblical passages to which he refers.

[69] Moscati (*Ancient Semitic Inscriptions*, p. 168) finds a mention of Aram on an inscription by Naramsin, and on a Drehem tablet of *c.* 2000 B.C.; also as a personal name on a slightly later Drehem tablet and on a Mari tablet of *c.* 1700 B.C.

[70] Otto Weber in his extensive notes on Knudtzon's edition of the Amarna Letters (1912) described the Akhlamu as Aramaic Nomad hordes which are first mentioned here, ignoring the biblical evidence. Similarly F. Rosenthal in the Article "Aram, Aramaens" in *NSHERK* makes no mention of the biblical testimony as to the time of the arrival of Aramaeans in Syria and Mesopotamia.

[71] Cf. Franz Delitzsch, *Com. on Job, in loco.*

[72] *BDB*, p. 808. No further light has been cast on the meaning by Ugaritic, cf. Gordon's *Ugaritic Textbook* (1965), p. 467.

[73] Albright, *FSAC*, p. 248f., cf. *FBM²*, p. 325, note 25.

[74] Martin Noth, *Das System der Zwolf Stamme Israels* (1930, p. 85f). He refers to Ewald; see also Bright, *A History of Israel*, p. 144. It is to be noted that Solomon's system of 12 monthly allotments clearly goes back to David (cf. 1 Chron. 27:1-15). But Noth apparently questioned as many critics still do the historical trustworthiness of Chronicles.

[75] In like manner Judges 15 is regarded by Alt and Noth as giving the administrative districts of the time of Josiah, i.e., of the seventh century (cf. G. E. Wright, *Biblical Archaeology*, p. 130 who dates it in the time of Jehoshaphat, ninth century). The fact that Deut. 27:15-26 lists twelve curses has led to its being called a "Dodecalogue" of Cursing and it is natural to observe that this corresponds to the twelve tribes. But this seems questionable as it might suggest that the twelve curses are to apply to the twelve tribes individually, one to each tribe. Yet we read that "all the people shall answer and say, Amen." If the number twelve has any special significance it is probably simply mnemonic.

[76] *ISBE*, p. 1514.

[77] Steindorff and Seele: *"When Egypt Ruled the East"²*, p. 252.

[78] *NBD*, p. 95.

[79] Unger, *Archaeology of the O.T.*, pp. 130f.

[80] The name Puti-el might be Hittite. We have pointed out that the name of the king of Jerusalem mentioned in the Amarna Letters which is usually read as Abduheba may also be read Putu-heba

[81] *Der Gott der Väter* (1929). Sèe the review by E. J. Young in *WTJ* (1940), pp. 25-40.

[82] Some earlier examples have since been cited.

[83] When John Bright tells us: "Whether or not Yahweh was worshipped before Moses is a question that cannot be answered" (*A History of Israel*, p. 116), it is clear that he does not consider such passages as Gen. 4:26; 8:20; 14:22; 24:3, 12; 27:7; 30:24; 38:7; 39:2, sufficiently dependable to justify the drawing of any inference as to the God whom the patriarchs worshipped. Eissfeldt holds that despite the fact that the sources of Genesis speak of the absoluteness of the God of the ancestors of Israel, it remains clearly evident (*deutlich erkennbar*) that the groups which invaded Canaan from the south in the time of Moses, reverenced (*verehrt haben*) another god than Abraham, Isaac and Jacob did. He claims that the Israelites of the pre-Mosaic period worshipped the *El*, whom the Ugaritic texts have shown to have been the chief god of the Canaanites. He finds this God referred to in the names of El 'Elyon, El 'Olam, El Rou, El Shaddaj, El Bethel, and El of Punel. And he insists that this El is distinct from Jahwe (*Die Genesis der Genesis*, 1958, pp. 63f.).

[84] *Israel from Its Beginnings* (1932), p. 161.

[85] *From Joseph to Joshua*, p. 109, also p. 1.

[86] *Prolegomena*, p. 441. For this theory of several invasions, cf. also Guthe's article "Israel" in *EBi*, col. 2225f.

[87] *Op. cit.*, p. 64.

[88] This splits the 40 years of wilderness wandering into a thirty-eight sojourn of the Southern Group at Kadesh and a two-year trek of the Egyptian Group from Egypt to Moab via Sinai. It involves the rejection of the forty-year figure of Num. 14:33f.; 32:13; Deut. 2:7; 8:2, 4; 29:5 (cf. Josh. 14:10); Ps. 95:10; Amos 2:10; 5:25; Acts 7:36, 42; 13:18; Heb. 3:9, 17, all of which refer to a forty-year wandering.

[89] The Habiru are mentioned in the El Amarna Letters written by Abdu-hiba of Jerusalem. The SA GAZ are mentioned in other letters. The identity of these invaders or marauders has been and still is a matter of dispute among scholars.

[90] The splitting of the forty years into thirty-eight years spent at Kadesh (*c.* 1440 B.C.) and two years in the desert after leaving Sinai (*c.* 1228 B.C.) introduces an interval of two centuries between these two portions of its forty years.

[91] Num. 14:39-45; Deut. 1:43f. The victory described in Num. 21:3 took place nearly forty years later and under quite different circumstances. It was no part of the Conquest, but simply a successful meeting of an attack. "Hormah" means "ban or destruction." The Hormah of Num. 21 may be quite distinct from the one mentioned in the other two passages.

[92] Commentary on Isaiah, *in loco*.

[93] G. B. Gray in *EBi*, col. 3777.

[94] Favored by Wellhausen in 1875 (*Prolegomena*, p. 440), it was first proposed by Ghillany (1862), adopted by Stade (1887), by Budde (1899) and so became widely accepted: e.g., by Oesterley and Robinson in *Hebrew Religion* (1930), pp. 110-15, 138f. It is rejected by Meek, König, Phythian-Adams, Buber, and Volz. G E. Wright holds that the evidence for it is "very tenuous" (*Biblical Archaeology*, p. 65). Cf. Rowley, *op. cit.*, p. 149; also *FBM²*, pp. 148, 207.

[95] Rowley argues that Jochebed was probably a kin of Jethro since Moses fled to Jethro, and that her name Jochebed (Yo, i.e., Yahweh, is honorable or glorious) may come through Kenite associations, direct or indirect (*FJJ*, p. 159f.). That this is an assumption read into the narrative with a view to establishing a link between Jethro and Yahwehism is clear when we compare the totally different story of Jacob's flight to his kindred at Haran (Gen 29:1-20). Obviously the writer of this account knew nothing of any kinship between Moses and Jethro. The words, "and Moses was content to dwell with the man" (v. 21) would be a strange way of describing the meeting of two kinsmen. Rather it seems to indicate that they were utter strangers.

[96] According to Budde, as quoted by Orr, if the Decalogue is regarded as Mosaic "it appears that there existed even in the earliest times, a conception of God so sublime that hardly anything could have remained for the prophets to do.

This of itself should suffice to show the impossibility of the Mosaic origin of the Ten Commandments" (*POT*, p. 120).

[97] Cf. *FBM*[2], pp. 137ff. More recently a third Decalogue, called by Pfeiffer "the old Canaanite decalogue" has been carved out of the Book of the Covenant (Exod. 23:12, 15-17; 22:29-30; 23:18-19). Cf. Pfeiffer, *Religion in the Old Testament*, p. 93 and also his *Introduction in loco*. Like the one discovered in Exod. 34 it is purely ritualistic and cultic.

[98] *Prolegomena*, p. 439f. For more recent pronouncements to much the same effect, see G. A. Barton, *The Religion of Israel* (1918), pp. 65f., 89f.; Geo. Harford in Peake's *Commentary*, pp. 184f.; S. L. Brown in *A New Commentary* edited by Gore, Goudge and Guillaume (1928). In opposition to the Critical view, cf. E. J. Young, *IOT* (1949), pp. 73f.

[99] *LOT*, pp. 35f.

[100] *Die Ursprünge des Israelitischen Rechts* (1934). In this he was preceded by Jirku and by Jepsen (cf. J. Coppens, *Histoire Critique des livres de l'ancien Testament*[3], p. 128). For a discussion of this theory, see also *FBM*[2], pp. 218-23.

[101] *A History of Israel*, p. 146.

[102] Nielsen, *Shechem*, p. 320.

[103] *Vide supa.*

[104] *ANET*, p. 95.

[105] Thus, according to the above mentioned ritual, 243 *sibtu*-loaves are to be baked daily. Of these 30 are to be placed on the tray for the god Anu (eight each for the two morning meals, seven each for the two evening meals), 30 each for Antu, Ishtar, and Nana, additional loaves for various shrines, a total of 168, while the other 75 are to be offered to the other deities of Erech (*ANET*, p. 343).

[106] The Egyptian system appears to have been even more elaborate than the Babylon, cf. Breasted, *The Development of the Religion of Ancient Egypt*, pp. 77f. Erman, *Die Aegyptische Religion*, pp. 49f.

[107] Cf. Exod. 16:35; Num. 11:6-9; Deut. 8:3, 16; Josh. 5:12. Cf. Ps. 78:24; Neh. 9:20; John 6:31; Heb. 9:4.

[108] Erman's statement is therefore especially noteworthy: "But the customary disposition made of the offerings was undoubtedly that one of which no mention is ever made, that the priests used them for their own support and that of their dependents as soon as they had remained a sufficiently long time before the god" (cf. Erman, *Die Religion der Aegypter*, p. 191). The Apocryphal story of *Bel and the Dragon* is probably quite true in so far as it illustrates the deceitful practices of the priests of paganism.

[109] Cf. Wellhausen, *Prolegomena*, p. 142, Note 2. Also the Article "Aaron" in *HDB, EBi*, and *FBM*[2], pp. 185-196.

[110] In Brightman, *Sources of the Hexateuch* (1918), p. 208n, the statement is made: "Aaron is missing from J; and is only incidental in E." Aaron is missing in J merely because Brightman eliminates all of the 13 occurrences in J. In E the word "incidental" is significant because in the stories of the golden calf (Exod. 32) and the challenge to Moses' authority (Num. 12), both of which are assigned to E and in which 12 of the 17 occurrences of Aaron in E are to be found, Aaron figures prominently in the narratives (cf. *FBM*[2], p. 194).

[111] *Op. cit.*, pp. 134, 143.

[112] The claim that these totals are "impossible" is argued quite fully for example by G. B. Gray in his commentary on Numbers (*ICC*, 1903). He gives Colenso "the great merit" of having demonstrated this.

[113] *ISBE*, p. 911f. By adding the figures for *elephs* (598) and those for hundreds and fifties (5,550) separately, the total of males is 5,550 which divided by 598 gives about 9½ males per *eleph*. So Petrie regarded the *eleph* as equivalent to "tent" or "family." But the arbitrariness of this solution is proved by the fact that when the 598 *elephs* are treated as thousands (598,000) and the 5,550 men are added to them the total is 603,550 which is the total given in Num. 2:32.

[114] *FSAC*[2], pp. 253, 291. See the brief discussion in *FBM*[2], pp. 274f. E. J. Kraeling appealing to Musil, the Czech explorer, arrives at approximately the same figure (*RMBA*, p. 101). Cf. G. E. Wright, *Biblical Archaeology* (1957), pp. 66f.; also G. E. Mendenhall, "The Census Lists of Numbers 1 and 26" (*JBL*, March, 1958, pp. 52-66). John Bright, *A History of Israel*, 1958, pp. 120f.) tells us: "The number that participated in the exodus was hardly more than a very few thousand; all of later Israel was scarcely descended from them." He quotes

A. Lucas' figure of 10,363; and adds: "The reader can figure that two and a half million people marching in an old-fashioned column of fours would extend some 350 miles!" (p. 121). This is clearly intended to make the account ridiculous. It is nowhere stated or suggested that they marched in "an old-fashioned column of fours." They may have crossed the Red Sea on a broad front of half a mile, for all we know to the contrary. On the other hand it is interesting to note that George Rawlinson apparently was not troubled by the size of the Israelite host at the time of the Exodus. With regard to Pharaoh's refusal of Moses' first request (Exod. 5:1) he says: "Menophthah not unnaturally, refused, fearing to lose the services of more than half a million of bondsmen, who if they once quitted the country and found themselves free, would not be likely to return" (*History of Ancient Egypt*, III, p. 344).

[115] In Old Testament times in Palestine figures were also used to write numbers just as had been the case for centuries in Egypt and Babylonia. We find them on ostraca dating from the time of Ahab. The use of letters of the alphabet (e.g., *aleph* for one, *yodh* for ten, and *kaph* for twenty) to designate numbers dates from a later time and is apparently due to Greek influence. But it is noteworthy that the St. Mark Isaiah scroll is exactly the same as the Masoretic Text in this respect. Thus, in 37:26 the enormous total "one hundred and eighty and five thousand" is spelled out in full. It is not given in figures.

[116] In his discussion of the Censuses, Gray made no mention of this important fact, probably because he held the figures to be "impossible" and the passages where they occur as nearly all (except Exod. 12:37f.) quite late (P) and therefore quite undependable.

[117] Breasted, *A History of Ancient Egypt*, pp. 236f.

[118] Deut. 4:37f.; 7:1; 9:1; 11:23-35. The brevity of the account of the destruction of the hosts of Sihon and Og in Num. 21:21-35 is a striking indication of the ease with which Israel's God could clear the way for his people's conquest.

[119] See above pp. 66-67.

[120] It is significant that while the grand total for the second census differs only slightly from the figure for the first census (601,730 as compared with 603,500), the figures for the individual tribes are all more or less different (an increase for Manasseh, Asher, Benjamin, Issachar, Zebulun, Judah, Dan; a loss for Simeon, Ephraim, Naphali, Gad and Reuben). The loss for Simeon is especially noteworthy, 59,300 reduced to 22,200, perhaps due in part to the sin of Baal-peor in which a prince of Simeon was the principal offender. The Census in Num. 1 is also much simpler than the one in Chap. 26. In the former, no tribal subdivisions are mentioned, and no names other than those of the tribal ancestors (12 plus Levi) are given. Chap. 26 on the other hand mentions the tribal divisions after the manner of Gen. 46 without, however, giving any figures for them.

[121] These figures show that the talent was reckoned as 3,000 shekels. They do not tell us the number of shekels in the mina or of minas in the talent.

[122] Verse 13f. states the problem with great plainness. It was impossible by any human standard. ,

[123] That the Israelites were to expect to suffer losses in battle is made clear by Deut. 20:1-19.

[124] G. B. Gray in his Commentary in *ICC* (p. 418) treats this passage as not history but as midrash and therefore worthless, a very convenient way of getting rid of unwelcome evidence.

[125] *ARI*, p. 201, note 13. According to the analysis generally accepted by critics the narrative Num. 13:1-14 belongs to P, and is therefore late and unreliable. Albright hesitates to regard it as historically dependable. But he ignores the question which then arises, What is its significance and how is its presence in this connection to be explained?

[126] As to its origin and authorship (prophetic or priestly, or both) there has been much dispute; but that at least in its present form it is late and non-Mosaic, there has been general agreement among the critics. Cf. Pfeiffer who calls it "a brilliant combination" etc. (p. 171).

[127] There are some indications that Moses proclaimed this law twice, first at, or on the march to, Kadesh (Num. 13:26) while the Israelites were awaiting the return of the spies, and in anticipation of the conquest which should have followed immediately on the receiving of a favorable report from the spies, and then a second time at the close of the forty years when the conquest was actually about to begin. (See *BCBS*, Vol. II, p. 9, which bases this claim on the cities

mentioned in 1:1-2). This theory is, however, not supported by the alleged "double allusion to the Cities of Refuge" (*ISBE*, p. 837) For 19:1-13 refers to the three cities to be appointed *west* of the Jordan, "in the midst of thy land" while 4:41-43 refers to the cities *east* of it.

[128] In the appendix to the Westcott and Hort edition of *The New Testament in Greek* about eighty "passages and phrases" are listed as quoted from Deuteronomy. It has often been noted that Jesus' three replies to Satan in the temptation are quoted from Deuteronomy. Compare especially Matt. 19:7-9 and 22:23-30, where laws which appear only in Deuteronomy are recognized both by Jesus and his critics as Mosaic.

[129] *Prolegomena,* p. 35.

[130] *LOT,* p. 191.

[131] *HDB,* article "Deuteronomy," pp. 598, 601.

[132] *Commentary on The Psalms* (English translation, 1883), Vol. III, p. 2.

[133] *The Psalms* (1902), p. 548.

[134] *Religion in the Old Testament,* edited by C. C. Forman, pp. 161-174. Probably no one has spoken more strongly of "the profound influence of the prophets on the Deuteronomic Code" than has R. H. Pfeiffer. He even tells us that "The epoch-making contributions of the prophets to the religious progress of mankind could be discovered and in a measure could be reconstructed, even if all their writing had perished . . . simply by comparing the ancient religion of Israel, as we have described it on the basis of the pre-exilic literature of the Old Testament preserved in the Pentateuch and the historical books, with the religion of the book found in the temple in 621 B.C., which form the bulk of Deuteronomy" (p. 118). Thus he cites "the doctrine of God" as stated in Deut. 10:12-18 as an example of "the profound influence of the prophets on the Deuteronomic Code" (p. 163). It would be hard to find more adequate evidence of the close connection between the Law as represented by Deuteronomy and the great prophets of the eighth and seventh centuries B.C., a connection which is stressed by the New Testament. This illustrates the vast importance of Deuteronomy to the student of the Bible. If Deuteronomy is accepted as Mosaic it reverses the whole situation as stated by Pfeiffer. It restores the biblical order, Moses and the prophets, an order which Driver, for example, cannot entirely ignore for he admits that Deuteronomy "was an emphatic reaffirmation of the fundamental principles which Moses long ago insisted on, loyalty to Jehovah and repudiation of all false gods" (*LOT,* p. 89), a statement which illustrates the weakness of the critical theory regarding Deuteronomy. For according to its own statements Deuteronomy was not a reaffirmation by others but a final affirmation by Moses himself of the law of God given through him at Sinai as a farewell exhortation and warning, a warning which was abundantly fulfilled in the later history of Israel. For Moses foretold in most emphatic terms and with heartbreaking sorrow the future falling away of Israel from the Law given at Sinai. Yet the critics have been insisting for nearly two centuries that Deuteronomy is not Mosaic.

[135] And the statement is added "these books inspired him to write the prophetic sermon of Moses, in all sincerity supplying a book which strangely did not exist" (p. 163.)

[136] *Ibid.,* p. 168.

[137] *Ibid.,* p. 170f.

[138] B. W. Anderson in his book, *Understanding the Old Testament* (1957), calls the books Joshua-Kings the "Deuteronomic History"; and he says of Judges: "The Deuteronomic 'theology of history' is found in capsule form in the introduction to the Deuteronomic section (Judg. 2:6; 3:6)," pp. 95f. According to Eichrodt, "Deutero-Isaiah may be regarded as in some respects the perfecter of Jeremiah's thought" (*TOT,* p. 62).

[139] *Religion,* p. 171. "The prophets represented a misunderstanding of the past, not a break with the past; they were heretics but not schismatics" (p. 134).

[140] *Op. cit.,* p. 133.

[141] *Op. cit.,* p. 164f.

[142] *Op. cit.,* p. 171.

[143] One element which must be eliminated is, of course, predictive prophecy. Pfeiffer holds that the prophets were not predictors: The chief and almost only function of the reforming prophets, beginning with Amos, was to proclaim to their people the nature and the will of Jehovah (p. 118). As an example of the elimination of prediction from Deuteronomy we note that Pfeiffer in his *Introduc-*

tion to the O.T., p. 184) treats most of Deut. 28:25-68 as postexilic. He says of vv. 47-57, "the siege and destruction of Jerusalem in 586 and the ensuing woes are clearly depicted"—in other words, a prophecy post eventum; and he refers to W. A. Irwin's article "An Objective Criterion for the Dating of Deuteronomy" (*AJSLL*, 1939, pp. 337-49). It is by such methods that Pfeiffer justifies his claim that "the prophet was not concerned with predicting the future" (*Religion*, p. 117).

[144] The discovery of treaties between ancient kings, especially the vassal treaties of Esarhaddon, published by Wiseman in 1958, has led to a careful study of these documents and to comparison of them with similar transactions recorded in the Old Testament. M. G. Kline (*Treaty of the Great King*, 1963) has drawn the conclusion that "Deuteronomy is a covenant renewal document which in its total structure exhibits the classic legal form of the suzerainty treaties of the Mosaic Age" (p. 28). This claim is based mainly on the fact that the "historical prologue," found in Deut. 1:6—4:49 and in other treaties of the time of Moses, is not found in the treaties of the later period, such as those of Esarhaddon. K. A. Kitchen, after a careful study of the treaties reaches the same conclusion as does Kline, that the evidence supports the early date of the Sinai covenant (*Ancient Orient and Old Testament*, 1966, pp. 90-102). Wiseman uses the term "vassal treaty" to describe the text "because of its nature as the imposition of certain obligations without agreement by, or benefits to, the subordinates of the Assyrian king, whether members of his own court or of territories subservient to him" (*op. cit.*, p. 27). By contrast, the pervasive theme of Deuteronomy is the blessing which will come to Israel through obedience to the covenant made with them by God. Chapters 27-28 contain both blessings and curses. In Esarhaddon's treaty there are no blessings; only oaths of obedience imposed in the name of the gods of Assyria (lines 25-413), followed by terrible curses for breach of covenant (lines 414-668). The spirit of the treaties or covenant is in this respect totally different.

Kline also points out that in the case of the Esarhaddon treaties there were two copies of each treaty, one for the king, the other for the vassal. He infers from this that the "two tables of stone" on which the Ten Commandments are written were *duplicates*, each containing all ten of the commandments. A serious objection to this novel interpretation lies in the fact that the two tables were both to be placed in the ark where they would be completely inaccessible to the people (Deut. 10:2, 5; 1 Kings 8:9; 2 Chron. 5:10). There is nothing to suggest that the tables were duplicates and that one, as a complete copy of the Decalogue, was to be placed in the ark, while the other was to be a public reminder to the people of the law which God had imposed on them and which they had solemnly promised to obey.

[145] One object of the Book of Ruth is clearly indicate that there was a remnant of faith even in that time of general apostasy.

[146] Pedersen, *Israel*, Vol. I, p. 147.

[147] *Ibid.*, Vol. II, p. 466.

[148] Exod. 34:14-17; Lev. 17:7, and many other passages.

[149] The land "flowing with milk and honey" (mentioned fourteen times in the Pentateuch, first in Exod. 3:8, 17) is given to them by their God, who is Lord of the whole earth. That all the blessings of agriculture come from him is pointed out again and again, e.g., Lev. 26:3-12; Deut. 7:12-14; 8:7-20; 28:3-5; 1 Kgs. 8:35f.; 18:1; Ps. 65:9; 67:6; 85:12; 104:14; 147:8f.; Isa. 30:23; 35 1f., 7; 55:1f.; Jer. 2:7, 13; 5:24; Hos. 2:8, 21; 14:4; Joel 2:19; Amos 4:6; 9:13 and many others.

[150] *Die Biblische und die Babylonische Gottesidee*, pp. 362f.

[151] Article, "The Crisis" in *Record and Revelation*, ed. by H. W. Robinson, p. 134.

[152] G. H. Davies in *Studies in Old Testament Prophecy*, edited by Rowley (1950) p. 37f. speaks of this as "another illustration of that transition from the Desert to the Sown, which has often been made at different times by different groups of the human race in widely separated parts of the world." If this change "has often been made," then the question must be faced, Why did this transition have such a uniquely different result in the case of Israel?

[153] According to Albright, "Given the initial tension of spirit which raised the faith of Israel so far above the pagan religions of that day, Palestine was thus an ideal land in which to develop increasing trust in Providence as against reliance

on the magic and divination which were the mainstay of surrounding peoples" (*AOP*, p. 255). But the following sentence is particularly significant: "Though archaeology can thus clarify the history and geography of ancient Palestine, it cannot explain the basic miracle of Israel's faith, which remains a unique factor in world history."

[154] Young (*IOT*, p. 153); Driver (*LOT*, pp. 183f.).

[155] In his *Israel* (pp. 408-13), Snaith in referring to Lods' theory (*OTMS*, p. 99) mentions Hempel, Hylander, and Press as accepting it. When proposed by Bernstein it was rejected by Morris Jastrow, Jr. (*JBL*, xix, 1900) and described as impossible by Karl Budde (*Kurzer Hand-Commentar*, 1902). Quite recently it has been stated by E. O. James as follows: "It is not improbable, in fact, that some of the incidents attributed to Samuel may have been told of Saul originally and subsequently transferred to Samuel by the anti-monarchical Deuteronomic school" and he cites the word-play on the name of Samuel as "being more relevant to the name of Saul" (*The Ancient Gods*, 1960, p. 253). This is only one of many illustrations of the way in which James uses radical criticism to fit the religion of Israel into the pattern of the religions of the Ancient Near East and make it a development according to which "the Christian concept of Deity represented the culmination of the long process of development and diffusion, of adaptation and amalgamation, and of syncretism and emergence on which this inquiry has been concentrated."

[156] See *FBM²*, p. 301.

[157] In this passage Ahimelech the son of Abiathar is mentioned. Probably he was representing his father temporarily for a reason that is not stated.

[158] *Prolegomena*, p. 126.

[159] Article "Zadok" (in *EBi*). Compare the very different article by Whitelaw in *ISBE*, p. 3131, for a discussion of the suggestion by Wellhausen that Zadok was "an adventurer, a soldier of fortune, who had climbed up into the priest's office, though by what means is not known." It is to be noted that the Zadok who is described as "a young man mighty of valor" (1 Chron. 12:28) is clearly represented as a Levite and probably as an Aaronite. Addis calls the steps taken by Nathan and Bathsheba to secure the succession for Solomon a "harem intrigue" and describes Adonijah as "the legitimate heir," a strange misinterpreting of the narrative! (*EBi*, col. 5374).

[160] In *Ezra den Skriftlaerde*, 1916, p. 109. When adopted by Bentzen, it was opposed by Budde (*ZAW*, 1934, pp. 42-50). It has been accepted by H. R. Hall, Dornseiff, Rowley, Nyberg, Nielsen and many others. Quite recently by John Bright.

[161] Article "Zadok and Nehushtan" (in *JBL*, 1939, pp. 113-141).

[162] There is nothing surprising in this. Eleazar had a son Phineas and Eli also a son with the same name. The genealogy of Heman contains three Elkanahs (1 Chron. 6:33-38). Jehoshaphat had a son Jehoram and a grandson Ahaziah. Ahab had a son Ahaziah who was succeeded by his younger brother Jehoram, Joash the son of Ahaziah of Judah and Joash the grandson of Jehu were contemporaries. Does this make any of these names questionable?

[163] He does not even mention the abundant evidence in the Middle Books of the Pentateuch (Exod., Lev., Num.) which proves that a priest must be a descendant of Aaron (see above), obviously because as a disciple of Wellhausen he holds it to be an assured result of criticism that belonging to P or H, they are late and undependable. This would apply also to 1 Chron. 12:28 which clearly treats Zadok as a leader among the Levites.

[164] The verb "left" (vs. 37) must be regarded as governing also the statements of verse 39f.

[165] The first is in Gen. 15:21.

[166] J. O. James in describing the ceremony when the ark was carried up to Jerusalem tells us that David "took over the priesthood of the god Zedek and placed himself at the head of the hierarchy with Zadok and Nathan as his *kohen* and *nabi* respectively" (*The Ancient Gods*, 1960, p. 125). In thus ignoring Abiathar and treating Zadok as a Jebusite, James shows that reckless disregard of the statements of the biblical text which this theory requires.

[167] In the Amarna Letters it is called Uru-salima, i.e., city of peace. Salem is also mentioned in Ps. 76:2. In Gen. 33:18 the rendering "Salem" is supported by *LXX* and *Vulg*. But "in peace" or "safely" is favored by *RV, RSV*, and *BV*. "In

health" is perhaps possible, the reference then being to the assumed healing of his lameness. But the assumption is doubtful (32:31f.).

[168] Twice in his letters to the Pharaoh, Abdu-hiba mentions the fact that he is a servant (*ardu*) of Pharaoh and that he owes his position "in the house of my fathers" not to his father or mother but to Pharaoh (*ANET*, pp. 487f.).

[169] Melchizedek may have been an Amorite. Cf. the name of a king of the First (Amorite) Dynasty of Babylon, Ammisaduga, which probably means "my kinsman is just."

[170] As an element in proper names "Adoni-" (lord) occurs only in five biblical names, two of which belong to the early period. Adoni-zedek, king of Jerusalem is included among the five kings of the Amorites (Josh. 10:1, 3, 5). Adoni-bezek (Judg. 1:4-8) is apparently included among the Canaanites and Perizzites against which Judah and Simeon fought when they sought to possess the land assigned to them. It is quite possible that *Adon* is an Amorite word which was adopted by both Phoenicians and Canaanites. (Cf. A. T. Clay, *Amurru*, p. 154). Cf. Otto Weber in Knudtzon, *Die El-Amarna-Tafeln*, p. 1163). The only connection of Adoni-bezek (Judg. 1:4-7) with Jerusalem lies in the statement that he was carried thither and died there. The location of Bezek is uncertain.

[171] Knudtzon, *E. A. Letter*, no. 287.

[172] The correct reading of this name is uncertain. *Heba* is apparently the name of the Hittite or Hurrian goddess Hepet. If the first part of the name which is not spelled out but written ideographically is also Hittite or Hurrian, it would then be read as *Putu;* if Accadian, it would be *Abdu*. The Abdu-heba of these Letters is perhaps 500 years later than Abraham. Adoni-zedek belongs to the time of Joshua (Josh. 10:1). Whether he is to be placed before or after Abdu-heba depends on the date to which we assign the Conquest. The names Melchizedek and Adoni-zedek are good Hebrew names.

[173] It is not to be confused with *Aliyan* which is a frequent epithet of Baal in the Ugaritic texts but comes from an entirely different root. *'Elyon* as a title of deity occurs most frequently in the Psalms. Cheyne considered it an evidence of late date. See R. D. Wilson "Names of God in the O.T." (*PTR* XVIII, pp. 483f.).

[174] de Vaux after discussing several theories regarding Zadok, notably the Jebusite theory which "enjoys great favour at the present," feels that "It is safer to admit that we do not know where Sadoq came from" (*Anc. Israel*, p. 374). When practically all the relevant data are rejected as undependable, the agnostic conclusion is obviously the safest. According to Albright, "There is no adequate reason to consider him as not an Aaronid" (*ARI*, p. 110); and he describes Rowley's article as "a learned but highly subjective discussion of the subject" (p. 205). Unfortunately the same criticism must be made of some of Albright's own theories.

[175] "Zadok and Nehushtan" (*JBL*, 1939, pp. 113ff.). In the Preface to *OTMS* (p. xviii) Dr. Rowley, as its editor, says of the conservative trend which he finds in recent years and attributes to archaeological discoveries, that it "is both other and firmer than the older conservatism, just because it is critically, and not dogmatically, based, and because it is based squarely on the evidence, instead of merely using the evidence as a support where it is convenient, and explaining it away where it is not." It seems to the present writer that this is a quite accurate statement of Dr. Rowley's own attitude, "using the evidence as a support where it is convenient, and explaining it away where it is not." Certainly it would be difficult to find a better example of explaining away the evidence where it is inconvenient than Dr. Rowley has given us in his treatment of Zadok and of Nehushtan. Such "conservatism" is very far from the conservatism of truly biblical scholarship.

[176] *ARI*, p. 129. He regards these names as hypocoristic and declares that they resemble scores of such names on Ugaritic tablets.

[177] Delitzsch speaks of them as "the four great Israelite wisemen in the time of Solomon" (*Commentary on Psalms, in loco*).

[178] So Keil, *Commentary on Kings*, pp. 55f. It is to be noted that the Levite who served Micah as priest and then became the priest of the Danites who migrated to the North is described as "a young man out of Bethlehem-Judah of the family of Judah who was a Levite" (Judg. 17:7). He was a Levite. But he had grown up in Judah and so is said to be of the family of Judah. Elkanah, the father of Samuel was a Levite (1 Sam. 1:11; cf. 1 Chron. 6:33-38). Yet he is called an Ephrathite. Similarly Heman and Ethan might be called Ezrahites or Zarhites, because they had dwelt among the Zarhites of the tribe of Judah.

[179] Exod. 23:21f.; 34:11-14; Num. 33:50-56; Deut. 7:1; 12:1-3; 20:17; 29:25ff.; Josh. 3:10.

[180] *Op. cit.*, p. 210. Also *ARI*, p. 127. Also Alleman & Flack, *O.T.Com.*, p. 153.

[181] So *AV, ARV, RSV.* Cf. "You must have one rule for the alien and the native" (Moffatt); "You must have the same statute for the resident alien as for the native born of the land" (Meek in *AT*); "all must abide by the same rule, both the foreigner and the native" (*BV*).

[182] In the line of Asaph there was an Ethni (possibly short for Ethan), son of Zerah, son of Adaiah, son of Ethan (1 Chron. 6:41f.). These names do not concern us except as they serve to show that Ethan (Ethni) may not have been a rare name in Levitical circles. Albright claims that "the name 'Ethan' actually does appear in the lists of personal names from fourteenth-century Ugarit *'Aty(a)* (whence 'Aytan) Ethan." He calls this a "characteristic transposition of the *yodh*" (*id.*, p. 227, n. 36). But the connection between a fourteenth century *'Aty(a)n* in Ugarit and a tenth century Israelite in Jerusalem is rather remote to say the least.

[183] *ANET*, p. 263. Discussed by Albright in *ARI*, pp. 12f., cf. p. 210. In *ANET*, J. A. Wilson translates this brief text and states that "Kerker (or Kurkur or Kulkul) seems to have been a woman minstrel for the Egyptian god Ptah in Palestine." He says nothing about Albright's claim that her name may be the same as that of Cholcol, the wise man with whom Solomon is compared.

[184] "Constantly" is rather a strong word to use for what was probably an unusual practice.

[185] *ARI*, p. 128.

[186] "The Sun cult and the Temple of Jerusalem" (*Myth and Ritual*, pp. 87f.).

[187] The incident described in Gen. 12:10-20 was apparently a brief one and it took place two centuries before Jacob went down to Egypt to sojourn.

[188] To treat this passage as evidence that the monarchs of Judah like those of Israel (1 Kings 12:33) and of other nations, sacrificed in person when they chose to do so down to the time of the captivity (1 Kings 9:25, 2 Kings 16:12f., cp. 2 Chron. 26:16ff.; Jer. 30:21) is not merely to place a meaning on 1 Kings 9:25 which is not necessary and is opposed to the definite statements of the law of Moses that only Aaronic priests might offer sacrifices, but it also ignores the fact that Uzziah was severely punished for his sacrilege and that Ahaz is described as an apostate.

[189] *NBCR*, p. 331, calls attention to the fact that this is the only place in the O.T. where sea is used in a figurative sense. But it is a natural not a mythological one, the word *apsu* is never used in the O.T. in the sense of sea. The size of the bath is uncertain because the only fragments of jars which are marked as baths are too fragmentary to make a correct estimate of its contents possible.

[190] 2 Chron. 4:5 gives 3000 baths, which means perhaps that the dual *('alpaim)* was later misread as plural (*alaphim*) and the figure three inserted. For a recent discussion of the size of the bath and of Solomon's sea, compare R. B. Y. Scott, "Weights and Measures in the Bible" (*BA*, May, 1959, pp. 25f., 29-32). Scott describes the calculation as "tentative." Estimates for the bath vary between *ca.* 5 gallons and twice that amount.

[191] *ARI*, p. 148f. It is to be noted that the word used to describe the great basin is the frequently occurring Hebrew word *yam* (sea) and not the Accadian word *apsu* which appears nowhere in the Old Testament. Whether the word *kiyor* is derived from Assyr. *kiuri* or *ki-ur* is at least doubtful (p. 151f.). The word may mean simply "round" and as such may be suitable to describe Solomon's "pulpit" and also the "lavers." Albright finds here "a rich cosmic symbolism" which was largely lost in later Israelite and Jewish tradition" (p. 154). The question is, whether it actually existed. In dealing with the altar in Ezekiel's Temple, he explains the word *'ar'el* or *har'el* by Accadian *arallu*, the word for the underworld, and in the expression "bosom of the earth" (Ezek. 43:13, 14, 17) rendered by *AV, ARV* "bottom," *RSV* "base," he finds confirmation of this mythological or cosmic meaning, all of which while showing Albright's great interest in comparative religion, is quite far-fetched and dubious.

[192] According to Albright, "The paganizing movement may be said to have been inaugurated by the building of the temple and to have been accelerated by Solomon's tolerance of pagan cults within the very shadow of the temple, continued and developed to a dangerous extent during the next two generations" (*ARI*, p. 155). But it is to be noted that he had already told us that, "Details of

cult, however, must remain in many cases doubtful because the Priestly Code restricts itself in principle to an account of the tabernacle service in so far as it could be reconstructed from tradition in the late seventh and the sixth centuries B.C." (*id.*, p. 142). Albright's claim that the temple was "a royal chapel" (cf. Amos 7:13) is refuted by 1 Kings 8:30-63 which clearly indicates that it was a place of worship for all Israel. But probably Albright regards the prayer of Solomon as "Deuteronomistic." He speaks of "the many vestiges of Canaanite cult" surviving among the people and of Solomon's "concessions" to them (*ARI*, p. 155). But the biblical narratives clearly indicate that these "concessions" were a later and terrible development, which came after the building of the house of the Lord, how long after we are not told (1 Kings 9:1-9). For on the contrary we read that the same sign of approval and acceptance, the "cloud" and the "glory" (1 Kings 8:10f.; 2 Chron. 5:13f.) was given to Solomon's temple as was given to the Mosaic tabernacle. Furthermore it is to be noted that, as pointed out in Oehler (*TOT*, p. 389), "The building of the temple took place with the cooperation of Nathan, that there is no trace of opposition to it on the part of the prophets, that Micah (4:1) and Isaiah (2:21) predict the highest glory for the mountain for the house of Jehovah."

[193] 1 Kings 5:1-12, 18; 7:13, 40, 45; give full credit to king Hiram and to Hiram his master workman.

[194] 1 Kings 3:12; 4:29-34; 5:12; 6:11-14. The praise of the Queen of Sheba (10:1-10) is a tribute to Solomon's wisdom and *originality*.

[195] The fact that this phrase, "under the sun," occurs once in the inscription of Tabnith and once in that of Eshmunazar II, both of which date from many centuries later than Solomon is a very weak argument for the late day of Ecclesiastes. G. A. Cooke (*A Text-Book of North-Semitic Inscriptions*, 1903) merely said of it, "The phrase is a favorite one with the author of Ecclesiastes" (p. 29). It may have originated with Solomon or be even more ancient. The expression is a natural one. It is used today by many people who do not think or know that they are quoting Ecclesiastes.

[196] The word *Elohim* is construed as a plural (gods). Cf. *LXX* and *Vulg.* There were two images because Jeroboam wanted to place one at either end of his kingdom. It is not likely that they were a male and a female (cf. Deut. 4:15). In Hosea 10:5 the noun is feminine. So Pusey renders there by "cow-calves." But the plural there is probably abstract.

[197] The terrible woe pronounced on Jeroboam and his house by Ahijah was by Jeroboam's contemporary and uttered to his wife. Ahijah's attitude was the same as was Hosea's, a century or more later.

[198] The only exceptions are Zimri, who is hardly more than mentioned, and Hosea as to whom the statement is made, "But not as the kings of Israel that were before him" (2 Kings 17:2), apparently to explain the reason for the omission of the usual denunciation.

[199] Albright speaks of this view as first proposed by Obbink (*FSAC*, pp. 299f.). In Kirkpatrick's article in *HDB*, which Albright describes as "excellent" not a word is said about an "invisible deity" of which the calves are only the pedestal.

[200] When Dr. Albright states that "conceptually there is, of course, no essential difference between representing the invisible deity as mounted on cherubim or as standing on a bull" (p. 306) he ignores the fact that nothing is said here about "an invisible deity." This is simply read into the narrative. The passage speaks here and in the case of Aaron's calf only of man-made images which were to be worshipped as gods.

[201] Compare especially Num. 7:89. It is only in the Bible that we read of this invisible God. The gods of the heathen were very visible!

[202] That idolatry was prevalent and popular when Rehoboam came to the throne is made clear by 2 Chron. 12:1. Compare 2 Kings 17:7-43 an indictment which includes Judah with Israel (vss. 13f.).

[203] How many examples of this have been discovered is not stated by Dr. Albright. There do not seem to have been very many. Whether the word "commonly" is fully warranted may be questioned. In *ANEP*, pp. 170 and 179, figures 500, 501, 531 are examples. Albright points out that most scholars have assumed the calves to have been direct representations of Yahweh as a bull god (*op. cit.*, p. 299), which he characterized as a "gross conception."

[204] The calves are referred to more than twenty times and always denounced

as the sin for which Jeroboam the son of Nebat was responsible. It was the great sin of which more than any other the Northern Kingdom was guilty.

[205] Writing in *HDB*, A. R. S. Kennedy was very emphatic that this was not idolatry: "It is needless to occupy space with proof of the absurdity of the opinion so long current in the Church, both Jewish and Christian, that we have here a species of avowed idolatry . . . it is now universally acknowledged that they were originally a sincere attempt to symbolize the true covenant God of Israel" (vol. I., p. 342). This is an expression of wishful thinking which is quite contrary to fact. The reason the opinion thus scathingly denounced was so long current and is so widely held today is that it is clearly taught in the Bible. To quote Charles Hodge: "The worship of the true God by images, in the eyes of the Hebrews, has ever been considered as much an act of idolatry as the worship of false gods" (*Systematic Theology*, Vol. III, pp. 292, 294).

[206] The utter absurdity of image worship is shown most convincingly in Isa. 44 which describes the making of an idol out of one part of a tree, the other part of which has been burned to give the worshipper warmth and to cook his food. The practice and the folly of it are denounced with the utmost severity and scorn. Isaiah knew idolatry first hand; he knew that the distinction between the image and the deity which it symbolized was rarely made, if ever. See Ps. 115:1-8; 135:15-18; Jer. 10:1-16 and many other passages.

[207] The Ugaritic myths (*ANET*, pp. 129-155) might well serve as an illustration of Ps. 50:21. "Thou thoughtest that I was altogether such an one as thyself." The gods are gluttonous, quarrelsome and licentious. The goddess Anath threatens her father benign El with physical violence if he does not have a house built for Bel (p. 137). Benign *El* gashes and flagillates himself as any hopeless heathen might do when he is informed of the death of his son, *Bel*. The goddess Anath causes the death of the lad Aqhat because he refuses to give her his bow (p. 153f.). The mythology of Ugarit sets a poor pattern for mortals to follow.

[208] The words of Hosea 13:2 "Let the men that sacrifice kiss the calves" suggest the familiarity with which the idolator was encouraged to treat his idol.

[209] It is to be remembered that the first third of the book of Numbers is assigned by the critics to P and regarded as late and unreliable.

[210] It is the attempt of the students of comparative religion to fit the religious history of Israel into the framework of the ethnic religions and interpret it by them, which is responsible for many of the false interpretations which they advance.

[211] Ezra arrived in Jerusalem in the fifth month of the seventh year of Artaxerxes (Ezra 7:7f.) and the problem of the foreign wives was disposed of by the first day of the first month (10:17). So the Book of Ezra tells only of the events of the first seven months after his arrival at Jerusalem.

[212] The mention of the seventh month in both Ezra 3:1 and Neh. 8:2 is apparently noteworthy since it calls attention to the fact that the two events took place at the time of the feast of tabernacles.

[213] The *LXX* inserts at Neh. 9:6 the words "and Ezra said," which indicates that Ezra was assumed to be one who offered the prayer which follows.

[214] It may seem strange that Ezra is not listed among those who sealed the covenant (Neh. 10:1f.). It may be that Seraiah was "the family name of the high priestly house to which Ezra and Eliashib belonged, one of whom—probably Ezra—affixed its seal" (*BCBS*, III, p. 500). This would account for the fact that neither Ezra nor Eliashib is listed among those who sealed.

[215] It is to be noted that in 1895 W. H. Kosters proposed (*EBi*, Col. 1487) that the "seventh year" be amended to read "thirty-second year" of Artaxerxes I (427 B.C.). Some scholars regard "thirty-seventh" as an "easier emendation" (*OTMS*, p. 114).

[216] The difference between these two views is to be carefully noted. While both place Ezra after Nehemiah, Kosters could and did claim that they were contemporaries and that both took part in the ceremonies in Neh. 8-10. But since the length of Nehemiah's absence from the city which is referred to in Neh. 13:6 is not known, those who claim that Ezra and Nehemiah "persistently ignore each other" can place Ezra's coming to Jerusalem during Nehemiah's absence.

[217] Batten's position is somewhat peculiar. In his articles published in 1902 in *HDB*, he accepted the traditional Ezra-Nehemiah sequence. But in his *Commentary* (*ICC*, 1912) he adopted van Hoonacker's theory in a slightly modified

form. He tells us: "Certainly we dare not follow Kosters ["Kosters" must here be a clerical error for "van Hoonacker"] and give Ezra's date as 398 B.C. for the 'seventh year' is entirely untrustworthy." Yet he concludes that Ezra's work was done "in the first quarter of the fourth century" (*Com.*, p. 47) which looks a good deal like a quibble. We note further that in the *Commentary* he scarcely mentions van Hoonacker and makes not the slightest mention of the fact that a decade earlier he had advocated the view that Ezra preceded Nehemiah. Since he had radically changed his position, it was, of course, necessary for him to state and defend his new position. But it is rather strange that he made no mention of this in the *Commentary*.

[218] *OTMS*, pp. 113f.

[219] G. E. Wright has stated the critical position accurately when he says that "perhaps a majority of scholars today believe that Ezra came to Jerusalem either in the seventh year of Artaxerxes II (Ezra 7:7) 398 B.C., not of Artaxerxes I (458 B.C.) or sometime after 432 B.C., that is, at the end of the reign of Artaxerxes I" (*Biblical Archaeology*, p. 208). But he makes no mention of the fact that many scholars have continued to hold the traditional view that Ezra preceded Nehemiah: e.g., J. D. Davis in *DDB*, R. D. Wilson in *ISBE*, E. J. Young in *IOT*, J. S. Wright in *NBC* and *NBD*, Whitcomb in *WBC*, Barabbas in *ZPBD*. It may also be noted that while Driver discussed it in *LOT* (1915) he did not accept it, nor did Oesterley in Peake's *Commentary* (1920).

[220] *ISBE*, p. 1084; *IOT*, p. 375; *NEB*, p. 408.

[221] Bright, *History of Israel*, p. 378. It is also argued that the mention of the wall in Ezra 9:9 refers to the wall built by Nehemiah and thus places Ezra after Nehemiah. But the word rendered by "wall" in *AV* is never used of Nehemiah's wall. It means fence or hedge and is probably used of the temple already built by Zerubbabel (Ezra 6:15). Cf. 1 Sam. 25:16. The fact that some who refer this to Nehemiah's wall feel obliged to delete the words "in Judah and" from the phrase "in Judah and Jerusalem" since Judah never was walled shows the weakness of this argument for the late date of Ezra.

[222] According to R. D. Wilson, "There is not the slightest proof that any of Ezra-Nehemiah is unhistorical, nor the least indication that all of it may not have been written as early as 405 B.C." (*ISBE*, p. 1084). See for example Dr. Wilson's study of Royal Names of the Persian Period in *SIOT*, pp. 68f.

[223] *ZAW*, 1934, p. 59; 1938, p. 67.

[224] *Ibid*, 1938, pp. 67, 84.

[225] *Ibid*, 1938, p. 72. Dornseiff is unwilling to see in Num. 25 an example and denunciation of religious prostitution. He tries to make it a denunciation of foreign marriages, which found its climax in Elijah's conflict with Jezebel. This is quite interesting because he argues that the failure of Leviticus to condemn mixed marriages, which Ezra opposed so vigorously, is fatal to the Wellhausen hypothesis that Leviticus was the Law-book of Ezra. "Damit bricht die Graf-Wellhausensche Pentateuchhypothese zusammen" (*ZAW*, 1938, p. 73).

[226] This is especially significant since of the 22,000 Levites numbered at Sinai (Num. 3:39) 8580 were within the age limits (30 to 50 years) for service in connection with the tabernacle, of whom probably one-third or nearly 3000 were Kohathites. Yet only five Kohathites were ordained to the priesthood, two of whom were slain for sacrilege. These facts make it easy for us to understand both the reason for the rebellion of Korah and his followers and its seriousness (Num. 16-18).

[227] *ZAW* (1935), p. 164. He refers to T. J. Meek's "striking observation" that Aaron's two sons, Nadab and Abihu, have names which suggest Jeroboam's sons (*AJSLL*, 1929, pp. 157ff.). See also *ZAW*, 1938, p. 64.

[228] *ZAW*, 1935, p. 164.

[229] Oesterley and Robinson, *Hebrew Religion*, p. 143, quoted and discussed in *FBM*², pp. 150f.

[230] Snaith in *Record and Revelation*, ed. by H. W. Robinson, p. 260.

[231] *ZAW*, 1937, pp. 134f., 1938, p. 65.

[232] *Ibid*, 1938, p. 84.

[233] Dornseiff finds in Phineas' mission to the men of Reuben, Gad and half-Manasseh (Josh. 22:13-34) an allusion to Ahab's conquest of Moabite territory in the days of Mesha (*ZAW*, 1938, p. 72). Similarly Eissfeldt argues that Gen. 27:39-40 which records the *prophecy* uttered by Isaac to and concerning Esau, and which Eissfeldt assigns to E, must be later than 1 Kings 11:14-22 which

speaks *historically* of an attempt by Edom to throw off the overlordship of Israel (*Die Genesis der Genesis,* 1958, p. 41).

234 Dornseiff is referred to repeatedly by Eissfeldt in *RAR,* but is ignored by North in *OTMS.*

235 *OTMS,* p. xxii.

236 Hitti, *Lebanon in History* (1957), pp. 126f.

237 *AOP* (1949), p. 233.

238 "Moreover we now know that the poetry of the Hebrew Bible, especially its older portions, swarms with allusions to the Canaanite verse of which the Ugaritic epics are merely samples" (*AOP,* p. 197). Cf. also Albright's essay on "The Psalm of Habakkuk" in *Studies in Old Testament Prophecy,* edited by Rowley (1950), pp. 6f.

239 *AOP,* p. 232f. Cf. *ANET,* p. 142.

240 *Op. cit.,* p. 142.

241 *Op. cit.,* p. 232. In *OTMS,* p. 32, Albright refers to it as "The song of Miriam (or Moses)."

242 *Ibid,* p. 233.

243 *ARV* renders by "cast up a highway," *RSV* by "lift up a song." Both renderings are appropriate in the context.

244 Cf. also Job 19:12; 30:12; Prov. 15:19 (*ARV*); Jer. 18:15; 50:26. In Exod. 9:17 and Prov. 4:8 the derived stems are used in the sense of "exalt (self)."

245 The rendering "upon the heavens" (*AV*) is derived, according to Franz Delitzsch from the Targum and Talmud, which use the word to designate one of the seven heavens (*Commentary on the Psalms,* pp. 274, 282f.). He supports the rendering "steppes" with an appeal to Isa. 40:3f.

246 It occurs ten or more times in the Baal-Anath series and once in the Tale of Aqhat (*ANET,* pp. 130-38, 153b.) A root written with "p" does occur in Hebrew in the forms *'aripah* (once) and probably also in *'araphel* (15 times), which may mean "cloud" or "thick darkness." But this is no sufficient reason for questioning the text of Ps. 68:4.

247 *AOP,* p. 233.

248 It is the rendering of *AV, ARV, RSV* and *BV.* C. H. Gordon (*Ugaritic Grammar,* p. 105) points to the expression "helpers of the war" (*AV,* 1 Chron. 12:1) as another case where the Ugaritic word "youths" may occur. But there also it is doubtful. The Greek (*LXX*) favors the rendering "helpers."

249 In these two cases the word is used as in Aramaic with the opposite sense, of shame or reproach, which is required by the context.

250 "Foreign Words in the Old Testament as an Evidence of Historicity" (*PTR,* 1928, pp. 177-247).

251 *Ibid,* pp. 217, 238.

252 *BDB* and many other Bible dictionaries refer to the cognate languages wherever they throw light on the meaning of words.

253 *AOP,* p. 233f.

254 *Ibid,* p. 234.

255 *Idem,* cf. *ANET,* pp. 137f.

256 *ANET,* p. 153, note 34.

257 *Ibid,* p. 1338, where it is used of the mounting of the goddess Asherah upon the back of a donkey (also p. 153).

258 *Ibid,* p. 139, where it describes the passionate grief of the chief god El.

259 *Ibid,* pp. 134f.

260 *Ibid,* p. 150; cf. Gordon, *Ugaritic Literature* (1949), p. 88.

261 *The Headings of the Psalms* (*PTR,* 1926, pp. 29f.). It apparently comes from a root *kshr* meaning "to be right" which is found in "Hebrew, Babylonian, New Hebrew, New Aramaic, and Syriac" (Wilson). Gordon prefers to derive it from a root *ktr* on the assumption that here the *sh* may as in Aramaic represent a *t.*

262 *The World of the Old Testament* (1958), p. 97. If there are "so many passages" which were first rendered intelligible through the Ugaritic, it is somewhat strange that here Gordon gives an example which he had already given in his *Ugaritic Handbook* (1947), p. 241, instead of a new example.

263 As another example of such alleged borrowings, Gordon claims the word used in vs. 14 for "gold" (*charus*). The choice of this word as proof of this contention is rather surprising. This word, which is probably derived from the Accadian in which it is the regular word for gold, occurs only here in the entire

Psalter, and elsewhere only in Proverbs (5 times) and in Zech. 9:3. The usual Hebrew word *(zahab)* occurs 385 times in the Old Testament, of which eight are in the Psalter, seven in Proverbs, and six in Zech. If parallels are to be sought, the unique phrase, "greenness of gold" suggests Babylonian origin, rather than Ugaritic.

[264] T. H. Gaster *(JQR,* 1946-71, pp. 55ff.) and F. M. Cross, Jr. *(BASOR,* no. 117, pp. 19-21).

[265] See above, pp. 203f.

[266] H. Ranke, *Early Babylonian Pers. Names,* gives a number of examples of such names.

[267] Its occurrence in Phoenician and Punic inscriptions has long been recognized. G. A. Cooke has given several examples in *North Semitic Inscriptions,* 1903, (pp 99f., also 91, n. 2, 154). We find the use of the Babylonian *ilani* (plural of *ilu)* seven times in the letter of Ammunira of Beruta *(E.A.,* 141), in which the king is called seven times, "my Lord, my Sun, my God" *(ilâni-ia);* also in E.A. 297, 298, 320 (rendered by "pantheon" by Albright in *ANET,* p. 490. It is to be noted, however, that *'elim* may also be derived from a root *'ul,* "to be strong, or prominent." Hence the rendering "mighty" *(AV,* cf. Luther) in some cases, is not impossible.

[268] *Eloah,* which would seem to be the natural singular of *Elohim* is largely restricted to the Book of Job (42 times out of 57). The reason for this is not known.

[269] It may be noted that in Ugaritic the verb "break" (vs. 5) would be written with *tau* and not as in Hebrew with *shin.*

[270] Cross claims to have found a further Canaanitism in the expression "beauty *(haderath)* of holiness." Because the word occurs in Ugaritic in a context which suggests the meaning "dream" or "vision" he would render here "Prostrate yourselves before Yahweh when he appears in holiness." Such a meaning in Ugaritic might suggest idolatry. It is no improvement on the usual interpretation. He also suggests that in Ps. 76 "the revision has progressed much further . . . kindreds of the people" being substituted for *"bene 'elim."* These "editorial" suggestions aim to trace the connection with the Canaanite "original," the one discovering a further Canaanitism, the other showing the elimination of it. On the other hand, the word *mabbûl* (vs. 10) is of interest. It occurs only here and in Gen. 6-11, where it is used of the Noachian deluge. Since at its first occurrence in Gen. 6:17 *mabbûl* has the definite article it cannot be rendered as in *AV* by "flood of waters." "Waters" must be an explanatory apposition. The verb does not occur in the transitive sense in Hebrew, but in Babylonian it has the meaning "destroy." So *mabbûl* means "destruction"; and the word which follows "waters" would define the instrument or cause of the destruction: "and behold I, even I, am sending the destruction, waters upon the earth." It appears then that *mabbûl* is probably a Babylonian word and not a Ugaritic word as those who claim that the psalm was an original Baal hymn might wish to believe (see article "The Flood of Waters" in *PTR,* vol. xvi, pp. 103-107).

[271] *OTMS,* p. 25.

[272] *AOP,* p. 242.

[273] *BASOR,* no. 117, pp. 19f. According to Albright "no genuine Canaanite hymns or psalms have yet been discovered" *(ARI,* p. 128). But he thinks we may rest assured that "the number of parallels would be many times what it is now, if we possessed the latter." But wishful thinking is not evidence!

[274] *AOP,* p. 235.

[275] *OTMS,* p. xv.

CHAPTER V

[1] We do not know when Isaiah died. But the words "and dwelt in Nineveh" (Isa. 37:37) which precede the account of Sennacherib's death may be regarded as intended to call attention to the fact that the defeated Assyrian monarch lived many years after the crushing and miraculous defeat which brought an end to his Palestine campaign.

[2] The words of the Rabshakeh "What confidence is this wherein thou trustest?" (Isa. 37:4) call to mind the contemptuous reply of Pharaoh to Moses: "Who is the Lord, that I should obey his voice to let Israel go. I know not the Lord." Sennacherib's spokesman claims that he does know him, that the Lord has sent

him against Israel, that Hezekiah has offended his own God and that Israel's God is weaker than the tribal gods whose cities his master has already captured. Thus it is the historical setting in Isa. 36 to 39, which provides the background for the wonderful promises and prophecies of Chapters 40 to 66.

3 Isaiah is fond of the rhetorical question which reaches its climax in the three synonymous verbs and are followed by the words, "that we may be like" and are preceded by the four emphatic I's of the preceding verse. Other examples are: 1:12; 10:3; 23:8; 27; 28:9; 33:14—about 50 occurrences in the book of Isaiah.

4 This does not include the cases where the pronoun is included in the form of the verb, but only those in which it is expressed independently, either as the subject of a nominal sentence or to emphasize the pronoun already expressed in the finite verb. It may be noted in this connection that both forms of the pronoun (*ani* and *anoki*) occur in both parts of Isaiah.

5 Cf. Isa. 2:8; 17:8; 37:19; also Deut. 4:28; Ps. 115:8; 135:15ff.; Hosea 14:3; Mic. 5:13; Jer. 1:16. The idols are the work of men's hands; his people are the work of God's hands (Isa. 29:23).

6 For a very fine discussion of this subject the reader is referred to P. Fairbairn, *Commentary on Ezekiel,* pp. 393-397.

7 In a treaty between Rameses II and the Hittite king Hattusilis we find the thousand gods of Egypt and the thousand gods of the Hittites invoked to bless those who keep and to curse those who break the treaty (*ANET,* p. 201, cf. Gurney, *The Hittites,* p. 199). The pantheons of Assyria and of Babylon were probably equally numerous.

8 In the fourteenth edition of the *EB* (1929) the article "Anthropoid Apes" lists twelve respects in which man differs from the apes. This statement does not appear in the corresponding article in the edition of 1963. Ever since Robertson Smith became the editor the *Britannica* has been a strong advocate of naturalistic evolution.

9 It suggests the annual procession of the gods along the great procession street of Babylon at the new year (*akitu*) feast.

10 Here as usually parentheses are used to indicate words which are supplied to complete the meaning, while italics are used for emphasis.

11 See the anonymous Psalm 115 with its echo in Ps. 135:15-21, which some would attribute to Isaiah. They certainly reflect the spirit of that great prophet of ethical monotheism. But compare Solomon's prayer (1 Kings 8:23) which is centuries earlier.

12 Delivered Sept. 18, 1902 and published in *PTR* vol. I (1903), pp. 239-55.

13 In his first lecture, delivered January 13, 1902, Delitzsch was able to make use only of "scattered fragments" of the Code of Hammurabi. The great stele which contained the whole of the Code was discovered by deMorgan at Susa just about the time that Delitzsch's first lecture was delivered, but before the discovery was known in Europe. Delitzsch referred to this fact in the second lecture which he delivered a year later.

14 In *The People and the Book* (1925), p. 190. But R. H. Pfeiffer in his *Introduction to the Old Testament* (1941) followed Wellhausen and Robertson Smith in emphasizing Bedawin origins.

15 Albright speaks of the language of Ras Shamra as "a very archaic Canaanite dialect akin to pre-Mosaic Hebrew" (*FSAC,* p. 12).

16 In his *Ugaritic Textbook* (1965), in discussing Linguistic Affinities, Gordon says: "The disagreement is gradually narrowing down to the question of whether Ugaritic is Canaanite or a separate NW Semitic language alongside Hebrew and Phoenician and Aramaic" and he adds "Thus the classification of Ugaritic tends to become a matter of arbitrary definition" (p. 144).

17 See Gen. 24:3; Exod. 20:3-5; 23:24f.; 34:12-17; Lev. 15:31; 18:3; Deut. 11:16; 12:2f., 29-31; 13:6-11; 27:5; Ps. 115; 147:19f.; Isa. 8:19-21; 44:9-20; Jer. 10:1-16 and many others; also Acts 10:28; 11:3; 2 Cor. 6:17. Israel is to be a "peculiar people" (Exod. 19:5; Deut. 14:2; 26:18).

18 Hegel, Max Mueller, Andrew Lang, Robertson Smith, Caird, Wm. James, Ladd.

19 Hooke, Oesterley, T. H. Robinson, A. R. Johnson, Gaster.

20 Mowinckel, Pedersen, Bentzen, Nyberg, Lindblom, Widengren, Engnell, Haldar, Hvidberg.

21 *Myth and Ritual,* p. 8; also *The Labyrinth, The Siege Perilous* and other of Hooke's numerous writings.

22 *Kingship and the Gods,* p. 405.

23 In Manson's *Companion,* p. 286.

24 *Ibid,* pp. 277, 282.

25 *Ibid,* p. 286.

26 Snaith in *RAR,* pp. 252f.

27 Engnell, *Divine Kingship,* p. 31, quoting Hooke, *Origins,* p. 23.

28 T. H. Robinson in *Myth and Ritual,* p. 185.

29 *OTMS,* p. 291.

30 C. H. Gordon opposes the view that Baal was a seasonal god. He denies that the annual performance of the ritual is proof of the annual death of Baal. He calls attention to the Gezer calendar which names all months after "useful agricultural events" (*Ugaritic Literature,* p. 3f.).

31 *Myth and Ritual,* p. 186.

32 A. Haldar, *The Notion of the Desert in Sumero-Accadian and West Semitic Religions* (1956).

33 Ps. 3:7; 7:6; 9:19; 10:12; 17:13; 44:26; 68:1; 74:22; 82:8; 132:8 (cf. 2 Chron. 6:41).

34 The words "go down" (e.g., Gen. 11:5; 18:21) and "go up" (e.g., Gen. 17:22; 35:13), "go forth" (2 Sam. 5:24), "return" (Num. 10:36) are all anthropomorphic expressions. But it is to be remembered that the language is figurative and that such expressions occur everywhere in the Old Testament and not merely in the Pentateuch. We find them, for example, in the psalm of Habakkuk. It is impossible to avoid the use of anthropomorphic language in speaking of God.

35 *Enuma Elish* originally covered seven large tablets and with more than 1,000 lines of text. The Fifth Tablet is almost entirely missing.

36 The translation in *ANET,* pp. 60-72 is by E. A. Speiser.

37 *Genesis and Semitic Tradition,* 1894.

38 T. G. Pinches, *The O.T. in the Light of the Historical Records of Assyria and Babylonia,* p. 48; A. Heidel, *The Babylonian Genesis,* 1942; E. A. Speiser in *ANET,* pp. 66-72.

39 *Israel and Babylon* (1925) pp. 166f.

40 *The Babylonian Genesis* (2nd ed. 1951), p. 97.

41 *Idem,* p. 139. This conclusion hardly accords with the statement of the preface that "The excavations ... have shown that the Old Testament is not an isolated body of literature but that it has so many parallels in the literature of the nations surrounding Israel that it is impossible to write a scientific history of the Hebrews or a scientific commentary on the Old Testament without at least a fair knowledge of the history and literature of Israel's neighbors" (p. v).

42 The word "deep" (*tehom*) has been regarded as derived from Babylonian *tiamat.* This was challenged by R. D. Wilson (*PTR,* I [1903] pp. 250, note), who regarded the roots as distinct. According to Heidel, "Though coming from the same root, the two words do not denote the same thing" (*op. cit,* p. 99).

43 In the article "Myth and Ritual Reconsidered," a paper read before the Oriental Society of the University of Manchester in 1954 (published in *The Siege Perilous,* p. 181).

44 Ps. 74:13-15 and 89:10 refer to the Exodus not to the Creation, as do Isa. 27:1f.; 51:9. Rahab, Leviathan and dragon (*tannin*) may be names borrowed from mythology. But in their contexts it is natural to see in them poetic allusion to the overthrow of Egypt in the time of the Exodus. Whether two or three enemies of God's people are referred to in Isa. 27:1 is a matter of dispute. *ARV* by rendering "and" finds three, which would be Babylon, Assyria, and Egypt. *AV* by rendering "even" apparently finds only two. *RSV* arbitrarily omits the "and" and apparently agrees with *AV.* (Cf. Paul Heinisch, *Theologie des AT.,* pp. 122f.)

45 T. H. Robinson, "Hebrew Myths" in *Myth and Ritual,* pp. 184f.

46 W. O. E. Oesterley, "Early Hebrew Festival Rituals" in *Myth and Ritual,* p. 122.

47 Halder, *Associations,* p. 153, By treating *qubbah* as referring to "the moveable tabernacle" makes the sinful act referred to in Num. 25:8 a violation of the tabernacle which was Israel's center of worship.

48 Exod. 19:15; 20:26; 28:42; Lev. 15:16-18; 22:3. Cf. 1 Sam. 21:4f.

49 A. R. Johnson, "The Psalms" in *OTMS,* p. 166.

50 *Ibid,* p. 190.

51 *Idem.*

52 In the words with which David received Nathan's prophecy (2 Sam. 7:18-29) regarding the kingship, we have the clearest proof that David recognized that while the kingship in Israel was a divine institution, the occupant of the throne was a man and might be a very weak and sinful man; and the record of the kings of Judah and Israel prove this conclusively (cf. also David's last words in 2 Sam. 23:1-7). Yet Engnell finds evidence of the divine kingship, as derived from the Canaanites, in Ps. 22:10; 71:6; 132:11; Isa. 44:2, 24; 49:1, 5 and he appeals to Ezek. 28:11f. as teaching his pre-existence and to Isa. 14:4f. as claiming this of the king of Babylon (*Divine Kinkship*, pp. 76).

53 *Gesammelte Studien* (1957), p. 209. He calls it "*Die auffäligste geschichtliche Tatsache in Blick auf das Königtum in Israel.*"

54 *Op. cit.* pp. 182f.

55 *Ibid,* p. 197.

56 *Divine Kingship,* p. 176.

57 *OTMS, p.* 181.

58 According to Oesterley, none of these rites was derived directly from Egypt, "they go back to an immemorial antiquity, to ages long anterior to the time of the Egyptians and Babylonians as we know them" ("Early Heb. Festival Rituals," in *Myth and Ritual,* p. 118).

59 According to Exod. 12:13, 23, 27, the verb is used of passing over or passing by the houses of the Israelites which had the blood stains on their doors. In Isa. 31:5 the figure of this first passover is apparently used of the sparing of Jerusalem. That this word had any connection with the verb "to be lame" is doubtful to say the least, and there is nothing to suggest it in the narrative. In 1 Kings 18 where it is used of the Baal-prophets, it seems in vs. 21 to have the sense of "straddle" two opinions, or skip from one to the other. In vs. 28, it may be used in the sense of "limp" to suggest the exhaustion which had followed their frenzied intercession. But this is the description of a pagan rite, which stands in such marked contrast to the conduct of Elijah that it is hard to believe that there is the slightest connection with the passover, as that feast is described in Exodus. David's dancing before the ark had no connection with the passover and different words are used to describe it, as is also the case in Exod. 15:20 when Miriam led the women in a triumphal dance. Dancing is referred to a few times (*ca.* 25) in the Old Testament and sometimes with approval. But it is nowhere directly connected with any of the feasts of the Lord. We are told, however, that the Israelites danced about the golden calf which Aaron had made (Exod. 32:19).

60 On the word *pasach*, in the light of comparative philology, cf. R. D. Wilson, "Babylon and Israel" in *PTR*, vol. I, pp. 249f.

61 Curt Kuhl, *The Prophets of Israel,* 1960, p. 51.

62 *ANET*, p. 139.

63 *Ibid.*, p. 124.

64 *Ibid.*, p. 142.

65 *Ibid.*, p. 136. Here we give Gordon's translation in *Ugaritic Literature.*

66 *Ibid.*, pp. 133f., 137.

67 *Ibid.*, p. 137, also Gordon's translation in *Ugaritic Literature,* p. 22. In defense or apology for such an attitude of one of the great goddesses of the Canaanite pantheon toward her father, the supreme god, Tor-il (Bull-god), Gordon reminds us that in the Gilgamesh Epic which was popular among the Babylonians for centuries, Ishtar, who is a kind of Babylonian counterpart of 'Anat, goes to Anu the god of heaven with threats of violence to secure the means of wreaking her wrath on Gilgamesh for his refusal to become her lover (Tablet VI, *ANET*, pp. 83f.). Compare also, legend of Aqhat which tells of 'Anat's slaying of Aqhat, p. 152. As compared with this bellicose attitude, the story in the Iliad of Hera, with the help of Sleep, beguiling Zeus from his watch on that the gods who want to help the Greeks may be able to do so, is quite mild and refined.

68 *ANET,* p. 139.

69 Gordon, *Ugaritic Literature,* p. 8

70 *Accadian and Hebrew Psalms,* p. 71, cf. p. 322. Widengren also claims that Jacob (Ps. 24:6) is a god, "a name for Jahve" (p. 321).

71 Engnell, *Divine Kingship,* p. 82.

72 Gordon, *Ugaritic Literature,* p. 63.

[73] Elsewhere, in a Baal Anat text they seem to be represented as the offspring of Aliyn Baal and Anat (*Ugar. Lit.*, p. 53).

[74] *Op. cit.*, p. 133.

[75] In *BASOR*, No. 93 (1944), pp. 17-20.

[76] In *ANET*, p. 136, Ginsberg renders rather freely:

> Take war [away] from the earth,
> Banish (all) strife from the soil;
> Pour peace into the earth's very bowels,
> Much amity into earth's bosom.

[77] *Ibid*, p. 17f. These words are repeated several times in the context, cf. *ANET*, pp. 136-137.

[78] Cf. Gordon, *Ugaritic Literature*, p. 19f.

[79] *ANET*, pp. 52-57. The Accadian version is given on pp. 106-109.

[80] *Introduction to the Old Testament* (1952), Part I, p. 188. This benediction is peculiar. The divine triad consists of Ea, the god of the sea and of wisdom. Damkina, his wife, who is rarely mentioned and Marduk who is the patron god of Babylon and represented as their son. It is quite different from the much older triad, Anu, Bel, Ea, which represents, as Jastrow has pointed out, sky, earth, sea. While triads do occur in the Babylonion religion, the conspicuous feature is the great number of gods in the pantheon, who are grouped in a great variety of ways.

[81] Article, "The Patriarchal Narratives" in *JNES* (1954), p. 57.

[82] Cf. A. T. Clay, *Amurru*, p. 16. The year 1857 was the year of the Sepoy Rebellion in India, of the Dred Scott Decision in Washington, of the Mountain Meadow Massacre in Utah. Thackeray's *Virginians* and Trollope's *Barchester Towers* appeared in that year (cf. *The World Almanac*).

[83] *ANET*, pp. 149-155.

[84] *Ibid.*, p. 149.

[85] *ANET*, pp. 151, 153. Instead of "beneath a mighty tree on the threshing-floor," C. H. Gordon renders "Alongside the dignitaries who are in the threshing-floor" (*Ugaritic Literature*), p. 88, 94. This rendering assigns to Daniel no such pre-eminent position as does Ginsberg's. Beasley-Murray refers to this passage in *NBC*, p. 653, apparently favoring the identification, but in the revised edition of *NBC* [1970] he also argues for the biblical Daniel (p. 672). This legend of *Aqht* like much of the Ugaritic poetry contains many repetitions; and these lines appear to be repeated in another place (p. 94). But the latter passage is badly mutilated.

[86] *Association of Cult Prophets* (1945), p. 149 n. 3. Haldar refers to an article published by H. Zimmern in 1928. It is possible of course that the Assyrian "woman at the window" represents Ashtarte who like her sacred harlots lures passers-by from her window. Pritchard in *ANEP*, p. 265a., refers to these three Old Testament passages. A number of such ivory plaques has been found recently at Fort Shalmaneser (Edw. Bacon, *Digging for History*, pp. 203f.)

[87] Mallowan.

[88] E.g., Engnell, *Divine Kingship*, pp. 135f., cf. p. 210; he feels that it may have cultic significance.

[89] *PTR*, Vol. IV, p. 297.

[90] Some years ago there was a vigorous debate over the word *sabbath*, whether its equivalent was to be found in the Babylonian word *shabbatum*. But Wardle's statement, made nearly fifty years ago, "at present no evidence has been produced to show that the Babylonians had any real equivalent of the Hebrew sabbath" (*Israel and Babylon*, p. 247) holds good today (cf. *NBD*, p. 1110).

[91] G. E. Wright tells us with regard to the Canaanite religion: "The amazing thing about the gods, however, is that there seems to have been no standard of morality governing their actions.... The lives of the gods were certainly on a moral level below that of the average of society as a whole, if we can judge from the ancient codes of law. They lived a life of their own, not to be questioned by man and scarcely providing a model to emulate" (*Biblical Archaeology*, p. 110). This is indicated very clearly, for instance, in the Ugaritic texts published in *ANET*, pp. 129-155. Their fertility rites, as examples of sympathetic magic, were sensual and sexual. They were corrupting and debasing. A man could easily be better than his religion. By contrast the demand of the Mosaic law was, "Be ye holy for I the Lord your God am holy" (Lev. 19:2); and this holiness was not

only ceremonial but ethical and set them apart from the religions of their neighbors (Lev. 18:3).

92 In discussing miracles, Eichrodt, *TOT*, Vol. II, pp. 163f., draws a sharp distinction between the non-miraculous view of many modern scientists and the biblical view. He accepts "the unbreakable natural order" and tells us that it is well known that "miracles such as the plagues of Egypt, the passage of the Red Sea, the feeding with manna, etc., are simply natural phenomena that have been elaborated in various ways in the oral tradition." On the other hand he tells us, "In contrast to our own scientific outlook, however, the Israelite does not think in terms of an unbreakable natural order such as would restrict even God's operation ... the Israelite rightly sees in God's sovereign control of nature, as manifested in his miracles, proof that the created order is totally dependent on the will of him who called it into being." This Israelite view, as Dr. Eichrodt calls it, is the biblical view taught equally in both Testaments. If this view is rejected in favor of the non-miraculous teaching of modern science, then it is to be recognized that when Dr. Eichrodt tells us that "the man who knows God hears his step in the tramp of daily events, discerns him near at hand to help, and hears his answer to the appeal of prayer in a hundred happenings outwardly small and insignificant," he is substituting subjective impressions for outward and objective realities. He is speaking as a mystic and has no real answer for "the man who can talk only of remarkable concidences, amazing accidents, or a peculiar turn of events." When with the anti-supernaturalist he has shut the door of the phenomenal world to God, he cannot expect his fellow disbeliever in the miraculous to hear the voice of God speaking to him through a crack or a key-hole. For the Bible believer there is no shut door; and the miracles recorded in scripture are the sufficient proof of the existence of a living, ever-present, and almighty God, "who alone doeth great wonders" (Psalm 136:4).

93 *Vide supra*, p. 34.

94 Vol. I, p. 501. This alleged "brittleness" is due to the rejection of prediction as a prominent and important element in biblical prophecy by the rationalistic critics of today. Instead of rejoicing in the predictive element as demonstrating that biblical prophecy is of God, they regard the predictive element as an obstacle to its acceptance which must be gotten rid of. The popularity and pressure of this view is illustrated by the fact that R. F. Harrison, who finds "almost no extraneous material at all in the prophecy of Isaiah" (*JOT*, p. 784), a statement which is a bold one to make in view of the wide acceptance of divisive theories concerning Isaiah, nevertheless feels constrained to regard the references to Cyrus by name in Isaiah 44:28; 45:1, "as constituting explanatory glosses imposed on the original text by a post-exilic copyist" (p. 794).

95 *Op. cit.*, I, p. 26. He declares that "Rationalism tore to shreds the inadequate attempts of orthodoxy to demonstrate the inner coherence of the Old and New Testaments by the collection of proof-texts and an extensive system of typology" (*id.*, p. 28). Yet he tells us that "in the encounter with the Christ of the Gospel there is the assertion of a mighty living reality bound up in the OT as pointing forward into the future" (p. 26). Is not this the very thing which the proof-text and the typology aim to establish?

96 *Op. cit.*, p. 25. This statement is made on the first page of Chapter I and is italicized for emphasis. It makes it clear that according to Eichrodt the main link between the two Testaments is to be found in comparative religion. For the author goes on to say: "Indeed it is in commanding such a wide panorama of the rich domain of man's religious activity that many will prefer to see the special significance of the faith of the OT." As to this it is to be noted the great aim of the OT is not to exhibit man's religious activity but God's redemptive revelation of himself to man.

97 *Id.*, Vol. I, p. 35.

98 *Id.*, Vol. I, p. 477.

99 *Biblical and Theological Studies*, p. 445.

CHAPTER VI

1 Biblical chronology resembles biblical history and biblical prophecy in one important respect. It is a wonderful combination of the clear and the obscure, the definite and the indefinite. Some facts are stated with great clearness, others are left for the Bible student to figure out for himself, still others are completely

omitted. A single example will suffice to illustrate. Exodus 12:40 tells us that Israel dwelt 430 years in Egypt, 1 Kings 6:1 that there were 480 years between the exodus and the foundation-laying of Solomon's temple. We might expect a statement in the New Testament as to the length of the interval between this event and the Advent. According to Ussher this interval was almost exactly one thousand years, but such a figure is nowhere given in the New Testament, and 4 B.C. for the birth of Jesus is an anomaly based on an ancient miscalculation, and December 25th for Christmas is probably incorrect also. We know in part but what we know is certain and it is sufficient for our needs.

2 In the article "Astronomy" in *EB* (1929), p. 578, he has stated that "the light which we see today left that nebula 900,000 years ago." In the article on "Chronology" J. H. Jeans is quoted as saying that the astronomer uses a clock that tells us "that light traveling 186,000 miles a second, takes about 140 million years to come to us from the most remote objects visible in the biggest telescope on earth" (p. 553). This instrument was the 100 inch Mount Wilson instrument.

3 See R. H. Robertson, article "Cosmology" in *EB* (1963 edition), p. 584.

4 H. R. Robertson, *op. cit.*, p. 587.

5 *EB* (1963).

5a *A Dictionary of Astronomy*, article by G. de VanCouleur.

5b Article "Cosmology" by G. Gamow, *EB* (1963, pp. 582f.)

6 G. Gamow, *Biography of the Earth: Its Past, Present, and Future* gives "the year 5,000,000,000 B.C." as "the earth's birth date" (Viking Press 1959 rev., p. 8) since it is based on rubidium-strontium decay, which involves no loss since both metals are solids. He holds the "big bang" theory of the origin of the stellar universe. But he has no answer to the question as to the cause of the bang or of the origin of the thing that banged.

7 Peking-man (1929) has been placed at 1,000,000, Java-man (1891), at 475,-000, Heidelberg (1907) at 300,000 years ago. See Will Durant, *The Story of Civilizations* 1935 (6th ed. 1942), pp. 90f.

8 See the article "Earliest Man on Earth," by Francis and Katherine Drake, *Reader's Digest,* Jan. 1964, pp. 157-163. "When samples of the volcanic minerals surrounding Zinj were checked for age by the University of California's new potassium-argon dating process, he was found to have been in his rocky coffin for 1,750,000 years — proof that Olduvia Man had pursued his *al fresco* life beside that unremembered African lake nearly one-and-a-half million years before Asia's Peking Man" (p. 159).

9 Geikie, Cunningham, *Hours with the Bible*, Vol. I, (1881, p. 70, cf. p. 42). Yet Geikie did not reach the same conclusions as to the existence of man. He tells us that "looked at, therefore, from every point of view, there seems no ground for placing the appearance of mankind on the earth further back than the Bible has assigned . . ." (p. 155; cf. p. 85f.), a decidedly inconsistent position.

9a The amazing speed of the Laser beam is a further illustration.

10 According to J. D. Davis the days were indefinite periods (*DDB*, p. 170) between which "long periods of time intervened" (*Ibid*, p. 152). The so-called "Framework Theory" which divides the Creative days into two parallel series of three days each, was accepted by S. R. Driver and Skinner and at least mentioned by J. D. Davis (*Op. cit.*, p. 153). It has recently been strongly advocated by Noordtzij and Ridderbos (see also *NBD*, p. 271) but rejected after careful examination by E. J. Young (*Studies in Genesis*, 1964), who argues that the six creative days stand in chronological sequence.

11 This position is maintained by Hepp, *Calvinism and the Theology of Nature* and by Aalders in *De Goddelijke Openbaring* (1932). The strength of this position is indicated by the fact that E. J. Young summarizes Aalders' two considerations advanced in its supports as follows: "(1) In the text of Genesis itself, he affirms, there is not a single allusion to suggest that the days are to be regarded as a form or mere manner of representation and hence of no significance for the essential knowledge of the divine creative activity. (2) In Exodus 20:11 the activity of God is presented to man as a pattern, and this fact presupposes that there is a reality in the activity of God which man is to follow. How could man be held accountable for working six days if God himself had not actually worked for six days?" And Young adds the following impressive comment, "To the best of the present writer's knowledge no one has ever answered these two considerations of Aalders" (*Studies in Genesis One*, p. 47).

12 *The Genesis Flood*, pp. 222-232.

13 Charles Hodge, *Systematic Theology*, vol. II, p. 92. He goes on to say, "It has therefore been almost the universal belief that the original state of man was as the Bible teaches, his highest state, from which the nations of the earth have more or less deteriorated" (p. 94). Cf. *Westminster Confession* IV, 2; *Shorter Catechism*, Q. 10. Also R. L. Dabney, *Syllabus and Notes* (1878), pp. 261-3 and Gosse, *Omphalos* of approximately the same date; also H. Bavinck, in *ISBE*, p. 1093.

14 Morris and Whitcomb, *op. cit.*, pp. 222f., 232f., 344f., 356f. The law of "apparent age," as illustrated by the maturity of Adam, appears clearly in the miracles of Jesus, referred to above.

15 Whitcomb and Morris account for this longevity as due to the effects of the protective blanket or canopy ("the waters above the firmament" — Gen. 1:7), which was removed when "the windows of heaven were opened" at the coming of the flood (7:11. *Op cit.*, pp. 399-405). This canopy they argue produced a uniform climate and may have shielded the earth from hurtful cosmic rays.

16 Argued in detail by W. H. Green in *BS* (April, 1890), B. B. Warfield in *PTR* (1911), reprinted in *Biblical and Theological Studies*, 1952; see also *FBM²*, pp. 295-298.

17 The *LXX* inserts a Cainan in the genealogy at 11:12 between Arphaxad and Shelah and this is supported by its inclusion in the genealogy in Luke 3:36.

18 Four kings (Ahaziah, Joash, Amaziah and Jehoiakim) are omitted in the genealogy in Matthew apparently to secure a uniform 3 x 14 pattern.

19 The figures given in *LXX* and *Sam.* vary by nearly 1000 years from the Hebrew. The vast figures given by Berosus (432,000) and the Sumerian King Lists, one of which is nearly the same as Berosus' and the other much smaller (241,200 years), rest on the somewhat questionable assumption that a *sar* is 3600 years.

20 See Whitcomb and Morris, *op. cit.*, pp. 154-69, 289-91. They mention also "the number of great dinosaur graveyards found in various parts of the world" (p. 280). In this book the reader will find a very thorough discussion of the whole subject.

21 The closest parallel in secular records, despite its pervasive polytheism, is the Sumero-Babylonian which resembles the biblical in a number of striking ways. The fullest account of this flood is given in the 11th tablet of the Gilgamesh Epic, which was discovered and published by George Smith nearly a century ago (1872) and frequently has been republished (e.g. in *ANET*, pp. 93-97), cf. also Finegan (*LAP*, pp. 25-30). For a detailed comparison of the two accounts cf. Unger, *AOT*, pp. 40-71.

22 In *FSAC* (1940) Albright makes no mention of the Deluge, but in the "Introduction" which he added to the paper-back edition (1957), we meet the following statement: "I see no reason any longer for refusing to connect the traditions of the Great Flood in most regions of Eurasia and America, including especially Mesopotamia and Israel, with the tremendous floods accompanying the following of the critical melting of the glaciers about 9000 B.C." (p. 9).

23 G. E. Wright in his *Biblical Archaeology* (1957) passes directly from Pre-historic Man (pp. 27-39) to the Founding Fathers (pp. 40-52) and discusses the Flood only incidentally in a subsequent chapter (pp. 118f.) where he deals with the influence of Babylon and Canaan on the development of Israel. He concludes that "the Flood story is an exaggeration of one such local inundation, or, much more probably, it is an old tradition, going back to the end of the Stone Age before the present bounds of the oceans were fixed."

24 The significance of the flood deposit discovered by Woolley in 1929 at Ur has been much debated. Many scholars regard it as evidence of a merely local inundation; and they consider the Noahic deluge as likewise local and deny its cosmic significance, despite the testimony of our Lord (Matt. 28:38) and his apostle (2 Peter 2:5). For a long list of scholars who accept and who reject, the identification with Noah's flood, cf. Whitcomb and Morris, *op. cit.*, pp. 111.

25 Patrick O'Connell in his recent book, *Science of Today and the Problems of Genesis* (1959) argues that the Flood at Ur destroyed the el Obaid (Neanderthal) civilization and produced the "hiatus" between the Mousterian and Aurignacian cultures which is widely recognized by archaeologists. He holds that this flood covered "all parts of the Continent of Europe that were free from ice, all parts of North Africa, and those parts of Asia west of the Himalaya system of mountains" (*Bk* II, p. viii). He holds further that the Neanderthal race was de-

stroyed by the flood, i.e., that the flood was total anthropologically (Noah and his family being the only survivors) but denies that it was total geographically. In addition to the evidence of flood deposits in various localities, O'Connell stresses the marked difference between antediluvian or pre-hiatus culture and the post-diluvian. He calls especial attention to three things as characteristic of the antediluvian culture: (1) hand-made pottery, the use of the potter's wheel being post-diluvian; (2) brightly-colored painted pottery which was wide-spread in the Obaid period and then disappeared; (3) the occasional use of hammered copper, smelted copper utensils appearing only after the flood.

26 That the Bible describes a universal Flood and that this understanding of it finds ample support in the recent findings in the field of geology, is argued convincingly by Whitcomb and Morris (op. cit., pp. 1-35).

27 G. F. Wright (Origin and Antiquity of Man, 1912) claimed that "while the antiquity of man cannot be less than ten thousand, it need not be more than fifteen thousand years" (p. 496) and he held that "eight thousand years of pre-historic time is ample to account for all known facts relating to his development," and that "post-glacial time may be limited to a few thousand years" (p. 494). O'Connell dates the Flood "about 7,000 B.C. or probably a little before it" (op. cit., p. 102). Whitcomb and Morris hold that "even the allowance of 5,000 years between the Flood and Abraham stretches Genesis almost to the breaking point" (op. cit., p. 489). S. J. Schultz gives the figure 8,000 to 10,000 B.C. (OTS, p. 16). Unger places the Flood "long before 4000 B.C." (op. cit., p. 102). The Sumerian King List (contained in part in ANET, p. 265, cf. Finegan LAP, pp. 25ff., 31-37) makes the interval from the time when "kingship was lowered from heaven" and the Flood 241,200 years, and the interval between the Flood and the Third Dynasty of Erech (Lugalzagisi) about 30,000 years. How little significance is attached to these figures by many archaeologists is indicated by the fact that Finegan reduces the 30,000 to about 500 (op. cit., p. 31) and dates the Early Dynastic Period which followed it ca. 2800-2366 B.C. which is approximately Albright's date (FSAC, p. 248), a couple of centuries earlier than Ed. Mayer's date and several centuries later than Kraeling's (RMBA, p. 58).

28 "Divided" is from a Hebrew root palag to divide. See, e.g., Kevan in NBC in loco. 2247 B.C. is Ussher's date for the birth of Peleg which would make the "in his days" of Gen. 10:25 refer to the time of his birth.

29 For a recent defense of this attempt to treat Hebrew as the original tongue of mankind, see Philip Bieberfeld, Universal Jewish History, Vol. I, (1948) pp. 50-55, 102-105, who apparently depends largely on Ahron Marcus' Barsilai Sprache. The evidence which he appeals to is hardly likely to commend this theory to sober and careful scholarship. Thus he argues that r is the letter of motion, that erets (earth) means "the rotating one."

30 The partial or total disappearance of case endings in many languages is a well-known illustration of this fact.

31 William Hales in his A New Analysis of Chronology (London, 1809), commends Ussher because "he happily rectified the vulgar error, that Abraham was born in the 70th year of his father's age" (Vol. I, p. 23). Hales makes Haran the eldest son since his daughter Sarai was only 10 years younger than Abram when she was married to him (Gen. 17:17). For a thorough discussion of the problem see E. J. Young, Thy Word Is Truth, pp. 175-9, who feels that no satisfactory solution of the problem is possible on the basis of our present knowledge.

32 In his elaborate work, Archaeologie Mesopotamienne, André Parrot has devoted nearly 100 pages to the various problems which enter into the determining of his date.

33 So Gurney, The Hittites, p. 62.

34 NBD, p. 214, places Abraham at ca. 2000-1850 B.C., which is about the tentative date given by Unger (AOT, p. 113), by Free (ABH, pp. 48f.); Thiele (ZPBD, p. 166) does not feel that the date of Abraham can be definitely determined largely because he attaches much importance to the variant figures given in the LXX. E. F. Campbell, Jr. has recently classified the datings for Hammurabi as "ultra high" (ca. 1900), "high" (1848-1806), "middle" (1792-1750), "low" (1728-1686), "ultra low" (ca. 1704-1662). These dates which vary by about two centuries are all advocated by recognized scholars (The Bible and the Ancient Near East, ed. by G. E. Wright, p. 217).

35 Steindorff and Seele, When Egypt Ruled the East², p. 252; the Merneptah

Stele mentions Israel as not in Egypt, but perhaps as not yet definitely settled in Canaan (*ANET*, p. 378).

36 See J. B. Lightfoot on *Galatians*, pp. 143f., also Fausset in *JFB in loco*. For other views see Henry Browne, Art. "Chronology" in Kitto-Alexander, *Cyclopaedia*, p. 509.

37 This is indicated by the fact that the various reading does not appear in the margin of ARV, AT, RSV, BV, NEB. *The Soncino Edition of the Pentateuch* (1960) and *The Torah, a New Translation*, published by the Jewish Publication Society of America (1962) likewise omit it. Davis argued strongly against it (*DBD*, pp. 194f.). Kitchen and Mitchell hold that 430 years for the sojourn "seems assured" (*NBD*, p. 214). According to Finegan "the Israelites entered Egypt around 1720 B.C., left that land about 1290 B.C. and entered Palestine approximately 1250 B.C." (*LAP*, p. 108), which assigns 430 years to the sojourn. Thiele is noncommittal, regarding the data insufficient for a definite conclusion (*ZPBD*, p. 167). These scholars adopt the late date of the Exodus. As we should expect, Unger (*AOT*, p. 135) and Free (*ABH*, pp. 81ff.) who hold to the early date of the Exodus accept the 430 years figure for the sojourn in Egypt as correct.

38 Genesis 14. The amount of historical and geographical detail in this chapter is surprising. We note in passing that this chapter has never been successfully assigned by the critics to any one of the main documents into which they divide the Pentateuch.

39 The use of the title Pharaoh has been proved for some kings of the 18th Dynasty. See R. D. Wilson, "Royal Titles in Antiquity" in *PTR*, 1904, pp. 635, 640, 644, 648; also Kitchen in *NBD*, p. 980.

40 *HAE*, p. 314.

41 In all the five occurrences in the Old Testament (Gen. 47:11; Exod. 1:11; 12:37; Num. 33:3, 5), this proper name is written the same way in the consonantal Hebrew text. The difference of pronunciation simply represents the difference in vocalization in the *MT*, which is reflected in AV, ARV, RSV, but is not found in *LXX* or *Vulg*.

42 Article "Rameses" in *EB* (1929). This article is unsigned but was probably written or at least approved by H. R. Hall or Llewellyn Griffith, who wrote the major articles on Ancient Egypt. The statement appears unchanged in the 1960 edition of the Encyclopaedia. Finegan describes it as "the basis" of this theory (*LAP*, p. 107). He claims that "Unless we are to regard Exodus 1:11 as an erroneous or anachronistic statement we must conclude that Rameses II was the Pharaoh of the oppression." But in developing his argument Finegan seems to ignore Gen. 47:11 completely. G. E. Wright in commenting on Gen. 47:11 tells us "The 'Rameses' here referred to was the name given to the same town, not in Joseph's day, but after 1300 B.C. when the city was rebuilt by the great Pharaoh, Rameses II, *ca.* 1290-1224 B.C." (*Bib. Arch.*, p. 56).

43 *ISBE*, pp. 1054, 2520.

44 There is no indication anywhere of a change of the name. That the name of Bethel was originally Luz is stated repeatedly (Gen. 28:19; Josh. 18:13; Judg. 1:23). The name Kirjath-arba (Gen. 23:2) clung to Hebron for centuries (Josh. 14:15; 20:7; Judg. 1:10; Neh. 11:25). Laish (or Leshem) was the original name of the city captured by the Danites and renamed Dan (Josh. 19:47; Jdgs. 18:29). Cf. Zephath changed to Hormah (Judg. 1:17), Kirjath-sepher changed to Debir (Josh. 15:15, 49; Jdgs. 1:11). Hermon called originally Sirion and Shenir (Deut. 3:9), also called Sion (4:48). Bethlehem is Ephrath (Gen. 35:19; 48:7). Esau is identified with Seir (Gen. 36:8, 9); but the name Seir is used centuries after Esau's day. Cf. Num. 32:38; Deut. 2:11, 20; 3:9. But nothing is said about an original or earlier name of the land of Ra'amses. The mention of Ra'amses as the place or region where Joseph settled his father at the command of Pharaoh is therefore *prima facie* evidence that the name Ra'amses was given to this region at least as early as the beginning of the sojourn, i.e., more than 400 years before the Exodus. To ignore this statement or to set it aside as an anachronism as Kraeling proposes is drastic to say the least. It is, of course, possible that a later name is used here, but this is an assumption and the fact that no change of the name is mentioned in the biblical narratives argues against such an assumption. Yet this objection to the late date for the Exodus is strangely ignored in this discussion.

45 G. E. Wright, *Biblical Archaeology*, pp. 57f. Kraeling favors the identification of Rameses with Tanis, but admits that "some scholars of great repute" are not

yet convinced, however, that Tanis is the city of Raamses, and seek the latter "at Qantir near Faqus." He would also locate Pithom at *Tell el Ertabeh*. But he makes the additional comment: "Some day, when that site has been excavated, we will know more about the city built by the Israelites" — a statement which justifies the hope that we may discover that the Pharaoh of the Oppression lived long before the time of Rameses the Great (*RMBA*, pp. 98f.).

46 This is true of advocates of the late and of the early date. Davis says of Rameses, "A town in Egypt. It was in the most fertile district of the country (Gen. 47:11) . . . the region where Pharaoh bade Joseph locate his father and brothers" (*DDB*, p. 646). Yet in opposing the early date of the Exodus based on the claim that the Habiru of the Amarna letters were the Hebrews, he says: "Rameses is a geographical designation (Exod. 1:11; 12:37) and the theory in question is unable to explain how it could have been so in the days of Amen-hetep II, or Thothemes IV, years before the first Ramses ascended to the throne of Egypt" (*ibid*, p. 196, note), a statement which ignores Gen. 47:11 and also the explanation given by Conder, cited above.

47 The *LXX* (Cod. B and A) gives 440. But there is apparently no good reason for preferring it to the 480 of *MT*. It may be due to failure to include in this total the 40 years of wandering in the wilderness.

48 According to M. G. Kline the statement in Exod. 1:11 instead of being as many assume a proof of the late date of the exodus is really an evidence for the early date: "For it is inconceivable that anyone should have described the magnificent operations of Ramses II at these sites, transforming one of them into the capital of Egypt, in the "store-cities" terms of Exod. 1:11. The Hebrew building and the Hebrew exodus must then precede Ramses II" (*WTJ*, Vol. XX, p. 65).

49 The use of the word "self-same" is noteworthy. It occurs 16 times and always with the word "day." It is used of the coming of the flood (Gen. 7:13), of the institution of circumcision (Gen. 17:23, 26), of the exodus from Egypt (Exod. 12:17, 41, 51), of Moses' death (Deut. 32:48), of the first passover in Canaan (Josh. 5:11), of the siege of Jerusalem by Nebuchadnezzar (Ezek. 24:2) and of the date of Ezekiel's final vision (40:1) — all important events; also of important holy days, "first fruits" (Lev. 23:14, 21), day of atonement (vss. 28-30) — all days and events requiring exactitude. Cf. also Josh. 10:27.

50 Keil, *The Book of Judges*, p. 289. It may be noted that Dispensationalists hold that the oppressions are not included in the 480 years, because God does not count time for Israel, when Israel is under foreign rulers and "not governed by God."

51 According to Josephus (*Antiq.* vi, 14:9; x.8.4) Saul's reign overlapped Samuel's judgeship 18 years. It is claimed that the text of 1 Sam. 13:1 is corrupt and that certain figures have been lost (cf. ARV, RSV, BV). Unfortunately the fragments of the Hebrew text of this book discovered in the Dead Sea Caves do not contain this passage. So it is to be noted that there is ancient evidence (*Symmachus*, the *Targum*, *Vulg.*, cf. S. R. Driver, *Notes on Samuel*) in support of the *MT*, which literally translated is, "a son of a year was Saul in his being (or becoming) king and he reigned two years over Israel and Saul chose . . .," which AV renders idiomatically by "Saul reigned one year and when he had reigned two years over Israel, Saul chose," etc. It cannot be justly claimed that this is "impossible Hebrew" (Driver). The rendering "being king" is just as possible as "becoming king." The most serious objection is that these words closely resemble the regnal formula, "X was the son of Y years when he became king and he reigned Z years," which occurs frequently in the historical books. But it is not necessary to assume this to be the case; and figures cannot be inserted without making changes in the Hebrew text. It would be natural to wish to find in these words the usual regnal formula, especially since the age of Saul when he became king and the length of his reign are not stated anywhere else in the Old Testament record. But this does not justify the claim that the text must be corrupt and that the literal rendering is impossible.

52 1 Kings 1:39; 2:12; 1 Chron. 29:20-23. Josephus' claim that Solomon reigned for 80 years (*Antiq.* viii, 7, 5), while accepted by Whiston, has probably no supporters today.

53 *LAP*, p. 108. The fact that the 480 years may be regarded as 12 times 40 is not a sufficient reason for calling it an "artificial" reckoning.

54 Cf. *NBD*, pp. 215, 898, for a defense of the view that a generation is treated in the Old Testament as 40 years.

Notes 479

[55] *Op. cit.,* p. 106.

[56] Both of the totals, 430 for the sojourn and 480 for the interval between sojourn and temple, have been drastically reduced by critical scholars. Thus Gressmann (1913) reduced the sojourn to 50 years and Simpson (1948) said of it, "hardly long enough for Moses to grow from infancy to maturity." Rowley makes it "about 130 years." Consequently, it is rather remarkable that in *NBD,* the substantial accuracy of the figure 430 for the sojourn is accepted (pp. 214a, 218b, 402) and that, as we have seen, the definition of a generation as 40 years is defended. Yet 1280 B.C. is described as "a good average date" for the exodus, which reduces the figure 480 to approximately 320 years (cf. p. 219), or by about one-third. Rowley then would be considerably below "the average," since he has reduced the figure still further to a total of about 260 years (*FJJ,* p. 162). Would it not be strange that one of the totals should be so accurate and the other so wide of the mark?

[57] Cf. M. G. Kline, Art. "Hebrews" in *NBD,* also his articles, "The HA-BI-ru, Kin or Foe of Israel" (*WTJ,* XX, 1957), in which he takes the position that the mention of the Habiru in the Amarna Letters refers to the oppression under Chushanrishathaim (Judg. 3:8f.).

[58] For a further discussion of this subject see Unger, *AOT,* pp. 140-152; Free, *ABH,* pp. 73-99. Cf. margin of *BV.* Edward Mack in *ISBE,* pp. 642f., dated the exodus *ca.* 1448, but limited the sojourn to 215 years.

[59] In *NBD* the date for Rehoboam is given as 931/30, "because the Hebrew year does not coincide with the January to December of our civil year." In these schedules and usually elsewhere in this volume only the first figure (e.g., 931) is given as sufficiently accurate for our purpose. Gehman (*Westminster Bible Dictionary,* 1944) lists 8 dates for Rehoboam's accession ranging between 945 and 925 (p. 104). It is dated 922 B.C. by Albright; and this reduction of some 9 years from the date given above is accepted by M. F. Unger (*IAD,* pp. 56-61).

[60] In *The Assyrian Eponym Canon* (1876) George Smith mentions three different attempts to find a gap in the Assyrian Canon but rejects them all (p. 72). W. J. Beecher in *The Dated Events of the O.T.* (1907) claimed that there was a gap of 51 years. But most scholars agree with Smith that there are no real gaps.

[61] Tiglath-pileser III calls himself the son of Adad-nirari III on an inscribed brick (in *ARA,* I, p. 294). The Babylonian King List and the Babylonian Chronicle call him Pulu: and in Ptolemy's Canon his name appears as Porus. But this name does not occur on any Assyrian royal inscriptions. He apparently assumed it when he made himself king of Babylon. In 1 Chron. we read that "the God of Israel stirred up the spirit of Pul king of Assyria and the spirit of Tiglath-pileser king of Assyria" to invade Israel. This statement is somewhat ambiguous since the "and" could also be rendered by "even." It is also to be noted that in 2 Kings 15, the king of Assyria is called Pul in vs. 19 and in vs. 29 Tiglath-pileser. This will be further discussed later. But it is clear that an Assyrian king called Pul came against Menahem.

[62] Thiele in *ZPBD,* article "Chronology." In *Mysterious Numbers,* rev. ed. 1965, Appendix D, he lists as "included in the total reign" (in Judah: Jehoshaphat 4; Azariah 24; Jotham 12; Manasseh 10; in Israel: Jeroboam II 12), as "co-regencies not included in total reign" (in Judah: Jehoram 6, Ahaz 4); also as "recorded reign partially overlapping a rival king" (in Israel: Omri 6, Pekah 12).

[63] Unfortunately there is a major flaw in Theil's chronology of this period which has often been pointed out. So it is rather surprising that W. H. Hallo in an article "From Qarqar to Carchemish" approves Thiele's Chronology because "it manages to account for all the chronological data in Kings and Chronicles without emendation." On the contrary, as will appear later, it is the fact that it does require emendation (a change of 12 years) which is the serious defect in his chronology of this period.

[64] *DDB,* p. 395. Gehman in *WDB* (p. 314) has eliminated the reference to the Commonwealth Period in England which appears in *DDB* (p. 395) to which Davis appealed as warrant for including Athaliah's reign in that of Joash; and he assigns Athaliah and Joash independent reigns of 6 years and 40 years respectively (p. 106), while giving Amaziah a 3 year co-reign with Joash.

[65] According to Keil, Amaziah's assassination followed immediately on his flight to Lachish (*Commentary on Kings,* p. 283f.). Ellison thinks that the writer of the narrative of Kings has conflated the two accounts into one: that Amaziah was first deposed and then, "when he tried increasingly to assert himself," they had

him assassinated (*NBC*, p. 325). The explanation is plausible. But the narrative says not a word about it.

[66] It is to be carefully noted that both Kings and Chronicles describe Jotham's status under Azariah as being "over the house judging the people of the land." They do not call him king during this period.

[67] According to J. A. Alexander, the reason Isaiah refers to the "year in which king Uzziah died" (6:1) instead of calling it the first year of Jotham was because the latter expression "would have been ambiguous, because his reign is reckoned from two different epochs, the natural death of his father and his civil death when smitten with the leprosy" (*Com. on Isaiah*, vol. I, p. 87). This is certainly the natural explanation of the "twenty years" of 2 Kings 15:30 and of the "sixteen years" of vs. 33. Yet this explanation is ignored by the critical commentators, probably because they want to make Jotham's "reign" overlap Uzziah's by much more than four years. The tendency with the advocates of the co-reign theory is to reduce Jotham's sole reign to a minimum or to eliminate it completely. According to Edward Mack, "for approximately 6 years the reigns of Uzziah, Jotham, and Ahaz were contemporaneous" (*ISBE*, p. 639). He gives Jotham no sole reign at all. (Cf. *NBD*, p. 220 for a similar view.) One of the most recent writers on the chronology of this period, H. Tadmor, in his article "Azriau of Yaudi" (*Scripta Hierosolymitana*, Vol. 8, pp. 233-271), gives a chronology of the years 748-732, which begins with the 38th year of Uzziah, ends with the death of Uzziah in the 11th year of Ahaz, and ignores Jotham completely (p. 263). Yet Jotham is mentioned in the succession of the kings of Judah in Isa. 1:1, 7:1, Hos. 1:1, Mic. 1:1, cf. 1 Chron. 3:12, Matt. 1:9. This treatment of Jotham is perhaps the greatest weakness in the co-reign theory.

[68] No one reading these biblical statements would imagine that Jotham was merely a shadow king who had no independent rule in Judah. We have become so accustomed to minimize or ignore Jotham in order to harmonize the biblical and the Assyrian chronologies that we are tempted to lose sight of Jotham entirely. He becomes the "forgotten man" in the history of Judah.

[69] It should not be forgotten that Jehoiada crowned Joash when he was only seven years old (2 Kings 11:21). According to the Middle Assyrian laws "a son at least ten years old might be given the bride intended for an older brother who had died" (*ANET*, p. 184, 43). It is a well-known fact that children mature earlier in oriental countries than in the Occident.

[70] That Hezekiah began his reform in the first year of his reign and invited the men of Manesseh and Ephraim to share in the passover (2 Chron. 29:17; 30:13) may be accounted for by the chaotic conditions in the Northern Kingdom when Hoshea was either shut up in Samaria or a hostage in the hands of the Assyrians. The Assyrian king may have permitted this as tending to undermine Hoshea's authority in Israel. And of course an earnest and pious king of Judah would want to share the blessing of a return to the God of their fathers with the men of the Ten Tribes.

[71] See *ANET*, p. 291 for Esarhaddon and p. 294 for Ashurbanipal.

[72] That the evidence for this co-reign theory is not easily detected in the biblical narratives is indicated by the fact that Keil in accounting for the regency of Joram with his father Jehoshaphat does not hesitate to say: "It is true that there is no analogy for this combination of the years in the reigns of two kings, since the other reductions of which different chronologists are fond are perfectly arbitrary and the case before us stands quite alone; but this exception to the rule is indicated clearly enough in the statement in ch. 8:16, that Joram began to reign while Jehoshaphat was (still) king" (*Com. on Kings*, p. 289).

[73] Both Kings (18:13) and Isa. 36:1 describe Sennacherib's invasion as taking place in the "fourteenth year" of Hezekiah. There are no manuscript variations. The account in 2 Chron. 32:1-22 is much briefer and gives no date.

[74] J. Barton Payne in an article entitled, "The relationship of the reign of Ahaz to the accession of Hezekiah" (*BS*, vol. 125 [1969], pp. 41-52) discusses three proposed datings for Ahaz (743-728, 735-719, 731-715) and, while favoring the first, finds no one of them entirely satisfactory. But he takes definite exception to Thiele's rejection of the synchronisms in 2 Kings 17 and 18.

[75] R. D. Wilson has shown conclusively that "a man who was not actually reigning at the time to which some event in his life is afterward referred might rightly be called king by a writer who was describing that event after the man had really been clothed with the royal dignity" (*SBD*, vol. i, p. 95).

[76] Sargon refers to a revolt in which Samaria took part in his second year, which was crushed at Qarqar, to an expedition against Carchemish in his fifth year, and to an expedition against Ashdod in his eleventh year (*ANET*, pp. 284-287). Sargon never mentions Sennacherib in these inscriptions.

[77] That Sennacherib makes no mention of his terrible defeat is, of course, to be expected. Assyrian kings never did that. That Hezekiah may have bought off Sargon as he later did Sennacherib is quite probable, though no mention is made of the fact.

[78] In opposition to Macadam's claim (*The Temples of Kawa*, I, pp. 18ff.) that Tirhakah was only a child of nine in 701 B.C., Kitchen, following Le Clant and Yoyette, holds that in 701 B.C. Tirhakah may have been twenty years old, quite capable of commanding an army for his brother Shebitku (cf. *AOOT*, pp. 82ff.). Since his father Pianchi was pharaoh as early as 740 B.C. Tirhakah may have been considerably older.

[79] This proposal was first made by Haynes in 1852. E. J. Young in accepting it claimed that it was probably a copyist's error; and that therefore its acceptance has no bearing on the inspiration of the original text. (*Com. on Isaiah*, Vol. II, p. 541). The same view has recently been expressed by Archer.

[80] In view of the wide acceptance of the theory of co-reigns, this is perhaps the most natural explanation for the critical scholar to give. That it is open to serious objection we have indicated above.

[81] *Standard Chronology of the Holy Bible* (1917), pp. 66ff.

[82] Thiele's claim is that "at some late date, long after the original records of the kings had been set in order and when the true arrangement of the reigns had been forgotten — certain synchronisms in 2 Kings 17 and 18 were introduced by some late hand, strangely out of harmony with the original pattern of reigns" and that after this correction is made, "it becomes possible to set forth an arrangement of reigns for the Hebrew kings in which we find both internal harmony with the facts of contemporary history." There is a strange inconsistency in this presentation. On the one hand Thiele tells us that "the work from beginning to end was done with great devotion and almost inconceivable accuracy." If such was the case it is hard to believe that a bungling editor living long after its completion was allowed to spoil this masterpiece of accuracy without apparently any protest or refutation. Thiele's final word in defense of his theory is especially regrettable: "And what shall we say, if here and there, an indication of some slight imperfection may come to light. This work was done by men, not God. These men were spokesmen for God, but they were not divine. God alone is infallible. Has any man ever lived who could not make a mistake? That the original records were exact in detail we have no reason to doubt. And that they were copied again and again with an almost uncanny degree of accuracy is altogether clear. But it is likewise clear that in connection with later editorial work on the involved chronological data misunderstandings could and did take place" (p. 197). "Almost inconceivable accuracy" and bungling editorial work by an ignorant editor of a later date do not harmonize readily. And the assertion that "only God is infallible" denies the possibility that divine inspiration can make fallible human beings infallible as writers and teachers. Furthermore the error of "twelve years" in a carefully constructed chronology is not "a slight imperfection." The more the general accuracy of the record is insisted upon, the harder does it become to admit that there are inaccuracies in it.

[83] Cf. Rowley, *FJJ*, p. 83: "An emendation that is born of a theory can never give any support to the theory."

[84] *DDB*, pp. 137, 307. Compare the parallel statement in *WDB*, pp. 107, 242.

[85] *ISBE*, p. 639.

[86] The indemnity which is mentioned in 2 Kings 18:15 is referred to in Sennacherib's *Annals* (cf. *ANET*, p. 288), and apparently refers to the same campaign.

[87] His untimely death at the age of 36 cut short the career of perhaps the ablest and most brilliant of the pioneers in the field of Assyriology. His discovery and publication of the Babylonian Deluge tablets was his most publicized work.

[88] *Op. cit.*, 185.

[89] *Ibid.*, p. 192.

[90] *Ibid.*, p. 154.

[91] *Ibid.*, pp. 189f.

[92] In *Die Keilinschriften und das Alte Testament*, which was promptly trans-

lated into English under the title *The Cuneiform Inscriptions and the Old Testament*.

93 The identity of Shalman (Hos. 14:14) is uncertain, as is also that of Jareb (5:13; 10:6). The mention of Asshur by Balaam (Num. 23:22, 24) is not surprising since his home was in the far north and he might have known something about that kingdom which in the days of Abraham was already powerful. But the prophecy is vague and does not expressly concern Israel, save as included under the general term Eber (Cf. Gen. 10:21ff.; 11:14-17).

94 To avoid confusion it should be carefully noted that the biblical dates given in this discussion are those of the Ussher Chronology, while the Assyrian and Syrian dates are given according to the Eponym Canon.

95 *ANET*, pp. 278f.

96 Unger places Irkanata, Shiana, Arvad, Ushana in Phoenicia, Que in Cilicia, Musri probably in Cappadocia (*IAD*, p. 68).

97 Gurney, speaking of the battle of Qarqar says: "The first effective opposition encountered by the Assyrians was that of the kings of Hamath and Damascus, who, by calling on the contingents of twelve subject princes, mainly from the Phoenician coastlands, were able to meet Shalmaneser at Qarqar in 853 B.C. . . ." (*The Hittites*, p. 44). Gurney's words certainly do not imply that he identified Ahabbu with Ahab of Israel. Ahab was certainly not a subject prince of Adad-idri.

98 Compare the names *Ahabi-ia* (my uncle) and *Ahat-abi-sha* (her aunt) given in Tallquist, *Bab, Namenbuch*, p. 3; also *Ahummisha* (brother of her mother) and *Ahat-abisha* (sister of her father), in *Nuzi Personal Names*, by Gelb, Purves & MacRae (p. 10). The number of non-Semitic names ending in -*pu* which are listed in this volume (pp. 201f.) is noteworthy. The spelling *A-ha-ab-bu*, with the double "b" is unusual for Semitic names, if the second element is the word *Abu* (father). It is to be noted also that the name could equally well be read as *A-ha-ap-pu*. There are a number of non-Semitic (Hurrian) names which end in -*pu* or -*ap-pu*. Purves defines these endings as "suffixal formatives" (Gelb, Purves and MacRae, *Nuzi Personal Names*, 1943, p. 192). There are about forty names with this ending listed in this volume. The study is restricted to personal names. But it may be noted that Purves lists the ending -*ia* as "the commonest suffix in final position" (p. 193), which might apply to the place name *Sir-'i-la-a-a*. Omri and *Ahab* are Arabic names according to M. Noth (*Die Isr. Personennamen*, pp. 63, 222). He still holds this view in *The History of Israel* (1958), p. 229) where he further remarks: "Was the striking prohibition contained in the deuteronomist 'royal law' against appointing a foreigner king (Deut. 17:15) based on the concrete case of Omrii" (p. 229n). But the name Omri occurs in 1 Chron. 7:8; 9:4; 27:18. Note also Amram, the name of Moses' father, which may have quite a different meaning: 'Am-ram."

99 So called by Adad-nirari III (*ANET*, p. 281), by Tiglath-pileser (*id*, pp. 283f.), and by Sargon (*id.*, pp. 284f.), i.e., for more than a century after the time of Omri. The name Sir'ilaia has not been found anywhere else on Assyrian inscriptions.

100 The statue of Shalmaneser discovered by Mallowan at Nimrud (*Iraq*, vol. 21, pp. 147-157) is quite fragmentary. The names of Adad-idri and Irhuleni appear on it but there is no indication that Ahabbu was also named on it.

101 Cf. Unger *IAD*, p. 152, who vigorously supports Albright's claim that the Ben-hadad of Ahab's, as well as of Asa's time is the Adad-idri of Shalmaneser's inscriptions.

102 Parrot places the death of Ahab in 850 about 4 years after the battle of Qarqar (*ninive et l'AT.*, pp. 68-9). Wright places it 3 years later, Kraeling two years. *JNES*.

103 *ANET*, p. 279.

104 Van der Meer, *The Chronology of Western Asia and Egypt*, p. 5.

105 As to the Eponym Canon he wrote: "looking at the imperfect state of our present knowledge of Assyrian history, the amount of evidence in favour of the accuracy of the Assyrian eponym canon appears to me remarkable and conclusive; and in the present state of the inquiry I see no reason for doubting that it is a correct chronological computation" (*op. cit.*, p. 153).

106 A notable exception was T. G. Pinches who collaborated with Rawlinson in the publication of his great collection of Assyrian texts. Pinches in *The Old Testament in the Light of the Historical Records of Assyria and Babylonia* (pub-

lished in 1902) discussed the problem in detail (pp. 327-332, cf. p. 245) and concluded: "nevertheless the chronological difficulty still remains." According to W. S. Auchincloss, "men of Ahab" need not mean that Ahab was present at Qarqar, or even still alive at that time, "men of Ahab" may be said of the Israelite contingent simply because they were part of a powerful fighting machine which Ahab had trained (*Standard Chronology of the Holy Bible*, p. 63).

[107] Luckenbill, *ARAK*, Vol. I, p. 211.

[108] On this fragment, the statement is made regarding Shalmaneser's 18th year: "at that time I received the tribute of the inhabitants of Tyre, Sidon and of *Ia-u-a* mar Humri."

[109] *ANET*, p. 282.

[110] See above, pp. 231ff. on the abbreviation of names.

[111] *Op. cit.*, p. 190. One reason for the general acceptance of this identification is that many Bible students have seen in it a welcome confirmation of the biblical record by contemporary sources and consequently have paid little or no attention to the serious consequences of these and other identifications, to the havoc which they have wrought with the generally accepted biblical chronology. The picture of Jehu son of Omri prostrating himself before Shalmaneser will be found in nearly every illustrated Bible or reference book. But the reader is not told of the obstacles in the way of this identification.

[112] *Ibid.*, p. 191.

[113] Jehu is called the son of Nimshi, Elisha is described as the son of Shaphat of Abel-Meholah, Hazael is simply Hazael, he needs no further description.

[114] Article, "Hadadezer or Ben-Hadad" and "The Statue of Shalmaneser at Asshur" in *PTR*, Vol. 17, pp. 173-189.

[115] *Op. cit.*, p. 191.

[116] *BASOR*, nos. 87 and 90.

[117] *ANET*, pp. 281f.

[118] See the lists given by Brinkman, in the Appendix to Oppenheim's *Ancient Mesopotamia*, pp. 344-347.

[119] Tallquist, *Neubabylonisches Namenbuch*, p. 306.

[120] Brinkman, as cited p. 340. Schrader in *KAT* (1872) argues that the name Pul stood for *apal* in Nabopolassar and for *pil* in Tiglath-pileser (pp. 126f.).

[121] Wiseman agrees (*NEB*, p. 1276) with Weidner that Tiglath-pileser was a son of Adad-Nirari III who died in 783. This would mean that he was at least forty years old when he succeeded Assur-Nirari V, in 744 B.C. This is not an improbable figure. He may of course have been considerably older. It may be noted, however, that some scholars still hold (e.g., Finegan, *LAP*, p. 173) that he was a usurper.

[122] Olmstead, *History of Assyria* (p. 172).

[123] Smith explained the fact that in 1 R, pl. 35 four inscriptions are described by Rawlinson as inscriptions of Pul which were later recognized as inscriptions of Adad-nirari as due to the mention of the fact that this king "subdued and took tribute from the land of Omri or Israel." But he adds that Rawlinson "afterwards abandoned this view when he discovered the eponym Canon."

[124] In 1 Chron. 5:26 we read that "the God of Israel stirred up the spirit of Pul king of Assyria, and the spirit of Tiglath-pileser king of Assyria and he carried them away, even the Reubenites, and the Gadites, and the half tribe of Manasseh. . . ." Here the statement is ambiguous. The "and" which connects the two royal names might be translated "even" and the fact that the verb is singular favors such a rendering and identification. Both *LXX* and *Vulg.* render by the simple "and" and treat the verb as singular, following the MT exactly. Here also express mention is made of the carrying away of the Transjordanic Tribes by Tiglath-pileser. On the other hand the fact that in 2 Kings 15:19 Pul is mentioned as aiding Menahem, while in vs. 29 Tiglath-pileser is said to have attacked Israel in the days of Pekah, would seem to imply that two different Assyrian kings are referred to; and the singular of the verb might be intended to indicate that it was the latter king who instituted the policy of wholesale deportations which seems to have been actually the case. That as king of Babylon, Tiglath-pileser was known as Pulu or Pul. The question is whether the reference in 2 Kgs. 15:19 to Pul, king of Assyria is to this same Pul. According to the Ussher chronology Menahem reigned in Samaria 10 years (772-761), which means that Menahem died some 13 years before Tiglath-pileser became king of Assyria and 32 years before he reigned under the name Pul in Babylon. Furthermore the mention of

Tiglath-pileser in the biblical record (vs. 29) while it follows closely on vs. 19 connect him with Pekah (759-39) and not with Menahem.

125 While Schrader made the suggestion that Pulu might be an abbreviation of Tiglath-pileser, he apparently did not consider the possibility that it might have been used also of an earlier king.

126 Smith held that the name we now read as Adad-nirari was to be read as Vulnirari and that the character *Vul* might have the phonetic value *Pul*. But he was mistaken as to this.

127 *ANET*, p. 282.

128 *Ibid.*, p. 283f.

129 Smith read the name *Ra-hi-a-nu*, a spelling which is followed by Oppenheim. It is to be noted therefore that the two characters *hi* and *a* when joined together have the phonetic value *sun* (see Delitzsch, *Assyr. Lesestücke*, p. 29). So the difference is accounted for by the chirography of the scribe.

130 *ANET*, pp. 283f.

131 Smith regarded the date as probably 738. Thiele placed the death of Menahem earlier (742-741), differing with Albright who claimed that Menahem was still alive in 738. Unger adopted Thiele's date (*IAD*, pp. 99, 175).

132 *Op. cit.*, p. 180.

133 *ANET*, pp. 282f.

134 2 Kings 14:28 which refers to the conquests of Jeroboam II of Israel, and includes Damascus and Hamath as having belonged to Judah must be a reference to the extent of the United Kingdom in the days of David and Solomon (1 Kings 8:65). For no king of Judah made any such claim, and if Oppenheim's reading of the mutilated passage in the *Annals.* "Azriau . . . a royal palace of my own [I built in his city . . .] is correctly restored and interpreted Azriau cannot be king Azariah of Judah. Tiglath-pileser did not invade Judah and if he had built a palace of his own in Jerusalem, we would certainly expect a reference to such a humiliating act in Kings or Chronicles.

135 In *NBD*, Wiseman apparently rejects the identification (p. 102) and accepts it (p. 1276), which shows how doubtful it is. This uncertainty finds even clearer expression in the article by Waite (p. 1307) in the same volume. Unger on the other hand finds no difficulty with the identification and calls Winckler's theory that Azriau of Yaudi had no connection with Azariah of Judah, an "unhappy" idea (*IAD*, pp. 96f.). Why Unger should be so zealous in opposing this identification is hard to understand, since Winckler's suggestion would lessen the congestion of co-reigns in this period materially. But it serves to illustrate how thoroughly committed most biblical scholars are today to the co-reign theory as providing the means of bringing, we feel justified in saying, of forcing the biblical chronology into agreement with the Assyrian. Unger accepts without question another "idea" of Winckler's, that the *Musri* mentioned along with Ahabbu on the Monolith inscription "probably refers to a small kingdom in the Cilician-Cappadocian region of Asia-Minor, rather than to the land of the Nile" (*Ibid.*, pp. 68, 152-3).

136 Thiele, as we have seen, gives Jotham an independent rule of eight years. But his chronology for this period is vitiated by his rejection of the synchronisms of 2 Kings 17 and 18.

137 *Op. cit.*, p. 180. These possibilities are not to be ignored. Unger claims that at least seven kings of Judah had more than one name; and he points out that Hazael's son, Benhadad II, as he calls him, the Birhadad of the Zakir stele "was commonly styled Mari' by the Assyrians, which was in all likelihood an abbreviation for a name like *Mari'-Hadad* (*IAD*, p. 152). This practice was by no means limited to kings. One of the most familiar examples is the use of Nathanael for Bartholomew in the New Testament.

138 *Op. cit.*, p. 181.

139 *Ibid.*, p. 182.

140 *Ibid.*, p. 184f. Smith assigned Pekah 30 years (759-29), instead of the 20 of the Bible (p. 155), which would include the 8 or 9 years of anarchy recognized by Ussher before Hoshea became established as king *ca.* 730, after killing Pekah in 739. But if Azriau is Azariah, the date of his death must be brought down from 758 to *ca.* 744 and Jotham's 16 years and Ahaz's 16 must be condensed into *ca.* 15 years. i.e., the two reigns must be reduced to less than one!

141 It is to be noted, however, that this does not explain the further statements that Pekah became king in the fifty-second year of Azariah and reigned *twenty*

years (vs. 27) and that Hosea then became king in the *twentieth* year of Jotham (vs. 30), which seems to mean that Jotham's reign overlapped Ahaz by four years.

142 According to Keil Jehosphaphat made Joram co-regent (2 Kings 3:1) in his 18th year (896) and abdicated (2 Kings 8:16) in his 23rd year (891), so that his abdication occurred two years before his death in 889. As to this Keil says: "It is true that there is no analogy for the combination of the years of the reigns of two kings, since the other reductions of which different chronologists are fond are perfectly arbitrary, and the case before us stands quite alone; but this exception to the rule is indicated clearly enough in the statement in 8:16, that Joram began to reign while Jehoshaphat was (still) king" (*Commentary on Kings*, p. 289 note). According to Ussher Jehoshaphat died in 889 and was succeeded by Joram "who had reigned four years along with his father." Ussher gives Jehoshaphat 25 years (914-889). Keil makes Joram regent for two years (891-889) and gives him a reign of 6 years (889-884), deducting the two years of co-reign from his total of eight.

143 Mack in *ISBE*, p. 639. According to Davis (*DDB*, pp. 137, 418) Jotham survived his father Uzziah "scarcely a year, it seems," which would reduce the triumvirate rule to less than a year. Thiele gives Jotham an independent reign of 8 years. But he accomplishes this by rejecting the synchronisms of 2 Kings 17-18, which are of prime importance for the determining of the chronology.

144 The fact that Isa. 7:1 passes from the death of Uzziah (6:1) to the days of Ahaz might seem to suggest that this interval is very short and thus to favor the view that Jotham had little or no independent reign. But it is to be noted that Isa. 1:1 and 7:1 take pains to mention Jotham, whose reign is given nine verses in 2 Chron. 27. His name as we have seen is never omitted in the genealogies of the kings.

145 *NBD*, p. 217.

146 There is nothing in the biblical narrative to suggest a co-reign except the statement which occurs in both Kings and Chronicles that Jotham after his father became a leper "was over the house judging the people of the land" (2 Kings 15:4; 2 Chron. 26:21), and it is followed in both passages by the statement that Azariah "slept with his fathers and was buried with his fathers . . . and Jotham, his son, *reigned* in his stead." The distinction could hardly be more clearly drawn between Jotham's *regency* after his father became a leper and his *reign* after his father was dead; and his reign is stated to have been sixteen years. The fact that this makes Isaiah's ministry a very long one, seventy to eighty years if it began in 758 and continued until after Sennacherib's death in 681, is not a sufficient reason for reducing it. Eli lived to be 98 and Jehoiada to 130.

147 *BETS*, Vol. 10, No. 4 (1967), p. 224.

148 *Op cit.*, p. 153.

149 Laessoe in discussing Assyrian Historiography, tells us: "The official inscriptions were never looked upon as written history: they were not compiled for the edification of posterity; least of all were they written with us in mind. In reporting his victories the king speaks to his god. . . ." This explains the inaccessibility of many such inscriptions of which he mentions the Behistun inscription of Darius as a striking example. The inscriptions "serve a definite purpose: they confirm the pact between king and god and glorify the god's power." So he concludes: "Their value as historical sources must be assessed in the light of these considerations" (*People of Ancient Assyria*, pp. 160f.). See above pp. 213f. See also Oppenheim's discussion of the subject "Historical Sources or Literature?" in his *Ancient Mesopotamia*, pp. 143-153. It begins with the striking statement: "Only few cuneiform texts expressly purport to write what in the traditional Western sense, we would call 'history' . . . in short nearly all these texts are as wilfully unconcerned with the 'truth' as any other 'historical text' of the ancient Near East" (see especially pp. 147f.).

150 *ANET*, p. 279.

151 *IAD*, p. 153.

152 *ISBE*, vol. I, p. 636.

153 *Westminster Confession of Faith*, chap. I, 10.

INDEX OF SUBJECTS AND PERSONS

Hazael, 419ff.
Hazor, 218
Hebron, 120
Heman, 132, 307-310
Herods, 3
Hezekiah, 101, 106f., 158, 341, 406-412, 425ff.
Higher Criticism, 4f., 240
History, 212-218, 372
History, Ancient May Not Mean Accurate, 214-217
History, Old Testament, Great Figures in, 19-33
History, Old Testament, Selective and Episodal, 19
History, Perplexing Problems of, 217
History, Prophecy and, 153
History, Sacred, 172, 174
History, Secular, 3f., 154, 172
History, Synchronous, 102
History, Telescoping, 118-125
Hittites, 192, 220, 228
Horeb, 72, 106
Hoshea, 100, 407, 423ff.
Hushai, 83f.
Hyksos Period, 213

Iaua, 400, 413, 417f., 429
Idolatry, 318
Ikhnaton, 226f.
Immanuel, 38f.
Individual Stressed, 110
Inexact or Incomplete Statements, 131-136
Inspiration, 10
Introduction, Old Testament, 1f., 6
Irony and Sarcasm, 43f.
Isaac, 64, 77, 113, 151f., 260-263
Isaiah, 235, 407f.
Isaiah Scroll, 197, 199
Ishbosheth, 83, 112, 155
Ishmael, 141
Ishtar, 368f.
Israel, 79-82, 263f., 326-333, 413f.

Jacob, 73, 82, 111, 113f.
Jacob, Sons of, 65f., 111
Jebus and Jebusites, 302ff.
Jehoahaz, 418
Jehoash, 156f., 404f., 407, 418
Jehoiachin, 101f.
Jehoiakim, 158, 167, 239
Jehoram, 400f., 403
Jehoshaphat, 403
Jehu, 167, 400, 413, 417f., 429
Jephthah, 115f.
Jeremiah, 9, 44f., 159, 195f.
Jericho, 184-187, 190f.

Jeroboam, 89, 138, 148f., 315-319, 405, 407
Jerusalem, 46f., 85f., 94, 180, 291, 303f.
Jesus, 38f.
Jethro, 82f.
Jews, 79ff.
Jezebel, 109f., 123
Jezreel, 167
Joash, 404f., 419
Job, 62f.
Joel, 63
Jonah, 84, 139f.
Jonathan, 115
Joram, 419
Jordan, 68f.
Joseph, 114, 146f., 234, 391ff.
Joshua, 68f., 109, 150, 183
Josiah, 148f.
Jotham, 157, 405f., 424-427
Jubilee, Year of, 146
Judges, 295-298, 396
Judgment, 12ff.

Kassite Period, 212f.
Kenites, 267, 271ff.
Kenites, God of, 271ff.
Kingdom, Divided, 398-429
Kingdom Period, 398
Kingship, 22f.
Kingship, Divine, 360-363
Kittim, 325
Korah, 142

Laban, 82
Lachish, 154, 180, 182ff., 193, 199
Lamech Scroll, 169
Language, Curiosities of, 209ff.
Laws and Customs, 218-224
Levi, 73, 110f.
Levites, 265
Literalism, 37ff.
Literary Form, 37-171

Man, Age of, 382
Man, Creation of, 82
Man, Fall of, 386f.
Manasseh, 158, 235, 407
Manna, 71f., 99
Marduk, 215f., 227, 356f., 359
Mari, 212, 217
Marriage, Sacred, 359f., 362
Massoretic Text, 165-170
Megiddo, 181
Melchizedek, 31, 258f., 304f.
Menahem, 413f., 421f.
Mephibosheth, 112, 135
Mesha Inscription, 180, 193

INDEX OF AUTHORS

494

INDEX OF BIBLICAL TEXTS